Frommer's®

Paris
from $95 a Day

10th Edition

by Haas Mroue

Here's what the critics say abou

"Amazingly easy to use. Very portable, very complete."

—*Booklist*

"Detailed, accurate, and easy-to-read information for all price ranges."
—*Glamour Magazine*

"Hotel information is close to encyclopedic."
—*Des Moines Sunday Register*

"Frommer's Guides have a way of giving you a real feel for a place."
—*Knight Ridder Newspapers*

Wiley Publishing, Inc.

About the Author

Haas Mroue studied at the American University of Paris for 2 years before graduating from UCLA Film School. He went on to receive an M.A. from the University of Colorado, Boulder. His travel articles, poems, and short stories have appeared in such publications as *Travel + Leisure, Interiors,* and *The Literary Review* among many others. His work has been broadcast on the BBC World Service and on the cable channel Starz! He has co-authored guidebooks for *National Geographic* and Berlitz. He's the author of *Frommer's Memorable Walks in Paris* and *Frommer's Amsterdam Day by Day,* and is a contributor to *Frommer's Europe from $85 a Day, Frommer's Gay & Lesbian Europe, Frommer's Argentina & Chile,* and *Frommer's South America.* When he's not on the road, he makes his home on the Olympic Peninsula in Washington.

Published by:

Wiley Publishing, Inc.

111 River St.
Hoboken, NJ 07030-5774

ISBN-13: 978-0-7645-9893-7
ISBN-10: 0-7645-9893-7

Editor: Marc Nadeau
Production Editor: Bethany J. André
Cartographer: Anton Crane
Photo Editor: Richard Fox
Production by Wiley Indianapolis Composition Services

For information on our other products and services or to obtain technical support, please contact our Customer Care Department within the U.S. at 800/762-2974, outside the U.S. at 317/572-3993 or fax 317/572-4002.

Wiley also publishes its books in a variety of electronic formats. Some content that appears in print may not be available in electronic formats.

Manufactured in the United States of America

5 4 3 2 1

Contents

6 Great Deals on Dining 106

7 Seeing the Sights 155

8 Paris Strolls 224

List of Maps

Acknowledgments

I would like to thank Veronique Surrel for her endless insights (and unfaltering enthusiasm), Brian Bost for the endless walks, Olivier Lacheze-Beer for his endless patience, and Patricia Stott for the endless laughter—my time in Paris would not have been the same without you.

—Haas Mroue

An Invitation to the Reader

In researching this book, we discovered many wonderful places—hotels, restaurants, shops, and more. We're sure you'll find others. Please tell us about them, so we can share the information with your fellow travelers in upcoming editions. If you were disappointed with a recommendation, we'd love to know that, too. Please write to:

Frommer's Paris from $95 a Day, 10th Edition
Wiley Publishing, Inc. • 111 River St. • Hoboken, NJ 07030-5774

An Additional Note

Please be advised that travel information is subject to change at any time—and this is especially true of prices. We therefore suggest that you write or call ahead for confirmation when making your travel plans. The authors, editors, and publisher cannot be held responsible for the experiences of readers while traveling. Your safety is important to us, however, so we encourage you to stay alert and be aware of your surroundings. Keep a close eye on cameras, purses, and wallets, all favorite targets of thieves and pickpockets.

Other Great Guides for Your Trip:

Frommer's France
Frommer's Paris
The Unofficial Guide to Paris
Frommer's Irreverent Guide to Paris
Frommer's Portable Paris
Paris For Dummies
Frommer's Memorable Walks in Paris
Suzy Gershman's Born to Shop Paris
The Unofficial Guide to Disneyland® Paris
Frommer's Provence & the Riviera

Frommer's Star Ratings, Icons & Abbreviations

Every hotel, restaurant, and attraction listing in this guide has been ranked for quality, value, service, amenities, and special features using a **star-rating system.** In country, state, and regional guides, we also rate towns and regions to help you narrow down your choices and budget your time accordingly. Hotels and restaurants are rated on a scale of zero (recommended) to three stars (exceptional). Attractions, shopping, nightlife, towns, and regions are rated according to the following scale: zero stars (recommended), one star (highly recommended), two stars (very highly recommended), and three stars (must-see).

In addition to the star-rating system, we also use **seven feature icons** that point you to the great deals, in-the-know advice, and unique experiences that separate travelers from tourists. Throughout the book, look for:

Finds	Special finds—those places only insiders know about
Fun Fact	Fun facts—details that make travelers more informed and their trips more fun
Kids	Best bets for kids and advice for the whole family
Moments	Special moments—those experiences that memories are made of
Overrated	Places or experiences not worth your time or money
Tips	Insider tips—great ways to save time and money
Value	Great values—where to get the best deals

The following **abbreviations** are used for credit cards:

AE	American Express	DISC	Discover	V	Visa
DC	Diners Club	MC	MasterCard		

Frommers.com

Now that you have the guidebook to a great trip, visit our website at **www.frommers.com** for travel information on more than 3,000 destinations. With features updated regularly, we give you instant access to the most current trip-planning information available. At Frommers.com, you'll also find the best prices on airfares, accommodations, and car rentals—and you can even book travel online through our travel booking partners. At Frommers.com, you'll also find the following:

- Online updates to our most popular guidebooks
- Vacation sweepstakes and contest giveaways
- Newsletter highlighting the hottest travel trends
- Online travel message boards with featured travel discussions

What's New in Paris

Paris is booming again. After tourism dropped during the Iraq war and for about a year after, hotels in the city are back to near-record highs, restaurants and cafes are full, and the city's sights are choked with visitors. Unfortunately, prices are up, up, up. Hotel owners and restaurateurs have taken advantage of this boom to raise prices more than the customary 5% per year. On several occasions, I found that hotels raised their prices over 15% in the past year and once-affordable restaurants are almost out of range for our budget in this book. And with the continued weak dollar, the city is at its most expensive. More than ever, it's paramount that you plan early and carefully when organizing your trip to Paris. Many hotels offer discounts from late July to end of August and again in January and February. Restaurants tend to be less busy in summer when many Parisians are away on holiday. Mid-winter is a great time to visit the city's attractions, when lines are short for most sights. Set your priorities and organize accordingly and you can stay within budget.

Planning Your Trip Airlines continue to shift around the various terminals at the sprawling Charles de Gaulles airport, north of Paris. American Airlines now arrives at terminal 2, as do Continental and British Airways. Be sure to check and double-check the terminal with your airline before heading out to the airport.

Getting Around Métro and bus tickets have gone up to 1.40€ ($1.75) in 2005. If you plan to make more than two trips per day on public transportation, then you should consider buying one of several discounted multiple-day passes. See p. 14.

Accommodations One of our favorite budget choices for many years, **Hotel Keppler,** has shut its doors and will reopen in 2007 as a luxury hotel. A new find is the recently opened **Hôtel Saint-Louis Bastille** (114 bd. Richard-Lenoir; ☎ 01-43-38-29-29) near the lively Oberkampf district in eastern Paris, steps from the Marais. The hotel's brand new rooms are modern and comfortable with a soothing lime-green decor. More and more hotels are adding free Internet in their lobbies for guests to use, and some are even adding WiFi access. Even the supercheap **Hôtel de Nevers** (53 rue de Malte; ☎ 01-47-00-56-18) will have wireless Internet access from its cozy lounge available as of early 2006. A terrific find for families is the **Hôtel de France** (102 bd. de la Tour Maubourg; ☎ 01-47-05-40-49) with its spacious doubles, triples, and connecting rooms. Some of the rooms have breathtaking views of the Invalides and all the way north to the Sacré-Coeur. The Art Deco **Hôtel Beaumarchais** (3 rue Oberkampf; ☎ 01-53-36-86-86) has just changed ownership. The new owner has turned the hotel's lobby into an art gallery. Exhibits change every 2 months and many of the exhibitors are hotel customers. If you're an artist, be sure to take a sample of your work with you to be considered for a future exhibit. **Hôtel Kensington** (79 ave. de la Bourdonnais;

© 01-47-05-74-00), steps from the Eiffel Tower, has some of the least expensive rooms in the swanky 7e arrondissement. Doubles are 70€ ($88) for a room with a double bed and bathroom with shower. The Latin Quarter's newest hotel is also one of the city's cheapest new additions. The **Hôtel du Commerce** (14 rue de la Montagne Ste Genevieve; © 01-43-54-89-69) opened in 2004 in a 600-year-old building, just a few minutes walk from Notre-Dame. Modern and colorful, the hotel's motto is "cheap doesn't have to be ugly." Double rooms begin at 49€ ($61).

Dining   More than ever, finding a bargain has become necessary to stay within the budget of this book. One of my favorite discoveries is a tiny restaurant near the Bastille that serves excellent French food with an emphasis on using Normandy and Mediterranean ingredients. **Au Trou Normand** (9 rue Jean Pierre Timbaud; © 01-48-05-80-23) has an amazingly priced 12€ ($14) two-course *prix-fixe* menu for lunch.

Overlooking the meandering Canal St Martin, **Poissons Rouge** (112 quai de Jemmapes; © 01-40-40-07-11) serves some of the best seafood in the city at the most affordable prices. The two-course lunch menu is only 14 ($17). Jack Nicholson, Diane Keaton, and Keanu Reeves shot several scenes of their movie *Something's Gotta Give* in the beautiful classic brasserie **Le Grand Colbert** (2–4 rue Vivienne; © 01-42-86-87-88), and despite a huge increase in popularity, the restaurant has not raised its prices much. Take advantage of the excellent three-course 19€ ($24) menu for lunch to relive those scenes for yourself. One of the best splurge choices in the city just became less expensive—an unheard of development. Celebrity Chef Alain Ducasse's **Aux Lyonnais** (32 rue St-Marc; © 01-42-96-65-04) restaurant focuses on the renowned cuisine of Lyon. The three-course menu that used to be 33€ ($41) is now 28€ ($35) and the food and the service are both as good as ever.

Seeing the Sights   The big cultural news in Paris is the frenzied construction and further delays on the immense museum project at Quai Branly, not far from the Eiffel Tower. Initially scheduled to open in 2004, the **Musée du Quai Branly** (55 quai Branly; © 01-56-61-70-00) will be dedicated to the arts and civilization from Africa, Asia, the Pacific Islands, and the Americas, and will be home to over 280,000 pieces of art. The exact opening date has not yet been determined but will occur sometime in mid-2006. President Jacques Chirac unveiled a new memorial in the old Jewish neighborhood of the Marais in January 2005. **Le Memorial de la Shoah** (17 rue Geoffroy-l'Asnier; © 01-42-77-44-72) is a Holocaust memorial in memory of the French children, women and men who were deported to Nazi camps from France between 1942 and 1944. The new **Musée Baccarat** (11 pl. des Etats Unis, 16e; © 01-47-70-64-30) opened its doors in 2004 in a beautiful villa in the very chic16e arrondissement. On display is a great collection of crystal ware used by celebrities through the years—from Czar Nicholas II of Russia to Princess Grace of Monaco. The museum shop is a great place to pretend that you're really interested in buying the 15,000€ ($18,750) crystal watches, or at least the 120€ ($150) crystal wine goblets.

The city's newest museum is dedicated to tennis. The **Tenniseum** (Stade Roland Garros, 2 av. Gordon-Bennett; © 01-47-43-48-48) is located just adjacent to the Roland Garros stadium, where the French Open is held in late May every year. In addition to antique tennis rackets and other equipment, the multimedia library holds hundreds of hours of archived tennis footage.

The Best of Paris from $95 a Day

Paris is a city of dreams. Its name calls up a parade of images and associations: the Eiffel Tower, the moonlit quais of the Seine, artists, accordions, and clouds of cigarette smoke. What's surprising is how well the city lives up to its mythic reputation. Though you won't see Gene Kelly dancing in the streets or run into Leslie Caron at the supermarket, you might actually hear an accordion playing as you stroll through a quiet market square, or see a rainbow arching over Parisian rooftops. The splendid Belle Epoque architecture still surrounds you; around every corner there seems to be yet another photo to be taken or poem to write. Yet Paris is not a museum. Underneath its velvet gown, it is a vibrant, modern city with its share of problems and annoyances. Still, if you squint your eyes on a rainy night, you might catch a glimpse of the Paris Brassaï photographed decades ago—a mysterious and lovely realm of the imagination.

Fortunately, this particular dream is not limited to pashas with bulging bank accounts. Though Paris is notoriously expensive, a little digging will reveal a healthy supply of reasonable hotels and restaurants. If you are willing to venture into street markets and public transportation, you can cut costs dramatically while getting a little closer to the Parisian's everyday life.

Many of the most impressive sights are free: the majestic sweep of the Champs-Elysées, the quiet grandeur of the place des Vosges, or the leisurely charm of the Jardin du Luxembourg. The city's magnificent churches are all free; it won't cost anything to spend an hour beneath the vaulted arches of Notre-Dame. Paris has dozens of affordable museums, from the mighty Louvre to the tiny doll museum, Musée de la Poupée. Choose your itinerary according to your interests. There's so much to see; don't try to do it all. Who cares if you see 35 museums or 13? Take time to sip an espresso or a glass of red wine at an outdoor cafe under the Parisian sky, and allow yourself to get lost down some ancient street where you'll find the ghost of Balzac, the flash of Yves St-Laurent, and cuisine of Alain Ducasse sharing the same sidewalk view.

Paris seduces. Her charm is effusive, yet she wields her power with an iron determination. From the place de la Concorde to the Opera Garnier to the basilica of Sacré-Coeur, she is a living work of art and, like all artists, can be decidedly temperamental. But you won't mind—you'll even understand—when you sip from her cup, break bread, and fall in love all over again.

1 Frommer's Favorite Affordable Experiences

- **Taking an Evening Cruise on the Seine.** Touristy, but it doesn't matter. The monuments that are impressive by day are floodlit at night, and Paris becomes glittering and romantically shadowy by turns. Gliding down the river under softly glowing bridges, with the towers of Notre-Dame against a dark sky and the Eiffel Tower transformed into a golden web of light, is a magical experience—until, that is, some visitors decide that shouting and doing the wave under each bridge is the best way to assert one's nationality. Word of advice: Save the displays for sporting events. For more information, see chapter 7.

- **Spending a Day at the Musée d'Orsay.** It holds the world's most comprehensive collection of Impressionist art, in addition to pre-Impressionists, post-Impressionists, and neo-Impressionists. See the sculptures on the ground floor, and then head upstairs for a look at the spectacular collection of van Goghs, some little-known Gauguins, and a roomful of Toulouse-Lautrec pastels. You'll leave refreshed and energized. See chapter 7.

- **Whiling Away a Weekend Afternoon in the Jardin du Luxembourg.** Enjoy the sun on your face while you lean back in an iron chair and watch neatly dressed, perfectly mannered Parisians of all ages sail toy boats, play tennis, ride ponies, and take beekeeping classes. Don't miss the working orchards, where fruit is carefully cultivated for the table of the French Senate and for local charities. See chapter 7.

- **Walking through the Marais.** Sprawling manors built by 17th-century nobles and narrow streets of fairy-tale quaintness coexist with artists and artisans who bring unique and sometimes whimsical style to the historic district. Stroll down **rue des Rosiers** in the heart of the old Jewish quarter, browse the antiques shops at **Village St-Paul,** and take a break in the tranquil **place des Vosges.** The bars and cafes on the main streets are lively at night and during the annual Fierté (gay pride) celebration; the side streets are so quiet, you can hear your footsteps echo in the dark. See chapter 7.

- **Tomb-Hopping in Père-Lachaise.** From Chopin to Jim Morrison to Maria Callas, this lush necropolis is a "who used to be who" of famous Parisians (or famous people who happened to die in Paris), and there's no wrong season or weather to visit. The bare trees of winter lend it a haunting quality; on rainy days, the cemetery is brooding and melancholy; on a summer day, it's the ideal place for a contemplative stroll. Best time to visit? November 1, All Saints' Day, when flowers decorate the tombs. See chapter 7.

- **Food Shopping, Parisian Style.** In an outdoor neighborhood market, you can observe the French indulging their passion for meat, dairy, fruit, fish, fowl, pâté, cheese, sausage, rabbit, and unusual animal parts: brains, kidneys, veal's head, tongue, and tripe. The merchants know their products and are happy to offer advice and even cooking tips. The markets on **rue Mouffetard** and **rue de Buci** are the best known; the ones on **rue Montorgueil** and **rue Cler** have an equally tempting array of produce and are less touristy.

- **Touring the Arcades.** You'll feel that shopping has been elevated to high art when you wander the iron-and-glass-covered passages that weave through the 2e arrondissement. Designed to shelter 19th-century shoppers from nasty weather, they now hold shops that sell stamps, old books, and discount clothing; designer boutiques; tea salons; homey brasseries; and even a wax museum (Grévin). Exploring these picturesque passages is a delightful way to while away a rainy afternoon. See chapter 7.

- **Watching the Sunset from the Pont des Arts.** Behind you are the spires of Notre-Dame; ahead is the river, with its bridges stretching toward the setting sun. On the bridge with you just might be a mime or someone dressed as a Louvre statue. See chapter 7.

- **Arriving in August.** It's a month when the city is shunned by tourists, abandoned by its residents. Even parking meters are free. The air begins to smell like air again, nightlife takes it down a notch, and parks and gardens are in full bloom. Although many restaurants close, enough remain open to give you a good choice of the local cuisine. The museums, the banks of the Seine, and the old neighborhoods are full of their usual charm, but without the bustle, what's left is beauty, art, and nature.

Although summers in Paris rarely reach the temperatures of more southern climes, 2003 proved to be the exception with an unprecedented heat wave. While the city government responded by creating an artificial beach, the high temperatures led to a number of heat-related fatalities. Air-conditioning is not a given in even the more luxe hotels, so keep that in mind when you're thinking about booking a late-summer vacation.

- **Strolling, Inline Skating, or Biking Along the Canal St-Martin.** Immortalized in the Marcel Carné film *Hôtel du Nord,* the canal runs through eastern Paris, a part of the city tourists rarely visit, which is a pity. The area closes to vehicle traffic on Sunday, and you can bike, *faire le roller* (skate), or scooter past footbridges connecting the tree-lined promenades on either side of the water. You'll see elderly men dozing in the sun as mothers watch their toddlers play. You might even take in a "spectacle" such as costumed actors evoking a Venetian scene on a line of boats floating past the *quartier.* The whole area relives the low-key tranquillity of prewar, working-class Paris.

- **Dancing in the Streets.** On June 21, the day of the summer solstice, everyone pours into the streets to celebrate the Fête de la Musique, and musicians are everywhere. Although the quality varies from don't-give-up-your-day-job to top-rung, it's exhilarating to join the parties in progress in every park, garden, and square. See "Paris Calendar of Events," in chapter 2.

2 Best Affordable Hotel Bets

- **Best for Business Travelers:** Ideally situated near one of the city's main business districts, the **Hôtel des Deux Acacias,** 28 rue de l'Arc de Triomphe, 17e (© **01-43-80-01-85**) is a quiet, well-run hotel with a lot of amenities for the money, including a second phone line in all rooms for Internet access. Its good address will impress your French business associates and show them that you're *malin* (shrewd). See p. 88.

- **Best for Romantic Atmosphere:** A short stroll from the Eiffel Tower, the **Hôtel du Champ de Mars,** 7 rue du Champ de Mars, 7e (© **01-45-51-52-30**), feels more like a luxury boutique hotel than a budget choice. Flowing

Impressions

Paris is a real ocean. Wander through it, describe it as you may, there will always remain an undiscovered place, an unknown retreat, flowers, pearls, monsters, something unheard of.

—Honoré de Balzac

curtains, fabric-covered headboards, throw pillows, and cushioned high-backed seats make each room ideal for a lazy breakfast in bed. With its 18th-century ceiling murals and wedding-cake plasterwork, **Hôtel St-Jacques,** 35 rue des Ecoles, 5e (ⓒ **01-44-07-45-45**), offers Second Empire romance at affordable rates. See p. 102 and 96.

- **Best for Families:** Spacious doubles with connecting doors can be found at **Hôtel de France,** 102 bd. de la Tour Maubourg, 7e (ⓒ **01-47-05-40-49**), which also features cribs and family-friendly management. See p. 100.

- **Best Overall Values:** On the Right Bank, **Hôtel Little Regina,** 89 bd. de Strasbourg, 9e (ⓒ **01-45-37-72-30**), near two of the city's train stations, offers incredible deals on spacious, recently renovated, and soundproofed rooms that come with new rugs and furniture, attractive burgundy wallpaper, ample wardrobe space, full-length mirrors, white-oak desks, and brand-new bathrooms with shower doors. On the Left Bank, **Grand Hôtel Lévêque,** 29 rue Cler, 7e (ⓒ **01-47-05-49-15**), boasts a fantastic location on a pedestrian-only street, steps from one of the most charming open-air markets in the city. The clean, well-maintained rooms are soundproofed and come with new air-conditioning units; rooms on the fifth floor have balconies with views of the Eiffel Tower. See p. 84 and 99.

- **Best Location:** Steps from the Ritz, **Hôtel Mansart,** 5 rue des Capucines, 1e (ⓒ **01-42-61-50-28**), is located in

the heart of the city, just off place de la Vendôme. From here, you are only a 10-minute walk from the Louvre, the Opéra, the Concorde, and the Left Bank. See p. 82.

- **Best for Travelers with Disabilities:** **Little Hôtel,** 3 rue Pierre Chausson, 10e (ⓒ **01-42-08-21-57**), is one of the only budget hotels in Paris to offer wheelchair-accessible rooms on the ground floor. The hotel is conveniently located near the Gare de l'Est and the Canal St-Martin. See p. 84.

- **Best Rooms with a View:** Would you like to gaze over the city's rooftops while you have your morning croissants and coffee? Splurge on a room with a view at the **Hôtel du Square d'Anvers,** 6 pl. d'Anvers, 9e (ⓒ **01-42-81-20-74**), overlooking a leafy park. From its top-floor rooms, you have a view that stretches from the Eiffel Tower to Sacré-Coeur. Up the hill, **Hôtel Regyn's Montmartre,** 18 pl. des Abbesses, 18e (ⓒ **01-42-54-45-21**), charges a little extra for the view from its fourth and fifth floors—and it's entirely worth it. See p. 83 and 91.

- **Best Splurge:** The **Hôtel du Bois,** 11 rue du Dome, 16e (ⓒ **01-45-00-31-96**), has it all: a fantastic location just off elegant boulevard Victor Hugo, handsome rooms (with Laura Ashley fabric, marble bathrooms, cable TV, and hair dryers), peace and quiet, and a friendly staff. It's popular with the French when they come to the capital to enjoy a dose of metropolitan life. See p. 90.

- **Best Youth Hostel:** In a historic mansion on a quiet side street in the Marais, **Youth Hostel le Fauconnier,** 17 rue de Fauconnier, 4e (✆ **01-42-74-23-45**), has a pleasant courtyard, and all rooms have private showers! Reserve well in advance. See p. 105.
- **Best for Nightlife Lovers:** Hôtel **Beaumarchais,** 3 rue Oberkampf, 11e (✆ **01-53-36-86-86**), is within walking distance of the city's three nightlife centers—the Bastille, the Marais, and rue Oberkampf. Air-conditioning and double-glazed windows allow you to sleep late, and the bold color scheme will give you a jolt of energy in the morning. See p. 87.
- **Best for a Taste of the Discreet Charm of the Bourgeoisie:** The **Hôtel Nicolo,** 3 rue Nicolo, 16e (✆ **01-42-88-83-40**), is in the heart of one of Paris's most expensive residential districts. If you'd like to live in gilded surroundings, even on a budget, you might enjoy the hotel's traditional French charm. See p. 90.
- **Best for Serious Shoppers:** The **Hôtel Chopin,** 10 bd. Montmartre, 9e (✆ **01-47-70-58-10**), is tucked away in the Passage Jouffroy shopping arcade. Across the street is the Passage des Panoramas; Galeries Lafayette, Au Printemps, and other department stores are only a short walk away. See p. 83.
- **Best Family-Run Hotels:** The very friendly and hard-working Eric and Sylvie Gaucheron own and run two hotels side by side, both highly recommended. The **Familia Hôtel,** 11 rue des Ecoles, 5e (✆ **01-43-54-55-27**), and the **Hôtel Minerve,** 13 rue des Ecoles, 5e (✆ **01-43-26-26-04**), are both excellent values and boast comfortable, lovingly maintained accommodations, some with hand-painted sepia frescoes and others with exposed beams and tiny balconies with views of Notre-Dame. See p. 92 and 93.

3 Best Affordable Restaurant Bets

- **Best Restaurant with a View:** In good weather, you'll have one of the loveliest views in Paris from an outdoor table at the **Restaurant du Palais-Royal,** 43 rue Valois, 1er (✆ **01-40-20-00-27**). The restaurant is in the Palais-Royal, so you'll overlook its beautiful, peaceful gardens while dining on fine dishes like grilled sole with a garnish of carrots, parsley, red pepper, and baby squid. See p. 117.
- **Best Cafes with a View:** Under the arcades, and facing the lovely place des Vosges with its shady chestnut trees, the **Café Hugo,** 22 pl. des Vosges, 4e (✆ **01-42-72-64-04**), is a great place to while away a summer afternoon. See p. 146.

Closer to the hubbub, chic **Café Marly,** 93 rue de Rivoli, cour Napoleon du Louvre, 1er (✆ **01-49-26-06-60**), overlooks I. M. Pei's glass pyramid at the Louvre and has ultracushy chairs for sitting back and contemplating architecture, art, and life. See p. 146.

- **Best Places for a Celebration:** If you want a glamorous night on the town, try the infinitely elegant **La Butte Chaillot,** 110 bis av. Keleber, 16e (✆ **01-47-27-88-88**), with its polished glass and leather interior, and exquisitely prepared dishes that are fresh, simple, and utterly delectable. See p. 128.

For something just as chic but a bit more trendy, head to **Georges,** Centre

Pompidou, 6th Floor, rue Rambuteau, 4e (© **01-44-78-47-99**). This creation of the Costes Brothers (of Hotel Costes) is one of the hottest spots in Paris, with a 360-degree view to kill—and its prices are surprisingly reasonable. See p. 121.

- **Most Typical Parisian Bistro:** Every Parisian has his or her pick, but almost everyone agrees that **Chardenoux,** 1 rue Jules-Valles, 11e (© **01-43-71-49-52**), belongs in the top 10. It's a small place in an out-of-the-way location, but the food is excellent and the Art Nouveau setting is gloriously, eternally Parisian. See p. 125.

- **Best Modern Bistro:** You'll have to book the minute you get to town if you want to sample the food at the almost hopelessly popular **Chez Casimir,** 6 rue de Belzunce, 10e (© **01-48-78-28-80**). It's worth the trip to this treasure close to the Gare du Nord, where you'll find traditional French cuisine with a twist in an animated setting. See p. 118.

- **Best for Business Meals: Bofinger,** 5–7 rue de la Bastille, 4e (© **01-42-72-87-82**). It's one of the prettiest restaurants in Paris, with a gorgeous domed stained-glass ceiling over the main dining room. It became part of the Brasserie Flo chain in 1996, and the food has never been better. See p. 121.

- **Best Brasserie:** For a taste of the real thing, go to **Brasserie Ile St-Louis,** 55 quai de Bourbon, 1er (© **01-43-54-02-59**), the last independent brasserie in Paris. Far from the polished restaurants that masquerade as true brasseries, this one has as its heart old Paris. See p. 112.

- **Best Place for a Late-Night Meal:** You can always wander into one of the all-night brasseries along rue Coquillière (on the northern edge of Les Halles) without a reservation. For

a Parisian experience with a splash of American literary history, head to **Closerie des Lilas,** 171 bd. du Montparnasse, 6e (© **01-40-51-34-50**). Ernest Hemingway wrote *The Sun Also Rises* here, and in his off time he hung out here with John Dos Passos. You'll need reservations. For a change of pace, try the bustling, bawdy **La Tour de Montlhéry,** 5 rue des Prouvaires, 1er (© **01-42-36-21-82**), open nonstop from 7am Monday to 7am Saturday. It's known for huge cuts of excellent meat and good house wines. Reservations are always required. See p. 139 and 116.

- **Best for Mingling with the Locals:** Parisians are avid bargain hunters, which explains the huge popularity of moderately priced eateries. On the Right Bank, near the Concorde and the U.S. consulate, **L'Escure,** 7 rue de Mondovi, 1e (© **01-42-60-18-91**), pulls in many of the local businesspeople at lunch and residents at dinner. On the Left Bank, **Bistro Mazarin,** 42 rue Mazarin, 6e (© **01-43-29-99-01**), attracts many locals associated with the shops or universities around the neighborhood; portions are large and prices are fair, and there's a terrace for outdoor dining. See p. 116 and 137.

- **Best for Celebrity Spotting: Le Relais Plaza,** 25 av. Montaigne, 8e (© **01-53-67-66-65**), at the venerable Hotel Plaza Athénée, has reopened and regained its place as the most star-studded and (somewhat) affordable eatery. Most recently, John Malkovich and Tom Hanks were spotted; years ago, it was Marlene Dietrich and Jackie Kennedy. See p. 128.

- **Best Breakfast:** The day sometimes starts with mealy croissants and watery coffee in budget accommodations; if you make the effort to come here, you'll wish that **Angelina,** 226 rue de Rivoli, 1er (© **01-42-60-82-00**), was next door to your hotel. This Belle Epoque palace with gold-trimmed mirrors serves buttery pastries and hot chocolate you'll never forget. See p. 149.

• **Best Afternoon Tea:** For a delightful timeout during an ambitious day of sightseeing, head to **Mariage Frères,** 30–32 rue du Bourg-Tibourg, 4e (✆ **01-42-72-28-11**). The Mariage family entered the trade in 1660, when Nicolas Mariage began importing tea from Persia for King Louis XIV. Take your pick from almost 500 teas in the attractive colonial-style salon at the back of the shop. See p. 150.

• **Best Sandwiches:** Italy is the inspiration for the focaccia-style bread and scrumptious fillings at **Cosi,** 54 rue de Seine, 6e (✆ **01-46-33-35-36**). To accompany the freshly baked bread, you can choose from an assortment of specialties, including arugula, mozzarella, Parmesan, Italian ham, roast tomatoes, and tapenade. See p. 137.

• **Best Picnic Fare:** Two excellent places for one-stop shopping are **La Grande Epicerie,** Bon Marché, 38 rue de Sèvres, 7e (✆ **01-44-39-81-00**); and **Lafayette Gourmet,** 52 bd. Haussmann, 9e (✆ **01-48-74-46-06**). The quiche from the Grande Epicerie Alsatian deli counter is a special treat. See p. 247.

• **Best Spot for a Family Meal:** The polite and efficient waiters at **Le Grand Colbert,** 2–4 rue Vivienne, 2e (✆ **01-42-86-87-88**), are used to Parisian family gatherings, especially on Sunday. This historic landmark dates back to the 1830s and shimmers with polished brass, old lamps, and frescoes. It's boisterous and lively, and children get to be a bit loud without upsetting the convivial atmosphere. See p. 118.

• **Best Wine Bar:** For excellent Rhône Valley wines and generous plates of cold cuts and cheese in a lively little dining room, visit **A la Cloche des Halles,** 28 rue Coquillière, 1er (✆ **01-42-36-93-89**). *Cloche* means "bell," and the name refers to the bell that tolled the opening and closing of the city's main market when it was nearby. Some old-market atmosphere survives here, including an interesting mix of people and a high level of conviviality. It's a great place for a light, very French lunch. See p. 151.

• **Best Cafe Food:** Although cafes all over town serve salads and omelets, the staff makes an extra effort at **La Chaise au Plafond,** 10 rue Trésor, 4e (✆ **01-42-76-03-22**), on a side street in the heart of the Marais. The offbeat decor—park benches and a ceiling painted black and white to resemble the markings on a cow—attracts a young crowd that delights in the big, fresh salads and thick *tartes.* See p. 147.

• **Best Foreign Meals:** A meal at **Le Manguier,** 67 av. Parmentier, 11e (✆ **01-48-07-03-27**), might be the only chance you'll ever have to try West African cooking. Among the better dishes are chicken *yassa* with lemons and onions, and *requin fumé* (smoked shark), if you're feeling adventurous. This lively place also serves potent, mostly rum-based cocktails and plays African music. At **Al Diwan,** 30 av. Georges V, 8e (✆ **01-47-20-18-17**), you can sample delicious, fresh, and affordable Lebanese cuisine just off the Champs-Elysées. See p. 132 and 125.

• **Best Student Hangout:** Parisian students have a keen eye for bargains, skimping on food so they can spend their parents' money in salsa bars. At **Restaurant Perraudin,** 157 rue St-Jacques, 5e (✆ **01-46-33-15-75**), in the heart of the Latin Quarter, students and professors get comfortable home cooking at rock-bottom prices. The 19€ ($24) lunch menu is hearty enough to see them through an afternoon of classes and an evening of carousing. See p. 136.

- **Best French Regional Restaurants:** Regional cooking has been enjoying a new vogue in Paris. Two of the best places to dine in the provinces without leaving town are: **ChantAirelle,** 17 rue Laplace, 5e (© **01-46-33-18-59**), to sample the sturdy fare of the south-central Auvergne region; and **Vivario,** 6 rue Cochin, 5e (© **01-43-25-08-19**), the oldest Corsican restaurant in

Paris, which serves hearty specialties from Napoleon's birthplace. See p. 136.

- **Best Deals:** The 12€ ($15) two-course lunch menu at **Au Trou Normand,** 9 rue Jean Pierre Timbaud, 11e (© **01-48-05-80-23**), may be the city's best deal. The 22€ ($28) three-course menu with wine at **L'Escure** (see above) provides delicious French cuisine that you don't often see at this price. The 33€ ($41) heavenly three-course gourmet menu at **Le Clos du Gourmet,** 16 av. Rapp, 7e (© **01-45-51-75-61**), will make you want to pinch yourself; no, you're not dreaming, these prices are real! See p. 124, 116, and 142.

2

Planning an Affordable Trip to Paris

Consider this chapter a tool kit to help you plan the most enjoyable and affordable vacation to the City of Light. We'll answer the questions you probably have concerning the what, when, where, and how of travel—from what documents you need, to how to get to Paris easily and economically. We'll tell you what you can expect to pay for rooms, a meal, a theater ticket. We provide tips for travelers with special needs and interests (students, families, travelers with disabilities, gay and lesbian travelers), as well as a calendar of special events.

1 The $95-a-Day Premise

Generally, you can count on Paris to be as expensive as two of the most costly American cities: New York and San Francisco. The raison d'être for this book is to help you get the best vacation for your money. "Affordable" doesn't mean shabby accommodations, bad food, and the feeling that you're being cheated out of the experience of Paris. Rather, it means seeking out the best values and refusing to overpay for mediocrity. Visiting Paris on a budget means you'll be living more like Parisians, who like to enjoy high standards without emptying their wallets.

First, let's deal with your expectations: Expect simple comforts in your **hotel.** The room will likely be quite small but cozy, the towels thinner than you're used to, and the decor basic—but usually somewhat charming. You will probably have a TV that gets a few French channels and an English news service (usually the BBC, sometimes CNN), a telephone, and a tiny bathroom with shower or antique tub and toilet.

Just because you'll be dining in a city famous for its food, don't expect to pay a fortune for it. While it is true you would be guaranteed the very best of haute French cuisine at one of the premier restaurants, if you do your homework, you can also eat some incredible French meals at restaurants that you can more readily afford. Peruse chapter 6, "Great Deals on Dining," and remember that a picnic is one of the best and cheapest ways to celebrate excellent French cuisine. You can put a meal together from the pâtés, cheeses, meats, wine, and fruit available at grocery stores, street markets, boulangeries, and *épiceries* throughout the city. You'll never be at a loss for a picnic location in Paris!

As for **sightseeing,** sometimes wandering down the ancient Parisian streets can be the greatest pleasure. The monuments commemorating the events that created Paris are free. The many museums offer reduced entrance fees at certain times and are free the first Sunday of every month. The parks, filled with sculptures and pastimes like puppet shows, are free, and even a stroll through the streets will expose you to buildings that resonate with literary and historical associations. In the evening, Paris opens up, and you can linger in a cafe over a glass of wine (cheaper than a soda or coffee) and people-watch, walk to your heart's content among the floodlit monuments, or stroll the bridges over the Seine.

The premise of this book is that two people traveling together can have an enjoyable, affordable vacation for $95 a day per person. That amount is meant to cover the per-person price of a double room and three meals a day, with the budget breaking down as follows: $55 for the room, $6 for breakfast, $10 for lunch, and $24 for dinner. This amount gives you more-than-adequate accommodations, a continental breakfast, picnic or low-cost lunch, and a fine evening meal. To save more and eat better, you can take advantage of the reasonable prix-fixe lunches offered throughout Paris and save your light meal for dinner. And you can modify the budget by opting to do it for less or more.

2 55 Money-Saving Tips

PLANNING & TRANSPORTATION

1. Knowledge is power. So **read as much as you can** about Paris before you go, ask friends who have been there, and get as much free information as possible from the Internet and tourist office.

2. **Plan well in advance.** Airlines and even car-rental firms and hotels need to sell their inventory of seats, cars, and rooms, and will reward the advance purchaser with a discount. A 14-day advance-purchase airfare is cheaper than a regular economy seat. If planning far ahead isn't an option, check for special offers on major airlines' websites, or on travel websites like www.lastminutetravel.com, www.cheaptickets.com, and http://smarterliving.com.

3. The most expensive part of any trip often is the airfare, so **scour newspapers and the Net** for the latest information. Airlines want to fill every flight, so they adjust their pricing frequently. Look for airlines that have just begun flying to Paris—they often launch the route with low fares.

4. Fly during the week rather than on weekends; it's cheaper. Also, you'll save on airfare and dining if you travel during the off season, approximately November to March.

5. **Consolidators,** also known as bucket shops, are great sources for international tickets. Start by looking in Sunday newspaper travel sections; U.S. travelers should focus on the *New York Times, Los Angeles Times,* and the *Miami Herald.* Several reliable consolidators are worldwide and available on the Net. **STA Travel** is the world's leader in student travel. It also offers good fares for travelers of all ages. **Flights.com** (© 800/TRAV-800; www.flights.com) started in Europe and has excellent fares worldwide, but particularly to that continent. The French operator **New Frontiers** ⚡ (© 800/677-0720) is more than a consolidator, offering a variety of low-cost flights and packages to France, as well as train travel, car rental, and lodging in hotels and apartments in Paris and the French provinces.

6. Consider **going as a courier** if you have plenty of time and are not traveling with a companion. Companies that hire couriers use your luggage allowance for their business baggage, and in return you get a deeply discounted ticket. You pay an annual fee to become a member of the **International Association of Air Travel**

Couriers (© **561/582-8320;** www.
courier.org) or the **Air Courier Association** (© **800/282-1202;** www.air
courier.org), which will provide you
with a daily list of low-fare courier
opportunities.

7. **Pack light.** You won't need a luggage
cart, and you'll be less likely to suc-
cumb to the desire for a taxi.

8. **Take the cheapest way into the city**
from the airport. You can save over
$60 by taking a train or bus instead
of a cab from Roissy–Charles de
Gaulle, and about $40 from Orly.

9. **Enjoy the price tag of a package
tour.** Sometimes the price of airfare,
transfers, and a week or more in a
hotel is little more than the cost of traditional airfare. You don't have to sign
up for the tour's features or join the
group activities unless you want to.

ACCOMMODATIONS

10. **Book early.** The best budget choices
fill up fast.

11. **What do you really need in your
hotel room?** Nearly all rooms in Paris
have a sink with hot and cold water.
If you don't mind sharing the facilities, you can stay in a lower-priced
room with a bathroom down the hall.

12. **Negotiate the room price,** especially
in the low season. Ask for a discount
if you're a student or over 60; ask for
a discount if you stay a certain number of days, say, 5 or more.

13. **Stay at a hotel that doesn't insist
you take breakfast,** which can add
$6 or more a day to your bill. Make
sure you aren't being charged for it.

14. If you're interested in experiencing the
life of the country, **sign up for a home-
stay program** such as **Servas** (© **212/
267-0252;** www.servas-france.org).

15. **Consider staying at a youth hostel**
or similar lodging. You don't necessarily have to bunk in with a bunch of
strangers; many hostels offer private
or family rooms, and many serve

meals and/or have public kitchens
and laundries.

16. A **home swap** or **short-term apartment rental** in Paris is a good option
if you don't need the services of a
hotel. One company that facilitates
home swapping is **Trading Homes
International** (www.HomeExchange.
com); for apartment rentals, try www.
lodgis.com.

17. **Don't call home from a hotel
phone** unless you know that you can
dial your "home direct" number to
reach your own operator. If you have
to make a call, use a public phone
booth to avoid hotel surcharges.
Another way to save money is to call
home and ask the person to call you
back; U.S. rates are much lower.

18. **Look for *télécartes* that give you
more for your money.** You'll be
hard-pressed to find a pay phone in
France that accepts coins; public
phones require that you insert a prepaid *télécarte* that has a microchip to
measure the connection time. Calls
to the United States between 8am
and 7pm use a *unité* every 14 sec-
onds; at other times it's every 17 sec-
onds. You can buy *télécartes* at any
post office or *tabac* (tobacco shop)
and some newsstands. Cashiers will
almost always try to sell you a card
from France Télécom, the French
phone company, for 7.50€ ($9.40)
or 15€ ($19). What tourists don't
know is that many *tabacs* and news-
stands sell *télécartes* issued by companies that have better rates than France
Télécom's. Look for *tabacs* that have
advertisements for Delta Multimedia
or Kertel, or ask for a *télécarte avec un
code.* The post office sells only France
Télécom *télécartes.*

DINING

19. If you're not opposed to picnicking,
patisseries, boulangeries, and **street
markets** are your best bets for quick,

cheap dining. Don't forget a cork-screw *(tire-bouchon)!* Boulangeries sell sandwiches, cold slices of pizza, and individual quiches for about 3.50€ ($4.40).

20. **Make lunch your main meal.** Many restaurants offer great deals on a fixed-price (prix fixe) lunch. After two or three courses at midday, you'll be happy to eat light at dinner.

21. **Seek out crêperies,** where you can enjoy meat- or vegetable-filled galettes and dessert crepes in Brittany-inspired surroundings. There are many off the boulevard du Montparnasse around the Square Delambre.

22. **Try ethnic neighborhoods** for tasty, inexpensive cuisine. You can get terrific Chinese food in the 13e arrondissement between the place d'Italie and the Porte de Choisy; try the 10e, 18e, and 20e for North African, Turkish, Vietnamese, and Thai.

23. **Chain restaurants** Hippopotamus, Léon de Bruxelles, and l'Ecluse offer good values. Pommes des Pains and Lina's are popular chains for sandwiches.

24. The *plat du jour* will usually be the cheapest main dish at a budget restaurant. If that's not enough food, order the *formule* or prix-fixe menus, which usually provide an appetizer and main dish or a main dish and dessert. Three-course menus include a starter, main dish, and dessert. Wine is usually not included, although some menus offer a *boisson,* which may be a glass *(verre du vin)* or small jug *(pot)* of wine. Coffee is almost always extra.

25. **Pay attention to the details of the menu.** On most menus the cheaper dishes are made of cheaper cuts of meat or organ meats, like brains, tripe, and so on. Andouillette is one such dish. It's not the "little" sausage you might expect, but a delicacy made of hog intestines.

26. **Wine is cheaper than soda.** Also, some mineral waters are less expensive than others. Unless you can really taste the difference, ask for tap water *(une carafe d'eau).*

27. **Don't eat breakfast at your hotel** unless you want to pay 4€ to 9€ ($5–$11) for the privilege. Grab a croissant or *pain au chocolat* from a boulangerie for 1.50€ ($1.90) and drink your coffee standing up at a cafe counter for another 1.50€ ($1.90).

28. **Know the tipping rules.** Service is usually included at restaurants; however, we still advise leaving a 4% to 7% tip, depending on the bill and quality of service. Most waiters and waitresses do this as a lifelong career; it's nice to show your appreciation.

29. **Have drinks or coffee at the bar.** You pay twice as much when you're seated at a table.

SIGHTSEEING

30. **Use the Métro or walk.** Take advantage of passes that lower the cost of a single ticket from 1.40€ to 1€ ($1.75–$1.25) if you buy a *carnet* of 10. If you plan to take more than seven trains in a day, it pays to get a **Mobilis** day card for 5.40€ ($6.75). It offers unlimited travel in the city center. If you know you'll be in Paris for up to 5 consecutive days, a **Paris Visite** pass may be a good idea. Heavily promoted by the RATP, the pass offers unlimited travel in zones 1 to 3 (outside the Paris city limits), plus free or discounted admission to some attractions—but make sure the attractions that interest you are included. There's also a pass that covers unlimited subway and bus travel in zones 1 to 8 (Paris and suburbs, including the airports, Versailles, and Disneyland Paris), but unless you're going to Disneyland, Versailles, or Fontainebleau, you won't need to go outside zone 3.

Buy Paris Visite passes at the airports, at any SNCF (major railroad) station, RER stations, and *tabacs* displaying the RATP logo. Not all Métro stations sell the passes. Fares range from 8.35€ ($10) for 1 day of travel in zones 1 to 3, to 53€ ($66) for 5 days' travel in zones 1 to 8.

31. **Check the calendar of events below.** Many festivals and fairs are free and offer an opportunity to participate in a uniquely Parisian event.

32. Instead of paying to look out over the **rooftops** of Paris, go to places that are free, such as the top floor of the department store La Samaritaine.

33. **Go to the parks.** They're lush, beautiful, and civilized.

34. **Tour the historic monuments** and **enjoy public art in the streets and parks.** History endures at sights like the place des Vosges and place de la Concorde. Statues can also give you a quick history course in the great figures and personalities that have shaped Paris, or maybe just afford you a chance to appreciate the male and female nude, such as the Maillol sculptures in the Tuileries.

35. **Hang out in the open-air food markets.** There's one in each arrondissement; they open at 8am. Some of our favorites are rue Montorgueil, rue Mouffetard, and rue de Buci. Go early, and remember that most markets are closed on Monday.

36. **Churches are free.** Take the opportunity to sit and contemplate, or attend a service. Many churches have dramatic interiors and famous artwork—paintings by Delacroix at St-Sulpice, sculptures by Coysevox at St-Roch, and etchings by Rouault at St-Séverin, to name only a few.

37. Consider buying the **Carte Musées et Monuments** (Museum and Monuments Pass), but only if you'll be visiting two or three museums a day.

The pass costs 18€ ($23) for 1 day, 36€ ($45) for 3 days, and 54€ ($68) for 5 days. Admission to the Louvre is 8.50€ ($11), and entrance fees for most other museums are 7€ to 8€ ($9–$10) or less; you do the math. The card gives you access to 65 museums and monuments, allowing you to go directly inside without waiting in line—a distinct benefit at the Louvre, for example.

38. **Visit the cemeteries.** Apart from their beauty, they're peaceful havens, and you may learn a little about French—and American—history. Worth exploring are Père-Lachaise, Montmartre, and Montparnasse (p. 164, 196, and 220).

39. Take advantage of the **reduced admission fee at museums,** which usually applies 2 hours before closing and all day Sunday.

40. If you're age **60 or over,** carry identification proving it and ask for discounts at theaters, museums, attractions, and the Métro.

41. If you're an auction buff, pick up a copy of the *Gazette de l'Hôtel Drouot,* which comes out every Friday, and check for **auctions** that interest you. The five major auction houses are Drouot Montaigne, Drouot Nord, Drouot Richelieu, the Salle des Ventes Saint Honoré, and the Salle des Ventes du Particulier.

SHOPPING

42. Paris is expensive, but there are many bargains. Take your time browsing through the little boutiques and flea markets and you'll be sure to find that perfect gift. Things like **film** and **toiletries,** including contact lens solution, are much more expensive in Paris than in the U.S. or the United Kingdom. Bring enough to get you through your trip.

43. You can secure a **tax refund** *(détaxe),* but only if you spend more than

185€ ($231) in one store. It's a complicated process, but when you spend that much, it's worth applying for the refund, usually 13% to 21% and usually credited to your charge card or sent to you a few months later. The major department stores have *détaxe* desks and will help you fill out the paperwork. At the airport, you present the paperwork to a French Customs officer who stamps the papers and returns them to you. You then mail the papers from the airport—the stamped envelope is included—and look for the refund, in euros, in about 3 months.

44. If **jewelry** is a pet purchase, explore the boutiques on the rue Tiquetonne and in the Passage du Grand Cerf. Also visit Tati Or (p. 243) and, for costume jewelry that looks like the real thing, try Bijoux Burma (p. 248).

45. **Perfume** made in France really *is* different from French perfume made elsewhere. In France, perfume is made with potato alcohol, which increases the scent and lengthens its endurance, making French-made perfume the best there is. Though the U.S. has tons of perfume discounters, they usually carry perfume made outside of France. Hotels, travel agents, and the welcome desks at department stores Au Printemps and Galeries Lafayette offer 10%-off coupons that you can use to buy perfume—if you buy more than 186€ ($233) worth, you'll also qualify for the value-added tax (about 13%) refund. If you have time, visit Catherine, 7 rue de Castiglione, 1er (p. 249), the favorite perfume discounter of Frommer's *Born to Shop* guru Suzy Gershman. The store will give you a discount and, if you qualify, you'll get your value-added tax rebate at the time of purchase.

46. Look for stylish, inexpensive clothes at the stores best described as upscale versions of the U.S. chain Target: Monoprix-Prisunic. For discounts on **fashion,** try the rue St-Placide.

47. For discounts on **china** and **other table goods,** check out the stores on the rue Paradis.

48. *Soldes* means "sales." The French government allows merchants to put their wares on sale below cost twice a year, in January and July.

49. To sample the **contemporary art scene,** stroll through the 11e arrondissement around the Bastille or along rue Quincampoix near the Centre Pompidou.

50. **Go to outdoor markets.** Even if you don't buy anything, the experience is fun. There are flea markets at Porte de Vanves, Porte de Montreuil, and Porte de Clignancourt, a flower market and a bird market on Ile de la Cité, a stamp market at Rond Point Clemenceau, and fresh produce markets everywhere.

51. For **antiques browsing,** go to one of the centers, like Le Louvre des Antiquaires, 2 pl. du Palais-Royal, 1er (p. 240); Village St-Paul, between rue St-Paul and rue Charlemagne, 4e (p. 240); or Le Village Suisse, avenue de la Motte-Picquet, 15e. Otherwise, explore the streets in the 6e arrondissement—especially rue Jacob, rue des St-Pères, and the rues de Bac and Beaune, which contain beautiful stores and galleries. The second floor of the Bon Marché's food store is also an air-conditioned antiques hall.

PARIS AFTER DARK

52. **Nightlife is expensive.** We'll share some tricks, but don't expect to save much. Allot some of your budget to go out on the town.

53. For **half-price theater** and other performance tickets, go to one of the kiosks by the Madeleine, on the lower level of Châtelet–Les-Halles Métro

interchange, or at the Gare Montparnasse. It's worth the legwork because you can see operas, classical concerts, and ballets in both the exquisitely redone Opéra Garnier (p. 252) and at the sparkling Opéra Bastille (p. 252) for as little as 23€ ($29).

54. **Low-cost concerts** (about 20€/$25 per person) are often given in churches. The weekly *Pariscope* magazine contains complete concert listings and can be found at every newsstand. Parts of *Pariscope* are in English.

55. At **clubs** you can save money by sitting at the bar instead of at a table. Some clubs are cheaper than others, and some are cheaper during the week.

3 Visitor Information

Your best source of information—besides this guide, of course—is the **French Government Tourist Office** (www.franceguide.com).

IN THE U.S. The **French Government Tourist Office** has offices at 444 Madison Ave., 16th Floor, New York, NY 10022-6903 (fax 212/838-7855); 676 N. Michigan Ave., Chicago, IL 60611-2819 (fax 312/337-6339); and 9454 Wilshire Blvd., Suite 715, Beverly Hills, CA 90212-2967 (fax 310/276-2835). To request information at any of these offices, dial the **France on Call** hot line at ℂ **410/286-8310.**

IN CANADA **Maison de la France/ French Government Tourist Office,** 1981 av. McGill College, Suite 490, Montréal PQ H3A 2W9 (fax 514/845-4868).

IN THE U.K. **Maison de la France/ French Government Tourist Office,** 178 Piccadilly, London W1V 0AL (ℂ **0891/ 244-123;** fax 0171/493-6594).

IN IRELAND **Maison de la France/ French Government Tourist Office,** 35 Lower Abbey St., Dublin 1, Ireland (ℂ **01/703-4046;** fax 01/874-7324).

IN AUSTRALIA French Tourist Bureau, 25 Bligh St. Level 22, Sydney, NSW 2000 Australia (ℂ **02/231-5244;** fax 02/231-8682).

IN NEW ZEALAND There's no representative in New Zealand; contact the Australian representative.

Tips **Paris, Je T'Adore**

Bonjour Paris (www.bparis.com) is one of the most comprehensive and fun sites about life in Paris, written from an American expatriate point of view. You'll find reviews of new restaurants, articles on bicycle fever, the French love affair, and inline skating on place des Vosges coexisting happily with guides to French cheese and wine and reviews of recent French films. Hotel recommendations and travel tips abound. Message boards debate cultural differences and offer readers restaurant, food, and wine picks. In the chat sessions you can learn to speak French better, get recipes, or talk about French literature, among other subjects. Suzy Gershman, author of Frommer's *Born to Shop* series, relates the latest trends in fashion and travel and her favorite finds.

IN PARIS   Once you reach Paris, the prime source of tourist information is the **Office de Tourisme et des Congrès de Paris,** 127 av. des Champs-Elysées, 75008 Paris (*©* **08-36-68-31-12;** fax 01-49-52-53-00; www.paris-touristoffice.com; Métro: Charles-de-Gaulle–Etoile or George V). Telephone access costs .35€ (45¢) per minute.

CITY GUIDES ON THE WEB

- **Paris France Guide (www.paris franceguide.com)**   Brought to you by the publisher of such magazines as *Living in France, Study in France,* and *What's On in France,* this site has lots of useful information about Paris, such as current articles and listings on nightlife, restaurants, events, theater, and music.
- **Paris Free Voice/thinkparis.com (parisvoice.com** or **thinkparis.com)** The online version of the monthly *Paris Voice* is hip and opinionated for "English-speaking Parisians." The calendar of events includes music, movies, and performance-art listings. Also included are restaurant reviews and guides like "Where to Kiss in Paris."
- **Paris Pages (www.paris.org)**   Unless you've got a high-speed connection, there's so much information on this site it sometimes takes ages to download. The lodging reviews are organized by area and the monuments that stand nearby. The city guide includes an event calendar, shop listings, a map of attractions with details about each, and photo tours.

- **Paris Tourist Office (www.paris-touristoffice.com)**   Here you'll find information on city events by week, month, favorites, and year, plus the closest Métro stops for museums, lodging, restaurants, and nightlife. Rent a scooter through its list of transportation services. Tour parks and gardens and discover Paris's trendy arrondissements.
- **Smartweb: Paris (www.smartweb.fr/ paris)**   This city guide shows the big attractions, such as the Louvre and Eiffel Tower, and includes history, photos, admission fees, and hours. Navigate the shopping and gallery listings organized by district and preview the airports' terminals. You can even see photos of the graffiti dedicated to Princess Diana on the torch and wall surrounding place de l'Alma, above the underpass where Diana was killed in a car accident on August 31, 1997.
- **RATP (www.ratp.fr)**   Métro, RER, and bus maps as well as street maps. Also helpful is the information on the lines, timetables, and journeys of Noctambus, which runs when the Métro is closed, between 1 and 5:30am. RATP links to Subway Navigator, which shows you how to get from one point to another on the Métro.
- **Mappy (www.mappy.fr)**   Excellent for maps and directions; you can find any address in Paris. It's very similar to MapQuest.

4 Entry Requirements & Customs

ENTRY REQUIREMENTS

For information on how to get a passport, see "Getting Your Passports," below—the websites listed provide downloadable passport applications as well as the current fees for processing passport applications.

CUSTOMS
WHAT YOU CAN BRING INTO FRANCE

Customs restrictions differ for citizens of the European Union and for citizens of non-E.U. countries. Non-E.U. nationals can bring in duty-free 200 cigarettes or 100 cigarillos or 50 cigars or 250 grams

Tips Passport Savvy

Allow plenty of time before your trip to apply for a passport; processing normally takes 3 weeks but can take longer during busy periods (especially spring). And keep in mind that if you need a passport in a hurry, you'll pay a higher processing fee. When traveling, safeguard your passport in an inconspicuous, inaccessible place like a money belt and keep a copy of the critical pages with your passport number in a separate place. If you lose your passport, visit the nearest consulate or embassy of your native country as soon as possible for a replacement.

For Residents of the United States: Whether you're applying in person or by mail, you can download passport applications from the U.S. State Department website at **http://travel.state.gov**. For general information, call the **National Passport Agency** (© 202/647-0518). To find your regional passport office, either check the U.S. State Department website or call the **National Passport Information Center** (© 900/225-5674); the fee is 55¢ per minute for automated information and $1.50 per minute for operator-assisted calls.

For Residents of Canada: Passport applications are available at travel agencies throughout Canada or from the central **Passport Office,** Department of Foreign Affairs and International Trade, Ottawa, ON K1A 0G3 (© 800/567-6868; www.ppt.gc.ca).

For Residents of the U.K.: To pick up an application for a standard 10-year passport (5-year passport for children under 16), visit your nearest passport office, major post office, or travel agency, or contact the **United Kingdom Passport Service** at © 0870/521-0410 or search its website at www.ukpa.gov.uk.

For Residents of Ireland: You can apply for a 10-year passport at the **Passport Office,** Setanta Centre, Molesworth Street, Dublin 2 (© 01/671-1633; www.irlgov.ie/iveagh). Those under age 18 and over 65 must apply for a €12 3-year passport. You can also apply at 1A South Mall, Cork (© 021/272-525), or at most main post offices.

For Residents of Australia: You can pick up an application from your local post office or any branch of Passports Australia, but you must schedule an interview at the passport office to present your application materials. Call the **Australian Passport Information Service** at © 131-232, or visit the government website at www.passports.gov.au.

For Residents of New Zealand: You can pick up a passport application at any New Zealand Passports Office or download it from its website. Contact the **Passports Office** at © 0800/225-050 in New Zealand or 04/474-8100, or log on to www.passports.govt.nz.

of smoking tobacco. You can also bring in 2 liters of wine and 1 liter of alcohol over 38.8 proof. In addition, you can bring in 50 grams of perfume, .25 liter of toilet water, 500 grams of coffee, and 100 grams of tea. Travelers 15 and over can also bring in 185€ in other goods; for those 14 and under, the limit is 93€.

E.U. citizens may bring any amount of goods into France as long as it is for their personal use and not for resale.

WHAT YOU CAN TAKE HOME FROM FRANCE

Those luscious persimmons you saw at the open-air market? Well, forget taking them or any other fresh fruit, vegetables, or meats to the U.S. Even cheese is problematic—only hard cheeses are allowed, and only those packed in labeled packages and sealed. What can you bring back? Coffee beans, roasted nuts, canned sauces, and canned fruits and vegetables; canned meats have to be shelf-stable without refrigeration, but determining that could get tricky if you get stopped. Truffles, however, are allowed.

Returning **U.S. citizens** who have been away for at least 48 hours are allowed to bring back, once every 30 days, $800 worth of merchandise duty-free. You'll be charged a flat rate of 4% duty on the next $1,000 worth of purchases. Be sure to have your receipts handy. On mailed gifts, the duty-free limit is $200. For specifics on what you can bring back, download the invaluable free pamphlet *Know Before You Go* online at **www.customs.gov** (click on "Travel," and then click on "Know Before You Go Online Brochure"). Or contact the **U.S. Customs Service,** 1300 Pennsylvania Ave. NW, Washington, DC 20229 (℡ **877/287-8867**) and request the pamphlet.

For a summary of **Canadian** rules, write for the booklet *I Declare,* issued by the **Canada Customs and Revenue Agency** (℡ **800/461-9999** in Canada, or 204/983-3500; www.ccra-adrc.gc.ca). Canada allows its citizens a C$750 exemption, and you're allowed to bring back duty-free one carton of cigarettes, one can of tobacco, 40 imperial ounces of liquor, and 50 cigars. You're also allowed to mail gifts to Canada valued at less than C$60 a day if they're unsolicited and don't contain alcohol or tobacco (write on the package "Unsolicited gift, under $60 value"). All valuables should be declared on the Y-38 form before departure from Canada, including serial numbers of valuables you already own, such as foreign cameras. *Note:* The C$750 exemption can only be used once a year and only after an absence of 7 days.

Citizens of the U.K. who are **returning from a European Union (E.U.) country** will go through a separate Customs exit (called the "Blue Exit") especially for E.U. travelers. In essence, there is no limit on what you can bring back from an E.U. country, as long as the items are for personal use (this includes gifts), and you have already paid the necessary duty and tax. However, Customs law sets out guidance levels. If you bring in more than these levels, you may be asked to prove that the goods are for your own use. Guidance levels on goods bought in the E.U. for your own use are 3,200 cigarettes, 200 cigars, 400 cigarillos, 3 kilograms of smoking tobacco, 10 liters of spirits, 90 liters of wine, 20 liters of fortified wine (such as port or sherry), and 110 liters of beer.

For more information, contact **HM Customs & Excise** at ℡ **0845/010-9000** (from outside the U.K., 020/8929-0152), or consult its website at www.hmce.gov.uk.

The duty-free allowance in **Australia** is A$400 or, for those under 18, A$200. Citizens can bring in 250 cigarettes or 250 grams of loose tobacco, and 1,125 milliliters of alcohol. If you're returning with valuables you already own, such as foreign-made cameras, you should file form B263. A helpful brochure available from Australian consulates or Customs offices is *Know Before You Go.* For more information, call the **Australian Customs Service** at ℡ **1300/363-263,** or log on to www.customs.gov.au.

The duty-free allowance for **New Zealand** is NZ$700. Citizens over 17 can bring in 200 cigarettes, 50 cigars, or 250 grams of tobacco (or a mixture of all three if their combined weight doesn't exceed 250g), plus 4.5 liters of wine and beer, or 1.125 liters of liquor. New Zealand currency does not carry import or export restrictions. Fill out a certificate of export, listing the valuables you are taking out of the country; that way, you can bring them back without paying duty. Most questions are answered in a free pamphlet available at New Zealand consulates and Customs offices: *New Zealand Customs Guide for Travellers, Notice no. 4.* For more information, contact **New Zealand Customs,** The Customhouse, 17–21 Whitmore St., Box 2218, Wellington (© **04/473-6099** or 0800/428-786; www.customs.govt.nz).

5 Money

Paris can be as expensive as London or New York. ATMs are visible throughout the city—look for the BNP (Banque Nationale de Paris) logos outside of buildings or on street corners; also, La Poste (post office) ATMs are yellow and found in and around all major post offices.

CURRENCY

It's a good idea to exchange at least some money—just enough to cover airport incidentals and transportation to your hotel—before you leave home, so you can avoid lines at airport ATMs. You can exchange money at your local American Express or Thomas Cook office or your bank. If your bank doesn't offer currency-exchange services, American Express offers travelers checks and foreign currency, though with a $15 order fee and shipping costs, at **800/807-6233** or www.americanexpress.com.

ATMs

The easiest and best way to get cash away from home is from an ATM (automated teller machine). The **Cirrus** (© **800/424-7787;** www.mastercard.com) and **PLUS** (© **800/843-7587;** www.visa.com) networks span the globe. Be sure you know your daily withdrawal limit before you depart. Also keep in mind that many banks impose a fee every time a card is used at a different bank's ATM, and that fee can be higher for international transactions (up to $5 or more). On top of this, the bank from which you withdraw cash may charge its own fee. To compare banks' ATM fees within the U.S., use www.bankrate.com. For international withdrawal fees, ask your bank.

TRAVELER'S CHECKS

Traveler's checks are something of an anachronism from the days before the ATM made cash accessible at any time. Traveler's checks used to be the only sound alternative to traveling with dangerously large amounts of cash. They were as reliable as currency, but, unlike cash, could be replaced if lost or stolen.

These days, traveler's checks are less necessary because most cities have 24-hour

---

Tips **Regarding the Euro**

As this book went to press, 1€ was worth approximately $1.25, down from a high of $1.35. Your dollars might not go as far as you'd expect but they'll go farther than they did just a few months ago. We list all prices in euros, followed by the U.S. dollar equivalent in parentheses. For up-to-the minute exchange rates between the euro and the dollar, check the currency converter website **www.xe.com/ucc.**

ATMs that allow you to withdraw small amounts of cash as needed. However, keep in mind that you will likely be charged an ATM withdrawal fee if the bank is not your own, so if you're withdrawing money every day, you might be better off with traveler's checks—provided that you don't mind showing identification every time you want to cash one.

You can get traveler's checks at almost any bank. **American Express** offers denominations of $20, $50, $100, $500, and (for cardholders only) $1,000. You'll pay a service charge ranging from 1% to 4%. You can also get American Express traveler's checks over the phone by calling © **800/221-7282;** Amex gold and platinum cardholders who use this number are exempt from the 1% fee.

Visa offers traveler's checks at Citibank locations nationwide, as well as at several other banks. The service charge ranges between 1.5% and 2%; checks come in denominations of $20, $50, $100, $500, and $1,000. Call © **800/732-1322** for information. AAA members can obtain Visa checks without a fee at most AAA offices or by calling © **866/339-3378. MasterCard** also offers traveler's checks. Call © **800/223-9920** for a location near you.

Foreign currency traveler's checks are useful if you're traveling to one country, or to the euro zone; they're accepted at locations, such as bed-and-breakfasts, where dollar checks may not be, and they minimize the amount of math you have to do at your destination. **American Express** offers checks in Australian dollars, Canadian dollars, British pounds, euros, and Japanese yen. **Visa** checks come in Australian, Canadian, British, and euro versions; **MasterCard** offers those four plus yen and South African rands.

If you choose to carry traveler's checks, be sure to keep a record of their serial numbers separate from your checks in the event that they are stolen or lost. You'll get a refund faster if you know the numbers.

CREDIT CARDS

Credit cards are a safe way to carry money, they provide a convenient record of all your expenses, and they generally offer good exchange rates. You can also withdraw cash advances from your credit cards at banks or ATMs, provided you know your PIN. If you've forgotten yours, or didn't even know you had one, call the number on the back of your credit card and ask the bank to send it to you. It usually takes 5 to 7 business days, though some banks will provide the number over the phone if you tell them your mother's maiden name or some other personal information. Your credit card company will likely charge a commission (1% or 2%) on every foreign purchase you make, but don't sweat this small stuff; for most purchases, you'll still get the best deal with credit cards when you factor in things like ATM fees and higher traveler's check exchange rates.

Establishments throughout Paris accept major credit cards, but their use, especially at budget restaurants and hotels, is not as widespread as it is in North America. Always check beforehand. The most widely recognized credit card is **Visa** (called **Carte Bleu** in France); establishments that display the **Eurocard** sign accept MasterCard. Diners Club and American Express are accepted at the more upscale restaurants, shops, and hotels. The exchange rate on a credit card purchase is based on the current rate when your bill is generated, not the rate when you made the purchase.

6 When to Go

The weather in Paris is famously unpredictable, so bring an umbrella if you plan to visit in the winter, spring, or fall. Although April in Paris may at times be too cold for some travelers, spring and fall are generally the best times to experience the city. Temperatures are usually mild, and the performing arts and other cultural activities are in full swing. In winter lack of sunshine, dampness, and cold winds can be disappointing, but there is so much to see and to do inside that you won't miss the picnics in the parks. You can often swing great deals on airfares, too.

Summer can be mild or extreme, depending on the year and your luck, and you'll have to deal with more tourists. Many Parisians, especially in August, head for the coast or the mountains. Cultural life dwindles, and many restaurants, cafes, and shops close for up to a month—what the French call the *fermeture annuelle* (annual closing). But it's a wonderful time to visit! The long hours of daylight give you more time to explore the city. You might also be able to negotiate a better deal with your hotel because you aren't competing with business travelers for rooms.

Paris's Average Daytime Temperature & Rainfall

	Jan	Feb	Mar	Apr	May	June	July	Aug	Sept	Oct	Nov	Dec
Temp. (°F)	38	39	46	51	58	64	66	66	61	53	45	40
Temp. (°C)	3	4	8	11	14	18	19	19	16	12	7	4
Rainfall (in.)	3.2	2.9	2.4	2.7	3.2	3.5	3.3	3.7	3.3	3.0	3.5	3.1

HOLIDAYS

France has lots of national holidays, most of them tied to the Catholic church calendar (Catholicism is the major religion in France). On these days, shops, businesses, government offices, and most restaurants are closed: New Year's Day (Jan 1); Easter Monday (late Mar or Apr); Labor Day (May 1); Liberation Day (May 8); Ascension Thursday (May or June, 40 days after Easter); Whit Monday, also called Pentecost Monday (51 days after Easter); Bastille Day (July 14); Assumption Day (Aug 15); All Saints' Day (Nov 1); Armistice Day (Nov 11); and Christmas Day (Dec 25).

In addition, schedules may be disrupted on Shrove Tuesday (the day before Ash Wednesday, in late winter) and Good Friday (late Mar or Apr).

PARIS CALENDAR OF EVENTS

When you arrive, check with the Paris Tourist Office and buy *Pariscope* (a weekly guide with an English-language insert), *Time Out,* or *L'Officiel des Spectacles* for dates, places, and other up-to-date information. Note that telephone access to the **Paris Tourist Office** (© 08-36-68-31-12) costs .35€ (45¢) per minute.

January

La Grande Parade de Montmartre. The big, brassy New Year's parade will make the mildest hangover hurt, but it shows that even a city renowned for elegance likes a little bit of Rose Bowl–style flash once a year. Elaborate floats represent everything from trade associations to the local firehouse, and there are majorettes and bands galore. The parade begins at 2pm from Porte St. Martin, 2e (Métro: Strasbourg-St-Denis) and winds its way to the Grand Boulevards. January 1.

Fête des Rois (Epiphany, or Three Kings Day). Wear a paper crown to celebrate the Feast of the Three Kings. On that day, it's traditional to eat a pie filled with almond paste, which conceals a charm usually made of ceramic (watch your teeth). It's sold at patisseries, and the crown comes with it. According to custom, whoever finds the charm becomes king or queen for the day. January 6.

La Mairie de Paris Vous Invite au Concert. A two-for-one special on a variety of jazz and classical concerts all over the city. The promotion lasts 2 weeks. Mid-January.

Commemorative Mass for Louis XVI. Yes, Parisians hold a Mass for a king their ancestors beheaded 200 years ago. It draws a full turnout of aristocrats and royalists, along with some far-right types. At the Chapelle Expiatoire, 29 rue Pasquier, 8e. Sunday closest to January 21.

February

Foire à la Feraille de Paris. Treasure hunters, here's your chance! This annual antiques and secondhand fair is held in the Parc Floral de Paris, a garden in the Bois de Vincennes in the 12e arrondissement that is pretty even in winter. For exact dates, call the **Paris Tourist Office** (see above).

Salon de l'Agriculture. Hundreds of farmers come to town to display their animals and produce. Regional food stands offer a great taste of corners of the country you may never get to visit, and the atmosphere is friendly and quintessentially French. At the Parc des Expositions de Paris, Porte de Versailles, 15e. For more information, call ✆ **01-49-09-60-00.** Last week of February to first week of March.

March

Foire du Trone. This annual carnival will chase away the end-of-winter blues with its fun Ferris wheel, rides and games, souvenirs, and fairground food. At the Pelouse de Reuilly in the Bois de Vincennes. Late March to end of May.

Prêt à Porter Fashion Shows. Although these shows are not open to the public, they're worth noting because hotels and restaurants are particularly booked up at this time. The same holds true for the autumn *prêt à porter* (ready-to-wear) shows, which are generally scheduled for early to mid-October. Mid-March.

La Passion à Ménilmontant. In a tradition that's been observed since 1932, actors and neighborhood residents perform the Passion Play (the events leading up to and including Christ's crucifixion) for a month around Easter. The play runs at the Théâtre de Ménilmontant, 20e. Call ✆ **01-46-36-98-60** for schedules and ticket prices. Mid-March to mid-April.

Le Chemin de la Croix (Stations of the Cross). Anyone can join the crowd that follows the Archbishop of Paris from the square Willette in Montmartre up the steps to the basilica of Sacré-Coeur and watch as he performs the 14 Stations of the Cross. 12:30pm on Good Friday. Call ✆ **01-53-41-89-00.** Métro: Anvers or Abbesses.

April

Poisson d'Avril (April Fool's Day). Local tradition is to stick a paper fish on the back of anyone unsuspecting, thereby awarding him or her a dunce cap. Phony newspaper articles are a tradition, too, so don't panic if you read about someone cloning sheep. (Hey, wait a minute . . .) April 1.

Paris Marathon. This popular race takes place around a variety of the city's monuments. Held on a Sunday, it attracts enthusiastic crowds. Starts at 9am, avenue des Champs-Elysées. ✆ **01-41-33-15-68;** www.parismarathon.com. First or second Sunday in April.

Foire de Paris. Parisians know spring has arrived when it's time for this huge fair. Hundreds of stands sell food and wine at excellent prices along with a variety of clothing and household goods. It's a great place to bargain hunt and people-watch. At the Parc des Expositions at the Porte de Versailles. © **01-49-09-61-21.** Late April to early May.

Grandes Eaux Musicales et les Fêtes de Nuit de Versailles. Try to get to at least one of these events during your visit. The Grandes Eaux Musicales bring the sounds of Bach, Mozart, or Berlioz to the fountains in the gardens of Versailles. They're held every Sunday from mid-April to mid-October, every Saturday June through August, and on national holidays in the same period. The Grandes Fêtes are a spectacular sound-and-light show with fireworks held one Saturday in June, three Saturdays in July, one Saturday in August, and two Saturdays in September. Château de Versailles, Versailles. For more information, visit www.chateau versailles.fr.

May

May Day. On the French version of Labor Day, you'll see people selling corsages made of the flower of the month, lily of the valley, all over the city. Banks, post offices, and most museums are closed. Although union membership has dwindled, there's a workers' parade that ends at the place de la Bastille. For more information, call the **Paris Tourist Office** (see above). May 1.

Vintage Car Rally, Montmartre. Held since 1924, this splendid array of antique cars makes its way through the streets of Montmartre starting at 10am in the tiny rue Lepic and ending at the place du Tertre. Sunday closest to May 15.

Les Cinq Jours Extraordinaire (The Five Extraordinary Days). These days *are* always extraordinary. The antiques shops in the rues du Bac, de Lille, de Beaune, des St-Pères, and de l'Université, and on the quai Voltaire, hold a free open house featuring some special

object that's been chosen according to the annual theme—one year it might be "Great Castles of Europe," the next "Voyages of Discovery." The whole quarter takes on a festive ambience, red carpets line the streets, and plants and flowers decorate shop fronts. © **01-42-61-18-77.** Third week of May.

D'Anvers aux Abbesses. Artists working in the Montmartre area open their studios to the public for 3 days. You just may meet the next Toulouse-Lautrec or Utrillo. Third week of May.

Journées Portes Ouvertes à Belleville. For two long weekends, more than 100 artists' studios in Belleville open to the public, offering a fascinating glimpse of contemporary painting and sculpture. Stop at 2 bd. de la Villette, 19e, for information and a map. Friday to Monday in mid-May.

French Open. One of tennis's Grand Slam events takes place in the Stade Roland Garros in the Bois de Boulogne on the western edge of the city, and tickets are much sought after. Unsold tickets go on sale 2 weeks before the tourney starts. The stadium is at 2 av. Gordon Bennett, 16e (© **01-47-43-48-00**). Last week in May and first week in June.

June

Fireworks at La Villette. Each year, a famous architect or designer is invited to create a fireworks display along the banks of the canal de l'Ourcq. Mid-June.

Festival Chopin à Paris. The Orangerie in the beautiful Bagatelle gardens on the edge of the Bois de Boulogne is the backdrop for this much-loved series of daily piano recitals. Mid-June to mid-July.

Fête de la Musique. Hear what all of France is listening to just by walking down the street. The entire country becomes a venue in celebration of the summer solstice; everything from jazz to the latest dance music is free in locations around Paris. There's usually a rock concert in the place de la République and a classical concert in the gardens of the Palais-Royal. ✆ 01-40-03-94-70. June 21.

Grand Prix de Paris. One of the most important and stylish horseracing events of the year in Paris is held at the Longchamp Racecourse in late June in the Bois de Boulogne. Late June.

Halle That Jazz. A lively, high-caliber jazz festival, held at the Grand Halle de la Villette in the Parc de la Villette, 211 av. Jean-Jaurès, 19e (✆ 01-40-03-75-03). Big-name talent might include Wynton Marsalis or Herbie Hancock. Late June to early July.

Fierté (Gay Pride). Fantastic floats, gorgeous drag queens, proud gays and lesbians, and the people and organizations that support them march in this huge, fun parade. It runs through the Marais and in other Paris streets, including the boulevard St-Michel. This event also includes art exhibits and concerts. For dates, call the Centre Gai et Lesbien (✆ 01-43-57-21-47). Usually last Sunday in June.

July

New Morning All-Stars' Festival. Every night at 8:30pm, the grand-daddy of Paris jazz clubs presents a different world-class talent. The club is at 7–9 rue des Petites-Ecuries, 10e. Call ✆ 01-45-23-51-41 for information. Daily in July.

Bastille Day. The French national holiday celebrates the storming of the Bastille on July 14, 1789. Festivities begin on the evening of the 13th with *bals,* or dances, held in fire stations all over the city. Some of the best are in the fire station on the rue du Vieux-Colombier near the place St-Sulpice,

6e; the rue Sévigné, 4e; and the rue Blanche, near the place Pigalle, 9e. The *bals* are free, though drinks aren't, and are open to all. On the 14th a big parade starts at 10am on the Champs-Elysées; get there early. Capping it all off is a sound-and-light show with terrific fireworks at the Trocadéro; it's extremely crowded, so many people watch the fireworks from the Champs de Mars across the river or from hotel rooms with views. July 13 and 14.

Paris, Quartier d'Eté. The emphasis during this festival is on open-air cultural events, including contemporary dance, music, and film. The outdoor cinema at the Parc de la Villette is a particularly popular part of this festival. ✆ 01-44-94-98-00. July 14 to August 15.

Tour de France. The most famous bicycle race in the world ends on the Champs-Elysées. Depending on the route, you can see the cyclists whir by elsewhere in Paris, too. Lance Armstrong has retired; who will take his place in 2006? Check the newspapers. ✆ 01-41-33-15-00. Ends in Paris usually on the third Sunday in July.

August

Fête de l'Assomption (Feast of the Assumption). Church services at Notre-Dame are the most popular and colorful on this important French holiday, and banners are draped from the church's towers to celebrate the day and a procession goes around the Ile de la Cité behind a statue of the Virgin Mary. ✆ 01-42-34-56-10. August 15.

September

Biennale des Antiquaires. One of the largest, most prestigious antiques shows in the world open to the public is held in even-numbered years. It runs in the Cour Carrée du Louvre, the underground exhibition space connected to the museum. For information, contact the **Paris Tourist Office** (see above). Early September.

Journées Portes Ouvertes. Hundreds of generally off-limits palaces, churches, and other official buildings throw open their doors for 2 days. Lines can be enormous, so plan what you want to see and show up early. A list and map of open buildings are available from the **Paris Tourist Office** (see above). Weekend closest to September 15.

Festival d'Automne. A wonderful arts festival held all over town is recognized throughout Europe for its programming and quality. Programs are available by mail so you can book ahead. Contact the Festival, 156 rue de Rivoli, 75001 Paris (℃ **01-53-45-17-00**). September 15 to December 31.

October

Fêtes des Vendanges à Montmartre. Celebrate the days when Montmartre was the city's vineyard. The wine produced from the neighborhood's one remaining vineyard, Clos Montmartre, is auctioned off at high prices to benefit local charities. (Word is that it's an act of charity to drink the stuff.) Locals dress in old-fashioned costumes, and the streets come alive with music. ℃ **01-46-06-00-32.** First or second Saturday of October.

Paris Auto Show. Held during even-numbered years in the exhibition halls at the Porte de Versailles, this show is an especially great place to check out the latest in European chrome. For more information, call the **Paris Tourist Office** (see above). Mid-October.

November

Mois de la Photo. Shows in many of the city's major museums and galleries celebrate the art of photography. Check listings in the weekly guide *Pariscope*. All month.

Beaujolais Nouveau. The sooner you drink it, the better—and to many, this means at midnight of the day the fruity red wine from north of Lyon is released to the public. Wine bars and cafes are packed, as are many bistros, so book ahead if you're going out to dinner. Third Thursday in November.

Festival d'Art Sacré de la Ville de Paris. A city-sponsored series of holiday concerts in the churches and monuments of Paris. November 25 to December 25.

Lancement des Illuminations des Champs-Elysées. The most glorious Christmas lights in Paris are the decorations hung in the trees lining this grand avenue. The annual inauguration of the lights makes for a festive evening, with jazz concerts and an international star du jour who pushes the symbolic button that lights up the avenue. For more information, call the **Paris Tourist Office** (see above). Late November.

December

La Crèche sur le Parvis. Each year a different foreign city installs a life-size manger scene in the plaza in front of the Hôtel de Ville (City Hall) at the invitation of the city of Paris. The crèche is open from 10am to 8pm. December 1 to January 3.

7 Health & Safety

STAYING HEALTHY

Unless you are arriving from an area known to be suffering from an epidemic, no inoculations are required to enter France.

Preservatifs (condoms) can be found at any pharmacy; machines in nearly every Métro station sell packages of four. Contraceptive *ovules* (suppositories) and *éponges* (sponges) are available in pharmacies. For questions and emergencies concerning sexuality, contraception, and abortion, contact the **Mouvement Français pour le Planning Familial,** 10 rue Vivienne, 2e (© **01-42-60-93-20;** Métro: Bourse).

GENERAL AVAILABILITY OF HEALTH CARE

If you do get sick or need a prescription refilled, you might want to ask the concierge at your hotel to recommend a local doctor—even his or her own. Or you can do as Parisians do: Call **SOS Médecins** (see "Fast Facts: Paris," in chapter 4) and ask for an English-speaking doctor. Most speak at least some English. The doctor will come to your hotel at any time of the day or night (usually within an hour of calling) for about $75. *Note:* In France some medications have different names than in North America (Tylenol, for example, is known as Panadol, but Advil is Advil.)

DIETARY RED FLAGS   Paris should not pose any major health hazards, although some travelers suffer from diarrhea caused by a change in normal intestinal bacteria. It's usually nothing to worry about; just take along some anti-diarrhea medicine. Although the water in France is considered safe, if you're prone to intestinal difficulties, you might want to consume mineral water only, at least for the first few days. Sometimes travelers find that a change of diet in France leads to constipation. If this occurs, eat a high-fiber diet and drink plenty of water.

WHAT TO DO IF YOU GET SICK AWAY FROM HOME

Medical care in France is very advanced; payment for foreign patients needs to be made at the time of care. Prescriptions are needed for most medications, although pharmacists here have the power to prescribe some antibiotics and other medications that only doctors can prescribe in the U.S. It doesn't hurt to talk first to a pharmacist before calling a doctor.

In most cases, your existing health plan will provide the coverage you need. Bring your insurance ID card with you when you travel.

If you suffer from a chronic illness, consult your doctor before your departure. For conditions like epilepsy, diabetes, or heart problems, wear a **MedicAlert Identification Tag** (© **800/825-3785;** www.medicalert.org), which will immediately alert doctors to your condition and give them access to your records through MedicAlert's 24-hour hot line.

Pack **prescription medications** in your carry-on luggage and carry them in their original containers, with pharmacy labels—otherwise they won't make it through airport security. Also bring along copies of your prescriptions in case you lose your pills or run out. Don't forget an extra pair of contact lenses or prescription glasses. Carry the generic name of prescription medicines, in case a local pharmacist is unfamiliar with the brand name.

Contact the **International Association for Medical Assistance to Travellers (IAMAT)** © **716/754-4883** or 416/652-0137; www.iamat.org) for tips on travel and health concerns in the countries you're visiting, and lists of local, English-speaking doctors. The United States **Centers for Disease Control and Prevention** (© **800/311-3435;** www.cdc.gov) provides up-to-date information on necessary vaccines and health hazards by region or country. Any foreign consulate can provide a list of area doctors who speak English. If you get sick, consider asking your hotel concierge to recommend a local doctor. You can also try the emergency room at a local hospital; many have walk-in clinics for emergency cases that are not life-threatening. You may not get immediate attention, but you won't pay the high price of an emergency room visit.

STAYING SAFE

Pickpocketing around major tourist sites (such as the Eiffel Tower and the Notre-

Dame) and in the Métro is the extent of any crime problem in Paris. It's generally a safe city, day and night, in most neighborhoods. Avoid walking alone (especially for female travelers) around Pigalle and Les Halles after midnight. Always keep your purse and backpack zipped and hug them securely around crowds and in the Métro. Thieves have been known to pick up a purse from a concert hall floor; keep your purse and shopping bags in your lap or under your feet, even at the symphony or the opera!

8 Specialized Travel Resources

TRAVELERS WITH DISABILITIES

Most disabilities shouldn't stop anyone from traveling. There are more options and resources out there than ever before.

When planning a trip to France, contact a **French Government Tourist Office** (see "Visitor Information," earlier in this chapter) for a publication with an English glossary called *Touristes Quand Même.* It provides a province-by-province overview of facilities for people with disabilities in the French transportation system and at monuments and museums.

Nearly all modern hotels in France have rooms modified for the needs of travelers with disabilities. Older hotels, unless they've been renovated, might not provide such features as elevators, special toilet facilities, or ramps. For a list of accessible hotels in France, write to **L'Association des Paralysés de France,** 22 rue de Père Guérion, 75013 Paris (℡ 08-00-85-49-76).

In France, high-speed and intercity trains are equipped for wheelchair access, and space is available in first class (at the price of a second-class ticket) for wheelchairs. Reserve well in advance. For further info, call French Rail, known as **SNCF,** or visit the helpful website (℡ 08-92-35-35-35; www.sncf.com/indexe.htm). Calls cost .35€ (45¢) per minute.

Public transportation in Paris isn't readily accessible to people with disabilities because most Métro stations don't have elevators or escalators. The newly built line 14 of the Métro is wheelchair accessible, as are the stations Nanterre-Université, Vincennes, Noisiel, St-Maur–Créteil, Torcy, Auber, Cité-Universitaire, St-Germain-en-Laye, Charles-de-Gaulle–Etoile, Nanterre-Ville, and several others. Bus no. 91, which links the Bastille with Montparnasse, is wheelchair accessible, as are new buses on order. Contact **Les Compagnons du Voyage** of the RATP, the Paris public transportation system (℡ 01-45-83-67-77; www.ratp.fr), for help in planning an itinerary.

Also contact the **Groupement pour l'Insertion des Personnes Handicapées Physiques (Help for the Physically Handicapped),** Paris Office, 98 rue de la Porte Jaune, 92210 St-Cloud (℡ 01-41-83-15-15).

Many travel agencies offer customized tours and itineraries for travelers with disabilities. **Flying Wheels Travel** (℡ 507/451-5005; www.flyingwheelstravel.com) offers escorted tours and cruises that emphasize sports and private tours in minivans with lifts. **Accessible Journeys** (℡ 800/846-4537 or 610/521-0339; www.disabilitytravel.com) caters to slow walkers and wheelchair travelers and their families and friends.

Organizations that offer assistance to travelers with disabilities include the **Moss Rehab Hospital** (℡ 800/CALL-MOSS; www.mossresourcenet.org), which provides a library of accessible-travel resources online; the **Society for Accessible Travel and Hospitality** (℡ 212/447-7284; www.sath.org; annual membership fees: $45 adults, $30 seniors and students), which offers a wealth of travel resources for all types of disabilities and informed recommendations on destinations, access guides, travel agents, tour operators, vehicle rentals, and companion services; and the **American Foundation for the Blind** (© **800/232-5463;** www.afb.org), which provides information on traveling with Seeing Eye dogs.

For more information specifically targeted to travelers with disabilities, the community website **iCan** (www.icanonline.net/channels/travel/index.cfm) has destination guides and several regular columns on accessible travel. Also check out the quarterly magazine *Emerging Horizons* ($15 per year, $20 outside the U.S.; www.emerginghorizons.com); **Twin Peaks Press** (© **360/694-2462**), offering travel-related books for travelers with special needs; and *Open World Magazine,* published by the Society for Accessible Travel and Hospitality (see above; subscription: $18 per year, $35 outside the U.S.).

GAY & LESBIAN TRAVELERS

France is one of the world's most tolerant countries toward gays and lesbians, and there are no special laws that discriminate against them. Sexual relations are legal for consenting partners 16 and over. However, one doesn't come of legal age in France until 18, so there could be problems with having sex with anyone under 18. Paris is the center of gay life in France; gay and lesbian establishments exist throughout the provinces as well.

"Gay Paree," with one of the world's largest homosexual populations, has dozens of gay clubs, restaurants, organizations, and services. Other than publications (see below), one of the best information sources on gay and lesbian activities is the **Centre Gai et Lesbien,** 3 rue Keller, 11e (© **01-43-57-21-47;** www.cglparis.org; Métro: Bastille). Well equipped to dispense information and coordinate the activities and meetings of gay people from virtually everywhere, it's open daily 2 to 8pm.

La France Gaie et Lesbienne (the France Queer Resource Directory; www.france.qrd.org) is a good resource.

For advice on HIV issues, call **F.A.C.T.S.** (© **01-44-93-16-69**) Monday, Wednesday, and Friday 6 to 10pm. The acronym stands for "Free AIDS Counseling Treatment and Support," and the English-speaking staff provides counseling, information, and doctor referrals.

Another helpful source is **La Maison des Femmes,** 163 rue Charenton, 12e (© **01-43-43-41-13;** http://maisondesfemmes.free.fr) Métro: Charonne), which offers information about Paris for lesbians and bisexual women and sometimes sponsors dinners and get-togethers. Call Monday, Wednesday, or Friday from 3 to 8pm for further information.

Gay magazines that focus mainly on cultural events include *Illico* (free in gay bars, about 2€/$2.50 at newsstands) and *e.m@le* (available free at bars and bookstores). Women might like to pick up a copy of *Lesbia,* at least to check the ads. These publications and others are available at Paris's largest gay bookstore, **Les Mots à la Bouche,** 6 rue Ste-Croix-la-Bretonnerie, 4e (© **01-42-78-88-30;** Métro: Hôtel-de-Ville). It's open Monday to Saturday 11am to 11pm, Sunday 3 to 8pm, and carries French- and English-language publications.

The International Gay & Lesbian Travel Association (IGLTA) (© **800/448-8550** or 954/776-2626; www.iglta.org) is the trade association for the gay and lesbian travel industry, and offers an online directory of gay- and lesbian-friendly travel businesses; go to its website and click on "Members."

Many agencies offer tours and travel itineraries specifically for gay and lesbian travelers. **Now, Voyager** (© **800/255-6951;** www.nowvoyager.com) is a well-known San Francisco–based gay-owned and -operated travel service. The following travel guides are available at most travel bookstores and gay and lesbian bookstores: *Frommer's Gay & Lesbian Europe,* an excellent travel resource;

PlanetOut (www.planetout.com), which offers electronic guidebooks packed with solid information on the global gay and lesbian scene; ***Spartacus International Gay Guide*** and ***Odysseus,*** both annual English-language guidebooks for gay men; the ***Damron*** guides, with separate, annual books for gay men and lesbians; and *Gay Travel A to Z: The World of Gay & Lesbian Travel Options at Your Fingertips,* by Marianne Ferrari (available from Amazon.com or Ferrari Publications; Box 35575, Phoenix, AZ 85069), a very good gay and lesbian guidebook series.

SENIOR TRAVEL

Mention the fact that you're a senior when you make your travel reservations. Discounts abound in Paris for seniors—from reduced museum admission to train tickets. France's consideration for seniors is apparent in the availability of a **Carte Senior.** With this card, travelers over 60 receive 20% to 50% discounts on train trips, except during holidays and periods of peak travel. The Carte Senior also allows some discounts on entrance to museums and historic sites. A card for an unlimited number of train rides, valid for 1 year, costs 50€ ($63) at any SNCF station. Be prepared to show an ID or a passport as proof of age when you buy the card.

Members of **AARP** (formerly known as the American Association of Retired Persons), 601 E St. NW, Washington, DC 20049 (© **800/424-3410** or 202/434-2277; www.aarp.org), get discounts on hotels, airfares, and car rentals. AARP offers members a wide range of benefits, including *AARP: The Magazine* and a monthly newsletter. Anyone over 50 can join.

Many reliable agencies and organizations target the 50-plus market. **Elderhostel** (© **877/426-8056;** www.elderhostel.org) arranges study programs for those 55 and over (and a spouse or companion of any age) in the U.S. and in more than 80 countries. Most courses last 5 to 7 days in the U.S. (2–4 weeks abroad), and may include airfare, accommodations in university dorms or modest inns, meals, and tuition.

Recommended publications offering travel resources and discounts for seniors include: the quarterly magazine ***Travel 50 & Beyond*** (www.travel50andbeyond.com); ***Travel Unlimited: Uncommon Adventures for the Mature Traveler*** (Avalon); ***101 Tips for Mature Travelers,*** available from Grand Circle Travel (© **800/221-2610** or 617/350-7500; www.gct.com); ***The 50+ Traveler's Guidebook*** (St. Martin's Press); and ***Unbelievably Good Deals and Great Adventures That You Absolutely Can't Get Unless You're Over 50*** (McGraw-Hill).

FAMILY TRAVEL

If you have enough trouble getting your kids out of the house in the morning, dragging them thousands of miles away may seem like an insurmountable challenge. But family travel can be immensely rewarding, giving you new ways of seeing the world through smaller pairs of eyes.

In Paris, sidewalks can be jammed with people at all hours; consider staying at a hotel next to a large park to give kids some space to run and play. The area around the Luxembourg gardens is especially kid-friendly, as the neighborhood is residential, youngish, and not very crowded. The same goes for the area around the Eiffel Tower, with the Champs de Mars providing a great outdoor space.

Booking a triple or quadruple room will almost always be less expensive than getting two rooms. Even better, travelers with kids might benefit most from renting their own apartments (see "Living Like a Parisian," in chapter 5) or check www.lodgis.com.

In France, children are prohibited from riding in the front seat of a car. Find out if the place at which you're staying stocks baby food, and if not, take some with you and plan to buy some.

Most hotels can arrange babysitting, but you should hold out as long as you can for a sitter with at least a rudimentary knowledge of English.

People under 18 are admitted free to France's national museums, but not necessarily to Paris's city museums.

If you have a child under 12 and will be traveling by rail, check out the **Carte Enfant Plus.** Available at any SNCF station, it offers a 50% discount for the child and up to four adult travel companions. It costs 65€ ($81) and is good for a month, but only a limited number of seats are available, and the discounts aren't offered for periods of peak travel or on holidays. Reserve in advance.

Familyhostel (℃ 800/733-9753; www.learn.unh.edu/familyhostel) takes the whole family, including kids 8 to 15, on moderately priced domestic and international learning vacations. Lectures, field trips, and sightseeing are guided by a team of academics.

You can find good family-oriented vacation advice on the Internet from sites like the **Family Travel Network** (www.familytravelnetwork.com); **Traveling Internationally with Your Kids** (www.travelwithyourkids.com), a comprehensive site offering sound advice for long-distance and international travel with children; and **Family Travel Files** (www.thefamilytravelfiles.com), which offers an online magazine and a directory of off-the-beaten-path tours and tour operators for families.

How to Take Great Trips with Your Kids (The Harvard Common Press) is full of good general advice that can apply to travel anywhere.

STUDENT TRAVEL

Paris, with its huge population of native and foreign students, has all sorts of organizations that provide information on discounts. **OTU Voyages,** 119 rue St-Martin, 75004 Paris (℃ 01-40-29-12-12; www.otu.fr; Métro: Châtelet), can help you find lodgings in hostels, economical hotels, or (usually in summer) University of Paris dorms (see chapter 5). It can also negotiate discounted rail, bus, and plane tickets; issue student IDs; and supply details about activities of special interest to young people. It's open Monday to Friday 10am to 6:30pm, Saturday 10am to 5pm.

It's a good idea to bring along an **International Student Identity Card (ISIC),** which offers substantial savings on rail passes, plane tickets, and entrance fees. It also provides you with basic health and life insurance and a 24-hour help line. The card is available for $22 from **STA Travel** (℃ 800/781-4040, and if you're not in North America, there's probably a local number in your country; www.sta travel.com), the biggest student travel agency in the world. If you're no longer a student but are still under 26, you can get an **International Youth Travel Card (IYTC)** for the same price from the same people, which entitles you to some discounts (but not on museum admissions).

In Paris, the STA travel offices are called Voyages Wasteels, and there are several branches. The most convenient is at 113 bd. Saint-Michel, 5e (℃ 01/43-26-93-92; www.wasteels.fr), where you can buy the ISIC for 15€ ($19).

If you're not a student but under 26, you can get a GO 25 card from the same organization. It gets you the insurance and some of the discounts, but not student admission to museums.

France's national train network, the SNCF, sells a **12–25 card.** Valid for 1 year, the card costs 50€ ($63) and offers 25% to 50% discounts to people 12 to 25. Even without the card, the 12-to-25 set can get 25% off on trains, except during peak travel periods and holidays. For more information, ask at any rail ticket office in France or contact the SNCF (© 01-47-23-54-02; www.sncf.fr).

Travel CUTS (© 800/667-2887 or 416/614-2887; www.travelcuts.com) offers similar services for both Canadians and U.S. residents. Irish students should turn to USIT (© 01/602-1600; www.usitnow.ie).

The Hanging Out Guides (www. frommers.com/hangingout), published by Frommer's, is the top student travel series for today's students, covering everything from adrenaline sports to the hottest club and music scenes.

9 Planning Your Trip Online

SURFING FOR AIRFARES

The "big three" online travel agencies, **Expedia.com, Travelocity,** and **Orbitz,** sell most of the air tickets bought on the Internet. (Canadian travelers should try expedia.ca and Travelocity.ca; U.K. residents can go to expedia.co.uk and opodo. co.uk.)

Each has different business deals with the airlines and may offer different fares on the same flights, so it's wise to shop around. Expedia.com and Travelocity will also send you **e-mail notification** when a cheap fare becomes available to your favorite destination. Of the smaller travel agency websites, **SideStep** (www.sidestep. com) has received the best reviews from Frommer's authors. It's a browser add-on that purports to "search 140 sites at once," but in reality only beats competitors' fares as often as other sites do.

Also remember to check **airline websites,** especially those for low-fare carriers such as EasyJet or RyanAir, whose fares are often misreported or simply missing from travel agency websites. Even with major airlines, you can often shave a few bucks from a fare by booking directly through the airline and avoiding a travel agency's transaction fee. But you'll get these discounts only by **booking online:** Most airlines now offer online-only fares that even their phone agents know nothing about. For the websites of airlines that fly to and from your destination, go to "Getting There," later in this chapter.

Great **last-minute deals** are available through free weekly e-mail services

provided directly by the airlines. Most of these are announced on Tuesday or Wednesday and must be purchased online. Most are only valid for travel that weekend, but some (such as Southwest's) can be booked weeks or months in advance. Sign up for weekly e-mail alerts at airline websites or check megasites that compile comprehensive lists of last-minute specials, such as **Smarter Living** (http:/smarterliving. com). For last-minute trips, **site59.com** in the U.S. and **lastminute.com** in Europe often have better deals than the major-label sites. U.K. travelers can try www.ebookers.com for the lowest fares to Paris, last minute or otherwise.

If you're willing to give up some control over your flight details, use an **opaque fare service** like **Priceline** (www. priceline.com; www.priceline.co.uk for Europeans) or **Hotwire** (www.hotwire. com). Both offer rock-bottom prices in exchange for travel on a "mystery airline" at a mysterious time of day, often with a mysterious change of planes en route. The mystery airlines are all major, well-known carriers—and the possibility of being sent from Philadelphia to Chicago via Tampa is remote; the airlines' routing computers have gotten a lot better than they used to be. But your chances of getting a 6am or 11pm flight are pretty high. Hotwire tells you flight prices before you buy; Priceline usually has better deals than Hotwire, but you have to play their "name our price" game. If you're new at this, the helpful folks at **BiddingFor-Travel** (www.biddingfortravel.com) do a

Frommers.com: The Complete Travel Resource

For an excellent travel-planning resource, we highly recommend Frommers.com (www.frommers.com). We're a little biased, of course, but we guarantee you'll find the travel tips, reviews, monthly vacation give-aways, and online-booking capabilities indispensable. Among the special features are our popular **Message Boards,** where Frommer's readers post queries and share advice (sometimes even our authors show up to answer questions); **Frommers.com Newsletter,** for the latest travel bargains and insider travel secrets; and **Frommer's Destinations Section,** where you'll get expert travel tips, hotel and dining recommendations, and advice on the sights to see for more than 3,000 destinations around the globe. When your research is done, the **Online Reservations System** (www.frommers.com/ book_a_trip) takes you to Frommer's preferred online partners for booking your vacation at affordable prices.

good job of demystifying Priceline's prices. Priceline and Hotwire are great for flights within North America and between the U.S. and Europe. But for flights to other parts of the world, consolidators will almost always beat their fares.

10 Getting There

BY PLANE

Flying time to Paris from London is 45 minutes; from Dublin, 1½ hours; from New York, 7 hours; from Chicago, 9 hours; from Los Angeles, 11 hours; from Atlanta, 8 hours; from Miami, 8½ hours; from Washington, D.C., 7½ hours; and from Sydney, 22 hours.

Air France (www.airfrance.com) is by far the largest airline operating to Paris. Its main hub is at the expansive postmodern Aerogare 2 at Charles de Gaulle and has six sub-terminals (2A, 2B, 2C, 2D, 2E, and 2F). Terminal 2E has now partially reopened after the roof collapsed in 2004; most flights from the U.S. land in either 2C, 2E, or 2F. You'll have to walk or take the underground moving escalators or a free shuttle van *(navette)* between these various terminals. Consult the airport's website (www.paris-cdg.com) for maps of the terminals and other detailed information.

Air France's main U.S. partner, Delta, operates out of terminal 2C; Air Canada uses 2A; British Airways uses 2D; American Airlines uses 2A; Continental uses 2C; Japan Airlines uses 2F.

Other international airlines fly into Terminal 1, including United, Lufthansa, Aer Lingus, British Midland, KLM, and South African Airways.

Charter airlines and EasyJet operate out of Terminal 3, known as T9.

Air France is the largest operator at Paris Orly Airport, although most of the flights here are domestic. The airline operates out of Orly Ouest (West Terminal), providing hourly "shuttle" flights to cities in France such as Nice, Bordeaux, and Toulouse, as well as some European destinations. Orly Sud (South Terminal) is used by some international airlines, charter airlines, and low-cost European airlines such as EasyJet.

Note: If you have a choice, flying into Orly is always more convenient than Charles de Gaulle: It's closer to the city and it's less expensive to reach central Paris.

Also consider flying into another European city and proceeding from there to Paris by train or bus. From Australia and the U.S., flights to Paris are generally more expensive than flights to London, so finding a cheap flight to London, then taking the train or even flying on a budget airline to Paris may be your best bet for the cheapest fare. That said, sometime during the fall and winter, airlines have sale fares to Paris that are the same price as flights to London—it's rare, but possible. Always check multiple websites before you decide whether to fly to London or Paris.

Most carriers offer a popular **advance purchase excursion (APEX)** fare that requires a 14-day advance payment and a stay of 7 to 30 days. In most cases this ticket is not refundable if you change flight dates or destinations.

FLYING FROM THE U.S. United (© 800/538-2929; www.united.com) flies nonstop from San Francisco, Chicago, and Washington Dulles. American (© 800/433-7300; www.aa.com) flies from New York's JFK, Chicago, and Dallas. U.S. Air (© 800/428-4322; www.usair.com) flies from Philadelphia. Continental (© 800/528-0280; www.continental.com) flies from Houston and Newark. Northwest (© 800/225-2525; www.nwa.com) flies from Detroit. Delta (© 800/241-4141; www.delta.com) flies from JFK, Atlanta, and Cincinnati.

Air France (© 800/237-2747; www.airfrance.com) flies to Paris daily from New York's JFK; Newark; Washington, D.C.; Boston; Miami; Chicago; Cincinnati; Atlanta; Houston; San Francisco; and Los Angeles. British Airways (© 800/247-9297; www.ba.com) flies to London nonstop from many U.S. cities and provides immediate onward connecting flights to Paris.

FLYING FROM THE U.K. EasyJet (© 0870-6000-000; www.easyjet.com) flies out of Luton and has up to five daily flights to Paris Charles de Gaulle; fares can be as low as $45 each way. British Airways (© 0845-773-3377; www.ba.com) and BMI (© 0870-607-0555; www.britishmidland.com) have both drastically lowered their fares to Paris to try and compete with EasyJet and have been offering flights from Heathrow and Gatwick for as low as $49 each way at press time. Air France (© 0845-0845-111; www.airfrance.com) has been lowering fares as well and flies to Charles de Gaulle from Heathrow. Nonstop flights to Paris are also available from Edinburgh, Bristol, Jersey, Leeds Bradford, Liverpool, Newcastle, Manchester and Southampton. Contact BMI, BA, or Air France (above).

From Dublin, rock-bottom fares are available on RyanAir (© 01-844-4400 in Ireland; www.ryanair.com) that flies five daily jets into Beauvais airport, an hour north of Paris. Aer Lingus (© 01-886-2222 in Ireland; www.aerlingus.com) has been trying to compete with RyanAir and has drastically reduced its fares from Dublin to Paris Charles de Gaulle.

FLYING FROM AUSTRALIA From Sydney, Emirates Airlines (© 02-929-09700 in Australia; www.emirates.com) has competitive rates (all flights connect in Dubai); but you must shop around and call various tour operators and consolidators to find the lowest fare. Qantas (© 13-13-13 in Australia; www.qantas.com.au) has good fares on its code-share flights operated by Air France. All flights make a refueling stop in Singapore.

GETTING INTO TOWN FROM THE AIRPORT

From both Charles de Gaulle and Orly, the most convenient way into central

Paris is on the Air France buses (you need not be flying Air France to use this service). See "Orientation," in chapter 4 for detailed information on this service.

From Charles de Gaulle, it's about a 45-minute drive to the city; it's 35 minutes from Orly.

GETTING THROUGH THE AIRPORT

You should be fine if you arrive at the airport **1 hour** before a domestic flight and **2 hours** before an international flight; if you show up late, tell an airline employee and he or she will probably whisk you to the front of the line.

Bring a **current government-issued photo ID** such as a driver's license or passport, and if you've got an e-ticket, print out the **official confirmation page;** you'll need to show your confirmation at the security checkpoint, and your ID at the ticket counter or the gate. (Children under 18 do not need photo IDs for domestic flights, but the adults checking in with them do.)

If you have trouble standing for long periods of time, tell an airline employee; the airline will provide a wheelchair. Speed up security by **not wearing metal objects** such as big belt buckles or earrings. If you've got metallic body parts, a note from your doctor can prevent a long chat with the security screeners. Keep in mind that only **ticketed passengers** are allowed past security, except for folks escorting passengers with disabilities, or children.

Federalization has stabilized **what you can carry on** and **what you can't.** The general rule is that sharp things are out, nail clippers are okay, and food and beverages must be passed through the X-ray machine—but that security screeners can't make you drink from your coffee cup. Bring food in your carry-on rather than checking it, as explosive-detection machines used on checked luggage have been known to mistake food (especially

chocolate, for some reason) for bombs. Travelers in the U.S. are allowed one carry-on bag, plus a "personal item" such as a purse, briefcase, or laptop bag. Carry-on hoarders can stuff all sorts of things into a laptop bag; as long as it has a laptop in it, it's still considered a personal item. The Transportation Security Administration (TSA) has issued a list of restricted items; check its website (www.tsa.gov/public/index.jsp) for details.

Passengers with e-tickets and without checked bags can still beat the ticket-counter lines by using **electronic kiosks** or even **online check-in.** Ask your airline which alternatives are available, and if you're using a kiosk, bring the credit card you used to book the ticket. If you're checking bags, you will still be able to use most airlines' kiosks; call your airline for up-to-date info. **Curbside check-in** is also a good way to avoid lines, although a few airlines still ban it; call before you go.

The TSA also asks that you **not lock your checked luggage,** so screeners can search it by hand if necessary. The agency says to use plastic "zip ties" instead, which you can get at hardware stores and can be easily cut off.

FLYING FOR LESS: TIPS FOR GETTING THE BEST AIRFARE

Passengers sharing the same airplane cabin rarely pay the same fare. Travelers who need to purchase tickets at the last minute, change their itinerary at a moment's notice, or fly one-way often get stuck paying the premium rate. Here are some ways to keep your airfare costs down:

- Passengers who can book their ticket **well in advance,** who can **stay over Saturday night,** or who **fly midweek** or **at less-trafficked hours** will pay a fraction of the full fare. If your schedule is flexible, say so, and ask if you can secure a cheaper fare by changing your flight plans.

- You can also save on airfares by keeping an eye out in local newspapers for **promotional specials** or **fare wars,** when airlines lower prices on their most popular routes. You rarely see fare wars offered for peak travel times, but if you can travel in the off-months, you may snag a bargain.

- Search **the Internet** for cheap fares (see "Planning Your Trip Online," earlier in this chapter).

- **RTV Voyages** has great deals on flights departing from Paris to many European and international destinations. Contact it at 8 rue Saint Marc, 2e (© **01-55-34-90-30;** fax 01-55-34-90-31).

- **Consolidators,** also known as bucket shops, are great sources for international tickets, although they usually can't beat the Internet on fares within North America. Start by looking in Sunday newspaper travel sections; U.S. travelers should focus on the *New York Times, Los Angeles Times,* and *Miami Herald. Beware:* Bucket shop tickets are usually nonrefundable or rigged with stiff cancellation penalties, often as high as 50% to 75% of the ticket price, and some put you on charter airlines with questionable safety records.

- **STA Travel** (© **800/781-4040;** www.sta.com) offers good fares for travelers of all ages. **Flights.com** (© **800/TRAV-800;** www.flights.com) started in Europe and has excellent fares worldwide, but particularly to that continent. It also has "local" websites in 12 countries. **Air Tickets Direct** (© **800/778-3447;** www.airtickets direct.com) is based in Montreal and leverages the currently weak Canadian dollar for low fares; it'll also book trips to places that U.S. travel agents won't touch, such as Cuba.

- Join **frequent-flier clubs.** Accrue enough miles and you'll be rewarded with free flights and elite status. It's free, and you'll get the best choice of seats, faster response to phone inquiries, and prompter service if your luggage is stolen, your flight is canceled or delayed, or if you want to change your seat. You don't need to fly to build frequent-flier miles—**frequent-flier credit cards** can provide thousands of miles for doing your everyday shopping.

LONG-HAUL FLIGHTS: HOW TO STAY COMFORTABLE

Long flights can be trying; stuffy air and cramped seats can make you feel as if you're being sent parcel post in a small box. But with a little advance planning, you can make an otherwise unpleasant experience almost bearable.

Tips **Travel in the Age of Bankruptcy**

At press time, two major airlines in the United States were struggling in bankruptcy court, and most of the rest weren't doing very well either. To protect yourself, **buy your tickets with a credit card,** as the Fair Credit Billing Act guarantees that you can get your money back from the credit card company if a travel supplier goes under (and if you request the refund within 60 days of the bankruptcy). **Travel insurance** can also help, but make sure it covers against "carrier default" for your specific travel provider. And be aware that if a U.S. airline goes bust midtrip, a 2001 federal law requires other carriers to take you to your destination (albeit on a space-available basis) for a fee of no more than $25, provided you rebook within 60 days of the cancellation.

- Your choice of airline and airplane will definitely affect your legroom. Among U.S. airlines, American Airlines has the best average seat pitch (the distance between a seat and the row in front of it). Find more details at www.seatguru.com, which has extensive details about almost every seat on six major U.S. airlines. For international airlines, research firm Skytrax has posted a list of average seat pitches at www.airlinequality.com.

- Emergency-exit seats and bulkhead seats typically have the most legroom. Emergency-exit seats are usually assigned the day of a flight (to ensure that the seat is filled by someone able-bodied); it's worth getting to the ticket counter early to snag one of these for a long flight. Keep in mind that bulkheads are where airlines often put baby bassinets, so you may be sitting next to an infant.

- To have two seats for yourself, try for an aisle seat in a center section toward the back of coach. If you're traveling with a companion, book an aisle and a window seat. Middle seats are usually booked last, so chances are good you'll end up with three seats to yourselves. And in the event that a third passenger is assigned the middle seat, he or she will probably be more than happy to trade for a window or an aisle.

- To sleep, avoid the last row of any section or a row in front of an emergency exit, as these seats are the least likely to recline. Avoid seats near highly trafficked toilet areas. You also may want to reserve a window seat so that you can rest your head and avoid being bumped in the aisle.

- Get up, walk around, and stretch every 60 to 90 minutes to keep your blood flowing. This helps avoid deep vein thrombosis, or "economy-class syndrome," a rare and deadly condition that can be caused by sitting in cramped conditions for too long.

- Drink water before, during, and after your flight to combat the lack of humidity in airplane cabins—which can be drier than the Sahara. Bring a bottle of water onboard. Avoid alcohol, which will dehydrate you.

BY CAR

You shouldn't drive in Paris: The traffic is terrible, and car rental, parking, and the price of gas can be quite expensive. However, if you're planning on striking out on your own for other parts of France or Europe, what follows are a few tips on getting the best price for a rental car.

To get the best deal, always reserve before leaving home and always ask for all-inclusive rates that include full insurance (including taxes, collision damage waiver, and theft insurance) and unlimited kilometers. The least expensive cars are stick shift and have no air-conditioning, such as the tiny Ford Fiesta, Renault Clio, or Opel Corsa. Automatic cars are slowly becoming more prevalent and it never hurts to ask for a rate quote for one—usually, it's about $60 more per weekly rental for an automatic with air-conditioning (a must in summer). Picking up a car in Paris and dropping it off in any other city in France usually does not incur drop-off charges (a move to encourage tourism countrywide). **AutoEurope** works with a variety of car-rental companies (including Avis and Europcar) to find you the lowest rates. In the U.S. contact AutoEurope at ℭ **888/223-5555** or www.autoeurope.com; in the U.K., ℭ **0800-169-9797** or www.auto-europe.co.uk.

For the best weekly rental rates, contact **Europe by Car** (in the U.S. ℭ **800/223-1516,** 212/581-3040, or 213/272-0424; www.europebycar.com). Europe by Car also has the least expensive rates for rentals of 21 days or more and the flexibility to pick up your car in France and drop it off at another French or European city.

If you arrive in Paris and must rent a car, remember that you'll be paying premium rates if you just call a rental agency. *Tip:* Find an Internet cafe and book your reservation online with one of the above-mentioned companies.

Driving a car in Paris is definitely *not* recommended. Parking is difficult, and traffic is dense and at times ruthless. If you do drive, remember that a ring road called the *périphérique* circles Paris—and that exits are not numbered. Avoid rush hours!

Few hotels, except the luxury ones, have garages, but the staff can usually direct you to one nearby. The major highways in Paris are the **A1** from the north (Great Britain and Belgium); the **A13** from Normandy and other points in northwest France; the **A109** from Spain and the southwest; the **A7** from the Alps, the Riviera, and Italy; and the **A4** from eastern France.

The **National Road Travel Information Center** (© **01-48-99-33-33**) can give you details about road conditions and weather in the Paris area (it can also answer questions about the best routes to take and so on). For road information throughout France, call © 08-36-68-20-00.

For maps, approximate driving times, and other road information in France, consult the AA Route Planner website at www.theaa.com.

BY TRAIN

If you're in Europe, you may want to go to Paris by train, especially if you have a **Eurailpass.** For information, call the national train network, **SNCF** (© **08-92-35-35-35**) between 6am and 10pm, and ask for someone who speaks English, or go to a travel agent or an information booth at the stations.

Coming from northern Germany or Belgium (and sometimes London), you'll most likely arrive at **Gare du Nord.**

Trains from Normandy come into **Gare St-Lazare,** in northwest Paris. Trains from the west (Brittany, Chartres, Versailles, Bordeaux) head to **Gare de Montparnasse;** those from the southwest (the Loire Valley, the Pyrenees, Spain) to **Gare d'Austerlitz;** those from the south and southeast (the Riviera, Lyon, Italy, Geneva) to **Gare de Lyon.** From Alsace and eastern France, Luxembourg, southern Germany, and Zurich, the arrival station is **Gare de l'Est.** All stations are next to a Métro station with the same name and taxis are available at the taxi stand just outside each station. All the above train stations are in the center of Paris.

FROM THE U.K. BY FERRY & TUNNEL

About a dozen companies run hydrofoil, ferry, and hovercraft across *La Manche* (the sleeve), as the French call the channel. Services operate day and night. Most carry cars, but some hydrofoils carry passengers only. Hovercraft or hydrofoils make the trip in just 40 minutes; the shortest ferry route between Dover and Calais takes about 1½ hours.

The major routes are between Dover and Calais and between Folkestone and Boulogne (about 12 trips a day). Depending on weather conditions, prices and timetables can vary. It's important to make a reservation, because ferries are crowded.

For information stateside, call **Britrail** (© **800/677-8585**) or **Britain Bound Travel** (© **800/805-8210**). In Britain, contact **Hoverspeed** (© **0870/524-0241;** www.hoverspeed.com).

Special fares are offered but frequently change. A good travel agent—say, in London—can sort out the ferry schedules, find a good option, and book your ticket.

The **Channel Tunnel,** or "Chunnel," opened in 1994, and the popularity of its **Eurostar** (www.eurostar.com) train service has had the effect of driving down prices on all cross-Channel transport.

This remarkable engineering feat means that if you take your car aboard Le Shuttle in Britain, you can be driving in France an hour later. Tickets can be purchased in advance or at the tollbooth. Eurostar tickets start at £59 (about $99) round-trip off season if you book way in advance (several months is best to get the lowest fare) and stay over the weekend, but prices rise in April and in June. The trip from London Waterloo to Paris Gare du Nord takes 2½ hours. Taking yourself and your car across the Channel starts at about £60 ($100) each way. For further information and reservations contact Le Shuttle (✆ **08-25-82-88-28;** www.euro tunnel.com). RailEurope (in the U.S. **877/257-2887;** www.raileurope.com) also has some of the lowest Eurostar rates; the earlier you book, the more you save. Round-trip second-class tickets start at £90 ($150) and round-trip first class begin at £170 ($284).

BY BUS

Buses connect Paris to most major European cities. European Railways operates **Europabus** and **Eurolines.** They do not have American offices, so travelers must make arrangements after arriving in Europe. In **Great Britain,** contact National Express Eurolines (✆ **08705/808-080;** www.nationalexpress.com). In **Paris** the contact is Eurolines, 28 av. du General de Gaulle, 93541 Bagnolet (✆ **08-92-69-52-52;** www.eurolines.fr); phone access costs .35€ (45¢) per minute. International buses serve **Gare Routière Internationale** (International Bus Terminal) at avenue Charles de Gaulle in the suburb of Bagnolet. It's across the *périphérique* from the Gallieni Métro station.

11 Packages for the Independent Traveler

Before you start your search for the lowest airfare, you may want to consider booking your flight as part of a travel package. Package tours are not the same thing as escorted tours. Package tours are simply a way to buy the airfare, accommodations, and other elements of your trip (such as car rentals, airport transfers, and sometimes even activities) at the same time and often at discounted prices—kind of like one-stop shopping. Packages are sold in bulk to tour operators—who resell them to the public at a cost that usually undercuts standard rates.

One good source of package deals is the airlines themselves. Most major airlines offer air/land packages, including **American Airlines Vacations** (✆ 800/321-2121; www.aavacations.com), **Delta Vacations** (✆ 800/221-6666; www.delta vacations.com), **Continental Airlines Vacations** (✆ 800/301-3800; www.cool vacations.com), and **United Vacations** (✆ 888/854-3899; www.unitedvacations.

com). Several big **online travel agencies**—Expedia.com, Travelocity, Orbitz, Site59, and Lastminute.com—also do a brisk business in packages.

Air France Holidays (✆ 800/237-2623 in the U.S.; www.airfranceholidays.com) has great all-around packages to Paris that combine convenient flight schedules with terrific hotels. **EasyJet** (in the U.K. ✆ **0870/6000-000;** www.easyjet.com) has a great website that allows you to create your own discount package by adding hotel and car to your flight; but this'll work only if you're planning to fly to Paris from London or some other European city.

Travel packages are also listed in the travel section of your local Sunday newspaper. Or check ads in magazines such as *Arthur Frommer's Budget Travel Magazine, Travel + Leisure, National Geographic Traveler,* and *Condé Nast Traveler.*

Package tours can vary by leaps and bounds. Some offer a better class of hotels than others. Some offer the same hotels for lower prices. Some offer flights on scheduled airlines, while others book charters. Some limit your choice of accommodations and travel days. You are often required to make a large payment upfront. On the plus side, packages can save you money, offering group prices but allowing for independent travel. Some even let you add on a few guided excursions or escorted day trips (also at prices lower than if you booked them yourself) without booking an entirely escorted tour.

Before you invest in a package tour, get some answers. Ask about the **accommodation choices** and prices for each. Then look up the hotels' reviews in a Frommer's guide and check their rates for your specific dates of travel online. You'll also want to find out what **type of room** you get. If you need a certain type of room, ask for it; don't take whatever is thrown your way. Request a nonsmoking room, a quiet room, a room with a view, or whatever you fancy.

Finally, look for **hidden expenses.** Ask whether airport departure fees and taxes, for example, are included in the total cost.

12 Escorted General-Interest Tours

Escorted tours are structured group tours with a leader. The price usually includes everything from airfare to hotels, meals, tours, admission costs, and local transportation.

The two largest tour operators conducting escorted tours of France and Europe are **Globus/Cosmos** (© **800/221-0090;** www.globusandcosmos.com) and **Trafalgar** (www.trafalgartours.com). Both companies have first-class tours that run about $100 a day and budget tours for about $75 a day. The differences are mainly in hotel location and the number of activities. There's little difference in the companies' services, so choose your tour based on the itinerary and preferred date of departure. Brochures are available at travel agencies, and all tours must be booked through travel agents.

Escorted tours—whether by bus, motorcoach, train, or boat—let travelers sit back and enjoy their trip without having to spend lots of time behind the wheel. All the little details are taken care of, you know your costs upfront, and there are few surprises. Escorted tours can take you to the maximum number of sights in the minimum amount of time with the least amount of hassle.

On the downside, an escorted tour often requires a big deposit, and lodging and dining choices are predetermined. As part of a cloud of tourists, you'll get little opportunity for serendipitous interactions with locals.

Before you invest in an escorted tour, ask about the **cancellation policy:** Is a deposit required? Can they cancel the trip if they don't get enough people? Do you get a refund if they cancel? If *you* cancel? How late can you cancel if you are unable to go? When do you pay in full? *Note:* If you choose an escorted tour, think strongly about purchasing trip-cancellation insurance, especially if the tour operator asks you to pay upfront. See "Travel in the Age of Bankruptcy," earlier in this chapter.

You'll also want to get a complete **schedule** of the trip to find out how much sightseeing is planned each day and whether enough time has been allotted for relaxing or wandering solo.

The **size** of the group is also important to know upfront. Generally, the smaller the group, the more flexible the itinerary, and the less time you'll spend waiting for people to get on and off the bus. What is the gender breakdown? Is this mostly a trip for couples or singles?

Discuss what is included in the **price.** You may have to pay for transportation to and from the airport. A box lunch may be included in an excursion, but drinks might cost extra. Tips may not be included. Find out if you will be charged if you decide to opt out of certain activities or meals.

If you plan to travel alone, you'll need to know if a **single supplement** will be charged and if the company can match you up with a roommate.

13 Tips on Accommodations

If you don't mind the occasional oddly shaped (and usually very tiny) room or lugging your baggage up some stairs, you'll find that staying in a hotel in Paris doesn't have to significantly lighten your wallet. Though they may lack 24-hour room service and complimentary shower caps, these small, mostly family-run lodgings offer some things that most luxury hotels can't supply: hominess, intimacy, and a degree of authenticity. In general, budget-priced French accommodations are reliably clean and comfortable. On the other hand, if you are used to the amenities offered for the same money in North American motels, you may be disappointed. Many hotels are in old buildings that date from a less expansive era; rooms tend to be smaller than you would expect, even in expensive places. Toiletries are minimal and towels are small and scratchy. Also, most budget hotels in Paris do not have air-conditioning, but then again, Parisian summers are not known for their high temperatures (a recent, and very uncomfortable, exception were the record-breaking hot temperatures in Paris in June 2005). Many hotels do offer cable or satellite TV, which generally means access to English-language channels like CNN and BBC.

For affordable **apartment rentals** in the heart of Paris, contact Lodgis Paris at www.lodgis.com (see chapter 5).

For **home swapping,** www.trading-homes.com advertises several apartments in Paris as well as a few houses in the suburbs close to the city.

The French star ratings, posted on the outside of all hotels, are based on the size of the rooms and the number of amenities and have nothing to do with quality. It is not unusual to find a well-kept two-star hotel that is far nicer than a dumpy three-star that happens to have hair dryers in all its bathrooms. Under French law, the more stars you have, the more you are allowed to charge. In this guide, most hotels have either two or three stars.

Unlike the U.S., where budget chains make up a large chunk of the market, there is no prevailing hotel chain in Paris. Timhotel has a few excellent budget hotels around the city, but they are a very small chain. We recommend Timhotel Montmartre (p. 91).

SAVING ON YOUR HOTEL ROOM

The **rack rate** is the maximum rate that a hotel charges for a room. Hardly anybody pays this price, however. To lower the cost of your room:

- **Ask about special rates or other discounts.** Always ask whether a room less expensive than the first one quoted is available, or whether any special rates apply to you. You may qualify for corporate, student, military, senior, or other discounts. Find out the policy on children—do kids stay free in the room or is there a special rate?

- **Book online.** Many hotels offer Internet-only discounts, or supply rooms to Priceline, Hotwire, or Expedia.com at rates much lower than the ones you can get through the hotel itself.

- **Look into long-stay discounts.** If you're planning a long stay (at least 5 days), you might qualify for a discount.

As a general rule, expect 1 night free after a 7-night stay.

- **Avoid excess charges and hidden costs.** When you book a room, ask whether the hotel charges for parking. Use your own cellphone, pay phones, or prepaid phone cards instead of dialing direct from hotel phones.

14 Tips on Dining

The Parisian's reverence for fine cuisine is almost religious. It is part of his or her heritage. Whether it's *choucroute* from the Alsatian region or *lapin à la moutarde,* it is quintessentially French, and it is all fabulous. Popular salads include salade niçoise (with tuna, olives, and anchovies) and *salade de chef* (with ham, Swiss cheese, salami, and hard-boiled egg). Popular main courses include *boeuf bourguignon* (tender chunks of beef simmered in red-wine sauce with potatoes and onions); cassoulet (a rich stew made of white beans, dry sausage, onion, and duck); *magret de canard* (sliced breast of fattened duck sautéed and usually served with a wine-and-peppercorn sauce); different kinds of fish (salmon, cod) grilled and served with a butter-lemon-wine sauce, rice, and vegetables; *lapin à la moutarde* (rabbit cooked with mustard, crème fraîche, and usually white wine); and *choucroute* (sauerkraut cooked with juniper berries and wine and served with pork). You will eat extremely well in Paris.

Parisians don't eat much of a breakfast; it's usually just a croissant with a small "café" (an espresso) or a café au lait on the run. For both lunch and dinner, however, the French sit down and have a full meal, either two or three courses. Lunch is eaten between noon and 2pm (usually 12:30pm is when a lunch appointment is made); dinner is between 8 and 10pm with 8:30pm as the most common time for a dinner reservation.

A 15% service charge is included in your bill and it's very common to leave a tip of 4% to 7% in cash. Note that credit card slips in France do not have an area to add a tip so you must have cash with you. If service is exceptionally unpleasant, however, Parisians don't leave a tip, and you might want to do the same.

Local beers are least expensive: 1664 and Kronenbourg are the most popular. European beers such as Heineken and Amstel are a bit more expensive, but widely available.

Wine is excellent in France; even the least expensive house wines are good. For an aperitif, many Parisians order a Ricard or pastis (a licorice drink that becomes milky when water is added).

Nobody drinks beer with a meal in France. Parisians drink beer as an aperitif before a meal, and wine with dinner. The French almost always order a bottle of mineral water whether or not they are having wine. Specify if you'd like *plat* (still) or *gazeuse* (fizzy).

In many cafes, it's less expensive to take your coffee or beer standing up at the counter rather than sitting down at a table. This does not apply to the more fancy cafes (such as Café Marly or Café Beaubourg).

15 Recommended Books & Films

GENERAL

Janet Flanner's *Paris Was Yesterday* (Harvest Books, 1989) is a collection of articles written for the *New Yorker* on aspects of the city's life in the 1920s and 1930s; it's full of themes you can still observe today. Dealing with the same period—and America's Lost Generation—is Ernest Hemingway's *A Moveable Feast* (Touchstone Books, 1996). For a French perspective on life in the first decades of the 20th century, read Simone de Beauvoir's *Memoirs of a Dutiful Daughter* (HarperCollins, 1974), an account of the author's bourgeois upbringing. Julian Green's *Paris* (M. Boyars, 1993) is a wonderful evocation of life around the city. More recently, American author Adam Gopnik's *Paris to the Moon* (Random House, 2001) is a collection of essays he wrote for the *New Yorker* about his life in Paris during the 1990s with his wife and daughter.

History buffs will enjoy Simon Schama's *Citizens* (Vintage Books, 1990), an account of the French Revolution. For a biography of Louis XIV, see Nancy Mitford's *The Sun King* (Penguin USA, 1995). Madame de Sévigné's *Selected Letters* (Penguin USA, 1982) is a marvelous introduction to 17th-century France. For an intelligent vision of the city, illustrated with paintings and photographs, read John Russell's *Paris* (Abrams, 1983).

THE ARTS

Much of Paris's beauty is in its art. Three excellent books discussing this perspective are *The History of Impressionism,* by John Rewald (Museum of Modern Art, 1973); *The French Through Their Films,* by Robin Buss (Ungar, 1988); and *The Studios of Paris: The Capital of Art in the Late Nineteenth Century,* by John Milner (Yale University Press, 1988).

Modern-architecture enthusiasts will want to see the bilingual *Guide to Modern Architecture in Paris,* by Hervé Martin. It includes photographs as well as maps.

FICTION, TRAVEL & BIOGRAPHY

Paris plays a role in the works of many French writers. The city is often a primary character in their books, as in Honoré de Balzac's *Père Goriot* and Victor Hugo's *Les Misérables* and *Notre-Dame de Paris* (the latter is translated into English

as *The Hunchback of Notre Dame*). Marcel Proust's *Remembrance of Things Past* examines the paths of the aristocracy and the bourgeoisie during the Belle Epoque. Shorter and equally sensual are Colette's novels, including *Chéri* and *Gigi*.

Perhaps the best-known novel by a foreign writer is Charles Dickens's *A Tale of Two Cities,* set during the French Revolution. Henry James contrasted American innocence and French experience in such works as *The American* and *The Ambassadors.* Henry Miller's *Tropic of Cancer* and any of the journals of his lover, Anaïs Nin, will lead you into the heart of bohemia. Canadian Mavis Gallant often sets her short stories in Paris, where she lives. Carlos Fuentes's *Distant Relations* (Farrar, Straus & Giroux, 1982) also takes place partially in Paris—at the Automobile-Club de France on place de la Concorde, and in houses near Parc Monceau and in the 7e arrondissement. Diane Johnson's French comedies of manners, *Le Divorce* (Plume, 1998) and *Le Mariage* (Plume, 2001) provide wonderful glimpses of American expatriate and bourgeoisie life in Paris.

Edmund White, the well-known gay American writer, lived on Ile St-Louis for many years and wrote his *Farewell Symphony* (Random House, 1998) there. It describes the artistic and literary gay and bisexual scene of the late 1980s and early 1990s in Paris. White also wrote *The Flaneur: A Stroll Through the Paradoxes of Paris* (Bloomsbury, 2001), an informal, personal guide to a Paris that most tourists never explore.

FILMS

Something's Gotta Give (2004, with Jack Nicholson and Diane Keaton) featured many beautiful scenes of Paris. The closing sequence was filmed at the lovely (and highly recommended) brasserie, Le Grand Colbert (p. 118).

For an edge-of-your-seat view of Parisian streets, train stations, bridges and tunnels, watch the *Bourne Supremacy* (2003, starring Matt Damon as CIA agent Jason Bourne).

Le Divorce (directed by James Ivory, 2003) was filmed almost entirely in Paris. Kate Hudson learns about French manners, customs, and Parisian society, and there are several beautiful scenes in the city's finest restaurants that will make your mouth water. *French Kiss* (directed by Lawrence Kasdan, 1993) provides a great tour of neighborhoods in Paris as the two stars, Meg Ryan and Kevin Kline, chase each other on foot and by taxi, motorcycle, and train. There are also several great scenes at one of the city's toniest hotels, The George V. The acclaimed French-Polish film, *Blue* (directed by Krzystof Kieslowski, 1993) also includes many excellent shots of the city's neighborhoods.

To see how the Champs-Elysées and other famous sites looked in the 1950s, check out the Jean-Paul Belmondo classic *Breathless* (directed by Jean-Luc Godard, 1959). For a steamier look at the city, *Last Tango in Paris* (directed by Bernardo Bertolucci, 1973) stars Marlon Brando and Maria Schneider and has lots of sensual scenes that take place throughout Paris.

3

Suggested Paris Itineraries

Seeing Paris in 1 to 3 days is possible, but calls for some discipline and fast moving on your part. Of course, to fuel you for the marathon visit, I suggest doing as the Parisians do and sitting down to a two- or three-course lunch to experience not only the French love affair with gastronomy, but the pleasure of taking at least an hour to rest and savor a meal.

Don't forget to wear comfortable shoes, as you will be on your feet a lot. Start your voyage of discovery right outside your hotel door.

1 The Best of Paris in 1 Day

Since time is wasting, arise early and begin your day with some live "theater" by walking the streets around your hotel—Right Bank or Left Bank, it doesn't matter at this point. This walk can acclimate you faster than anything to the sights, sounds, and smells of the City of Light, and it gets you centered before you catch a taxi or hop aboard the Métro for a ride underground to your first attraction.

Instead of having breakfast in a stuffy hotel dining room, why not duck into a cafe for breakfast? It doesn't matter which one. On virtually every street in Paris you'll find a cafe, often more than one.

Any neighborhood will provide a slice of Parisian life, as you order breakfast as thousands of locals do. Sit back, enjoy, and breathe deeply before beginning your descent on Paris. **Start:** *Métro to Palais Royal-Musée du Louvre.*

❶ Musée du Louvre ★★★
You know you have to see the Louvre, one of the world's greatest art museums. You wouldn't dare go home without that citadel having been stormed. Since it opens at 9am, be among the first in line.

With your clock ticking, at least call on the "great ladies of the Louvre": the *Mona Lisa* with her enigmatic smile, the sexy *Venus de Milo,* and *Winged Victory* (alas, without a head). Try to allot at least 2 hours of viewing time for some world-class masterpieces. See p. 166.

Around 11am, go for a walk along:

❷ The Quays of the Seine ★★★
After leaving the Louvre, walk south toward the river and head east for a stroll along the Seine. You'll encounter the most splendid panoramic vistas that Paris has to offer. Trees shade the banks of the river, and 14 bridges span the Seine. So much of the city's fortune has depended on this river, and you'll be in the very nerve center of Paris life as you stroll along. So much the better if you buy a book from one of the vendors—called *bouquinistes*—or else a little painting from a sidewalk artist.

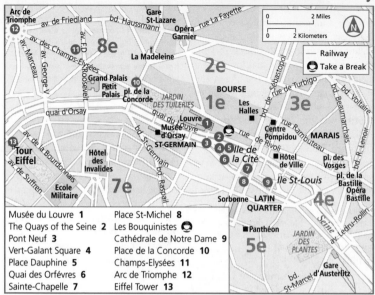

| 0 | 2 Miles |
| 0 | 2 Kilometers |

— Railway
🟢 Take a Break

Musée du Louvre **1**
The Quays of the Seine **2**
Pont Neuf **3**
Vert-Galant Square **4**
Place Dauphine **5**
Quai des Orfévres **6**
Sainte-Chapelle **7**

Place St-Michel **8**
Les Bouquinistes 🟢
Cathédrale de Notre Dame **9**
Place de la Concorde **10**
Champs-Elysées **11**
Arc de Triomphe **12**
Eiffel Tower **13**

You'll see Paris's greatest island in the Seine, the Cité, emerging before you. Cross over the:

③ Pont Neuf

The oldest and most evocative of the bridges of Paris, Pont Neuf (p. 173) dates from 1578 and looks much as it did then. From the bridge, the view down (or up) the river is perhaps the most memorable in Paris.

Walk down the steps, emerging on your right along Pont Neuf to:

④ Vert-Galant Square

The steps take you behind the statue dedicated to Henri IV to Vert-Galant Square (p. 173) at the western tip of Ile de La Cité. The square takes its designation from the nickname given Henry IV, meaning "old spark." The square is the best vantage point for viewing Pont Neuf and the Louvre.

As you stand on this square, you'll be at the "prow" of Cité if you liken the island to a giant ship. After taking in that view, continue east, pausing at the:

⑤ Place Dauphine

This square—perfect for a picnic—was named in honor of the Dauphin, the future Louis XIII. It faces the towering mass of the Conciergerie (p. 172), whose gloomy precincts and memories of the French Revolution you can save for another visit to Paris.

With time moving on, head east along:

⑥ Quai des Orfèvres

This Seine-bordering quay leads east to Notre-Dame. It was the former market of the jewelers of 17th and 18th century Paris. Marie Antoinette's celebrated necklace, subject of countless legends, was fashioned here.

The quay leads you to:

⑦ Sainte-Chapelle

This Gothic chapel (p. 169) is sublime, its upper chapel like climbing into Tiffany's most luxe jewel box. As the colored light from the 13th century bathes you, take in what is perhaps the most brilliantly colored "walls of glass" in the world. We rank taking in the deep glow of these astonishing windows as one of the great joys of a visit to the City of Light. The windows, the oldest in Paris, are not just known for the vividness of their brilliant colors, but for the vitality of their characters, depicting everybody from the Adam and Eve to St. John the Baptist and the life of the *Virgin*. In essence, the glass panels are a veritable illustrated Bible story book.

After a visit, it's time for lunch. Since first-day visitors might not have time to absorb Left Bank life, here's your chance.

Continue east along Quai des Orfèvres until you come to the Pont St-Michel. Cross the bridge to the Left Bank of Paris, arriving at the Latin Quarter centering around:

❽ Place St-Michel

One of the inner chambers of Left Bank life, this square was named in memory of the ancient chapel of St-Michel that stood here once upon a time. The square, a bustling hub of Sorbonne life, centers around a fountain from 1860 designed by Gabriel Davioud, rising 229m (751 ft.) high and stretching out to 4.6m (15 ft.), a "monster" spouting water. A bronze statue depicts Saint Michael fighting the dragon.

Why not splurge for lunch at a lovely restaurant overlooking the river and the booksellers? Walk a few minutes down the quai (heading away from Notre Dame).

☕ ❾ LES BOUQUINISTES ⭐⭐

This chic restaurant takes its name after the *bouquinistes* (booksellers) who line the banks of the Seine in this neighborhood of Paris. The food here is delicate and divine. Specials include a delectable pan-fried foie gras, roasted Pyrenees lamb with shallot confit, or a ravioli of smoked tuna. Take advantage of the two-course special lunch menu for 24€ ($30).

52 Quai des Grands-Augustins, 6e. ℂ 01-43-25-45-94. See p. 139.

After lunch, walk back to place St-Michel. Still on the Left Bank, continue east along quai St.-Michel until it becomes quai de Montebello. At the "green lung" or park, square Rene Viviani, pause to take in the most dramatic view of Notre-Dame across the Seine. Then cross the bridge, Pont au Double, to visit the cathedral itself.

❿ Cathédrale des Notre-Dame ⭐⭐⭐

In so many ways, the exterior is more exciting than the vast and hollow interior, which since its denuding during the French Revolution is almost tomblike. One of the supreme masterpieces of Gothic art, Notre-Dame still evokes Victor Hugo's novel, *The Hunchback of Notre Dame*. You stand in awe, taking in the majestic and perfectly balanced portals. These portals were a Bible in stone for the illiterate. After a walk through the somber interior, climb the towers (around to the left facing the building) for a close encounter with tons of bells and the most eerie inspection of what are history's most bizarre gargoyles, some looking so terribly impish it's as if they're mocking you. See p. 162.

After Notre-Dame, take Métro to the:

⓫ Place de la Concorde ⭐⭐⭐

This octagonal traffic hub, built in 1757, is dominated by an Egyptian obelisk from Luxor, the oldest object made by humans in Paris, circa 1200 B.C. In the Reign of Terror at the time of the French Revolution, the dreaded guillotine was erected on this spot to claim thousands of heads. For a spectacular view, look down the Champs-Elysées.

The grandest walk in Paris begins here leading all the way to the Arc de Triomphe (see below). It's a distance of about 3.2 km (2 miles), and is the most popular walk in Paris.

But since your afternoon is short, you may want to skip most of it, taking the Métro to Franklin-D-Roosevelt, then continuing west from here. At least you'll see the busiest and most commercial part of the:

⑫ Champs-Elysées ★★★

Called "the highway of French grandeur," this boulevard was designed for promenading. It's witnessed some of the greatest moments in French history and some of its worst defeats, such as when Hitler's armies paraded down the street in 1940. Louis XIV ordered the construction of the 1.8 km (1 mile) avenue in 1667. Without worrying about any particular monument, stroll along its avenue of sidewalk cafes, automobile showrooms, airline offices, cinemas, lingerie stores, and even hamburger joints. The Champs has obviously lost its *fin-de-siècle* elegance as evoked by Marcel Proust in *Remembrance of Things Past.* But then, what hasn't?

At the end of the broad boulevard, you approach:

⑬ Arc de Triomphe ★★★

The greatest triumphal arch in the world, the 49m (161-ft.) arch can be climbed for one of the most panoramic views of Paris. The arch marks the intersections of the 8th, 16th, and 17th arrondissements. From the monument, a dozen avenues, each clogged with traffic, radiate out. The arch is imbedded with sculpture, including François Rude's famous *La Marseillaise,* depicting the uprising of 1792. See p. 160.

After a visit, and with the afternoon fading, take the Métro to the Champ de Mars-Tour Eiffel for an ascent up the:

⑭ Eiffel Tower ★★★

It's open until 11pm or midnight, so don't worry about missing it. This close encounter with this tower, a 10,000-ton dark metal structure, is more inspiring up close than when seen from afar. A source of wonder since the 1889 World Exposition, this 317m (1,040-ft.) tower was the world's tallest building until the Chrysler Building went up in New York in 1930. Hopefully, you'll be here as the sun sets over Paris and your day 1. If the fading afternoon is clear, you can see for 65km (40 miles). See p. 164.

2 The Best of Paris in 2 Days

If you've already made your way through "The Best of Paris in 1 Day," you'll find that your second full-day tour takes in other fascinating sections of Paris, including Ile St-Louis (the most beautiful island in the Seine) and Montmartre, the hill crowning Paris, and such major attractions as an array of the greatest works of the Impressionists in the Musée d'Orsay along with Napoleon's Tomb and other amusements. ***Start:*** *Pont-Marie Métro stop.*

❶ Ile St-Louis ★★

The neighboring island to La Cité is Ile St-Louis (p. 174), lying to the larger island's immediate east. Beautiful antique town houses with charming courtyards, tree-shaded quays opening onto the Seine, mansions that once housed such famous literati as Voltaire and his mistress, antique shops, and little restaurants and cafes fill the narrow streets of this platinum island of expensive real estate. Wandering its streets and quays in the early morning before the museums and attractions open is a great way to break in your second day in Paris. After arriving at Pont-Marie on the Right Bank, head south across the bridge, Pont-Marie, to Ile St-Louis. Cut immediately to your right and walk along Quai de Bourbon. We suggest that you circle the entire Seine-bordering quays, including those south of the island, Quai d'Orléans and Quai de Béthune. When you reach Square Barye in the far southeastern corner, take in the scenic view down river before crossing by Pont de Sully. At this point you can cut inland and walk the entire length of rue St-Louis-en-l'Ile, which will take you along the "main street," the most historic of the island.

After your stroll, take the Métro to Solférino. Walk north, towards the Seine on rue de Bellechasse to:

❷ Musée d'Orsay ✶✶✶

This splendid museum will take up the rest of your morning, at least 2 hours. It shelters the world's greatest collection of the Impressionists, including all the old masters such as Manet, Monet, and van Gogh. You'll even get to see the fabled painting of *Whistler's Mother*—and it's by an American. This former railway station also presents a vast array of sculpture and decorative arts with other departments devoted to architecture, photography, and cinema. Most of the works span the period from 1848 to 1914 and the beginning of World War I. To speed you on your way, English language information is available at the entrance. Audio guides offer analyses of more than 50 masterpieces on display. See p. 166.

Since it's time for lunch, we suggest you eat on-site.

📷 RESTAURANT DU MUSÉE D'ORSAY

Serving first-class cuisine, this elegant restaurant should be visited if only for its setting, although the food is excellent. Gabriel Ferrier designed this Belle Epoque room with its panoramic vista of the Seine and its splendid chandeliers. Main dishes are reasonably priced at 9€ to 15€ ($11–$19). Lunch is also offered Tuesday to Sunday 11:30am to 2:30pm, afternoon tea Friday to Wednesday 3:30 to 5:30pm, and dinner only Thursday 7 to 9:30pm. If you want something cheaper, you can patronize **Café des Hauteurs** on the fifth floor behind one of the former train station's huge iron clocks. It is open Tuesday to Wednesday and Friday to Sunday 10am to 5pm, Thursday 10am to 9pm. For food on the run, patronize a self-service food stand directly above the cafe; it's open Tuesday to Sunday 11am to 5pm. 1 rue de Bellechasse, 7e. ✆ **01-40-49-48-14.**

After lunch, take the Métro to:

❸ Hôtel des Invalides/Napoleon's Tomb ✶✶✶

Still beloved by many French people in the way that some Germans still worship Hitler, the little megalomaniac who tried to conquer Europe lies locked away (or at least his remains) in six coffins of red Finnish porphyry—a lot of tombs for such a small man. All his remains are here with one exception: Someone cut off his penis and made off with it. After seeing the tomb in Église du Dome, you can leave at once or else take a quick look at the **Musée de l'Armée** located here. This is a gaudy celebration of French military history, but most first-timers to Paris skip it. See p. 218.

From Invalides take the Métro over to the Right Bank, getting off at the Alma-Marceau stop. Here you can embark on one of the:

❹ Bateaux-Mouches Cruises of the Seine

There's not really a better way to enjoy Paris than from the deck of one of these scenic boat tours that take in Paris from the riverbank point of view, including the most dramatic vistas of Notre-Dame. Tours depart every 20 to 30 minutes during the day and are in English, lasting about 75 minutes. First you sail east all the way to Ile St-Louis, returning west past the Eiffel Tower.

As the afternoon fades, head for "the top of Paris," the legendary Montmartre district, reached by Métro going north to the stop at Abbesses.

❺ Basilique du Sacré-Coeur ✶✶

Before heading for the church, you can wander around the legendary square, **place du Tertre** (p. 198 of our walking tour of Montmartre). Dozens of young artists are waiting for you to give them the nod to paint your portrait. This may sound corny to some sophisticated travelers, but thousands upon thousands of visitors view one of these portraits as their

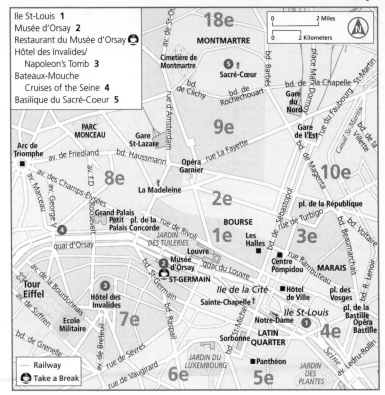

Ile St-Louis **1**
Musée d'Orsay **2**
Restaurant du Musée d'Orsay ☕
Hôtel des Invalides/
   Napoleon's Tomb **3**
Bateaux-Mouche
   Cruises of the Seine **4**
Basilique du Sacré-Coeur **5**

most memorable souvenir of Paris. Perhaps your portrait will be painted by tomorrow's Toulouse-Lautrec. The Church of the Sacred Heart, its many cupolas, is a brilliant white and as much a part of the Paris skyline as the Eiffel Tower. Ascend to the dome at 80m (262 ft.) for one of the greatest panoramas in all of Europe, extending for 48km (30 miles) on a clear afternoon. After coming down from the dome, we always like to sit with dozens of other visitors on the steps of Sacré-Coeur, watching the afternoon fade and the lights go on all over Paris.

3 The Best of Paris in 3 Days

Having survived 2 days in the capital of France, you are by now a veteran Parisian. Now it's time to hit the road, Jack (or Jill), and head for the single most glorious monument to pomp and pomposity that France ever saw erected to royal pretensions and kingly vanity. *Start: RER line C to Versailles Rive Gauche station.*

❶ Château de Versailles ✸✸✸

There is nothing in all of Paris to equal this regal wonder, former stamping ground of everyone from Madame de Pompadour, the royal mistress, to Marie Antoinette, the Austrian princess doomed to marry a French king about to lose his head. The palace opens at 9am, so try to get here at that time because it will take a minimum of 3 hours to see just some of the highlights. If you move with a certain speed, you'll still have time to get back to Paris to sample more neighborhoods and attractions before night falls.

A first-time visitor will want to concentrate on the **Grands Appartements**, the glittering **Hall of Mirrors**, and the **Petits Appartements**, where Louis XV died in 1774 of smallpox. Other "don't miss" attractions include the **Opéra** that Gabriel designed for Louis XV in 1748 and the **Royal Chapel** that Hardouin-Mansart didn't live to complete. There's more. For your final hour, wander through Le Nôtre's "Garden of Eden"—in other words, the **Gardens of Versailles**, paying a visit to the **Grand Trianon**, where Nixon once slept in a room where Madame de Pompadour died, and the **Petit Trianon**, which Louis XV used for his trysts with his mistress, Madame du Barry. See p. 266.

Note: Should you regard your time too precious for a sit-down meal, you can have a fast lunch on the run and save those dwindling hours to see more of Paris itself. You could visit a deli in the morning before leaving Paris and secure the makings of a *piquenique,* which you can enjoy by the canal in the Gardens of Versailles after you tour the palace. Within various corners of the gardens you'll also encounter snack bars discreetly tucked away. There's even a McDonald's, *quelle horreur,* on the walk back from the palace to the train station, which you'll need to visit anyway to take the RER back to Paris.

Once in Paris, take the Métro to Hôtel-de-Ville, to have lunch at Trumilou below, or skip that and go directly to the Centre Pompidou, a few minutes walk away:

TRUMILOU ☆
Just behind the Hôtel de Ville and serving lunch until 3pm is this gem of a place. Very French and very proper, you can take advantage of the amazingly priced 15€ ($19) two-course lunch menu or the 18€ ($23) three-course menu. The duck with prunes or baked cod with new potatoes will hit the spot after the appetite you've worked up in Versailles. The figs stewed in a light cream sauce is divine for desert. 84 quai de l'Hotel-de-Ville, 4e. ⓒ 01-42-77-63-98. See p. 123.

Walk past the Hotel de Ville and make a right towards Les Halles and you will find the:

❸ Centre Pompidou ☆☆

The exterior is controversial, called either daringly innovative and avant-garde, or else "the eyesore of Paris." But inside virtually everyone agrees that this museum dominating Beaubourg is a repository of one of the world's greatest collections of modern art. Amazingly, more art lovers visit Pompidou per day than they do the Louvre or the Eiffel Tower. Head inside past the fire-eaters, caricaturists, portrait-painting artists, street musicians, and a motley crew of "rebels." Beginning with Rousseau's *Snake Charmer* and ending with the latest acquisition from the 21st century, you can view the greatest modern artists of the 20th century: the inevitable Picassos, but also Chagall, Francis Bacon, Calder, Magritte, Matisse, Mondrian, Pollock, Kandinsky—and the beat goes on. Allow at least 2 hours. See p. 184.

Take the Métro to:

❹ Place des Vosges ☆☆☆

Having tasted the glories of such districts as Montmartre and Ile St-Louis, it's time to discover the charms of one of Paris's most enchanting neighborhoods, the Marais. Place des Vosges, one of the world's most perfectly designed and harmonious squares, is found at the very

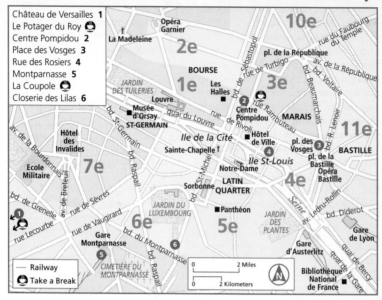

Château de Versailles **1**
Le Potager du Roy ☕
Centre Pompidou **2**
Place des Vosges **3**
Rue des Rosiers **4**
Montparnasse **5**
La Coupole ☕
Closerie des Lilas **6**

center of the Marais. For those with extra time, we've designed a complete walking tour of the Marais (p. 224). But most 3-day visitors, especially if they visited Versailles, will not have time to see the entire district.

The oldest square in Paris is flanked by 36 matching pavilions with red and gold brick and stone facades. Architecturally, this square represents the first time in Paris that an arcade was used to link houses. Balconies were also designed for use for the first time—not just for decorative reasons. The most famous resident of this square (no. 6) was the French writer, Victor Hugo, who lived here from 1833 to 1848 until Napoleon III came to power and Hugo fled into voluntary exile to the Channel Islands. His home is now a museum (p. 187), which at this point may have to be saved until your next trip to Paris.

Arm yourself with a good map and spend at least an hour wandering the narrow Marais streets to the west of place des Vosges. You can make discoveries on every block, as you explore trendy cafes and funky shops.

At the northern tier of the place des Vosges, head west along rue des Francs Bourgeois, one of the most historic streets in Marais. At some point, dip south to visit the parallel street:

❺ Rue des Rosiers

"The Street of Rose Bushes" remains from the heyday of the old Jewish ghetto that once flourished here. The street, deep in the heart of the Marais, is still packed with kosher butchers, bakeries, and falafel shops. In the 1960s the waves of North African Sephardim radically changed the street. After an attempt at extermination in World War II, Jewish families are still surviving in the Marais. A synagogue is at 25 rue des Rosiers.

One more famous neighborhood awaits discovery; take the Métro to Montparnasse-Bienvenüe.

❻ Montparnasse ✈

Once Montparnasse was the retreat of bohemian artists and the working class. Today it's been as successfully gentrified with urban renewal projects as the Marais. The former stamping ground of such expats as Gertrude Stein and her lover, Alice B. Toklas, the district today teems with cafes (many of literary fame), cinemas, and nightclubs, along with artisan shops and bars. For a description of some of the highlights of the area, see coverage beginning on p. 219. For the best overview, take an elevator to the 56th floor of **Tour Montparnasse** (*©* **01-45-38-52-56**), which when it was built was accused of bringing Manhattan to Paris. The tower, completed in 1973, rises 206m (676 ft.) above the Parisian skyline.

After taking in the view, descend on the most famous cafe of Montparnasse.

---

7 LA COUPOLE *☕*

One doesn't see as many writers and publishers as before, but this is still the best viewing platform for Montparnasse life. In this citadel to the bohemian life of Paris in the 1920s and 1930s, Hemingway, Picasso, and Louis Armstrong once scribbled, sketched, or composed here. Chanteuse Josephine Baker would show up accompanied by her lion cub, and Jean-Paul Sartre would dine here. Eugène Ionesco always ordered the *café liegeois*. Henry Miller came for his morning porridge, and the famous Kiki of Montparnasse picked up tricks here to service back in her hotel room. James Joyce patronized the joint, and so did F. Scott Fitzgerald, when he didn't have much money; when the royalty check came in, he fled to the Ritz Bar. Join the local fauna for the memories if for no other reason.

102 bd. du Montparnasse, 14e. *©* **01-43-20-14-20**. See p. 148.

You can order drinks here and sit back to enjoy the cafe scene in Montparnasse, perhaps not as colorful as in days gone by but still a lively, bustling place to be at night.

For dinner on your final night, head for a restaurant that is a virtual sightseeing attraction as well as a place for food.

After taking the Métro Port Royal or Vavin, descend on this legend that has been wining and dining some of the most famous figures of the past 2 centuries since it opened back in 1847, the:

8 Closerie des Lilas *☕☕*

It is "The Pleasure Garden of the Lilacs," a virtual French monument. Follow the sounds of a jazz pianist and enter its hallowed precincts, heading for the *bateau* (boat) section for a champagne julep (the bartender's special). You can dine more expensively in the main restaurant with formal service, or else enjoy the more democratically priced brasserie. Should you be on the strictest of budgets, you can order a coffee or a beer at the bar and soak up the atmosphere, the way Hemingway did between royalty checks when he was broke and having to kill a pigeon in the park for his dinner. Today the lilacs of its namesake no longer bloom; Trotsky has long been assassinated, and Henry James a mere skeleton of himself (if that). But young Parisians, including rising film stars, models, the pretty, and the chic, still patronize the place, giving you a close encounter with Paris after dark. And, yes, it's still going in August when the rest of the town shuts down. Have a nightcap at the bar and promise a return to Paris.

Getting to Know the City of Light

Vaguely egg-shaped, the geometry of Paris is defined by its arrondissements and the Seine, which arcs through the city on its way towards the Atlantic. The river splits the city in two, the northern side being the Rive Droite, or Right Bank, and the southern the Rive Gauche, or Left Bank. The logic of these names seems arbitrary unless you can position yourself in the direction that the river flows. The Right Bank takes up the lion's share of the city, if you include the parks of Bois de Vincennes and Bois de Boulogne, which are inside the city boundaries. Beyond the natural dividing line carved by the river, there are 20 administrative districts, or *arrondissements*. Each has its own town hall, mayor, central post office, police and fire station, and ambience.

Spiraling outward from the city center, the districts begin with the 1er arrondissement, which includes the Louvre and Sainte-Chapelle, and end with the 20e, which encompasses Père-Lachaise cemetery. The Right Bank is made up of arrondissements 1 through 4, 8 through 12, and 16 through 20. The Left Bank holds 5 through 7 and 13 through 15.

You'll be able to tell where you are in a few ways. Most street signs contain the arrondissement number above the street name. Locating the Seine will help you get your bearings, as will picking out certain monuments: Remember, the Eiffel Tower and the Tour Montparnasse are on the Left Bank, while the Sacré-Coeur and the Louvre are on the Right Bank. Notre-Dame, at the center of Paris, sits on an island in the Seine, the Ile de la Cité. On the other side of the bridge behind the cathedral lies the river's other island, Ile St-Louis.

The Ile de la Cité is Paris's historic center; the Romans and later the nascent French monarchy set up shop on this strategic site. Pieces of the ancient Gallo-Roman settlement survive in an archaeological crypt next to Notre-Dame, while the Conciergerie and Sainte-Chapelle are the last remainders of the Capetian palace that once stood on the Ile.

The city spread north from the Right Bank and south from the Left Bank; the Right Bank became a place of merchants and markets and, later, the home of royalty. The Left Bank became home to intellectuals and the Sorbonne. The grandeur of the Louvre and mansions in the Marais expressed the prestige of an increasingly wealthy and influential city. The kings abandoned the Marais in the 17th century, but the ancient Jewish community remained, and some kosher shops and synagogues are still there—surrounded by trendy restaurants, boutiques, and bars. The vista that stretches from the pyramid of the Louvre through the Tuileries Gardens to the Champs-Elysées and the Arc de Triomphe follows the westward movement of 18th- and 19th-century aristocracy. This area contains some of the most expensive real estate and most elegant shops in the city.

Who's Rude?

Are Parisians rude? There's no doubt that they can be a little frosty, particularly around major tourist sights. Even Parisians lament the fact that their cohabitants refuse to roll out the welcome mat. Some of it stems from a tradition of formality, some from an innate crustiness, and some from a completely different interpretation of the term "customer service." It is interesting to note that to many Parisians, particularly shopkeepers, it is the tourists who are rude. When sloppily dressed foreigners barge into their carefully tended stores and begin to snoop around and demand things without even offering a simple "bonjour" to the management, this gets their hackles up. You would be amazed what a polite "bonjour, madame" will do to that crabby woman behind the croissant counter. If you throw in a respectful "merci" and "bonne journée" at the end of your transaction, she just might get downright, well, friendly!

While the Right Bank was developing into a bastion of money and power, the Left Bank became known for more intellectual pursuits. A Benedictine abbey flourished at St-Germain-des-Prés in the Middle Ages, while the Sorbonne drew scholars from all over Europe to the Latin Quarter. The thriving intellectual life gave rise to bookstores and cafes where lively minds congregated to discuss the issues of the day. In the 1920s and 1930s, artists and writers flocked to the cafes of Montparnasse; they returned after World War II to the cafes along the boulevard St-Germain, where Sartre expounded his existentialist philosophy. The University of Paris (the Sorbonne), in the Latin Quarter, ensures a young, bohemian presence even as the neighborhood becomes known more for shopping than intellectual life.

Also on the Left Bank is the Faubourg St-Germain, home of 18th-century aristocracy and now the site of embassies and ministries.

In the 19th century, the city absorbed the outlying villages. Montmartre mixed its vineyards and windmills with cabarets and music halls, luring a new generation of artists—van Gogh, Renoir, Toulouse-Lautrec, and, later, Picasso, Braque, and Juan Gris. In the southwest, the villages of Passy and Auteuil were annexed to create a chic residential district, the 16e arrondissement. In the east, the cemetery of Père-Lachaise was constructed where the villages of Belleville, Ménilmontant, and Charonne joined. Baron Haussmann designed the Grands Boulevards to open up the old streets, and the system of arrondissements was instituted.

1 Orientation

ARRIVING

BY PLANE

Paris has two airports that handle international traffic: Charles de Gaulle and Orly. The outlying Beauvais Airport (70km/43 miles from Paris; ✆ **08-92-68-20-66;** www. aeroportbeauvais.com) is used by the budget operator RyanAir for all its European flights and by a few charter airlines. A bus service for 10€ ($13) operates between the airport and Porte Maillot in the city, 20 minutes after the arrival of flights and 3 hours, 15 minutes before each departure. For flight information, contact RyanAir at ✆ **08-92-23-23-75,** or www.ryanair.com.

AEROPORT CHARLES DE GAULLE   The larger, busier, and more modern airport, commonly known as CDG and sometimes called Roissy–Charles de Gaulle (② **01-48-62-22-80** or 08-92-68-15-15; www.adp.fr), is 23km (14 miles) northeast of downtown. Terminal 1 (Aérogare 1) is used only for international flights by a variety of foreign airlines, including United, KLM, and Lufthansa; Terminal 2 (Aérogare 2) serves Air France, domestic and intra-European airlines, and a growing number of foreign airlines, including Air Canada, Continental, and Delta. Terminal 2 is divided into halls A through F. Because the halls are far apart, it makes sense to know from which hall your flight will leave. Terminal 3, a more remote terminal sometimes referred to as T9, caters only to charter airlines and all EasyJet flights. A free shuttle bus *(navette)* connects the three terminals.

There are several ways of getting to and from the airport. The easiest and most comfortable choice is the **Air France buses** (② **08-92-35-08-20**) that run from the two main terminals—and you don't have to fly Air France to use the service. Buy tickets on the bus. **Line 2** runs every 15 minutes from terminals 1 and 2 to the Porte-Maillot Métro station, next to Paris's huge convention center on the western end of the city, and to place Charles-de-Gaulle–Etoile and the Arc de Triomphe. The 40-minute trip costs 10€ ($13) one-way, 17€ ($21) round-trip. This service is available from 5:45am until 11pm. **Line 4** runs every 30 minutes from terminals 1 and 2 to Gare Montparnasse, near the Left Bank, and Gare de Lyon, near the Marais. The journey takes about 50 minutes and costs 12€ ($15) one-way or 20€ ($25) round-trip. It runs from 7am to 9pm. **Line 3** operates every 30 minutes and connects Charles d -Gaulle and Orly from Terminal 1, Porte 34, arrivals level, and Terminal 2 at Porte B2 and Porte C2. The hour-long trip costs 16€ ($20) one-way (round-trips not available). Infants travel free on Air France buses and there are discounted rates for children under 11. Groups of four passengers or more can receive a 15% discount off the one-way fares.

A less expensive way is the **Roissybus** (② **08-92-68-77-14**), which leaves every 15 minutes for place de l'Opéra; it takes 45 to 50 minutes and costs 8.30€ ($10). It departs from Terminal 1 at Porte 30, arrivals level; Terminal 2 at Porte A10; Porte D12; and Hall F, Port H, arrivals level. Buses run from 5:45am to 11pm.

The **RER Line B suburban train** (www.ratp.fr), which stops near terminals 1 and 2, is also a good bet if you don't have a lot of luggage. A free **shuttle bus** connects all three terminals to the RER train station. From the station, trains depart about every 15 minutes for the half-hour trip into town, stopping at the Gare du Nord, Châtelet–Les Halles Métro interchange, and RER stations St-Michel, Luxembourg, Port-Royal, and Denfert-Rochereau, before heading south out of the city. A ticket into town on the RER is 7.75€ ($9.70).

A **taxi** into town from Charles de Gaulle takes 40 to 50 minutes and costs about 45€–50€ ($56–$63) from 7am to 7pm, about 40% more at other times. Taxis are required to turn on the meter and charge the price indicated (plus a 1€/$1.25 supplement for each piece of baggage—see "Getting Around," later in this chapter). Check the meter before you pay—rip-offs of arriving tourists are not uncommon. If you feel that you might have been overcharged, demand a receipt (which drivers are obligated to provide) and contact the **Préfecture of Police** (② **08-91-01-22-22**). Good luck.

AEROPORT D'ORLY   Direct flights from the United States no longer arrive here, but a handful of European carriers, charter flights, and some international airlines fly into **Orly** (② 01-49-75-15-15; www.adp.fr), 14km (8 ¾ miles) south of the city. The airport has two terminals: French domestic flights land at Orly Ouest, and intra-European and intercontinental flights at Orly Sud. Shuttle buses connect these terminals, and other shuttles connect them to Charles de Gaulle every 30 minutes or so.

The cheapest trip into town is on **Jetbus** (② 01-69-01-00-09). It connects Orly with the Métro station Villejuif–Louis Aragon, which is in a southern suburb of Paris, and costs 5.30€ ($6.65) for the 15-minute journey. The bus leaves every 12 to 15 minutes from Exit H in Orly Sud and from Exit C, arrivals level, in Orly Ouest.

Air France coaches (you need not be an Air France passenger) run to the downtown terminal at Invalides every 15 minutes. **Line 1** leaves from Exit D on the arrivals level at Orly Ouest and Exit K at Orly Sud. The trip takes 35 minutes and costs 7.50€ ($9.40) one-way, 13€ ($16) round-trip. You can request that the bus stop at Montparnasse-Duroc (the stop is right in front of the Duroc Métro station). This service operates from 5:45am to 11pm. **Line 3** runs between Orly and Charles de Gaulle; see "Aéroport Charles de Gaulle," above.

An airport **shuttle bus,** Orly-Rail, leaves every 15 minutes for the RER Pont de Rungis–Aéroport d'Orly station, where you can board a Line C train that stops at several downtown stations, including St-Michel, Invalides, and Gare d'Austerlitz (35 min.). This airport shuttle leaves from Orly Sud Exit F on Platform 1 and from Exit G on the arrivals level at Orly Ouest. It costs 5.50€ ($6.90).

You can also take the **Orlyval** service at the RER Line B. From Orly Sud it departs from Exit K near the baggage-claim area and from Exit W or Exit J on the departures level at Orly Ouest. You'll connect at the Antony RER station. The trip to Châtelet takes about 30 minutes and costs 8.85€ ($11). You can avoid the line by buying your Orlyval tickets from a machine if you have French coins.

The **Orly Bus** (from Exit J arrivals level at Orly Ouest and from Exit H Platform 4 at Orly Sud) goes to Denfert-Rochereau and costs 5.80€ ($7.25).

A **taxi** into the city costs about 36€ ($45) and takes 30 to 40 minutes.

AIRPORT SHUTTLES   Cheaper than a taxi for one or two people but more expensive than airport buses and trains is the **Paris Airport Shuttle** (② 01-43-90-91-91; www.paris-airport-shuttle.com). An excellent choice for those who overpack, this service requires advance reservation (reservation@paris-airport-shuttle.com). A minivan will meet you at Orly or Charles de Gaulle to take you to your hotel for 19€ ($24) per person for parties of two or more, 25€ ($31) for a single.

The **Blue Shuttle** (② 01-30-11-13-00; www.airport-shuttle.fr) offers a similar service, and also requires reservations. It costs 29€ to 32€ ($36–$40) for one person, 39€ to 45€ ($49–$56) for two, 55€ to 61€ ($69–$76) for three, and 70€ to 81€ ($87–$101) for four, depending on the time of day. (The lower fare applies from 6am–4pm, the higher fare applies from 4pm–6am). You can save up to 5€ ($6.25) on the above rates if you make your reservation online.

Both companies have toll-free numbers that you call once you arrive at the airport to confirm your arrival and location of pickup. Be sure to ask for this number when you make your reservations and call as soon as you land, before collecting your luggage, to lessen the amount of time you spend waiting around.

VISITOR INFORMATION

The prime source of information is the **Office de Tourisme et des Congrès de Paris,** 127 av. des Champs-Elysées, 8e (② 08-92-68-31-12; fax 01-49-52-53-00; www.paris bienvenue.com; Métro: Charles-de-Gaulle–Etoile or George V). It's open daily 9am to

Getting the Picture

We strongly recommend supplementing the maps in this book with a pocket-sized *Plan de Paris* book or the *Paris Pratique Par Arrondissement,* which Parisians themselves often carry. They are available at any bookstore and at most news-stands for about 6€ ($7.50).

8pm (Nov–Apr, Sun 11am–7pm). For a fee, the staff will make a same-day room reservation for you. The charge is 2€ ($2.50) for hostels and *foyers* (homes), 3.50€ ($4.40) for one-star hotels, 4.50€ ($5.65) for two-star hotels, and 6.50€ ($8.15) for three-star hotels. There are information offices at the airports; the staff will help you make a hotel reservation, but they work only with hotels that charge more than 50€ ($62) a night.

In slow periods, hotels with unsold rooms often sell them at a huge discount through the Office de Tourisme, providing you with a good way to stay in a three-star hotel at a two-star price. The office is very busy in summer, with lines sometimes stretching outside.

The Office de Tourisme has **auxiliary offices** at the Eiffel Tower (May–Sept only, daily 11am–6:40pm) and at the Gare de Lyon (year-round, Mon–Sat 8am–8pm). At the main office you can also reserve concert, theater, or cabaret tickets without an extra fee.

CITY LAYOUT

To get your bearings, visit Notre-Dame as soon as you can; this will bring to you to the heart of the city and help you understand that the Seine is Paris's most important "street." Even better, climb up to the tower and take advantage of the view to orient yourself according to your map. Now you will have a point of reference; the magnificent cathedral is visible from many parts of the city.

MAIN ARTERIES & STREETS   When Baron Haussmann overhauled Paris in the 19th century, he cut through the dense city and created the Grands Boulevards: Haussmann, Malesherbes, Sébastopol, Magenta, Voltaire, and Strasbourg. He also created avenue de l'Opéra and the 12 avenues that radiate from the Arc de Triomphe. These remain the largest roads inside Paris proper.

The main streets on the Right Bank are the broad **avenue des Champs-Elysées,** beginning at the Arc de Triomphe and running to place de la Concorde, and the narrower **rue de Rivoli,** from place de la Concorde to place de la Bastille. **Boulevards St-Michel and St-Germain** (also part of Haussmann's grand plan) are the main streets of the Left Bank.

Streets change names as they make their way through the city. If you come to a corner and don't see the street name you expect, look on the opposite corner.

FINDING AN ADDRESS   Finding the right neighborhood is usually easy. The last three digits in the postal code indicate the arrondissement; 75005 means the 5e arrondissement ("75" is for Paris), 75019 means the 19e, and so on.

Addresses often include the name of the nearest Métro station. You'll find good neighborhood maps *(plans du quartier)* in the Métro station that will help you locate your street. Addresses on streets that run parallel to the Seine generally follow the direction of the river (east to west). For perpendicular streets, the lowest numbers are closest to the Seine.

STREET MAPS   There's a foldout sheet map included with this book. Maps printed by the *grands magasins* (department stores) are usually available free at hotels, and they're good for those visiting Paris for only a few days and hitting only the major attractions.

ARRONDISSEMENTS IN BRIEF

1er Arr. (Right Bank, Musée du Louvre/Palais-Royal/Les Halles) One of the world's great art museums, the **Louvre,** still lures visitors to the 1er arrondissement. The **rue de Rivoli** rolls through the neighborhood, lined with elegant arcades that shelter a combination of high-end shops and over-priced trinket stores. The **Jardin des Tuileries** extends out from the Louvre, and harbors a number of sculptures, as well as the **Jeu de Paume** museum. For an extra dose of grandeur, visit the **place Vendôme,** home of Cartier, Boucheron, and the Ritz Hotel. For more plebian shopping, try the **Forum des Halles,** a mall and entertainment center surrounded by greenery—but be aware that the area becomes rather unsavory at night. This arrondissement tends to be crowded, and hotels are pricier in high season.

2e Arr. (Right Bank, Grands Boulevards) Home to the **Bourse** (stock exchange), this district is bordered by the **Grands Boulevards** and rue Etienne Marcel. Often overlooked by tourists, the 2e nonetheless presents some interesting contrasts. On weekdays, the shouts of brokers—*J'ai!* or *Je prends!*—echo across place de la Bourse until it's time to break for lunch. Much of the eastern end of the arrondissement **(Le Sentier)** is devoted to the wholesale outlets of the garment district; meandering 19th-century **arcades** honeycomb the center. Though not that exciting, the 2e is still central, and hotels can be cheaper in this neighborhood.

3e Arr. (Right Bank, Le Marais) Now one of the hippest neighborhoods in Paris, **Le Marais** (the swamp) fell into decay for years after its 17th-century aristocratic heyday. Over the centuries, salons in the Marais resounded with the witty, remarks of Racine, Voltaire, Molière, and Madame de Sévigné. One of the Marais's chief attractions today is the **Musée Picasso,** with treasures that the artist's estate turned over to the French government in lieu of huge inheritance taxes. Paris's oldest Jewish neighborhood is around rue des Rosiers, and rue Vieille-du-Temple is home to many gay bars and boutiques. Although a few old buildings still stand, the traditional working-class neighborhood of Beaubourg, to the west, was largely destroyed to make way for the Pompidou center (see below). This is a great area to stay in—if you can find a vacant hotel room.

4e Arr. (Right Bank, Ile de la Cité/Ile St-Louis, Centre Pompidou) As you walk through the aristocratic town houses, courtyards, and antiques shops on the **Ile St-Louis,** try to picture it as it used to be: a cow pasture. Now it's part of an arrondissement that seems to have it all, including **Notre-Dame** on **Ile de la Cité.** Unfortunately, the whole area is touristy and overrun. Seek out Ile de la Cité's gems of Gothic architecture, **Sainte-Chapelle** and **Notre-Dame,** look for the flower markets, and see the nation's law courts, which have a long tradition of dispensing justice French style. It was here that Marie Antoinette was sentenced to death in 1793. The 4e is also home to the **Centre Georges Pompidou,** one of the country's top tourist attractions. Finally, after all this pomp and glory, you can retreat to **place des Vosges,** a square of perfect harmony and beauty where Victor Hugo lived from 1832 to 1848 and penned many of his masterpieces. Like the 3e, this arrondissement is in high demand, so book your hotel early.

5e Arr. (Left Bank, Latin Quarter)

The **Quartier Latin** (Latin Quarter) is the intellectual heart and soul of Paris. Bookstores, schools, churches, clubs, student dives, and Roman ruins characterize the district. Beginning with the founding of the **Sorbonne** in 1253, the *quartier* was called "Latin" because students and professors spoke the scholarly language. As the center of what was called "bohemian Paris," it formed the setting for the Puccini opera *La Bohème.*

You'll follow in the footsteps of Descartes, Verlaine, Camus, Rimbaud, Sartre, James Thurber, Elliot Paul, and Hemingway as you explore this district. But don't expect to run into their modern equivalents at the McDonald's on boulevard St-Michel. Changing times have brought chain stores and fast food to the "Boul'mich," and tourists have taken over the rue de la Huchette. However, you can still find a spot for contemplation at the **Jardin des Plantes,** and lovely views from the top of the **Institut du Monde Arabe.** Stroll along **quai de Montebello,** and inspect the inventories of the *bouquinistes* in the shadow of Notre-Dame, who sell everything from antique prints to yellowing copies of Balzac's *Père Goriot.* The 5e also stretches down to the **Panthéon,** which was constructed by a grateful Louis XV after he recovered from gout. It's the resting place of Rousseau, Léon Gambetta, Emile Zola, Louis Braille, Victor Hugo, Voltaire, and Jean Moulin, the Resistance leader tortured to death by the Gestapo.

Centrally located and packed with monuments, the 5e is popular with tourists. If you want to avoid the crowds, head east and seek out hotels near rue des Ecoles and the Jardin des Plantes.

6e Arr. (Left Bank, St-Germain/Luxembourg Gardens)

This is the heart of Paris publishing and, for some, the most colorful quarter of the Left Bank. Waves of young artists still emerge from the **Ecole des Beaux-Arts.** Strolling the boulevards of the 6e, including St-Germain, has its own rewards—including window-shopping some of the most chic designers around; but the secret of the district is in its narrow streets and hidden squares. Everywhere you turn you encounter historical and literary associations, none more so than on rue Jacob. At no. 7, Racine lived with his uncle as a teenager; Richard Wagner resided at no. 14 from 1841 to 1842; Jean Ingrès lived at no. 27 (now the publishing house Editions du Seuil); and Hemingway occupied a tiny room at no. 44. Today's "big name" is likely to be Spike Lee checking into his favorite, La Villa Hôtel, at no. 29.

Delacroix kept his atelier in the 6e, and George Sand and her lover, Frédéric Chopin, visited him there to have their portraits done. His studio is now open to the public. **Rue Monsieur-le-Prince,** historically a popular street for Paris's resident Americans, was frequented by Martin Luther King Jr., Richard Wright, James McNeill Whistler, Henry Wadsworth Longfellow, and Oliver Wendell Holmes. The 6e takes in the **Luxembourg Gardens,** a 148-hectare (60-acre) playground where Isadora Duncan went dancing and where a destitute Hemingway looked for pigeons to cook for lunch. Before their falling-out, he took his son to visit Gertrude Stein and Alice B.

Paris Arrondissements

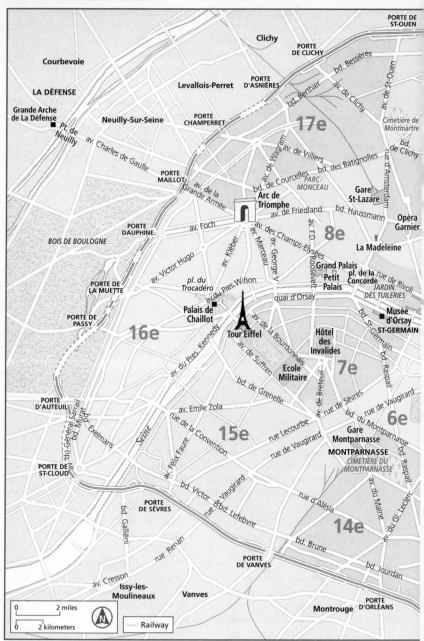

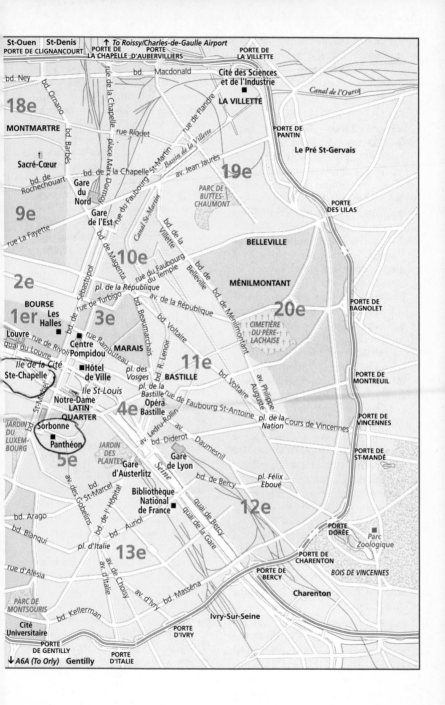

St-Ouen St-Denis ↑ To Roissy/Charles-de-Gaulle Airport
PORTE DE CLIGNANCOURT PORTE DE PORTE PORTE DE
LA CHAPELLE D'AUBERVILLIERS LA VILLETTE

bd. Ney   bd. Macdonald Cité des Sciènces
                                            et de l'Industrie
bd. Ornano   LA VILLETTE   Canal de l'Ourcq

18e   rue de Flandre   PORTE DE
                                                                  PANTIN
MONTMARTRE   rue Riquet   Le Pré St-Gervais
                        place Max Dormoy

Sacré-Cœur
bd. de   bd. de la Chapelle St-Martin av. Jean Jaurès 19e
Rochechouart   Gare   Bassin de la Villette
                 du
                 Nord   PARC DE
                                                                  BUTTES-   PORTE
9e   Gare   Canal St-Martin   CHAUMONT   DES LILAS
                de l'Est
rue La Fayette   BELLEVILLE

                          bd. de Magenta bd. de la Villette

2e   rue du Faubourg bd. de Belleville   MÉNILMONTANT
                          du temple
       BOURSE   pl. de la République   20e   PORTE DE
1er   Les   rue de Turbigo av. de la République   BAGNOLET
      Halles   3e   bd. Voltaire
Louvre   rue de Rivoli rue Rambuteau   CIMETIÈRE
quai du Louvre   Centre   bd. R. Lenoir DU PÈRE-
Ile de la Cité Pompidou   MARAIS   pl. des   LACHAISE
Ste-Chapelle   Hôtel   Vosges   11e   PORTE DE
                de Ville   BASTILLE   MONTREUIL
       Notre-Dame Ile St-Louis pl. de la bd. Voltaire
       LATIN   pl. de la Bastille av. Philippe
       QUARTER   4e Bastille rue de Faubourg St-Antoine Auguste PORTE DE
JARDIN Sorbonne   Opéra   pl. de la   VINCENNES
DU   Bastille   Nation Cours de Vincennes
LUXEM-   Panthéon   av. Ledru-Rollin av.
BOURG   JARDIN bd. Diderot Daumesnil PORTE DE
         5e   DES   ST-MANDÉ
                  PLANTES Gare   Seine
          av. des d'Austerlitz Gare   pl. Félix
          bd.   de Lyon bd. de Bercy Eboué
          St-Marcel Bibliothèque
bd. Arago bd. de l'Hôpital National
                   de France   quai de Bercy 12e
bd. Blanqui bd. Auriol   quai de la Gare
          pl. d'Italie   PORTE
                   13e   DORÉE   Parc
rue d'Alésia av. de Choisy   Zoologique
                   av. d'Italie PORTE DE
          av. d'Ivry bd. Masséna CHARENTON BOIS DE VINCENNES
PARC DE   PORTE DE
MONTSOURIS bd. Kellerman   BERCY   Charenton
Cité
Universitaire   Ivry-Sur-Seine
   PORTE   PORTE
   DE GENTILLY   D'IVRY
↓ A6A (To Orly) Gentilly PORTE
                           D'ITALIE

63

Toklas, at 27 rue de Fleurus. Stein also entertained Max Jacob, Apollinaire, T. S. Eliot, and Matisse. An excellent spot to stay; book early for a hotel in this area.

7e Arr. (Left Bank, Eiffel Tower/ Musée d'Orsay) The city's most famous symbol, the **Eiffel Tower,** dominates the 7e, a district of respectable residences and government offices. Part of the **St-Germain** neighborhood is here as well. The **Hôtel des Invalides,** which contains both **Napoleon's Tomb** and the **Musée de l'Armée,** is also in the 7e. The **Musée Rodin,** 77 rue de Varenne, is where the sculptor lived until his death, and includes some of his greatest works. The museum's garden is breathtaking in the warmer months.

Rue du Bac was home to the heroes of Dumas's *The Three Musketeers* and to James McNeill Whistler. After selling *Portrait of the Artist's Mother* (better known as *Whistler's Mother*), he moved to 110 rue du Bac, where he entertained Dégas, Henry James, Manet, and Toulouse-Lautrec.

Even visitors with no time to explore the 7e rush to its second major attraction, the **Musée d'Orsay,** the showcase of 19th-century French art and culture. The museum is in the old Gare d'Orsay, which Orson Welles used as a setting for his film *The Trial,* based on the book by Franz Kafka.

If you'd like to be next to the Eiffel Tower, this is the place to stay. The neighborhood around Rue Cler's open market is charming but expect to share much of the area with other visiting Americans.

8e Arr. (Right Bank, Champs-Elysées/Madeleine) The grandest boulevard of them all, the **Champs-Elysées,** plows through this district, drawing busloads of tourists from around the world. Stretching from the **Arc de Triomphe** to the obelisk on **place de la Concorde,** the Champs-Elysées has long been cited as the metaphor for the Parisian love of symmetry. However, by the 1980s, it had become a garish strip, with too much traffic, fast-food joints, and panhandlers. In the 1990s, Mayor (later President) Jacques Chirac launched a cleanup. Sidewalks have been widened, trees planted, streetlights upgraded, and timeless legends like the Hôtel Georges V and Fouquets have been given an overhaul. There are still too many megastores and overpriced tourist restaurants, but no one will deny that it's a vast improvement. Whatever you're looking for, in the 8e it will be the city's best, grandest, and most impressive. It has the best restaurant in Paris (Taillevent), the sexiest strip joint (Crazy Horse Saloon), the most splendid square in France (place de la Concorde), the best rooftop cafe (at La Samaritaine), the grandest hotel in France (the Crillon), the most impressive triumphal arch on the planet (Arc de Triomphe), the world's most expensive residential street (av. Montaigne), the world's oldest Métro station (Franklin-D-Roosevelt), the most ancient monument in Paris (the 3,300-year-old Obelisk of Luxor), and on and on. Hotel seekers will need to look hard to find a bargain in this pricey neighborhood.

9e Arr. (Right Bank, Opéra Garnier/Pigalle) The 9e is never boring. Everything from the classy **Opéra Garnier** to the strip joints of **Pigalle** (the infamous "Pig Alley" for World War II GIs) falls within the 9e, which was radically altered by Baron Haussmann's 19th-century redevelopment. (The Grands Boulevards radiating through the district are among the most obvious of his labors.) The boulevards were the place to see and be seen, and their cafes, music halls, and theaters were the cultural hub of the city. Today they are mostly filled with car traffic, but there is still some strolling to be done at the *grands magasins* **Printemps** and **Galeries Lafayette.** Boulevard des Italiens is the site of the **Café de la Paix,** which opened in 1856 and was once the meeting place of Romantic poets, including Théophile Gautier and Alfred de Musset. Later, Charles de Gaulle, Marlene Dietrich, and two million Americans showed up.

Place Pigalle is still sex-shop central, but nearby, a tamer crowd frequents the **Folies-Bergère,** where cancan dancers have been high kicking since 1868. If this is your cup of tea, get in line behind the tour bus contingent. The **Opéra Garnier** (which now presents dance performances) has been hailed as the epitome of Second Empire opulence. Renoir hated it, but several generations later, Chagall did the ceilings. Pavlova danced *Swan Lake* here, and Nijinsky took the night off to go cruising.

Though the neighborhood is not exciting, there are some lovely pockets of old Paris, such as the houses and neoclassical mansions in the New Athens area around rue Notre-Dame-de-Lorette. This is a good area in which to stay if you'd like to be near Montmartre but not too far from the city center. Steer clear of place Pigalle when picking a hotel.

10e Arr. (Right Bank, Gare du Nord/Gare de l'Est) Home of two huge train stations, porn theaters, and an unappealing commercial zone, the 10e is not exactly a tourist's dream destination. However, a few bright spots line the Canal St-Martin in the east. The canal's bridges and promenades are attracting low-key hipsters, and cafes and boutiques are popping up along the tree-lined **quai de Valmy** and **quai de Jemmapes.** Two classic

old restaurants provide more reasons to venture into the 10e: **Brasserie Flo,** 7 cour des Petites-Ecuries (go there for *la formidable choucroute,* sauerkraut garnished with everything), and **Julien,** 16 rue du Faubourg St-Denis—called the poor man's Maxim's because of its Belle Epoque interiors and moderate prices. The hotels near the stations can be convenient and comfortable, if your travel plans dictate your choice of accommodations.

11e Arr. (Right Bank, Place de la Bastille) The place de la Bastille is famous for a building that vanished over 200 years ago: the Bastille prison. A symbol of all that was arbitrary and unfair about the French monarchy, it was the first target of the angry mob that took to the streets on July 14, 1789, the start of the French Revolution. They succeeded in liberating the seven people imprisoned there and pulled down the fortress, stone by stone. To commemorate the bicentennial of this event, the **Opéra Bastille** was constructed, nearly causing another revolution in the process. Referred to by some as "the hippopotamus," the huge gray structure had a profound effect on this working-class neighborhood, which suddenly sprouted bars, clubs, restaurants, and hoards of young people.

Even when the district wasn't fashionable, visitors flocked to **Bofinger,** 5–7 rue de la Bastille, to sample its Alsatian *choucroute* (sauerkraut, usually topped by cuts of pork but also available here with seafood). Today, many of the 20-somethings have moved farther north to **rue Oberkampf,** which is now lined with a new generation of bars and restaurants.

For the daytime visitor, the 11e has few landmarks or museums, but it is pleasant to wander around the passages of the **Faubourg St-Antoine,** which still hold ateliers of furniture makers and craftsmen. Night owls will appreciate a hotel in this area, as the Métro stops running at around 12:45am.

12e Arr. (Right Bank, Bois de Vincennes/Gare de Lyon) The 12e has had a major overhaul over the last few years. The mostly industrial areas have been transformed into modern housing and two lovely parks, the **Parc de Bercy** and the **Promenade Plantée,** a promenade that spans the length of an old train viaduct and continues through tunnels and bowers to the **Bois de Vincennes.** The Bois, a sprawling park on the city's eastern periphery, is a longtime favorite of French families, who enjoy its zoos and museums, its royal château and boating lakes, and the **Parc Floral de Paris.** The 19th-century **Gare de Lyon** also lies in the 12e; be sure to go upstairs and sneak a peak at the magnificent decor of **le Train Bleu,** a sumptuous restaurant where the likes of Sarah Bernhardt, Edmond Rostand, Coco Chanel, and Jean Gabin used to dine. The nearby **Marché d'Aligre** is a great stop for gourmets and bargain hunters; the huge open-air market includes both festive vegetable stalls and a small flea market. This quiet district is a good place to stay if you need to take a train from the Gare de Lyon.

13e Arr. (Left Bank, Gare d'Austerlitz) A victim of rampant urban development during the '60s and '70s, the landscape of the 13e has been scarred by ugly apartment towers and shopping centers. However, not even concrete can completely squash a Parisian neighborhood; the 13e has become a hub for Paris's Asian community. Vietnamese restaurants and Chinese markets sit next to Cambodian Buddhist temples and Laotian drugstores. Dragons can be seen snaking down the avenue d'Ivry and avenue de Choisy during Chinese New Year festivities. Although high-rises dominate much of the neighborhood, a small section of village life survives in a cozy network of streets and passages surrounding rue Butte-aux-Cailles. The opening of the **Bibliothèque Nationale de France** has begun to lure businesses and shops to the barren eastern end of the 13e, which is undergoing massive construction in the **Tolbiac** area. Travelers from Spain and Portugal arrive at the **Gare d'Austerlitz,** which looms over the Seine. Nearby, the **Manufacture des Gobelins,** 42 av. des Gobelins, is the tapestry factory that made the word "Gobelins" internationally famous. During the reign of Louis XIV, some 250 Flemish weavers launched the industry to compete with the tapestries produced in southern Belgium (Flanders). Not a great place for a hotel, except along the northern border with the 5e.

14e Arr. (Left Bank, Montparnasse) Some of the world's most famous literary cafes, including La Rotonde, Le Select, La Dôme, and La Coupole, are in the northern end of this arrondissement, near the Rodin statue of Balzac at the junction of boulevard Montparnasse and boulevard Raspail. Known as **Montparnasse,** it was the stomping ground of the "lost generation": Gertrude Stein, Alice B. Toklas, Hemingway, and other American expats who gathered here in the 1920s. After World War II, it ceased to be the center of intellectual life in Paris, but the memory lingers in its cafes. Henry Miller, plotting *Tropic of Cancer,* came to La Coupole for his morning porridge. So did Josephine Baker (with a lion cub on a leash), James Joyce, Man Ray, Matisse, and Ionesco. Jean-Paul Sartre came here and stayed—he's buried in the **Cimitière de Montparnasse,** a few streets from the famous cafes. Today, many cafes remain, if their clientele has changed—but the real transformation happened in the early '70s, when someone decided to rip out the old train station and build a 53-story glass-and-steel office tower. This attempt to "modernize" disemboweled the neighborhood, but it does offer a great view from the top floor—the only place in Paris where you can't see the Tour Montparnasse! Hotel seekers might not consider this the most exciting district, but this area is centrally located and good for connections to several buses, the Métro, and train lines.

15e Arr. (Left Bank, Gare Montparnasse/Institut Pasteur) A mostly residential district beginning at **Gare Montparnasse,** the 15e stretches all the way to the Seine. In size and population, it's the largest *quartier* of Paris, but draws few tourists. It has few attractions, aside from the **Parc des Expositions** and the **Institut Pasteur.** In the early 20th century, the artists Chagall, Léger, and Modigliani lived in this arrondissement in an atelier known as "the Beehive." Staying in this district will mean a lot of time on public transportation, unless you stay near its northeast border with the 6e and 7e.

16e Arr. (Right Bank, Trocadéro/Bois de Boulogne) Benjamin Franklin lived in Passy, one of the 18th-century villages that make up this district. Highlights include the **Bois de Boulogne,** the **Jardin du Trocadéro,** the **Musée de Balzac,** the newly reopened **Musée Guimet,** and the **Cimetière de Passy,** resting place of Manet, Talleyrand, Giraudoux, and Debussy. One of the largest arrondissements, the 16e is known for its exclusivity, its BCBG *(bon chic, bon genre)* residents, its upscale rents, and posh (and, according to critics, rather smug) residential boulevards. Prosperous and conservative addresses include avenue d'Iéna and avenue Victor Hugo. Avenue Foch, the widest boulevard in Paris, was home to Aristotle Onassis, Shah Mohammad Reza Pahlavi of Iran, Maria Callas, and Prince Rainier of Monaco. The arrondissement also includes what some visitors consider the best place in Paris from which to view the Eiffel Tower, **place du Trocadéro.** Hotel prices can run sky-high here, and this district is a little out of the way for short-term visitors.

17e Arr. (Right Bank, Parc Monceau/Place Clichy) On the northern periphery of Paris, the 17e incorporates neighborhoods of bourgeois respectability (in its western end) and less affluent, more pedestrian neighborhoods (in its eastern end). Most of the arrondissement is residential, and rather dull. However, the **Batignolles** area around avenue de Clichy has perked up; keep an eye out for new bars and restaurants on rue des Dames. This out-of-the-way area is not great for bedding down unless you stay near Etoile.

18e Arr. (Right Bank, Montmartre) The 18e is the most famous outer quarter of Paris, containing **Montmartre,** the **Moulin Rouge,** the **Basilica of Sacré-Coeur,** and **place du Tertre.** Utrillo was a native son, Renoir and van Gogh lived here, and Toulouse-Lautrec adopted the area as his own. Picasso painted some of his most famous works at the **Bateau-Lavoir** (Boat Washhouse) on place Emile-Goudeau. Max Jacob, Matisse, and Braque were all frequent visitors. Today, place Blanche is known for its prostitutes, and place de Tertre is filled with sketch artists and souvenir shops. The quieter north, east, and west sides of the hill retain traces of the old days and are well worth exploring. The city's most famous flea market, **Marché aux Puces de la Porte de St-Ouen,** lies on the northern edge of the district. You can find some hotels with marvelous views up here; however, keep in mind that you are a good distance from the center of town.

19e Arr. (Right Bank, La Villette) This working-class arrondissement got a new blast of life when the massive **Parc de La Villette** opened in 1997 on the site of the city's old slaughterhouses. The complex includes the enormous **Cité des Sciences et de l'Industrie,** a science museum; the **Cité de la Musique,** which includes a concert hall and museum; a giant metal sphere with an IMAX-like movie theater; and lawns, gardens, and lots of kids stuff. Mostly residential and not upscale, this arrondissement is one of the most ethnically diverse in Paris, the home of people from all parts of the former French Empire. Another highlight is **Les Buttes-Chaumont,** a park with a man-made mountain and pond where kids can enjoy puppet shows and donkey rides. Parts of this district can get scary at night; in general, this is not a good place to bed down.

20e Arr. (Right Bank, Père-Lachaise Cemetery) An influx of artists looking for cheap apartments and studios has given this old immigrant quarter new cachet. Once known only for **Père-Lachaise Cemetery**—the resting place of Edith Piaf, Marcel Proust, Oscar Wilde, Isadora Duncan, Sarah Bernhardt, Gertrude Stein, Colette, Jim Morrison, and many others—the 20e boasts a blend of cultures that makes it one of the city's more exotic regions. On the streets of Belleville, you'll find turbaned men selling dates; numerous Chinese, Vietnamese, and Thai restaurants; and kosher couscous for the benefit of a Sephardic Jewish community transplanted from Algeria and Tunisia. Overlooking it all is the new **Parc de Belleville,** 11 acres of gardens and paths on a hill with a spectacular view of Paris. Though fascinating during the day, parts of this far-flung arrondissement are dark and deserted at night; look for a hotel closer to the center of town.

2 Getting Around

BY PUBLIC TRANSPORTATION

SAVING MONEY If you plan to use public transportation frequently and are staying in town for a week or more, consider the **Carte Orange.** Parisians use the weekly or monthly pass, which is economical—16€ ($20) for a week's unlimited travel *(coupon hebdomadaire)* or 52€ ($65) for a month *(coupon mensuel)* covering zones 1 and 2. The pass is good on the Métro, RER, and buses.

The only catch is that the weekly pass starts on a Monday, so it won't be worthwhile if you are staying for a week starting on Friday, for example. Similarly, the monthly pass starts on the first of the month. To get either, you must supply a photo of yourself. You can find photo booths in train stations and many Métro stations, department stores,

---

Tips Striking Out with Mass Transit

Strikes are a national pastime in France, and from time to time they hit the Métro system. They usually only affect certain lines and only last a day or so, and are generally announced in the papers at least a day before. If you enter a Métro station and notice a lot of hand-wringing and grumbling, see if the information monitor mentions a "Movement Social" (that's the RATP euphemism for "strike"); it will list the lines affected.

and Monoprix stores. The booths will give you four black-and-white pictures for about 5€ ($6.25). The weekly Carte Orange is on sale Monday through Wednesday morning; the monthly card is on sale starting on the 20th day of the preceding month.

Otherwise, a 10-ticket *carnet* (booklet) for 11€ ($13) is a good deal because a single ticket costs 1.40€ ($1.75). Get *carnets* at all Métro stations as well as *tabacs* (cafes and kiosks that sell tobacco products). Prices for the **Paris Visite** card start at 8.35€ ($11) a day. It does offer free or discounted admission to some attractions and unlimited travel and airport connections, but make sure the attractions are ones that interest you. A less expensive option is the 1-day **Mobilis** card for 5.40€ ($6.75). Mobilis gives you unlimited access to public transit in Paris proper (that is, zones 1 and 2), but no discounts.

BY METRO & RER   The best way to get around Paris is to walk, and entire neighborhoods—such as the Latin Quarter and the Marais—can be easily negotiated this way. For longer distances, the Métro, or subway, is best. See the Paris Métro map on the inside back cover of this book.

Fast, quite safe, and easy to navigate, the Métro opened its first line in 1900. The newest line is the futuristic and fast Météor, which connects the Bibliothèque Nationale with the Madeleine. The **RATP (Régie Autonome des Transports Parisiens)** operates the Métro and city buses, as well as the Réseau Express Régional (RER), which links downtown Paris with its airports and suburbs. The Métro has 16 lines and 380 stations, so there's bound to be one near your destination. It connects with the RER at several stations. Both trains run from 5:30am to around 12:45am. After that, you can wait in line for a taxi (there is a severe shortage), walk, or try the night bus, Noctambus. Noctambuses run on the hour from 1 to 5:30am from Châtelet-Hôtel de Ville, but their purpose is to take passengers from Paris to the suburbs, so they won't always be going your way. The Métro and the RER operate on a zone-fare system, but you probably won't travel any farther than the first two zones.

At the station, insert your ticket in the turnstile, pass through the entrance, and take your ticket out of the machine. You must keep your ticket until you exit the train platform and pass the *limite de validité des billets*. An inspector may ask to see your ticket at any time, and if you fail to produce it, you'll be subject to a 50€ ($63) fine that you must pay on the spot. When you ride the RER, it is especially important to keep your ticket because you have to insert it in a turnstile to leave the station. If you have a Carte Orange, just keep using the same ticket each time you enter the turnstile.

Some older Métro stations are marked by elegant Art Nouveau gateways reading METROPOLITAIN; others are marked by big yellow M signs. Every Métro stop has maps of the system, which are also available at ticket booths. Once you decide which line you need, make sure you are going in the right direction: On Métro line 1, "Direction: Esplanade de la Defense" indicates a westbound train, "Direction: Château de

Vincennes" is eastbound. To change train lines, look for the CORRESPONDANCE signs; blue signs reading SORTIE mark exits.

Near the exits there is usually a *plan du quartier,* a detailed pictorial map of the streets and buildings surrounding the station, with all exits marked. It's a good idea to consult the *plan du quartier* before you climb the stairs, especially at large stations; you might want to use a different exit to reach the other side of a busy street or wind up closer to your destination.

For more information on public transportation, stop in at the **Urbiel/RATP center** on place de la Madeleine, 1er (℃ **08-92-68-77-14;** www.ratp.fr; Métro: Madeleine), or call ℃ **08-92-68-41-14** for information in English.

BY BUS   The bus system is convenient and can be an inexpensive way to sightsee. Each bus shelter has a route map, which you'll want to check carefully. Because of the number of one-way streets, the bus is likely to make different stops depending on its direction. Métro tickets and passes are valid for bus travel, or you can buy your ticket from the conductor. Single tickets are 1.40€ ($1.75). *Carnets* cannot be bought onboard. Tickets must be punched in the machine and held until the end of the ride. Passes will also get you on the **Balabus** line (℃ **08-92-68-77-14**), which does a tourist circuit from the Gare de Lyon to the Grande Arche de la Defense; this service only runs on Sundays and holidays from April to September. A one-way trip equals three Métro tickets; pass holders ride free.

BY TAXI

Parisian taxis are fairly expensive, but you should know a few things in case you need one. First, look for the blue taxi sign denoting a taxi stand; although you can hail taxis in the street (look for a taxi with a white light on; an orange light means it's occupied), most drivers will not pick you up if you are near a taxi stand. Check the meter carefully, especially if you are coming from an airport; rip-offs are common. If you feel that you may have been overcharged, demand a receipt (which drivers are obligated to provide) and contact the **Préfecture of Police** (℃ **08-91-01-22-22**). For one to three people, the drop rate in Paris proper is 2€ ($2.50); the rate per kilometer is .62€ (80¢) from 7am to 7pm; otherwise, it's 1.06€ ($1.35). The rate per kilometer from the airport is 1.06€ ($1.35) during the day and 1.24€ ($1.55) at night (and all day Sun and public holidays). You will pay supplements from taxi ramps at train stations and at the Air France shuttle-bus terminals (1€/$1.25) for each piece of luggage, and, if the driver agrees to do so, 4€ ($5) for transporting a fourth person. It is common practice to tip your driver .50€ to 1€ (65¢–$1.25), except on longer journeys when the fare exceeds 15€ ($19); in these cases, a 5% to 10% tip is appropriate. Within central Paris, the average taxi fare is usually 9€ to 14€ ($11–$18).

Tips **Safety First**

Most of the time, the Métro is quite safe. Precautions are in order in the northern parts of the city, in deserted stations, and in long corridors between stations late at night. As a tourist, you are a special mark. You may feel safer riding in the first train car, where the engineer is. Watch out for pickpockets on platforms and trains.

BY CAR

Streets are narrow, and parking is next to impossible. Nerve, skill, ruthlessness, and a copilot are required if you insist on driving in Paris.

A few tips: Get an excellent street map and ride with another person, because there's no time to think at intersections. You usually must pay to park on the street. Depending on the neighborhood, expect to pay 1€ to 3€ ($1.25–$3.75) an hour for a maximum of 2 hours. Place coins in the nearest meter, which issues you a ticket to place on your windshield. You can also buy parking cards at the nearest *tabac* for meters that accept only cards. Parking is free on Sundays, holidays, and for the entire month of August.

Drivers and all passengers must wear seat belts. Children under 12 must ride in the back seat. Drivers are supposed to yield to the car on the right, except where signs indicate otherwise, as at traffic circles. Watch for the gendarmes, who lack patience and who consistently countermand the lights. Horn blowing is frowned upon except in emergencies. Flash your headlights instead.

BY BICYCLE

Long accustomed to darting through traffic, bicyclists are gaining new respect and a few amenities. Out of concern for pollution, city planners have been trying to encourage more cycling by setting aside more than 161km (100 miles) of bicycle lanes throughout Paris. The main axes run north-south from the Bassin de La Villette along the Canal St-Martin through the Left Bank and east-west from Château de Vincennes to the Bois de Boulogne and its miles of bike lanes. For more information and a bike map, pick up the *Plan Vert* from the tourist office, or *Mini Paris Vélo* map, on sale at many bookstores around the city for 4€ ($5).

Some sections along the Seine are closed to cars and open to pedestrians and cyclists from 10am to 5pm Sundays from March to November. It might not make much of a dent in the air quality, but it's a lovely way to spend a Sunday afternoon.

To rent a bicycle, contact **Maison Roue Libre,** 1 Passage Mondetour, 1e (© **08-10-44-15-34;** www.rouelibre.fr), a cycling center run by the RATP at Les Halles. They rent bikes for 9€ to 14€ ($11–$18) per day, 9€ ($11) for 3 hours, or 4€ ($5) for 1 hour, and can supply loads of biking info for Paris and the surrounding area. Hours are 9am to 7pm daily.

From April to September, Roue Libre has smaller outlets in several areas around the city, including Place de la Concorde and Bercy, where you may pick up your bike. Contact the main office above for details. ID and a deposit are required for all rentals. Roue Libre also runs **bike tours** (see "Organized Tours," in chapter 7).

FAST FACTS: Paris

American Express Amex operates a 24-hour phone line (© **01-47-14-50-00**) that handles questions about American Express services (banking, wire transfers, or emergencies that include lost or stolen Amex cards) in greater Paris. Tours, mail drop, money exchange, and wire-transfer services are available at 11 rue Scribe, 9e (© **01-47-14-50-00**; Métro: Opéra), and at 38 av. Wagram, 8e (© **01-42-27-58-80**; Métro: Ternes). Both are open for banking services Monday to Saturday from 9am to noon and from 2 to 5pm. Foreign exchange and participation in the company's many guided bus tours are offered Monday to Saturday from 9am to 6pm, and Sunday (rue Scribe branch only) from 10am to 4:30pm.

Babysitters **Allo Maman Poule?**, 7 villa Murat, 16e (© **01-45-20-96-96**), has babysitters who speak English, and they are accustomed to serving Paris hotels. The hourly rate is 15€ ($19; 3-hr. minimum) plus an agency fee of 13€ ($16). These rates are for up to two children. If you plan to stay out past 11pm, the agency will ask that you also pay the babysitter's taxi, approximately 12€ ($15).

Banks Banks in Paris are open Monday to Friday from 9am to 5pm. A few are open on Saturday. Ask at your hotel for the location of the bank nearest you. Shops and most hotels will cash your traveler's checks, but not at the advantageous rate a bank or foreign-exchange office will give you, so if you don't have access to your funds through an ATM, make sure you've allowed enough funds for *le weekend.*

Business Hours The **grands magasins** (department stores) are generally open Monday through Saturday 9:30am to 7pm; some **smaller shops** close for lunch and reopen around 2pm, but this is rarer than it used to be. Many stores stay open until 7pm in summer; others are closed on Monday. Most large **offices** remain open all day, but some close for lunch. **Banks** are normally open weekdays 9am to noon and 1 or 1:30 to 5pm. Many banks also open on Saturday from 9am to noon and 1 to 4pm.

Currency Exchange Banks and *bureaux de change* (exchange offices) almost always offer better exchange rates than hotels, restaurants, and shops. ATMs offer the best rates; make sure your bank card is on a major network (see "ATMs," in chapter 2.) For good rates and quick service, try the **Comptoir de Change Opéra,** 9 rue Scribe, 9e (© **01-47-42-20-96**; Métro: Opéra; RER: Auber). It is open weekdays from 9am to 6pm, Saturday from 9:30am to 4pm. The *bureaux de change* at all train stations (except Gare de Montparnasse) are open daily; **Exchange Corporation France,** 63 av. des Champs-Elysées, 8e (© **01-53-76-40-66**; Métro: Franklin-D-Roosevelt), and 140 av. des Champs-Elysées, 8e (© **01-40-75-00-49**; Métro: Charles-de-Gaulle–Etoile), keep long hours. (See "Money," in chapter 2, for exchange rates.)

Dentists You can call your consulate and ask the duty officer to recommend a dentist. For dental emergencies, call **SOS Dentaire** (© **01-43-37-51-00**), available daily from 9am to midnight. The cost ranges from 40€ to 55€ ($50–$69) depending on your location and time of day.

Doctors **SOS Médecins** (✆ 01-47-07-77-77) is a very reliable 24-hour service. Doctors usually arrive within 1 hour of your call and most speak at least some English. The cost is 35€ ($44) between 9am and 7pm and 59€ ($73) from 7pm to 9am.

Drugstores Pharmacies are marked with a green cross and are often very expensive; it's cheaper to buy your toiletries elsewhere. After regular hours, ask at your hotel where the nearest 24-hour *pharmacie* is. You'll also find the address posted on the doors or windows of other drugstores in the neighborhood. One all-night drugstore is the **Pharmacie Derhy,** in La Galerie Les Champs, 84 av. des Champs-Elysées, 8e (✆ 01-45-62-02-41; Métro: George V).

Electricity The French electrical system runs on 220 volts. Adapters are needed to convert the voltage and fit sockets and are cheaper at home than in Paris. Make sure you have an adapter that converts voltage; if you plug in a 110 hair dryer in a 220 socket, you can forget about the blow-dried look for the rest of your trip. Many hotels have two-pin (in some cases, three-pin) sockets for electric razors.

Embassies & Consulates If you have a passport, immigration, legal, or other problem, contact your consulate. Call before you go—they often keep strange hours and observe French and home-country holidays. Here's where to find them: **Australia,** 4 rue Jean-Rey, 15e (✆ 01-40-59-33-00; Métro: Bir-Hakeim); **Canada,** 35 av. Montaigne, 8e (✆ 01-44-43-29-00; Métro: Franklin-D-Roosevelt or Alma Marceau); **New Zealand,** 7 rue Léonard-de-Vinci, 16e (✆ 01-45-01-43-43; Métro: Victor-Hugo); **Great Britain,** 16 rue d'Anjou, 8e (✆ 01-44-51-31-02; Métro: Madeleine); and **United States,** 2 rue St-Florentin, 1er (✆ 01-43-12-22-22; Métro: Concorde).

Emergencies Call **112** or **17** for the **police.** To report a **fire,** dial ✆ **18.** For an **ambulance,** call ✆ **15** for **SAMU** (*Service d'aide médicale d'urgence,* or "emergency services"). For help in English, call **SOS Help** (✆ 01-47-23-80-80) between 3 and 11pm. The main police station, 1 rue de Lutèce, 4e (✆ 01-53-71-53-71; Métro: Cité), is open 24 hours a day.

Hospitals Two hospitals with English-speaking staff are the **American Hospital of Paris,** 63 bd. Victor-Hugo, Neuilly-sur-Seine (✆ 01-46-41-25-25), just west of Paris proper (Métro: Les Sablons or Levallois-Perret), and the **British Hospital of Paris,** 3 rue Barbes Levallois-Perret (✆ 01-46-39-22-22), just north of Neuilly (Métro: Anatole-France). The American Hospital is quite expensive; French hospitals and doctors' fees are much cheaper. Open Monday to Saturday from 8am to 7pm, **Central Médical Europe,** 44 rue d'Amsterdam, 9e (✆ 01-42-81-93-33; Métro: Liège or St-Lazare), maintains contacts with medical and dental practitioners in all fields. Appointments are recommended. An additional clinic is the **Centre Figuier,** 2 rue du Figuier, 4e (✆ 01-49-96-62-70; Métro: St-Paul). Call before visiting.

Internet Access Cybercafes abound all over Paris, but few have English keyboards. For a complete listing of Internet cafes, go to www.cybercaptive.com or www.cybercafe.com. One of the most popular is **Luxembourg Micro,** 81 blvd. Saint-Michel, 5e (✆ 01-46-33-27-98; www.luxembourg-micro.com; Métro: Luxembourg), open daily 9am to 11pm. To surf the Web or check your e-mail, you'll find English keyboards at the **Cyber World Cafe,** 20 rue de l'Exposition, 7e (© **01-53-59-96-54;** Métro: Ecole-Militaire), open Monday to Saturday from noon to 10pm and Sunday from noon to 8pm.

Laundry & Dry Cleaning To find a laundry, ask at your hotel or consult the Yellow Pages under *Laveries.* Take as many .50€, 1€, and 2€ pieces as you can. Washing and drying 6 kilos (13 lb.) costs from around 4€ to 7€ ($5–$8.75). Dry cleaning is called *nettoyage à sec* or *pressing.*

Liquor Laws Supermarkets, grocery stores, and cafes sell alcoholic beverages. The legal drinking age is 18. Persons under 18 can be served an alcoholic drink in a bar or restaurant if accompanied by a parent or legal guardian. Wine and liquor are sold every day of the year. *Be warned:* The authorities are very strict about drunk-driving laws. If convicted, you face a stiff fine and a possible prison term of 2 months to 2 years.

Lost & Found Be sure to tell all of your credit card companies the minute you discover your wallet has been lost or stolen and file a report at the nearest police precinct. Your credit card company or insurer may require a police report number or record of the loss.

Use the following numbers in Paris to report your lost or stolen credit card: **American Express** (call collect) © **336/393-1111; MasterCard** © **08-00-90-13-87; Visa** © **08-00-90-11-79;** they may be able to wire you a cash advance or deliver an emergency card in a day or two.

If you've lost all forms of photo ID, call your airline and explain the situation; they might allow you to board the plane if you have a copy of your passport or birth certificate and a copy of the police report you've filed.

If you need emergency cash over the weekend, when all banks and American Express offices are closed, you can have money wired to you via **Western Union** (© **800/325-6000;** www.westernunion.com).

Mail Large **post offices** are open weekdays 8am to 7pm, Saturday 8am to noon; small post offices may have shorter hours. There are many post offices (PTT) around the city; ask anybody for the nearest one. Air-mail letters and postcards to the United States cost .90€ ($1.15); western Europe, .60€ (75¢); eastern Europe .70€ (90¢); and Australia or New Zealand, 1.05€ ($1.30).

The **main post office** is at 52 rue du Louvre, 75001 Paris (© **01-40-28-20-40;** Métro: Louvre-Rivoli). It's open 24 hours for urgent mail, telegrams, and telephone calls. It handles Poste Restante mail—sent to you in care of the post office; be prepared to show your passport and pay .50€ (60¢) for each letter. If you don't want to use Poste Restante, you can receive mail in care of **American Express.** Holders of American Express cards or traveler's checks get this service free; others have to pay a fee.

Newspapers & Magazines Many newsstands carry the latest editions of the *International Herald Tribune*—it costs a whopping 2€($2.50) and is published Monday through Saturday—and the major London papers. The weekly entertainment guide *Pariscope,* which comes out on Wednesday, has an English-language insert with information on cultural events. You can also get the *New York Times* in some of the bigger English-language bookstores.

Police Dial ⓒ **112** or **17** in emergencies; otherwise, call ⓒ **08-91-01-22-22**. There's also a website: www.prefecture-police-paris.interieur.gouv.fr.

Restrooms Public restrooms are plentiful, but you usually have to pay for them. Every cafe has a restroom, but they are supposed to be for customers only. The best plan is to ask to use the telephone; it's usually next to the *toilette*.

Smoking Although restaurants are required to provide nonsmoking sections, you may find yourself next to the kitchen or the restrooms. Even there, your neighbor will probably light up and defy you to say something. Large brasseries, expensive restaurants, and places accustomed to dealing with foreigners are most likely to be accommodating. Smokers generally get the last word; the best strategy for avoiding smoke is to sit outside.

Taxes As a member of the European Community, France routinely imposes a 20.6% value-added tax (VAT) on many goods and services. The tax on merchandise applies to clothing, appliances, liquor, leather goods, shoes, furs, jewelry, perfume, cameras, and even caviar. You can get a refund—usually 13%—on certain goods and merchandise, but not on services. The minimum purchase is 185€ ($231) in the same store for nationals or residents of countries outside the European Union. See chapter 9, "Paris Shopping," for details on the refund process.

Telephone & Fax All **public phone booths** take only telephone debit cards, called *télécartes,* which can be bought at post offices and at *tabacs.* You insert the card into the phone and make your call; the cost is deducted from the "value" of the card recorded on its chip, or *puce.* The *télécarte* comes in 50- and 120-unit denominations, costing 7.50€ ($9.40) and 15€ ($19), respectively, and can be used only in a phone booth. Ask for a *télécarte France Télécom* (made by France Télécom, the French national telecommunications company).

Another kind of telephone card is a little more labor intensive, but cheaper, especially for international calls. Instead of inserting the card into a public phone, you dial a free number and tap in a code. The cards come with directions, some in English, and can be used from public and private phones (such as your hotel room) unlike the *télécartes.* Tell the cashier at the *tabac* that you would like a *carte téléphonique avec un code,* and which country you want to call (some cards specialize in certain regions). Delta and GTS Omnicom are two good cards for calling North America and Europe.

A word of warning about phone charges: Many businesses and services now charge for information given over the phone. Numbers beginning with **0802, 0803,** and **0892** cost .16€ (20¢), .22€ (27¢), and .35€ (44¢) per minute, respectively. Whenever possible, try to find phone numbers within the same organization that you can call without paying a fee. Also watch out for numbers beginning with **06**—it indicates that you are calling a cellular phone, which costs more in France, unless you are calling from another cellular phone.

For placing **international calls from France,** dial 00, then the country code (for the United States and Canada, 1; for Britain, 44; for Ireland, 353; for Australia, 61; for New Zealand, 64), then the area or city code, and then the local number (for example, to call New York, you'd dial 00 + 1 + 212 + the seven-digit phone number). For **calling from Paris to anywhere else in France** (called *province*), just dial the number; the area code will always be included in the number you are given. The country is divided into zones with prefixes beginning with 01, 02, 03, 04, and 05. Paris is 01.

If you're **calling France from the United States,** dial the international prefix, 011; then the country code for France, 33; followed by the number but leaving off the initial zero (for example, if you are calling a number in Paris, you would dial 011 + 33 + 1 and the remaining eight digits).

Avoid making phone calls from your hotel room; many hotels charge at least .50€ (62¢) for local calls, and the markup on international calls can be staggering.

You can send **fax** messages at the main post office in each arrondissement of Paris, but it's often cheaper to ask at your hotel or to go to a neighborhood printer or copy shop.

Time Paris is 6 hours ahead of Eastern Standard Time and 9 hours ahead of Pacific Standard Time; when it's noon in New York, it's 6pm in Paris, and when it's noon in Los Angeles, it's 9pm in Paris.

Tipping Service is supposedly included at your hotel, but it is still customary to tip the **bellhop** about 1€ ($1.25) per bag, more in expensive (splurge) hotels. If you have a lot of luggage, tip a bit more. It's not customary to tip housekeepers unless you do something that requires extra work. Tip 2€ to 4€ ($2.50–$5) if a **reception staff member** performs extra services.

Although your *addition* (**restaurant bill**) or *fiche* (**cafe check**) will bear the words *service compris* (service charge included), it's customary to leave a small tip. Generally, 5% is considered acceptable. Remember, a 15% service charge has supposedly already been paid for.

Taxi drivers appreciate a tip of .30€ to .75€ (38¢–94¢). On longer journeys, when the fare exceeds 15€ ($19), a 5% to 10% tip is appropriate. At the theater and cinema, tip .50€ (62¢) if an usher shows you to your seat. In **public toilets,** there is often a fee for using the facilities. If not, the attendant will expect a tip of about .50€ (62¢). Put it in the basket or on the plate at the entrance. **Porters** and **cloakroom attendants** are usually governed by set prices, which are displayed. If not, give a porter 1€ to 1.50€ ($1.25–$1.90) per suitcase, and a cloakroom attendant .50€ to 1€ (62¢–$1.25) per coat.

Water Tap water in Paris is perfectly safe, but if you're prone to stomach problems, you may prefer to drink mineral water. If you stop at a supermarket (such as a Francprix or Monoprix), the price of a bottle of Evian or Volvic will be about 1€ ($1.25). Buy it anywhere else and you'll end up paying up to 4€ ($5) per bottle!

5

Accommodations You Can Afford

You'd be surprised what comfortable accommodations the budget traveler can find in Paris. If you don't mind the occasional oddly shaped (and usually tiny) room or lugging your baggage up some stairs, you'll find that staying in a hotel in Paris doesn't have to significantly lighten your wallet. These small, mostly family-run lodgings offer some things that most luxury hotels can't supply: hominess, intimacy, and a degree of authenticity.

Don't be afraid to ask for what you want when making reservations. Tell the management you want a large room, a quiet room, a room with a view, a bathroom with a tub, or simply the most recently renovated room. Ask to see your room before checking in, and if you don't like it, ask to see another.

If room size is important, you would do better to reserve a triple or suite in a modest hotel than a double in a higher-priced one. Budget triples are generally larger than comparably priced doubles. Also, if you're looking for a double room, note that a double bed is cheaper than two twin beds, but the twin beds are likely to be in a larger room.

Rooms facing the street tend to get more light, but can be noisier. Hotels often have double-paned windows, but noise can be a problem in lively areas. If you are a light sleeper, ask for a room on the courtyard, and pack earplugs. Also, if you're coming in midsummer, finding a room with air-conditioning will prevent you from having to keep the windows open.

Though generally quite clean, bathrooms in Parisian hotels can be a bit of an adventure. They usually range in size from tiny to small. Some rooms have only a sink or a shower; most have a toilet with a shower or a tub. If you do get a full (toilet and shower or tub) bathroom, it will always have a sink. Rooms without facilities can be a bargain if you don't mind sharing a bathroom with other guests (there is usually a charge for the shower). More hotels are adding full bathrooms. Rooms with a tub tend to be nicer (and more expensive), but if you take this option, you may have to deal with a hand-held shower and no curtain—so watch where you aim! The hotels described in this chapter offer private full bathrooms unless specified.

Breakfasts, unless otherwise noted, are continental, meaning croissants, rolls, jam, and a hot beverage. A "buffet breakfast" will usually be an expanded version, including cereal, yogurt, and sometimes cheese or ham. There is usually a small supplement of 1€ to 2€ ($1.25–$2.50) for having breakfast delivered to your room. If you are anxious to get going and are not a big eater, you will usually spend less at a nearby cafe or bakery.

Blow dryers and irons are often available at the front desk. Almost every hotel that doesn't have a safe in the room will have one at reception. For online addicts, a few hotels are beginning to include phone jacks in rooms that accept North

American phone plugs (RG-45), and others have modem jacks for French phone plugs. Be sure to bring appropriate adapters.

High season is generally late spring to early summer and early fall; during these periods reserve at least 2 months in advance. April, June, and September are the busiest months. Often, hotels are booked solid during this time, so reserving 3 to 5 months in advance would be even better.

The dead of winter and August are lighter months. During annual trade shows and events, like the Foire de Paris in late April or the Fête de la Musique in June, hotels are booked solid. Mid-September to mid-October is one of the busiest times for conventions, so hotel space is scarce. We suggest reserving up to 4 months in advance if you're visiting during these busy periods.

Check the "Paris Calendar of Events" in chapter 2, "Planning an Affordable Trip to Paris," to ensure that you plan your trip for a time when the city won't be full to bursting.

If you do come to town without a reservation, try to arrive early in the day and head to one of the tourist offices in the airports, at the train stations, or at 127 av. des Champs-Elysées. For a small fee, the staff will book a room for you.

Be flexible about what part of the city you stay in. Paris is relatively small and public transportation is excellent. Even on the fringes, you aren't more than 30 minutes from the center of town, where hotel rates are highest. Most listings are for places within our $95-a-day guidelines; options that fall outside those limits are **"Super-Cheap Sleeps"** or **"Worth a Splurge."**

The prices are correct as of fall 2005, but are, of course, subject to change. All rates below include tax.

1 On the Right Bank

1ER ARRONDISSEMENT

You can't get much more central than the 1er arrondissement. The Parisii tribesmen camped out around here, and you too may decide that this is your preferred place to stay. The chic shopping areas around place Vendôme and rue St-Honoré are in this area, as well as some of the city's most famous monuments (the Louvre, Notre-Dame, Sainte-Chapelle). The Tuileries gardens and place de la Concorde are also here. Just remember that you will be surrounded by hoards of other tourists with the same idea.

Hôtel Londres St-Honoré *Finds*   On a tiny side street off *très chic* rue St-Honoré lined with swanky boutiques, you'll find this tidy hotel perfect for the visitor on the run. Rooms are not especially large or bright but are clean and somewhat charming with whitewashed walls and white bedspreads (though the blankets are a bit old and worn), and some have exposed wood beams. Stay here for the excellent location, quiet atmosphere, and friendly staff. If this hotel is full, you might try the sister property a few steps away at **no. 25. Hôtel St-Roch** (✆ **01-42-60-17-91**), which has 21 rooms and similar rates.

13 rue St-Roch, 75001 Paris (corner of 300 rue St-Honoré). ✆ **01-42-60-15-62**. Fax 01-42-60-16-00. hotel.londres. st.honore@gofornet.com. 29 units. 70€–86€ ($88–$108) single; 90€–98€ ($113–$123) double; 100€–108€ ($125–$135) twin; 120€ ($150) triple. Breakfast 7€ ($8.75). MC, V. Métro: Tuileries. **Amenities:** Elevator. *In room:* Satellite TV, minibar, hair dryer.

Hôtel Louvre Forum ✦   On a quiet street, this comfortable hotel provides modern, clean rooms in bright, tasteful colors. Best of all, it's steps from the Louvre. All the rooms have been renovated in the last few years and have new wood furniture and new bathrooms. Space can be tight in the rooms on the lower floors. The service, like the lobby, is practical, stylish, and not particularly welcoming, but the hotel's location and condition are ample compensation.

25 rue du Bouloi, 75001 Paris. (✆) **01-42-36-54-19**. Fax 01-42-33-66-31. www.hotel-louvre-forum-paris.com. 27 units. 78€ ($98) single; 88€–98€ ($110–$123) double. Breakfast 9€ ($11). AE, DC, MC, V. Métro: Louvre-Rivoli. **Amenities:** Elevator. *In room:* TV, minibar, hair dryer, safe.

Hôtel Louvre Richelieu *Value* This hotel offers great rates for this location—halfway between the Louvre and the Opéra. The restored stone walls of the entry corridor lead you to the second-floor lobby, where you are greeted by Joel, the affable proprietor. All the rooms were slowly renovated between 2003 and 2005; the work is now complete and the rates have remained unchanged. The new decor boasts rich blues and golds with sleek lighting fixtures and new bathrooms. Rooms with twin beds are surprisingly spacious and have high ceilings that help compensate for the lack of light. There is no elevator and none of the rooms has a TV. A computer in the lobby is available for guests to log on to the Internet for a small fee.

51 rue de Richelieu, 75001 Paris. (✆) **01-42-97-46-20**. Fax 01-47-03-94-13. www.louvre-richelieu.com. 14 units, 12 with bathroom. 62€ ($78) single with sink, 86€ ($108) single with bathroom; 74€ ($93) double with sink, 86€ ($108) double with bathroom; 90€ ($113) twin with bathroom; 111€ ($139) triple with bathroom; 128€ ($160) quadruple with bathroom. Breakfast 6€ ($7.50). MC, V. Métro: Palais-Royal–Musée du Louvre, Pyramides.

Hôtel Montpensier *Value* This sprawling hotel was once the residence of Mademoiselle de Montpensier, cousin of Louis XIV, but the high ceilings and enormous staircase are all that is left of its grandeur. The lobby was renovated in 2005 and boasts a white-oak reception and a cozy sitting area with leather sofa and chairs, giving the hotel more of a luxury-hotel feel. Unfortunately the rooms on the first two floors are somewhat drab; try requesting one of the rooms on the fifth floor that have more character, with slanted, beamed ceilings and views of Parisian rooftops. The hotel began a renovation in 2003, redecorating a few rooms per year. At press time, only 15 rooms were completely refurbished (freshly painted with new carpets) and come with bright yellow and orange tile in the new bathrooms. Request one of the "new" rooms at check-in, as they can't be guaranteed when making your reservation. If the rest of the rooms are a bit worn, the friendly service is usually top-notch.

12 rue de Richelieu, 75001 Paris. (✆) **01-42-96-28-50**. Fax 01-42-86-02-70. www.montpensierparis.com. 43 units, 35 with bathroom, 4 with toilet and sink. 61€ ($76) single or double with sink; 81€ ($101) double with toilet and sink, 95€ ($119) double with bathroom; 115€ ($144) triple with bathroom; 129€ ($161) quadruple with bathroom. Shower 4€ ($5). Breakfast 7€ ($8.75). AE, MC, V. Métro: Palais-Royal–Musée du Louvre. **Amenities:** Elevator. *In room:* TV, hair dryer.

SUPER-CHEAP SLEEPS

Hôtel Henri IV *Moments* One of Europe's most famous and crowded budget hotels (book far in advance) occupies a great location on place Dauphine—the northernmost tip of Ile de la Cité, across from the St-Germain neighborhood. The 17th-century building was designed for a more petite population, so don't be surprised to find halls, stairs, and rooms somewhat miniature. The cozy rooms are past their prime; many find them romantically evocative, others just run-down. There are five newer rooms with bathrooms; two have tubs. All the other rooms come with a sink. Several rooms have views of place Dauphine. Rooms don't have phones and there is no elevator, but the hotel has plenty of atmosphere. Advance view requests cannot always be honored; preference goes to longer stays.

Accommodations on the Right Bank (1–4, 8–11 & 16–18e)

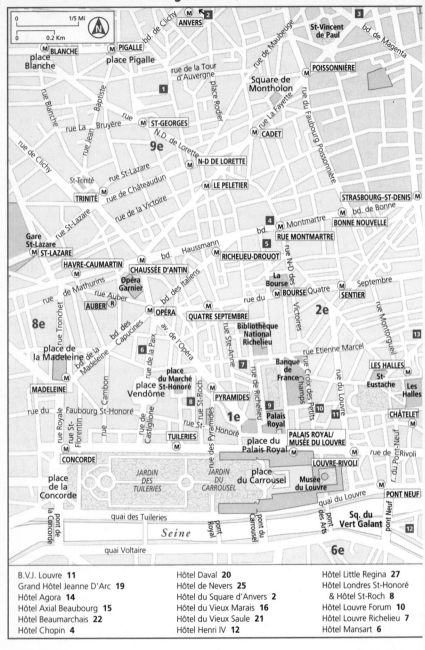

B.V.J. Louvre **11**	Hôtel Daval **20**	Hôtel Little Regina **27**
Grand Hôtel Jeanne D'Arc **19**	Hôtel de Nevers **25**	Hôtel Londres St-Honoré
Hôtel Agora **14**	Hôtel du Square d'Anvers **2**	& Hôtel St-Roch **8**
Hôtel Axial Beaubourg **15**	Hôtel du Vieux Marais **16**	Hôtel Louvre Forum **10**
Hôtel Beaumarchais **22**	Hôtel du Vieux Saule **21**	Hôtel Louvre Richelieu **7**
Hôtel Chopin **4**	Hôtel Henri IV **12**	Hôtel Mansart **6**

Hôtel Montpensier **9**
Hôtel Navarin et d'Angleterre **1**
Hôtel Notre-Dame **25**
Hôtel Saint-Louis Bastille **24**
Hôtel Sévigné **18**
Hôtel Tiquetonne **13**

Hôtel Vivienne **5**
Little Hôtel **26**
New Hôtel **3**
Résidence Alhambra **23**
Youth Hostel le Fauconnier **17**

25 pl. Dauphine, 75001 Paris. © **01-43-54-44-53**. 21 units, 5 with bathroom, 5 with shower only. 24€–27€ ($30–$34) single without shower; 31€–43€ ($39–$54) double without shower, 46€–55€ ($58–$69) double with shower, 69€ ($86) double with bathroom; 49€–55€ ($61–$69) triple without shower; 71€ ($89) triple with shower; 55€ ($69) quad without shower. Rates include breakfast. MC, V. Métro: Pont-Neuf.

WORTH A SPLURGE

Hôtel Agora ⟨R⟩   Don't be put off by the ugly green wallpaper in the entry—this charming hotel is favored by film crews and visiting notables who come for the lovely rooms, central location, and reasonable prices. Rooms are furnished with antiques and include touches such as marble mantle pieces, floral prints, and painted tabletops. Fifth-floor rooms have views of the cathedral of St-Eustache, and all look out on the street. Double-glazed windows muffle some of the noise of Les Halles, which can get a little seedy at night. If you request the smaller double when making your reservations, you'll get the best value for your money at 97€ ($121 is a steal in this neighborhood). Claustrophobes should avoid the elevator.

7 rue de la Cossonnerie, 75001 Paris. © **01-42-33-46-02**. Fax 01-42-33-80-99. www.parisby.com/agora. 29 units (most with shower only). 68€–116€ ($85–$145) single; 97€–136€ ($121–$170) double; 149€ ($186) triple. Breakfast 8€ ($10). AE, MC, V. Métro: Châtelet. **Amenities:** Small elevator. *In room:* TV, safe.

Hôtel Mansart ⟨R⟩⟨R⟩ *(Finds)*   This elegant hotel's location may be the best in Paris. Behind the Ritz and steps away from the swanky place Vendôme, the Mansart offers old-world luxury at bargain prices. A renovation was completed in 2003; an attractive lobby leads to the traditionally decorated rooms of varying sizes. Frequent promotional rates in the dead of winter and July and August reduce the smallest rooms to a steal at 135€ ($169). The more spacious doubles come with two windows, marble-topped dressers, full-length mirrors, and heavy drapes. All bathrooms are white and sparkling. The breakfast room has comfortable chairs and white tablecloths. The hotel is named after Jules Harouin-Mansart, the architect who designed place Vendôme and the Palace of Versailles for Louis XIV.

Tips   **Living Like a Parisian**

Renting a furnished apartment is one of the best ways to experience life as a Parisian. **Lodgis Paris** (47 rue Paradis, 10e; © 01-70-39-11-11; fax 01-70-39-11-15; www.lodgis.com) has an incredible selection of budget apartments throughout the city. All are privately owned dwellings in residential buildings and come completely furnished with a kitchen, bathroom, and linens. Rates range from about 375€ to 500€ ($469–$625) for a studio for two people per week, and 450€ to 750€ ($563–$938) for a one-bedroom for up to four people. Most apartments come with TV, stereo, and utensils, and some have dishwashers and washing machines.

The rates are quite a bargain and more travelers are choosing this option for the privacy and wealth of amenities it provides. Remember, however, that you won't have any services and you'll have to clean the apartment on the day of your departure. The agency will help you arrange for a cleaning service (about 45€/$56), if you prefer.

5 rue des Capucines, 75001 Paris. ✆ **01-42-61-50-28.** Fax 01-49-27-97-44. www.esprit-de-france.com. 57 units. 165€–186€ ($206–$233) double; from 255€ ($319) suite. Breakfast 10€ ($13). AE, MC, V. Métro: Tuileries or Concorde. **Amenities:** Elevator. *In room:* Satellite TV, minibar, hair dryer.

2 & 9E ARRONDISSEMENTS

Though not packed with monuments, this area is a good place to stay for those who want to be away from the tour buses but still centrally located. Die-hard shoppers will enjoy the Printemps and Galeries Lafayette department stores on boulevard Haussmann, and history buffs can wander around New Athens in the 9e, where many artists and writers of the Romantic period lived and worked.

Hôtel Chopin 🌟 *Finds*   This alluring hotel stands at the far end of the Passage Jouffroy, a covered shopping arcade just off one of the Grands Boulevards. Both were built in 1846 and have since been classified as national monuments. Behind the glass-and-wood facade lies an inviting lobby, where there's a piano in honor of the hotel's namesake. Comfortable, attractive rooms are decorated in splashy fabrics and include sparkling, modern bathrooms. The management does a great job keeping the rooms looking fresh; several of the rooms were completely refurbished in 2005 with new mattresses and carpets. Each year the hotel renovates a few rooms to keep them all fresh. Because rooms overlook the glass-topped arcade rather than the street, they are all quiet enough for you to leave the windows open if you wish. The few rooms behind the elevator bank don't get as much light, but they are also cheaper. Reserve early as this hotel is very popular with returning guests.

10 bd. Montmartre or 46 Passage Jouffroy, 75009 Paris. ✆ **01-47-70-58-10.** Fax 01-42-47-00-70. 36 units, 35 with bathroom. 58€ ($73) single without bathroom, 65€–73€ ($81–$91) single with bathroom; 75€–88€ ($94–$110) double; 100€ ($125) triple. Breakfast 7€ ($8.75). AE, DC, MC, V. Métro: Grands Boulevards. **Amenities:** Elevator. *In room:* TV.

Hôtel du Square d'Anvers 🌟 *Finds*   Overlooking the leafy park Anvers, this charming hotel is tucked away on a quiet street. Most rooms overlook the park and are small but bright and come with attractive yellow wallpaper and simple furnishings. The bathrooms on the first five floors were redone in 2002 with orange tile and are attractive (bathrooms on the sixth floor will be renovated in the next 2 years). The sixth-floor rooms are more spacious and have tiny balconies with glorious views of Paris—from the Eiffel Tower to the Sacré-Coeur. There's a lovely garden where breakfast is served in summer and a bright living room where you can relax in winter. The management tries hard to make guests feel welcome.

6 pl. d'Anvers, 75009 Paris. ✆ **01-42-81-20-74.** Fax 01-48-78-47-45. www.hotel-paris-montmartre.com. 28 units. 90€–110€ ($113–$138) single; 100€ ($125) double; 120€ ($150) double with views on 6th floor. Breakfast 7€ ($8.75). MC, V. Métro: Anvers. **Amenities:** Elevator. *In room:* Satellite TV, hair dryer.

Hôtel Navarin et d'Angleterre *Value*   Nestled in a quiet, villagelike neighborhood at the foot of Montmartre, this hotel has been managed by the Maylin family for more than 25 years. The lobby is breezy and inviting; the rooms are in good, if not mint, condition. All rooms have French windows that let in ample light, but those facing the street are noticeably brighter. Bathrooms are clean, but small. During the warmer months, breakfast is served on a garden patio with an acacia tree. If you book a room facing the garden, you'll be wakened by singing birds.

8 rue de Navarin, 75009 Paris. ✆ **01-48-78-31-80.** Fax 01-48-74-14-09. Navarin-anglettere@wanadoo.fr. 26 units, 24 with bathroom, 2 with toilet only. 58€ ($73) single with toilet only, 68€ ($85) single with bathroom; 64€ ($80) double with toilet only, 78€ ($98) double with bathroom; 94€ ($118) triple with bathroom. Breakfast 8€ ($10). MC, V. Métro: St-Georges or Notre-Dame de Lorettes. **Amenities:** Elevator. *In room:* TV.

Hôtel Vivienne *(Kids)*   If you like modern, sparkling hotels, then this is a good choice. Just up the street from the Bourse on a block lined with numismatic shops and money-changers, this comfortable hotel offers soundproofed rooms steps from the arcades branching off from the Passage des Panoramas. The new lobby with attached breakfast area is attractive and modern and offers Internet access to guests for a small fee. Rooms vary in size from adequate to huge; some of the rooms were renovated in 2003 with work continuing slowly until 2006. Ask for one of the newer rooms when making reservations. All bathrooms have just been redone, and a few rooms have terraces big enough for an alfresco breakfast. Cribs are available and kids under 10 stay free. A computer with free Internet is in the lobby for guests.

40 rue Vivienne, 75002 Paris. (℃ **01-42-33-13-26.** Fax 01-40-41-98-19. paris@hotel-vivienne.com. 45 units, 30 with bathroom, 14 with shower only. 54€ ($68) single with shower only; 69€ ($86) double with shower only, 81€–104€ ($101–$130) double with bathroom. Breakfast 7€ ($8.75). Children under 10 stay free in parent's room. MC, V. Métro: Bourse or Grands Boulevards. **Amenities:** Elevator. *In room:* Satellite TV, dataport, hair dryer.

SUPER-CHEAP SLEEPS

Hôtel Little Regina *(Kids) (Value)*   Run by the Corbel family since the 1960s, this hotel's warm atmosphere and relatively spacious rooms are a great bargain. The recently renovated rooms are soundproofed and have new rugs and furniture, burgundy wallpaper, ample wardrobe space, full-length mirrors, and white-oak desks. New cotton bedspreads cover comfortable beds. The sparkling bathrooms have all been redone and come with shower doors (a rarity in Paris and even rarer in budget hotels). Breakfast can be served in your room, or you can amble downstairs and check out the new breakfast area. The hotel's proximity to the train stations keeps the streets hopping with people until late into the night. Upon arrival, show your Frommer's guide to Mr. Corbel and he'll offer a 10% discount.

89 bd. de Strasbourg, 75009 Paris. (℃ **01-40-37-72-30.** Fax 01-40-36-34-14. www.littleregina.com. 34 units. 60€ ($75) single; 75€ ($94) double; 85€ ($106) triple. Breakfast 6€ ($7.50). AE, MC, V. Métro: Gare de l'Est. **Amenities:** Elevator. *In room:* TV, hair dryer.

Hôtel Tiquetonne *(Value)*   This welcoming hotel is on a street lined with body-piercing parlors, fine food stores, and jewelry shops, and is right around the corner from the hip Passage du Grand Cerf. Large, well-lit rooms contain medium-firm beds, writing tables, and comfortable chairs. Rue Tiquetonne is a pedestrian zone, so rooms facing the street are quiet. Rooms on the upper floors are a little smaller, but have nice views of rooftops. The friendly owner, Mme Sirvain, would be happy to answer any questions you have about the neighborhood.

6 rue Tiquetonne, 75002 Paris. (℃ **01-42-36-94-58.** Fax 01-42-36-02-94. 46 units, 32 with bathroom. 30€ ($38) single without bathroom, 40€–50€ ($50–$63) single with bathroom; 50€ ($63) double with bathroom. Breakfast 6€ ($7.50). Shower 5€ ($6.25). MC, V. Métro: Etienne Marcel. **Amenities:** Elevator.

10E ARRONDISSEMENT

This is a good area in which to stay if you have train connections at either Gare du Nord or Gare de l'Est. It's also close to the Canal St-Martin, a little-visited waterway with lovely arched bridges and the locale of the film classic *Hôtel du Nord.*

Little Hôtel   An easy walk to the Canal St-Martin, this pleasant hotel is on a quiet street near the Gare de l'Est. Well-kept rooms have new wallpaper, and furniture and carpets are in good shape. The bathrooms are spotless and recently tiled, though some fixtures are old. The hotel has two wheelchair-accessible rooms on the first floor and renovated its vaulted cellar as a breakfast room.

3 rue Pierre Chausson, 75010 Paris. ✆ **01-42-08-21-57.** Fax 01-42-08-33-80. hotellittle@aol.com. 37 units. 55€ ($69) single; 70€ ($88) double; 85€ ($106) triple. Breakfast 5€ ($6.25). AE, DC, MC, V. Métro: Jacques Bonsergent or République. **Amenities:** Elevator, wheelchair-accessible rooms. *In room:* Satellite TV.

New Hôtel   This hotel's management aims to please. Automatic glass doors open into a lobby that includes a miniwaterfall, a soda machine, and Internet access (.10€/15¢ per min.). Downstairs, the vaulted breakfast room offers bacon and eggs as well as croissants. The six-story hotel provides tidy, if slightly fading, rooms with modern furniture. Rooms overlooking the street have two windows and are the brightest. Most have hair dryers, and about half have air-conditioning for an extra charge. Some rooms have small, vertiginous balconies.

40 rue de St-Quentin, 75010 Paris. ✆ **01-48-78-04-83.** Fax 01-40-82-91-22. www.newhotelparis.com. 41 units. 65€–75€ ($81–$94) single, 75€–93€ ($94–$116) single with A/C; 70€–80€ ($88–$100) double, 75€–98€ ($94–$123) double with A/C; 99€–106€ ($124–$133) triple with A/C; 106€ ($133) quad, 110€–130€ ($138–$163) quad with A/C. Breakfast 5€ ($6.25); hot breakfast an extra 2€ ($2.50). AE, DC, MC, V. Métro: Gare du Nord. **Amenities:** Elevator, nonsmoking rooms. *In room:* A/C available in most rooms, satellite TV, hair dryers in most rooms.

3, 4 & 11E ARRONDISSEMENTS

Crisscrossed with narrow, medieval streets and dotted with 17th-century mansions, the Marais is one of the hippest neighborhoods of Paris. Here you can find boutiques and restaurants, a happening gay scene, several museums, and the remnants of the city's Jewish quarter. Hotels book up fast and this is the most challenging area in which to find hotels within our budget. Farther east, the Bastille area offers a wealth of nightspots and a huge modern opera house—an architectural masterpiece or an eyesore, depending on your outlook.

Grand Hôtel Jeanne D'Arc ★ *Finds*   Reserve well in advance for this great little hotel near all the major attractions in the area. It's a favorite with the fashion industry during show season. Housed in an 18th-century building on the place Marché St-Catharine (a lovely square lush with Chinese mulberry trees), the lobby includes a wild mirror framed in mosaics; the walls in the breakfast room are hand-painted by local artists. Rooms are colorful, decent-size, and have large bathrooms, but none have views of the square.

3 rue de Jarente, 75004 Paris. ✆ **01-48-87-62-11.** Fax 01-48-87-37-31. www.hoteljeannedarc.com. 36 units. 58€–70€ ($73–$88) single; 82€–96€ ($103–$120) double; 115€ ($144) triple; 145€ ($181) quad. Breakfast 6€ ($7.50). MC, V. Métro: St-Paul or Bastille. **Amenities:** Elevator. *In room:* Satellite TV, hair dryer, safe. Cribs available upon request.

Hôtel Daval *Kids*   An oasis of calm in a lively neighborhood, this hotel was renovated a few years ago and has been kept in pristine condition since. Rooms are decorated in a contemporary style with shades of blue. The best look out on a courtyard; street-side rooms are noisy, but double-glazed windows and air-conditioning muffle the commotion. Doubles are good-sized, triples large enough for a family. Skip the expensive breakfast; cafes and bakeries abound nearby.

21 rue Daval, 75011 Paris. ✆ **01-47-00-51-23.** Fax 01-40-21-80-26. hoteldaval@wanadoo.fr. 23 units, all with shower only. 71€ ($89) double; 82€ ($103) triple; 100€ ($125) quad. Breakfast 8€ ($10). AE, DC, MC, V. Métro: Bastille. **Amenities:** Elevator. *In room:* A/C, satellite TV, hair dryer, safe.

Hôtel du Vieux Saule ★   Smart travelers make tracks for this lovely hotel in the northern Marais that offers not only air-conditioning and Internet access (free for guests in the salon) but a sauna as well. The cheerful, smallish rooms come with satellite TV, a trouser press, and small irons with ironing boards. Deluxe rooms on the top floor are large and have slanted ceilings and big bathrooms. The buffet breakfast is served in a vaulted cellar and includes cereals and nut breads, as well as baguettes and croissants. You may wish to skip the expensive breakfast and find a cafe tucked away in this neighborhood laced with tiny, narrow streets left over from the medieval era.

6 rue de Picardie, 75003 Paris. ℰ **01-42-72-01-14.** Fax 01-40-27-88-21. www.hotelvieuxsaule.com. 31 units. 91€ ($114) single; 106€–151€ ($133–$189) double. Breakfast 10€ ($13). AE, DC, MC, V. Métro: République or Filles du Calvaire. **Amenities:** Free sauna; laundry service; elevator; nonsmoking rooms. *In room:* A/C, satellite TV w/pay movies, hair dryer, iron, safe, trouser press.

Hôtel Notre-Dame *(Value)*   On a quiet side street a short walk from place de la République and the Marais, this hotel offers pleasant, large rooms at reasonable prices. The carpets in all rooms were replaced in early 2005 and there are full-length mirrors, and double-glazed windows. Mattresses are fairly new and medium-firm. Rooms with bathrooms have TVs, and those on the sixth floor have small balconies. The English-speaking staff is friendly.

51 rue de Malte, 75011 Paris. ℰ **01-47-00-78-76.** Fax 01-43-55-32-31. www.hotel-notredame.com. 46 units, 30 with bathroom. 38€ ($48) single with sink; 45€ ($56) single with shower only; 60€ ($75) single with bathroom; 60€ ($75) double with shower only; 67€–72€ ($84–$90) double with bathroom; 86€ ($108) triple with bathroom. Breakfast 6.50€ ($8.15). AE, MC, V. Métro: République. **Amenities:** Elevator. *In room:* TV (in rooms with baths only).

Hôtel Sévigné *(Finds)*   Just off the rue de Rivoli in the Marais, this comfortable hotel offers a great location and clean, well-kept rooms. Rooms facing the street have some great views of the Church of St-Paul for those who don't mind a bit of noise. Windows are double-glazed and mattresses are firm. Some rooms on the second, third, and fifth floors have narrow balconies.

2 rue Malher, 75004 Paris. ℰ **01-42-72-76-17.** Fax 01-42-72-98-28. www.le-sevigne.com. 30 units. 63€–78€ ($79–$98) single; 74€–86€ ($93–$108) double; 121€ ($151) triple. Breakfast 6.40€ ($8). MC, V. Métro: St-Paul. **Amenities:** Elevator. *In room:* Satellite TV.

Résidence Alhambra *(Value)*   This hotel was totally renovated in 2002 and is fresh and inviting. In the summer you can eat breakfast among the roses in the back garden. The simple, modern rooms have newer mattresses, bright yellow curtains and bedspreads, and some have balconies over the garden. Rooms facing the street get little noise, and those facing the garden get none. Small families can take advantage of good-size triples. The hotel is within easy walking distance to the Marais, Bastille, and Oberkampf areas.

11 bis and 13 rue de Malte, 75011 Paris. ℰ **01-47-00-35-52.** Fax 01-43-57-98-75. www.hotelalhambra.fr. 58 units. 63€ ($79) single; 70€–74€ ($88–$93) double; 85€–106€ ($106–$133) triple; 119€ ($149) quad. Breakfast in breakfast room 6.20€ ($7.75), in room 6.80€ ($8.50). AE, DC, MC, V. Métro: Oberkampf (exit Crussol). **Amenities:** Elevator. *In room:* Satellite TV, dataport.

SUPER-CHEAP SLEEPS

Hôtel de Nevers *(Value)*   Don't mistake this hotel for another in the 7e with the same name. The ebullient Alain Bourderau, his wife, Sophie, and their cats will enthusiastically welcome you to this well-tended hotel. A 1930s vintage wood-paneled elevator brings you to basic, average-size rooms papered with floral prints. The triples on the sixth floor have skylights, sloping ceilings, and views over the rooftops. Double rooms with twin beds are a little bigger, but the beds are quite narrow. The walls are thin, so if you're a light sleeper, bring earplugs. There is not one TV to be found in this hotel, but there is a computer with free Internet access for guests in the cozy lounge, where wireless Internet will be available as of early 2006. The owners will generously recommend their favorite cafes and restaurants in the area.

53 rue de Malte, 75011 Paris. ℂ **01-47-00-56-18.** Fax 01-43-57-77-39. www.hoteldenevers.com. 32 units, 20 with bathroom, 3 with shower only. 35€ ($44) single or double with sink, 45€ ($56) single or double with shower only, 49€ ($61) single or double with bathroom; 76€–78€ ($95–$98) triple with bathroom. Breakfast 4.50€ ($5.65). Shower 4€ ($5). MC, V. Métro: République. **Amenities:** Elevator.

WORTH A SPLURGE

Hôtel Axial Beaubourg 𝕯𝕯   If you like sleek, modern hotels, this is a great choice in a neighborhood known for its more traditional offerings. Its modern, air-conditioned interior is reminiscent of a luxury hotel. Some rooms come with wood-beamed ceilings; all come with dark green drapes and bedspreads and high-thread-count cotton sheets. The bathrooms are sparkling and modern, if a bit small. Skip the pricey continental breakfast and amble down to one of several neighborhood cafes just a few steps away.

11 rue du Temple, 75004 Paris. ℂ **01-42-72-72-22.** Fax 01-42-72-03-53. www.axialbeaubourg.com. 39 units. 112€–130€ ($140–$163) single; 160€–210€ ($200–$263) double. Continental breakfast 11€ ($14). AE, DC, MC, V. Métro: Hôtel-de-Ville. **Amenities:** Laundry; dry cleaning; elevator. *In room:* A/C, satellite TV, dataport, minibar, safe.

Hôtel Beaumarchais 𝕯𝕯 *(Value)*   Situated at the start of ultracool rue Oberkampf, this hotel offers high style for a reasonable price. The small, minimalist rooms are decorated with hypermodern furniture in bold primary colors, gooseneck lamps, and rugs that could have been designed by Jackson Pollock. Windows have recently been soundproofed and air-conditioning units have been added in all but three rooms. The bathrooms are also ultramodern with walls that are covered in tile shards and mirror pieces. Breakfast is served in the lovely courtyard during summer. The lobby doubles as art gallery with paintings rotated every 2 months. In fact, the affable owner, himself an artist, frequently exhibits the art of his customers. So if you're an artist, bring samples of your work (or at least photographs) if you're interested in having your art hung on these walls. There's wireless Internet in the lobby, too. The friendly staff can book tours, obtain theater tickets, and make restaurant reservations, for no additional charge.

3 rue Oberkampf, 75011 Paris. ℂ **01-53-36-86-86.** Fax 01-43-38-32-86. www.hotelbeaumarchais.com. 31 units. 90€ ($113) single; 110€ ($138) double. Continental breakfast in breakfast room or courtyard 10€ ($13), in room 11€ ($14). AE, MC, V. Métro: Filles du Calvaire or Oberkampf. **Amenities:** Elevator. *In room:* A/C, satellite TV, hair dryer, dataport, safe.

Hôtel Saint-Louis Bastille 𝕯 *Finds*   This new hotel is housed in a seven-story building that was originally constructed in the 18th century using stones salvaged from the Bastille prison. Several of the charming rooms have wood-beamed ceilings; all come with tiled floors giving them a fresh, inviting feel. Walls and bedspreads are a neutral color and add a sense of Zen to the atmosphere. The marble bathrooms, though on the small side, are a luxury in a hotel at this price and come with glass-shower doors. The basement breakfast room has exposed stone and old-world ambience. You can order drinks in the cozy lobby lounge.

114 bd. Richard-Lenoir, 75011 Paris. ℂ **01-43-38-29-29.** Fax 01-43-38-03-18. www.saintlouisbastille.com. 27 units. 80€ ($100) single; 100€–120€ ($125–$150) double. Extra bed 15€ ($19). Breakfast 7.50€ ($9.40). AE, MC, V. Métro: Oberkampf. **Amenities:** Lounge; laundry service; concierge; elevator. *In room:* Satellite TV, hair dryer, dataport, safe.

Hôtel du Vieux Marais 𝕯 *Finds*   This charming hotel is a gem. Its sparkling rooms are spacious and chic, with white-oak furniture, plush leatherette upholstery, and tons of closet space. The bathrooms are tiled in rough marble squares, and the ultramodern shower has no curtains—or walls, for that matter. Rooms facing the courtyard are darker, but look out on a garden, and the air-conditioning ensures a good night's sleep on warm nights.

8 rue du Plâtre, 75004 Paris. © **01-42-78-47-22.** Fax 01-42-78-34-32. www.vieuxmarais.com. 30 units. 92€–108€ ($115–$135) single; 108€–140€ ($135–$175) double. Extra bed 23€ ($29). Continental breakfast 9.50€ ($12). MC, V. Métro: Hôtel-de-Ville. **Amenities:** Elevator. *In room:* A/C, satellite TV, dataport, hair dryer, safe.

8, 16 & 17E ARRONDISSEMENTS

The grandeur of this area makes you half expect to hear trumpets blowing each time you round the corner. The Arc de Triomphe and Trocadéro are two of the landmarks. It's a good place to stay if you have limited time and want to concentrate on Paris's most famous sites. This is one of the city's most luxurious neighborhoods. Not surprisingly, very few are hotels within our budget, but this is the area with one of the best splurge choices in Paris.

Hôtel des Deux Acacias ⭐ *Finds* On a quiet side street, a few minutes' walk from the Arc de Triomphe, you'll find this gem of a hotel. Extensive renovations were completed in 2002 and everything here still sparkles. Rooms have been papered in bright colors with matching drapes and wicker furniture, and bathrooms are new with tasteful tiles and large mirrors. An extra phone line has been added in each room for Internet access—unusual in a small hotel. Breakfast is served in the airy dining room, where dinner can also be served if ordered in advance. The management works hard to make guests feel welcome.

28 rue de l'Arc de Triomphe, 75017 Paris. © **01-43-80-01-85.** Fax 01-40-53-94-62. www.2acacias.com. 31 units. 78€ ($98) small single; 93€–112€ ($116–$140) single or double; 120€ ($150) triple; 150€ ($188) quad. Breakfast 8€ ($10). AE, MC, V. Métro: Charles-de-Gaulle–Etoile; use av. Carnot exit. **Amenities:** Elevator. *In room:* Satellite TV, dataport, hair dryer.

Hôtel des Deux Avenues ⭐ The street market full of fresh food and beckoning vendors at the foot of this hotel is one of its best features. After stuffing yourself with cheese and *sausisson sec* (dry cured pork), settle into this friendly hotel that has a fresh, inviting feel. It is bright and modern, with small, comfortable rooms done in pastels. Bathrooms are in mint condition. No units have remarkable views, but four front rooms have narrow balconies. Rooms with bathtubs and/or twin beds are larger and have minibars, and the spacious rooms on the top floor are *mansardé*—the ceilings slant with the angle of the mansard roof. A 10% to 20% discount is offered in January, February, and mid-July to late August.

38 rue Poncelet, 75017 Paris. © **01-42-27-44-35.** Fax 01-47-63-95-48. www.hotel-des-deux-avenues.com. 34 units. 87€–97€ ($109–$121) single; 97€–103€ ($121–$129) double; 100€–130€ ($125–$163) triple. Extra bed 23€ ($29). Breakfast 8€ ($10). MC, V. Métro: Charles-de-Gaulle–Etoile or Ternes. **Amenities:** Elevator. *In room:* Satellite TV, hair dryer.

Hôtel Riviera *Value* Just 5 minutes from the Arc de Triomphe, this attractive hotel is in a prime location for the tourist on the run. The immaculate, renovated rooms come in a wide range of colors and decors, with matching bedspreads and drapes. Unfortunately, the staff here can be grumpy and indifferent. Don't expect any smiles or friendly service—but the rooms give you excellent value for your euro. *Caution:* If you are looking for a quad, look elsewhere—quads here are triples with an extra mattress. A nice touch here is the choice of nonsmoking rooms. State your preference at the time of reservation.

Accommodations on the Right Bank (8 & 16–17e)

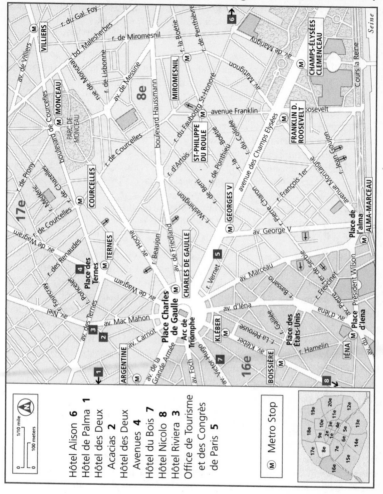

Hôtel Alison **6**
Hôtel de Palma **1**
Hôtel des Deux Acacias **2**
Hôtel des Deux Avenues **4**
Hôtel du Bois **7**
Hôtel Nicolo **8**
Hôtel Riviera **3**
Office de Tourisme et des Congrès de Paris **5**

Ⓜ Metro Stop

55 rue des Acacias, 75017 Paris. ☎ **01-43-80-45-31.** Fax 01-40-54-84-08. www.hotelriviera-paris.com. 26 units, a few with shower only. 50€ ($63) single with shower only; 63€–78€ ($79–$98) single with bathroom; 70€–87€ ($88–$109) double with bathroom; 97€ ($121) triple with bathroom; 104€ ($130) quad with bathroom. Breakfast 6.50€ ($8.15). AE, MC, V. Métro: Ternes or Charles-de-Gaulle-Etoile. **Amenities:** Elevator. *In room:* Satellite TV, dataport, hair dryer, safe.

WORTH A SPLURGE

Hôtel Alison 🐾 *Kids*   Surrounded by the rue St-Honoré shopping district and several embassies, this hotel has a sleek, upscale ambience. The large, well-appointed rooms are furnished in a modern style, with black furniture and light walls. Closet space is plentiful and Roger & Gallet toiletries grace gleaming bathrooms with wall-mounted showers. The two sets of adjoining rooms on the top floor are great for families or small groups. The management is gracious and the lobby is plush and inviting, with a small bar and 1980s-style decor.

21 rue de Surène, 75008 Paris. ℂ **01-42-65-54-00.** Fax 01-42-65-08-17. www.hotel-alison.com. 35 units. 78€–90€ ($98–$113) single; 110€–142€ ($138–$178) double. Breakfast 8€ ($10). AE, DC, MC, V. Métro: Madeleine or Concorde. **Amenities:** Elevator. *In room:* Satellite TV, dataport, minibar, hair dryer, safe, trouser press.

Hôtel du Bois 🏆🏆 *Finds*   A magnificent location and discreet elegance keep this gem of a place buzzing with returning guests, many of them French. On a side street that juts out onto the chic boulevard Victor-Hugo, the Hôtel du Bois has warmly decorated rooms, plush with amenities found in deluxe hotels. The Laura Ashley wallpaper, flowery curtains, and crimson bedspreads compliment the heavy mahogany furniture and sparkling white bathrooms. The English-speaking staff is efficient and friendly and is always ready to help with directions. Mornings, you could skip breakfast and walk down to one of the city's most renowned patisseries, **Le Nôtre,** 2 blocks away, and pick up croissants. Then walk a few minutes further to a Trocadéro cafe overlooking the Eiffel Tower. *Note:* To avoid stairs with your luggage, be sure to arrive at the rue du Dôme address.

11 rue du Dôme (at 29 av. Victor-Hugo), 75016 Paris. ℂ **01-45-00-31-96.** Fax 01-45-00-90-05. www.hoteldubois. com. 41 units. 110€ ($138) small single; 129€–149€ ($161–$186) standard double; 165€ ($206) deluxe double. Extra bed 50€ ($63). Breakfast 12€ ($15). AE, MC, V. Métro: Kleber or Victor-Hugo. RER: Etoile. **Amenities:** Elevator. *In room:* Satellite TV, minibar, hair dryer, safe.

Hôtel Nicolo *Finds*   If you don't mind being slightly out of the center, Hôtel Nicolo is a terrific value, located in posh Passy, a residential district. Past a courtyard, the lobby resembles the salon of an elegant house, with tasteful furniture, plants, and flowers. The atmosphere carries over to the exquisitely decorated rooms, all renovated over the past few years. They are spacious and include carved headboards from India and Southeast Asia, armoires, and white walls hung with tasteful artwork. The sparkling bathrooms were overhauled in 2002. Since the hotel is off the street, every room is quiet. On its business card the hotel claims to be *"calme et confortable";* it is. The only drawback is the outlying location, but the Métro and a street crowded with shops and boutiques are nearby.

3 rue Nicolo, 75016 Paris. ℂ **01-42-88-83-40.** Fax 01-42-24-45-41. hotel.nicolo@wanadoo.fr. 28 units. 100€ ($125) single; 115€–166€ ($144–$208) double. Breakfast included. Rates 20% lower in Aug. AE, DC, MC, V. Métro: Passy. **Amenities:** Elevator. *In room:* Satellite TV, hair dryer, safe.

18E ARRONDISSEMENT

If you can dodge the tour buses on the place du Tertre and wander into quiet side streets, you will discover why so many artists, writers, and poets found inspiration in this villagelike area above the rest of the city. Though not close to the center of town, the neighborhood's character and views can make it worth the haul.

Ermitage Hôtel *Finds*   This house was built in 1890 by a gentleman for his *dame de coeur*—he must have loved her very much. On a quiet street behind Sacré-Coeur, this delightful hotel retains much of its 19th-century charm and feels like a private residence. Each room is furnished differently, with touches such as lace curtains, canopied beds, period wallpaper, and old photos. The hallways are painted in deep blues and reds, and art and antiques are displayed throughout. Try to get one of the rooms on the top floor with a view of Paris, or one of the two on the ground floor that open onto a garden terrace and wake up to the sound of birds singing. There is no elevator and none of the rooms have TVs.

24 rue Lamarck, 75018 Paris. ℂ **01-42-64-79-22.** Fax 01-42-64-10-33. www.ermitagesacrecoeur.fr. 12 units. 68€–78€ ($85–$98) single; 72€–88€ ($90–$110) double; 113€ ($141) triple; 134€ ($168) quad. Rates include continental breakfast. No credit cards. Métro: Lamarck-Caulaincourt. *In room:* Hair dryer.

Hôtel Regyn's Montmartre ✯ (Value)   If you are willing to fork out an extra 20€ to 44€ ($25–$55) for the rooms on the top floors of this well-kept establishment, you will get wonderful views of the Eiffel Tower or Sacré-Coeur. Hôtel Regyn's is on the place des Abbesses at the bottom of the Butte in a lively neighborhood filled with shops, cafes, and grocery stores. The rooms have medium-firm beds and are in excellent condition—all the bathrooms are modern and clean. Double-glazed windows at the front should keep out noise from weekend revelers who gather in the square, or you can opt for a quieter room on the garden-courtyard.

18 pl. des Abbesses, 75018 Paris. ✆ **01-42-54-45-21.** Fax 01-42-23-76-69. www.regynsmontmartre.com. 22 units. 50€–92€ ($63–$115) single; 60€–84€ ($75–$105) double; 104€ ($130) double with view. Breakfast 7€ ($8.75) in breakfast room, 8€ ($10) in room. AE, MC, V. Métro: Abbesses. **Amenities:** Elevator. *In room:* TV, hair dryer, safe.

Hôtel Utrillo (Finds)   You decide: Does an in-house sauna make up for a lack of storage space? (It certainly relaxes aching muscles!) Within walking distance of both Sacré-Coeur and the nightlife around Pigalle, this hotel offers bright, tidy rooms with quilted bedspreads and new wooden furniture. The bathrooms have recently been retiled and several larger sixth-floor rooms have nice views of Parisian rooftops and, if you stick your head out the window, the Eiffel Tower.

7 rue Aristide Bruant, 75018 Paris. ✆ **01-42-58-13-44.** Fax 01-42-23-93-88. www.hotel-paris-utrillo.com. 30 units, most with shower. 64€ ($80) single; 76€–82€ ($95–$102) double; 96€ ($120) triple. Extra bed 12€ ($15). Breakfast 6.50€ ($8.15). AE, MC, V. Métro: Abbesses. **Amenities:** Sauna, elevator. *In room:* Satellite TV, minibar, hair dryer.

WORTH A SPLURGE

Hôtel Prima Lepic ✯   This gleaming hotel underwent a major renovation in 2002 but has managed to keep the old Montmartre feel of the rooms. The colorful decor includes old-fashioned flowered wallpaper with matching curtains and bedspreads, as well as plush carpets and spiffed-up bathrooms. Rooms on the fifth floor have south-facing balconies with great views. The more expensive rooms have bathtubs and face the street. The least expensive doubles are those with no view at (106€/$133), which is still a relatively good bargain. Be sure to check the "promotional" Internet-only rates that are usually offered at a 10% discount.

29 rue Lepic, 75018 Paris. ✆ **01-46-06-44-64.** Fax 01-46-06-66-11. www.hotel-paris-lepic.com. 38 units. 92€ ($115) single; 106€–135€ ($133–$169) double; 188€ ($235) triple. Extra bed 25€ ($31). Breakfast 8€ ($10). MC, V. Métro: Abbesses or Blanche. **Amenities:** Elevator. *In room:* Satellite TV, dataport, hair dryer.

Timhotel Montmartre ✯   The best thing about this classy hotel is the views—many rooms have great views of the neighborhood, and some on the top floors have panoramas that include the Eiffel Tower and Sacré-Coeur. Part of a well-run chain, everything in this place—including the corridors—is superclean. Rooms get lots of light and are decorated in light blues and bright yellows. Bathrooms are tiled, and showers have glass doors. The hotel is next door to the Bateau Lavoir (the boat wash), for those who want to imagine themselves rubbing shoulders with Picasso, Modigliani, and other artists who once lived there.

11 rue Ravignan (pl. Emile Goudeau), 75018 Paris. ✆ **01-42-55-74-79.** Fax 01-42-55-71-01. www.timhotel.com. 60 units. 115€–130€ ($144–$163) single or double; 150€ ($188) single or double with view; 170€ ($213) triple, 200€ ($250) triple with view. Breakfast 9€ ($11). AE, DC, MC, V. Métro: Abbesses. **Amenities:** Elevator. *In room:* Satellite TV.

2 On the Left Bank

5E ARRONDISSEMENT

If you are looking for a lively spot from which to base your operations, try the Latin Quarter. The 5e, particularly around place St-Michel, is hopping year-round and at all hours of the day and night. The 6e, for comparison if you're choosing one or the other, is a little quieter and a little classier, and loaded with places to eat and drink. Both are near the center of the city.

Familia Hôtel ★★ *Finds*   Owner Eric Gaucheron will just about do back flips to please guests at this charming hotel, which has been lovingly maintained and renovated. Every part of this hotel is meticulously maintained. Window boxes full of flowers, *toile de Jouy* (fabric printed with a scenic design), wallpaper, exposed beams, and stone walls are some of the touches found in the rooms, many of which have balconies with views of the Latin Quarter. From the fifth and sixth floors, you can see Notre-Dame. Some rooms have sepia murals of Parisian scenes, some have ceramic tile, some have exposed stone walls; all rooms have ceiling fans. In early 2005 new bedspreads and curtains were added. Bathrooms are small but sparkling and the majority of them are marble. The friendly, English-speaking staff can help with directions and they have maps and brochures at the front desk.

11 rue des Ecoles, 75005 Paris. © **01-43-54-55-27.** Fax 01-43-29-61-77. www.hotel-paris-familia.com. 30 units. 78€ ($98) single; 78€–125€ ($98–$156) double; 149€ ($186) triple. Breakfast included. AE, DC, MC, V. Métro: Cardinal Lemoine or Jussieu. **Amenities:** Elevator. *In room:* Satellite TV, minibar, hair dryer.

Grand Hôtel de Suez ★   Many guests return to this old standby for its good-size rooms and reasonable prices. Rooms are attractively papered and curtained in warm pastel colors and white oak furniture; carpets are in reasonable condition. Beds are medium-firm, storage space is ample, and the bathrooms have recently been retiled. Most rooms are quiet, but don't even think of opening the windows to the street-side balconies—the boulevard St-Michel is as noisy as a carnival. This hotel wins the prize for the least expensive hotel breakfast in Paris—it's definitely worth your while to eat in.

31 bd. St-Michel, 75005 Paris. © **01-53-10-34-00.** Fax 01-40-51-79-44. www.hoteldesuez.fr. 49 units. 80€–105€ ($100–$131) single; 85€–120€ ($106–$150) double; 115€–150€ ($144–$188) triple. Continental breakfast 4€ ($5). AE, DC, MC, V. Métro: St-Michel. **Amenities:** Elevator. *In room:* Satellite TV, dataport, hair dryer.

Hôtel Carofftel ★   On the edge of the Latin Quarter, within walking distance of the outdoor market on rue Mouffetard, this hotel is quieter than those closer to the action. Rooms vary in size, but all are in excellent condition, with reading lamps, luggage racks, double-glazed windows, and full-length mirrors. Some rooms have small balconies. Phone jacks in the rooms will accept American computer hookups; whether you can actually get online is less certain. The hotel offers a 10% discount from the third week in July to the end of August.

18 av. des Gobelins, 75005 Paris. © **01-42-17-47-47.** Fax 01-45-35-00-57. www.hotelcarofftelgobelins.com. 23 units. 63€ ($79) single; 76€–89€ ($95–$111) double; 108€ ($135) triple. Continental breakfast 7€ ($8.75). MC, V. Métro: Gobelins. **Amenities:** Elevator. *In room:* Satellite TV, dataport, hair dryer.

Hôtel des Trois Collèges ★   Located in the thick of university life, this hotel has a nice *salon du thé*, or tearoom, which serves light lunches, tea, and coffee. The top-end rooms provide the best value—they're more spacious and newer than less-expensive units, with big, tiled bathrooms, beamed ceilings, and views of the Sorbonne and the Panthéon. All are comfortably furnished in modern style. Top-floor rooms are the brightest and offer some views of the rooftops—but they cost 36€ ($45) more, and unless you're spending ample time in your room, it's not really worth the splurge. The staff is efficient and friendly.

16 rue Cujas, 75005 Paris. ✆ **01-43-54-67-30**. Fax 01-46-34-02-99. www.3colleges.com. 44 units. 71€ ($89) single; 91€–99€ ($114–$124) double; 150€ ($188) triple. Breakfast 8€ ($10). AE, DC, MC, V. Métro: St-Michel or Cluny–La Sorbonne. **Amenities:** Laundry service; elevator; tearoom. *In room:* Satellite TV, hair dryer.

Hôtel du Collège de France ⚜

The lobby of this hotel has a medieval theme and is filled with plush armchairs and artwork. The 16th-century building was raised on the site of an 11th-century fort. Rooms are anything but ancient. They are modern, large, and attractive, with simple furniture and full-length mirrors. Bathrooms are not new, but very clean and well kept. The fifth-floor rooms have small balconies and views of the Collège de France. The hotel is on a quiet street, minutes away from boulevard St-Michel. The young, friendly Marc family run the hotel and will welcome you with a smile. In 2005, all the rooms were equipped with free DSL and WiFi.

7 rue Thénard, 75005 Paris. ✆ **01-43-26-78-36**. Fax 01-46-34-58-29. www.hotel-collegedefrance.com. 29 units. 70€–83€ ($88–$104) single; 78€–110€ ($98–$138) double. Extra bed 17€ ($21). Buffet continental breakfast 8€ ($10). AE, DC, MC, V. Métro: Maubert-Mutualité. **Amenities:** Babysitting; elevator. *In room:* Satellite TV, hair dryer, dataport.

Hôtel Esmeralda *(Moments*

If you're a big fan of Shakespeare and Co., this hotel, just 45m (148 ft.) away, is for you. It's also a favorite of a lot of others, and you may have to book months in advance. The Esmeralda is a funky, ramshackle hotel with a winding wooden staircase, dogs and cats dozing in the lobby, and lovely views of Viviani square; if you stick your head out the window, you'll get a fantastic shot of Notre-Dame. Velvet coverings and pseudo-antique furniture create a hippie-esque warmth that almost makes up for the dark rear rooms. The front rooms have modern bathrooms with tubs, and some are exceptionally large. Service here is spotty and somewhat indifferent, so bring your patience with you.

4 rue St-Julien-le-Pauvre, 75005 Paris. ✆ **01-43-54-19-20**. Fax 01-40-51-00-68. 19 units, 16 with bathroom. 35€ ($44) single with sink; 65€ ($81) single with bathroom; 80€–95€ ($100–$119) double with bathroom; 110€ ($138) triple with bathroom; 150€ ($188) quad with bathroom. Breakfast 6€ ($7.50). MC, V. Métro: St-Michel.

Hôtel Marignan ⚜ *(Value*

Owners Paul and Linda Keniger are so welcoming, they will let you use the kitchen and the washing machine. You can also bring your own food into the dining area. The lobby is papered with handy tips for travelers, and there's a computer in the basement for guests to use the Internet for a small fee. The Kenigers have invested much time and energy in renovating this hotel, keeping much of the building's architectural detailing, such as ceiling moldings and mantle pieces. Mattresses are firm, bathrooms expertly tiled—the communal showers and toilets are a pleasure. The least expensive rates at this hotel are in effect from the end of October to the end of February.

13 rue du Sommerard, 75005 Paris. ✆ **01-43-54-63-81**. www.hotel-marignan.com. 30 units, 10 with bathroom, 15 with toilet only. 45€–58€ ($56–$73) single; 55€–90€ ($69–$113) double; 75€–110€ ($94–$138) triple; 85€–130€ ($106–$163) quad. Continental breakfast included. No credit cards. Métro: Maubert-Mutualité or St-Michel. **Amenities:** Internet/computer room. *In room:* Hair dryer.

Hôtel Minerve ⚜⚜

Owners Eric and Sylvie Gaucheron run this establishment with the same enthusiasm as they do their Hôtel Familia next door. Applying the same attention to detail, they have created a more upscale bargain establishment and added air-conditioning in 2005. The rooms are larger and more plush; the more expensive

Accommodations on the Left Bank (5–7 & 13–14e)

Métro Stop
RER Stop

0   1/5 Mi
0   0.2 Km

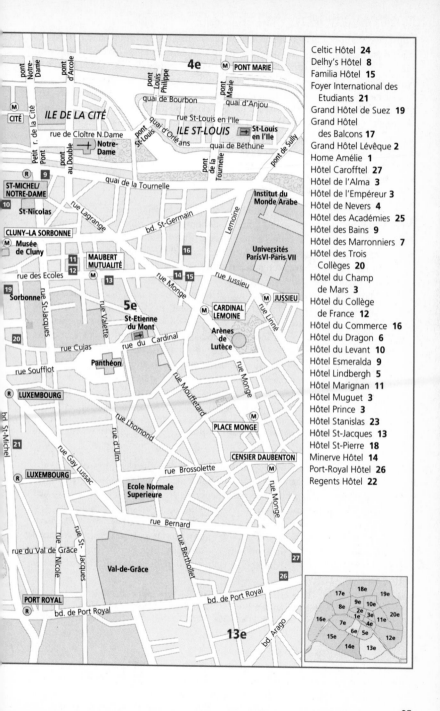

ILE DE LA CITÉ

ILE ST-LOUIS

4e

Notre-Dame

5e

St-Etienne du Mont

Panthéon

Arènes de Lutèce

Val-de-Grâce

13e

Celtic Hôtel **24**
Delhy's Hôtel **8**
Familia Hôtel **15**
Foyer International des
  Etudiants **21**
Grand Hôtel de Suez **19**
Grand Hôtel
  des Balcons **17**
Grand Hôtel Lévêque **2**
Home Amélie **1**
Hôtel Carofftel **27**
Hôtel de l'Alma **3**
Hôtel de l'Empéreur **3**
Hôtel de Nevers **4**
Hôtel des Académies **25**
Hôtel des Bains **9**
Hôtel des Marronniers **7**
Hôtel des Trois
  Collèges **20**
Hôtel du Champ
  de Mars **3**
Hôtel du Collège
  de France **12**
Hôtel du Commerce **16**
Hôtel du Dragon **6**
Hôtel du Levant **10**
Hôtel Esmeralda **9**
Hôtel Lindbergh **5**
Hôtel Marignan **11**
Hôtel Muguet **3**
Hôtel Prince **3**
Hôtel Stanislas **23**
Hôtel St-Jacques **13**
Hôtel St-Pierre **18**
Minerve Hôtel **14**
Port-Royal Hôtel **26**
Regents Hôtel **22**

units have wood-beamed ceilings, stone walls, mahogany furnishings, and rich fabrics on the walls. Sepia frescos decorate several of the rooms, and 10 have balconies with tables and chairs overlooking the street; no. 103 has a patio overlooking the courtyard where there's a new and huge mural. The triples are good for families, with the kids' beds somewhat separate. The sparkling bathrooms come with glass shower doors. The 1866 staircase has been restored and there are over 60 antique tapestries throughout the hotel. The charming breakfast area downstairs has exposed stone while the conference room has more antique tapestries.

13 rue des Ecoles, 75005 Paris. ✆ **01-43-26-26-04.** Fax 01-44-07-01-96. www.hotel-paris-minerve.com. 54 units. 84€–130€ ($105–$163) double; 150€ ($188) triple. 10% discount offered mid-July to late Aug, early Jan to mid-March. Expanded continental breakfast 8€ ($10). Parking 20€ ($25). AE, DC, MC, V. Métro: Cardinal Lemoine or Jussieu. **Amenities:** Elevator; conference room. *In room:* A/C, satellite TV, hair dryer.

Hôtel St-Jacques
A sleek new lobby, lounge, and breakfast room were added in 2005 to this beautifully preserved hotel. The rooms were overhauled in 2003 and are still in great shape; several rooms have restored 18th-century ceiling murals. Most of the ceilings have wedding-cake plasterwork; traditional furniture enhances the romantic effect. The hallways have been painted with *trompe l'oeil* marble and draperies. The rooms are spacious and well lit, with fabric-covered walls and ample closet space; no. 23 has gold "royalty" bedspreads and no. 25 is done in a pinkish pastel color. Several rooms have balconies with views of Notre-Dame and the Panthéon; bathrooms are immaculate and roomy, and some come with glass doors instead of shower curtains. Twenty-first-century amenities include a modem plug, and you can request a fax machine with its own phone number for your room. If you don't mind climbing one flight of stairs, the rooms on the top floor are less expensive and have great views. The new lounge-bar includes a piano that plays electronically while guests sip drinks in the early evening. The hotel is planning to add air-conditioning to all the rooms in 2006.

35 rue des Ecoles, 75005 Paris. ✆ **01-44-07-45-45.** Fax 01-43-25-65-50. www.paris-hotel-stjacques.com. 38 units. 55€–84€ ($69–$105) single; 95€–124€ ($119–$155) double; 152€ ($190) triple. Breakfast 8.50€ ($11). AE, DC, MC, V. Métro: Maubert-Mutualité. **Amenities:** Bar, lounge, elevator. *In room:* Satellite TV, fax (on request), dataport, hair dryer, safe.

Port-Royal Hôtel
This family-run hotel is a budget traveler's dream. It has the rates of a motel but the perks of a high-class hotel. The lobby is spacious and air-conditioned, halls are freshly painted, and all the rooms are in mint condition, decorated with colorful wallpaper and antiques. Many rooms have nonworking fireplaces, and several bathrooms have been redone with tiles by Kenzo and have towel warmers. There is a breakfast/TV room, and a courtyard for an outdoor breakfast. Communal bathrooms are spotless. The location is away from the center, but for this quality and price it's worth the walk. The hotel does not accept credit cards, but there is a bank with a 24-hour ATM a few doors down.

8 bd. Port-Royal, 75005 Paris. ✆ **01-43-31-70-06.** Fax 01-43-31-33-67. www.portroyalhotel.fr.st. 46 units, 21 with bathroom. 39€–46€ ($49–$58) single with sink, 51€ ($64) double with sink, 82€–87€ ($103–$109) single or double with bathroom. Shower 2.50€ ($3.15). Breakfast 5.50€ ($6.90). No credit cards. Métro: Gobelins. **Amenities:** Elevator. *In room:* Towel warmer.

SUPER-CHEAP SLEEPS
Hôtel du Commerce
This newly opened hotel is very well located on a small side street a few minutes walk from Notre-Dame. Housed in a 600-year-old building, the hotel's motto is "cheap doesn't have to be ugly." Rooms are basic but attractive and range in size and price from the tiny with a single bed and no bathroom (toilets are

available on each floor and showers behind the lobby) to a spacious double with bathroom and air-conditioning. The hotel does not serve breakfast, but a communal table with coffeemakers, microwave, and vending machine is available so you can purchase and make your own meals and snacks. The showers behind the lobby are very clean. There are no phones or TVs but the hotel provides free Internet for guests near the breakfast table. There's no elevator and the stairs are quite steep up to the fifth floor. The hotel, as you can imagine, caters mostly to a young and cool European crowd.

14 rue de la Montagne Ste Genevieve, 75005 Paris. (C) 01-43-54-89-69. Fax 01-43-54-76-09. www.commerce-paris-hotel.com. 33 units. 29€ ($36) single with sink; 39€–49€ ($49–$61) single with shower or toilet; 49€ ($61) double with shower or toilet; 59€ ($74) double with bathroom; 89€–99€ ($111–$124) luxury double with air-conditioning. 2€ ($2.50) shower. MC, V. Métro: Maubert Mutualité.

WORTH A SPLURGE

Hôtel du Levant 🏔 *Kids*   In a lively pedestrian area near place St-Michel, this hotel offers a bit of luxury in the midst of budget restaurants and souvlaki joints. Its large rooms have firm mattresses, plush carpeting, and ample closet space. About half have neo–Art Deco furniture, a modern design, and minibars; the others are more traditional. Some of the new bathrooms have granite or marble tiles, and all have good toiletries. The hot breakfast buffet is served in a pretty room with a mural, framed artwork, and photographs portraying old Paris. Triples and quads are well suited for families.

18 rue de la Harpe, 75005 Paris. (C) 01-46-34-11-00. Fax 01-46-34-25-87. www.hoteldulevant.fr. 47 units. 69€ ($86) single; 111€–150€ ($139–$188) double; 165€–206€ ($206–$258) triple; 220€ ($275) family room (quad); 285€–303€ ($356–$379) suite. Rates include buffet breakfast. AE, MC, V. Métro: St-Michel. *In room:* A/C, satellite TV, dataport, hair dryer, safe.

6E ARRONDISSEMENT

Postwar St-Germain was home to intellectuals like Sartre and de Beauvoir, who thought deep thoughts at the Café de Flore. Today you're more likely to find boutiques than philosophers in this pricey neighborhood. It's getting harder to find hotels within our budget here, but it's a great place to hang your hat for the night.

Delhy's Hôtel *Value*   This backpacker's classic has upgraded—but the rooms still don't have toilets. The building's 500-year-old beams have been exposed, and some rooms have been redone. Rooms on the lower floors are dark. The best rooms face the street, which is virtually traffic-free. Shower-free rooms are cheaper, but the communal shower is on the ground floor and there is no elevator.

22 rue de l'Hirondelle, 75006 Paris. (C) 01-43-26-58-25. Fax 01-43-26-51-06. delhys@wanadoo.fr. 21 units, none with bathroom, 7 with shower only. 44€ ($55) single without shower, 67€ ($84) single with shower; 59€–65€ ($74–$81) double without shower, 73€–80€ ($91–$100) double with shower; 94€–114€ ($118–$143) triple with shower. Continental breakfast included. Communal shower 4€ ($5). MC, V. Métro: St-Michel. *In room:* Satellite TV.

Hôtel des Académies *Value*   This no-frills hotel may remind you of a visit to your grandmother's apartment. The small "lobby" on the first floor has a daybed, a birdcage, a clock, and various bits of homey clutter. The rooms are a little worn but clean and exceptionally low-priced for the location—near Montparnasse and a 10-minute walk from the Jardin du Luxembourg. There's no elevator, but rooms on the fourth and fifth floors are cheaper, so the climb pays for itself. The hotel is managed by an elderly couple who love dogs and insist on quiet after 10pm.

15 rue de la Grande-Chaumière, 75006 Paris. (C) 01-43-26-66-44. Fax 01-43-26-03-72. hotel.academies@wanadoo.fr. 21 units, 12 with bathroom, 5 with shower only. 50€ ($63) single with sink and toilet; 64€ ($80) single or double with shower only, 68€ ($85) single or double with bathroom. Breakfast 7€ ($8.75). MC, V. Métro: Vavin.

Hôtel du Dragon *Moments*   In the heart of St-Germain, this 17th-century hotel has a lot to offer. The formerly sparse and slightly monastic rooms have been renovated with sparkling new bathrooms and contain wood armoires, bed frames, and tables in French country style. There is a patio for summer breakfasts, and a piano in the lounge. Rooms facing the courtyard get plenty of light. There is no elevator, but the top floor has air-conditioning, which could make up for the climb.

36 rue du Dragon, 75006 Paris. ℂ **01-45-48-51-05.** Fax 01-42-22-51-62. www.hoteldudragon.com. 28 units, 27 with bathroom, 1 with shower only. 79€ ($99) single with shower only; 99€ ($124) single or double with bathroom. Continental breakfast 8€ ($10). AE, MC, V. Métro: St-Germain-des-Prés or Sèvres-Babylone. *In room:* A/C (top floor only), satellite TV, dataport, hair dryer.

Hôtel St-Pierre *Value*   If you get a room facing the street in this stylish hotel, you will see what is left of a 13th-century convent—next to the former lodgings of celebrated actress Sarah Bernhardt. Rooms tend to be smallish, but the higher-price doubles are good-size, and the one with the tub is large, with double sinks in the bathroom. Air-conditioning was added to the majority of the rooms in 2004 and free DSL Internet connections were added to all rooms in 2005. The fabrics, wallpaper, and rugs are in good condition and the bathrooms are in great shape. Closets are ample and windows are double-glazed. The communal toilets on each of the seven floors are immaculate. This hotel wins the prize for the least expensive double room in Paris with air-conditioning, but be warned that at press time a few rooms remain without air-conditioning. so be sure to state your preference at the time of reservation.

4 rue de l'Ecole de Médecine, 75006 Paris. ℂ **01-46-34-78-80.** Fax 01-40-51-05-17. www.stpierre-hotel.com. 50 units, 45 with bathroom, 5 with shower only. 61€ ($76) single with shower only; 70€ ($88) single with bathroom; 61€ ($76) double with shower only, 80€ ($100) double with bathroom. Breakfast 5.50€ ($6.90). AE, MC, V. Métro: Odéon. **Amenities:** Elevator. *In room:* A/C (in most rooms), satellite TV, dataport, free DSL Internet connection, hair dryer.

Hôtel Stanislas *Value*   This family-owned hotel has some of the nicest staff in Paris. Across from a polytechnic institute, it has a small cafe (where you can get breakfast or a snack until midnight) that's often crowded with students, many of whom the employees know by name. The rooms are in good condition and generally large. Mattresses can be a little soft, and there's no elevator. Breakfast is served until noon, a nice touch if you want to sleep in or feel jet-lagged.

5 rue du Montparnasse, 75006 Paris. ℂ **01-45-48-37-05.** Fax 01-45-44-54-43. www.hotel-stanislas.com. 18 units. 58€–61€ ($73–$76) single; 60€–63€ ($75–$79) double. Breakfast 6€ ($7.50). AE, MC, V. Métro: Notre-Dame-des-Champs. *In room:* Satellite TV, hair dryer.

Regents Hôtel *Finds*   This is a charming hotel on a quiet side street. A stone's throw from the Jardin du Luxembourg, it was completely renovated a few years ago and is quite elegant. The decor evokes the south of France, with yellow-and-blue bedspreads and wood-framed mirrors in most rooms; the bathrooms are sparkling and newly tiled. Breakfast is served in the garden overflowing with plants during summer. Hot and cold beverages are served in the cozy indoor lounge. Top-floor rooms have a narrow balcony with delightful views over the rooftops. Don't expect any extra services from the somewhat surly staff, but the wonderful location and quiet atmosphere will help you overlook their shortcomings.

44 rue Madame, 75006 Paris. ℂ **01-45-48-02-81.** Fax 01-45-44-85-73. regents.hotel@wanadoo.fr. 34 units. 80€ ($100) single or double; 100€–110€ ($125–$138) double with balcony. Breakfast 7€ ($8.75). AE, MC, V. Métro: Rennes or St-Sulpice. **Amenities:** Elevator; lounge. *In room:* Satellite TV, hair dryer.

WORTH A SPLURGE

Grand Hôtel des Balcons ★ *Value*   Denise and Pierre Corroyer take pride in this gracious hotel, which has modern light-oak furnishings, bright fabrics, and new beds. The stairwells have 19th-century stained-glass windows, and their Art Nouveau design is echoed in the lobby furnishings (you can't miss the statue of Venus in the breakfast room). All rooms facing the street have small balconies. Although most rooms are small, clever use of space allows for large closets and full-length mirrors. Bathrooms are small but well designed, and come equipped with a clothesline. The higher-priced doubles, triples, and quads are big and luxurious; some have double-sink bathrooms and a separate toilet. The lounge has free tea and coffee, and if it's your birthday, the breakfast buffet is free.

3 Casimir Delavigne, 75006 Paris. ⓒ **01-46-34-78-50.** Fax 01-46-34-06-27. www.paris-hotel-grandbalcons.com. 50 units. 80€–120€ ($100–$150) single; 100€–150€ ($125–$188) double; 180€ ($225) triple or quad. Buffet breakfast 10€ ($13). AE, DC, MC, V. Métro: Odéon, RER: Luxembourg. **Amenities:** Elevator. *In room:* Satellite TV, dataport, hair dryer.

Hôtel des Marronniers ★★ *Finds*   You might miss the entrance to this delightful hotel—it's in the back of a courtyard on a street lined with antiques stores. Rooms have exposed beams, period furniture, and fabric-covered walls in rich reds or blues. Some bathrooms have ceramic tiling over the tub, and rooms facing the garden have a view of the steeple of St-Germain-des-Prés. The off-street location makes this hotel incredibly peaceful. Book 3 months in advance.

21 rue Jacob, 75006 Paris. ⓒ **01-43-25-30-60.** Fax 01-40-46-83-56. www.hotel-marronniers.com. 37 units. 110€ ($138) single; 153€–173€ ($191–$216) double; 208€ ($260) triple. Extra bed 38€ ($48). Breakfast 10€ ($13), in room 12€ ($15). MC, V. Métro: St-Germain-des-Prés. **Amenities:** Elevator. *In room:* A/C, TV, hair dryer.

7E ARRONDISSEMENT

The upside: If you stay in this swanky neighborhood, you will be close to the Eiffel Tower and you'll be in a charming residential neighborhood. The downside: You will not be alone. With the Musée d'Orsay and the Invalides in the vicinity, this elegant arrondissement is in constant demand—so book early.

Grand Hôtel Lévêque ★ *Value*   As you enter, you will pass a collection of framed pages from guidebooks (including this one) hailing the virtues of this venerable establishment. On a colorful market street that is car-free, this large hotel offers good-size rooms with decent, if not inspired, decorations. All rooms come with both fans and air-conditioning. The bathrooms are small but in excellent condition and come with shower doors. Staff members are friendly and helpful; if you ask, they may be able to give you a higher-priced room on the fifth floor with a balcony and partial view of the Eiffel Tower. For the price, this is a great deal.

29 rue Cler, 75007 Paris. ⓒ **01-47-05-49-15.** Fax 01-45-50-49-36. www.hotel-leveque.com. 50 units. 57€ ($71) single; 87€–93€ ($108–$116) double; 110€ ($138) twin; 125€ ($156) triple. Continental breakfast 8€ ($10). AE, MC, V. Métro: Ecole-Militaire or Latour-Maubourg. **Amenities:** Elevator; soda and ice machines. *In room:* A/C, satellite TV, hair dryer, safe (3€/$3.75).

Hôtel Amélie ★ *Kids*   Hôtel Amélie is as pretty on the outside as its name suggests, with flowerpots brimming with bouquets at each window. The interior is modest, with small, pleasant rooms. Closets are small, but the bathrooms boast sparkling blue and white tiles and good-quality toiletries. Rooms facing the courtyard are brighter than those facing the street; many have yellow walls and blue bedspreads. Despite the central location, the atmosphere is peaceful, almost serene. There is no elevator. The

Orvilles, the young couple who own the hotel, have kids of their own and are friendly to visitors with little ones. Be sure to inquire about the promotional rates (usually a discount of about 10%–15%) offered in August and January.

5 rue Amélie, 75007 Paris. ☎ **01-45-51-74-75.** Fax 01-45-56-93-55. www.hotelamelie.fr. 16 units. 78€–85€ ($98–$106) single; 88€–95€ ($110–$119) double; 96€–103€ ($120–$129) twin. Breakfast 7€ ($8.75). AE, DC, MC, V. Métro: Latour-Maubourg. *In room:* Satellite TV, dataport, minibar, hair dryer.

Hôtel de France ✸ *Kids*   This meticulously managed hotel has some of the most breathtaking views over the golden domed Invalides, across the street. Many of the modern rooms are quite spacious with light wood beds, dark burgundy drapes and bedspreads, and marble sinks in the white bathrooms. The single rooms overlooking the courtyard are a bargain at 75€ ($94) in this swanky residential neighborhood. Most rooms are very bright with large windows; those on the sixth floor have views all the way to Sacré-Coeur. Connecting rooms are available for families—very rare in budget hotels. The copious buffet breakfast includes freshly cut fruit salad, eggs, and sausages.

102 bd. de la Tour Maubourg, 75007 Paris. ☎ **01-47-05-40-49.** Fax 01-45-56-96-78. www.hoteldefrance.com. 60 units. 75€ ($94) single; 92€–95€ ($115–$119) double; 104€–107€ ($130–$134) triple; 148€ ($185) quad. Breakfast 9€ ($11). AE, MC, V. Métro: Ecole Militaire. **Amenities:** Elevator; lounge; bar. *In room:* Satellite TV, minibar, hair dryer.

Hôtel de l'Alma ✸ *Value*   This cozy hotel is on what may be one of the narrowest (and quietest) streets in Paris, a few minutes' walk from the rue Cler market. The hotel is very slowly being renovated. Carpets and bedspreads in all rooms were changed in 2005 while work on the bathrooms continue. At press time, only about 10 rooms were fully renovated. Though rather small, rooms are clean and bright with colorful wallpaper and white bathrooms. The new rooms have heavy fabrics with deep burgundy and blue colors, writing desks, new mattresses, and new fixtures in the bathrooms. Top-floor rooms have rooftop views, and no. 64 boasts a view of the Eiffel Tower but usually costs an additional 20€ to 30€ ($25–$37), though it never hurts to ask at check-in for a complimentary upgrade. Breakfast is served in the small garden in summer, and an Internet cafe is a few doors down. Many of the guests are young Americans, affiliated with the American University nearby. When reserving, be sure to identify yourself as a Frommer's reader to qualify for a discount.

32 rue de l'Exposition, 75007 Paris. ☎ **01-47-05-45-70.** Fax 01-45-51-84-47. 32 units. Special rate for Frommer's readers: 85€ ($106) single; 95€ ($119) double; 120€ ($150) triple. Breakfast included. AE, DC, MC, V. Métro: Ecole-Militaire or Alma Marceau. **Amenities:** Elevator. *In room:* Satellite TV, minibar.

Hôtel de l'Empereur   Napoleon would be proud. Every bed in this hotel has an insignia on the headboard of the emperor's famous hat, and many rooms have a view of the dome of Les Invalides—the site of his tomb. The rooms are a good size and trimmed in green and gold with armchairs and wrought-iron sconces. The bathrooms are clean and tidy. The imperial theme extends all the way to the carpet in the lobby, which is covered with laurel crowns.

2 rue de Chevert, 75007 Paris. ☎ **01-45-55-88-02.** Fax 01-45-51-88-54. www.hotelempereur.com. 38 units, all with shower or bath. 80€ ($100) single; 90€–100€ ($112–$125) double; 120€ ($150) triple; 140€ ($175) quad. Breakfast 8€ ($10). AE, DC, MC, V. Métro: Latour-Maubourg. **Amenities:** Elevator; laundry service. *In room:* Satellite TV, hair dryer.

Hôtel de Nevers ✸   Paris never ceases to surprise—tucked away in St-Germain-des-Prés's chic shopping area, this restored 17th-century house provides simple rooms at prices that are reasonable for this area. In the wood-beamed lobby, thick with North

Accommodations on the Left Bank (7e)

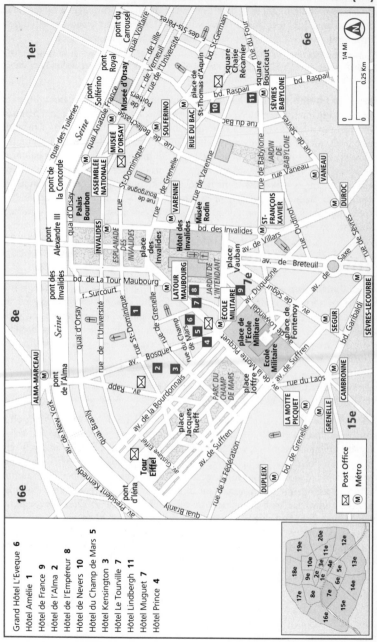

Grand Hôtel L'Eveque **6**
Hôtel Amélie **1**
Hôtel de France **9**
Hôtel de l'Alma **2**
Hôtel de l'Empéreur **8**
Hôtel de Nevers **10**
Hôtel du Champ de Mars **5**
Hôtel Kensington **3**
Hôtel Le Tourville **7**
Hôtel Lindbergh **11**
Hôtel Muguet **7**
Hôtel Prince **4**

☒ Post Office
Ⓜ Métro

African rugs, you can chat with the friendly staff. You'll be escorted up a winding stair-case to meticulously maintained rooms with wood bureaus and wood-framed mirrors. Some rooms on the fourth floor have small terraces. There is no elevator.

83 rue de Bac, 75007 Paris. ℂ **01-45-44-61-30.** Fax 01-42-22-29-47. 11 units. 83€ ($104) single; 83€–93€ ($104–$116) double. Extra bed 21€ ($26). Breakfast 6€ ($7.50). MC, V. Métro: Rue du Bac. *In room:* TV, minibar, hair dryer.

Hôtel du Champ de Mars 🗲🗲 *Finds*   This hotel is a gem tucked around the cor-ner from a market street near the Eiffel Tower. The owners, Françoise and Stéphane Gourdal, put a lot of work into choosing fabrics, wallpaper, and carpets. The entire place, from the elegant facade to the cloth-covered chairs in the breakfast room, is as chic as you'd find in a luxury boutique hotel. All the rooms were overhauled during the winter of 2005 with fresh paint and carpets. Flowing curtains, fabric-covered headboards, throw pillows, and high-backed seats make each room charming and comfortable. Bathrooms are in mint condition, with large towels and good lighting; those with tubs have wall-mounted showers. Reserve at least 2 months in advance as this hotel is very popular with visiting Americans.

7 rue du Champ de Mars, 75007 Paris. ℂ **01-45-51-52-30.** Fax 01-45-51-64-36. www.hotelduchampdemars.com. 25 units. 73€ ($91) single; 79€–83€ ($99–$104) double; 100€ ($125) triple. Continental breakfast 6.50€ ($8.15). MC, V. Métro: Ecole-Militaire. RER: Pont de l'Alma. **Amenities:** Elevator. *In room:* Satellite TV, hair dryer.

Hôtel Kensington *Value*   This simple hotel has a wonderful location on a leafy, tree-lined street a few steps from the Eiffel Tower. The basic rooms are soundproofed and colorful; some come with pastel bedspreads and curtains; others have a blue-and-white motif. The bathrooms are large and most come with tubs. The attractive breakfast room has wrought-iron chairs and modern IKEA-style wooden tables. All in all a com-fortable place to call home in Paris, at a terrific bargain.

79 av. de la Bourdonnais, 75007 Paris. ℂ **01-47-05-74-00.** Fax 01-47-05-25-81. www.hotel-kensington.com. 25 units. 55€ ($69) single; 70€–75€ ($88–$94) double; 85€ ($106) twin; 96€ ($120) triple. Extra bed 12€ ($15). Breakfast 6€ ($7.50). AE, MC, V. Métro: Ecole Militaire. **Amenities:** Elevator. *In room:* Satellite TV.

Hôtel Prince 🗲   In a stately building near the Eiffel Tower, the Hôtel Prince offers modern, soundproof accommodations with big bathrooms. Lively orange-and-yellow curtains brighten the rooms, which vary in size but are all comfortable and well kept. All have a restored stone wall, luggage racks, and ample closets; some have small bal-conies. If you're too worn out from sightseeing to stagger out the door for meals, the hotel will arrange for a local restaurant to deliver a meal. A ground-floor room has facilities for travelers with disabilities. Air-conditioning is available in a few rooms but those may only be available at check-in; ask the receptionist when you arrive.

66 av. Bosquet, 75007 Paris. ℂ **01-47-05-40-90.** Fax 01-47-53-06-62. www.hotel-paris-prince.com. 30 units. 69€ ($86) single; 89€–109€ ($111–$136) double; 115€ ($144) triple. Cold buffet breakfast 7.50€ ($9.40). AE, DC, MC, V. Métro: Ecole-Militaire. **Amenities:** Elevator. *In room:* Satellite TV, minibar, hair dryer.

WORTH A SPLURGE

Hôtel Lindbergh 🗲   This hotel has two themes: aviation and fine accommodations at fair prices. It features photos of Charles Lindbergh and Antoine de St-Exupéry, the pilot author of *Le Petit Prince.* Completely renovated in the past few years, rooms range from simple and sweet (with colorful bedspreads and matching bathrooms) to refined and elegant, with stylish touches such as floor-length curtains, fabric head-boards, and fluffy white comforters. The owners are friendly and eager to talk about the photographs in the homey lobby area, a lovely place to relax and read.

5 rue Chomel, 75007 Paris. (C) **01-45-48-35-53**. Fax 01-45-49-31-48. www.hotellindbergh.com. 26 units. 99€–160€ ($124–$200) single or double; 126€–180€ ($158–$225) triple; 136€–190€ ($170–$238) quad. Breakfast 8€ ($10). AE, MC, V. Métro: Sèvres-Babylone. **Amenities:** Elevator. *In room:* Satellite TV, dataport, hair dryer.

Hôtel Muguet ★★ *Finds*   You would think this hotel was renovated just yesterday—every detail is spick-and-span and in great condition. Rooms are light and airy, with wood furniture and print drapes. If you get a room that faces the courtyard, you will look out on a garden. Single rooms are pretty small but most doubles are quite spacious, though the showers are tiny. The staff is friendly and ultraefficient, and the location is on a quiet street around the corner from the Invalides and the Eiffel Tower. A self-service laundromat is a few steps from the hotel and several nice cafes within a 3-minute walk. The air-conditioning is a great perk on a warm summer's day.

11 rue Chevert, 75007 Paris. (C) **01-47-05-05-93**. Fax 01-45-50-25-37. www.hotelmuguet.com. 48 units. 95€ ($119) single; 110€–125€ ($13–$156) double; 160€ ($200) triple. Breakfast 8.50€ ($11). AE, MC, V. Métro: Latour-Mauborg or Ecole-Militaire. **Amenities:** Elevator. *In room:* A/C, satellite TV, dataport, hair dryer, safe.

14E ARRONDISSEMENT

In the 1920s, this neighborhood was a favorite haunt of artsy American expats like Henry Miller and Man Ray. Today a skyscraper looms over this area, but it still bustles with a huge train station and great shopping on rue de Rennes.

Hôtel des Bains *Finds*   This quiet hotel is a budget traveler's delight, offering excellent quality and value. A walk from the attractive lobby through the courtyard brings you to a separate building with a winding staircase that leads to three brand-new suites (each on its own floor), with large bathrooms and ample storage space—a boon for families. The elevator in the main building runs to a landing between floors, so you will have to manage some stairs. The rooms were overhauled in 2002 and have either carpeted or frequently waxed wooden floors, desks with reading lights, and bright bedspreads and draperies. Bathrooms are well maintained; some showers have smoked-glass doors. Book early.

33 rue Delambre, 75014 Paris. (C) **01-43-20-85-27**. Fax 01-42-79-82-78. des.bains.hotel@wanadoo.fr. 42 units. 76€ ($95) single or double with 1 bed; 79€ ($99) twin; 91€ ($114) suite for 2, 119€ ($149) suite for 3, 142€ ($178) suite for 4. Buffet breakfast 7.20€ ($9). Métro: Vavin or Edgar-Quinet. **Amenities:** Elevator. *In room:* Satellite TV, hair dryer, safe, trouser press.

SUPER-CHEAP SLEEPS

Celtic Hôtel *Value*   In a central Montparnasse location not far from the Square Delambre, the Gare Montparnasse, and the Cimitière de Montparnasse, this hotel is a very good deal. It has cozy features such as (nonworking) fireplaces in many of the surprisingly large rooms. Fifth-floor rooms offer superb views of the Eiffel Tower from narrow balconies. There is no elevator.

15 rue d'Odessa, 75014 Paris. (C) **01-43-20-93-53** or 01-43-20-83-91. Fax 01-43-20-66-07. hotelceltic@wanadoo.fr. 29 units, 21 with bathroom, 5 with shower only. 43€ ($54) single with sink; 56€ ($70) single or double with shower; 59€ ($74) single or double with bathroom. Breakfast 3€ ($3.75). Shower 3€ ($3.75). MC, V. Métro: Montparnasse or Edgar Quinet. *In room:* Satellite TV.

3 Hostels & Dorms

Paris has plenty of hostels (*auberges de jeunesse*) and *foyers* (literally "homes") to accommodate students and young travelers. Over the last few years, the quality of these has improved to the point where some can compete with a basic budget hotel. Most offer large, shared rooms, and smaller, more private ones for a higher price. Few have private bathrooms, so be prepared to share. You can usually count on cleanliness and a certain amount of congeniality. While some hostels are in large and impersonal buildings, others are in historic buildings that are both comfortable and handsome. Many welcome travelers of all ages, though there may be restrictions when it comes to sharing rooms.

Hostels in Paris are an especially good deal for solo travelers. Hostels are a great place to meet travelers from all over the world. While there are still a few hostels in Paris that have lockout times, many are now open 24 hours a day. Still, if you are a night owl, be sure to check open hours before you commit.

Another positive development is that hostels are starting to take reservations in advance—but there are still some that don't. In that case, the best strategy is to show up as early as possible in the day. You can also call ahead to find out what your chances are for getting a bed.

If you arrive late in the day, head to one of the offices of **OTU Voyages** at 119 rue St-Martin in the 4e (Métro: Châtelet), 39 rue George Bernanous in the 5e (Métro: Port Royal), or 2 rue Malus in the 5e (Métro: Place-Monge). All three locations have the same phone number: ℭ **01-40-29-12-12;** www.otu.fr. Its staff will help you find lodgings in hostels, budget hotels, or (in summer) University of Paris dorms. It will also negotiate discount rail, bus, and plane tickets; issue student IDs; and provide details about activities of special interest to young people. It's open Monday to Friday 10am to 6:30pm, Saturday 10am to 5pm.

The **Office de Tourisme et des Congrès de Paris,** 127 av. des Champs-Elysées, 75008 Paris (ℭ **01-49-52-53-35;** Métro: Charles-de-Gaulle–Etoile or George V), will book you a bed in a hostel for a 1€ ($1.25) fee.

Auberge Internationale des Jeunes *Value*

Near place de la Bastille and the nightlife along rue de Charonne, this hostel was renovated in the mid-1990s and offers a higher level of comfort than most Paris hostels. Most rooms contain two to four beds, and about half have bathrooms. Common showers and toilets are on each floor. The hostel is open 24 hours and has an Internet connection (.15€/20¢ per min.).

10 rue Trousseau, 75011 Paris. ℭ 01-47-00-62-00. Fax 01-47-00-33-16. www.aijparis.com. 50 units, 22 with bathroom. 13€–17€ ($16–$21) per person depending on the season. Rates include bed sheet, showers, and breakfast. MC, V. Métro: Ledru-Rollin.

B.V.J. Louvre

Run by the Union des Centres de Rencontres Internationales de France, this hostel is friendly, and its location is excellent. Each room has 2 to 10 beds, and showers and toilets are on each floor. It's open 24 hours.

UCRIF also runs **B.V.J. Quartier Latin,** 44 rue des Bernardins, 5e (ℭ **01-43-29-34-80;** Métro: Maubert-Mutualité), in the Latin Quarter. All rooms have showers, with toilets down the hall. There are some singles, costing 35€ ($44), and double rooms are 28€ ($35) per person; a bed in a room with 10 others is 26€ ($33). Breakfast is included.

20 rue Jean-Jacques-Rousseau, 75001 Paris. ℭ 01-53-00-90-90. Fax 01-53-00-90-91. www.bvjhotel.com. 204 beds. 25€–28€ ($31–$35) per person. Rate includes continental breakfast. MC, V. Métro: Palais-Royal–Musée du Louvre.

Foyer International des Etudiants

Open to travelers in the summer, this university residence is across from the Luxembourg gardens and is quite comfortable. Reservations are recommended and must be made via regular mail.

93 bd. St-Michel, 75005 Paris. ℭ 01-43-54-49-63. www.fie.fr. 160 beds. 30€ ($38) single; 22€ ($28) per person double. Rates include showers and breakfast. No credit cards. Closed Oct–June. Métro: Luxembourg.

Youth Hostel le Fauconnier *(Finds* Run by the Maisons Internationales de la Jeunesse et des Etudiants, this hostel is in a historic *hôtel particulier,* or private home, on a quiet street in the Marais. All rooms have private showers, and some rooms are singles or doubles—unusual for hostels. Be warned, however, that this hostel is often overrun by groups, so book in advance. Doors close at 1am.

Other MIJE hostels are nearby: **Maubuisson,** 12 rue des Barres, 4e, with 111 beds; and **Fourcy,** 6 rue de Fourcy, 4e, with 190 beds. The rates are identical to Le Fauconnier. Reservations and information are available at the numbers listed below.

11 rue du Fauconnier, 75004 Paris. (C) **01-42-74-23-45.** Fax 01-40-27-81-64. www.mije.com. 135 beds. 25€–28€ ($31–$35) per person in multibed room; 32€–38€ ($40–$48) twin; 42€–49€ ($53–$61) single. Rates include continental breakfast. No credit cards. Maximum stay 7 nights. Métro: St-Paul or Pont-Marie.

6

Great Deals on Dining

The Parisian's reverence for fine cuisine is almost religious. It is part of his or her heritage. Whether it's *choucroute* (sauerkraut) from the Alsatian region or *agneau de lait Pyrénées rôti* (roast lamb) from the southwest, it is quintessentially French, and it is all fabulous. The millennium seems to have ushered in a renewed excitement in French dining, ignited by some star chefs including the Costes brothers, whose flagship restaurant at their eponymous hotel is thriving, along with Georges, Café Marly and l'Esplanade, to name a few of their spots. Michelin star Alain Ducasse has brought reputation to trendy restaurants like Spoon, Food, and Wine, where he offers a variety of *cuisine internationale* and boasts an extensive foreign wine list. And, of course, there are the more low-key, traditional chefs—like Thierry Breton of Chez Michel and Philippe Tredgeu of Chez Casimir—who are more interested in classic French dining, assuring the Parisian and tourist alike that traditional—and excellent—French fare will never die out.

It is true, the French are reserved, and nowhere is this more evident than when you are in one of their holy places: a restaurant. This can make the French dining experience daunting, but don't be intimidated: It's all part of the act, and your waiter is just playing his role. To open a dialogue simpatico, smooth your way with such phrases as "Bonjour, Monsieur." It's a little bit of *politesse* that works like "open sesame." Do *not* address your server as *garçon*. Remember, behind your server's protective mask lies a well of passion, knowledge, and pride, because he is your liaison to the most sacred cathedral of all—*La Cuisine*.

For the French, dining is an art, and they give it due respect. So whether they're lunching at a family brasserie or a place that serves haute cuisine, the French will take time to eat their *feuilleté au fromage* (cheese pastry) and *confit de canard*. Honoring this tradition, most shopkeepers close their stores from 1 to 3pm to savor their noontime repast.

While lunch is important, dinner is *le plus important,* so if you were galloping through the Louvre all day and grabbed a crepe on the street for lunch, unwind during dinner at a leisurely French pace. Even if you're not feeling flush, you can find a restaurant that offers a wonderful meal at an affordable price, particularly since so many places offer a prix-fixe menu called *formule* or *menu du jour.* Ethnic restaurants are inexpensive and worth trying for some spice in your life.

With so much emphasis on cuisine, it may be surprising that you find a slender population. That is because French chefs use only the freshest ingredients and portions are sensible. In the unlikely event that you have leftovers, *don't* ask for a doggie bag (it's just not done here).

If you're feeling a bit bohemian, be creative: Picnic! Go to a *fromagerie* for cheese, a boulangerie for a baguette, and a charcuterie for some pâté, sausage, or salad. Add a bottle of Côtes du Rhône, and head for the Pont des Arts; nothing is more romantic than toasting the most beautiful city in the world on this magnificent bridge under a moonlit sky. *Bon appétit!*

1 Eating Like a Parisian

The key to fine dining on a budget is to eat where Parisians eat and to stay away from most restaurants around major tourist attractions. Opt for restaurants in neighborhoods where people live and work, which must keep their prices and quality competitive to satisfy their regular customers.

Eat the way Parisians eat and you'll also save money. If you must have eggs, bacon, and toast for breakfast, you'll pay dearly. Instead, save your appetite for lunch and enjoy a light meal of café au lait and croissants or a buttered baguette called a *tartine*. Unless the price of your hotel room includes breakfast, go to a cafe and stand at the counter. The experience is inimitably Parisian. You'll rub shoulders with workers downing shots of Calvados with their espresso, and executives perusing the morning *Figaro* before work. The price will also be about 40% to 50% lower at the counter than for sit-down waiter service.

DINING ESTABLISHMENTS   Bistros, brasseries, and restaurants offer different dining experiences. The typical **bistro** used to be a mom-and-pop operation with a menu of Parisian standbys like *oeuf mayonnaise, boeuf bourguignon* (cubes of beef in red wine, onions, and mushrooms), and *tarte tatin* (an apple tart). Today many bistros have expanded on the classics but retained the tradition of hearty, relatively low-priced dishes in a convivial atmosphere. Tradition is strong, though. Take the case of *oeuf mayonnaise* (basically a hard-boiled egg with Hollandaise sauce): The old favorite is held in such regard that it has an organization dedicated to its "protection"—the Association de Sauvegarde de Oeuf Mayonnaise. It awards prizes every year.

Brasserie means "brewery" and refers to Alsatian specialties, which include beer, Riesling wine, and *choucroute* (sauerkraut, usually topped by cuts of pork). Most brasseries are large, cheerful places that open early and close late; many no longer specialize in Alsatian fare. Brasseries began as independent enterprises and remained so for more than a century, then began to fall to corporate acquisition in the 1970s. Today, all brasseries (except Brasserie Ile St-Louis in the 1er, p. 112) are part of one chain. While this does not detract from the charm of the legendary eateries, watch out for mundane and repetitive food—it's out there. At brasseries you can usually get a meal at any time of day, even when restaurants and bistros are closed, and the food is relatively inexpensive.

Restaurants are where you go to savor French cuisine in all its glory. Classic dishes are expertly interpreted, and new taste sensations are invented. Dining is more formal than in bistros or brasseries, and service is slower. Like bistros, restaurants serve lunch between noon and 2:30pm and dinner between 7:30 and 10pm. Parisians usually dine between 8:30 and 9pm.

THE CUISINE   The genius of French cuisine has always been the variety of the regional tables, and they are well represented in Paris. Regional restaurants provide a gastronomic tour of France—oysters and crepes from Brittany, fondue from the Savoy, cassoulet from the southwest, and Provençal dishes based on tomatoes, herbs, and olive oil. Wine lists showcase local products, sometimes at excellent prices.

Every so often, even French people need a break from French food. The most popular ethnic dish is couscous from North Africa—steamed semolina garnished with a ladleful of broth, stewed vegetables, and meat. Chinese, Thai, Vietnamese, Indian, Tex-Mex, and Russian restaurants are also popular, although not necessarily cheaper than their French counterparts. Lebanese food is the latest ethnic cuisine in Paris, with 150 Lebanese restaurants operating in the city.

Vegetarianism has not caught on, but it is usually possible to get a veggie meal no matter where you eat. *Oeuf mayonnaise,* onion soup, omelets, salads, and cheese platters are staples in most bistros and brasseries, and most chefs have no problem putting together vegetable platters derived from their regular menus.

DRINKS   French wine is, of course, excellent. Moreover, having wine with your meal is less expensive than having juice or soda. The *menu du jour* at many establishments includes red or white wine. The standard measure is a quarter-liter carafe *(un quart).* If wine is not included, you can order *vin ordinaire* (house wine) or a Beaujolais or Côtes du Rhône, which are reasonably priced.

Coffee is never drunk during a meal. *Café* or *espresso* means an espresso; *café au lait* is a larger cup of espresso and steamed milk. If you would like to dilute your espresso with a little milk, ask for *café noisette.* For decaffeinated coffee, ask for *un deca;* decaffeinated herbal tea is *infusion.*

TIPPING   Although a service charge of 15% (or more) will be included in your total bill, we recommend leaving an extra 4% to 7% tip, depending on the service. Remember, this is a lifelong career for most servers.

Cheap Streets: The Lowdown

- **Rue des Rosiers,** in the Marais. People have been known to trudge across town for the two-fisted pita-bread sandwiches sold on this street. Stuffed with falafel, eggplant, and salad, then topped with your choice of sauce, this must be the best 5€ ($6.25) meal in town.

- **Avenue d'Ivry** and **avenue de Choisy,** 13e. Far off the tourist track, the Vietnamese, Chinese, and Thai restaurants along these avenues cater to the local Asian population. Prices are low and quality is high.

- **Métro Belleville,** 11e. The streets radiating out from this station are the northern headquarters for Asian cuisine. Whether at an unassuming little spot or a large Chinese-style brasserie, you can usually slurp down noodle soup at any hour of the day and into the night.

- **Boulevard de Belleville,** 11e. You'll find a lot of reasonably priced and fine, if not outstanding, couscous places. Middle Eastern snacks, pastries, and a glass of mint tea make an exotic and inexpensive meal.

- **Rue de Montparnasse,** 14e. The street between boulevard Edgar Quinet and boulevard du Montparnasse is a Crêperie Row of inexpensive Breton eateries. Whether sugared with syrups and jam (crepes) or stuffed with vegetables and meat (galettes), they make a tasty light meal for less than 10€ ($13).

- **Rue Ste-Anne,** 9e. Sushi is expensive in Paris, but because this street lies in the same neighborhood as many Japanese businesses, you'll find the freshest fish and most authentic dishes at prices that are more moderate than elsewhere.

2 Restaurants by Cuisine

AFRICAN/SENEGALESE

Le Manguier ✦, 11e (p. 132)

ALSATIAN

Bofinger ✦✦, 4e (p. 120)

Brasserie Flo ✦, 10e (p. 119)

Brasserie Ile St-Louis ✦, 1er (p. 112)

Chez Jenny ✦, 3e (p. 123)

ARGENTINIAN

El Palenque, 5e (p. 132)

AUVERGNE

ChantAirelle ✦, 5e (p. 136)

BASQUE

Auberge de Jarente, 4e (p. 120)

BELGIAN

Bouillon Racine, 6e (p. 137)

BISTRO

Au Pied du Fouet, 7e (p. 140)

Au Relais–Le Bistrot d'Edouard ✦, 18e (p. 129)

Au Rendez-Vous des Camionneurs, 14e (p. 143)

Bar des Théâtres, 8e (p. 126)

Bistro Mazarin ✦, 6e (p. 137)

Bistrot de Beaubourg, 4e (p. 120)

Camille, 3e (p. 121)

Chardenoux ✦, 11e (p. 125)

Dame Jeanne ✦, 11e (p. 124)

La Formi Ailée, 5e (p. 132)

L'Ebauchoir, 12e (p. 124)

Le Café du Marche ✦, 7e (p. 142)

L'Ecailler du Bistrot, 11e (p. 124)

Le Coude Fou, 4e (p. 122)

Le Galopin ✦, 10e (p. 118)

Le Père Claude ✦, 15e (p. 144)

Le Polidor ✦, 6e (p. 138)

Le Tambour, 2e (p. 119)

Restaurant Perraudin ✦, 5e (p. 136)

Rotisserie Armaillé ✦✦, 17e (p. 128)

BRASSERIE

Bofinger ✦✦, 4e (p. 120)

Brasserie Balzar ✦, 5e (p. 136)

Brasserie Flo ✦, 10e (p. 119)

Brasserie Ile St-Louis ✦, 1er (p. 112)

Chez Jenny ✦, 3e (p. 123)

Closerie des Lilas ✦✦, 6e (p. 139)

Le Grand Colbert ✦✦, 2e (p. 118)

Les Grandes Marches ✦, 12e (p. 125)

Vagenende ✦, 6e (p. 139)

BRAZILIAN

Boteco, 11e (p. 132)

BRETON

A la Bonne Crêpe, 6e (p. 137)

Les Muses ✦, 8e (p. 128)

CAFES

Au Bistrot de la Place, 4e (p. 145)

Café Baci ✦, 3e (p. 145)

Café Beaubourg ✦, 4e (p. 145)

Café Charbon, 11e (p. 145)

Café Concert Ailleurs, 4e (p. 145)

Café de Flore ✦, 6e (p. 147)

Café de la Place, 14e (p. 147)

Café de l'Industrie, 11e (p. 146)

Café Etienne Marcel ✦, 2e (p. 146)

Café Hugo ✦, 4e (p. 146)

Café Lateral ✦, 17e (p. 146)

Café Mabillon, 6e (p. 147)

Café Marly ✦, 1er (p. 146)

Café Roussillon, 7e (p. 147)

Cyber World Café ✦, 7e (p. 148)

Fouquet's, 8e (p. 146)

La Chaise au Plafond, 4e (p. 147)

La Chope, 5e (p. 147)

La Coupole, 14e (p. 148)

La Palette ✦, 6e (p. 148)

Le Café de l'Esplanade ✦, 7e (p. 148)

Les Deux Magots ✦, 6e (p. 148)

Les Editeurs ✦, 6e (p. 148)

L'Eté en Pente Douce, 18e (p. 147)

CAFETERIAS

Empire State, 17e (p. 112)

Flunch-Fontaine Innocents, 1er (p. 112)

CORSICAN

Vivario ✦, 5e (p. 136)

CREPES

A la Bonne Crêpe, 6e (p. 137)
Les Muses ✦, 8e (p. 128)

DELI

Jo Goldenberg, 4e (p. 121)

EUROPEAN

Jo Goldenberg, 4e (p. 121)

FONDUE

Chez Les Fondus ✦, 18e (p. 129)

FRENCH

Auberge de la Reine Blanche, 4e
    (p. 123)
Au Bon Accueil ✦, 7e (p. 142)
Au Pied de Cochon, 1er (p. 116)
Au Poulbot Gourmet ✦, 18e (p. 130)
Au Rendez-Vous des Chauffeurs, 18e
    (p. 129)
Aux Charpentiers, 6e (p. 137)
Aux Lyonnais ✦✦✦, 2e (p. 119)
Au Trou Normand ✦, 11e (p. 124)
Aux Marches du Palais ✦✦, 16e
    (p. 126)
Aux Troix Bourriques, 5e (p. 132)
Bon 2 ✦, 2e (p. 117)
Café Constant ✦✦, 7e (p. 140)
Chartier ✦, 9e (p. 118)
Chez Casimir ✦, 10e (p. 118)
Chez Clément, 2e, 8e, 11e (p. 111)
Chez Germaine, 7e (p. 140)
Chez Marie, 18e (p. 130)
Chez Michel ✦, 10e (p. 119)
Closerie des Lilas ✦✦, 6e (p. 139)
Georges ✦, 4e (p. 121)
Hippopotamus, 5e (p. 111)
Julien ✦, 10e (p. 120)
La Butte Chaillot ✦✦, 16e (p. 128)
La Fontaine de Mars ✦, 7e (p. 140)
La Petite Hostellerie, 5e (p. 133)
La Poule au Pot, 1er (p. 116)
La Serre ✦, 7e (p. 140)
La Tour de Montlhéry, 1er (p. 116)
Le Bistrot du Dome, ✦,14e (p. 143)
Le Café du Commerce ✦, 15e
    (p. 144)
Le Caveau du Palais, 1er (p. 113)

Le Clos du Gourmet ✦✦, 7e (p. 142)
Le Coupe Chou ✦, 5e (p. 133)
Le Felteu ✦, 4e (p. 122)
Le Liteau, 8e (p. 126)
Le Moulin de la Galette ✦, 18e
    (p. 130)
Leo Le Lion ✦✦, 7e (p. 142)
Le Petit Keller ✦, 11e (p. 125)
Le Petit Machon, 1er (p. 113)
Le Petit Prince de Paris, 5e (p. 133)
Le Petit St-Benoît, 6e (p. 138)
Le Petit Vatel, 6e (p. 138)
Le Relais Plaza ✦✦, 8e (p. 128)
Les Bouquinistes ✦✦, 6e (p. 139)
L'Escure ✦, 1er (p. 116)
Les Temps des Cerises, 4e (p. 122)
Poissons Rouge ✦, 10e (p. 117)
Restaurant du Palais-Royal ✦✦, 1er
    (p. 117)
Restaurant Paul ✦, 1er (p. 117)
Robert et Louise ✦, 3e (p. 123)
Trumilou ✦, 4e (p. 123)

GREEK

Restaurant Orestias, 6e (p. 138)

INDO-PAKISTANI

Vallée du Kashmir, 14e (p. 143)

INTERNATIONAL

Bon 2 ✦, 2e (p. 117)
Chez Prune ✦, 10e (p. 112)
La Grande Armée ✦, 17e (p. 126)
Le Fumoir ✦, 1er (p. 113)
Georges ✦, 4e (p. 121)
Spoon, Food, and Wine ✦✦, 8e
    (p. 129)
Ze Kitchen Galerie ✦, 6e (p. 139)

ITALIAN

Le Bugatti, 15e (p. 143)
Le Moulin de la Galette ✦, 18e
    (p. 130)

LEBANESE

Al Diwan ✦, 8e (p. 125)

LYONNAISE

Aux Lyonnais ✦✦✦, 2e (p. 119)
L'Assiette Lyonnaise, 8e (p. 126)
Le Petit Machon, 1er (p. 113)

MIDDLE EASTERN
L'As du Falafel, 4e (p. 121)

MORROCAN
Chez Omar ✿, 3e (p. 121)

NORMAN
Au Trou Normand ✿, 11e (p. 124)
Aux Troix Bourriques, 5e (p. 132)

NORTH AFRICAN
Le 404 ✿, 3e (p. 122)

PATISSERIES & BOULAN-
GERIES
Au Délice de Sèvres, 7e (p. 154)
Au Panetier, 2e (p. 153)
Bonneau, 16e (p. 153)
BoulangEpicier ✿, 8e (p. 153)
Boulangerie des Martyrs, 9e (p. 154)
Eric Kayzer ✿, 5e (p. 154)
Eric Kayzer Organic, 5e (p. 154)
Le Moulin de la Vierge ✿, 15e
(p. 154)
Le Notre Paris Patissier ✿, 16e
(p. 154)
Poilâne ✿, 6e (p. 154)
Poujauran, 7e (p. 154)

SANDWICHES
Cosi ✿, 6e (p. 137)
Lina's Sandwiches, 1er, 9e (p. 112)

SEAFOOD
Le Bistrot du Dome, ✿, 14e (p. 143)
L'Ecailler du Bistrot, 11e (p. 124)
Léon de Bruxelles, 8e (p. 112)
L'Ostréa, 1er (p. 116)
Poissons Rouge ✿, 10e (p. 117)

SOUTHWEST
Auberge de Jarente, 4e (p. 120)
Le Gros Minet, 1er (p. 113)

TAPAS
Juveniles, 1er (p. 112)

TEA SALONS
A la Cour de Rohan, 6e (p. 150)
Angelina ✿, 1er (p. 149)
A Priori Thé ✿, 2e (p. 149)
Instant Delices, 1er (p. 149)
Ladurée ✿, 8e (p. 149)
Les Enfants Gatés, 4e (p. 150)
Mariage Frères ✿, 4e (p. 150)
Salon de Thé de la Mosqué de Paris,
5e (p. 150)
Tea Caddy, 5e (p. 150)

VEGETARIAN
Le Grenier de Notre-Dame ✿, 5e
(p. 133)

WINE BARS
A la Cloche des Halles, 1er (p. 151)
Aux Négociants, 18e (p. 151)
Bistro du Peintre, 11e (p. 151)
Chai 33 ✿, 12e (p. 151)
Clown Bar, 11e (p. 151)
La Tartine, 4e (p. 152)
L'Ecluse Saint-Michel, 6e (p. 152)
Le Griffonnier, 8e (p. 152)
Le Sancerre ✿, 7e (p. 152)
Mélac, 11e (p. 152)
Taverne Henri IV, 1er (p. 152)

3 The Best of the Budget Chains

Paris has several good chains, the best of which is the **Chez Clément** group. Their specialty is spit-roasted meat, with sweet spices, honey, or dried fruit. The Grand Rotisserie—salad, beef, pork, chicken, and mashed potatoes for 15€ ($19)—is a good deal. It has eight branches, including 123 av. des Champs-Elysées, 8e (⓸ **01-40-73-87-00**); 17 bd. des Capucines, 2e (⓸ **01-53-43-82-00;** Métro: Opéra); and 21 bd. Beaumarchais, 11e (⓸ **01-40-29-17-00;** Métro: Bastille or Breguet-Sabin). All are open daily from noon to 1am.

You'll see the red awnings of **Hippopotamus** all over town. These places prepare decent red-meat dishes accompanied by fries and salad and served in a pleasant atmosphere. The extended hours are a convenience as well—you can get a hot meal here when most other places are closed. Try the one at 9 rue Lagrange, 5e (**© 01-43-54-13-99;** Métro: Maubert); it's open Sunday to Thursday 11:30am to midnight, Friday and Saturday 11:30am to 1am.

Lina's Sandwiches packs an assortment of fillings onto bread and rolls in American-deli style. Add soup or salad and finish with a brownie. Among its locations are 30 bd. des Italiens, 9e (**© 01-42-46-02-06;** Métro: Opéra), and 7 av. de l'Opéra, 1er (**© 01-47-03-30-29;** Métro: Pyramides).

Léon de Bruxelles, Belgium's answer to T.G.I. Friday's, specializes in steamed mussels rather than fries and burgers. The chain serves 13 styles of the crustacean, all with *frites,* in a cavernous environment that echoes with rounds of "Joyeaux Anniversaire" ("Happy Birthday") sung at party tables. There is a branch at 63 av. des Champs-Elysées, 8e (**© 01-42-25-96-16;** Métro: Charles-de-Gaulle–Etoile).

Though the ambience can be uninspiring, some cafeterias offer good food at moderate prices. In the Les Halles neighborhood, try **Flunch-Fontaine Innocents,** 5 rue Pierre Lescot, 1er (**© 01-42-33-54-00;** Métro: Etienne Marcel). Near the Arc de Triomphe there's the modern **Empire State,** 41 av. Wagram, 17e (**© 01-43-80-14-39**).

4 On the Right Bank

1ER ARRONDISSEMENT

Brasserie Ile St-Louis ✷ ALSATIAN/BRASSERIE   This is Paris's last independent brasserie, open since 1870, with food to remember and a view to kill. These loud, big spaces, brimming with cheer and good food, once thrived throughout the city; many survive, but as parts of chains. Brasserie Ile St-Louis, owned by the same family for over 60 years, now stands alone. The favorite haunt of writer James Jones, who kept a *chope* (mug) at the bar, it's directly off the footbridge from Ile de la Cité to Ile St-Louis, with an unparalleled view of the eastern tip of Ile de la Cité (including the back of Notre-Dame). The vista is delightful from the summer terrace over the water. And the food is quintessentially Alsatian—*choucroute* with heaps of tender, biting sauerkraut and meaty slices of ham.

55 quai de Bourbon, 1er. © **01-43-54-02-59.** Main courses 12€–26€ ($15–$33). MC, V. Fri–Tues noon–1am; Thurs 6pm–1am. Métro: Pont Marie.

Chez Prune ✷ *Value* INTERNATIONAL   Half restaurant and half bar, this fun and boisterous place is always crowded with young locals. The atmosphere is best at lunch when the scene is lively but not loud. The eclectic menu changes daily and may include a salmon with mango butter or lamb stewed with garlic cream and served with polenta. The salads are excellent and fresh. Try the seafood with fresh octopus. At night, light "bar snacks" are served until closing. This eatery wins the prize for the cheapest coffee in Paris (if you take it standing up at the bar) for a mere 1€ ($1.25).

71 quai de Valmy, 10e. © **01-42-41-30-47.** Main courses 12€–16€ ($15–$20). MC, V. Daily 8am–1:45am. Métro: Republique.

Juveniles *Finds* TAPAS   Close to the Palais Royal, you'll find Paris's best spot for tapas. Juveniles, a small, attractive wine bar owned by Englishman Tim Johnson, is always hopping and has a fun, laid-back atmosphere. Recommended dishes include *gambas grillés au basilic* (grilled jumbo shrimp with basil), grilled squid, and chorizo. Or you can order from the a la carte menu, which features cheese plates, lamb curry, and daily specials. Juveniles specializes in French, Australian, and Spanish wines, so try something you've never heard of—you may be pleasantly surprised. You can choose from at least 12 kinds of wine by the glass.

47 rue de Richelieu, 1er. ℂ 01-42-97-46-49. 2-course menu with wine and coffee 15€ ($19); 3-course dinner menus 17€ ($21) and 23€ ($29); tapas 6€–10€ ($7.50–$13); main courses 10€–15€ ($13–$19). AE, MC, V. Mon–Sat noon–11pm. Métro: Palais-Royal–Musée du Louvre.

Le Caveau du Palais *Finds* FRENCH

In the heart of charming, tree-lined place Dauphine, a secluded park at the tip of Isle de la Cité, lies this well-kept Parisian secret. The restaurant is a favorite with local residents, as it was for Yves Montand and Simone Signoret. Low ceilings, stone walls surrounding an open kitchen, and the welcoming smiles of owners Bernard and Maïté Dieuleveut create a cozy atmosphere. In the spring, customers sit outside along the park while workers on break from the Monnaie de Paris (the French mint) play boules. Begin a memorable meal with sumptuous *foie gras cru de canard au naturel.* After a fine Sauternes, dive into the house specialty *côte de boeuf* (grilled giant ribs), prepared for two. *Confit de canard et pommes Sarladaise,* duck served with crispy potato bits sautéed in foie gras drippings, is another must. Round out your meal with a good glass of house wine for 4€ ($5).

19 pl. Dauphine, 1er. ℂ 01-43-26-04-28. Main courses 16€–28€ ($20–$35). AE, DC, MC, V. Mon–Sat 12:15–2:30pm and 7:15–10:30pm. Métro: Pont Neuf.

Le Fumoir ✦ INTERNATIONAL

This trendy restaurant-cafe-bar-tearoom-library is notable for its concept, but the food is pretty good, too. Subtle lighting and newspapers around the bar set an academic tone, meant to prepare you for the rear library, where you can browse, exchange, or borrow books. The menu spans the globe, with tidbits like sushi, bruschetta, roast potatoes with tomato-apricot chutney, and a variety of large salads. The international theme extends to the drinks menu, which includes *mate* (a tealike South American drink), carrot juice, margaritas, and teas and cocktails. Play chess, gaze at the Louvre, and have fun looking serious. Although the bar stays open until 1:30am, the kitchen closes at 11:30pm, so be sure to arrive before then if you plan to eat late here.

6 rue de l'Amiral Coligny, 1er. ℂ 01-42-92-00-24. Weekly 2-course lunch menu 19€ ($24); Sun brunch 21€ ($26); dinner menu 28€ ($35); salads 8€–11€ ($10–$14); main courses 14€–27€ ($18–$34). AE, V. Daily 11am–1:30am. Métro: Louvre-Rivoli.

Le Gros Minet *Value* SOUTHWEST

This is a pretty restaurant with French country linens that adorn the tables. And the food is wonderful and a good bargain, too. The menu changes regularly, but if it's available, start with the mouthwatering *feuilleté au fromage,* a flaky, crispy crust filled with warm Emmental cheese, followed by the *Jambonette de dinde,* which includes minced potatoes cooked in garlic, or the delicious *blanquette de veau.* Complete your meal with the fabulous homemade chocolate mousse.

1 rue des Prouvaires, 1er. ℂ 01-42-33-02-62. 3-course lunch menu 15€ ($18); 3-course dinner menu 22€ ($28). MC, V. Tues–Fri noon–2pm; Mon–Sat 7–11pm. Closed for lunch Aug. Métro: Châtelet.

Le Petit Machon *Value* FRENCH/LYONNAIS

Sleek and modern, with a wood bar and mirrored ceiling, this restaurant serves good Lyonnais cuisine. Start with regional specialties *saucisson chaud pommes à l'huile* (warm sausage with potatoes in oil) or salad with Roquefort and walnuts. Follow with *noisette d'agneau* (sliced lamb) in asparagus cream sauce, ham with lentils, or *merlu* (a whitefish similar to hake) in a delicate cream sauce. The adventurous gastronome might try *oreilles de cochons* (pigs' ears). Service is hurried but friendly.

Where to Dine on the Right Bank (1–4 & 9–12e)

Au Pied de Cochon **18**
Au Trou Normand **42**
Auberge de Jarente **33**
Auberge de la Reine
  Blanche **32**
Aux Lyonnais **5**
Bistro de Beaubourg **21**
Bofinger **35**

Bon 2 **6**
Brasserie Flo **2**
Brasserie Ile St-Louis **29**
Camille **31**
Chardenoux **39**
Chartier **3**
Chez Casimir **1**
Chez Jenny **41**

Chez Michel **1**
Chez Omar **40**
Chez Prune **43**
Dame Jeanne **37**
Georges **22**
Jo Goldenberg **30**
Julien **4**
Juveniles **10**

L'As du Fallafel **28**
L'Ebauchior **37**
L'Ecailler du
  Bistrot **39**
L'Escure **9**
L'Ostréa **14**
La Poule au Pot **15**
La Tour de Montihéry

BELLEVILLE Ⓜ
rue St-Maur
GARE de l'EST
GARE DE L'EST
Ⓜ
JARDIN VILLEMIN
Hôpital St-Louis
rue St-Maur
du Temple
COURONNES
bd. de Belleville Ⓜ
MÉNILMONTANT Ⓜ
10e
Canal St-Martin
44
av. Parmentier
GONCOURT Ⓜ
St-Joseph
Fontaine au Roi
Ⓜ Métro Stop
Ⓡ RER Stop
---- Railway
bd. de
rue du Faubourg St-Martin
CHÂTEAU D'EAU
Strasbourg
43
JACQUES BONSERGENT Ⓜ
rue de Faubourg
rue de la
ST-MAUR Ⓜ
RÉPUBLIQUE Ⓜ
place de la République
av. de la République
PARMENTIER Ⓜ
rue Oberkampf
11e
ouvelle
bd. St-Martin
bd. Voltaire
bd. du Temple
OBERKAMPF Ⓜ
rue St-Martin
TEMPLE Ⓜ
41
42
ST-AMBROISE Ⓜ
Conservatoire des Arts et Métiers
rue de Turbigo
Square du Temple
FILLES DU CALVAIRE Ⓜ
rue St-Sébastien
RICHARD LENOIR Ⓜ
rue Réaumur
40
rue de Temple
bd. Richard
rue du Chemin Vert
39→
RÉAUMUR-SÉBASTOPOL Ⓜ
ARTS ET MÉTIERS Ⓜ
3e
rue Charlot
rue de Turenne
ST-SÉBASTIEN FROISSART Ⓜ
rue St-Sabin
BREGUET SABIN Ⓜ
rue Sedaine
rue Beaubourg
23
ÉTIENNE MARCEL Ⓜ
rue des Archives
rue Amelot
38→
bd. de Sébastopol
RAMBUTEAU Ⓜ
rue Rambuteau
Musée Picasso
rue Vieille du Temple
27
CHEMIN VERT Ⓜ
bd. Beaumarchais
22
Centre Pompidou
rue du Renard
Musée Carnavalet
rue des Francs Bourgeois
31
place des Vosges
rue des Tournelles
BASTILLE Ⓜ
rue St-Denis
21
26
28
30
33
35 place de la Bastille
36 BASTILLE Ⓜ
37→
HÔTEL DE VILLE Ⓜ
rue St-Antoine
25
4e
ST-PAUL Ⓜ
BASTILLE Ⓜ
Opéra Bastille
av. Victoria
Hôtel de Ville
St-Germain l'Auxerrois
24
rue St-Paul
34
bd. Henri IV
bd. Bourbon
bd. de la Bastille
12e
quai de l'Hôtel de Ville
quai des Célestins
PONT MARIE Ⓜ
SULLY-MORLAND Ⓜ
Ste-Chapelle
CITÉ Ⓜ
ÎLE DE LA CITÉ
r. d' Arcole
pont Louis Philippe
pont Marie
r. des Deux Ponts
32
ÎLE ST-LOUIS
pont de Sully
Notre-Dame
pont St-Louis

Le 404 **23**
Le Caveau du Palais **19**
Le Coude Fou **25**
Le Felteu **26**
Le Fumoir **13**
Le Galopin **45**
Le Grand Colbert **8**

Le Gros Minet **17**
Le Petit Keller **38**
Le Petit Machon **12**
Le Tambour **7**
Les Grandes Marches **36**
Les Temps des Cerises **34**
Poissons Rouge **44**

Restaurant du Palais-Royal **11**
Restaurant Paul **20**
Robert et Louise **27**
Trumilou **24**

> ### *Tips* Three-Course Meals after Midnight
>
> If you're jet-lagged or want more than a snack in the middle of the night, there are three excellent choices in Paris, all near Métro Les Halles. **La Poule au Pot** (9 rue Vauvilliers, 1er; ✆ **01-42-36-32-96**) is open Tuesday to Sunday 7pm to 5am and has been serving traditional French cuisine since 1935 in a charming Art Deco setting. The 30€ ($38) three-course menu might include confit of duck, *filet mignon au poivre,* or trout with champagne. Main courses run about 16€ to 24€ ($20–$30). More affordable and open daily 24 hours, the ever-popular **Au Pied de Cochon** (6 rue Coquillière, 1er; ✆ **01-40-13-77-00**) boasts an excess of marble, murals, sconces, and chandeliers, as well as lots of tourists. You can have a plate of half a dozen oysters or onion soup to start. Follow with grilled salmon *entrecôte maître d'hôtel* (in rich red-wine sauce), or the restaurant's specialty and namesake, *pied de cochon* (pigs' feet). Finish with scrumptious profiteroles. Main courses are 13€ to 29€ ($16–$36). At **La Tour de Montlhéry** (5 rue des Prouvaires, 1er; ✆ **01-42-36-21-82**) the atmosphere is fabulously old Paris with hams and sausages dangling from the beams and red-and-white-checked tablecloths. Main courses are 13€ to 23€ ($16–$29) and it's open around the clock Monday to Friday but closed mid-July to mid-August. All three restaurants accept MasterCard and Visa.

158 rue St-Honoré, 1er. ✆ **01-42-60-08-06**. 3-course menu 19€ ($24); main courses 11€–15€ ($14–$19). V. Tues–Sun noon–2:30pm and 7–10:30pm. Métro: Palais-Royal–Musée du Louvre.

L'Escure ✿ *Finds* FRENCH   Don't let the armored vehicles on the street corner dissuade you from coming here. This wonderful restaurant is a few steps from the U.S. consulate and has been serving country French cuisine in a homey setting since 1919. The waitstaff is older, friendly, and refreshingly attentive and efficient. At lunch the place is filled with businessmen who consume a three-course meal—with wine—in less than an hour. Dinner is a more leisurely affair; a few tables are available for sidewalk dining in warm weather. Portions are large. You may begin with a chicken-liver terrine or a simple tomato salad followed by a tender boeuf bourguignon, or poached haddock. The homemade cassoulet with green beans is delicious. For dessert, try the exquisite pear tart.

7 rue Mondovi, 1er. ✆ **01-42-60-18-91**. 3-course menu with wine 22€ ($28); main courses 14€–18€ ($18–$23). MC, V. Mon–Fri noon–2:15pm and 7–10:30pm. Métro: Concorde.

L'Ostréa SEAFOOD   An aquarium and model ships along the stone walls set a marine mood for a fine fish dinner. Fresh baby shrimp and periwinkles are on the table for nibbling before the generous portions of fish and seafood arrive. The smoked-haddock appetizer served with *chèvre chaud,* apples, and sliced grapefruit is a standout; the tureen of fish soup is a meal in itself. The restaurant also offers six varieties of herring and four of mussels. The higher-priced delicacies constitute a splurge, but with careful selection, you can have an excellent two-course meal for around 24€ ($30).

4 rue Sauval, 1er. ℂ **01-40-26-08-07.** Main courses 10€–19€ ($13–$24); seafood delicacies 23€–62€ ($29–$78). MC, V. Mon–Fri noon–2:30pm; Mon–Sat 7:30–11pm. Closed Aug. Métro: Louvre-Rivoli.

Poissons Rouge ⭐ *(Finds* SEAFOOD/FRENCH   Overlooking the Canal St Martin, this lovely restaurant serves some of the best seafood in the city. The young and friendly waiters will recommend one of two *plats du jour* (usually one beef, one fish), and several other fish specials written on a large blackboard. Start with the mussels in a tomato-basil broth and move onto the *brochette de thon* (tuna on skewers) with fragrant rice and seasonal vegetables. In summer, a refreshing watermelon soup is served for dessert; otherwise, the crème brûlée is divine. There are several good wine selections at under 20€ ($25) a bottle. The bargain 14€ ($18) two-course menu includes one of the two *plats du jour* and your choice of either an appetizer or a dessert.

112 quai de Jemmapes, 10e. ℂ **01-40-40-07-11.** 2-course menu 14€ ($18); main courses 13€–16€ ($17–$20). MC, V. Tues–Sun noon–2:30pm and 7:30–11pm. Métro: Republique or Goncourt.

Restaurant Paul ⭐ *(Moments* FRENCH   Charismatic owners Thierry and Chantal make diners feel at home in this intimate, relaxed restaurant on the first floor of an 18th-century town house. The couple's affection for their restaurant, which they remodeled with wood banquettes and hand-painted murals of Parisian scenes, is palpable, and they extend that enthusiasm to their customers, many of whom have become regulars. Start with an invigorating lentil salad, tossed with marinated *lardons* (bits of cured ham), or a terrine of salmon, asparagus, and dill. Main dishes include haddock covered with butter-tarragon cream sauce, and a delicate casserole of tender veal and mushrooms with rice. End your evening with warm *tarte de pomme* (an apple pastry) in a room full of jovial people and empty plates.

15 pl. Dauphine and 52 quai des Orfèvres, 1er. ℂ **01-43-54-21-48.** Main courses 15€–21€ ($19–$26). AE, MC, V. Tues–Sun noon–2:30pm and 7–10pm. Métro: Pont Neuf or Cité.

WORTH A SPLURGE
Restaurant du Palais-Royal ⭐⭐ *(Moments* FRENCH   Tucked away in one of the most romantic locations in Paris—the arcade that encircles the gardens inside the Palais-Royal—this charming restaurant serves excellent modern bistro cooking in pleasant surroundings. Sit at the terrace on warm, sun-filled days and begin your meal with marinated leeks in beet-juice vinaigrette, or scallop salad. Main dishes are seasonal but might include grilled tuna steak with a Basque relish, or roast baby lamb. The desserts are delicious. Order carefully, as some of the main courses are expensive; several bottles of good wine are under 25€ ($31). Service can be brusque, but with a setting this beautiful, you'll be tempted to overtip even the most harried of waiters. In midsummer be sure to call a few days ahead and request a table on the terrace. If you're lucky, the moon will rise while you dine, splashing your table with romantic light.

43 rue Valois, 1er. ℂ **01-40-20-00-27.** Main courses 18€–46€ ($23($57). AE, DC, MC, V. Mon–Fri 12:30–2:30pm; Mon–Sat 7:30–10:30pm. Métro: Palais-Royal–Musée du Louvre.

2, 9 & 10E ARRONDISSEMENTS
Bon 2 ⭐ FRENCH/INTERNATIONAL   This ultrahip loungey restaurant is filled with young professionals in the early evenings after the Bourse has closed. They come after work for drinks and stay for the steak tartare with fries, or roasted chicken with mashed potatoes. Several Asian-influenced specials are offered such as seared tuna with sesame and soy sauce. You can sit indoors in the dimly lit but elegant space with its

enormous bar and dark-wood furniture or on the large sidewalk overlooking the place Bourse, watching the players of the French stock market walk by.

2 rue du quatre Septembre, 2e. ℂ 01-44-55-51-55. Main courses 13€–20€ ($16–$25); weekend brunch menu 17€ ($21). MC, V. Daily 11:45am–midnight. Métro: Bourse.

Chartier ℛ 𝒱𝒶𝓁𝓊𝑒 FRENCH   Think dark wood, mirrors, brisk waiters, and hazy lighting in this former workers' 1890 canteen that can seat a few hundred rowdy, yet well-behaved, diners. With the ghosts of Parisians past everywhere, there is a sense of intrigue that has been captured in several French films, notably *Borsalino,* with Alain Delon and Jean-Paul Belmondo. There are about 100 items on the menu, including 16 main courses like *poulet rôti* (roasted chicken), a variety of steaks and frites, and turkey in cream sauce. Appetizers here are incredibly affordable (about 4€/$5), so this is definitely a place to have a reasonable three-course meal even though it has no prix-fixe menu.

7 rue du Faubourg-Montmartre, 9e. ℂ 01-47-70-86-29. Reservations required for large groups. Main courses 8€–13€ ($10–$16). V. Daily 11:30am–3pm and 6–10pm. Métro: Grands Boulevards.

Chez Casimir ℛ FRENCH   This small, cozy restaurant serves light, healthy, and delicious cuisine. The credit goes to chef Philippe Tredgeu, who works magic in his kitchen preparing inventive, upscale dishes using market-fresh ingredients. Start with refreshing *crème de petit pois au Parmesan*—cold pea soup with slices of Parmesan cheese served with toasted bread (take as much as you want from the pot placed on your table), then have *filet de rascasse avec des spaguetti de courgettes* (scorpionfish filet served with spaghetti-style cooked zucchini, fresh-cut tomatoes, and a touch of vinegar). For dessert, indulge in homemade pastry topped with raspberries and vanilla cream. The wine list is affordable, with prices starting at 8€ ($10) for half a bottle.

6 rue de Belzunce, 10e. ℂ 01-48-78-28-80. Reservations recommended for dinner. Main courses 13€–19€ ($15–$24). No credit cards. Mon–Fri noon–2pm; Mon–Sat 7–11:30pm. Métro: Gare du Nord.

Le Galopin ℛ 𝐹𝒾𝓃𝒹𝓈 BISTRO   This gem, nestled in an unassuming neighborhood, serves excellent traditional French food in a homey, casual atmosphere. The menu, which changes daily, is written on a chalkboard hanging at the back of the rustic dining room. Many members of the friendly staff speak English. Appetizers may include moist, delicate *terrine campagne,* or fresh mushrooms in light cream sauce, followed by tuna steak in herb-sprinkled sauce Provençal or delicious *rôti de veau* (roasted veal). Fresh ratatouille and tasty carrot salad garnish many dishes. If *pot-au-feu* is on the menu, it's a must. There's enough tasty marrow to top a crisp slice of bread. Patrons make a heartfelt effort to sing along to the traditional live French music on weekends. Dinner on weekends costs 10% more to cover the cost of the musicians.

34 rue Ste-Marthe, 10e. ℂ 01-53-19-19-55. 2- and 3-course lunch menus 8€–11€ ($10–$14); 2- and 3-course dinner menus 13€–19€ ($16–$24). AE, DC, MC, V. Tues–Sun noon–2:30pm; Tues–Fri and Sun 8–11pm; Sat 8pm–midnight. No Sun brunch in summer. Métro: Belleville.

Le Grand Colbert ℛℛ CLASSIC BRASSERIE   Jack Nicholson, Keanu Reeves, and Diane Keaton dined here in the last scene of *Something's Gotta Give* in 2004, putting this historic place on the Hollywood map. It's a beautiful, grand old Belle Epoque brasserie where the very proper Parisians go for their Sunday lunch *en famille.* A national historic landmark dating back to the 1830s, the place shimmers with polished brass, old lamps, and frescoes. Service is old-world polite, proper, and unrushed. Skip the pricey seafood platters (around 33€/$41), and indulge in a variety of French favorites such as the warm chèvre salad or haddock with a wine-butter sauce; the grilled lamb with *dauphinois* potatoes is exquisite. Finish off with a fluffy baba au rhum.

2–4 rue Vivienne, 2e. ✆ 01-42-86-87-88. Reservations recommended. 3-course weekday lunch menu 19€ ($24); 3-course menu 30€ ($38); main courses 15€–29€ ($19–$36). AE, MC, V. Daily noon–3pm and 7:30pm–1am. Métro: Bourse.

Le Tambour ⓥalue BISTRO   Tucked between the journalist hangout of rue de Louvre and the arcades of Les Halles, this old-time bistro is a monument to Parisian eccentricity and charm. The eclectic decorations include worn bookshelves full of ancient texts, a huge subway map, and front tables covered in tile mosaics. The beret-wearing owner stands at the front bar and bellows "Bonjour!" to each person who enters. To get to the side dining area, patrons must walk behind the bar. All of this is great fun. The food—hearty fare at wonderful prices—includes tasty quiches with salad, warm *boudin* (blood sausage), and sumptuous *poulet rôti.*

41 rue Montmartre, 2e. ✆ 01-42-33-06-90. 2-course lunch menu 10€ ($13); main courses 10€–13€ ($13–$16) at lunch, 11€–19€ ($14–$24) at dinner. V. Daily noon–3pm and 7:30pm–4am. Métro: Châtelet–Les Halles or Sentier.

WORTH A SPLURGE
Aux Lyonnais ✸✸✸ ⓥalue FRENCH/LYONNAIS   This brainchild of Alain Ducasse, open since 2002, still offers, hands down, the best Lyonnais food in the city. Ducasse groomed a young and talented chef to oversee this elegant but casual bistro. The setting is simple and lovely—an 1890s bistro that has kept its redwood facade and bistro sign. Lots of pretty tile from Provence, floral patterned moldings, and "art pompier" light fixtures add to the decor. The service is exceptionally friendly and efficient. In addition to the changing menu, for appetizers you'll most likely find a pot of homemade foie gras served with cornichons or a dozen tender escargots in a garlicky butter sauce. Move on to the *quenelles* (fish dumplings) baked in a red sauce, or the roasted Cornish hen with mushrooms, tomatoes, and onions. Save room for the St-Marcellin cheese on a shallot-rubbed slice of baguette or the exquisite soufflé with pear liqueur. Several good wines are under 25€ ($31) a bottle, and a very laid-back and friendly sommelier will help you make the best choice. The 28€ ($35) three-course menu is a steal.

32 rue St-Marc, 2e. ✆ 01-42-96-65-04. Reservations required 2 weeks in advance. 3-course menu 28€ ($35); main courses 18€–31€ ($23–$39). AE, DC, MC, V. Tues–Fri noon–2:30pm and 7:30–10:30pm; Sat 7:30–11pm. Métro: Grands Boulevards.

Brasserie Flo ✸ ⓂＯments ALSATIAN/BRASSERIE   Founded in 1886 by an Alsatian named Flöderer, this is one of the city's oldest restaurants and one of the prettiest, with its early-20th-century stained-glass windows and beautiful wooden interior. Owner Jean-Paul Bucher bought it in 1968 and went on to become the brasserie king of Paris, with more than a dozen establishments to his name. It is the perfect place to celebrate a special occasion and feast on the renowned *choucroute* or wonderful seafood, although *poisson* tends to be quite expensive—six plump Breton oysters will set you back 18€ ($23). The excellent 35€ ($44) three-course menu includes a half-bottle of wine—your choice of white, rosé, or red.

7 cour des Petites-Ecuries, 10e (Note: It's "cour," not the nearby "rue" des Petites-Ecuries). ✆ 01-47-70-13-59. 2-course menu 25€ ($31); 3-course dinner menu with wine 35€ ($44); main courses 16€–26€ ($20–$32). AE, DC, MC, V. Daily noon–3pm; Tues–Sat 7:15pm–1am; Sun–Mon 7:15pm–12:30am. Métro: Château d'Eau.

Chez Michel ✸ ⒻＩnds FRENCH   Tucked behind the 19th-century St-Vincent de Paul church, Chez Michel takes bistro standards and modernizes them in a way foodies will love. From a grilled sardine salad to veal stew with leeks, owner Thierry Breton (who was

President Mitterrand's chef for a time) offers imaginative food and well-chosen wines. Choices are limited, but you can be assured that everything's fresh and lovingly prepared.

10 rue de Belzunce, 10e. ✆ **01-44-53-06-20.** Reservations recommended. 3-course menu 33€ ($41). MC, V. Mon–Fri 7–11pm; Tues–Fri noon–2pm. Closed 3 weeks in Aug, 1 week at Christmas. Métro: Gare du Nord.

Julien ✦ FRENCH This restaurant's breathtaking Art Nouveau interior is a national historic landmark and is reason enough to make this a top dining choice. At the turn of the 20th century, Julien was a workers' canteen that served not-so-hot food at prices poor folk could afford. Today it's no longer a bargain joint, but relatively speaking it's still not outrageous, considering the wonderful food. Start with smoked salmon with blinis and crème fraîche, and follow with cassoulet, chateaubriand with béarnaise sauce, or sole with sorrel sauce. Finish with the dark, rich chocolate gateau with coffee crème anglaise.

16 rue du Faubourg-St-Denis, 10e. ✆ **01-47-70-12-06.** 2-course menu with wine 25€ ($31); 3-course menu with wine 35€ ($44); main courses 14€–27€ ($18–$34). AE, DC, MC, V. Daily noon–3pm and 7pm–midnight. Métro: Strasbourg-St-Denis.

3 & 4E ARRONDISSEMENTS

Auberge de Jarente *(Finds)* BASQUE/SOUTHWEST Serving specialties from the Basque region, where cooks use olive oil, tomatoes, and all kinds of peppers, this cozy spot offers a change from cream sauces. The prix-fixe menus might include charcuterie or goat cheese on toast served with fig chutney to start. For a main course, choose among several Basque dishes, such as cassoulet or duck confit, and *cailles* (quail) *à la façon du chef,* which is quite good. If you choose carefully, you can dine relatively cheaply off the a la carte menu, too. While the food is pleasant and fairly priced, the charming service and rustic decor (including a cavelike, cozy downstairs) are what make a visit worthwhile.

7 rue de Jarente, 4e. ✆ **01-42-77-49-35.** 3-course lunch menu with wine 14€ ($18); 3-course dinner menus 19€ ($24), 21€ ($26) with half bottle of wine; main courses 12€–18€ ($15–$23). MC, V. Tues–Sat noon–2:30pm; Tues–Fri 7:30–10:30pm; Sat 7:30–11pm. Closed 1st 3 weeks of Aug. Métro: Bastille or St-Paul.

Bistrot de Beaubourg *(Value)* CLASSIC BISTRO This cheap bistro, a few steps from the Centre Pompidou, attracts a hip, intellectual crowd. Join an animated discussion of the latest controversial author or music trend, and admire the theater and literature posters on the walls. The cooking is hearty and filling. Try dishes like chitterling sausage or braised beef with noodles. Wash it down with the good house wine—after all, your throat may be dry from all the talking!

25 rue Quincampoix, 4e. ✆ **01-42-77-48-02.** Main courses 8€–12€ ($10–$15); *plats du jour* from 5.80€ ($7.25). MC, V. Daily noon–2am. Métro: Hôtel-de-Ville.

Bofinger ✦✦ *(Moments)* ALSATIAN/BRASSERIE Just a few steps from place Bastille, this classic Alsatian brasserie, which opened in 1864, is now one of the best-loved restaurants in the city, with its numerous rooms done in wonderful Belle Epoque decor (dark wood, gleaming brass, bright lights, glass ceiling, and waiters with long white aprons—and solicitous manners). The menu features many Alsatian specialties, such as *choucroute* (sauerkraut with smoked ham), as well as its famed oysters and foie gras. The prices are moderate for Paris, but it doesn't matter—you'd pay a lot more for a sampling of this cuisine. If you feel like something a little smaller and intimate, try Le Petit Bofinger across the street.

5–7 rue de la Bastille, 4e. (𝄐) **01-42-72-87-82.** Weekday lunch menu 23€ ($29); lunch and dinner menu with half bottle of wine 35€ ($44); main courses 14€–28€ ($18–$35). AE, MC, V. Mon–Fri noon–3pm and 6:30pm–1am; Sat–Sun noon–1am. Métro: Bastille.

Camille BISTRO   Neither the *potage de légume* (vegetable stew) nor the *filet de cabillaud au jus de moules* (cod with mussels) are the best in town and the service is a bit brusque, but it's still fun to come to this bistro with its rustic stone walls warmed by pretty lighting. Plus, it's on the best shopping street in the Marais! With a menu that changes daily, this place is hit-or-miss cuisine-wise.

24 rue des Francs-Bourgeois, 3e. (𝄐) **01-42-72-20-50.** 2-course lunch menu 18€ ($23); main courses 12€–16€ ($15–$20). AE, DC, MC, V. Daily 8am–midnight. Métro: St-Paul.

Chez Omar 𝄐 (Value) MOROCCAN   Most Parisians will tell you that Chez Omar has the best couscous in the city. Open for almost 30 years, it's often packed with devoted followers, sometimes waiting in line for an hour just to score their favorite sidewalk table. No reservations are accepted. Even indoors, this bustling brasserie has a distinct Mediterranean energy—a frenzy more reminiscent of Marseille or Naples than Paris. The food here is excellent—freshly prepared and it shows: thick-cut vegetables accompany your choice of beef, chicken, or spicy merguez sausage with a steaming bowl of couscous. There's not much else on the menu to speak of other than couscous. The service can be a bit brusque when the restaurant is full (which is often). The house wine is good and reasonably priced at 12€ ($15) a half bottle. Finish off your meal with Morroccan almond sweets and a cup of fragrant mint tea.

47 rue de Bretagne, 3e. (𝄐) **01-42-72-36-25.** Main courses 12€–16€ ($15–$20). No credit cards. Mon–Sat noon–3pm and 7:30–11:30pm; Sun 7:30–11pm. Métro: Arts et Metier.

Georges 𝄐 INTERNATIONAL/FRENCH   If you're in the mood to immerse yourself in hip, mod Paris with a view to kill, then come to Georges on top of the Centre Pompidou. The food is a little expensive and the waitresses may look and act like bored models, but who cares when you can sit in one of the Costes brothers' wildly colorful rooms with shapes resembling something like cavities with a 360-degree view of Paris?

Centre Pompidou, 6th Floor, rue Rambuteau, 4e. (𝄐) **01-44-78-47-99.** Main courses 14€–28€ ($18–$35). AE, DC, MC, V. Wed–Mon noon–2am. Métro: Rambuteau.

Jo Goldenberg (Moments) EUROPEAN/DELI   A Paris institution, Jo Goldenberg deserves a stop, even if it's only to step into the sumptuous delicatessen in the front, where sausages dangle and baklava beckons. The quintessential Jewish/Eastern European restaurant, Jo Goldenberg has a convivial atmosphere. Photos of famous patrons, including François Mitterrand, and paintings by up-and-coming artists surround the red banquettes. Specialties include *poulet paprika,* goulash, moussaka, and Wiener schnitzel. Deli offerings include pastrami and corned beef—allegedly invented here by Goldenberg senior in the 1920s. Adding to the festive air, Gypsy musicians begin playing around 9pm. As you leave, Jo Goldenberg hands out gifts, including a calendar of Jewish holidays, a neighborhood map, and a drawing of the Hebrew alphabet for kids.

7 rue des Rosiers, 4e. (𝄐) **01-48-87-20-16.** Main courses 12€–15€ ($15–$19). AE, DC, MC, V. Daily 9am–midnight. Métro: St-Paul.

L'As du Falafel MIDDLE EASTERN   One of the neighborhood's most popular falafel bars has installed a seating area in the rear, making it more comfortable to feast on the vegetarian kosher treats—if you can get a table. Sunday afternoons are particularly crowded.

34 rue des Rosiers, 4e. ☎ **01-48-87-63-60.** Falafel sandwiches 5€ ($6.25). MC, V. Sun–Thurs noon–midnight; Fri noon–4pm. Métro: St-Paul.

Le Coude Fou MODERN BISTRO   The atmosphere at this small bistro is warm and laid-back—contrasting with the food, which is quite *soigné.* The 23€ ($26) weekday dinner menu (served Mon–Thurs) offers a choice of three appetizers, main courses, and desserts that might include a salad of goose filets, *pavé de saumon,* and crème brûlée. On the a la carte menu, the *tartare de daurade et saumon* topped with watercress sauce is a treat. Follow with *filet de canette aux copeaux de foie gras cru* (duck filet with slices of raw foie gras) or *filet de daurade aux épices* (daurade filet in spices), and finish with divine *fondant* au chocolat.

12 rue du Bourg-Tibourg, 4e. ☎ **01-42-77-15-16.** 2-course weekday lunch menu 17€ ($21) and 20€ ($24); 3-course weekday dinner menu 24€ ($30); main courses 15€–17€ ($19–$21). AE, MC, V. Sun–Fri noon–2am; Sat noon–3pm and 7:30pm–2am. Métro: St-Paul.

Le Felteu CLASSIC FRENCH   If there ever was a more hidden hole-in-the-wall, I have yet to find it. This is truly a gem. The aging interior with its wrinkled faux leather banquettes, peeling wallpaper and nonchalant waiter may initially put you off your dinner. But wait. When the food comes out (beautifully laid out on sparkling white plates) it is the most *correcte,* lovingly prepared French food you may experience on your entire trip. There's no menu. The waiter will shuffle over to you with a blackboard on which the specials are scribbled. If you're lucky there'll be the delicious house rabbit terrine with cornichons, green salad and fresh village bread; the *soupe à l'oignons* is also divine. The food is classic and a bit heavy, great for a cold winter's night. For the main course, the roasted lamb served with gratin dauphinois is excellent; the blood sausage with baked apples is also very good. For dessert, you can never go wrong with the luscious mousse au chocolat. The house Cabernet Franc goes for 12€ ($15) bottle.

15 rue Pecquay, 4e. ☎ **01-42-72-14-51.** *Plat du jour* 12€ ($15); main courses 11€–16€ ($14–$20). No credit cards. Mon–Sat 7:30–11pm. Métro: St Paul.

Le 404 NORTH AFRICAN   It would be hard to find better couscous dishes than the specialties at this restaurant, owned by the popular French comedian Smain. The semolina is rolled by hand, making the pasta unusually light and fluffy. The steaming broth has a hint of sweet spices that enhance the flavor of the fresh vegetables. Portions are enormous; try the lamb *tajine,* or Couscous 404, which features a succulent array of skewered spicy sausage, lamb, and vegetables. The wood-screened windows, dim lighting, and soft North African music make you feel as though you've entered a harem.

69 rue des Gravilliers, 3e. ☎ **01-42-74-57-81.** Reservations recommended. Lunch menu 17€ ($21); main courses 10€–24€ ($13–$30); weekend brunch 21€ ($26). AE, DC, MC, V. Daily noon–3pm (brunch Sat–Sun until 4pm) and 8pm–2am. Métro: Arts et Métiers.

Les Temps des Cerises *(finds)* FRENCH   This bistro is charged with history—it's been in business since 1900 in an 18th-century building that once was a convent. It's a classic bar-bistro, with mosaic-tile floor, pewter bar, and walls covered with artwork. Look out for the certificate for its efforts to "protect" the *oeuf mayonnaise.* Locals gather to chat over a glass of wine or coffee. It's packed at lunch, but it's a bargain and service is extremely fast. A choice of menus (which don't include a beverage) might tempt you with anything from sardines and egg mayonnaise to start, then sausage with red beans, or steak with shallot sauce and braised endive. The wines can be expensive, but you can always select one of the chalkboard specials or the inexpensive house wine.

31 rue de la Cerisaie, 4e. ✆ **01-42-72-08-63.** Lunch 14€ ($18); main courses 12€–15€ ($15–$19). No credit cards. Mon–Fri 7:45am–8pm (lunch 11:30am–2:30pm). Closed Aug. Métro: Bastille or Sully-Morland.

Robert et Louise ✿ *Moments* FRENCH   In 1962, when both Robert and Louise where young and in love, they opened this cozy restaurant that specializes in grilled meats. Robert died in 2003 and Louise is older now. Their children have taken over, but Louise can still be spotted late in the evening nursing a glass of wine at the tiny bar. Basically you order your cuts of entrecôte or *poulet* (steak or chicken breast) and they grill it for you as you watch. Your choice of fried or roasted potatoes, or salad comes with your main course. Half bottles of wine are 7€ ($8.75). A great meal at a bargain price can be had here. This is not a good place for a romantic dinner, as often, you'll be joined by strangers at your table (when the place fills up it's only polite to let everybody sit down). It's that kind of place; friendly, laid-back and with delicious straightforward cuisine.

64 rue Vieille du Temple, 3e. ✆ **01-42-78-55-89.** Main courses 18€ ($23). No credit cards. Mon–Sat 11:30am–3pm and 7:30–10:30pm. Métro: St-Paul or Chemin Vert.

Trumilou ✿ *Value* FRENCH   With copper pots lining the walls, red leatherette banquette seats, and white linen tablecloths, you'll appreciate the (French) country style, as do a lot of Parisians. Whether it's the *paysan* decor and cuisine, or the view of the Seine or the arches of Notre-Dame, this is one of the most popular restaurants around Paris's Hôtel de Ville (city hall). Your meal might start with a pâté from Auvergne. The prix-fixe menus always include a grilled fish, or try *manchons de canard à l'ancienne* (old-fashioned duck). Neck of lamb (served medium rare unless you specify otherwise) is tender and juicy, and *canard aux pruneaux* (duck with prunes) is a house specialty. Finish off with the luscious *gratin de figues* (figs baked in a light cream sauce).

84 quai de l'Hôtel-de-Ville, 4e. ✆ **01-42-77-63-98.** Reservations recommended Sat–Sun. 2-course menu 15€ ($19); 3-course menu 18€ ($23); main courses 13€–18€ ($16–$23). MC, V. Daily noon–3pm and 7–11pm. Métro: Hôtel-de-Ville.

WORTH A SPLURGE
Auberge de la Reine Blanche *Moments* FRENCH   For truly French fare, try this restaurant in the heart of Ile St-Louis, tucked away in a 17th-century building. Tiny models of antique furnishings adorn the walls, and at night candles illuminate the tables. The robust menu offers frogs' legs in Provençale sauce or Burgundy snails by the dozen. Main courses include coq au vin and the house specialty, *le magret de canard au miel* (duck breast in honey). The service is efficient and friendly.

30 rue St-Louis-en-l'Ile, 4e. ✆ **01-46-33-07-87.** 2-course lunch menu 16€ ($20); 3-course dinner menu 20€ ($25). AE, MC, V. Fri–Tues noon–3pm; Thurs–Tues 7–11pm. Métro: Pont Marie.

Chez Jenny ✿ ALSATIAN/BRASSERIE   Whether it's the trays of lusciously arranged shellfish or the platters of *choucroute*, something about brasseries seems to keep everyone in good spirits. Surrounded by paneling dating from 1932, cheerful women in traditional costumes serve solid brasserie fare. Herring, quiche, onion soup, and *choucroute* are on the menu, as well as a wide assortment of fish and shellfish. After the meal, wander upstairs to check out the exquisite marquetry. Don't miss the tiles in the *toilettes,* which have wood stalls.

39 bd. du Temple, 3e. ✆ **01-42-74-75-75.** 2-course menu 24€ ($30); 3-course menu with wine and coffee 32€ ($40); main courses 14€–27€ ($18–$34); seafood platters 25€ ($31) and 35€ ($44). AE, DC, MC, V. Sun–Thurs noon–midnight; Fri–Sat noon–1am. Métro: République.

11 & 12E ARRONDISSEMENTS

Au Trou Normand ✷ *Value* NORMAN/FRENCH   This miniscule restaurant serves up excellent homemade cuisine. With space for only about eight tables, be prepared to sit very close to other diners—mostly youngish locals, who all seem to know each other. The fresh, imaginative cuisine has a touch of Normandy and a touch of the Mediterranean. The red-checkered tablecloths might remind you of a small village restaurant. You'll be served a dish of herbed olives with a hunk of farm bread as you peruse the menu. Appetizers include a delicate *tartare de saumon* (salmon tartare), which is served with ripe cherry tomatoes; or the house chicken-liver pâté with cornichons. For the main course, the turkey *osso buco* is a lighter variation on the Italian version and comes with grilled courgettes and fluffy white rice. To round out your meal try the fruit sorbets or end with a cheese course—marinated goat cheese in olive oil and mild chiles. You can't go wrong with a carafe of house wine at 6€ ($7.50).

9 rue Jean Pierre Timbaud, 11e. ✆ 01-48-05-80-23. 2-course lunch menu 12€ ($15). Main courses 11€–18€ ($14–$23). MC, V. Daily noon–3pm and 7:30–11pm. Métro: Oberkampf.

Dame Jeanne ✷ MODERN BISTRO   Dame Jeanne proves that gourmet dining at an affordable price is not impossible. Chef Francis Lévêque relies on talent and imagination to create memorable dishes at fair prices. The seasonal-fruit-and-vegetable menu might include dishes like *fricassée de légumes au lard et à l'estragon* (sautéed vegetables with cured ham and oregano) and desserts like caramelized brioche topped with sweetened banana. The more expensive menus might offer risotto accented with tapenade, topped with diced, steamed salmon. The reasonably priced wine list begins with Dame Jeanne's *découvertes*—lesser-known wines—for 15€ ($19) a bottle. The interior is decorated in autumnal colors illuminated by soft golden lighting, and the service is friendly.

60 rue de Charonne, 11e. ✆ 01-47-00-37-40. 2-course menu 23€ ($29); 3-course menu 29€ ($36); seasonal-fruit-and-vegetable menu 20€ ($25). MC, V. Tues–Sat noon–2:15pm; Tues–Thurs 7:30–11pm; Fri–Sat 7:30–11:30pm. Métro: Ledru-Rollin.

L'Ebauchoir BISTRO   Food is plentiful and the atmosphere laid-back in this colorful restaurant. A mural pays homage to the Bastille neighborhood's working-class roots, and the space is large enough to be a bit noisy. Friendly waiters rush to show the day's offerings written on a chalkboard. The superb food makes up for the decibel level. Appetizers may include warm foie gras or stuffed ravioli, followed by smoked tuna with fennel, or steak in red-wine bordelaise sauce. For dessert, the *meuille feuille* (a flaky, multilayered pastry) is divine.

45 rue de Citeaux, 12e. ✆ 01-43-42-49-31. 2-course lunch menu 14€ ($18); main courses 15€–23€ ($19–$29). MC, V. Mon–Sat noon–2:30pm; Mon–Thurs 8–10:30pm; Fri–Sat 8–11pm. Métro: Faidherbe-Chaligny.

L'Ecailler du Bistrot SEAFOOD/BISTRO   This tiny, handsome nautical-themed restaurant could almost be in Nantucket, with its blue, white, and yellow striped napkins and blonde wood. But it's definitely in France, and makes a proud display of its wine collection including Riesling, Brouilly, and Sancerre. The eight wonderful varieties of oysters are from Normandy, Brittany, and Marennes. Other seafood includes crisp steamed shrimp served with a light salad, and smoked salmon and tuna. The house wine is surprisingly good; you pay only for what you drink out of the bottle. Everything is available for takeout—a rarity in Paris.

22 rue Paul Bert, 11e. ✆ 01-43-72-76-77. 2-course lunch 16€ ($20); dinner seafood platters 32€ ($40); oysters by the half dozen or dozen 16€–26€ ($20–$32); main courses 14€–19€ ($18–$24). MC, V. Tues–Fri noon–2:30pm; Tues–Sat 7:30–11:30pm. Métro: Charonne.

Le Petit Keller ⭐ *(Value)* FRENCH   You'll feel a little retro when you walk into this neighborhood spot with its green and red Formica tables and parquet floors. In the artsy 11e arrondissement, youngish locals come here for simple, copious grub. Every day is a surprise because the menu changes daily, but if it's available, try the tomato stuffed with goat cheese, rotisserie chicken in country sauce, duck in honey-and-fig sauce, and *fondant au chocolat crème anglaise.*

13 rue Keller, 11e. ℂ 01-47-00-12-97. 2-course lunch menu 14€ ($18); 3-course menu 19€ ($24). MC, V. Mon–Sat noon–2:30pm; Mon–Fri 7:30–11pm. Closed 1 week in early August. Métro: Bastille.

WORTH A SPLURGE

Chardenoux ⭐ CLASSIC BISTRO   Ask a Parisian for a list of his or her favorite bistros, and this small, charming place will invariably be mentioned. From the etched plate-glass windows to the swirling stucco decorations on the walls and ceiling, the decor is the essence of old Paris. (It has been appointed a *Monument Historique.*) Service is friendly and English-speaking. A variety of regional dishes appears on the menu—try *oeufs en meurette,* a Burgundian dish of poached eggs in a sauce of red wine and bacon, or *boeuf en daube,* braised beef as it's done in Provence. Desserts are homey and delicious, especially the fruit tarts and nougat in raspberry sauce.

1 rue Jules-Valles, 11e. ℂ 01-43-71-49-52. Main courses 16€–24€ ($20–$30). AE, MC, V. Mon–Fri noon–2pm; Mon–Sat 8–11:30pm. Métro: Charonne.

Les Grandes Marches ⭐ MODERN BRASSERIE   This classic brasserie recently got a makeover and is now as sleek and modern as the Opéra Bastille next door. The marble floors clash slightly with the Art Deco pastel motif, funky pinkish chairs, and photographs on the walls, but it all comes together to create an ambience of ultramodernism. If you score a table overlooking place de la Bastille, you'll be set for an amazing evening of people-watching. The food is excellent even if the service is a bit slow. The oysters are plump and delicious and the most popular appetizer. For the main course, the *foie de veau* (veal liver) is thick and tender, baked in a red-wine sauce, and served with mashed potatoes and sautéed endives. If you've been hesitant to be adventurous elsewhere, here's your chance. There are at least five choices each of fish, meat, and chicken dishes and a selection of reasonably priced wines, including half bottles.

6 pl. de la Bastille, 12e. ℂ 01-43-42-90-32. 2-course lunch menu with wine 25€ ($31); 3-course dinner menu with wine 35€ ($44); main courses 18€–27€ ($23–$34). AE, DC, MC, V. Daily noon–3pm and 7pm–1am. Métro: Bastille.

8, 16 & 17E ARRONDISSEMENTS

Al Diwan ⭐ *(Finds)* LEBANESE   Don't head upstairs to the pricey restaurant; stay on the ground floor in the casual, delicious, and affordable bistro. The decor is nondescript, but if you score a table by the window, you'll have a great view of avenue Georges V. The Lebanese food here is authentic, fresh, and prepared with care. Start with a *fatoush* salad (tomatoes, romaine, parsley, and green onions tossed in a pomegranate dressing) or puréed lentil soup. Then move on to one of the fantastic main courses such as *sayadiyeh,* a flaky whitefish with saffron rice drizzled with a lemony tahini dressing, or *kibbe* balls (ground lamb, mild spices, and bulgur wheat) simmered in a yogurt-and-mint sauce. For dessert, an array of pastries is on hand to delight, but for something light, try the *moghli*—a yummy (nondairy) rice pudding made with caraway and anise and sprinkled with dried coconut.

30 av. George V, 8e. ℂ 01-47-20-18-17. 2-course menu 25€ ($31); main courses 11€–23€ ($14–$29). MC, V. Daily noon–3pm and 7–11pm. Métro: Georges V.

Aux Marches du Palais 🎯🎯 *Finds* FRENCH   Tucked away at the bottom of the steps next to the Palais du Tokyo, this *very* French restaurant prides itself on its *cuisine traditionelle*. In summer, the outdoor terrace is pleasant for a leisurely meal; the chic indoor tables boast white tablecloths. This is one of the most affordable but elegant (without being at all stuffy) traditional French restaurants in the city. The excellent house-made chicken-liver terrine is served in a *verrine*—a glass jar used to preserve the intensity of the flavors. The smoked salmon appetizer served with blinis, stewed apples, and lime is unusual and delicious (and well priced at 8€/$10). Main courses include tender cod in garlic-cream sauce with steamed new potatoes, a delicate leg of lamb with fresh carrots and rosemary, and a Dover sole. The restaurant prides itself on its crème brûlée infused with a hint of cardammon and the fluffy mousse au chocolat. The house wines are excellent and affordable at 9€ ($11) a half bottle.

5 rue de la Manutention, 16e. ✆ **01-47-23-52-80.** Main courses 12€–18€. ($15–$23). AE, DC, MC, V. Mon–Fri noon–3pm and 7:30–10:30pm; Sat 7:30–11pm. Métro: Iena.

Bar des Théâtres *Finds* BISTRO   Habitués have dubbed Bar des Théâtres the "Temple of Steak Tartare." Established in 1945 by the same family that runs it today, Bar des Théâtres is a charming secret in one of the city's most exclusive neighborhoods. Drawing from the Théâtre des Champs-Elysées across the street, and the nearby *bateaux mouches,* it attracts actors, singers, musicians, and tourists. Customers may prepare their own steak tartare in the kitchen if they wish. Caviar and foie gras also top the menu. With so much social and culinary entertainment, you'll forget all about the theater next door.

6 av. Montaigne, 8e. ✆ **01-47-23-34-63.** Reservations recommended. Main courses 12€–22€ ($15–$28). MC, V. Daily 6am–2am. Métro: Alma-Marceau.

La Grande Armée 🎯 INTERNATIONAL   Yet another Costes brother creation, this massive cafe/bar/restaurant is great for a late supper close to the Champs-Elysées. The dimly lit and very loungey interior hops with the fashion crowd who come to drink heavily and eat light. In summer, sidewalk tables offer dining alfresco. The chicken Caesar and warm chèvre with spinach salads are the two most popular items, followed by sautéed shrimp. The cheeseburger is pricey (18€/$23) but excellent, served with crispy fries and real Dijon mustard. For dessert, there is a great selection of ice creams and sorbets.

3 av. de la Grande Armée, 17e. ✆ **01-45-00-24-77.** Main courses 19€–32€ ($24($40); salads and light meals 11€–17€ ($14–$21). AE, MC, V. Daily noon–2am. Métro: Charles-de-Gaulle–Etoile.

L'Assiette Lyonnaise *Value* LYONNAISE   Jam-packed at lunch, this friendly little place does a good job with such Lyonnais dishes as *quenelles* (fish dumplings), hot dried sausage, and lentil salad. Finish with tarte tatin and cream sauce. Considering its proximity to the Champs-Elysées, prices are reasonable.

21 rue Marbeuf, 8e. ✆ **01-47-20-94-80.** Main courses 9€–14€ ($11–$18). AE, DC, MC, V. Daily noon–3pm and 7pm–midnight. Métro: Franklin-D-Roosevelt.

Le Liteau *Value* FRENCH   It's almost unthinkable to have a 20€ ($25) three-course meal just half a block off the Champs-Elysées. Le Liteau offers just that—no ambience or decor to speak of, just decent food at incredible prices. Service is friendly and efficient. Dinners choose from 10 appetizers, 10 main courses, and 6 desserts. You might begin with a herring filet and warm potatoes drizzled with an olive oil vinaigrette, or a *soupe de poissons* (fish soup with garlic croutons). For the main course, the

Where to Dine on the Right Bank (8 & 17e)

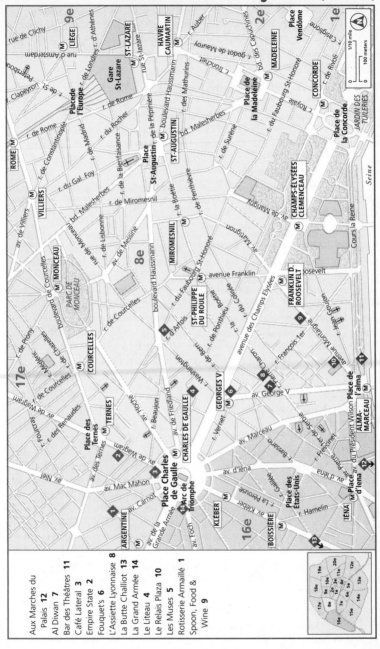

salmon escalope with lemon butter is excellent, as are the mussels simmered in a white-wine sauce. For dessert, you can opt for a slice of ripe brie or Camembert, or try the chilled nougat with raspberry purée, or the sorbet du jour.

12–16 rue Washington, 8e. ☎ 01-42-89-90-43. 3-course menu 20€ ($25). MC, V. Mon–Sat noon–2:30pm and 7–10:30pm. Métro: Georges V.

Les Muses ★ *Value* BRETON/CREPES   Owner Madame Rous will greet you, seat you, and serve you with a smile in this cozy Breton crepe restaurant. I dine here often to enjoy her hospitality and the wonderful crepes filled with meat, seafood, or vegetables, garnished with portions of salad or crudités followed by a sweet dessert crepe. Wash it all down with a bowl of cider. *Crepes de froment* are made of wheat flour; *galettes de sarrasin* are buckwheat griddlecakes. The prices are awesome—and it's just 2 blocks from the Champs-Elysées!

45 rue de Berri, 8e. ☎ 01-45-62-43-64. 2-course crepe meal with cider 7.90€ ($9.90); main-course crepes 2€–5.80€ ($2.50–$7.25); dessert crepes 2.50€–5.80€ ($3.15–$7.25). MC, V. Mon–Fri 11:30am–8:30pm. Métro: St-Philippe-du-Roule or George V.

WORTH A SPLURGE

La Butte Chaillot ★★ *Finds* FRENCH   Elegant, discreet, and modern, this swanky restaurant makes you feel as if you're spending much more than you are. The service is top-notch and the glass tables, leather chairs, and thick cloth napkins add to the sleek plushness. This is a wonderful place to celebrate a special occasion. The food is delicate, refined, and exquisite. Simplicity is the theme here: Steamed cod with balsamic drizzle and crunchy vegetables; thyme-roasted chicken with apple compote and mashed potatoes; grilled leg of lamb with sautéed green beans and cherry tomatoes. The thinly sliced apples on the *très delicat* apple tart are a must for dessert. After dinner take a stroll to Trocadéro and watch the Eiffel Tower light up.

110 bis av. Keleber, 16e. ☎ 01-47-27-88-88. Reservations recommended. 3-course menu 32€ ($40); main courses 20€–27€ ($25–$34). AE, DC, MC, V. Daily noon–3pm and 8–10:30pm. Métro: Trocadéro.

Le Relais Plaza ★★ *Moments* FRENCH   Marlene Dietrich came for lunch every day and sat at the sole table by the window. Jackie Kennedy ate here, too. So did Sophia Loren, Kim Basinger, Valentino, and Liza Minelli, among many other luminaries. Most recently, it was John Malkovich and Tom Hanks (not together). After a complete makeover, Le Relais Plaza reopened last year and has regained its place in Paris as *the* place for a discreet meal. Here you'll find elegant older ladies sipping white wine and chatting quietly, or businessmen having a power lunch. Service is utterly good. And the food is *très français et très correcte* (very French and very proper). The specialty is *escalope de veau* (a thin but large slice of veal filet lightly breaded and fried and served with a linguine marinara) and *foie de veau* (veal liver) sautéed in red-wine sauce and served with mashed potatoes. For dessert, the homemade sorbets are divine.

Attached to the Hôtel Plaza Athénée, 25 av. Montaigne, 8e. ☎ 01-53-67-66-65. Reservations required. 3-course lunch menu 43€ ($54); main courses 29€–38€ ($36–$48). AE, DC, MC, V. Daily noon–2:30pm and 7:30–10:30pm. Métro: Alma-Marceau or Franklin-D-Roosevelt.

Rotisserie Armaillé ★★ *Finds* MODERN BISTRO   Jacques Cagna is a celebrity chef with a highly regarded restaurant in St-Germain-des-Prés. This "baby bistro" is his nod to the current mood for fine dining at a prix fixe. Although the decor is pleasant, with light-wood paneling and plaid upholstery, his modern approach to hearty bistro dishes is what draws crowds of businesspeople for lunch and the local chic set for dinner. Fresh warm bread accompanies starters like *terrine de laperau aux parfums d'agrumes* (terrine of baby rabbits with citrus zest), and main courses of *squab aux raisins de Smyrnes* or tuna carpaccio. The rack of lamb with rosemary and crystallized tomatoes melts in your mouth, and the sea-bass filet with spicy chorizo is exquisite. Wild snails from Burgundy and fresh oysters are also available. For dessert, the roasted green apple is divine. Service is rapid and friendly.

6 rue d'Armaillé, 17e. ℂ **01-42-27-19-20.** Reservations required. 3-course lunch menu 30€ ($38); 3-course dinner menu 40€ ($50); main courses 24€–29€ ($30–$36). AE, DC, MC, V. Mon–Fri noon–2:30pm; Mon–Sat 7:30–11pm. Métro: Charles-de-Gaulle–Etoile or Argentine.

Spoon, Food, and Wine 🌟🌟 INTERNATIONAL   With its ultramodern white interior, great service, and pretentious crowd, this sleek restaurant feels like it belongs in London or New York. Celebrated chef Alain Ducasse's menu encompasses a variety of international dishes, and the customer chooses (from a list of enticing choices) the condiments, side dishes, and vegetables to complement the main dish. Take, for example, spareribs—try a marmalade of stewed meat, red wine, tomato, and olives beside a heaping portion of Maxim's potatoes. Spoon also boasts a diverse wine list, with 120 selections from South Africa, Argentina, and New Zealand. For dessert, opt for the oozing, warm chocolate "pizza" over bubble-gum ice cream or, if you can't choose, order the selection of five "mini" desserts (a miniature baba au rhum, slice of cheesecake, chocolate-chip cookies, and whatever else the pastry chef has made that day).

14 rue de Marignan, 8e. ℂ **01-40-76-34-44.** Reservations recommended 1 week in advance. Main courses 26€–38€ ($32–$47). Mon–Fri 11:45am–2:30pm and 6:30–11:30pm. AE, MC, V. Métro: Franklin-D-Roosevelt.

18E ARRONDISSEMENT

Au Relais–Le Bistrot d'Edouard 🌟 CLASSIC BISTRO   If the sight of Montmartre has tapped hidden emotions and your desire to be taken care of is strong, let Chef Edouard Martinez warm you with his extraordinary bistro cuisine, like *salade de gesiers de canard confits* (salad with sautéed gizzards) or an egg mayonnaise specialty, and *magret de canard* or *brandade* as main dishes. The food is made with love, and the cozy atmosphere with its red tablecloths and close-together tables in this two-room bistro make this a perfect choice.

48 rue Lamarck, 18e. ℂ **01-46-06-68-32.** 2-course lunch menu 11€ ($14); 3-course dinner menu 22€ ($28). Tues–Sat noon–2:30pm and 6:30–10:30pm. MC, V. Métro: Lamarck-Caulaincourt.

Au Rendez-Vous des Chauffeurs *(Value)* FRENCH   Cheap family-style restaurants are a dying breed in Paris, which is one reason this friendly place with blue-checked tablecloths is so popular with locals. The 14€ ($18) menu offers excellent value at noon and in the evening before 8:30pm; afterward, you'll have to order a la carte. The kitchen turns out solid basics like a delicious country terrine, followed by roast chicken or lamb stew, and old-fashioned desserts like apricot tart. Although it's a little out of the way, this is a good stop if you're hitting the flea market at Clignancourt.

11 rue des Portes-Blanches, 18e. ℂ **01-42-64-04-17.** 2-course lunch menu 10€ ($13); 3-course prix-fixe menu with 1 drink (before 8:30pm; not available Sun) 14€ ($18); main courses 12€–16€ ($15($20). MC, V. Fri–Tues noon–2:30pm and 7:30–11pm. Métro: Marcadet-Poissonnièrs.

Chez Les Fondus 🌟 *(Value)* FONDUE   Be prepared to wait even if you have reservations for this popular and fun place. Two long wooden tables occupy the tiny space, and you'll have to jump over the table to get into the inside seats. Chatting with your neighbors is an inevitable part of the evening where the wine flows freely. As soon as you're seated, you'll be served red wine in baby bottles (included in the meal price). The waiters don't let you drink from a glass (those are the rules) and they are boisterous and loud. Dinner is your choice of fondue bourguignonne (meat) or *savoyarde* (cheese), with dried sausage as an appetizer. Most of the diners are young and intent on having a good time. The cheese fondue is tasty but too heavy for some; the meat is tender and comes with several sauces. For dessert, you'll get a whole frozen orange filled with sorbet.

17 rue des Trois-Frères, 18e. ℰ **01-42-55-22-65.** Reservations recommended. 3-course menu with wine 17€ ($21). No credit cards. Tues–Sat 7pm–midnight. Métro: Abesses or Anvers.

Chez Marie *(Value)* FRENCH   At the base of the steps heading to place du Tertre, you'll find some of the cheapest eats in a neighborhood that's not exactly known for bargain dining. The food is passable (and that's more than you can say for a lot of the "cuisine" by Sacré-Coeur), the owners are charming and friendly, and the room is cozy. Seating is on wood benches, with red-and-white picnic tablecloths and wallpaper in the distant style of Toulouse-Lautrec (some of the subjects are laughing cats). Stick to the basics, like lamb and frites or duck confit, and you'll leave full and content with money in your wallet.

27 rue Gabrielle, 18e. ℰ **01-42-62-06-26.** 2-course menu 11€ ($14); 3-course menus (including aperitif) 17€ and 22€ ($21 and $28); main courses 9€–22€ ($11–$28). AE, DC, MC, V. Daily noon–3:30pm and 7pm–1:30am. Closed Jan. Métro: Abesses.

WORTH A SPLURGE

Au Poulbot Gourmet *(Finds)* FRENCH   This intimate restaurant with chic leather banquettes and white linen tablecloths is usually filled with a local crowd savoring moderately priced classic cuisine. Chef Jean-Paul Langevin brings tremendous finesse to the preparation and presentation of dishes such as *noisette d'agneau* (lamb slices) served with delicate splashes of mashed potatoes and spinach, and *marmite de poissons,* assorted fresh fish in light saffron sauce. As an appetizer, *oeufs pochés* with smoked salmon is a standout. For dessert, try *charlotte glacée.* Surrounded by sweet cream sauce topped with an intricate web of chocolate syrup, it almost looks too pretty to eat. Check out the photos of old Montmartre and the drawings by illustrator Francisque Poulbot on the walls.

39 rue Lamarck, 18e. ℰ **01-46-06-86-00.** 2-course weekly lunch menu with wine and coffee 18€ ($23); 3-course menu 36€ ($45); a la carte main courses 16€–27€ ($20–$34). MC, V. Mon–Sat noon–1:30pm and 7:30–10pm; Oct–May Sun noon–1:30pm. Métro: Lamarck-Caulaincourt.

Le Moulin de la Galette *(Finds)* ITALIAN/FRENCH   Under the Moulin de la Galette windmill, one of the last windmills in Paris and a favorite subject of Renoir, rests this glossy, poised restaurant. It was a favorite haunt of French-Egyptian singer Dalida, and fans come to eat fine Italian fare and gaze at her pictures and portraits gracing the walls. The lunch menu (appetizer and main course, or main course and dessert) is a great deal and includes wine. The wide range of dishes includes classic French preparations such as steamed sea bass. Italian specialties include a medley plate of veal tortellini, Spanish ricotta ravioli, and crab *ventrilli.* Lovely front and back terraces afford romantic dining.

83 rue Lepic, 18e. ℰ **01-46-06-84-77.** 2-course lunch menu with wine 25€ ($31); main courses 16€–29€ ($20–$36). Tues–Sun noon–3pm; Tues–Sat 7:30pm–midnight. MC, V. Métro: Abesses.

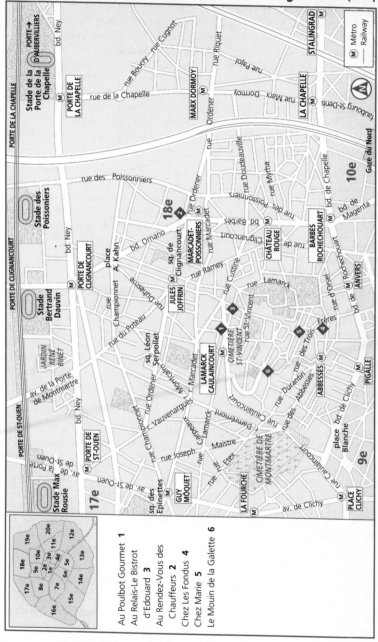

Au Poulbot Gourmet **1**
Au Relais-Le Bistrot
d'Edouard **3**
Au Rendez-Vous des
Chauffeurs **2**
Chez Les Fondus **4**
Chez Marie **5**
Le Mouin de la Galette **6**

11 & 20E ARRONDISSEMENTS

Boteco *Value* BRAZILIAN Boteco, in the heart of the rue Oberkampf, draws a lively crowd with lively food. The hearty platters of Brazilian treats may include a dollop of rice or a crunchy salad. The national dish, *feijoada* (black bean and pork stew), is excellent. For a lighter dish, try chicken tart with palm hearts. Order a mean Brazilian *caipirinha* (a cocktail made of sugar cane and rum) to accompany your meal. The atmosphere is convivial—diners sit at long wood tables in the colorful interior or out on the sidewalk terrace. Although it's open longer hours, food is served only from noon to midnight. The 10€ ($13) two-course prix fixe is a steal for lunch.

131 rue Oberkampf, 11e. ✆ **01-43-57-15-47**. 2-course lunch menu 10€ ($13); main courses 8€–15€ ($10–$19). No credit cards. Daily 9am–2am. Métro: Parmentier or Oberkampf.

Le Manguier ✶ *Value* AFRICAN/SENEGALESE With a huge fishnet hanging from a blue ceiling and tables covered in cloths of African design, Le Manguier is a wonderful, lively restaurant. At African restaurants, you don't just eat—you linger, enjoying the music and the atmosphere. The cocktails, such as the potent Le Dakar with rum and spices, are delicious. The menu doesn't list all that is available, so ask your waiter for suggestions. Fish dishes, like *requin fumé* (smoked shark), are very good.

67 av. Parmentier, 11e. ✆ **01-48-07-03-27**. 3-course lunch menu 15€ ($19); main courses 11€–14€ ($14–$18). AE, MC, V. Mon–Sat 11am–3pm and 7pm–1am. Métro: Parmentier.

5 On the Left Bank

5E ARRONDISSEMENT

Aux Trois Bourriques FRENCH/NORMAN Nestled on a peaceful street, this appealing restaurant—with red tablecloths, stone walls, and beamed ceilings—serves fine Normandy-inspired food. On the 15€ ($19) menu, you might find *pintade à la Normande* (guinea hen flavored with apples or Calvados) and beef *en daube* (rich, flavorful stew). If you're in the mood to splurge, the 29€ ($36) menu might offer *tournedos à la Normande* or *au poivre*, followed by a cheese course. Banana flambé or crepe flambé makes a fine finish to any meal.

5 rue des Grands Degrés, 5e. ✆ **01-43-54-61-72**. Fax 01-43-29-61-78. Main courses 12€–17€ ($15–$21); menus 15€ ($19), 22€ ($28), and 29€ ($36). MC, V. Wed–Sun noon–2pm; Tues–Sun 7–10pm. Métro: St-Michel.

El Palenque *Value* ARGENTINIAN You'll find some of the most succulent beef in Paris here. With its white stucco walls, pictures of tango dancers, saddles hanging overhead, and sweet smell of *carne,* you'll feel like you've been transported to Argentina for the night—and it tastes great. The specialty is *parrillas,* grilled meats from Argentina. The surprisingly wide menu offers *asado de tira* (ribs) for only 12€ ($15). *Parrillada completa*—a medley of blood sausage, veal sweetbreads, ribs, and kidneys—is pricier (about 20€/$25 per person) but worth it. It maintains a great selection of South American wines.

5 rue de la Montagne Ste-Geneviève, 5e. ✆ **01-43-54-08-99**. Reservations recommended. Main courses 12€–23€ ($15–$29). No credit cards. Mon–Sat noon–2pm and 7:30–11pm. Métro: Maubert-Mutualité.

La Formi Ailée BISTRO With its 7.5 meter (25-foot) ceilings, books lining the walls, cool aqua marble tables, and a little annex upstairs, this feels more like a tea salon than a bistro, so bring your laptop or a book and enjoy a leisurely homemade lunch or snack while you gaze out the window that looks onto rue Fouarre. Light dishes include *St-Pierre aux figues sur tartine* (warm goat cheese on toast with figs, green salad, and berries); heartier fare might be Norwegian salmon served with spinach pie and white cheese. Original desserts like lemon tart with prunes top off the eclectic menu.

8 rue du Fouarre, 5e. ☎ 01-43-29-40-99. Main courses 8€–13€ ($10–$16). MC, V. Daily noon–midnight. Métro: Maubert-Mutualité.

La Petite Hostellerie (*Value*) FRENCH   It's usually crowded and service is harried at times, but this cozy place is still a good choice, located on a fun, happening (if touristy) street in the 5e. The food is hearty and the price will make digestion a pleasant process. The 9.95€ ($12) menu has a variety of choices. You can begin with *soupe à l'oignon,* followed by *coq au vin,* and finish with chocolate profiteroles. The more expensive menus include more elaborate appetizers and a cheese course. The house wine is 5€ ($6.25) a half bottle.

35 rue de la Harpe (just east of bd. St-Michel), 5e. ☎ 01-43-54-47-12. Prix-fixe 2-course meal 7.50€ ($9.40); 3-course menus 9.95€ ($12), 14€ ($18), and 20€ ($25). AE, DC, MC, V. Daily noon–2pm and 6:30–11pm. Métro: St-Michel or Cluny-Sorbonne.

Le Coupe Chou 🍴 FRENCH   If medieval Parisian ambience is what you're looking for, come here, where you'll enjoy sumptuous French bistro cuisine in a series of intimate rooms lit by candles and firelight. Simple puréed vegetable soup or the heartier *Salade Coupe Chou* make an excellent start, followed by a perfect duck breast or succulent leg of lamb. As you enjoy coffee or an *eau de vie* in the salon after dinner, you will have forgotten about the other Americans surrounding you and believe you're living in the *vrai quartier Latin.*

11 rue de Lanneau, 5e. ☎ 01-46-33-68-69. 2-course menu 24€ ($30); 3-course dinner menu 32€ ($40); main courses 15€–21€ ($19–$26). AE, DC, MC, V. Mon–Sat noon–2pm; daily 7pm–11pm. Métro: Maubert-Mutualité.

Le Grenier de Notre-Dame ★ (*Finds*) VEGETARIAN   You may feel like you've just entered a green house, with everything from the tablecloths to the walls to the outdoor patio blanketed in various shades of the verdant color, but it goes with the cuisine you'll find here, which is worth a try. Especially recommended is *cassoulet végétarien,* with white beans, onions, tomatoes, and soy sausage; couscous and cauliflower au gratin are also delicious. And don't forget desserts, such as *tarte de tofu,* for which Le Grenier has a well-deserved reputation. The wine list includes a variety of organic offerings.

18 rue de la Bûcherie, 5e. ☎ 01-43-29-98-29. 3-course lunch menu 16€ ($20); 3-course dinner menu 18€ ($23); main courses 11€–15€ ($14–$19). MC, V. Sun noon–3pm; Mon–Thurs 12:30–3pm; Fri–Sat noon–2:30pm; Sun–Thurs 7–10:30pm; Fri–Sat 7–11pm. Métro: Maubert-Mutualité.

Le Petit Prince de Paris (*Finds*) FRENCH   Not to be confused with Au Petit Prince, this chic find in the 5e serving traditional French cuisine is popular among the hip, Sorbonne crowd who have a few bucks to spare, as well as young businessmen trying to impress their dates. With its smoky mirrors and discreet lighting illuminating its burnt sienna walls, this sexy place fills up quickly so it's best to make a reservation—although the owners may accommodate you at the last minute, particularly if you make an effort to speak to them in French. *One caveat:* With only two waiters tending to this three-room restaurant, it's best not to be in a hurry—but the food is worth the wait. Not only are the dishes pretty to look at, they taste divine, too. The *confit de canard* is cooked to perfection with yummy mashed potatoes on the side, or a sumptuous salmon tartare.

Where to Dine on the Left Bank (5–6 & 14e)

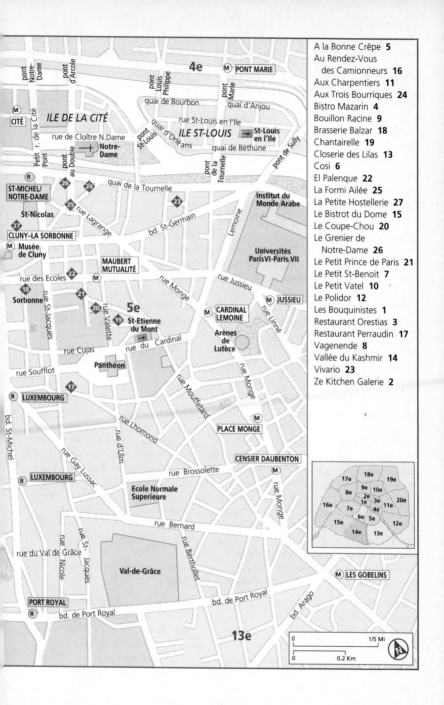

4e

Ⓜ PONT MARIE

pont Notre-Dame
pont d'Arcole
pont Louis Philippe
pont Marie

quai de Bourbon
quai d'Anjou

Ⓜ CITÉ
rue de la Cité

ILE DE LA CITÉ

rue St-Louis en l'Ile

ILE ST-LOUIS
🚈 St-Louis en l'Ile

rue de Cloître N.Dame
quai d'Orléans
quai de Béthune

Petit r. Pont au Double
pont St-Louis

✝ Notre-Dame

pont de la Tournelle
pont de Sully

Ⓜ ST-MICHEL/ NOTRE-DAME
Ⓡ
❷⓺
❷⓸
quai de la Tournelle

St-Nicolas
❷⓹ rue Lagrange
❷⓷

Institut du Monde Arabe

❷⓻ CLUNY-LA SORBONNE

bd. St-Germain

Lemoine

Ⓜ Musée de Cluny

MAUBERT MUTUALITÉ

Universités Paris VI-Paris VII

rue des Ecoles ❷⓶ Ⓜ
rue Monge
rue Jussieu

Ⓜ JUSSIEU

❶⓼
Sorbonne
❷⓵
rue St-Jacques

❷⓪ rue Valette
5e
❶⓽ St-Etienne du Mont

Ⓜ CARDINAL LEMOINE

rue Linné

Arènes de Lutèce

rue Cujas
rue du Cardinal

Panthéon
rue Soufflot

Ⓡ LUXEMBOURG

rue Mouffetard

rue Monge

rue Lhomond
rue d'Ulm

Ⓜ PLACE MONGE

CENSIER DAUBENTON
Ⓜ

bd. St-Michel
Ⓡ LUXEMBOURG
rue Gay Lussac

rue Brossolette

rue Monge

Ecole Normale Superieure

rue Bernard
rue Berthollet

rue du Val de Grâce
rue St-Nicole

Val-de-Grâce

Ⓜ LES GOBELINS

PORT ROYAL
Ⓡ bd. de Port Royal
bd. de Port Royal
bd. Arago

13e

17e 18e 19e
9e 10e
8e 2e 3e 20e
16e 1e 11e
7e 6e 4e
15e 5e 12e
14e 13e

0 ————— 1/5 Mi
0 ————— 0.2 Km
N

12 rue de Lanneau, 5e. ℂ 01-43-54-77-26. 2-course menu 16€ ($20); 3-course menu 23€ ($29); main courses 14€–21€ ($18–$26). MC, V. Sun–Thurs 7:30pm–midnight; Fri–Sat 7:30–11:30pm. Métro: Maubert-Mutualité.

Restaurant Perraudin 𝕲 CLASSIC BISTRO   The first reason to come here? If you present your Frommer's guide, you get a free aperitif known as a *communard,* kir made with red bordeaux. The second reason? The service is some of the best in the city, the food is great, and on the walls are pictures of turn-of-the-20th-century Paris when the restaurant opened—*très* cool. It was already a classic when Hemingway ate here. The bargain lunch menu offers a choice of three appetizers, two main courses, and cheese or dessert. You might start with tomatoes and mozzarella, then have ham with endives or roast beef, followed by baba au rhum. Classic dishes like duck confit and *gigot d'agneau* with gratin Dauphinois are on the a la carte menu.

157 rue St-Jacques, 5e. ℂ 01-46-33-15-75. 3-course lunch 19€ ($24); 3-course gastronomic menu 27€ ($34); main courses 12€–15€ ($15–$19). No credit cards. Tues–Fri noon–2:15pm; Mon–Sat 7:30–10:15pm. Métro: Luxembourg.

Vivario 𝕲 CORSICAN   The oldest Corsican restaurant in Paris is an excellent spot to sample the robust flavors of Napoleon's birthplace. Corsican cuisine relies upon the earthy charcuterie, cheese, and wine the fertile island produces. Many ingredients come straight from Corsica to the dim, cavelike restaurant, with stone walls and ceiling beams. To start, opt for rich traditional soup, teeming with beans, vegetables, and generous pieces of dried prosciutto. Follow with *cabri rôti à la Corse* (roast goat) or eggplant with cheese and spicy tomato sauce. Chewy whole-wheat baguettes accompany the meal, which might end with a selection of Corsican cheeses or *the* Corsican dessert—Fiadone tarte made with mild *bruccio,* the island's famous pungent cheese.

6 rue Cochin, 5e. ℂ 01-43-25-08-19. Main courses 10€–21€ ($13–$26). AE, MC, V. Tues–Fri noon–2pm; Mon–Sat 7:30–10pm. Métro: Maubert-Mutualité.

WORTH A SPLURGE

Brasserie Balzar 𝕲 *(Moments* BRASSERIE   In the heart of the Latin Quarter, this lovely old brasserie has welcomed many of France's intellectuals, including Sartre and Camus, and is still a great place if you feel like contemplating over a meal or a highball. Also, the tall mirrors allow you to discreetly spy on the other diners, making this a good place for people-watching. The wood tables are close together, but not uncomfortably so, and the staff is friendly and willing to accommodate your every need (including explaining the menu in English). Many of the regulars go for *poulet rôti avec frites* (roast chicken with french fries) or *choucroute garni,* but you can also try steak au poivre and a few fish dishes. There's no prix-fixe menu except after 10:30pm, but portions are copious. For dessert, try *tarte au citron* (lemon tart) or *gâteau au chocolate amère* (bittersweet chocolate cake).

49 rue des Ecoles, 5e. ℂ 01-43-54-13-67. 3-course menu available 10:30pm–midnight 25€ ($31); main courses 12€–19€ ($15($24). AE, MC, V. Daily noon–midnight. Métro: Cluny-Sorbonne.

ChantAirelle 𝕲 *(Finds* AUVERGNE   With foliage everywhere, including vines climbing the 7.5m (25-ft.) wall in its pretty backyard terrace, and the sounds of bells tolling from the nearby church, you may think you've found a secret garden in the bustling city. Portions are large, so only order an appetizer (like the famous charcuterie) unless you're ravenous. Main courses like wonderful poached pikeperch filet on green lentils and grilled country ham in a garlic-cream sauce are lovely, or try hearty *potée* (a tureen filled with pork, cabbage, potatoes, turnips, and leeks in broth). Although most dishes use ham or pork, vegetarians will enjoy the *croustade forestière* (assorted mushrooms and eggs poached with Fourme d'Ambert cheese). The best Auvergne wine is the Chateaugay, a fine fruity red.

17 rue Laplace, 5e. © **01-46-33-18-59.** Lunch menus 15€ ($19) and 20€ ($25); dinner menu 28€ ($35); main courses 13€–22€ ($16–$28). MC, V. Mon–Fri noon–2pm; daily 7–10:30pm. Closed for dinner Dec 24 and all day Dec 25 and 1 week in mid-August. Métro: Maubert-Mutualité.

6E ARRONDISSEMENT

A la Bonne Crêpe *(Value* BRETON/CREPES   It's hard to resist eating at this cozy spot, since you can smell the mélange of sugar, spice, and everything nice coming from this restaurant all the way down the street. And why resist? The crepes are wonderful, and you can watch the chef make them on an open stove in front of you while you sip cider and admire the pottery that decorates the walls. Crepes with cheese, meat, seafood, or other hearty fillings make up the main course, and sweet crepes filled with jam or chocolate are a wonderful dessert.

11 rue Grégoire-de-Tours, 6e. © **01-43-54-60-74.** 2-course weekday lunch with main-course crepe and glass of cider or wine 9.50€ ($12) and 11€ ($14) Sat and Sun; crepes a la carte 4€–8€ ($5–$10); bottle of cider 8€ ($10). No credit cards. Mon–Sat noon–2pm and 7–11pm. Closed last 2 weeks of Aug. Métro: Odéon.

Aux Charpentiers FRENCH   During the Middle Ages and Renaissance, the carpenters' guildhall was next door to this restaurant, and it gave Aux Charpentiers its name. If you ask Parisians for a good budget restaurant, 9 out of 10 times they'll name this bistro, in business for 130 years. The walls are decorated with photographs and illustrations of master carpentry, including models of wooden vaults and roof structures. The clientele is mostly local, and the prices are reasonable for traditional hearty dishes such as steak with Roquefort sauce or duckling with olives and port.

10 rue Mabillon, 6e. © **01-43-26-30-05.** *Plats du jour* 15€–17€ ($19–$21); 3-course dinner menu with ¼ liter of wine 26€ ($33); main courses 14€–23€ ($18–$29). AE, DC, MC, V. Daily noon–3pm and 7–11:30pm. Métro: Mabillon.

Bistro Mazarin *⊛ (Value* BISTRO   Not far from the St-Germain church, this charming bistro attracts the locals who work in this historic neighborhood. In either of two dining rooms, whose wood paneling has been congenially battered over the years, you can order classics like *petit sale* of pork (salt pork), prepared like a stew; boeuf bourguignon; a midwinter selection of fresh oysters; veal chops sautéed with butter-and-lemon sauce; and a satisfying combination of lentils with charcuterie and herbs. The portions are large, and everything can be washed down with reasonably priced wine. The heaters on the flowery sidewalk provide enough warmth so you can take your meal outdoors in any season.

42 rue Mazarine, 6e. © **01-43-29-99-01.** Main courses 11€–16€ ($14–$20). AE, MC, V. Daily noon–3pm and 7:30pm–midnight. Métro: Odéon.

Bouillon Racine *(Moments* BELGIAN   This gorgeous Belgian brasserie with its tiled floor and tables, iridescent lime-green walls, and shimmering mirrors is worth coming to just to admire its breathtaking Belle Epoque style. But fortunately the food is really good, too, and the selection of beer even better. In the late afternoon you'll often find businessmen discussing pressing matters, while a few tables over will be a group of seasoned Parisian ladies playing bridge.

3 rue Racine, 6e. © **01-44-32-15-60.** 2-course lunch menu 16€ ($20); 3-course menu 26€ ($32); main courses 14€–21€ ($18–$26). AE, MC, V. Daily noon–1am. Métro: Cluny-Sorbonne or Odéon.

Cosi *⊛* SANDWICHES   Walking into Cosi is like finding yourself in the midst of a Mediterranean spring day with its cornflower blue, coral, and lemon-covered walls.

Opera plays in the background. The sandwiches are sublime, too. You can get everything from baked salmon, roasted eggplant, smothered onions, and roast beef, to mozzarella and tomatoes, all served on focaccia. Add soup, a glass of wine, and a slice of chocolate cake and you'll be in the heaven. You can take your food out or eat upstairs, surrounded by photos of opera singers.

54 rue de Seine, 6e. ☎ **01-46-33-35-36.** Sandwiches 5€–9€ ($6.25–$11). No credit cards. Daily noon–11pm. Métro: Odéon.

Le Petit St-Benoît *Value* FRENCH   In summer the doors are flung open on this crowded dining room, with tile floors and red tablecloths. The food is cheap and well prepared, but not original. You might start with coquilles St-Jacques and follow with *pavé de rumpsteak aux chanterelles* (rump steak with mushrooms) or *canard aux navets* (duck with turnips). Finish with a delicious apple or lemon tart.

4 rue St-Benoît, 6e. ☎ **01-42-60-27-92.** Main courses 9€–12€ ($11–$15). No credit cards. Daily noon–2:30pm and 7–10:30pm. Métro: St-Germain-des-Prés.

Le Petit Vatel *Value* FRENCH   Since 1914 (and through a series of owners), this has remained one of Paris's most charming cost-conscious eateries. With hanging lamps and a handful of photos commemorating earlier incarnations, its pocketsize dining room contains only 22 seats (plus a few on the sidewalk in summer). The daily specials are based on simple dishes that reflect the traditions of Toulouse and France's Mediterranean coast. They include several robust soups and a Catalan platter *(pamboli)* with slices of grilled bread garnished with country ham, mountain cheese, spicy tomato sauce, and olive oil. The place is crowded and popular thanks to its no-nonsense prices and rib-sticking cuisine.

5 rue Lobineau, 6e. ☎ **01-43-54-28-49.** 2-course lunch menu 13€ ($16); main courses 8€–11€ ($10–$14). MC, V. Tues–Sat noon–3pm and 7pm–midnight. Métro: Mabillon or Odéon.

Le Polidor ❧ CLASSIC BISTRO   This 150-year-old bistro has a festive air, with people sitting elbow to elbow at picnic-style tables covered with red-and-white-checkered tablecloths and walls lined with smoky mirrors with the daily specials written on them. The cooking is earthy and homey, with all desserts and ice creams made on the premises. Begin with spinach salad with nut oil, followed by solid plates of *rognons en madere* (kidneys in Madeira sauce), *blanquette de veau,* boeuf bourguignon, or ragout of pork. Save room for a selection from the array of fresh tartes and pies.

41 rue Monsieur-le-Prince, 6e. ☎ **01-43-26-95-34.** 2-course weekday lunch menu 12€ ($15); 3-course dinner menu 19€ ($24); main courses 8€–13€ ($10–$16). No credit cards. Mon–Sat noon–2:30pm and 7pm–midnight; Sun 7–11pm. Métro: Odéon.

Restaurant Orestias GREEK   When you're in the mood for something other than French fare and want to pay practically nothing, come here. You may feel like you're back at summer camp sitting at the long wooden tables, but if you happen to glance up, you'll notice the murals depicting ancient Greece—reminding you that you're an adult and the home of Plato is a lot closer than Boy or Girl Scout camp. The kitchen turns out basic Greek dishes such as stuffed grape leaves with salad, souvlakia, and baklava, as well as roast chicken, lamb chops, and steak with potatoes, peas, and rice. You can't expect frills and thrills at these prices, but the ingredients are fresh and the dishes are hearty.

4 rue Grégoire-de-Tours, 6e. ☎ **01-43-54-62-01.** 2-course menu 8.50€ ($11); 3-course menu 15€ ($19); main courses 7€–11€ ($8.75–$14). MC, V. Mon–Sat noon–2:30pm and 5:30–11:30pm. Métro: Odéon.

WORTH A SPLURGE

Closerie des Lilas BRASSERIE/FRENCH   If you're looking for a romantic experience with some American literary history thrown in, look no further. Literary greats Hemingway, James, and Dos Passos sat out under the shady lilac bushes, while Lenin and Trotsky debated politics over chess. Hemingway wrote a large chunk of *The Sun Also Rises* while standing at the bar; Gertrude Stein and Alice B. Toklas were regulars. Closerie consists of a dark, romantic restaurant and a cheaper, brighter brasserie that serves more traditional French fare. A meal may start with a staple such as *oeufs dur* (eggs with mayonnaise), oysters in season, *terrine de fois gras canard avec toasts* (terrine of duck liver with toasted bread), or the classic *steak tartare avec frites maison*. Dinners may include tender *selle d'agneau rôti en croute dorée* (roasted lamb flank in a golden crust), *filet de boeuf au poivre*, or *homard Breton à votre façon* (Brittany lobster cooked the way you choose). Finish with cafe and patisser*ies* du jour or crêpes Suzette. Reservations are essential; even though the brasserie is open until 1am, Closerie has never been more popular.

171 bd. du Montparnasse, 6e. ℂ 01-40-51-34-50. Reservations required. Main courses 18€–30€ ($23–$38). AE, DC, MC, V. Daily noon–1am. Métro: Port-Royal.

Les Bouquinistes FRENCH   Chic and always crowded, this popular restaurant caters to the in-the-know tourist and trendier Parisians. After you've bought an Albert Camus from *les vrais bouquinistes* (booksellers), head to this elegant restaurant overlooking the Seine, ask for a table by the large picture windows, and watch the city go by. The food is delicate and divine. To begin, try the ravioli of smoked tuna and sea bream or the delectable pan-fried *foie gras* with chestnuts. For your main course, the roasted Pyrenees lamb with baby potatoes and shallot confit is a must. Seafood and meat selections, including giant tempura prawns seasoned with ginger and perfect *tendrons de veau* (veal ribs) served with stewed red cabbage in blackcurrant cream are delicious. Try the excellent-for-the-price dish named for the chef, Guy Savoy, and follow his recommendation for the house dessert wine.

52 quai des Grands-Augustins, 6e. ℂ 01-43-25-45-94. Reservations recommended. 2-course lunch menu 24€ ($29); main courses 19€–30€ ($24–$38). AE, DC, MC, V. Mon–Fri noon–2:30pm; daily 7pm–midnight. Métro: St-Michel.

Vagenende BRASSERIE   The rich, dark wood, smoky glass mirrors, and red velvet banquette seats will transport you back to the Belle Epoque, and the *confit de canard* with *pommes persillade* (potatoes in a parsley vinaigrette) will transport you to heaven. This brasserie is a cut above the rest, yet keeps its prices reasonable. Founded in 1904 as a *bouillon* (canteen or soup kitchen) by M. Chartier—of the 9e arrondissement restaurant of the same name—Vagenende evolved into a brasserie now classified as a *Monument Historique*.

142 bd. St-Germain, 6e. ℂ 01-43-26-68-18. 3-course lunch menu 19€ ($24); 23€ ($29) 3-course dinner menu; main courses 16€–23€ ($20–$29). AE, DC, MC, V. Daily noon–1am. Métro: Odéon.

Ze Kitchen Galerie INTERNATIONAL   This trendy place used to be crowded every night of the week. It's recently lost some of its allure to the "see and be seen" crowd but it's still serving imaginative cuisine in a fantastic setting. The sleek, ultra-modern black-and-white interior is complemented with contemporary art on the walls and trendy waitstaff. Diners are encouraged to order any combination of food in any order from four different categories: soup and salad, seafood, pasta, and grilled meats. The menu changes often, depending on the season. The fish choice may be cod roasted with coriander; the meat may be a grilled quail with polenta. Order carefully from the extensive wine list as you can easily overspend here. Service is mostly efficient but not especially friendly.

4 rue des Grands-Augustins, 6e. ℂ **01-44-32-00-32.** Reservations recommended. Main courses 15€–27€ ($17–$34). AE, DC, MC, V. Mon–Fri noon–2:30pm; Mon–Sat 7–10:45pm. Métro: St-Michel.

7E ARRONDISSEMENT

Au Pied du Fouet   CLASSIC BISTRO   This minuscule place in one of the most expensive parts of Paris is extremely popular with people who could pay much more. The cooking's homey and appetizing, if never surprising. Start with a salad of hot shredded cabbage with bacon, followed by chicken livers, and then a slice of runny Camembert or maybe an apple tart. Coffee's taken at the bar to make way for the next round of hungry, pennywise diners.

45 rue de Babylone, 7e. ℂ **01-47-05-12-27.** Main courses 9€–11€ ($11–$14). No credit cards. Mon–Sat noon–2:30pm; Mon–Fri 7–9:45pm. Closed 1 week in mid-Aug. Métro: Vaneau.

Café Constant   CLASSIC FRENCH   This may very well be the Left Bank's best-kept secret. Recently opened by award-winning Chef Christian Constant (who runs the swanky Le Violin d'Ingre down the street), this simple cafe serves traditional French cuisine at very reasonable prices. Appetizers are 8€ ($10) and main courses are 12€ ($15). Desserts are 6€ ($7.50). Simple. The *terrine de foie gras canard maison* is, as stated, made lovingly in this kitchen. The very French *pied de porc* is served with a house-made apple purée. Classic dishes such as boeuf bourguigon, sole meuniere, and *magret de canard* are also frequently featured on the ever-changing menu. Desserts also tend to lean towards the very traditional—this is the place to have a wicked crème caramel.

139 rue St Dominique, 7e. ℂ **01-47-53-73-34.** Main courses 12€ ($15). MC, V. Mon–Sat noon–2:30pm and 7:30–10:30pm. Métro: Ecole Militaire.

Chez Germaine *(Value)* FRENCH   Chez Germaine takes up a space not much larger than your hotel room. The crowd of discerning regulars is a tip-off that you'll get a quality meal at a great price. The menu changes regularly, but you'll usually find *lentilles vinaigrette,* calves' liver, and crème caramel. To discourage lingering, smoking is not allowed, and you'll have to go elsewhere for coffee.

30 rue Pierre-Leroux, 7e. ℂ **01-42-73-28-34.** 3-course prix-fixe menu with wine 13€ ($16); main courses 7€–9€ ($8.75–$11). No credit cards. Mon–Sat noon–2:30pm; Mon–Fri 7–9:30pm. Closed Aug. Métro: Duroc.

La Fontaine de Mars *(star)* FRENCH   This cozy restaurant is quintessentially Parisian with its red-and-white-checkered tablecloths and its windows overlooking pretty Rue Dominique, and the *grandes matrons* perched on their balconies across the way, eyeing the goings on in this busy street. The food is homey, scrumptious, and filling; no need to order an appetizer. Try the roast duck with garlic potatoes and mushrooms (16€/$20) or the duck and sausage stew with white beans, bacon, and tomato sauce (21€/$24). During the summer you can do your daydreaming on their lovely patio overlooking the fountain.

129 rue St-Dominique, 7e. ℂ **01-47-05-46-44.** Reservations required during warmer months. Main courses 15€–24€ ($19–$30). V. Daily noon–3pm and 7:30–11pm. Métro: Ecole-Militaire.

La Serre *(star)* FRENCH   This tiny, friendly restaurant on one of the city's narrowest streets is a good bargain. You can easily have a gourmet two-course meal for 20€ ($25). Begin with the unusual but delicious *profiteroles d'escargots* (9€/$11) and move on to the salmon filet with leeks (11€/$14). The homemade desserts include a luscious

Where to Dine on the Left Bank (7 & 15e)

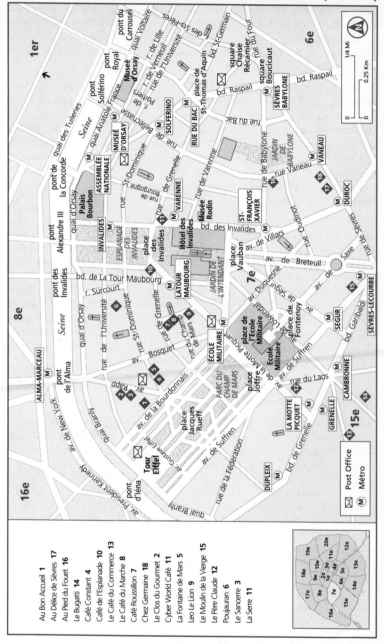

Au Bon Accueil 1
Au Délice de Sèvres 17
Au Pied du Fouet 16
Le Bugatti 14
Café Constant 4
Café de l'Esplanade 10
Le Café du Commerce 13
Le Café du Marche 8
Café Roussillon 7
Chez Germaine 18
Le Clos du Gourmet 2
Cyber World Café 11
La Fontaine de Mars 5
Leo Le Lion 9
Le Moulin de la Vierge 15
Le Père Claude 12
Poujauran 6
Le Sancerre 3
La Serre 11

☒ Post Office
Ⓜ Métro

141

mousse au chocolat. Service is pleasant and the international crowd is on the young side. Tables are very close together, so this restaurant is not recommended for a quiet, romantic meal.

29 rue de l'Exposition, 7e. © **01-45-55-20-96**. Main courses 11€–15€ ($14–$19). MC, V. Tues–Sun 7–10:30pm. Métro: Ecole-Militaire.

Le Café du Marche ⭐ *(Value)* BISTRO   Overlooking the rue Cler open-air market, this popular cafe/bistro serves surprisingly good food for the price. Examples of the 11€ ($14) *plat du jour* include a pork curry with rice or a cod filet with sautéed baby potatoes. Both the Caesar salad with chicken and the warm chèvre salad are big enough for a light meal (10€/$13). The atmosphere is local and neighborhoody—but service can be slow. Forget dessert here and stroll down the street to pick up fresh berries, chocolate, or a pastry.

38 rue Cler, 7e. © **01-47-05-51-27**. *Plat du jour* 11€ ($14); main courses 10€–12€ ($13–$15). MC, V. Daily 11am–11pm. Métro: Ecole-Militaire.

WORTH A SPLURGE

Au Bon Accueil ⭐ FRENCH   Au Bon Accueil has an understated elegance and an outdoor patio with a spectacular view of the Eiffel Tower. If you're yearning for something a little more private and romantic, try the back room—perfect for a tête-à-tête. The menu changes daily according to what the chef finds in the markets. On the prix-fixe menu, start with *filets de sardines mi-cuites à l'huile et romarin méli mélo de legumes provencaux* (sardines lightly grilled in oil with a blend of vegetables from Provence). Follow with *steak de thon poélé et son caviar d'aubergine aux olives* (seared tuna steak with eggplant caviar and olives). Divine, if pricey, main dishes include scallops with asparagus, and whole lobster from Brittany roasted in herbs and tomatoes. The fantastic desserts include fig tart and crème brûlée made with walnuts.

14 rue de Monttessuy, 7e. © **01-47-05-46-11**. Reservations recommended. 3-course lunch menu 27€ ($34); 3-course dinner menu 31€ ($39); main courses 23€–39€ ($29–$49). MC, V. Mon–Fri noon–2:30pm and 7:30–10:30pm. Métro: Alma-Marceau.

Le Clos du Gourmet ⭐⭐ *(Finds)* FRENCH   As close to perfect as possible, this place is a gourmand's dream. Settle into the expansive dining room with large windows overlooking an upper-crust residential street, and order a glass of champagne while you peruse the menu. Diners have seven appetizers, seven main courses, and seven desserts from which to choose. You may begin with a *crème d'asperges blanches, croûtons dorés romarin* (cream of white asparagus soup with toasted rosemary croutons), or the *escalope de foie gras* drizzled with maple syrup and served with baby spinach and beet salad. Move on to a salmon filet served on a bed of puréed green peas or the *poulette du Gers rotie au vin d'Arbois* (Cornish hen from Gers roasted in Arbois wine) served with a watercress dressing. For dessert, the *meringue crème légère à la pistache* (meringue with a light pistachio cream) is delightful, while the cappuccino crème brûlée is delicate and unique. Dessert wines are on offer for 4€ ($5) a glass. Service is friendly and polite.

16 av. Rapp, 7e. © **01-45-51-75-61**. Reservations recommended. 3-course menu 33€ ($41). MC, V. Tues–Sat noon–2:30pm and 7:30–10:30pm. Métro: Alma-Marceau.

Leo Le Lion FRENCH   If you've ever wondered how it is to dine in an elegant Parisian home, you're about to find out. Françoise is a gracious hostess, her husband Didier a proper French chef, and Frederic an animated waiter who will look after you.

A tiny place with no more than 10 tables, the decor feels like somebody's chic living room: wood chairs, velvet banquettes, thick tablecloths, and candles on every table. The food is incredibly good. It's very French, very proper, very carefully prepared *cuisine du marché,* based on what's fresh at the market. Always amazing is the foie gras appetizer (served with raspberry coulis in summer), pickled herring with greens of the day, and a soup. Fish reigns supreme here. Choices may include baked eel with berries or roasted cod with fennel and cream sauce; and there's always a *magret de canard* and a meat choice. For dessert, the tarte tatin flambéed with Calvados is exquisite. Reasonable wine selections start at 22€ ($28) a bottle.

23 rue Duvivier, 7e. ☎ **01-45-51-41-77.** Reservations recommended. Main courses 16€–22€ ($20–$28). AE, DC, MC, V. Tues–Sat 7:30–10:30pm. Closed Aug. Métro: Ecole-Militaire.

14E ARRONDISSEMENT

Au Rendez-Vous des Camionneurs CLASSIC BISTRO   Although the name translates to "The Meeting Place of the Truck Drivers," the reference is more to the convivial atmosphere than the clientele. The friendly *patronne,* Monique, spoils the crowd of local regulars. Husband Claude runs the kitchen and sends out appetizing dishes like roast chicken, lamb stew, and pork chops. All are generously garnished, usually with mashed potatoes and a vegetable.

34 rue des Plantes, 14e. ☎ **01-45-40-43-36.** 3-course menu 15€ ($19). No credit cards. Mon–Fri noon–2:30pm and 7:30–9:30pm. Closed Aug. Métro: Alesia.

Vallée du Kashmir INDO-PAKISTANI   Parisian palates are too finely tuned to withstand fiery spices, which means that Asian restaurants must temper their cuisine to suit local tastes without sacrificing authenticity. This tiny, popular restaurant has found the right formula. A combination of sweet spices, hot spices, or dried fruit is applied to chicken, lamb, fish, rice, and vegetable dishes, with delicious results. An aperitif and *papadum* whet the appetite. Follow with crisply fried *samosa* or *oignon bhaja,* then delicately seasoned chicken Kashmir.

10 rue d'Odessa, 14e. ☎ **01-42-79-92-23.** Lunch menus 7.50€ ($9.40) and 9€ ($11); dinner menus 16€ ($20), 17€ ($21) and 20€ ($25). MC, V. Daily noon–2:30pm and 7:30–11:30pm. Métro: Montparnasse-Bienvenüe.

WORTH A SPLURGE

Le Bistrot du Dome FRENCH/SEAFOOD   This bistro annex of one of the most famous seafood restaurants in the city is a great place to get a first-rate meal on a budget. The ambience is light and airy; ceramic tiles with fish designs cover the walls, and soft lights dangle from ceilings adorned with faux grapevines. Daily blackboard specials vary with the season, and the friendly staff is happy to describe the options. Signature first courses include salmon tartare, baby clams with thyme, and grilled baby squid. Main dishes range from *solettes meunière* to tangy *daurade beurre citronne.* In summer, with the breeze blowing through the front windows, you can imagine that you're dining by the sea.

1 rue Delambre, 14e. ☎ **01-43-35-32-00.** Reservations recommended. Main courses 17€–26€ ($21–$33). AE, MC, V. Daily noon–2:30pm and 7:30–11pm. Métro: Vavin.

15E ARRONDISSEMENT

Le Bugatti ITALIAN   If you're in the mood for a low-key Italian meal in a middle-class Parisian neighborhood, come to Le Bugatti. The food is good but the reason you're coming is for the warm ambience and excellent service; you'll probably be served by the owner, Giuseppe Dandachi, who has pictures of Marilyn, his favorite gal, all over the wall. His smile will put you at ease and is a truly welcoming sight after a day of Paris shopping and stopping.

1 rue du Docteur Jacquemaire–Clémenceau, 15e. ℂ **01-42-50-37-40.** Main courses 10€–17€ ($13–$21). No credit cards. Daily 7:30–11:30pm. Métro: Commerce.

Le Café du Commerce FRENCH   After you've done the Eiffel Tower and shopped till you dropped, stop here for a great meal at a bargain price. You'll love the ambience, complete with smoky mirrors, stained-glass windows, and photos of great scribes who supposedly wrote their *oeuvres* on the premises. Maybe the three floors wrapping around the green-filled atrium inspired them. Or maybe it was the cheap house wine. The menu includes *escargots en Caquelon* as a main course, and *plats* of *tartare de boeuf* and *la cuisse de canard confite*. The wine list is extensive. As in many Paris restaurants, you have to ask for the dessert selection: Profiteroles—puff pastries filled with ice cream and topped with hot chocolate—are a good bet. Smoking is forbidden in the first-floor dining section, and watch out for the free-flying birds in the atrium.

51 rue du Commerce, 15e. ℂ **01-45-75-03-27.** *Plat du jour* 13€ ($16); main courses 13€–18€ ($16–$23). AE, DC, MC, V. Daily noon–11:30pm. Métro: Emile-Zola, Commerce, or La Motte–Picquet.

WORTH A SPLURGE
Le Père Claude CLASSIC BISTRO   You may feel like you've just walked into a 1970s movie with the rust-colored walls, shag carpeting, and faux Romanesque murals everywhere, but don't let that scare you away, because the food is sublime. Plus, interesting people in the know, like President Jacques Chirac and Don King, have been spotted dining here. Go figure. You can begin with warm sausage with pistachio and apples, or mussel soup with saffron. The rotisserie behind the bar signals that the house specialty is roasted meat, but seafood lovers won't be disappointed in *assiette de pecheur aux pâtés fraîches* (fisherman's plate with fresh terrine). *Panaché de viandes* is an assortment of perfectly roasted meat served with a comforting heap of mashed potatoes. Make sure you specify how you want the beef cooked, or it will be served the way the French like it—very, very rare. After dinner you can stroll up avenue de La Motte-Picquet and take in a view of the dazzlingly illuminated Eiffel Tower.

51 av. de la Motte-Picquet, 15e. ℂ **01-47-34-03-05.** 2-course menu 28€ ($35); 3-course menu 32€ ($40); main courses 17€–28€ ($21–$35). AE, MC, V. Daily 11:30am–2:30pm and 7:30–11pm. Métro: La Motte-Picquet–Grenelle.

6 The Best Cafes

To a Parisian, a cafe is a combination of club, tavern, and snack bar. You can read your newspaper, meet a friend, do your homework, or write your memoirs. Often people meet at cafes to relax and talk before going to a show.

Cafes aren't restaurants, although some serve meals. They aren't bars, although they offer alcoholic drinks. And they aren't coffee shops in the American sense, because you can order a bottle of champagne as readily as a hot chocolate.

The cafe is a Parisian's home away from home, even if it originated in Vienna. So if you're an American but feel like emulating a Frenchman, then you should go to one, too; it's like a microcosm of city life here with all its *café*, red wine, croque-monsieurs, deep conversation, and smoke.

Cafes are a great respite from the museum trot or Paris rain because you can sit for hours—but be polite and order a few café crèmes, and leave a generous tip.

Many older cafes are filled with ancient men, there from the wee hours of the morn, sipping their first coffee of the day or something a little stronger, like a wake-me-up beer, in between smoking cigarettes. These are great places to come and practice your French with the regulars, but they sometimes feel like an old-man's club. If you're a woman traveling alone, or feel like something more modern, then head for a newer, hip cafe, many of which are popping up all over Paris. They'll serve the same basic fare, which is not quite up to the standards of a restaurant, but can be quite hearty, and you'll watch as a new generation of Parisians defines the cafe experience.

THE RIGHT BANK

Au Bistrot de la Place   This is definitely not an "old-man bar" with its cool orange and yellow papier-mâché lamp coverings that emit a sexy, low light—certain to inspire some profound thoughts for your epic novel. Plus, the bistro food here is great, even if the service is not. If you're just a tad hungry, come when it's not mealtime to enjoy a leisurely drink or pastry on the terrace, which looks onto place du Marché Ste-Catherine, the site of an 18th-century market.

2 pl. du Marché Ste-Catherine, 4e. ⓒ 01-42-78-21-32. MC, V. Daily noon–3pm and 7–11pm; tearoom 9:30am to early afternoon. Métro: St-Paul.

Café Baci ⭐ *(Finds)*   The newest and most elegant "Café in the Marais" boasts beige leather stools, heavy chandeliers, and Venetian prints on its walls. A well-heeled Parisian crowd fills this place, especially on weekends. The food is good, if a bit over-priced, and the atmosphere is sensual and romantic. There are two floors here—the downstairs tends to be quieter. Live music (and sometimes impromptu dancing) erupt upstairs late in the evening.

36 rue de Turenne, 3e. ⓒ 01-42-71-36-70. MC, V. Tues–Sun noon–10:30pm. Métro: St-Paul.

Café Beaubourg ⭐   *Hip* is the word for this funky, Art Deco hot spot next to the Centre Pompidou. Designed by Christian de Portzamparc, the wide, bi-level space is cool and elegant, with circular columns that soar up to an illuminated ceiling. The walls, filled with books, prompt conversation. The decor suits the excellent French fare at reasonable prices. The *hachis parmentier* (shepherd's pie) is prepared to perfec-tion, the *comté* cheese will melt in your mouth, and quiche Lorraine is a light mouth-ful of flavor. Desserts are a steal at 6€ ($7.50). In the summer, sit in a chair on the terrace and become a main attraction yourself.

100 rue St-Merri, 4e. ⓒ 01-48-87-63-96. AE, DC, MC, V. Sun–Thurs 8am–1am; Fri–Sat 8am–2am. Métro: Ram-buteau or Hôtel-de-Ville.

Café Charbon   With a back room that plays live music several nights a week, this popular cafe has become one of the hottest spots in East Paris. You won't mind the crowds either; you'll be mesmerized by this turn-of-the-20th-century dance hall's Art Nouveau interior including its delicately hanging lamps, smoky mirrors, hand-painted murals, and cathedral ceilings—a convenient place for the cigarette smoke to go. Dur-ing the day or early evening, it's a little more subdued.

109 rue Oberkampf, 11e. ⓒ 01-43-57-55-13. MC, V. Daily 9am–2am. Métro: Parmentier.

Café Concert Ailleurs   Forget about Piaf and Brel in this funky cabaret, and listen to a new generation of songsmiths. This relaxed space, run by an artists' collective, attracts bohemians of all ages who are interested in up-and-coming artists. Drinks run 3€ to 5.50€ ($3.75–$6.90).

13 rue Jean de Beausire, 4e. ⓒ 01-44-59-82-82. Daily 2pm–2am. Métro: Bastille.

Café de l'Industrie Whether it's the jazz playing in the background or the photos of Brazilian women and children that line the wooden walls, you'll want to spend some time at this cafe. Filled with plants and Venetian blinds that give it a vaguely colonial flavor, this is a refuge from crowded place Bastille, a few blocks away. Plus, the food, including salads, pastas, and *plats* is good, too, and the prices are very reasonable; *quelle dommage* that it's closed on Saturdays! Drink prices start at 3€ ($3.75).

16 rue St-Sabin, 11e. ℂ **01-47-00-13-53.** MC, V. Daily 10am–2am. Métro: Bastille.

Café Etienne-Marcel ✦ *Finds* The Costes brothers empire has spread to this out-of-the-way neighborhood, a 15-minute walk from the Marais and Bastille. It used to be hard to find an elegant cafe around here, but not anymore. A young and trendy crowd gathers here in the early evenings to sit on the weirdly 1970s large fiberglass chairs and people-watch. As with most Costes cafes, light meals are delicious and reasonable, around 11€ to 15€ ($14–$19).

34 rue Etienne Marcel, 2e. ℂ **01-45-08-01-03.** MC, V. Daily 8am–2am. Métro: Etienne-Marcel.

Café Hugo ✦ *Finds* Finally, an affordable option overlooking the glorious place des Vosges. Café Hugo has a large terrace under the arcades and it's open daily from 8am to 2am, making it an ideal stop whenever you're in the Marais. Sandwiches are cheap, 3.50€ to 4€ ($4.40–$5), and the omelets cost 5€ to 7€ ($6.25–$8.75). You can make a great meal out of the salad niçoise (9.50€/$12), followed by a sweet crepe for dessert (4€/$5).

22 pl. des Vosges, 4e. ℂ **01-42-72-64-04.** MC, V. Daily 8am–2am. Métro: St-Paul.

Café Lateral ✦ *Finds* Strictly for locals-in-the-know, this cafe is hidden a few minutes' walk from the Champs-Elysées. The handsome interior is all dark wood and there's a small terrace for outdoor seating. Parisians who wouldn't be caught dead on the Champs-Elysées come here for *un café* (2.50€/$3.15) and a *tartine* (1.40€/$1.75) in the morning or a glass of Stella beer (4.10€/$5.15) or a glass of Côtes du Rhône (3.60€/$4.50) in the afternoon. The food is also good and reasonable; main courses are 11€ to 17€ ($14–$21). The specialty is the steak tartare (14€/$18), prepared many different ways—the most popular is the gratinée, half-cooked and served with fresh basil and mozzarella. They also have a two-course menu for lunch for 16€ ($20). Note that after 10pm a .50€ (65¢) surcharge is added to all items.

4 av. Mac-Mahon, 17e. ℂ **01-43-80-20-96.** www.cafelateral.com. AE, MC, V. Daily 7am–2am. Métro: Charles-de-Gaulle.

Café Marly ✦ The rich, scarlet entranceway sets the tone for this magnificent cafe that stares onto the Louvre's glass pyramid. You can afford a light meal here; the prices are reasonable considering its proximity to the *Mona Lisa*. During the warmer months you can sit on the patio and sip a drink while you watch the mobs waiting to get into the museum. It's easy to miss this well-hidden cafe nestled in the heart of Paris's art world. For a light lunch fare, the *petites ravioles "comme à la maison"* for 15€ ($19) is an ample portion of pasta in delicate cream sauce. The simple *salade melée aux herbes,* at 10€ ($13), is a generous serving of the freshest frisée and mesclun, lightly touched with crisp lemon vinaigrette. After 8pm, seating is for dinner only.

93 rue de Rivoli, cour Napoleon du Louvre, 1er. ℂ **01-49-26-06-60.** AE, DC, MC, V. Daily 8am–2am. Métro: Palais-Royal–Musée du Louvre.

Fouquet's A great place to meet for a drink at its swanky bar, the early-20th-century Fouquet's is a Champs-Elysées institution. Patrons have included James Joyce,

Charlie Chaplin, Marlene Dietrich, Winston Churchill, and Franklin D. Roosevelt. It's also a nice place to dine, but you'll pay out the wazoo.

99 av. des Champs-Elysées, 8e. ✆ **01-47-23-70-60**. AE, MC, V. Daily 8am–2am. Métro: George V.

La Chaise au Plafond   You'll smell La Chaise's tarts and treats from down rue Trésor, and you won't be able to resist. Tucked away on a little street in the heart of the Marais, this friendly, stylish place is a perfect spot for a timeout after visiting the Musée Picasso. It also serves good salads and sandwiches at reasonable prices.

10 rue Trésor, 4e. ✆ **01-42-76-03-22**. MC, V. Daily 9am–2am. Métro: Hôtel-de-Ville.

L'Eté en Pente Douce   To escape the tourists on place du Tertre, head down the eastern steps under the Sacré-Coeur. You'll find yourself on a leafy square, popular with a local crowd. The terrace of L'Eté en Pente Douce, underneath two trees, faces the stairs and iron lamps painted by Utrillo. The interior is brightly decorated with mosaics, objets d'art, and a lovely painted ceiling. Between lunch and dinner, the restaurant serves a tempting array of pastries and sandwiches.

23 rue Muller, 18e. ✆ **01-42-64-02-67**. MC, V. Daily noon–midnight. Métro: Château-Rouge.

THE LEFT BANK

Café de Flore ✮ *Moments*   You have to at least check it out because after all, Sartre is said to have written his trilogy *Les Chemins de la Liberté (The Roads to Freedom)* at his table here. Other regulars included André Malraux and Guillaume Apollinaire. In the heart of the lovely St-Germain-des-Prés neighborhood, the cafe is still going strong, and even though the famous writers have moved on, a group of new Anglo-Saxon scribes meet here fairly regularly on Monday nights to discuss emerging works. Care to join them?

172 bd. St-Germain, 6e. ✆ **01-45-48-55-26**. AE, V. Daily 7:30am–1:30am. Métro: St-Germain-des-Prés.

Café de la Place   Not all of Montparnasse has yielded to fast food and traffic. This old-fashioned cafe overlooking a tree-lined square has become a popular spot for young neighborhood residents. There's a menu of inexpensive bistro specialties, or you can opt for a sandwich and a glass of wine.

23 rue d'Odessa, 14e. ✆ **01-42-18-01-55**. MC, V. Mon–Sat 7:30am–2am; Sun 10am–11pm. Métro: Edgar-Quinet.

Café Mabillon   This feels like an overpriced place you might find on the Upper West Side of Manhattan, but if you're searching for "young and new," as in techno music at night and something a little lighter during the day, then stop here for a café crème or something stronger. One plus, however, is it's open nearly 24 hours, so when you've had a late night and are starving at 3am but can't find any place to *mange*, it might be the only place close to satisfy your hunger.

164 bd. St-Germain, 6e. ✆ **01-43-26-62-93**. MC, V. Daily 7:30am–6am. Métro: Mabillon.

Café Roussillon   Recently opened, this traditional French cafe with breezy, modern touches is located on a great corner in the 7e, on the edge of the outdoor market at rue Cler. It's a wonderful place to people-watch as you sip your café crème on the outdoor patio and daydream your afternoon away.

186 rue de Grenelle, 7e. ✆ **01-45-51-47-53**. MC, V. Mon–Thurs 7am–midnight; Fri–Sat 7am–2am; Sun 7am–4pm. Métro: Ecole-Militaire.

La Chope   Hemingway didn't drink here and Sartre didn't write here, but this cafe is worth a stop for its location on top of rue Mouffetard, right on pretty place de la

Contrescarpe. The square centers on four lilac trees and a fountain, and is small enough that you can enjoy a peaceful espresso without cars whizzing by.

2–4 pl. de la Contrescarpe, 5e. ② 01-43-26-51-26. V. Daily 8am–2am. Métro: Cardinal Lemoine.

La Coupole *Moments* This Paris institution has been packing them in since Henry Miller came here for his morning porridge. The cavernous interior is always jammed and bristling with energy. Japanese businesspeople, French yuppies, models, tourists, and neighborhood regulars keep the frenzied waiters running until 2am. You won't know which is more interesting, the scene on the street or the parade that passes through the revolving doors. And the food is good.

102 bd. du Montparnasse, 14e. ② 01-43-20-14-20. AE, DC, MC, V. Daily 8:30am–1am. Métro: Vavin.

La Palette *Finds* The service is brusque, but then, what's new? Still one of our favorites, this is a great place to take your paper, laptop, or inner self and sit on the patio watching the ebb and flow of life on the Left Bank. As per the name, a lot of artsy types come here, so you'll feel right at home (they love everyone). The interior is decorated with murals, and a palette hangs over the bar. The fare is cafe-style—open-face ham sandwiches and the like—at reasonable prices.

43 rue de Seine, 6e. ② 01-43-26-68-15. MC, V. Mon–Sat 8am–2am. Métro: Mabillon.

Le Café de l'Esplanade A little pretentious and a bit of a scene, this hip cafe, owned by the Costes brothers, adds some color to this staid neighborhood and is a great place to unwind after a day of touring or snoring. With its dim lighting and modern lounge feel, it's fun to sit inside. But don't, because the best view is from its patio, where you can sip a nice glass of wine—or eat a complete meal—while you watch a magnificent sunset over Les Invalides.

52 rue Fabert, 7e. ② 01-47-05-38-80. AE, DC, MC, V. Daily 8:30am–2am. Métro: La Tour Maubourg.

Les Deux Magots Like its neighbor the Café de Flore, Deux Magots was a hangout for Sartre and de Beauvoir. Sartre wrote at his table every morning. With prices that start at 4.30€ ($5.40) for coffee and 2€ ($2.50) for a croissant, it's an expensive place for literary pilgrims, but a great spot to watch the nightly promenade on the boulevard St-Germain and worth the splurge.

6 pl. St-Germain-des-Prés, 6e. ② 01-45-48-55-25. AE, DC, V. Daily 7:30am–1:30am. Métro: St-Germain-des-Prés.

Les Editeurs *Finds* This new, chic and happening place is named for the editors from nearby publishing houses. The location is perfect for people-watching, either from the sidewalk terrace or from the expansive windows. A full breakfast is served daily with your choice of eggs, juice, croissant, and café au lait for 16€ ($20); sandwiches and light meals are 8€ to 13€ ($10–$16).

4 carrefour de l'Odéon, 6e. ② 01-43-26-67-76. www.lesediteurs.fr. AE, MC, V. Daily 8am–2am. Métro: Odéon.

CYBERCAFES
Cyber World Café Useful if you're having e-mail withdrawal, especially since it's one of the few places with English keyboards. The rates are 2€ ($2.50) for 10 minutes, 5€ ($6.25) for 30 minutes, and 7€ ($8.75) for 1 hour.

20 rue de l'Exposition, 7e. ② 01-53-59-96-54. Mon–Sat noon–10pm; Sun noon–8pm. Métro: Ecole-Militaire.

7 Salons de Thé (Tea Salons)

A good cup of tea is hard to find in Paris. The French have never favored the stuff, preferring to fortify themselves with powerful little blasts of coffee. Tea lovers will find in tea salons a wide range of blends, steeped to perfection. In contrast to the smoke and bustle that characterize most cafes, tea salons are refined and often elegant establishments. The pastry selection is usually excellent, but full meals tend to be expensive.

THE RIGHT BANK

Angelina 🎯 When you sit down in this Belle Epoque palace of pastry and sip a hot chocolate the likes of which you've never had before, you might mistake the gold gilded mirrors and arched entrance for the Pearly Gates. Don't be intimidated by the tourists who frequent this famous tea salon—the experience is worth it, and the space is big enough to lose yourself in the sweets. The variety of pastries includes éclairs, brioche, and apricot tarte with powdered sugar. While coffee and tea aren't cheap at 4€ to 6€ ($4.60–$6.90), you get about two servings in a small pitcher, making them good deals. The main dishes can be pricey, so stick to sweets and lighter fare.

226 rue de Rivoli, 1er. ✆ 01-42-60-82-00. Pot of tea (for 1) 6.50€ ($8.15); pastry 3€–6€ ($3.75–$7.50); light fare 7€–13€ ($8.75–$16); main courses 12€–21€ ($15–$26). MC, V. Daily 9am–5:45pm (lunch 11:45am–3pm). Métro: Concorde or Tuileries.

A Priori Thé 🎯 *Finds* You can enjoy the beautiful Galerie Vivienne and a good repast at A Priori Thé, a cleverly named tearoom that serves a large assortment of teas, coffees, light meals, tarts, salads, and desserts. The American management has created a harmonious and appealing blend of Parisian and New World styles. The emphasis is on light sauces and fresh ingredients. Teatime delights include a variety of tarts—chocolate, lemon-cheese, and orange—as well as scones, muffins, cookies, and brownies. Call ahead for a reservation if you're coming for weekend brunch, and be prepared for brusque service during the rush. Afternoons are much quieter.

35–37 Galerie Vivienne (enter at 6 rue Vivienne, 4 rue des Petits-Champs, or 5 rue de la Banque), 2e. ✆ 01-42-97-48-75. Continental breakfast 9€ ($11); light lunch or supper 12€–16€ ($15–$20); Sat brunch 22€ ($28); Sun brunch 24€ ($30). MC, V. Mon–Fri 9am–6pm; Sat 9am–6:30pm; Sun 12:30–6:30pm. Métro: Bourse, Palais-Royal–Musée du Louvre, or Pyramides.

Instant Delices *Finds* Off fashionable rue St-Honoré, this tiny teahouse has hardwood floors and tables and serves up creative and delicious salads such as the Caesar with potato pancake croutons and roast chicken, or the green salad with white-wine rabbit terrine. If you're planning a picnic, this is a good place to stop for a variety of yummy platters they pack for the tourist on the run.

21 rue St-Roch, 1er. ✆ 01-42-60-90-29. 2-course menu with wine 19€ ($24); light fare and salads 8€–13€ ($10–$16). No credit cards. Mon–Fri 11am–10pm. Métro: Tuileries.

Ladurée 🎯 When you're tired of the typical, austere Paris cafe and want a little luxury without spending a fortune, go to Ladurée. You'll feel relaxed as soon as you walk in its beautiful entrance with its famous macaroons, *marron glacée,* and chocolates exquisitely displayed in *la vitrine.* Its richly paneled and gilded room with rows of tiny black marble tables and antique chairs is a great place to rest your tired feet. The teas are lovely, but the hot chocolate is a must! Its original location, founded during the Belle Epoque, is known as the most refined tearoom in Paris and is located at 16 rue Royale, 8e (✆ **01-42-60-21-79**).

75 av. des Champs–Elysées, 8e. (✆) **01-40-75-08-75.** Beverages 4.50€–7€ ($5.65–$8.75); light meals from 11€ ($14). MC, V. Mon–Sat 8:30am–7pm. Métro: Franklin-D-Roosevelt.

Les Enfants Gatés   This tearoom's central location makes it the perfect place to unwind after a day of sightseeing. Sink into a wicker chair, sip tea, and indulge your neocolonial fantasies under the ceiling fans. Potted palms and a tape of twittering birds help set the mood. A wide selection of teas, pastries, and wines, plus several vegetarian dishes attracts a loyal clientele. The weekend brunch is a good deal, but you'll have a hard time finding a seat.

43 rue des Francs-Bourgeois, 4e. (✆) **01-42-77-07-63.** Beverages 3€–4€ ($3.75–$5); pastries 5€–6€ ($6.25–$7.50); light meals 7€–13€ ($8.75–$16); brunch 18€ ($23). MC, V. Sat–Mon 11am–8pm; Wed–Fri noon–8pm. Métro: St-Paul.

Mariage Frères 🐾   A cornucopia of heavenly scents for your olfactory sense, this piece of paradise in a sky-lit room is a must for any tea lover. Plus, the service is as heavenly as the desserts and assortment of teas. If you like green tea, then the Japanese Matcha is a must—it may look like a witch's brew with its dark, green broth bubbling over, but it's reputed to be excellent for your complexion. We also took lovely waiter Jean-Marc's suggestion and had a *coup du soleil,* a tart so good as to make you weep. Another specialty is the scones. The Mariage family has been importing tea since the 17th century, and you have a choice of more than 475 varieties that you can also purchase at their store, in addition to chocolates, jellies, gingerbread, and tea-making instruments; but go early, the line gets long. There are also branches at 13 rue des Grands-Augustins, 6e (✆) **01-42-72-28-11;** Métro: St-Michel), and 260 rue du Faubourg–St-Honoré, 8e (✆) **01-40-51-82-50;** Métro: Tuileries).

30–32 rue de Bourg-Tibourg, 4e. (✆) **01-42-72-28-11.** Pot of tea 6€–9€ ($7.50–$11); lunch 13€–19€ ($16–$24); brunch 24€ ($30); afternoon tea 23€ ($29). AE, MC, V. Store daily 10:30am–7:30pm; tearoom daily noon–7pm. Métro: Hôtel-de-Ville.

THE LEFT BANK

A la Cour de Rohan   With the theme from *The Godfather* drifting through the window from an accordion down the cobblestone street, you'd think you were in Sicily. But the luscious banana chocolate pie is definitely not Italian! The chocolate pie is a big hit here, too. Order a pot of green tea and do some people-watching in this cluttered yet elegant salon.

59–61 rue St-André-des-Arts, 6e. (✆) **01-43-25-79-67.** Pot of tea 5.50€–8€ ($6.90–$10); lunch pastries 7€ ($8.75), evening pastries 9€ ($11); brunch menus 13€ ($16), 27€ ($34), and 30€ ($38); 2-course lunch menu 18€ ($23); weekend dinner menus 20€ ($25) and 30€ ($38). V. Sun–Thurs noon–7:30pm; Fri–Sat noon–11:30pm. Métro: Odéon or St-Michel.

Salon de Thé de la Mosqué de Paris *(Moments)*   After we've steamed in the Turkish baths and gotten an unparalleled massage in the mosque, we walk into the tea salon with its exotic and tantalizing *Arabian Nights* decor and enjoy mint tea served in beautifully etched glasses to complete an afternoon of self-indulgence. If you're hungry, there are plenty of yummy Turkish treats to try.

39 rue Geoffroy-St-Hilaire, 5e. (✆) **01-43-31-18-14.** Glass of tea 2.80€ ($3.50); pastries 3€ ($3.75). MC, V. Daily 10am–10pm. Métro: Monge.

Tea Caddy   With its beamed ceiling, comfortable atmosphere, and tables nestled close together, this tearoom is a cozy spot. It serves a variety of teas and coffees, scones, toast, and dishes like omelets and croque-monsieurs.

14 rue St-Julien-le-Pauvre, 5e. ℂ **01-43-54-15-56**. Pastries and light main courses 5€–11€ ($6.25–$14). AE, MC, V. Daily noon–7pm. Métro: St-Michel.

8 Wine Bars

Wine bars are great places to sample fine wines normally available only by the bottle. Most wine bars serve one or two *plats du jour* in traditional bistro style, but the best choices are usually pâtés, terrines, and cheeses. Although prices for these light meals are high, quality is usually first rate. Most wine bars are busiest at lunch and again in the late afternoon and early evening.

A la Cloche des Halles   A true Parisian relic, this is a great place to improve your Franglais and learn a little something about Parisian history from one of the regulars. Outside the restaurant you'll see the bell that tolled the opening and closing of the vast food market once in this neighborhood. On the interior are wooden tables and basic eats. Try the *terrine de campagne* or quiche, accompanied by a bottle of wine. It's convivial and fun but noisy and crowded. If you can't find a seat, you can usually stand at the bar and eat.

28 rue Coquillière, 1er. ℂ **01-42-36-93-89**. Wine from 3€ ($3.75) a glass; *plat du jour* 6€–11€ ($7.50–$14). No credit cards. Mon–Fri 8am–10pm; Sat 10am–5pm. Métro: Les Halles or Palais-Royal–Musée du Louvre.

Aux Négociants   A discerning crowd of regulars keeps this tiny wine bar near Montmartre humming. On the wall next to the bar hangs a photo of bushy-haired Robert Doisneau. The photographer was a regular here way back when. The pâtés and terrines are homemade and served with chewy *pain poilâne*.

27 rue Lambert, 18e. ℂ **01-46-06-15-11**. Wine from 2.90€ ($3.65) a glass; cheese or pâté with bread 5€ ($6.25). No credit cards. Mon–Fri noon–3pm; Tues–Thurs 6:30–10:30pm. Métro: Château-Rouge or Lamarck-Caulaincourt.

Bistro du Peintre   The zinc bar, wood paneling, and superb Belle Epoque style would make this wine bar a highlight even if the selection were not so reasonably priced. Bastille bohemian types—painters, actors, and night crawlers—gather nightly at the bar or tables on the large terrace.

116 av. Ledru-Rollin, 11e. ℂ **01-47-00-34-39**. Wine from 2.50€ ($3.15) a glass; light meals 5€–16€ ($6.25–$20). MC, V. Daily 7am–midnight. Métro: Ledru-Rollin.

Chai 33 🏴 *Kids*   Seriously out of the way (in Bercy), this hip wine bar is in the up-and-coming area that used to be the city's old wine district. It's worth a trek on warm days where you can sit outdoors on their terrace and sample one of many wines and champagnes by the glass. The food is good, although the 27€ ($34) Sunday brunch is overpriced. There's a kids' menu (11€/$14) and you'll find lots of French families here on weekends. Since cour St-Emilion is a pedestrian-only street, children can safely play as parents sip their wine.

33 cour St-Emilion, 12e. ℂ **01-53-44-01-01**. Wine from 5.50€ ($6.90) a glass; light meals 11€–21€ ($14–$26). AE, MC, V. Tues–Sun noon–midnight. Métro: Cour St-Emilion.

Clown Bar   Near the Cirque d'Hiver, the Clown Bar is decorated with a mélange of circus posters and circus-themed ceramic tiles. The wine list features an extensive selection of French offerings. The food is passable but not as original as the decor.

114 rue Amelot, 11e. ℂ **01-43-55-87-35**. Wine from 3€ ($3.75) a glass; *plat du jour* 14€ ($18). No credit cards. Mon–Sat noon–2:30pm and 7pm–1am. Métro: Filles du Calvaire.

La Tartine   About as smoky as a Parisian cafe can get, La Tartine, with its ancient wooden tables crammed next to each other and dimly lit low-hanging chandeliers, is a perfect place to drink some cheap wine and write your novel—or just people-watch. The crowd is eclectic, from working-class Parisians to beautiful visiting models. One caveat—if you're hungry, this is not the place for you; only sandwiches and other cold entrees are served.

24 rue de Rivoli, 4e. © 01-42-72-76-85. Wine from 2.50€ ($3.15) a half glass; light meals from 8.50€ ($11). No credit cards. Wed–Mon noon–10pm. Métro: St-Paul.

L'Ecluse Saint-Michel   Dim lighting illuminates the rust-colored walls and red velvet chairs, making this a perfect harbor from the Paris rain—or the Seine—when it gets rough. You can choose from 20 wines by the glass, and snack on such fare as carpaccio, salads, and soups. It's good for late-night dining.

15 quai des Grands-Augustins, 6e. © 01-46-33-58-74. Wine from 2.50€ ($3.15) a glass; light meals 7€–18€ ($8.75–$23). MC, V. Daily 11:30am–1:30am. Métro: St-Michel.

Le Griffonnier   Modern and well lit, Le Griffonnier offers a change from the folkloric decor of most wine bars. It's noted as much for its first-rate kitchen as for its wine cellar. You can sample bistro specialties such as *confit de canard maison,* or try a plate of charcuterie, terrines, and cheese, usually from the Auvergne region. Hot meals are served only at lunch and on Thursday evenings.

8 rue des Saussaies, 8e. © 01-42-65-17-17. Wine from 3€ ($3.75) a glass; *tartines* 5€ ($6.25); *plat du jour* 15€ ($19). AE, MC, V. Mon–Fri 7:30am–9 or 10pm. Métro: Champs-Elysées–Clemenceau.

Le Sancerre ✪   The food is exceptional at this rustic wine bar, across the street from Paris's most beautiful example of Art Nouveau architecture, designed by Jules Lavirotte in 1901. Try the quiche Sanceroise filled with bacon, cheese, and other heavenly ingredients, or one of the delicious omelets that come with a yummy side of fried potatoes. The ubiquitous andouillette, the sausage that is decidedly an acquired taste, is also on hand. The selection of Loire wines is very good—including, of course, its flagship: Sancerre.

22 av. Rapp, 7e. © 01-45-51-75-91. Wine from 3€ ($3.75) a glass; omelets and quiches from 9€ ($11). V. Mon–Fri 8am–10pm; Sat 8am–4pm. Métro: Alma-Marceau.

Mélac   Mélac is like a beacon in the night on this dismal street in the 11e. It's worth the trek if you crave a Parisian wine bar experience *extraordinaire.* With a few hundred types of wine from which to choose and some of the barrels lying around for proof, you'll love hanging out here with a friend to contemplate the meaning of life. If this makes you hungry, you can order a hot *plat du jour* or feast on a selection of first-rate pâtés, terrines, charcuterie, and cheeses all day. Personal touches abound from the owner, mustachioed Jacques Mélac, who loves his customers and . . . his name.

42 rue Léon Frot, 11e. © 01-43-70-59-27. Wine 4€–6€ ($5–$7.50) a glass; light meals 6€–14€ ($7.50–$18). V. Tues–Sat 9am–10:30pm; Mon 9am–2pm. Métro: Charonne.

Taverne Henri IV   An old wine bar with a lot of relics—and artists—smoking up a storm makes this a fun place to visit when you're strolling on the Pont Neuf. The food is nothing special but it's cheap; maybe settle for a coffee or a glass of wine, and soak in the old Paris bar atmosphere.

13 pl. du Pont Neuf, 1er. © 01-43-54-27-90. Wine from 3.50€ ($4.40) a glass; sandwiches 5€ ($6.25). No credit cards. Mon–Fri noon–10pm; Sat noon–4pm. Métro: Pont Neuf.

9 Patisseries & Boulangeries

It's easy to wake up early when the smells of freshly baked baguettes, croissants, *pain au chocolat*, and fruit tarts come wafting through your open window. With boulangeries on almost every street corner in Paris, just follow your nose when you want a delicious snack.

The boulangerie is an integral part of a Parisian's daily life. In the morning you'll see French businessmen in line next to laborers, both buying their morning croissants. In the afternoon stores fill with French girls and boys waiting to pick up their *famille's* dinner baguette. On Saturday you'll often find grandfathers and grandmothers purchasing tarts and cakes for the Sunday family dinner.

Perhaps the reason bread bears an almost religious significance for the French is because their history is so closely linked to it. Boulangeries have been around for a long time—since the 8th century when King Pépin "The Short" declared baking a trade. Originally, boulangeries served primarily *pain de compagne,* a round, crusty loaf made with basic ingredients (flour, yeast, and water), catering to the poor and working class. Baguettes were more expensive, so only the moneyed classes could afford them, and pastries were only available to the wealthy, who hired professional *patissiers* to make the goods in their homes.

But after the French Revolution (when Marie Antoinette ill advisedly said of the peasants, "Let them eat cake"), this all changed. Patissiers opened shops on Paris streets, and came into their own. Boulangeries still thrived because many workers could still not afford the baguettes and sugary baked goods of the patisseries. Today most boulangeries are patiseries as well, and affordable for all, a living work of art that you should put on your "must-see" list in Paris.

(Information from *Paris Boulangerie, Patisserie: Recipes from 13 Outstanding French Bakeries,* by Linda Dannenberg; Clarkson Potter, 1994.)

RIGHT BANK

Au Panetier   This boulangerie is known for its old-fashioned, rustic breads and rich pastries. Compare the Parisian baguette to the crispy country-style one, or sample the five-grain bread. The chocolate and coffee éclairs are famous.

10 pl. des Petits Pères, 2e. © 01-42-60-90-23. Mon–Fri 8am–7:15pm. Métro: Bourse.

Bonneau *(Finds)*   Just steps from the Roland Garros tennis stadium and the Bois de Boulogne, this boulangerie puts on its own show. As you stand at the counter, your mouth watering, television monitors broadcast the scene in the back kitchen. From the dizzying variety of breads, try the lard or olive *fougasse* (originally from the southeast of France), or bread baked with *levain* and *sel de guérande.* The Baron (chocolate mousse) is the house specialty.

75 rue d'Auteuil, 16e. © 01-46-51-12-25. Tues–Sun 6:30am–8:30pm. Métro: Michel-Ange Auteuil.

BoulangEpicier ✿   BoulangEpicier is the newest of Paris's upscale boulangeries. The collaborative effort of Alain Ducasse and master baker Eric Kayzer, the boulangerie allows customers to watch the bread-making process, as the oven is at the center of the store. The creations are inventive and unusual, including organic seaweed bread. Over 350 gourmet products are on sale as well, such as walnut oil from the Dordogne, eggplants marinated in olive oil from Naples, and yellow wine vinegar from the Jura region of France.

73 bd. de Courcelles, 8e. © 01-46-22-20-20. Mon–Sat 7:30am–8pm. Métro: Ternes or Courcelles.

Boulangerie des Martyrs   For nearly half a century, this boulangerie near place St-Georges has turned out some of the best *banettes* (miniature baguettes) in town. The Flute Paysanne is a rye specialty. The brioches, made with milk leavening, are divine.

10 rue des Martyrs, 9e. ✆ **01-48-78-20-17**. Wed–Mon 6:45am–8:30pm. Métro: Notre-Dame-de-Lorette.

Le Notre Paris Patissier ✿   The most glamorous of the city's patisseries is on avenue Victor Hugo, although several other branches are scattered throughout the city. You'll find the usual offerings of pastries, tarts, and sandwiches, plus a deli area where you can pick up gourmet dishes to go. Everything is beautifully presented and delicately prepared. Try the miniature croissants and miniature *pains au chocolat* (both 1€/$1.25), among other mini choices that are perfect for those who want to try just a bite of everything.

48 av. Victor Hugo, 16e. ✆ **01-45-02-21-21**. Tues–Sun 8am–8pm. Métro: Victor Hugo.

LEFT BANK

Au Délice de Sèvres   This boulangerie between Montparnasse and Les Invalides offers an array of homemade baguettes, from traditional Parisian to olive. Different varieties of the warm, crusty breads are made with nuts, grapes, or rye. The chocolate pastries alone, including the Samba (flaky layers of dough filled with dark and milk chocolate), are worth a trip from anywhere.

70 rue de Sèvres, 7e. ✆ **01-47-34-65-00**. Tues–Sun 6:30am–9pm. Métro: Vaneau.

Eric Kayzer ✿   You'll have to stand in line, but the bread is worth the wait at this grand boulangerie near boulevard St-Germain and the Latin Quarter. Try one of the special breads made with plums, figs, apricots, oranges, or walnuts and grapes. The country bread baked with *levain* and *sel de guérande* is excellent. If you prefer organic bread, go to the sister boulangerie (see below).

8 rue Monge, 5e. ✆ **01-44-07-17-81**. Wed–Mon 6:30am–8:30pm. Métro: Maubert-Mutualité.

Eric Kayzer Organic *(finds)*   Less crowded than the nearby boulangerie Eric Kayzer, this establishment produces some of Paris's best organic bread as well as the top croissant (according to a citywide survey). It also features delicate pastries and hot dishes, which you can eat on the premises or take out.

14 rue Monge, 5e. ✆ **01-44-07-17-81**. Tues–Sun 8am–8pm. Métro: Maubert-Mutualité.

Le Moulin de la Vierge ✿   This expansive boulangerie overwhelms you with the smells of warm, freshly baked bread. The Fougass bread, made with olives and anchovies, rivals the country bread with *levain* as customers' favorite. The store also stocks delicious jams, including apricot, blackberry, and pear.

166 av. de Suffren, 15e. ✆ **01-47-83-45-55**. Mon–Sat 7am–8pm. Métro: Sèvres-Lecourbe.

Poilâne ✿   This specialty boulangerie is the source of the eponymous bread found in Paris's better food shops and restaurants. In addition to the wonderfully chewy *pain poilâne,* they make delectable apple tarts with a *pure beurre* melt-in-your-mouth crust. How do Parisians of this chic quartier stay so thin?

8 rue du Cherche-Midi, 6e. ✆ **01-45-48-42-59**. Mon–Sat 7:15am–8:15pm. Métro: St-Sulpice or Sèvres Babylone.

Poujauran   Don't be intimidated by the long line. Not only is it a sign that locals love this place, but it moves quickly. This is a real treat in a neighborhood that tends to take advantage of tourists. To complement the scrumptious bread, they also sell fine wines (the two go together, don't they?). Also available is a special cornbread for foie gras.

20 rue Jean Nicot, 7e. ✆ **01-47-05-80-88**. Mon–Sat 8am–8:30pm. Métro: La Tour Maubourg.

7

Seeing the Sights

If you are overwhelmed by the number of must-see sights in the City of Light, take heart: Simply walking down Parisian streets may very well fulfill your deepest French fantasies. Peeking at pastries in shop windows, noticing the swirls of the Belle Epoque architecture, or watching children play in a public garden could be some of your more lasting memories.

It's hard to resist the temptation to try to cram every monument and museum into one visit, but if you do, you will end up exhausted, and may not even remember a lot of what you saw. Take your time. Most sights in Paris are hundreds of years old, and they aren't going anywhere soon. What you miss will just give you a good excuse to come back.

Of course you should see the Eiffel Tower. But you should also linger over a cup of coffee in a neighborhood cafe, or stroll the banks of the Seine at sunset. Make a list of sights you can't miss, and see them first. Then improvise. Keep in mind that the weather may do some planning

for you. Two thousand one was a particularly rainy year for a city not known for its blue skies, the summer heat in 2003 broke all records, and the spring of 2005 was exceptionally dry and sunny.

Take advantage of clear days for strolls, and save the rainy ones for visiting museums (*Note:* Most museums close on Mon or Tues, and admission is discounted 1 day of each week or free on the first Sun of every month.)

Enjoy the adventure of getting lost. In nearly every neighborhood you'll stumble across alleys and passages, small parks with elegant iron fences, winding old streets, and arresting architecture. Of course, you'll want to bring a map so you can get back to your hotel before your loved ones begin to think you've gone native.

So relax and enjoy. It's hard to do this city the wrong way. Just remember to wear good walking shoes, to stop and appreciate all the beauty, and to indulge your curiosity. And don't forget that umbrella.

1 Attractions by Type

MUSEUMS

Centre Georges Pompidou ✿✿, 4e (p. 184)

Cité de la Musique ✿, 19e (p. 206)

Cité des Sciences et de l'Industrie ✿, 19e (p. 207)

Espace Montmartre Salvador-Dalí, 18e (p. 196)

Explore Paris, 9e (p. 180)

Fondation Cartier pour l'Art Contemporain, 14e (p. 220)

Grévin, 9e (p. 181)

Jeu de Paume ✿, 1er (p. 176)

Le Memorial de la Shoah (Holocaust Memorial) ✿, 4e (p. 186)

Maison de Balzac ✿, 16e (p. 199)

Maison de l'Air, 20e (p. 207)

Maison de Victor Hugo ✿, 4e (p. 187)

Maison Européenne de la Photographie ✿, 4e (p. 187)

Musée Baccarat ✿✿, 16e (p. 200)

Top Paris Attractions

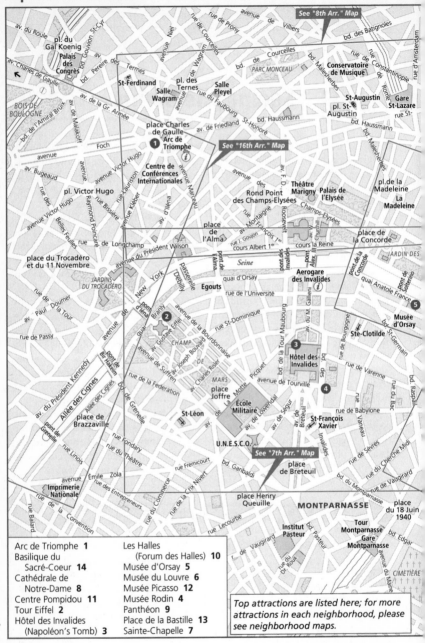

Arc de Triomphe **1**
Basilique du
  Sacré-Coeur **14**
Cathédrale de
  Notre-Dame **8**
Centre Pompidou **11**
Tour Eiffel **2**
Hôtel des Invalides
  (Napoléon's Tomb) **3**

Les Halles
  (Forum des Halles) **10**
Musée d'Orsay **5**
Musée du Louvre **6**
Musée Picasso **12**
Musée Rodin **4**
Panthéon **9**
Place de la Bastille **13**
Sainte-Chapelle **7**

Top attractions are listed here; for more attractions in each neighborhood, please see neighborhood maps.

MONTMARTRE

place Pigalle
bd. de Clichy
bd. de Rochechouart
rue de Dunkerque

Gare du Nord

St-Joseph

St-Georges

av. Trudaine

rue Condorcet

asino e Paris

Ste-Trinité

See "18th Arr." Map

St-Vincent de Paul

rue de Chabrol

Gare de l'Est

place du Colonel Fabien

PARC DES BUTTES-CHAUMONT

azare

Notre-Dame de Lorette

Folies Bergère

St-Laurent

bd. Haussmann

See "1st Arr." Map

Opéra Garnier

bd. des Italiens

bd. Montmartre

St-Joseph

place de l'Opéra

bd. des Capucines

rue du 4 Septembre

Bourse des Valeurs

rue de Bonne Nouvelle

bd. St-Martin

place de la République

See "3rd–4th Arr." Map

place Vendôme

rue St-Augustin

rue des Petits Champs

avenue de la République

St-Roch

Palais Royal

place A.-Malraux

Conservatoire des Arts et Métiers

rue de Turbigo

LE MARAIS

St-Ambroise

JILERIES

place du Carrousel

Musée du Louvre

Bourse du Commerce

rue de Rivoli

Forum des Halles

Archives Nationales

St-Denis

bd. Voltaire

quai des Tuileries

Théâtre du Châtelet

St-Merri

Hôtel de Ville

rue St-Antoine

place des Vosges

Théâtre de la Bastille

ole Nationale des Beaux-Arts

ST-GERMAIN-DES-PRÉS

Seine

St-Gervais

St-Paul

place de la Bastille

St-Germain

ILE DE LA CITÉ

Notre-Dame

ILE ST-LOUIS

St-Louis

Opéra Bastille

e du Four

rue de Vaugirard

Palais du Luxembourg

Sorbonne

bd. St-Germain

QUARTIER LATIN

Institut du Monde Arabe

avenue Daumesnil

JARDIN DU LUXEMBOURG

Panthéon

Université Paris VII

Gare de Lyon

Université Paris V

JARDIN DES PLANTES

Gare d'Austerlitz

U MONTPARNASSE

St-Médard

Université Paris III

Observatoire de Paris

See "5th–6th Arr." Map

bd. Arago

0 .28 Miles
0 .45 Kilometers

157

ARCHITECTURE, HISTORIC BUILDINGS & MONUMENTS

Paris's Top Free (or Almost) Attractions

- The **rooftops** of Paris, which can be seen from many vantage points, several for free, like La Samaritaine department store, the Institut du Monde Arabe, and Sacré-Coeur.

- The **neighborhood markets,** such as the Latin Quarter's **rue Mouffetard, rue de Buci** in St-Germain, **rue Lepic** in Montmartre, **rue Montorgueil** near the Bourse, and **rue Daguerre** in Montparnasse.

- The **bird** and **flower markets** on the Ile de la Cité and the **Marché aux Puces** at Porte de Clignancourt (Paris's largest flea market).

- The **churches** of Paris, which have been central to the life of the city. In addition to Notre-Dame and Sacré-Coeur, visit St-Eustache (in the heart of Les Halles), St-Séverin, St-Germain-des-Prés, St-Etienne du Mont, and St-Sulpice for its Delacroix paintings and magnificent organ.

- The **cemeteries** of Paris—especially the famous **Père-Lachaise.** The **Cimetière de Montmartre** and **Cimetière de Montparnasse** also contain the graves of famous writers, artists, and composers.

- **The Louvre on Sunday,** when admission is half price—or, if you're lucky, the first Sunday of the month, when it's free.

- The city's gorgeous gardens and parks. The most famous is the **Jardin des Tuileries.** The **Bois de Boulogne** is the largest, and the **Jardin du Luxembourg** the most beloved. The **Jardins des Plantes,** the oldest public garden in Paris, is a riot of color and variety.

- The **Seine** and its **bridges.** Take a day to stroll along the *quais* (riverbanks)—it's one of the world's most romantic walks.

- The **antiques stores** and **art galleries** that line rue de Beaune, rue Jacob, rue de Seine, rue Bonaparte, and streets in the St-Germain area.

- The **arcades** winding through the 2e and 9e arrondissements. These 19th-century iron-and-glass–covered passages are ideal for rainy-day shopping.

- The many and various **squares** of Paris: **Place de la Contrescarpe** in the Latin Quarter and the magnificent **place des Vosges** in the Marais are great places to sit and watch life pass by. **Square du Vert-Galant** on the Ile de la Cité is ideal for a picnic by the water.

CHURCHES

Basilique du Sacré-Coeur ✦✦ , 18e (p. 162)

Cathédrale de Notre-Dame ✦✦✦ , 4e (p. 162)

La Madeleine ✦, 8e (p. 192)

Sainte-Chapelle ✦✦✦ , 4e (p. 169)

St-Etienne du Mont ✦✦ , 5e (p. 213)

St-Eustache ✦ , 1er (p. 178)

St-Germain-des-Prés ✦✦ , 6e (p. 215)

St-Germain-l'Auxerrois ✦, 1er (p. 179)

St-Gervais–St-Protais, 4e (p. 190)

St-Merri, 4e (p. 191)

St-Paul–St-Louis ✦, 4e (p. 191)

St-Pierre de Montmartre ✦, 18e (p. 198)

St-Roch ✦, 1er (p. 180)

St-Séverin ✦, 5e (p. 213)

St-Sulpice ✦, 6e (p. 216)

PARKS & GARDENS

Bois de Boulogne ✦✦ , 16e (p. 199)

Bois de Vincennes ✦, 12e (p. 206)

Champ de Mars, 7e (p. 216)

Jardin d'Acclimatation ✦, 16e (p. 199)

Jardin des Plantes ✦, 5e (p. 209)

Jardin des Tuileries ✦✦✦ , 1er (p. 175)

Jardin du Luxembourg ✦✦✦ , 6e (p. 165)

Jardin du Palais-Royal, 1er (p. 178)

Jardin Shakespeare, 16e (p. 199)

Parc de Bagatelle ✦✦ , 16e (p. 199)

Parc de Bercy ✦, 12e (p. 208)

Parc des Buttes-Chaumont, 19e (p. 209)

Parc de la Villette ✦✦ , 19e (p. 208)

Parc Floral de Paris ✦, 12e (p. 206)

Parc Monceau ✦✦ , 8e (p. 195)

Parc Montsouris, 14e (p. 221)

Promenade Plantée, 12e (p. 206)

CEMETERIES

Catacombes, 14e (p. 219)

Cimetière de Montmartre ✦, 18e (p. 196)

Cimetière de Montparnasse, 14e (p. 220)

Cimetière du Père-Lachaise ✦✦✦ , 20e (p. 164)

2 The Top 10 Sights

The following sights are the most celebrated in Paris. The city is much more than the sum of its highlights, but these are the attractions that have entered our collective subconscious. No photograph, movie, or guidebook can prepare you for the majesty of Notre-Dame, the grand sweep of the Eiffel Tower, or the boundless treasures of the Louvre.

Arc de Triomphe ✦✦✦   The largest triumphal arch in the world was created by one of the greatest egos ever: Napoleon I. The emperor commissioned the Arc in honor of his Grande Armée and its 128 victorious battles, whose names are inscribed on its sides. Based on the smaller Arch of Titus in Rome, Architect Jean-François Chalgrin began construction in 1806, but the arch was far from finished by the time France's imperial army was swept from the field at the Battle of Waterloo in 1814; it was not completed until 1836. Although it has come to symbolize France and her greatness, it has also witnessed some defeats, as in 1871 and 1940, when German armies marched through the arch and down the Champs-Elysées.

In August 1944, General de Gaulle came here after the liberation of Paris; the black-and-white pictures taken then are powerful symbols of the end of fascism and war. Napoleon's funeral cortege passed below the arch in 1840, but Victor Hugo was the only person ever to lie in state beneath it. Crowds gathered here and up and down the Champs-Elysées after France won the World Cup in 1998, and again to celebrate the turning of the 21st century.

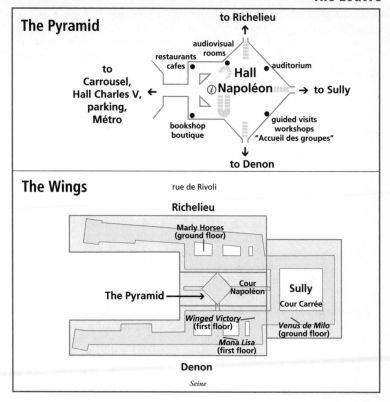

Beneath the arch, under a tricolor flag, burns the eternal flame for France's Unknown Soldier. It is lighted every evening at 6:30. The inscription reads: ICI REPOSE UN SOLDAT FRANÇAIS MORT POUR LA PATRIE, 1914–1918 ("Here rests a French soldier who died for his country"). Remembrance ceremonies are held on Armistice Day, November 11, and other national holidays.

Several outstanding 19th-century sculptures cover the arch. The most famous is Rude's *La Marseillaise,* on the bottom right on the Champs-Elysées side, representing volunteer soldiers' departure for the front in 1792.

To reach the stairs and elevators that climb the arch, do *not* try to cross the traffic circle—take the underpass near the Métro entrances. Twelve avenues radiate from place Charles-de-Gaulle, formerly place de l'Etoile, one of the busiest traffic hubs in Paris. Watch in amazement as cars careen around the arch yet somehow manage not to collide. From the top, 49m (161 ft.) up, you can see in a straight line the Champs-Elysées, the obelisk on place de la Concorde, and the Louvre. On the opposite side is the Grande Arche de la Défense, a modern cube-shaped structure so large that Notre-Dame could fit beneath it. You can also see the tree-lined avenue Foch, leading to the Bois de Boulogne.

Pl. Charles-de-Gaulle, 8e. ☎ **01-55-37-73-77.** Admission 7€ ($8.75) adults, 4.50€ ($5.65) ages 18–25, free for children under 18. Apr–Sept daily 10am–11pm; Oct–Mar daily 10am–10:30pm. Closed major holidays. Métro: Charles-de-Gaulle–Etoile.

Basilique du Sacré-Coeur ★★   The sensual yet exotic white dome of Sacré-Coeur is almost as familiar as the Arc de Triomphe and the Eiffel Tower; and it, too, is a romantic symbol of Paris. Made famous by Utrillo and other Montmartre artists, Sacré-Coeur is a vaguely Byzantine-Romanesque church built from 1876 to 1919. Construction began after France's defeat in the Franco-Prussian War; Catholics raised money to build this monument to the Sacred Heart of Jesus. Climb the 237 steps to climb to get up to the dome; the view is fabulous: almost 50km (30 miles) across the rooftops of Paris on a clear day. You can ease the ascent by taking the elevator up from the Métro and riding the *funiculaire* (which is a sort of tram drawn up and down the side of the hill by cables) to the church. For the staircase-phobic, the panorama from the front of the church is pretty spectacular if you don't mind fending off trinket vendors.

On the other side of Sacré-Coeur is place du Tertre; Vincent van Gogh lived off the place and used it as a scene for one of his paintings. Its charm is long gone and the square is swamped with tourists and quick-sketch artists in the spring and summer. Avoid the hoards and follow any of the small streets winding downhill from the rear of the church to find the quiet side of Montmartre and a glimpse of what Paris looked like before busy Baron Haussmann built his boulevards.

25 rue du Chevalier-de-la-Barre, 18e. © **01-53-41-89-00**. Admission to basilica free; to dome and crypt 5€ ($6.25) adults, 2.80€ ($3.50) students under 25. Basilica daily 6am–10:30pm; dome and crypt daily 10am–5:30pm (to 7pm June–Sept). Métro: Abbesses. Take elevator to surface and follow signs to *funiculaire,* which runs to the church (fare: 1 Métro ticket).

Cathédrale de Notre-Dame ★★★   A circular bronze plaque in front of the cathedral marks the spot, **Point Zéro,** from which all distances in France have been measured since 1768. In many ways, Notre-Dame *is* the center of France. Its Gothic loftiness dominates the Seine and the Ile de la Cité, as well as the history of Paris. Napoleon, wishing to emphasize the primacy of the state over the church, crowned himself emperor here, then crowned his wife Joséphine empress. When Paris was liberated during World War II, General de Gaulle rushed to the cathedral after his return, to pray in thanksgiving.

Construction of Notre-Dame started in 1163, but its grounds were sacred long before. Where the cathedral now stands, the Romans built a temple; a Christian basilica and then a Romanesque church succeeded it. As the population grew in the 1100s, Maurice de Sully, bishop of Paris, ordered a brilliant and still unknown architect to build a cathedral. The building was completed in the 14th century.

Parisians, like other urban dwellers in the Middle Ages, learned religious history by looking at the statuary and the stained-glass windows of their cathedral. Built in an age of illiteracy, the cathedral tells the stories of the Bible in its portals, paintings, and stained glass.

Notre-Dame was pillaged during the Revolution: Citizens mistook statues of saints for representations of kings and, in their fervor, took them down. (Some of the statues were found in the 1970s in the Latin Quarter and can be seen in the Musée de Cluny.)

Nearly 100 years later, architect Viollet-le-Duc began Notre-Dame's restoration. Writer Victor Hugo and artists such as Ingres called attention to the state of disrepair into which the cathedral had fallen, raising awareness of its value. Whereas 18th-century neoclassicists had virtually ignored the creations of the Middle Ages—and even replaced the stained glass at Notre-Dame with clear glass—19th-century romantics saw that remote period with new eyes and greater appreciation. Besides bringing new

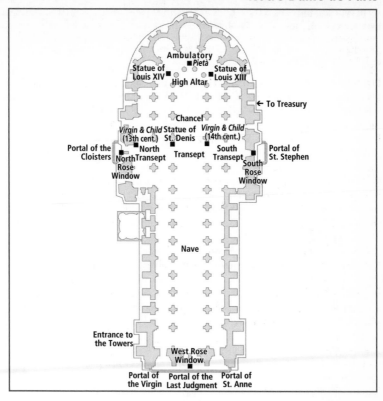

Ambulatory
Pietà
Statue of Louis XIV
Statue of Louis XIII
High Altar
← To Treasury
Chancel
Virgin & Child (13th cent.)
Statue of St. Denis
Virgin & Child (14th cent.)
Portal of the Cloisters
North Transept
Transept
South Transept
Portal of St. Stephen
North Rose Window
South Rose Window
Nave
Entrance to the Towers
West Rose Window
Portal of the Virgin
Portal of the Last Judgment
Portal of St. Anne

life to the rose windows and the statues, Viollet-le-Duc designed Notre-Dame's spire, a new feature. Also in the 19th century, Baron Haussmann (Napoleon III's urban planner) evicted the residents of the area. The houses were torn down to permit better views of the edifice. Colored paving stones on the parvis trace the outline of the old neighborhood and its main street, rue de Neuve Notre-Dame.

Today, the art of Notre-Dame continues to awe over 12 million yearly visitors. In fact, it's one of the top three most visited sights in all of France. The west front contains 28 statues representing the monarchs of Judea and Israel. The three portals depict, from left to right, the Coronation of the Virgin; the Last Judgment; and the Madonna and Child, surrounded by scenes of Mary's life. The impressive interior, with its slender, graceful columns, holds as many as 6,000 worshipers. The three rose windows—to the west, north, and south—are masterful, their colors a glory to behold on a sunny day.

For a look at the upper parts of the church, the river, and much of Paris, climb the 402 steps to the top of the south tower. (The cleaning of the facade continues through 2006, so expect some views to be obstructed until then.) Lightweights can climb to the first balcony, a mere 255 steps. Allow around 1½ hours, including a visit to the tower, but not including the lines.

6 pl. du Parvis Notre-Dame, Ile de la Cité, 4e. ⓒ **01-42-34-56-10**. Free admission to the cathedral; admission to the tower 6.10€ ($7.65) adults, 4.10€ ($5.15) students 18–25, free for kids under 18. Cathedral hours: Daily 7:45am–6:45pm. Treasury: Mon–Sat 9:30am–5:30pm. 6 Masses celebrated on Sun, 4 on weekdays, 1 on Sat. Tower hours: daily Oct 1–Mar 31 10am–4:45pm; Apr 1–Sept 30 9am–6:45pm. Free guided visits of the cathedral in English Wed–Thurs noon; Sat 2:30pm. Métro: Cité or St-Michel. RER: St-Michel.

Cimetière du Père-Lachaise 🟊🟊🟊

Tombstones and memorials might not seem like star-attraction fodder, but this cemetery truly is not to be missed. If you have any artistic or literary heroes, one of them is bound to be here. Chopin, Bizet, Proust, Balzac, Corot, Delacroix, Pissarro, Modigliani, Molière, Sarah Bernhardt, Isadora Duncan, Simone Signoret, Yves Montand, and, of course, Jim Morrison (whose gravesite gets its own guard to protect it from the fervor of his fans) are just some of the luminaries resting in this peaceful spot. Beyond hero worship, the cemetery offers an atmosphere belonging to a more tranquil, romantic era. Quiet alleyways wind through lush greenery and statues. The tombs are often topped with exquisite marble and stone figures, or tiny, phone booth–size chapels with mosaics and stained-glass windows. Flowers droop from urns and memorials, and Oscar Wilde's gravestone is covered with lipstick kisses.

Legends abound. The 18th-century bronze tomb of murdered journalist Victor Noir is reputed to give women fertility when rubbed (the polished sheen of certain parts of his statue is testament to its lore). The tragic love story of Abélard and Héloïse is lesser known these days, but in the 19th century their tombs were magnets for disappointed lovers. "Go when you will, you find somebody snuffling over that tomb," wrote Mark Twain in *The Innocents Abroad.* Also at Père-Lachaise are several moving memorials to the Holocaust.

Admission is free, but get a map because the winding cobblestone paths have a mazelike quality, and many graves are tricky to locate. A free map is available at the entrance, but you can buy one on the street outside for 2€ ($2.50) that is easier to read (or use the one on p. 171). Allow at least 2 hours to visit. The city offers a number of guided tours of Père-Lachaise, including one in English on Saturdays at 3pm from June to August (ⓒ **01-40-71-75-60**).

16 rue du Repos, 20e. ⓒ **01-55-25-82-10**. Free admission. Mar 16–Nov 5 Mon–Fri 8am–6pm, Sat 8:30am–6pm, Sun 9am–6pm; Nov 6–Mar 15 Mon–Fri 8am–5:30pm, Sat 8:30am–5:30pm, Sun 9am–5:30pm. Métro: Père-Lachaise.

Eiffel Tower (Tour Eiffel) 🟊🟊🟊

What is now the icon of all that is French created as much controversy in its time as Pei's pyramid at the Louvre did in the 1980s. Artists and writers such as Maupassant, Verlaine, and Huysmans (who called it a "hollow candlestick") thought it was an abomination. Charles Garnier, architect of the Opéra, was among several who signed a protest petition. But others found the tower a source of inspiration, as evidenced by its appearance in the paintings of Rousseau, Utrillo, Chagall, and Delaunay. Since then, its popularity has soared and now it is virtually impossible to think of Paris without imagining the Eiffel Tower's elegant silhouette.

Seven hundred entrants competed in the project to design a monument for the 1889 *Exposition Universelle* (World's Fair), and engineer Gustave Eiffel won. At first, many thought his 295m (968-ft.) tower couldn't be built, and in fact the job took more than 2 years. Upon completion, the Eiffel Tower was the tallest human-built structure in the world. The Prince of Wales (later Edward VII) and his family were the first visitors to ascend the tower, and it quickly became a magnet for publicity stunts. In 1923, for instance, Pierre Labric (who later became mayor of Montmartre) went down the tower's steps on his bicycle.

Politics have also played a role in its life. During the war, the Germans hung a sign on it that read DEUTSCHLAND SIEGT AUF ALLEN FRONTEN ("Germany is victorious on all fronts"). In 1958, a few months before Fidel Castro's rise to power, Cuban revolutionaries hung their red-and-black flag from the first level; and in 1979, an American from Greenpeace hung one that read SAVE THE SEALS. In 1989 an 89-minute show of music and fireworks celebrated the tower's centennial; in the 1990s, it counted down the days until the millennium.

Probably the best approach is to take the Métro to the Trocadéro station and walk from the Palais de Chaillot to the Seine. Besides fabulous views, especially when the Trocadéro fountains are in full force on summer evenings, you get a show from the dancers and acrobats who perform around the Palais de Chaillot.

The best view is, of course, from the top level, where historians have re-created the office of engineer Gustave Eiffel. On a clear day, you can see the entire city. The vast green esplanade beneath the tower is the Champs de Mars, which extends to the 18th-century Ecole Militaire (Military Academy) at its southeast end. This formal lawn was once a parade ground for French troops, and is now the site of special holiday *fêtes* and concerts.

Don't miss the tower at night, one of the great sights of Paris. The gold lighting highlights the lacy delicacy of the steelwork in a way that daylight doesn't. Skip the tour buses and pickpockets on Trocadéro and head to Ecole Militaire for a more tranquil view.

Champ de Mars, 7e. ⓒ 01-44-11-23-45. www.tour-eiffel.fr. Admission 4.10€ ($5.15) for elevator to 1st level (56m/184 ft.), 7.50€ ($9.40) to 2nd level (114m/374 ft.), 11€ ($14) to highest level (318m/1,043 ft.), 3.80€ ($4.75) for stairs to 1st and 2nd levels. Discounted admission for children under 12. Daily Sept to mid-June 9:30am–11pm; late June to Aug 9am–midnight. Fall and winter, stairs close at 6:30pm. Métro: Trocadéro, Bir-Hakeim, or Ecole-Militaire. RER: Champ-de-Mars.

Jardin du Luxembourg ⭐⭐⭐ (Kids)

The French love of order and harmony is expressed in these formal gardens, commissioned by Marie de Medici in the 17th century. Long gravel walks shaded by trees lead to a central pond and fountain. On the way, flowerbeds and statues create a calm, inviting space.

On the first warm day of the year, you'll see Parisians flocking to the park for serious bouts of reading, sunbathing, or people-watching. Sunday-afternoon band concerts draw a crowd in the summer, and the Medici Fountain is a cool, shady spot on a hot day. Children love the park, too, especially for the *parc à jeux* (playground), the toy sailboats in the central pond, and the *théâtre des marionettes* (puppet theater), where the ancient Guignol characters live on. Besides pools, fountains, and statues, there are tennis courts and spaces for playing boules. In the southwest corner is an orchard where several hundred species of apple and pear trees blossom each spring. A fenced-in area in the northwest corner houses beehives, and a beekeeping course is taught on weekends in the spring and summer.

The **Palais du Luxembourg,** at the northern edge of the park, was built for Marie de Medici, who was homesick for the Palace Pitti in Florence. Marie, who believed in the divine rights of royalty, engaged Rubens to do a series of paintings on her life—he finished under threat of execution—in which she appears as the best thing to happen to France since bread. (The paintings are now in the Louvre.) Upon the queen's banishment in 1630, the palace passed along to various royals until the Revolution, when it was used as a prison. The American writer Thomas Paine was incarcerated here in 1793 when he fell out of favor with Robespierre. He narrowly escaped execution. The palace is now the seat of the French Senate, but is not open to the public. The *orangerie* holds the **Musée de Luxembourg,** which presents temporary exhibits several times per year. 6e. ℂ **01-42-34-23-62.** Museum information ℂ 01-42-34-25-95. Garden daily 8am–dusk. Métro: Odéon. RER: Luxembourg.

Musée d'Orsay ✸✸✸ In 1986 a renovated train station and the best art of the 19th century were combined to create one of the world's great museums.

The Compagnie des Chemins de Fer d'Orléans constructed the fabulous iron-and-glass monument to the industrial age in 1900, but after only 39 years, it was virtually abandoned. Years later, Orson Welles's film of Kafka's *The Trial* captured its sorry state. In the 1970s, it was classified as a historical monument. Work began in 1983 to transform the station into a museum for 19th-century art.

For years, Paris's collections of 19th-century art had been distributed among the Louvre, the Musée d'Art Moderne, and the small Galerie Nationale du Jeu de Paume, with its Impressionist masterpieces. In 1986 the collections were transferred to the Orsay. Thousands of paintings, sculptures, objets d'art, items of furniture, architectural displays, even photographs and movies illustrate the diversity and richness of the century. They encompass Impressionism, realism, Postimpressionism, and Art Nouveau.

Exhibits cover three floors. On the ground floor you will find Ingres's *La Source,* Millet's *L'Angelus,* the Barbizon school, Manet's *Olympia,* and other works of early Impressionism. Impressionism continues on the top level, with Renoir's *Le Moulin de la Galette,* Manet's *Déjeuner sur l'Herbe,* Degas's *Racing at Longchamps,* Monet's *Cathedrals,* van Gogh's *Self-Portrait,* and Whistler's *Portrait of the Artist's Mother.* There are also works by Gauguin and the Pont-Aven school, Toulouse-Lautrec, Pissarro, Cézanne, and Seurat. Symbolism, naturalism, and Art Nouveau are represented on the middle level; the international Art Nouveau exhibit includes wonderful furniture and objets d'art as well as Koloman Moser's *Paradise,* an enticing design for stained glass.

If you need a break between exhibits, stop by the lovely cafe on the fifth floor for a freshly baked fruit tart and coffee.

Three to four hours should be sufficient to see a good chunk of the collection here.

62 rue de Lille and 1 rue Bellechasse, 7e. ℂ **01-40-49-48-48.** www.musee-orsay.fr. Admission 7.50€ ($9.40) adults, 5.50€ ($6.90) 18–24 and for all on Sun, free for children under 18. Tues–Wed and Fri–Sat 10am–6pm; Thurs 10am–9:45pm; Sun 9am–6pm. June 20–Sept 20 museum opens at 9am. Métro: Solférino. RER: Musée-d'Orsay.

Musée du Louvre ✸✸✸ You could visit the Louvre every day for a month and not see all its 35,000 treasures. To have an enjoyable, nonexhausting experience, you'll need to limit your focus or plan more than one trip.

The Louvre bookstore in the Carrousel de Louvre sells comprehensive guides and maps in English; brochures for "visitors in a hurry," and a guidebook, *The Louvre, First Visit* are good bets. You can also try the 90-minute tour of the most popular works (*Visite Découverte;* ℂ **01-40-20-52-09**), which will give you a quick orientation to the museum's layout. You can set your own pace with the "audiotour," which you can rent for 5.50€ ($6.90) at the entrance to any of the wings. It has an English-language option and is designed to last 4 hours.

If you choose to go it alone, focus on a particular department, collection, or wing. The departments are: Egyptian antiquities; Oriental antiquities; Greek, Etruscan, and Roman antiquities; sculptures; paintings; graphics and the graphic arts; and art objects, spread across three wings: Sully, Denon, and Richelieu.

First-timers usually head to the three most famous works: *Mona Lisa, Winged Victory of Samothrace,* and *Venus de Milo.* Finding your way is easy; signs mark the route, and the flow of other tourists carries you along. In the Denon wing, the *Winged Victory of Samothrace,* dating from the 2nd century B.C., is a masterpiece of Hellenic art. Before you climb the staircase topped by this magnificent sculpture, follow the sign that directs you to *Venus de Milo* (in the Sully wing), sculpted in the 1st century B.C. as the quintessence of feminine grace and sensuality. Don't miss the fragments from the 5th-century-B.C. Parthenon. Also in the Sully wing are the *Seated Scribe* and the crypt of Osiris, the 18th-century rococo paintings of Fragonard and Boucher, and Ingres's *Turkish Bath.*

En route from *Winged Victory* to *Mona Lisa,* you will pass David's *Coronation of Napoleon* opposite his *Portrait of Madame Récamier.* Stop and admire Ingres's *Grand Odalisque.* In 2005, Leonardo da Vinci's *La Gioconda (Mona Lisa)* returned to her usual digs, the Salle des Etats, after getting a makeover. (Don't worry, she remained on display while her home was renovated and was, as usual, the center of attention.) As shutterbugs crowd around the portrait, the famous Florentine gazes out at the throng. The secret of her tantalizing smile is a technique known as *sfumato,* which blends the borders of the subject into the background. The artist blurred the outlines of her features to make the corners of her mouth and eyes fade away, making her expression ever changeable and mysterious.

Da Vinci became so enamored of the painting that he carted it around with him on his travels. In 1516, François I invited the painter and his portrait to his château in the Loire valley; he eventually bought *Mona Lisa.* The painting was stolen from the Louvre in 1911 and finally discovered in Florence in 1913. Now, a guard and bullet-proof glass protect the lady from further such adventures.

Tips   Some Louvre Tips

Long lines outside the Louvre's pyramid entrance are notorious, but here are some tricks for avoiding them:

- Enter through the underground shopping mall Carrousel du Louvre.
- Enter through the staircases *(Porte des Lions)* next to the Arc du Carrousel.
- Enter directly from the Palais-Royal–Musée du Louvre Métro station.
- Buy a **Carte Musées et Monuments** (Museum and Monuments Pass), which allows direct entry through the priority entrance at the Passage Richelieu, 93 rue de Rivoli. The pass costs 18€ ($23) for 1 day, 36€ ($45) for 3 days, and 54€ ($68) for 5 days. The pass is also good for dozens of other museums in Paris.
- Order tickets via the Internet at www.louvre.fr, or by phone through FNAC (✆ **08-92-68-36-22,** toll number), and pick them up at any FNAC store (except FNAC photo shops). There is an added service charge of 1€ ($1.25). Or walk into the nearest FNAC and purchase tickets at the *billeterie.* You'll find a branch of FNAC at 71 bd. St-Germain, 5e (✆ **01-44-41-31-50;** Métro: Cluny). You can also buy tickets at Virgin Megastore, Bon Marché, Printemps, Galeries Lafayette, and BHV.

No such security paraphernalia mars enjoyment of other examples of Italian Renaissance art calmly hanging in the nearby *Salle des Sept Cheminées*. Here you will find da Vinci's *Virgin with the Infant Jesus and St. Anne* and *The Virgin of the Rocks*, as well as Titian's *Open Air Concert*, Raphael's *La Belle Jardinière*, and Veronese's massive *Marriage at Cana*. Other highlights of the Denon wing include Velasquez's infantas, Ribera's *Club Footed Boy*, Botticelli's frescoes, Michelangelo's *Slaves*, Canova's *Psyche Revived by the Kiss of Cupid*, and works by Murillo, El Greco, and Goya.

The inauguration of the Richelieu wing in 1993 opened several acres of new space, allowing display of some 12,000 works of art in 165 airy, well-lit rooms. Before heading into the galleries, look in at the adjoining cour Marly, the glass-roofed courtyard that houses Coustou's rearing *Marly Horses*. The *Code of Hammurabi* in the Babylonian collection, Rubens's Medici cycle, Rembrandt's self-portraits, Holbein's *Portrait of Erasmus*, and van Dyck's portrait of Charles I of England are among the works in the Richelieu wing. For a change of pace, see the apartments of Napoleon III (open mornings only), furnished in over-the-top Second Empire style.

In 1997, 9,941 sq. m (107,000 sq. ft.) of exhibition space devoted to Egyptian art and antiquities opened in the Sully and Denon wings. The display now totals 7,000 pieces, the largest exhibition of Egyptian antiquities outside Cairo.

In 2000 an exhibit featuring 120 pieces from the earliest civilizations in Africa, Asia, Oceania, and the Americas opened on the ground floor. It will be in the Louvre until mid-2006, when Musée de Quai Branly, to which it belongs, opens.

The building itself has evolved over the centuries. In 1190, King Philippe Auguste ordered construction of a castle and fortifications. The Louvre became a royal residence in 1528, when François I demolished the keep and began building a palace. Construction included the beginnings of the Louvre's Cour Carrée ("square courtyard," the easternmost courtyard), one of the highest achievements of French Renaissance architecture. In 1654, architect Claude Perrault built the Colonnade, a majestic facade that surrounds the outside of the Cour Carrée.

In the 17th century, Louis XIV moved the court to Versailles, and the Louvre's regal connection again faded. It wasn't until the French Revolution that the palace found its true calling, when the National Assembly called for the creation of a public museum in the Louvre. In 1793 the new museum's doors opened.

The museum and its collections have continued to grow. In 1983, President François Mitterrand placed architect I. M. Pei in charge of a renovation of the Louvre. Pei's glass pyramid, which now serves as the museum's entrance, was as controversial as the restoration, but Mitterrand persevered. Like other monuments that initially faced strong opposition, the pyramid, completed in 1989, has gradually won over most critics. Whether by day, when the pyramid gathers and reflects the sunlight, or by night, when floodlights make the courtyard sparkle, the monument has taken its place among the beauties of Paris.

Rue de Rivoli, 1er. 🕐 **01-40-20-51-51** for recorded message, 01-40-20-53-17 for information desk. www.louvre.fr. Admission 8.50€ ($11) adults, 6€ ($7.50) Wed and Fri 6–9:45pm; free 1st Sun of month and for children under 18. Mon 9am–6pm; Wed 9am–9:45pm; Thurs 9am–6pm; Fri 9am–9:45pm; Sat–Sun 9am–6pm. Métro: Palais-Royal–Musée du Louvre.

Musée National Auguste-Rodin ★★★
Auguste Rodin's legendary sensuality, which outraged 19th-century critics, is expressed in a collection that includes his greatest works.

The Kiss immortalizes in a sensuous curve of white marble the passion of doomed 13th-century lovers Paolo Malatesta and Francesca da Rimini. In the courtyard,

> **Tips   Great Spots for Getting That Panoramic Shot**
>
> The roofscape of Paris is every photo-jockey's dream shot. You'll have to pay entrance fees for most places listed, but the price is small and the memory, and your photos, will last a lifetime. The highest lookout spot is the 318m (1,043-ft.) platform on the **Eiffel Tower.** The second-highest perch is the outdoor terrace on the 56th floor of the **Tour Montparnasse.** The **Grande Arche de la Défense** affords a magnificent view of the triumphal way designed by Le Nôtre in the 17th century, with its series of landmarks—the Arc de Triomphe, place de la Concorde, the Tuileries, and the cour Napoleon at the Louvre. Great views can also be had from **Sacré-Coeur** and the **Arc de Triomphe,** and don't forget the **tower of Notre-Dame.** Other less obvious spots include two department stores: **La Samaritaine** (usually free but temporarily closed for emergency renovations; see chapter 9 for details), which provides exceptional views of the Conciergerie, Notre-Dame, the Pont Neuf, and the Institut de France; and **Le Printemps** (free), which looks out over the Opéra and La Madeleine. There's a good view of the islands from the **Institut du Monde Arabe.** Breathtaking views can also be had from the *funiculaire,* run by Paris's urban transit system, that travels up the side of the Montmartre Butte in the 18e, and from the top of the **Centre Pompidou** (free).

Burghers of Calais is a commemoration of the siege of Calais in 1347, after which Edward III of England kept the town's six richest burghers as servants. Also in the courtyard is *The Thinker.* The *Gates of Hell* is a portrayal of Dante's *Inferno.* Intended for the Musée des Arts Décoratifs, the massive bronze doors were not completed until 7 years after the artist's death.

Studies done by Rodin before he executed his sculptures take up some of the 16 rooms. Particularly interesting is the evolution of his controversial nude of Balzac, which was his last major work. Don't miss the portrait heads of his many female friends, as well as the work of his mistress, Camille Claudel.

The museum is in the 18th-century Hôtel Biron, which was a convent before it became a residence for artists and writers. Matisse, Jean Cocteau, and the poet Rainer Maria Rilke lived and worked in the mansion before Rodin moved there in 1908. The government bought the studio in 1911 and, after his death (in 1917), transformed it into a museum devoted to France's greatest sculptor. The garden surrounding the museum is almost as big a draw as the sculptures themselves; be sure to budget time for a leisurely stroll and give yourself at least 2 hours in all.

Hôtel Biron, 77 rue de Varenne, 7e. ℂ **01-44-18-61-10.** www.musee-rodin.fr. Admission 5€ ($6.25) adults, 3€ ($3.75) 18–24 and for all on Sun, free for children under 18, 1€ ($1.25) for garden only. Apr–Sept Tues–Sun 9:30am–5:45pm; Oct–Mar Tues–Sun 9:30am–4:45pm. Garden closes at 6:45pm in summer, last admission at 5:15. Métro: Varenne.

Sainte-Chapelle ⭐⭐⭐   Sainte-Chapelle is an explosion of color. As you enter the lower chapel, you will be surrounded by arches and columns painted in golds, reds, and blues, covered by a starry sky painted on the ceiling. But the real treat awaits when you climb the short, narrow staircase to the upper chapel. The sunlight streaming through its brilliantly hued stained-glass windows is an unforgettable sight, and you are surrounded by the reds and blues of the glass, as if you had just walked inside a magnificent piece of jewelry.

St. Louis IX (both king and saint) had the "Holy Chapel" built to house the relics of the crucifixion, including the Crown of Thorns (now in Notre-Dame). The king bought them from the emperor of Constantinople for an astronomical sum—more than twice the cost of the construction of the Sainte-Chapelle itself.

Built with unusual speed between 1246 and 1248, Sainte-Chapelle was a notable feat. Supporting the roof with pillars and buttresses allowed the architect, Pierre de Montreuil, to brighten the interior with fifteen 15m-high (50-ft.) windows. Old and New Testament scenes are illustrated over 612 sq. m (6,588 sq. ft.) of stained glass, to be read from bottom to top and from left to right. The 1,134 scenes trace the biblical story from the Garden of Eden to the Apocalypse.

The 17th and 18th centuries were not kind to Sainte-Chapelle; a fire in 1630 did extensive damage, as did the anticlerical fervor of the French Revolution. Fortunately, plans to raze it were shelved, and renewed interest in the medieval era during the 19th century led to a restoration. Two-thirds of the stained glass is original; the rest is reconstructed. Allow 1 hour to take in this masterpiece.

4 bd. du Palais, Palais de Justice, Ile de la Cité, 4e. ℂ **01-53-73-78-50.** www.monum.fr. Admission 6.10€ ($7.65) adults, 4.10€ ($5.15) 18–25, free for children under 18. Combined Sainte-Chapelle and Conciergerie ticket 9€ ($11). Daily 9am–6pm Apr–Sept; 9:30am–4:30pm Oct–Mar. Closed holidays. Métro: Cité or St-Michel. RER: St-Michel.

3 Ile de la Cité & Ile St-Louis

ILE DE LA CITE 𝒦𝒦

Little is known about the Parisii, the Celtic tribe of fishermen who built their huts on the Ile de la Cité around 250 B.C. Living on an island allowed the tribe to fish in peace—at least until the Romans came along in 52 B.C. and conquered them, naming the island Lutecia. After barbarians destroyed much of Lutecia in A.D. 280, the Romans rebuilt it and called it Paris in honor of its original inhabitants.

In the mid–5th century, the city's survival, always dramatically secured, was attributed to a young girl from Nanterre named Geneviève. As Attila the Hun stormed toward Paris with 700,000 troops, she calmed the terror-stricken Parisians with a promise that divine intervention would protect them. Sure enough, as he approached the little island, Attila mysteriously turned and headed south. Geneviève became the city's patron saint. In the 6th century, Paris began to thrive under the rule of King Clovis. By the 9th century, the city-island was strong enough to withstand an assault and siege by the Normans.

The Merovingian kings and later the Capetians felt secure within the arms of the Seine. They made the island their royal residence and administrative headquarters. The Ile de la Cité blossomed in the 13th century as **Notre-Dame** arose, closely followed by **Sainte-Chapelle** and the royal palace of the **Conciergerie** (see below). At the end of the 14th century, the royal residence moved to the Right Bank, but the island remained a judicial and administrative center. While tourists admire the splendid Gothic art of Notre-Dame and Sainte-Chapelle, Parisians are likely to be found either in the law courts of the Palais de Justice or tangling with French bureaucracy in the Prefecture.

When you are done gasping at the monuments, wander the narrow streets and imagine the days when the entire city was on this bit of land. These days, a large chunk

Pére-Lachaise Cemetery

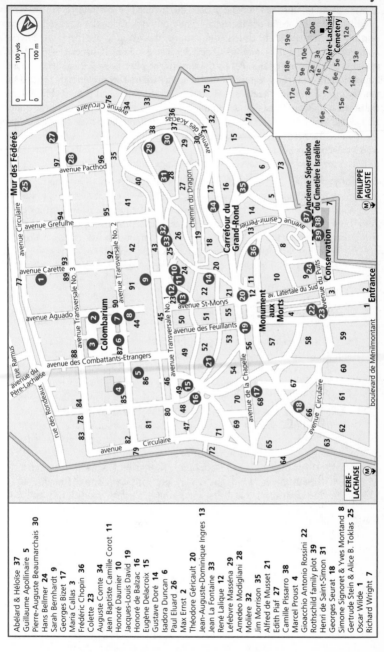

Abélard & Héloïse **37**
Guillaume Apollinaire **5**
Pierre-Auguste Beaumarchais **30**
Hans Bellmer **24**
Sarah Bernhardt **9**
Georges Bizet **17**
Maria Callas **3**
Frédéric Chopin **36**
Colette **23**
Auguste Comte **34**
Jean Baptiste Camille Corot **11**
Honoré Daumier **10**
Jacques-Louis David **19**
Honoré de Balzac **16**
Eugène Delacroix **15**
Gustave Doré **14**
Isadora Duncan **6**
Paul Eluard **26**
Max Ernst **2**
Théodore Géricault **20**
Jean-Auguste-Dominique Ingres **13**
Jean La Fontaine **33**
René Lalique **12**
Lefebvre Masséna **29**
Amedeo Modigliani **28**
Molière **32**
Jim Morrison **35**
Alfred de Musset **21**
Edith Piaf **27**
Camille Pissarro **38**
Marcel Proust **4**
Gioacchino Antonio Rossini **22**
Rothschild family plot **39**
Henri de Saint-Simon **31**
Georges Seurat **18**
Simone Signoret & Yves Montand **8**
Gertrude Stein & Alice B. Toklas **25**
Oscar Wilde **1**
Richard Wright **7**

171

of the island is taken up by the **Palais de Justice,** or law courts, which Balzac described as a "cathedral of chicanery." The building's style is neoclassical, the proportions monumental. The courts admit visitors daily 9am to 6pm; you can enter the building free. The main entrance is next to that for Sainte-Chapelle, which is surrounded by this grand edifice. Across the street is the place Louis-Lépine, where there is a **flower market** every day except Sunday, when a **bird market** occupies the space. Once you've stopped to smell the roses, walk toward Notre-Dame and pass the **Hôtel-Dieu,** the oldest hospital in Paris, founded in the 7th century. The inner courtyard was remodeled in the 19th century and is a quiet place to relax. Behind the cathedral on the tip of the island is **Le Memorial de la Déportation,** which commemorates the French Jews who were sent to concentration camps during World War II. The sculpture is by Desserprit. The memorial can be visited daily from 10am to noon and 2 to 7pm.

Conciergerie 🀫🀫   If you know anything about the French Revolution, you will want to see this infamous edifice. Built in the Middle Ages as a royal palace, it was used as an administrative office of the Crown; torture was frequent at its western tower, the Tour Bonbec. Ravaillac, Henri IV's murderer, was a prisoner here before an angry crowd tore him apart. But the Conciergerie is most famous for its days as a prison during "the Terror" of the French Revolution, when 4,164 "enemies of the people" passed through. More than half headed for the guillotine on place de la Révolution (now pl.

Finds **Pretty Place Dauphine**

This peaceful, triangular park is one of Paris's best-kept secrets. Laid out by Henri IV in 1607 in honor of the Dauphin (the future Louis XIII), place Dauphine was built on what was the site of three converging islands that originally surrounded the Ile de la Cité but disappeared under successive landfills. As one of the most prominent royal squares, place Dauphine was second in importance only to place Royale, now known as place des Vosges. Built in the fashionable design of brick and stone, the square was closed at one end (where the Palais de Justice now stands) and structured in arcades to provide secrecy for the clusters of negotiating bankers.

In the 19th century, place Dauphine suffered under the reconstructive efforts of Haussmann, as did much of ancient Paris. Only one of the original facades remains, at no. 14. Today, intimate restaurants, art galleries, and a small hotel (appropriately named Henri IV) flourish in the place. The strong community influence is palpable among its inhabitants, who maintain the beauty of the 18th-century buildings with intense loyalty.

Residents, including several "discreet" movie stars, refer to themselves as "islanders" and call traipsing across the river a trip to the "Continent." The Palais de Justice has made the place a favorite reprieve for attorneys, judges, and police officers. On sunny days, workers from the Monnaie de Paris come to the square to play a lively game of *pétanque* (boules).

Long an inspiration for artists and writers, place Dauphine is particularly stirring when the sun sets; the shadows suggest calm and reverie as benches fill with lovers and poets touched by the history of the square.

de la Concorde). Besides revolutionary ringleaders Danton and Robespierre, Charlotte Corday and the poet André Chenier were imprisoned here. Marie Antoinette awaited her fate in a tiny, fetid cell. When she was taken to her execution, the queen was forced to ride backward in the cart so she would have to face a jeering, taunting crowd.

Marie Antoinette's cell is now a chapel, and the dank cells have been transformed with exhibits and mementos designed to convey a sense of prison life in a brutal era. The Gothic halls built by Philip the Fair in the 14th century are impressive examples of medieval secular architecture. Allow 1½ hours.

Palais de Justice, Ile de la Cité, 1er. ℂ 01-53-73-78-50. Admission 6.10€ ($7.65) adults, 4.10€ ($5.15) 18–25, free for children under 18. Combined Sainte-Chapelle and Conciergerie ticket 9€ ($11). Apr–Sept daily 9:30am–6:30pm; Oct–Mar daily 10am–5pm. Métro: Cité, Châtelet–Les Halles, or St-Michel. RER: St-Michel.

La Crypte Archéologique   In 1965 excavations for a parking lot under the parvis revealed Gallo-Roman ramparts, 3rd-century rooms heated by an underground furnace system called a hypocaust, and cellars of medieval houses. The excavations were turned into this museum. When you go down to the crypt, you'll be at the island's original level. Over the centuries, builders erected new structures over the ruins of previous settlements, raising the Ile de la Cité about 6.9m (23 ft.). To help you visualize the buildings that stood here, there are scale models showing how Paris grew from a small settlement to a Roman city, and photographs of the pre-Haussmann parvis. History buffs will take at least 45 minutes to look through the exhibit, others can allow a half hour.

Pl. du Parvis Notre-Dame, 4e. ℂ 01-55-42-50-10. Admission 3.30€ ($4.15) adults 27–60; 1.60€ ($2) for those 14–27; over 60 $2.20 ($2.75); free for children under 14. Tues–Sun 10am–5:30pm. Métro: Cité.

PONT NEUF ✪✪

At the exit from place Dauphine at the western tip of the Ile de la Cité, a statue of Henri IV on horseback marks the middle of the Pont Neuf. Ironically, the "new bridge" is the oldest bridge in Paris. Henri III laid the first stone in 1578. The Pont Neuf had two unique features for its time: It was not flanked with houses and shops, and it was paved. Though the structure of the bridge has barely changed, it has recently been cleaned, and the alabaster-white stone has regained its luminous beauty.

At the Hôtel Carnavalet, a museum in the Marais (p. 183), is a painting called *Spectacle of Buffons,* showing what the bridge was like between 1665 and 1669. Duels were fought on the structure, great coaches belonging to the nobility crossed it, and peddlers sold their wares. With all those crowds, it attracted entertainers, such as Tabarin, who sought a few coins from the gawkers. The Pont Neuf is decorated with corbels, a mélange of grotesquerie and fantasy.

While the view of the Louvre and Institut de France from the bridge is superb, to see the Pont Neuf itself, walk along the Passerelle des Arts, the parallel pedestrian bridge. From there, away from the clutter, noise, and exhaust of vehicular traffic, enjoy an unobstructed view of the most exquisite bridge in Paris, as well as the lovely park tucked in its underbelly, the Square du Vert-Galant.

SQUARE DU VERT-GALANT

Beloved King Henri IV deserved, at least, the designation of a park to mark his legacy. The park lies at the base of the stairs that descend from the middle of Pont Neuf, behind the statue of the king; the garden is as close to the river as you can get without actually being in it. The square is at the level of the Ile de la Cité during the Gallo-Roman period, about 6.9m (23 ft.) lower than it is now.

Fun Fact **Bridge over the River Seine**

The city of Paris recently implemented a program to illuminate all bridges across the Seine, making an after-dark stroll along the river particularly lovely. In addition to the Pont Neuf, there is the Pont Royal (1685–89), where Parisians celebrated festivities for centuries; the Passerelle des Arts, also called Pont des Arts (1804), a footbridge that crosses from the Institut on the Left Bank to the Louvre on the Right Bank; the Pont Mirabeau (1895–97), adorned by four bronze statues and immortalized by Apollinaire; and the Pont Alexander III (1896–1900). The new Passerelle Solférino pedestrian bridge linking the Musée d'Orsay with the Tuileries Garden has reopened after a false start in 1999; its original metallic surface was exceedingly slippery when wet.

Vert Galant, or the "Old Spark," was a fond nickname for Henri IV. The king, known for his gentle manners, was married twice: first to Marguerite de Valois, known as the Reine Margot, then to Marie de Medici. As his sobriquet suggests, the king was also famous for the mistresses he kept in his court. Perhaps it's due to his memory that the square has become a favorite rendezvous for lovers. The view on both banks, from the gargoyles of the Pont Neuf to the majestic Louvre, is breathtaking. The greenery, flowerbeds, and benches make this a great picnic spot (you can pick up drinks and snacks next to the park at the embarkation point for the tourist boats). Still, the best time to enjoy one of Paris's most romantic spots is at dusk, when a symphony of lights illuminates the city.

THE OTHER ISLAND IN THE SEINE: ILE ST-LOUIS ✹✹✹

As you walk across the little iron footbridge from the rear of Notre-Dame toward the Ile St-Louis, you'll enter a world of tree-shaded quays, restaurants, antiques shops, and stately town houses with courtyards. In contrast to its sister island, the Ile de la Cité—the site of Lutèce, the first settlement in Paris—Ile St-Louis is a relatively recent creation. The result of a contract between Louis XIII and the architect Christophe Marie in 1614, the island was developed when Marie was given 10 years to build mansions for the bourgeoisie. The land was then two islands known as l'Ile Nôtre Dame and the Prés aux Vaches—the cow meadow. Construction, which began with the creation of a bridge to link the two islets, was completed half a century later. The unity of the classical architecture gives the island the image of a cozy, aristocratic village, with a steep church spire emerging from the heart of it all. The illustrious quarter drew its name from the sumptuous feast King St-Louis threw on the very same pasturelands in 1267 in celebration of his entry into the Crusades.

Because of its ideal location, relative privacy, and luxurious estates, rich and famous Parisians have always clamored for an address on the island. Plaques on the facades of houses identify the former residences of various celebrities, including Marie Curie (36 quai de Béthune, near Pont de la Tournelle). Voltaire and his mistress lived in the **Hôtel Lambert,** 2 quai d'Anjou, where they engaged in legendary quarrels. The mansion, which also housed the Polish royal family for over a century, is now home to the Rothschilds, one of the wealthiest families in France. Down along the corner of quai d'Orléans and rue Budé, James Jones, the American author of *From Here to Eternity,* owned an apartment in the 1960s and '70s, where he completed the novel *The Thin Red Line.*

Farther along, at 9 quai d'Anjou, stands the house where painter, sculptor, and lithographer Honoré Daumier lived between 1846 and 1863. Here he produced hundreds of lithographs satirizing the bourgeoisie and attacking government corruption. His caricature of Louis-Philippe landed him in jail for 6 months.

Today, Ile St-Louis is one of the most expensive quarters in Paris. A stop at Berthillon, the famous ice-cream and sherbet shop, and the Brasserie Ile St-Louis makes the visit complete. The view of the back of Notre-Dame from the island's entrance is lovely.

4 1er Arrondissement: The Louvre, Tuileries & Les Halles

In 1527, François I announced that the Louvre would be his palace on the Seine, and the neighborhood hasn't been the same since. He began embellishments that continued during the reigns of a succession of kings, and endowed the whole quarter with a lasting aura of prestige. The classical refinement of the **Louvre** (see "The Top 10 Sights," above) is echoed in the **Jardin des Tuileries** (which once adjoined a palace), Cardinal Richelieu's stately **Palais-Royal,** the **place Vendôme,** and the long stretch of arcades making up rue de Rivoli. Even the repertoire of the **Comédie-Française** is classical: Corneille, Molière, and Racine.

Shopping runs the gamut from Cartier on place Vendôme to Eiffel Tower key rings along rue de Rivoli, with the underground shopping mall of Les Halles focusing on the middle range. Although the shopping center is creepy and unsafe at night, the streets around Les Halles often go strong long after the rest of Paris is asleep. Connected to Les Halles by a Métro station is **Châtelet,** the city's geographic center and a hub for its lively theater, music, and jazz scene. An underground network of passages, moving walks, stairs, escalators, and open spaces connect the Les Halles and Châtelet Métro stops to make one giant station referred to as Châtelet–Les Halles.

Simpler pleasures of this neighborhood include a stroll along the quai de la Mégisserie, where the daily pet **market** used to spill out onto the sidewalks. Today, due to hygiene laws, the birds, squirrels, cats, and dogs are mostly in shops, but it's still fun to browse. The **Passerelle des Arts** (1804), a footbridge, is perhaps the most romantic bridge in Paris; a stroll at sunset is not to be missed. If the rain chases you indoors, check out **Galerie Véro-Dodat,** a covered arcade built in 1826, between rue Bouloi and rue Jean-Jacques-Rousseau, where you'll find an antique-doll repair shop, galleries, and a cafe.

Jardin des Tuileries ✦✦✦ *(Moments)*   A study in geometric elegance, this classical French garden is the city's most visited park. Tourists and Parisians come here for the fountains, the flowers, and the pathways, laid out in precise lines. On sunny days, the green metal chairs around the main fountain are filled with travelers, students, and businesspeople enjoying a peaceful moment. The benches in various corners of the park make great picnic spots for the après-museum crowd.

The name derives from *tuiles* (tiles)—the clay earth found here that was once used to make roof tiles. The gardens were laid out in the 1560s to complement Catherine de Medici's Tuileries Palace, which burned down in the 19th century. In 1664, Le Nôtre, creator of French landscaping, redesigned a large section of the garden in the classical style, adding octagonal pools surrounded by statues and terraces. The garden took some hits during World War II, but was restored. In 1990 the Tuileries got a major overhaul and today it is as stunning as ever. The **Jeu de Paume** (see below) is at the garden's western edge, and its eastern border opens on to the courtyard and pyramid of the **Louvre.**

Those naked ladies hiding in the bushes near the Arc du Carrousel are a collection of bronzes by Aristide Maillol. An impressive array of sculpture, both classical and modern, is scattered throughout the gardens, including works by Jean Dubuffet, Alberto Giacometti, David Smith, Max Ernst, Henry Moore, and Henri Laurens. Depending on your mood, you could spend a good couple of hours here.

Quai des Tuileries, 1er. ℂ **01-40-20-90-43.** Daily Apr–Sept 7am–9pm; Oct–Mar 7:30am–7:30pm, closing call 30 min. before. Métro: Tuileries or Concorde.

Jeu de Paume ✪ The Jeu de Paume was built in 1861 during the reign of Napoleon III as a place to play *jeu de paume,* a forerunner of tennis. During World War II, the Nazis used it as a warehouse for artworks they considered "degenerate." In 1947 the building was turned into a showcase for Impressionist art, and became the world center for Impressionism until the collection was transferred to the Musée d'Orsay in 1986. Following a $12.6-million face-lift, the building was transformed into a state-of-the-art exhibition space with huge spaces and a video-screening room and is now home of the National Center for Photography. It is devoted to visiting exhibits of photography from around the world.

1 pl. de la Concorde, 1er. ℂ **01-47-03-12-50.** www.jeudepaume.org. Admission $6€ ($7.50). Tues noon–9:30pm; Wed–Fri noon–7pm; Sat–Sun 10am–7pm. Métro: Concorde.

Musée de la Mode et Textile ✪ In the same building as the Musée des Arts Décoratifs, this new museum is devoted to the history of fashion. Only a portion of the 16,000 costumes and 35,000 accessories in the collection make up the changing thematic exhibitions. The restored clothing on display ranges from the 18th century to the Belle Epoque (the minuscule waistlines are the size of your wrist) to France's finest couturiers—Chanel, Dior, Schiaparelli, Lanvin, Balenciaga, Gaultier, and Lacroix. It's a must for couture aficionados, who will linger over the displays. The rest of us can get through in under an hour.

107 rue de Rivoli, 1st and 2nd floors, 1er. ℂ **01-44-55-57-50.** www.ucad.fr. Admission 6€ ($7.50) adults, 4.50€ ($5.65) ages 18–25, free under 18. Admission includes entry to the Musée des Arts Décoratifs and Musée de la Publicité. Tues–Fri 11am–6pm; Sat–Sun 10am–6pm. Métro: Palais-Royal–Musée du Louvre or Tuileries.

Musée de la Publicité Opened in November 1999, this high-tech museum brags that it is the only advertising museum in the world. Its temporary exhibits run for about 2 months. The museum relies on video displays, industrial lighting, and techno music to highlight advertising history and the techniques of selling products such as Louis Vuitton bags, Chanel perfume, and Citroen cars. As you enter, sit at one of the computers and browse through ads, posters, and promotional campaigns for just about any product you can think of. The museum also has a media library. Allow 45 minutes.

107 rue de Rivoli, 3rd floor, 1er. ℂ **01-44-55-57-50.** www.ucad.fr. Admission 6€ ($7.50) adults, 4.50€ ($5.65) 18–25, free under 18. Admission includes entry to the Musée des Arts Décoratifs and Musée de la Mode et Textile. Tues–Fri 11am–6pm; Sat–Sun 10am–6pm. Métro: Palais-Royal–Musée du Louvre or Tuileries.

Musée des Arts Décoratifs ✪✪ Though it is housed in one of the long arms of the Louvre, the revamped Musée des Arts Décoratifs is a separate entity. The museum, which has a stunning collection of more than 200,000 art objects, is still undergoing renovation. Although salons from the 17th to the 20th centuries won't open until May 2006, the exhibits from the Middle Ages to the Renaissance are absolute marvels. Stunning examples of glassware, frescos, carved wood panels, armoires, tapestries, choir stalls, triptychs, and polyptychs fill the halls. Amidst such impressive displays,

Attractions in the 1er

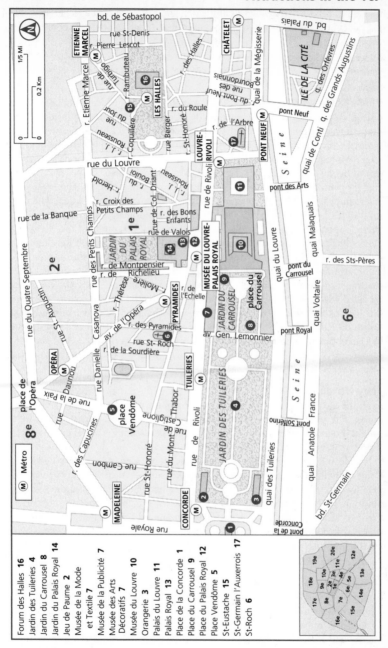

Forum des Halles **16**
Jardin des Tuileries **4**
Jardin du Carrousel **8**
Jardin du Palais Royal **14**
Jeu de Paume **7**
Musée de la Mode
et Textile **7**
Musée de la Publicité **7**
Musée des Arts
Décoratifs **7**
Musée du Louvre **10**
Orangerie **3**
Palais du Louvre **11**
Palais Royal **13**
Place de la Concorde **1**
Place du Carrousel **9**
Place du Palais Royal **12**
Place Vendôme **5**
St-Eustache **15**
St-Germain l'Auxerrois **17**
St-Roch **6**

it's hard to believe that nearly half of the museum has yet to open. The limited size of the present display is a boon for time-pressed tourists; allow around 1 hour to take in these treasures.

107 rue de Rivoli, 3rd floor, 1er. (✆ **01-44-55-57-50.** www.ucad.fr. Admission 6€ ($7.50) adults, 4.50€ ($5.65) 18–25, free for under 18. Admission includes entry to the Musée de la Mode et Textile and Musée de la Publicité. Tues–Fri 11am–6pm; Sat–Sun 10am–6pm. Métro: Palais-Royal–Musée du Louvre or Tuileries.

Palais-Royal 🏛🏛 Though you can't enter the building, which houses government offices, Palais-Royal is worth the visit for its beautiful gardens and historic signifi-cance. It was the residence of Cardinal Richelieu, Louis XIII's prime minister; after the cardinal's death it was passed to the king. Louis XIV spent part of his childhood here, where as a toddler he reportedly almost drowned in the fountain. The palace was later owned by the duc de Chartres et Orléans (see "Parc Monceau" on p. 195), who cov-ered his debts by encouraging the opening of cafes, gambling dens, and other public entertainment in the galleries lining the interior courtyard and garden. The duke's royal status kept out the police, and the liberal atmosphere soon made the Palais a haven for party animals and revolutionaries. It was here that on July 12, 1789, Camille Demoulins called the people of Paris to arms and ignited the French Revolution.

By the mid-1800s the glory days were over, and the Palais lost a great deal of its lus-ter, though few of its bordellos. The 20th century was kinder to the building, and its apartments sheltered luminaries such as Collette and Jean Cocteau. Today the galleries are filled with pricey shops—stamp, antique jewelry, and toy collectors will have a field day, as will fashion victims and vintage-clothing fans. Be sure to pause in the **Jardin du Palais-Royal** at the center of the enclosure. A controversial 1986 sculpture by Daniel Buren covers the courtyard: 280 prison-striped columns, oddly placed.

Rue St-Honoré, 1er. Gardens daily Apr–May 7am–10pm; June–Aug 7am–11pm; Sept 7am–9pm; Oct–Mar 7:30am–8:30pm. Métro: Palais-Royal–Musée du Louvre.

Place Vendôme 🏛🏛🏛 The grandeur of the 17th-century place Vendôme epito-mizes the age of Louis XIV, when grace and harmony were the dominant architectural values. The recognizable names on the square—Hôtel Ritz, Cartier, Van Cleef & Arpels, Boucheron—create an aura of opulence. Among the residents of place Vendôme was Chopin, who died at no. 12 in 1849.

Napoleon commissioned the **column** in the center, modeled on Trajan's column in Rome, to honor those who fought and won the battle of Austerlitz. Austrian cannons were used in its construction. Napoleon's statue has graced the top of the column at times; in 1815 royalists substituted a fleur-de-lis, symbol of France's monarchy. A statue of Henri IV also stood here. During the months of the Paris Commune, the issue was temporarily resolved when the column was destroyed; it was re-erected dur-ing the Third Republic.

Rue de Castiglione, 1er. Métro: Tuileries, Concorde, or Madeleine.

St-Eustache 🏛🏛 This magnificent church looms over the gardens that top the Forum des Halles shopping center. Built between 1532 and 1637, it combines Gothic construction with Renaissance decoration in a soaring, light-filled structure. Modeled on the design of Notre-Dame, St-Eustache has had an illustrious lineup of parishioners. Molière and Mme de Pompadour were baptized here, and Molière's funeral was held here in 1673. It was the first church to contain the tombs of celebrated Parisians, most notably Colbert, Louis XIV's finance minister, who is buried in a black-marble tomb embellished with sculptures of Abundance, Fidelity, and Colbert, all by Coysevox.

Notice the nearby *Disciples d'Emmaüs,* from the school of Rubens. The organ is one of the finest in Paris and has been restored and modernized. Franz Liszt used to play here; the current church organist is Jean Guillou, who gives a free concert every Sunday at 5:30pm. The acoustics are so good that the church is often used for recordings. Allow 45 minutes to take in one of the city's most beautiful churches.

2 rue du Jour, 1er. © **01-42-36-31-05.** www.st-eustache.org. Mon–Sat 9am–7pm; Sun 9am–12:45pm and 2:30–7pm. Métro: Les Halles.

St-Germain-l'Auxerrois ⭐   Begun on the site of an 8th-century church, St-Germain-l'Auxerrois is a mélange of architectural styles. The Romanesque tower was built in the 12th century, the chancel is 13th-century Gothic, the porch 15th-century flamboyant Gothic, the rose windows are from the Renaissance, and the entire church was restored in the 19th century. The facade is a petrified zoo of carved birds, vultures, monkeys, wolves, bears, and dogs. The interior contains excellent carved pews from the 17th century.

The church's history is as eventful as its architecture. When the monarchy moved to the Louvre in the 14th century, St-Germain became the royal church. It welcomed Henri III, Henri IV, Marie de Medici, and Louis XIV. On August 24, 1572, the bells of St-Germain signaled the St. Bartholomew's Day Massacre. The scheming Catherine de Medici had persuaded her son, Charles IX, to sign the order for the massacre of the Huguenots (Protestants), some 50,000 of whom were slaughtered in Paris and the provinces. Hear the bells ring a more palatable tune at the free concert every Wednesday from 1:30 to 2pm.

2 pl. du Louvre, 1er. © **01-42-60-13-86.** Daily 8am–8pm. Métro: Louvre-Rivoli.

Fun Fact   **Baron Haussmann: The Man Who Transformed Paris**

Georges Eugène Haussmann created much of the Paris we see today. He transformed the city in the 1850s and 1860s from a medieval town to a 19th-century metropolis. He razed most of old Paris, widened the streets, and laid out a series of boulevards leading from the railroad stations on the city's periphery into its heart. Politics were at the heart of the decision: Revolutionary mobs were easier to control in large avenues than in tiny alleyways. Along their routes he created open spaces like place de l'Opéra and place de l'Etoile (now pl. Charles-de-Gaulle).

Haussmann was born in Paris in 1809. He entered the civil service and went to the provinces, where he gained a reputation as a tough administrator capable of crushing socialism and republicanism wherever he found it. In 1853, Napoleon III appointed him prefect of the Seine, and he began the work of revising Paris. His lack of tact and his conviction that he was absolutely right were notorious. Although his actions swept away most of the densest old neighborhoods, filled with mansions and private gardens, the straight, broad avenues he created have proved adaptable to different periods and fashions. That is more than can be said for some urban designs today.

St-Roch ✯ This 17th-century church has the richest trove of painting and sculpture in Paris outside a museum. Beginning on the right aisle, notice the bust of *maréchal François de Créqui* by Geneviève, *Cardinal Dubois and Priests* by Coustou, and paintings by Louis Boulanger in the fourth chapel. At the entrance to the choir is Falconet's sculpture, *Le Christ au Jardin des Oliviers.* Other highlights include *La Nativité* by Anguier (on the altar), the bust of Le Nôtre by Coysevox, and the monument to the painter Mignard by Girardon (both on the left aisle).

On October 5, 1795, Napoleon secured an impressive victory around the church, launching his rise to power. The revolutionaries got wind of a royalist plot to topple their hold on power. Bonaparte was given the task of defending the Tuileries palace, the seat of government, from a 30,000-man army of rebels. Demonstrating a masterful use of artillery, Napoleon positioned 40 guns along the streets around the church so cleverly that the rebel force was routed in a few minutes. Later, asked to acknowledge the cheers of the revolutionary convention, Napoleon refused to take the stage—probably his last display of modesty.

296 rue St-Honoré, 1er. Daily 8am–7pm. Métro: Tuileries or Palais-Royal–Musée du Louvre.

5 2, 9 & 10e Arrondissements: The Opéra, Bourse & the Grands Boulevards

Tracing the outline of long-gone medieval ramparts, the Grands Boulevards stretch from the reclining nymphs and Corinthian columns of the **Opéra Garnier** to the fast-food chains and neon of the **place de la République.** In the late 18th and early 19th centuries, the Grands Boulevards were filled with theaters, cafes, and intrigue—in short, *the* place to be. Baron Haussmann's remodeling scooped a good deal of the life out of the area; by the 1920s, the elegant *boulevardiers* who used to stroll along the bustling avenues had moved on to more fashionable neighborhoods. Today the boulevards are busy, if less chic, and one can still do lots of shopping at *grands magasins* like **Printemps** and **Galeries Lafayette.** Though this area is not action-packed, if you wander away from the big avenues, there is plenty of interest. **New Athens** near place St-Georges in the 9e was the stomping ground of the stars of the Romantic movement; George Sand, Delacroix, Chopin, and others stayed in the neoclassical buildings sprinkled around this villagelike neighborhood. Rue du Faubourg St-Denis in the 10e may not be family-friendly, but it is colorful: a weird mélange of clothing wholesalers, sex shops, and outrageously dressed prostitutes. A more wholesome stroll can be had along the locks and bridges of the **Canal St-Martin,** where new cafes and shops are sprouting along the quais. Nineteenth-century **arcades** zigzag through the 2e arrondissement from the boulevards south to the **place des Victoires.** Flower vendors, cheese shops, butchers, and bakers crowd the pedestrian area of **rue Montorgueil.** The outdoor market has been a gastronomic center since the 13th century and is now one of the liveliest and least touristy street markets in the city. This is also a great place to find a good meal. Look inside Patisserie Stohrer, 51 rue de Montorgueil, at the delicately painted ceiling done in 1864 by Paul Baudry, who also painted the interior of the Opéra.

Explore Paris *(Kids)* Yes, it's touristy, but it does offer an easy and interesting overview of the French capital—a nice way to introduce the city to kids. It used to be called "Paris Story" until June 2005, when they changed the name but not the venue. Victor Hugo will be your guide for this multimedia presentation of the history of Paris. By late 2005, five additional video presentations will be available allowing you to truly explore Paris. The show runs for 1 hour and 10 minutes and is available with simultaneous English translation.

11 bis rue Scribe, 9e. ℭ **01-42-66-62-06.** www.paris-story.com. Admission 10€ ($13) adults, 6€ ($7.50) students and children 6–18, free for children under 6. Daily hourly shows 9am–7pm. Métro: Opéra or Chaussée d'Antin.

Grévin (Kids) Naomi Campbell and Arnold Schwarzenegger have joined a gang of some 300 re-creations at this wax museum, whose inhabitants range from Leonardo da Vinci to Lara Croft. After a 6-month spruce up, Grévin has dropped its first name (Musée) and added 80 new characters, a new lobby, and a boutique. Established in 1882, the waxworks is also known for its animated tableaux that tell the history of France; you can see the assassination of Henri IV and Joan of Arc about to be burned at the stake. You can also visit a wax vision of the future. Allow 1 hour.

10 bd. Montmartre, 9e. ℭ **01-47-70-85-05.** www.musee-grevin.com. Admission 17€ ($21) adults, 9€ ($11) children. Mon–Fri 10am–5:30pm; Sat–Sun 10am–6pm. Métro: Grands-Boulevards.

Musée de la Vie Romantique Fans of George Sand will get a kick out of this museum, which re-creates rooms from her home in Nohant and displays mementoes and letters. The museum is in a lovely house set back from the street and has a small garden; it belonged to painter Ary Scheffer, another figure of the Romantic period. Scheffer's studio is also displayed. You can have tea in the greenhouse and garden during the summer months.

16 rue Chaptal, 9e. ℭ **01-48-74-95-38.** Admission 5€ ($6.25) adults, 3.50€ ($4.40) seniors (over 60), 2.50€ ($3.15) ages 7–26, free for children under 7 and Sun before 1pm. Tues–Sun 10am–6pm. Closed holidays. Métro: St-Georges or Pigalle.

Musée des Monnaies, Médailles et Antiques The National Library of France's 10 million books were removed to the giant new Bibliothèque François Mitterrand in 1998; but the old building still shelters special collections, including this display of archaeological objects, cameos, bronzes, medals, and coins. Originally assembled by the French kings, some of the exceptional objects include the Treasure of Berthouville, a collection of Gallo-Roman money; the Cameo of Sainte-Chapelle, a huge, multi-colored cameo from the 1st century that shows the emperor Tiberius receiving Germanicus; the silver cup of Ptolémées; and the Treasure of Childéric, one of the oldest remnants of the French monarchy. The library also offers temporary exhibits throughout the year. Allow at least 45 minutes for the museum.

Bibliothèque Nationale de France, 58 rue de Richelieu, 2e. ℭ **01-53-79-83-40.** Admission 4€ ($4.60) adults, 2.50€ ($3.15) students. Mon–Sat 1–5pm; Sun noon–6pm. Métro: Pyramides or Palais Royal.

Musée du Parfumerie Fragonard This museum is in the lobby of what was once the 19th-century theater where French icon Arletty got her start. Established by the Fragonard perfume company, it introduces you to perfume history and manufacture. Displays include copper containers with spouts and tubes that were used in the distillation of oils and scents, and a small but impressive collection of perfume bottles. After your visit, sniff out the ground-floor shop, where you'll find a vast array of Fragonard scents. You'll leave smelling better than ever. Thirty minutes should be enough time for the museum and shop.

39 bd. des Capucines, 2e. ℭ **01-47-42-04-56.** Free admission. Mon–Sat 9am–5:30pm. Open Sun Apr–Oct 9:30am–4pm. Métro: Opéra.

Musée National Gustave Moreau This house and studio display the works of the symbolist painter Gustave Moreau (1826–98), who embraced the bizarre and painted mythological subjects and scenes in a sensuous, romantic style. Among the works displayed are *Orpheus by the Tomb of Eurydice* and *Jupiter and Semele*. Moreau taught at the Ecole des Beaux-Arts, and his influence can be seen in the works of Rouault, the first curator of this little-visited museum. Moreau fans should allow at least 1 hour; others can do with less time.

14 rue de la Rochefoucauld, 9e. ⓒ 01-48-74-38-50. www.musee-moreau.fr. Admission 4€ ($5) adults, 2.60€ ($3.25) ages 18–25 and for all on Sun, free for children under 18. Wed–Mon 10am–12:45pm and 2–5:15pm. Métro: St-Georges or Trinité.

Opéra Garnier (Palais Garnier) 👁👁   In 1861 the city planners held a competition to choose the best design for a new opera house. An unknown named Charles Garnier, whose design mixed elements of 17th-century Spanish style with an Italian Renaissance facade, won the contest. "What kind of strange style is this?" Empress Eugénie allegedly complained. "It's neither Greek nor Roman." "It is the style of Napoleon III, Madame," replied Garnier, and, indeed, the Opéra epitomizes the extravagance of Second Empire style. From the gold dome on the roof to the marble staircase in the lobby, the building is a mass of baroque riches, including a panoply of sculptures of composers, Greek gods, and the arts.

For the price of admission, you can visit the entire opera house, including the velvet-and-gold auditorium with its exquisite Chagall ceiling (unless a rehearsal is in progress), the spectacular mirrored ballroom where galas are still held, the museum of the Opéra, and the downstairs carriage room where turn-of-the-20th-century horse-drawn buggies deposited their elegant passengers.

Is there a phantom of the opera? The inspiration for Gaston Leroux's 1911 novel undoubtedly came from the building's vast subterranean caverns, which enclose an underground lake that was constructed to help stabilize the building.

Pl. de l'Opéra, 9e. ⓒ 01-40-01-22-63. www.opera-de-paris.fr. Admission for visits 7€ ($8.75) adults, 3.50€ ($4.40) students, free for children under 10. Daily 10am–4:30pm. Métro: Opéra.

THE ARCADES

Picture shopping in the early 19th century: People, horses, and carriages crowd the unpaved, dirty, badly lit streets. When it rains, everything turns to mud. When covered arcades were built and filled with shops, they were a huge success.

These iron-and-glass galleries—which could be considered the Western world's first shopping malls—are still a delight, particularly on rainy days. They range from chic and luxurious to somewhat seedy, but most have enough quirky and interesting storefronts to intrigue veteran shoppers and those who just come to *lèche-vitrine* (literally, to lick the windows, or window-shop).

The arrondissement with the greatest concentration of arcades is the 2e. Each has its own character. **Passage Choiseul,** 40 rue des Petits-Champs (Métro: Quatre-Septembre), dates from 1824 and is the longest and most animated arcade. Shoe stores and used-book shops mix with a bagel cafe and an old toy store displaying an extensive teddy bear collection. French writer Louis-Ferdinand Céline grew up here and included it in his books *Journey to the End of Night* and *Death on the Installment Plan*. **Passage des Panoramas,** 11 bd. Montmartre and 10 rue St-Marc (Métro: Grands-Boulevards), opened in 1800 and was enlarged with the addition of galleries Variétés, St-Marc, Montmartre, and Feydeau in 1834. This passage offers the largest choice of dining options—Korean food, a cafeteria, tea salons, bistros—as well as outlets for stamps, clothes, and knickknacks. Across the street is **Passage Jouffroy,** 10 bd. Montmartre or

9 rue de la Grange-Batelière (Métro: Grands-Boulevards), built between 1845 and 1846. The richness of its decoration—as well as the fact that it was the first heated gallery in Paris—made Passage Jouffroy an immediate hit. The arcade has a variety of midrange stores, including one that specializes in dollhouses. The **Passage Verdeau,** 31 bis rue du Faubourg-Montmartre (Métro: Le Peletier), was built at about the same time as the Passage Jouffroy and has a classier air than its neighbor. Old postcards and books are specialties here, along with photo galleries and restaurants. The most gorgeous interior is that of **Galerie Vivienne,** 4 pl. des Petits-Champs, 5 rue de la Banque, and 6 rue Vivienne (Métro: Bourse), which opened in 1826. The neoclassical style of this arcade (a national monument) has attracted art galleries, a tea salon, and boutiques selling rare books, silk flowers, and wine paraphernalia. The classical friezes, mosaic floors, and arches have been beautifully restored and linked to the adjoining **Galerie Colbert,** built in 1826 to capitalize on the success of the Vivienne gallery. The Passage Colbert has a large rotunda and is decorated in Pompeian style. Check out Le Grand Colbert, a Belle Epoque restaurant with an entrance in this arcade. The **Passage du Grand Cerf,** 10 rue Dussoubs (Métro: Etienne-Marcel), is of a more hip bent, with jewelry designers, trendy clothing stores, and an ad agency.

For a change of pace, visit **Passage Brady,** 46 rue du Faubourg St-Denis (Métro: Strasbourg St-Denis), which has become an exotic bazaar. Indian restaurants and spice shops scent the air of this arcade, which opened in 1828.

6 3, 4 & 11e Arrondissements: The Marais, Beaubourg & Bastille

The Marais has always been a mixed bag—palaces next door to modest homes, royalty next to the working classes. Today, it is still a mix, with different ingredients. The remnants of the old Jewish quarter butts up against a thriving gay scene, cool boutiques on **rue des Francs Bourgeois** flank the 17th-century glory of the **place des Vosges.** As you head west, the Marais segues into the **Beaubourg** neighborhood, which centers its frenetic energy around the multicolored tubes and piping of the **Centre Pompidou.** At night the action turns back east to Marais and the streets around the Bastille.

The neighborhood got its start in the 13th century when several religious congregations decided to set up shop. Not long after, Charles of Anjou, king of Naples and Sicily, moved in and the neighborhood acquired cachet. By the 14th century, Charles V had extended the city's fortifications east to the Bastille and built a palace next to **Village St-Paul.** Other kings decided the Right Bank wasn't for them, and things stayed quiet until 1604, when Henri IV transformed the Marais into a glittering center of royal power. Dozens of mansions and palaces were built by the nobility. But even before the razing of the Bastille in 1789 scared them off, the aristocracy was gravitating to Versailles. The Marais fell into lingering decay until various restoration projects in the early 1960s.

The mansions of the Marais are a reminder of the 17th century, but the bistros and bars have become the hub of young, *branché* (trendy) Parisians. The "look" is casual, the ambience artsy, and the boutiques lining rue Vieille-du-Temple casually chic. As you head north toward République, the neighborhood loses some luster, but the narrow streets and old-fashioned stores give you an idea of what the Marais was like before the *bobos* (bourgeois bohemians) moved in. Before the restoration, many of the *hôtels particuliers* (private mansions) had been used as warehouses and ateliers for small manufacturers, and others were demolished. Today, most of those remaining have been restored and many are museums and administrative offices. Be sure to poke your head into the courtyards of these buildings and take a minute to marvel at their elegance.

More wandering is to be done in the old Jewish neighborhood around **rue des Rosiers.** Although many of the ground-floor shops have metamorphosed into fancy designer salons, the old delicatessens, falafel stands, and kosher goods stores still display signs in Hebrew as well as French. The street closes down on Friday night, when the faithful head to synagogues in the neighborhood, including one designed by Guimard on **rue Pavée.**

A lesser-known find in the Marais is **Village St-Paul** (Métro: St-Paul), an enclosed 17th-century village that is now an outdoor arts fair. It's easy to walk past the entrance to this town-within-a-town tucked between rue St-Paul, rue Jardins St-Paul, and rue Charlemagne; look for the signs inside the narrow passageways between the houses. You'll find yourself in a cluster of interlocking courtyards lined with shops that display antiques, paintings, and bric-a-brac. The haphazard arrangement of courtyards dates from the 14th century, when they were the walled gardens of King Charles V. Flea markets are held each spring and fall, drawing vendors from the Paris region. The stores are open Thursday through Monday 11am to 7pm. The high stone wall you see on rue Jardins St-Paul is part of Philippe-August's 13th-century fortification; the other part of the wall survives in the Latin Quarter on rue Clovis.

Further east, Carl Ott's futuristic **Opéra Bastille** (Métro: Bastille) may not be everyone's idea of an opera house, but it did a lot for the neighborhood. Soon after its opening in 1989, the narrow side streets around the opera house began to pulsate with a new beat—and it's not opera. Rue de la Roquette, rue de Charonne, and rue de Lappe are a strange blend of neon, cobblestones, fast food, bistros, art galleries, and tapas bars. The action starts after sundown and peaks on weekend nights. Recently, many of the black-clad, intense 20-somethings who gravitated to the Bastille in the early 1990s have stormed on to rue Oberkampf.

Centre Georges Pompidou   The "guts" are on the outside of the Centre National d'Art et de Culture Georges Pompidou, designed by British architect Richard Rogers and Italian architect Renzo Piano in the late 1960s. The architects won a competition held by President Pompidou in the late 1960s to design the building as part of a redevelopment plan for the neighborhood. As with much of Parisian architecture, it was despised by many at first, but over the years, Parisians have come to love—or at least accept—the very 1970s building, with its "exoskeletal" architecture and bright colors.

The center houses an impressive collection of modern art, a cinema, a library, and spaces for dance and music. Temporary exhibits often include video and computer art. Works from the Musée National d'Art Moderne (the national modern art collection) take up two floors. The Brancusi Atelier features nearly 150 drawings, paintings, and sculptures by sculptor Constantin Brancusi.

Since its opening in 1977, more than 160 million people have visited the Centre Pompidou—and the building began to crumble under the weight of its popularity. It underwent a renovation that cost more than $100 million and reopened on January 1, 2000. Even if you don't visit the museum, you can take an escalator to the top floor for a breathtaking (and free) view of Paris. Don't miss the nearby Igor Stravinsky fountain, with its fun sculptures by Tinguely and Niki de Saint Phalle that include red lips dripping water and a twirling, grinning skull. Allow about 1½ hours to visit the center.

Attractions in the 3 & 4e

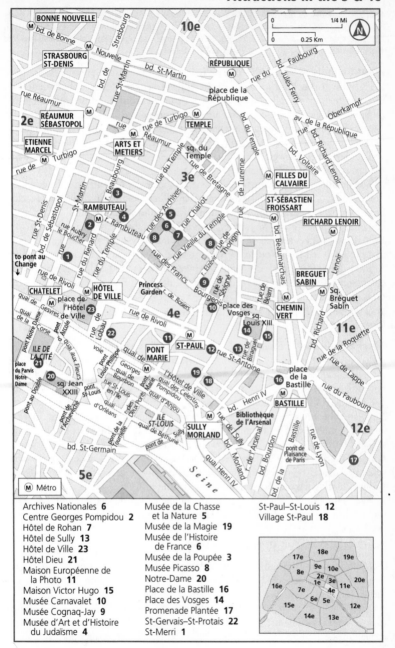

| 0 | | 1/4 Mi |
| 0 | 0.25 Km | |

BONNE NOUVELLE
Ⓜ bd. de Bonne Nouvelle

10e

STRASBOURG
ST-DENIS

RÉPUBLIQUE
Ⓜ

bd. St-Martin

place de la
République

rue Réaumur

2e

RÉAUMUR
SÉBASTOPOL
Ⓜ

rue de Turbigo Ⓜ

TEMPLE

ÉTIENNE
MARCEL
Ⓜ Turbigo

ARTS ET
MÉTIERS
Ⓜ

sq. du
Temple

rue de Bretagne

3e

FILLES DU
CALVAIRE Ⓜ

RAMBUTEAU
Ⓜ

r. Rambuteau

ST-SÉBASTIEN
FROISSART

RICHARD LENOIR
Ⓜ

to pont au
Change
↓

rue de Rivoli

CHÂTELET
Ⓜ

HÔTEL
DE VILLE
Ⓜ

Princess
Garden

BREGUET
SABIN

Sq.
Bréguet
Sabin Ⓜ

place de
l'Hôtel
de Ville

rue de Rivoli

4e

place des
Vosges

CHEMIN
VERT Ⓜ

11e

ÎLE DE
LA CITÉ

place
du Parvis
Notre
Dame

sq. Jean
XXIII

PONT
MARIE
Ⓜ

ST-PAUL
Ⓜ

rue St-Antoine

place
de la
Bastille

rue du Faubourg

l'Hôtel
de Ville

ÎLE
ST-LOUIS

SULLY
MORLAND
Ⓜ

Bibliothèque
de l'Arsenal

BASTILLE
Ⓜ

12e

bd. St-Germain

Seine

5e

pont de
Plaisance
de Paris

Ⓜ Métro

Archives Nationales **6**
Centre Georges Pompidou **2**
Hôtel de Rohan **7**
Hôtel de Sully **13**
Hôtel de Ville **23**
Hôtel Dieu **21**
Maison Européenne de
la Photo **11**
Maison Victor Hugo **15**
Musée Carnavalet **10**
Musée Cognaq-Jay **9**
Musée d'Art et d'Histoire
du Judaïsme **4**

Musée de la Chasse
et la Nature **5**
Musée de la Magie **19**
Musée de l'Histoire
de France **6**
Musée de la Poupée **3**
Musée Picasso **8**
Notre-Dame **20**
Place de la Bastille **16**
Place des Vosges **14**
Promenade Plantée **17**
St-Gervais–St-Protais **22**
St-Merri **1**

St-Paul–St-Louis **12**
Village St-Paul **18**

185

Pl. Georges-Pompidou, 4e. 🕐 **01-44-78-12-33**. www.centrepompidou.fr. Admission to museum 7€ ($8.75) adults, 5€ ($6.25) ages 13–26, free for children under 13. Admission to special exhibits (museum entry included) 9€ ($11) adults, 7€ ($8.75) ages 13–26, free for children under 13. Centre: Wed–Mon 11am–10pm. Museum: Wed–Mon 11am–9pm. Métro: Rambuteau, Hôtel-de-Ville, or Châtelet–Les Halles.

Hôtel de Sully ✻ The Hôtel de Sully is one of the most impressive mansions in the Marais. It was built in 1624 for the affluent banker Mesme-Gallet. Henri IV's minister, the duc de Sully, beautified it with painted ceilings and painted and gilded pilasters. The facades and courtyard are richly ornamented in Renaissance style, with bas-reliefs representing the elements and the seasons. Sully was 74 when he bought the house, but he had a very young wife. "Here's so much for the household, so much for you, and so much for your lovers," he'd say when he gave her money, asking only that her lovers not loiter on his stairway.

The building is now home to the Caisse Nationale des Monuments Historiques et des Sites (National Historical Monuments and Sites Commission), and occasionally hosts photography exhibitions. The building is open to the public on the third week-end of September during the Journées Portes Ouvertes, but be prepared for long lines. Even if you can't get in, walk through the courtyard to the garden in the back—a great place to rest tired feet. Next to the Orangerie on the far side of the garden is a little archway that leads to place des Vosges. Between the courtyard and the garden is a fas-cinating bookstore that retains the painted ceiling beams that were a feature of 17th-century mansions.

62 rue St-Antoine, 3e. 🕐 **01-44-61-20-00**. Admission to courtyard free. Mon–Fri 8am–7:30pm; Sat–Sun 9am–7pm. Métro: St-Paul or Bastille.

Hôtel de Ville ✻✻ Even though you can't tour the inside of Paris's City Hall, sim-ply staring at the swirls and curlicues on the facade of this huge neo-Renaissance wed-ding cake is an excellent visit. The current version was built between 1874 and 1882, but earlier buildings that stood here witnessed many great and dire moments. In July 1789, Louis XVI was forced to kiss the new French flag. The blue and red stood for Paris, and the white represented the monarchy. In subsequent revolutions, in 1848 and 1870, mobs occupied the building, and in 1870 the building that had been con-structed by François I was burned down. The place in front was also used for execu-tions from 1313 to 1830, when witches, Huguenots, and criminals such as Ravaillac (Henry IV's assassin) were dispatched. As befits the city's municipal building, 146 stat-ues representing famous Parisians adorn the facade.

Note: Hôtel de Ville is not open to the public except during the Journées Portes Ouvertes in September (see "Paris Calendar of Events," in chapter 2) or for special exhibits.

Pl. de l'Hôtel de Ville, 4e. 🕐 **01-42-76-43-43**. Métro: Hôtel-de-Ville.

Le Memorial de la Shoah (Holocaust Memorial) ✻ President Jacques Chirac unveiled this new memorial in January 2005 with a wall filled with 76,000 names of the children, women, and men who were deported to Nazi camps from France between 1942 and 1944. A permanent exhibit chronicles the history of Jews in Europe using original documents, films and multimedia. Over 55,000 photographs are on display in the reading room. The space also is used to host lectures and talks about Jewish history.

17 rue Geoffroy-l'Asnier, 4e. 🕐 **01-42-77-44-72**. www.memorialdelashoah.fr. Free admission. Sun–Wed and Fri 10am–6pm; Thurs 10am–10pm. Métro: St-Paul or Pont-Marie.

Maison de Victor Hugo ✿ Victor Hugo occupied this sprawling apartment from 1832 to 1848. You will see some of his furniture, his drawings, his inkwell, first editions of his works, a painting of his funeral procession at the Arc de Triomphe in 1885, and drafts of his writing, scrawled on scrap paper and the backs of envelopes. There are also portraits of his family, including Adèle, the subject of François Truffaut's excellent film *L'Histoire d'Adèle H.* The Chinese salon from Hugo's house on Guernsey has been reassembled here. Allow at least an hour to see the museum and to climb all the stairs.

6 pl. des Vosges, 4e. ✆ **01-42-72-10-16**. Admission 5.50€ ($6.90) adults, 2.50[eu]($3.10) ages 13–27; free for children under 13 and for all on Sun 10am–1pm. Tues–Sun 10am–5:40pm (window closes at 5:15pm). Métro: St-Paul.

Maison Européenne de la Photographie ✿ Photography buffs will adore this sleek museum, devoted entirely to the art of the camera. Housed in two renovated 18th-century town houses, the museum has ever-changing exhibits, an excellent video library where you can look up thousands of photographs, a projection room, and permanent collections of Polaroid art. Depending on the show, allow around 2 hours. In November 2006, the museum will host the biennial "Month of Photography."

5–7 rue de Fourcy, 4e. ✆ **01-44-78-75-00**. www.mep-fr.org. Admission 5€ ($6.25) adults, 2.50€ ($3.15) ages 8–26 and seniors (over 60), free for children under 8. Free to all Wed after 5pm. Wed–Sun 11am–8pm. Métro: St-Paul or Pont-Marie.

Musée Carnavalet–Histoire de Paris ✿✿✿ Also known as the Musée Historique de la Ville de Paris, this museum details the history of the city of Paris from prehistoric times to the present. Two mansions house the museum: the 16th-century Hôtel Carnavalet and the Hôtel Le Peletier de St-Fargeau. Their current look dates to the 17th century, when the architect François Mansart was hired to enlarge and modernize the original structure. The statue in the center of the sumptuous main courtyard is a bewigged Louis XIV by Coysevox.

Perfectly preserved period salons, including Louis XV's and Louis XVI's 18th-century blue and yellow rooms, contain ornate furnishings and art. The Cabinet doré de l'hotel La Riviére, with its ceiling painting of Apollo and Aurora by Charles Le Brun, is a spectacular exhibit of beauty and excess. For similar grandeur, don't miss the other ceiling painted by Le Brun, which depicts Psyché with the Muses. Several rooms are devoted to the Revolution, including models of the Bastille, and Marie Antoinette's personal items, including a lock of hair. In the basement, you'll find a collection of prehistoric artifacts, including ancient coins, bronze figures, bowls, and Roman bas-reliefs. The beautiful interior garden, accessible only through the museum, is a sublime spot to contemplate the 3,000 years of history you've just stepped through.

You will need at least 2 or 3 hours to get through this vast collection—note that the museum commentary is all in French, so it's well worth it to buy a guidebook in English at the museum bookshop before you enter.

23 rue de Sévigné, 3e. ✆ **01-44-59-58-58**. Admission 5.50€ ($6.90) adults, 2.50€ ($3.15) ages 14–26; free for children under 14. Temporary exhibits (including entry to permanent collection) 6€ ($7.50) adults, 3.80€ ($4.75) students. Free Sun 10am–1pm. Tues–Sun 10am–5:40pm. Métro: St-Paul.

Musée Cognacq-Jay La Samaritaine department store founder Ernest Cognacq and his wife amassed this collection of 18th-century rococo art. Although perhaps not in the same class as the grand museums in the neighborhood, it provides a window into the aristocratic lifestyle that flourished before the Revolution. Shelves of porcelain and porcelain figures, rich cabinets, and furniture are on display in the 16th-century Hôtel Donon. Works by Boucher, Fragonard, Rubens, Van Loo, Watteau, and Tiepolo grace

Louis XV and Louis XVI paneled rooms. Outside lies a little manicured garden (open May–Sept). The museum presents temporary exhibits two to three times a year. One hour should give you a good taste of the highbrow side of the 18th century.

8 rue Elzévir, 3e. ℂ 01-40-27-07-21. Admission 5€ ($6.25) adults, 4€ ($5) ages 7–26 and seniors over 60, free for children under 6. Tues–Sun 10am–5:40pm. Métro: St-Paul or Chemin-Vert.

Musée d'Art et d'Histoire du Judaïsme ⋆⋆   Don't be put off by the airport-level security at the entrance—this recent addition to the city's museum scene is worth having your purse X-rayed. Occupying the 17th-century Hôtel de Saint-Aignan, this gracefully displayed collection traces the development of Jewish culture in France and Europe. The collection includes medieval gravestones, illuminated manuscripts, exquisitely carved Renaissance torah arks, and 18th-century paintings and drawings depicting religious ceremonies and Bible stories. The beautifully crafted religious objects, including torah ornaments, prayer shawls, menorahs, and numerous *rideaux d'arche sainte* (ark curtains), reflect both the Sephardic and Ashkenazi traditions. The museum also presents newly available documents relating to the Dreyfus affair. Make sure to take the free, informative audio tour. The exhibits end with a collection of works by Jewish artists, including paintings by Modigliani, Soutine, Zadkine, and Chagall. Allow at least 2 hours, as there is lots of reading to be done.

Hôtel de St-Aignan, 71 rue du Temple, 3e. ℂ 01-53-01-86-60. www.mahj.org. Admission 6.80€ ($8.50) adults, 4.50€ ($5.65) ages 18–26, free for children under 18. Mon–Fri 11am–6pm; Sun 10am–6pm (window closes at 5:15pm). Métro: Rambuteau or Hôtel-de-Ville.

Musée de la Chasse et la Nature   Closed since early 2005 for renovations, at press time the museum was scheduled to open in mid-2006. The collection is not expected to change.

Hunters and their prey, weapons, and exploits are chronicled here in exhibits that can be fascinating or repulsive. Bears and wolves with horrific fangs and a variety of antlered creatures have been stuffed and displayed. Rembrandt's drawing of a lion, Desportes's painting of a wild-boar hunt, and works by Breughel, Chardin, and Rubens are among the hunting scenes. The museum also traces the development of weapons, many of them exquisitely designed. You'll see Marie Antoinette's elegant hunting rifle and Napoleon's carbine inset with gold and silver.

The museum is in a beautiful mansion designed by Mansart (the architect of Versailles) between 1651 and 1655 for Jean-François de Guénégaud des Brosses. After falling into disrepair, it was restored by the Sommer Foundation in 1966 and is now a fine example of classical 17th-century architecture. Notice the grand interior staircase and the garden visible from some of the windows. Unless you are a weapons maven, 1 hour should be more than enough.

60 rue des Archives, 3e. ℂ 01-53-01-92-40. www.chassenature.org. Admission 5€ ($6.25) adults, 2.50€ ($3.15) students and children under 16. Tues–Sun 9am–5:15pm. Métro: Rambuteau or Hôtel-de-Ville.

Musée de la Magie (*Kids*   Magicians operate this temple of magic and escort you through a collection of trick mirrors, animated paintings, talking genies, and the history of illusion. While they won't disclose any secrets, you will have your senses tickled through many interactive displays. Try inserting your hand in the open mouth of a lion and see if, indeed, he is just an illusion. Live magic shows are performed throughout the afternoon. For those entranced by a visit, a shop in the front stocks all the tools you need to cast spells—benevolent French ones, that is. Allow an hour and a half, including a show.

11 rue St-Paul, 4e. ℂ **01-42-72-13-26.** www.museedelamagie.com. Admission 7€ ($8.75) adults, 5€ ($6.25) children under 13. Wed and Sat–Sun 2–7pm. Métro: St-Paul.

Musée de la Poupée *Kids* Hidden at the back of an alley decked with greenery, this museum has a collection of more than 500 French dolls dating from 1800 to the present day. The antique beauties peek coyly out of exquisite period clothing; the dolls are displayed with matching furniture and even furry dog and cat friends. The 36 themed windows feature dolls made out of porcelain, papier-mâché, fabric, rubber, and, more recently, plastic. The museum offers temporary exhibits twice a year. Be sure to check out the boutique and doll hospital—a nice place to shop for gifts. Allow about 40 minutes.

Impasse Berthaud (off rue Beaubourg), 3e. ℂ **01-42-72-73-11.** Admission 6€ ($7.50) adults, 4€ ($5) ages 18–25 and over 60, 3€ ($3.45) ages 3–17. Daily 10am–6pm. Métro: Rambuteau.

Musée de l'Histoire de France/Archives Nationales ⭐ François de Rohan, prince de Soubise, bought this palace in 1700. A scion of one of the most powerful families of the 18th century, he received many gifts from Louis XIV—not only for his position but for the many "favors" his wife, Anne de Rohan-Chabot, bestowed on the king. Perhaps evading her royal obligations, Anne moved to the mansion and, wanting to make it palatial, brought in the architect Delamair in 1704. He built a palace, beginning with the courtyard enclosed by a 56-column peristyle and a promenade. Reclining figures of Prudence and Wisdom and children representing artistic spirits adorn the facade. Feeling cramped in his parents' home, the couple's son, the future Cardinal de Rohan, had Delamair build another palatial mansion next door, the Hôtel de Rohan.

Since 1808, when Napoleon ordered the acquisition of the Soubise-Rohan estates to house Empire records, the mansions have contained the National Archives. On the first floor of the Hôtel de Soubise is the Musée de l'Histoire de la France, where you can get a glimpse of the Rohan lifestyle by visiting the apartments of the Princess of Soubise. Because the museum is not heavily frequented, you may have the rooms almost to yourself. A few of the museum's historical documents are still on display, including Henry IV's Edict of Nantes (which guaranteed religious liberties), the order to demolish the Bastille, and the will of Louis XVI. Even if you skip the museum, the courtyard is worth a visit—during business hours you can wander through the lovely gardens enclosed by the National Archives complex. The museum visit should take under an hour.

Hôtel de Soubise, 60 rue des Francs-Bourgeois, 3e. ℂ **01-40-27-60-96.** Admission to museum 3.50€ ($4.40) adults, 2.50€ ($3.15) ages 18–24 and seniors (over 60), free for children under 18. Mon and Wed–Fri 10am–12:30pm; daily 2–5:30pm. Courtyard Mon–Fri 9am–7pm; Sat–Sun 1:45–5:45pm. Métro: Rambuteau or Hôtel-de-Ville.

Musée National Picasso ⭐⭐ Hôtel Salé, or the Salted Mansion, got its name from its owner, Aubert de Fontenay, a salt tax collector. The splendidly renovated 17th-century *hôtel particulier* boasts a magnificent staircase and courtyard.

The Hôtel Salé's present claim to glory is Picasso. It houses the world's largest collection of the Spanish master's art. In 1973, following the artist's death, his heirs donated his personal art collection to the state in lieu of inheritance taxes. The Musée Picasso grew out of those holdings. The collection includes more than 200 paintings, almost 160 sculptures, 88 ceramics, and more than 3,000 prints and drawings (many of them too fragile for permanent display). Works can be viewed chronologically; budget at least a few hours here. Because the works are exhibited in rotation, you can pay a visit to this museum on each trip to Paris and see something different each time. The museum also displays works by artists collected by Picasso, including Corot,

Cézanne, Braque, Rousseau, Matisse, and Renoir. Allow 2 hours for your visit here. In summer, the garden cafe is very pleasant for a quick snack.

Hôtel Salé, 5 rue de Thorigny, 3e. ⓒ **01-42-71-25-21.** www.musee-picasso.fr. Admission 6.70€ ($8.40) adults, 5.20€ ($6.50) ages 18–25, free for children under 18. Free to all first Sun of each month. Apr–Sept Wed–Mon 9:30am–6pm, Oct–Mar Wed–Mon 9:30am–5:30pm. Métro: Chemin-Vert, St-Paul, or Filles du Calvaire.

Place de la Bastille ✷✷   Ignore the traffic and try to imagine place de la Bastille just over 200 years ago, when it contained eight towers rising 30m (98 ft.). It was here, on July 14, 1789, that a mob attacked the old prison, launching the French Revolution. Although the Bastille had fallen into disuse, it symbolized the arbitrary power of a king who could imprison anyone for any reason simply by issuing a *lettre de cachet*. Prisoners of means could buy a spacious cell and even host dinner parties. The less fortunate disappeared within the prison's recesses and sometimes drowned when the Seine overflowed its banks. Even though the revolutionary mob discovered only seven prisoners, attacking the prison was a direct assault on royal power. "Is it a revolt?" Louis XVI allegedly asked after learning of the Bastille's fall. "No, sire," came the reply. "It is a revolution."

The Bastille was razed in 1792. In its place stands the **Colonne de Juillet,** a 51m (167-ft.) column commemorating another revolution that took place in 1830.

Pl. de la Bastille, 11e. Métro: Bastille.

Place des Vosges ✷✷✷   This stunning square was one of the first of its kind in Paris. In the 17th century, on the site of the Hôtel des Tournelles, Henry IV put his place Royale, deciding that the surrounding buildings should be "built to a like symmetry." The royal association was evident in the white fleurs-de-lis crowning each row of rose-colored brick houses, and the square became the center of courtly parades and festivities. After the Revolution, it became place de l'Indivisibilité and later place des Vosges, in honor of the first *département* in France that completely paid its taxes. Among the figures connected with the square are Mme de Sévigné, who was born at no. 1 bis, and Victor Hugo, who lived at no. 6 (his house hosts a museum; see the listing for Maison de Victor Hugo, above).

The promenades and romantic duels of the 17th century are long gone, and antiques dealers, galleries, booksellers, tearooms, and cafes occupy the arcades. Live music echoes through the arches in summer. If you're lucky, you'll hear the enchanting melody of a male opera singer who sings Soprano. Children romp and older residents chat—an evocative slice of Parisian life.

Pl. des Vosges, 3e. Métro: St-Paul.

St-Gervais–St-Protais   In the 6th century, a basilica was erected here to saints Gervase and Protase, Roman officers martyred by Nero. The church was reconstructed in the 13th and 17th centuries, but little remains of the older structure. Métezeau built the classical facade in 1621. With Doric, Ionic, and Corinthian orders, it was the first of its kind in Paris. From 1656 to 1826, members of the great Couperin family of organists played here.

The interior is bright, with Gothic vaulting, stained-glass windows, and carved stalls, all dating from the 16th and 17th centuries. German artillery hit the nave of the church on March 29, 1918, causing 100 deaths; it has been well reconstructed.

In the center of St-Gervais square in front of the church, you'll see a small elm. Until the Revolution, debts and claims were settled under an elm here. Judges held court in the square, and the parish priest published their edicts. A promise made "under the elm" was supposed to be inviolable.

Pl. St-Gervais, 4e. Daily 7:30am–6:30pm. Métro: Hôtel-de-Ville.

St-Merri   "Merri" is short for Médéric, an 8th-century Benedictine abbot buried here. His tomb became a pilgrimage site, and a church was constructed in the 13th century. The expanding population of the quarter eventually required a larger structure, and work began in 1520. Although Renaissance style was in full bloom at the time, this church is a throwback to the Gothic style that had flourished a century earlier. Inside you'll find 16th-century stained-glass windows and a magnificent organ loft built by Germain Pilon. The 19th-century murals that decorate the interior chapels depict the lives of the saints, but it is hard to see them in the gloom. The church is in need of renovations, and donations are eagerly accepted. Camille Saint-Saëns used to play the organ here, and the church frequently stages concerts.

76 rue de la Verrerie, 4e. (✆) **01-42-71-93-93**. Daily 9am–7pm. Free guided tour Sun at 4pm in French. Métro: Châtelet–Les Halles.

St-Paul–St-Louis 🕭   Built between 1627 (Louis XIII laid the first stone) and 1641 by the Jesuits, St-Paul–St-Louis is a beautiful example of the baroque art of the Counter-Reformation, with sweeping alabaster ceilings and an imposing organ. On May 9, 1641, Cardinal Richelieu said the first Mass here, and the church became the favorite place of worship for the Marais's elegant inhabitants. Madame de Sévigné and Victor Hugo were parishioners. Henry II's mausoleum was here for many years, along with the hearts of Louis XIII, Louis XIV, and other aristocrats. Although most of the art originally housed here was taken during the Revolution, Delacroix's *Christ in the Garden of Olives* remains. Hugo donated the holy water fonts on each side of the entrance. Free guided tours of the church (in French) are given the second Sunday of every month at 3pm.

99 rue St-Antoine, 4e. (✆) **01-42-72-30-32**. Fri–Wed 9am–7pm, Thurs 9am–10pm.Métro: St-Paul.

7 8 & 17e Arrondissements: The Champs-Elysées & Environs

Within the past few years, the most famous boulevard in the world has had a face-lift. With enlarged sidewalks, rows of newly planted trees, and a law prohibiting parking in the street, the Champs-Elysées now resembles the grand promenade it was always intended to be.

In celebration of France's winning the 1998 World Cup soccer championship, more than one million people packed the street in triumph—drinking, dancing, and singing until dawn. To the ecstatic joy of fans of *le foot,* France went on to win the European Cup in 2000, sparking similar festivities. In the spring of 2005, Paris staged a massive show on the Champs-Elysées to show off its bid to host the 2012 Olympic Games. It lost to London. And of course, the Champs-Elysées is where the Tour de France ends on the third Sunday of July.

With its stunning entrance at the Arc de Triomphe, the Champs-Elysées is France's favorite show-off spot. Almost all big military events take place here, as does the Bastille Day celebration. A legacy of the Mitterrand administration, the giant hollow cube of **La Grande Arche de la Défense** hovers behind Napoleon's monument, lining up in synch with the Arc de Triomphe, the obelisk at the **place de la Concorde,** and the pyramid at the Louvre.

Famous for its movie theaters and touristy stores, the Champs-Elysées has become more of an attraction than a neighborhood. Yet, on the streets branching off the boulevard, there's a sense of moneyed splendor—from the grand couture houses (Lacroix, Dior, Valentino) on **avenue Montaigne** to the presidential residence, **Palais de l'Elysée,** on the Faubourg St-Honoré. Unlike other Parisian neighborhoods whose charms are hidden in a haphazard arrangement of old streets and narrow passages, the avenues from the Champs-Elysées to the **Parc Monceau** were designed to flaunt the wealth of their inhabitants. The "elysian fields" was originally a pathway bordered by trees, until urbanization overtook the neighborhood during the Second Empire. In the 19th century, city planners and developers capitalized on the aristocracy's slow movement west by building the spacious avenues that typify this neighborhood. New money replaced old as bankers and industrialists built ornate residences in the stylish district.

Cafes, restaurants, and theaters sprang up to entertain a new clientele. The Champs-Elysées is still in the entertainment business, though the audience is mostly tourists and out-of-towners, and the show is the brash, jazzed-up multiplexes, megastores, and McFoods that have sprung up along the boulevard. Despite the glitz, the promenade still has a certain glamour, especially at night.

A few blocks from the boulevard is **Place de l'Alma** (Métro: Alma-Marceau), which has been turned into an unofficial shrine to Diana, Princess of Wales, killed in an auto accident on August 31, 1997, in the nearby underpass. The bronze flame in the center, a replica of the flame in the Statue of Liberty, was a gift to the city of Paris from the *International Herald Tribune* in 1989, in honor of Franco-American friendship and France's bicentennial. The many bouquets and messages surrounding the flame and scrawled on the outside of the tunnel reflect the devotion the princess inspired.

La Grande Arche de la Défense ⟨✦⟩

This 35-story cube was built for the bicentennial of the French Revolution in 1989, and it could be one of the world's most bizarre office buildings. Designed by Danish architect Johan Otto von Spreckelsen as the centerpiece of the La Défense suburb, the view from the top offers a spectacular vista down avenue Charles-de-Gaulle to the Arc de Triomphe, the Champs-Elysées, and the Louvre. The arch's monumental size and angular geometry are—you guessed it—not to everyone's taste. Still, even curmudgeons will be impressed when this otherworldly edifice is lit up at night. On weekend nights in the summer, free jazz concerts are held here.

1 parvis de la Défense. ℂ 01-49-07-27-57. Admission 7€ ($8.75) adults, 5.50€ ($6.90) students 15–26, 4.50€ ($5.65) children 6–14, free for children under 6. Oct–Mar daily 10am–7pm; Apr–Sept daily 10am–8pm. Métro: Grande-Arche-de-la-Défense. RER: La Défense–Grande Arche.

La Madeleine ⟨✦⟩

Resembling a Roman temple, the church dominates the short rue Royale, which culminates in place de la Concorde. Although the first stone was laid in 1764, the death of the architect and then the Revolution interrupted its construction. After that, no one could figure out what to do with it until 1806, when Napoleon decided to make it into a temple to the glory of the Grande Armée. The building owes its neo-Roman look to this idea, but the emperor's number was up before the temple was ready. Finally, in 1842, under the Restoration, the Madeleine was consecrated as a church.

Climb the steps leading to the facade and look back: You can see rue Royale, place de la Concorde and the obelisk, and, across the Seine, the dome of the Assemblée Nationale. The inside is gloomy due to the lack of windows, but if you look hard, you will find Rude's *Le Baptême du Christ,* to the left as you enter.

Pl. de la Madeleine, 8e. ℂ 01-44-51-69-00. Métro: Madeleine.

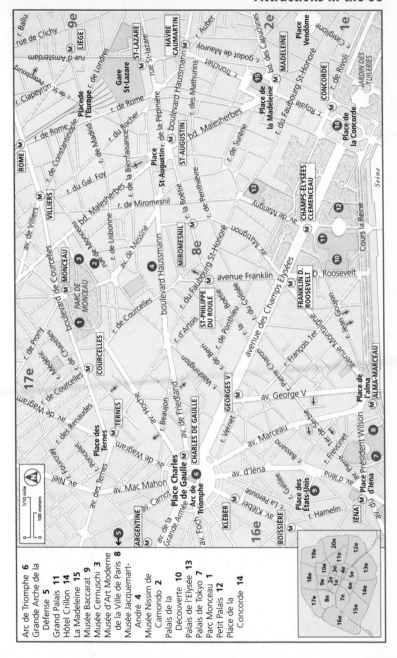

Arc de Triomphe **6**
Grande Arche de la
Défense **5**
Grand Palais **11**
Hôtel Crillon **14**
La Madeleine **15**
Musée Baccarat **9**
Musée Cernuschi **3**
Musée d'Art Moderne
de la Ville de Paris **8**
Musée Jacquemart-
André **4**
Musée Nissim de
Camondo **2**
Palais de la
Découverte **10**
Palais de l'Elysée **13**
Palais de Tokyo **7**
Parc Monceau **1**
Petit Palais **12**
Place de la
Concorde **14**

Le Grand Palais 🎦★★   This magnificent exhibition hall was built for the Exposition Universelle in 1900, along with its little sister, le Petit Palais. A mélange of glass, iron, and stone, the Grand Palais, which was designed by Charles Girault, is a prime example of the Belle Epoque in full bloom. The building is still used as an exhibition hall, and presents temporary exhibitions of art-world all-stars such as Gauguin (1989), Poussin (1994), Signac (2001), and Chagall (2003). The western half of the building houses the Palais de la Découverte (see below). The central hall is closed for renovation until 2006, but two the others remain open.

3 av. du Général Eisenhower, 8e. © **01-44-13-17-24.** Admission 10€ ($13). Call ahead for reduced admission prices for temporary exhibits. Wed–Mon 10am–10pm. Métro: Franklin-D-Roosevelt.

Musée Cernuschi 🎦   This smallish museum, just steps from the Parc Monceau, focuses on the art and archaeology of China. Initially opened in 1898, it's one of the city's oldest museums. After extensive renovations, the building reopened in June 2005 with a larger ground floor, and a new mezzanine and basement area for temporary exhibits. Nineteenth-century financier and humanist Henri Cernuschi assembled the excellent permanent collection, which is displayed in his sumptuous mansion. Ceramics, bronzes, funerary statues, Buddhist sculptures, and contemporary paintings are among the objects on offer. Two exquisite pieces are worth seeking out: a 5th-century bodhisattva and an 8th-century Tang silk painting, *Horses and Their Grooms.* The museum also presents temporary exhibits on China and other Asian cultures.

7 av. Velasquez, 8e. © **01-45-63-50-75.** Admission 6€ ($7.50) adults, 4€ ($5) students and seniors over 60, free for children under 8. Free to all Sun 10am–1pm. Tues–Sun 10am–5:40pm. Métro: Villiers or Monceau.

Musée Jacquemart-André 🎦★★   The combination of an outstanding art collection and a splendid 19th-century mansion makes this museum one of the jewels of Paris. Edouard André was the last child of a prominent banking family, and Nélie Jacquemart a well-known portraitist. Upon their marriage in 1881, they commissioned architect Henri Parent to build this impressive showcase, then set about filling it with French, Flemish, and Italian paintings, furniture, and Beauvais tapestries. Their taste was exquisite. Highlights of the collection include a fresco by Jean Baptiste Tiepolo, Fragonard's *Portrait d'un Vieillard,* Elisabeth Vigée-Lebrun's portrait of *Catherine Skavronskaia,* Rembrandt's portrait of an anxious *Docteur Tholinx,* van Dyck's *Time Cutting the Wings of Love,* and several rooms filled with paintings of the Italian Renaissance, including Botticelli's *Virgin and Child.* As you wander the ornate rooms, pause in the "winter garden," a tour de force of marble and mirrors that flanks an unusual double staircase. After losing out to Charles Garnier in the design competition for the Opéra, Parent evidently wished to prove that his own talent was nothing to be trifled with. Make sure to take advantage of the fascinating free audio tour; give yourself at least 2 hours to soak up the museum and its atmosphere. The beautiful restaurant on the ground floor makes an excellent lunch stop.

158 bd. Haussmann, 8e. © **01-45-62-11-59.** www.musee-jacquemart-andre.com. Admission 9.50€ ($12) adults, 6.50€ ($8.15) students and children under 18. Daily 10am–6pm. Métro: Miromesnil.

Musée Nissim de Camondo 🎦 *Finds*   Count Moïse de Camondo was mad about the 18th-century decorative arts, and he furnished this exquisite mansion accordingly. Built in 1914, it was inspired by the Petit Trianon at Versailles. Go up the marble staircase to sun-drenched salons filled with gilded mirrors, ornate fireplaces, stunning oil paintings, Savonnerie carpets, and Beauvais tapestries, including one that depicts La

Fontaine's "Fables." A special room holds the Buffon service, a spectacular set of Sèvres china—every piece is decorated with a different species of bird. Presented as a working home, visitors are allowed to visit not only the formal rooms, but also the kitchen and an enormous bathroom that is the size of a New York City studio apartment. Count de Camondo bequeathed the mansion and its contents to France, which inherited it upon his death in 1935. He stipulated that the museum should be named after his son, Nissim, killed in World War I. His daughter, Béatrice, her husband, and her children perished in Auschwitz in 1945. Allow around 1 hour.

63 rue de Monceau, 8e. (℃) **01-53-89-06-50**. www.ucad.fr. Admission 6€ ($7.50) adults, 4.50€ ($5.65) ages 18–25, free for under 18. Wed–Sun 10am–5:30pm. Métro: Villiers or Monceau.

Palais de la Découverte ⭐ *Kids*   This wonderful science museum is in part of the Grand Palais (see above). Your hair will stand on end in the electrostatics room, and kids will have a ball exploring dozens of other scientific exhibits. This is a funhouse of things to do: displays to light up, machines to test muscle reactions, and live experiments to watch. The planetarium takes you on a 45-minute voyage through the universe.

Grand Palais, av. Franklin-D-Roosevelt entrance, 8e. (℃) **01-56-43-20-21**. www.palais-decouverte.fr. Admission 6.50€ ($8.15) adults, 4€ ($5) students and children 8–17. Planetarium supplement 3.50€ ($4.40). Tues–Sat 9:30am–6pm; Sun 10am–7pm. Métro: Franklin-D-Roosevelt.

Parc Monceau ⭐⭐ *Kids*   This lovely park was commissioned by Louis Philippe Joseph, duc de Chartres et Orléans, an aristocrat whose democratic ideals led him to renounce his nobility and adopt the name Philippe-Egalité after the Revolution. (He was later guillotined.) The painter Carmontelle designed several structures for this whimsical park, including a windmill, a Roman temple, a covered bridge, a waterfall, a farm, medieval ruins, and a pagoda. The place became known as "Chartres's folly." Garnerin, the world's first parachutist, landed here. In the mid–19th century, the park was redesigned in the English style. Once a favorite place for Marcel Proust to stroll, it contains Paris's largest tree, an Oriental plane with a circumference of almost 7m (23 ft.).

Bd. de Courcelles, 8e. (℃) **01-42-27-08-64**. Nov–Mar 7am–8pm; Apr–Oct 7am–10pm. Métro: Monceau.

Place de la Concorde ⭐⭐⭐   The place de la Concorde, at the end of the Champs-Elysées, is a stunning example of artistic, dynamic urban design. During the day, wild traffic whizzes past the formidable administrative buildings toward the Champs-Elysées or Pont de la Concorde. The place takes on a mystical aura when the sun begins to set and the obelisk becomes a piercing silhouette against the sky, its lines mirrored by the Eiffel Tower in the distance.

This is one of the centers of Paris. On its perimeter stands the **Hôtel Crillon,** where Benjamin Franklin and Louis XVI signed the Treaty of Friendship and Trade, recognizing the United States of America, in February 1778. Soon thereafter, the octagonal space, designed by Gabriel under Louis XV, became place de la Révolution. The guillotine was installed here, and among the heads severed was that of Louis XVI. From 1793 to 1795, 1,343 people were guillotined—Marie Antoinette, Mme du Barry, Charlotte Corday, Danton, Robespierre, and Alexandre de Beauharnais among them. After the Reign of Terror, in hopes of peace, the square was renamed place de la Concorde.

The **Egyptian obelisk** comes from the temple of Ramses II in Thebes, and is more than 3,000 years old. It was a gift to France from Egypt in 1829.

Pl. de la Concorde, 8e. Métro: Concorde.

8 18e Arrondissement: Montmartre

There are two Montmartres: one is crowded with tourists, tour buses, and "artists" vying to sketch your portrait. The other is a quiet, lovely place with old windy streets, vine-covered buildings, and even a **windmill** or two lurking on a hillside. How to get from one to the other? It's not that hard—just follow any street that leads away from the hoards around the **place du Tertre** and **Sacré-Coeur** until the noise fades into the distance. This should take no more than a few minutes, particularly if you head toward the rear and the sides of the basilica. This is also true of the streets around **place des Abbesses** and **rue Lepic** (those windmills are at 75 rue Lepic). In these streets you will begin to understand what drew all those artists to this high hill in what was then the outskirts of the city—cobbled lanes, majestic panoramas, and an almost rustic atmosphere that can make you forget you are in the nation's capital. Keep in mind that the last of those famous artists moved out of the neighborhood around 50 years ago, and adjust your expectations accordingly. You may not see the Montmartre of Utrillo and Picasso, but you might just happen into the Montmartre of today.

Though quiet now, Montmartre has had a turbulent history, beginning with its name. Historians believe the name refers to the martyrdom of St. Denis, who was reputedly decapitated on the hill. Legend has it that he picked up his head and walked 6.4km (4 miles) before finally collapsing. The village was occupied by Henri IV in the 16th century and by the Russians and the English in the early 19th century before becoming part of Paris in 1860.

In the late 19th century, Montmartre became a mecca for painters, poets, and musicians. Composers Berlioz and Offenbach, writers Henri Murger and Tristan Tzara, and painters Henri Toulouse-Lautrec and Maurice Utrillo were among the artists who gathered at the Lapin Agile and Moulin Rouge cabarets. Later, Picasso painted *Les Demoiselles d'Avignon* at his studio in the **Bateau-Lavoir.** The building still stands in the charming **place Emile Goudeau,** a good spot to sit and soak up the scenery.

Cimetière de Montmartre ⊛   The graves of artist Edgar Degas; composers Hector Berlioz, Léo Delibes, and Jacques Offenbach; writers Théophile Gautier, Stendhal, and Emile Zola; cartoonist Francisque Poulbot; and filmmaker François Truffaut are here. You can pick up a map at the main entrance, 20 av. Rachel, for a general idea of where to find them. The cemetery was founded in 1798 on the site of gypsum quarries. Allow at least 1 hour.

Rue Caulaincourt or av. Rachel, 18e. Métro: Place de Clichy.

Espace Montmartre Salvador-Dalí   Dalí's flirtation with commercialism lives on in this tourist-filled space, years after his death. Some 330 works by the Spanish artist are on display, including watercolors, sculptures, lithographs, and collages, but none of his paintings. There are also several pieces of furniture based on his designs. The furniture, like the lithographs, is for sale; the gift shop is almost as big as the museum. The steep entry price should limit this visit to serious Dalí fans, who will need an hour or so to see the museum and shop.

11 rue Poulbot, 18e. 🕐 **01-42-64-40-10.** www.dali-espacemontmartre.com. Admission 7€ ($8.75) adults, 6€ ($7.50) seniors (over 60), 5€ ($6.25) ages 8–26, free for children under 8. Sept–June daily 10am–6:30pm; July–Aug daily 10am–9:30pm. Métro: Abbesses or Anvers.

Musée de l'Erotisme *(Finds)*   Yes, this is a real museum, even if it is sandwiched in between various sex shops in the red-light district along boulevard de Clichy. Definitely

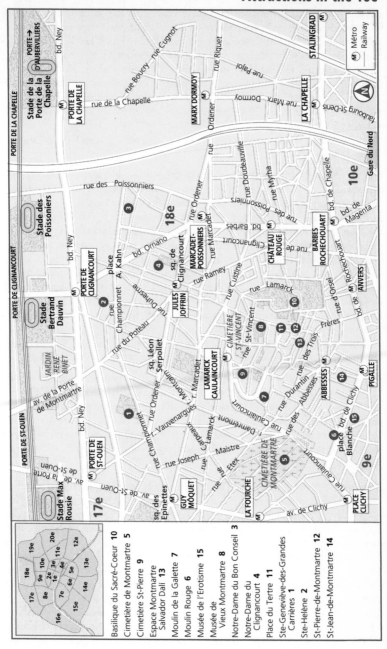

Métro Ⓜ
Railway

Basilique du Sacré-Coeur **10**
Cimetière de Montmartre **5**
Cimetière St-Pierre **9**
Espace Montmartre
Salvador Dali **13**
Moulin de la Galette **7**
Moulin Rouge **6**
Musée de l'Erotisme **15**
Musée de
Vieux Montmartre **8**
Notre-Dame du Bon Conseil **3**
Notre-Dame du
Clignancourt **4**
Place du Tertre **11**
Ste-Geneviève-des-Grandes-
Carrières **1**
Ste-Helène **2**
St-Pierre-de-Montmartre **12**
St-Jean-de-Montmartre **14**

not family fare, the museum attempts to offer a comprehensive survey of erotic art. The objects and paintings are spread over seven floors, starting on the ground floor with a collection that includes African wood sculptures, Japanese prints, and Peruvian ceramic pots. Though you will be amazed at the acrobatics represented, you may be frustrated at the lack of coherent labeling—then again, it is pretty obvious what is going on. Higher floors include antique collections of naughty cards, modern art, and temporary exhibits. Mostly merely titillating, there is one section that is actually quite poignant—photos and documents on the long-vanished bordellos of Paris and Marseilles, and the women who worked there.

72 bd. de Clichy, 18e. ☎ 01-42-58-28-73. Admission 7€ ($8.75) adults, 5€ ($6.25) students; children under 18 not admitted. Daily 10am–2am. Métro: Blanche.

Musée du Vieux Montmartre   This 17th-century building was converted into artists' studios in 1875. In 1876, Renoir rented a space, where he finished *Le Moulin de la Galette* and entertained Paul Gauguin and Vincent van Gogh.

The museum charts Montmartre's history. It includes the legend of St-Denis, and the foundation of the Society of Jesus (Jesuits) by Loyola. Also captured here are the neighborhood's not-so-saintly cabarets; you'll see a Montmartre-style bistro, complete with piano. The museum also features a re-creation of the manufacture of Clignancourt pottery, and Delâtre's engraving studio. An entire room is devoted to former inhabitants Suzanne Valadon; her husband, Utter Utrillo; their son, Maurice Utrillo (who later had his own studio here); Fauvist painter Raoul Dufy; and painters Emile Bernard and Auguste Renoir. The city of Paris bought the house in 1922 from actress Rose de Rosimund.

12 rue Cortot, 18e. ☎ 01-49-25-89-37. Admission 5€ ($6.25) adults, 3.50€ ($4.40) students and those in groups larger than 15, free for children under 10. Tues–Sun 11am–5:30pm. Métro: Lamarck-Caulaincourt or Abbesses.

Place du Tertre *(Overrated*   Perhaps if you got here at dawn, you would be able to appreciate the beauty of this rustic village square high above the city, surrounded by 18th-century houses. But usually you will be faced with scads of artists begging to do your portrait, dozens of trinket shops selling Eiffel Tower key rings, and crowds in a density comparable with that of the Métro at rush hour. This is quite possibly the most tourist-laden spot in the city. If this doesn't bother you, dive in and enjoy—if it does, skip it.

18e. Métro: Abbesses.

St-Pierre de Montmartre ☆   This church, one of the oldest in Paris, has been at the center of Montmartre life for nearly 9 centuries. Consecrated in 1147 by Pope Eugene III, the Eglise St-Pierre stands on the site of an early sanctuary to St-Denis that replaced a Gallo-Roman temple. It is also the last trace of the original Benedictine Abbey of Montmartre, which achieved tremendous influence before it was destroyed in the Revolution. The revolutionaries turned it into a Temple of Reason, the occupying Allies of 1814 used it to store provisions, and during the Commune of 1870, it was used as a munitions depot. Renovation began in 1905, and the church reopened for worship in 1908. Although the entrance was reconstructed in the 18th century, the chancel and the nave date from 1147. The four 6th-century columns in the choir stall are believed to have come from the original temple. In the left aisle is the tombstone of the abbey's founder, Queen Adélaide, wife of Louis VI. The stained-glass windows were made by Max Ingrand in 1954; earlier ones were destroyed during World War II.

2 rue du Mont-Cenis, 18e. Daily 8:30am–7pm. Métro: Lamarck-Caulaincourt.

9 16e Arrondissement: Trocadéro & Le Seizième

The 16e is one of the city's most residential arrondissements, as well as the most prestigious—and has been since before Benjamin Franklin stayed here. Aristocrats and merchants, attracted by the beauty of the land between the Seine and the **Bois de Boulogne,** and by its location on the road to Versailles, built country houses in the villages (now neighborhoods) of **Chaillot, Passy,** and **Auteuil.** Most of the houses didn't survive the real estate boom that began in the 19th century, but Art Nouveau master Hector Guimard left some superb examples of his architecture on rue La Fontaine, especially the Castel Béranger at no. 14. The district is home to several museums, including the **Musée Guimet,** which has a stunning collection of Asian art. A relic of the Universal Exposition of 1937, the grand **Palais de Chaillot** and **place du Trocadéro** offer the ultimate view of the Eiffel Tower. If an excess of grandeur has tired you, take advantage of the lush parks and gardens of the **Bois de Boulogne** for rest and relaxation.

Bois de Boulogne   This legendary park (see map on p. 201) got its start as a royal forest and hunting ground. Napoleon III donated it to the city, and Baron Haussmann transformed it, using London's Hyde Park as his model. He also laid out avenue de l'Impératrice (now av. Foch), from the Arc de Triomphe to the Bois.

Today the Bois is a vast reserve of more than 880 hectares (2,174 acres). It offers space for jogging, horseback riding, bicycling (rentals are available), and boating on the two lakes. Also here are the famous Longchamp and Auteuil racecourses and the beautiful **Jardin Shakespeare** in the Pré Catelan, a garden containing many of the plants and herbs mentioned in Shakespeare's plays. The Bois's **Jardin d'Acclimatation** (see below) is Parisian children's favorite amusement park.

Be sure to visit the **Parc de Bagatelle** , a gorgeous park-within-a-park. The thematic gardens surround a château, built by Comte d'Artois in 66 days in 1775, after he made a bet with his sister-in-law Marie Antoinette. The rose gardens are sublime; some 10,000 rose bushes encompass 1,000 varieties. There is also a pond of water lilies—the garden's designer was a friend of Monet.

As the sun sets, prostitutes move in (notably along the Porte Dauphine entrance), so the Bois is best enjoyed in daylight.

Bois de Boulogne, 16e. Métro: Les Sablons, Porte-Maillot, or Porte-Dauphine; Parc de Bagatelle, Bois de Boulogne, 16e. ℂ **01-40-67-97-00.** Admission 2€ ($2.50) adults, 1€ ($1.25) students 7–26; free for children under 7. Daily 9am–dusk. Métro: Porte-Maillot.

Jardin d'Acclimatation   This is a great place to take kids when they've had one too many museums. It contains an enchanted river (boat ride), a minicar racetrack, a carousel, rides, Guignol puppet shows, circus acts, and a small zoo. A little train will take you to the park from the Porte Maillot entrance.

Bois de Boulogne, 16e. ℂ **01-40-67-90-82.** www.jardindacclimatation.fr. Admission 2.70€ ($3.40) adults and children 3 and over, free for children under 3. Oct–May daily 10am–6pm; June–Sept daily 10am–7pm. Métro: Sablons.

Maison de Balzac   Balzac lived in this rustic cabin with a romantic garden from 1840 to 1847, hiding from creditors by living under an assumed name, M. de Breugnol. (That didn't stop him from buying a jewel-encrusted cane, which apparently was the talk of Paris. It's exhibited here.) His study is preserved, and portraits, books, letters, and manuscripts are on display. Give yourself around 45 minutes to enjoy this lovely house.

47 rue Raynouard, 16e. (*)* **01-55-74-41-80.** www.balzac.paris.fr. Admission 3.30€ ($4.15) adults, 2.20€ ($2.75) seniors (over 60), 1.60€ ($2) ages 8–26, free for children under 8. Tues–Sun 10am–6pm. Closed holidays. Métro: Passy or La-Muette.

Musée Baccarat   This fantastic museum moved its collection in 2004 to the sumptuous minimansion once owned by Marie-Laure de Noailles (1902-71) who hosted "salons" for artists such as Dalíand Mondrian, and threw the most lavish parties. Philippe Starck was hired to renovate the entire building and now its interior design, like its collection, is stunning. You feel as if you've walked into a very exclusive club when you enter the building—with red carpet and fireplaces on each side of the entrance hall. Mirrors, tables and chairs with crystal bases, and low-hung crystal chandeliers adorn the place. (Baccarat was founded in 1794 and is named after a village in Eastern France where the crystal items are cut by hand to this day.)

On the ground floor lies a small boutique where serious crystal lovers place thousands of euros worth of orders (the least expensive item, a small wine glass, sells for 115€/$144). Purses with crystal buttons, watches with crystal, belts with crystal—you get the picture (if you're curious, the watches cost around 15,000€/$18,750). Upstairs, "Le Crystal Room" restaurant has become all the rage in Paris for its chic decor (crystal again) and 100€/$125 dishes (there's a 6-week wait-list to dine here). Next door to the restaurant is the small museum (though the entire place is like a museum, the actual museum is a small room upstairs that is home to the incredible collection of crystal products), many designed for the world fairs over the years. Here, you can see a cognac snifter that once belonged to Princess Grace of Monaco; a 1909 specially designed wine glass for Tzar Nicolas of Russia and a tumbler for Aristotle Onassis from 1953, among many other items. Be sure to visit the toilets—themselves full of black crystal and chandeliers.

You can enter the boutique for free if you'd like to take a peek at the place without paying the admission price for the museum. You just won't have access to the historical collection.

11 pl. des Etats Unis, 16e. (*)* **01-47-70-64-30.** www.baccarat.fr. Admission 8€ ($10). Mon–Sat Apr–Oct 9:30am–12:30pm and 2–6:30pm; Nov–Mar 10–noon and 2–6pm.

Musée d'Art Moderne de la Ville de Paris *(★)*   Many don't know that Paris has two modern art museums; this one is often overshadowed by the Musée National d'Art Moderne at the Centre Pompidou, and was closed in 2005 for renovations. It will reopen in late 2005 with a Pierre Bonnard exhibit. Primarily known for its temporary exhibitions, this huge space also accommodates a somewhat sparse permanent collection, including a sampling of works from the major 20th-century art movements. It has a good collection of the works of George Rouault, Robert and Sonia Delaunay, and Raoul Dufy, including Dufy's *La Fée Electricité (The Good Fairy Electricity)*, one of the largest pictures in the world. The museum also holds two of Matisse's set of three triptychs, *La Dance*. The building, which looks like something out of the movie *Metropolis*, was constructed in 1937 for the Exposition Universelle.

11 av. du Président Wilson, 16e. (*)* **01-53-67-40-00.** www.paris.fr/musees/MAMVP. Admission 4.50€ ($5.65) adults, 2.50€ ($3.15) ages 14–26 with ID, free for 13 and under. Tues–Fri 10am–6pm; Sat–Sun 10am–7pm. Métro: Iéna or Alma-Marceau.

Musée de la Marine *(★)*   This fascinating museum traces the history of navigation, sailing, and maritime culture since the 17th century, including topics such as shipbuilding, navigational instruments, explorers' routes, steamships, fishing, sea rescue,

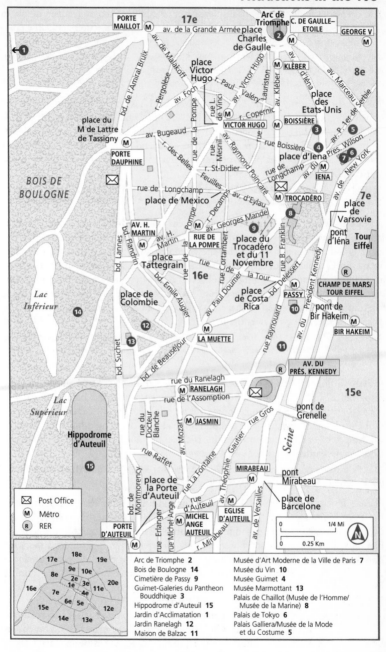

Attractions in the 16e

PORTE MAILLOT Ⓜ

17e

av. de la Grande Armée

Arc de Triomphe ❷

place Charles de Gaulle

C. DE GAULLE–ETOILE

GEORGE V Ⓜ

❶

bd. de l'Amiral Bruix

av. de Malakoff

r. Pergolèse

av. Foch

place Victor Hugo

r. Paul Valéry

av. Victor Hugo

av. Raymond Poincaré

r. L. de Vinci

rue L. de Vinci

Ⓜ KLÉBER

av. Kléber

av. d'Iéna

av. Marceau

8e

place des Etats-Unis

av. P. 1er de Serbie

VICTOR HUGO

Ⓜ BOISSIÈRE

❸

❺

place du M de Lattre de Tassigny

Ⓜ PORTE DAUPHINE

av. Bugeaud

r. des Belles Feuilles

rue de la Pompe

r. du Mesnil

r. Copernic

r. St-Didier

rue Boissière

❹

place d'Iéna

av. Prés. Wilson

❼ ❻

Ⓜ IENA

av. du Pdt Wilson

av. de New York

7e

BOIS DE BOULOGNE

✉

rue de Longchamp

place de Mexico

r. Decamps

av. d'Eylau

av. Georges Mandel

av. du Prés. Wilson

✉ TROCADÉRO

❽

place de Varsovie

pont d'Iéna

Tour Eiffel

AV. H. MARTIN Ⓜ

av. H. Martin

RUE DE LA POMPE

❾

place du Trocadéro et du 11 Novembre

r. Franklin

Lac Inférieur

bd. Lannes

bd. Flandrin

rue de la Pompe

rue Cortambert

place Tattegrain

rue de la Tour

16e

place de Costa Rica

R CHAMP DE MARS/ TOUR EIFFEL

place de Colombie

bd. Émile Augier

av. Paul Doumer

bd. Delessert

PASSY Ⓜ

❿

pont de Bir Hakeim

❷ ❸

Ⓜ LA MUETTE

av. du Président Kennedy

⓫

Ⓜ BIR HAKEIM

bd. Suchet

bd. de Beauséjour

R AV. DU PRÉS. KENNEDY

Lac Supérieur

rue du Ranelagh

Ⓜ RANELAGH

rue de l'Assomption

✉

15e

pont de Grenelle

Hippodrome d'Auteuil

rue du Docteur Blanche

Ⓜ JASMIN

rue du Mozart

rue Gros

rue Gautier

Seine

⓯

rue Raffet

rue La Fontaine

av. Théophile Gautier

MIRABEAU Ⓜ

pont Mirabeau

place de Barcelone

place de la Porte d'Auteuil

rue d'Auteuil

Ⓜ

EGLISE D'AUTEUIL

av. de Versailles

bd. de Montmorency

rue Erlanger

rue Michel Ange

MICHEL ANGE AUTEUIL

PORTE D'AUTEUIL Ⓜ

r. Mirabeau

✉	Post Office
Ⓜ	Métro
R	RER

Map index

17e	18e	19e
9e	10e	
8e	2e	11e	20e
16e	1e	3e	
7e	4e	
6e	5e	12e
15e		
14e	13e	

Arc de Triomphe **2**
Bois de Boulogne **14**
Cimetière de Passy **9**
Guimet-Galeries du Pantheon Bouddhique **3**
Hippodrome d'Auteuil **15**
Jardin d'Acclimatation **1**
Jardin Ranelagh **12**
Maison de Balzac **11**

Musée d'Art Moderne de la Ville de Paris **7**
Musée du Vin **10**
Musée Guimet **4**
Musée Marmottant **13**
Palais de Chaillot (Musée de l'Homme/ Musée de la Marine) **8**
Palais de Tokyo **6**
Palais Galliera/Musée de la Mode et du Costume **5**

and deep-sea diving. Numerous displays cover everything from Melanesian canoes to supertankers. Highlights include an extensive model-ship collection and some fabulous ship's prows. The gift shop stocks unusual nautical souvenirs.

Palais de Chaillot, 17 pl. du Trocadéro, 16e. ℂ 01-53-65-69-69. www.musee-marine.fr. Admission 9€ ($11) adults over 25, 7€ ($8.75) students 18–25, 5€ ($6.25) children 6–17, free for children under 6; 29€ ($36) "Tarif Equipe" ("Crew Fare") for a group of 5 including at least 2 children. Wed–Mon 10am–5:50pm. Métro: Trocadéro.

Musée de l'Homme   The Museum of Mankind has not been renovated in some time since the collection will be moving to Quai Branly nearby when it opens in mid-2006. Though a bit old-fashioned, it can still fascinate. The collection contains objects from all over the world that are extremely beautiful and quite rare, such as a stone seat built by native peoples in the Caribbean. It's unclear as yet what will become of this museum once Quai Branly opens.

17 pl. du Trocadéro, 16e. ℂ 01-44-05-72-72. www.mnhn.fr. Admission 7€ ($8.75) adults 27 and over, 5€ ($6.25) ages 18–26, free for children under 18. Wed–Fri 9:45am–5:15pm; Sat–Sun 10am–6:30pm. Métro: Trocadéro.

Musée du Vin   This museum is in an ancient stone-and-clay quarry that 15th-century monks used as a wine cellar. It makes a good introduction to the art of winemaking—if you can get over the weirdness of posed wax figures representing "all stages in the life of wine," with displays of tools, beakers, cauldrons, and bottles in a series of exhibits. The quarry is right below Balzac's house (see above), and the ceiling contains a trap door he used to escape from his creditors. The visit lasts about an hour; the museum offers several packages that include admission and various wine and cheese tastings, and even an entire lunch.

Rue des Eaux, 5 sq. Charles Dickens, 16e. ℂ 01-45-25-63-26. www.museeduvinparis.com. Admission (including glass of wine) 8€ ($10) adults, 7€ ($8.75) seniors over 60, 5.70€ ($7.15) students under 26. Tues–Sun 10am–6pm. Métro: Passy.

Musée Galliera/Musée de la Mode et du Costume   You'll understand the importance of the fashion industry to this city when you see the Italian Renaissance palace in which this museum is housed. Three statues under the central arches represent Painting, Architecture, and Sculpture. Frequently changing exhibitions illustrate the history of French fashion from the 18th century to the present. You can take a break in the garden after your visit.

10 av. Pierre-Premier-de-Serbie, 16e. ℂ 01-56-52-86-00. Admission 8€ ($10) adults, 6€ ($7.50) seniors over 60, 4€ ($5) ages 13–26. Tues–Sun 10am–6pm. Métro: Iéna or Alma-Marceau.

Musée Marmottan Monet ⭐⭐ (Finds)   Located between the Ranelagh garden and the Bois de Boulogne, the Musée Marmottan Monet celebrates the painter Claude Monet and contains an outstanding collection of his water-lily paintings. The problem of rendering the delicate flowers floating on a reflective pool obsessed the artist during his years at Giverny. This museum also displays his more abstract representations of the Japanese Bridge at Giverny, as well as *Impression: Rising Sun,* the painting from which the term "Impressionist" derived. Monet's personal collection is also here. It includes works by his contemporaries Pissarro, Manet, Morisot, and Renoir.

The museum is in a 19th-century mansion that belonged to the art historian Paul Marmottan. When Marmottan died in 1932, he donated the mansion and his collection of Empire furniture and Napoleonic art to the Académie des Beaux-Arts. Claude Monet's son and heir bequeathed his father's collection to the Marmottan. Subsequent donations have expanded the collection to include more Impressionist paintings and

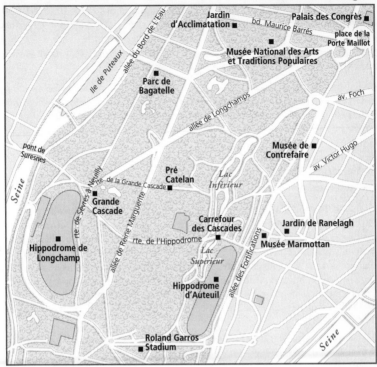

the stunning Wildenstein collection of late medieval illuminated manuscripts. Give yourself 2 hours for this beautiful museum.

2 rue Louis-Boilly, 16e. ℂ **01-44-96-50-33**. www.marmottan.com. Admission 7€ ($8.75) adults, 4.50€ ($5.65) ages 8–25, free for children under 8. Tues–Sun 10am–6pm. Métro: La-Muette.

Musée National Des Arts Asiatique—Guimet 🕊🕊   At the entrance to this airy museum you will be greeted by a giant seven-headed stone serpent from Cambodia, which leads the way to an enormous room full of peaceful, smiling statues from Southeast Asia. A beautiful portrait of the Khmer monarch Jayavarman VII is just one of the museum's highlights, which also include a sublime 11th-century dancing Shiva from southern India, a life-size Chinese ceramic of the Buddhist disciple Luohan, and some spectacular Tibetan mandalas. Be prepared to spend several hours marveling over these and other treasures such as Korean masques, Japanese prints, and Nepalese jewel-encrusted crowns. Don't miss the cupola on the top floor with its magnificent carved lacquer screens from China.

Emile Guimet was a 19th-century industrialist and scholar with a fascination for the religions of the Eastern world. During his travels, he began collecting religious objects with the goal of opening a museum devoted to the subject. The museum was a huge success, and the collection grew and evolved; after Guimet's death, the focus changed from religion to art and culture, and the institution is now one of the largest Asian art museums outside of Asia. As an acknowledgement of the founder's intentions, the

Guimet also offers the **Galeries du Panthéon Bouddhique** at 19 av. d'Iéna (② **01-40-73-88-11;** free admission), a collection of art objects relating Buddhism in China and Japan.

6 pl. d'Iéna, 16e. ② 01-56-52-53-00. www.museeguimet.fr. Admission 8€ ($10) adults, 5.50€ ($6.90) ages 18–25 and for all on Sun, free for under 18. Wed–Mon 10am–6pm. Métro: Iéna.

Palais de Chaillot *(Moments*   This monumental building, which has two huge curved wings that stretch out like embracing arms, was constructed for the Exposition Universelle in 1937. Hovering over the site of what was once a Medici palace, the Palais de Chaillot now holds the Musée de l'Homme and the Musée de la Marine (see above), as well as the Cinémathèque Française and the Théâtre de Challiot. Its terraces afford great views of the Eiffel Tower, the Champs de Mars, the Ecole Militaire, and the Trocadéro fountains.

Pl. du Trocadéro, 16e. Métro: Trocadéro.

Palais de Tokyo   After a complete renovation, the Palais de Tokyo reopened in 2002 as a space devoted to temporary exhibits of contemporary art. Encompassing one side of the huge building that also holds the Musée d'Art Moderne de la Ville de Paris, this vast space is now used as a flexible environment for art installations and exhibitions, as well as musical events and films. The temporary exhibits here are often controversial, political, and thought provoking. Occasionally (and understandably), parts of the museum are off-limits for those under 18. The coffee shop is a popular spot with art students for lunch, and the bookshop has a great collection of books and unique postcards.

13 av. du Président Wilson, 16e. ② 01-47-23-54-01. www.palaisdetokyo.com. Admission 6€ ($7.50) adults, 4.50€ ($5.65) students and children under 18. Tues–Sun noon–12am. Métro: Iéna or Alma-Marceau.

Tenniseum (Tennis Museum) *(★ *(Finds*   This new museum is located adjacent to the famous clay courts of Roland Garros, home of the French Open in late May and early June each year. The collection focuses on the history of tennis with antique tennis rackets and related items (such as the first ball machine circa 1928). You can watch over 400 hours of tennis footage, from 1897 to the present in the excellent multimedia space. You can also tour the stadium and buy official Roland Garros products at the museum boutique. Note that the museum is closed from third week of May until the second week of June each year during the French Open.

Stade Roland Garros, 2 av. Gordon-Bennett, 16e. ② 01-47-43-48-48. Admission. 7.50€ ($9.40). Apr–Oct (except May 21–June 7) Tues–Sun 10am–6pm; Nov–Mar Wed 10am–6pm; Fri–Sun 10am–6pm. Métro: Porte d'Auteuil.

10 12, 19 & 20e Arrondissements: Eastern Paris

Long ignored by both hipsters and city administrators, the eastern reaches of Paris have been experiencing a flurry of interest over the past few years. Young artists and real estate mavens are infiltrating the older neighborhoods, and families are moving into the new apartment buildings that have sprouted near the Seine. Though not as glamorous as other parts of the city, these arrondissements contain some of the last remaining pockets of *Paris populaire,* the down-to-earth Paris of working-class people, most of whom have been chased out of the city by rising rents. It is also an area that has experienced a lot of urban renewal, not always done with a delicate touch. Mixed into this cultural stew of old and new is a healthy dose of energy from the area's vibrant immigrant population.

Attractions in the 12 & 19–20e

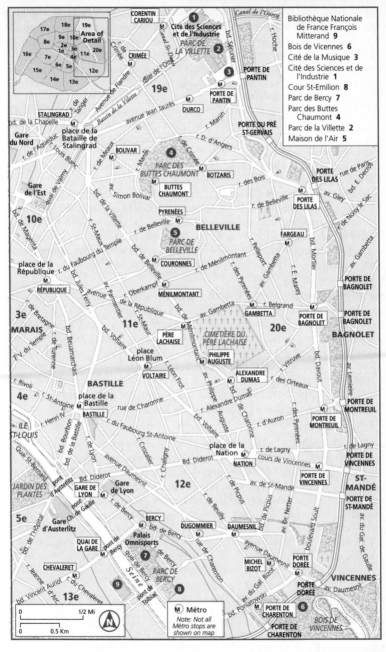

Bibliothèque Nationale de France François Mitterand **9**
Bois de Vicennes **6**
Cité de la Musique **3**
Cité des Sciences et de l'Industrie **1**
Cour St-Emilion **8**
Parc de Bercy **7**
Parc des Buttes Chaumont **4**
Parc de la Villette **2**
Maison de l'Air **5**

Ⓜ Métro
Note: Not all Métro stops are shown on map

0   1/2 Mi
0   0.5 Km

Just about every uprising in the city's history sprang from this area, including the Revolution of 1789. If you poke around the streets and passages of the **Faubourg St-Antoine,** you will find there are still plenty of furniture makers and craftsmen; the **Viaduct des Arts** with its crafts galleries and workshops is an homage to many endangered skills and arts. On top of the Viaduct is the **Promenade Plantée,** a lovely narrow garden that extends the length of this old train track from the place de la Bastille to the huge park **Bois de Vincennes.**

While some may wince at the modern buildings in the 12e arrondissement's Reuilly and Bercy neighborhoods, no one can complain about the new **Parc de Bercy,** with its tree-shaded pathways, themed gardens, and lake. The park affords an excellent view of the new **Bibliothèque Nationale de France** across the Seine. Next to the park, old wine warehouses have been renovated and reborn as the **Cour St-Emillon,** a collection of terraced restaurants and chic boutiques.

Continents collide in **Belleville,** a neighborhood in the 20e where Chinese grocery stores are frequented by African women swathed in bright fabrics, Jewish bakeries are next door to Arab restaurants, and Caribbean music pulses in a Greek kabob house. Nearby in the 19e, the wacky **Parc de la Villete** offers green lawns, a music complex, and a giant science museum, **La Cité des Sciences et de l'Industrie.** Crisscrossing the park, and the area, are Paris's three **canals,** where you can take a cruise—a unique way to see this unique part of the city.

Bibliothèque Nationale de France   With its looming glass towers shaped like open books, this national library is the grandest of the Grand Projects commissioned by former president François Mitterrand. It's one of the largest libraries in the world. The reading rooms are austere but comfortable, and the collections include films, photos, recordings, and videos. A gallery section has rotating exhibits of rare books and manuscripts. Although city planners boasted of its high-tech search-and-retrieve capabilities, technological glitches have proved frustrating to both researchers and staff. Part of the library is open to the public; special exhibits are held several times a year.

Quai François Mauriac, 13e. ℂ **01-53-79-59-59.** www.bnf.fr. Admission 3€ ($3.75). Tues–Sat 10am–8pm; Sun noon–6pm. Métro: Quai de la Gare.

Bois de Vincennes   This park was once a hunting ground for kings, and the largest green area in Paris. Its lake, where you can rent boats, its *parc zoologique,* and a petting zoo make this a favorite spot for families. There is also a Buddhist center, complete with temple. The park has its own castle, the Château de Vincennes, where early monarchs like Charles V and Henri III sought refuge from wars. In 1917, Mata Hari was executed here. Most of the building is used as administrative offices; there is a tour, but with the dungeon closed for renovations, there's not much to see. The Bois houses the **Parc Floral de Paris,** which has a butterfly garden, library, and, in the summer, free concerts. The 1999 *tempête* hit the Bois de Vincennes hard, but even though it will take a long time before all the trees grow back to their full splendor, this is still a beautiful place to spend a sunny afternoon.

Bois de Vincenes, 12e. Métro: Porte-Dorée or Château de Vincennes; Parc Zoologique, Bois de Vincennes, 53 av. St-Maurice, 12e. ℂ **01-44-75-20-10.** Admission 6€ ($7.50) adults, 4.50€ ($5.65) ages 4–16 and seniors (over 60), free for children under 4. Daily 9am–6pm. Métro: Porte-Dorée; Parc Floral de Paris, Esplanade du Château de Vincennes, ℂ 01-55-94-20-20. Admission 2€ ($2.50) adults, 1€ ($1.25) ages 6–18 and seniors over 60, free for children under 6. Daily 9:30am–dusk. Métro: Château de Vincennes.

Cité de la Musique   This ultramodern complex in the Parc de la Villette (see below) includes a music conservatory, a documentation center, concert halls, and the

Musée de la Musique. All are architecturally astounding, but the music museum is the gem. Wide, sweeping halls full of light embrace a collection of more than 900 instruments dating from the Renaissance, including Italian lutes, harpsichords, glass flutes, and a 1.8m (6-ft.) bassoon. A portable headset plays extracts from major works and offers commentary (in English) that places the instruments in historical context. Check out the copies of handwritten musical scores by major composers including Beethoven, Debussy, Bach, and Ravel, whose beautiful script is almost as inspired as his music. Allow 2 hours.

221 av. Jean-Jaurès, 19e. © 01-44-84-45-45. www.cite-musique.fr. Admission 6.10€ ($7.65) adults, 4.60€ ($5.75) students, 2.30€ ($2.90) children 6–18, free for children under 6. Tues–Sat noon–6pm; Sun 10am–6pm. Métro: Porte de Pantin.

Cité des Sciences et de l'Industrie   This massive museum is housed in a building that was the subject of one of the biggest financial scandals of the century. Built as a high-tech abattoir to replace the slaughterhouses in the area, the project consumed enormous amounts of money and was obsolete before it was finished. Now the mammoth structure is a wonderful science and industry museum that includes a planetarium, a 3-D cinema, and interactive exhibits designed for 3- to 5-year-olds and 5- to 12-year-olds at the **Cité des Enfants.** The main museum is called **Explora** and includes models and interactive games that demonstrate scientific principles, as well as exhibits covering the universe, the earth, the environment, space, computer science, and health. There are two *médiathèques* (multimedia centers), one for children and one for adults. Outside, a gigantic metal sphere called the **Géode** shows films on a huge screen. Also outside, kids can climb into an actual submarine, the *Argonaute.* Located in the Parc de la Villette, there is plenty of access to cafes, restaurants, and places to rest tired feet. During school vacations, call ahead to reserve for Cité des Enfants. Depending on your stamina, you could spend a day here.

30 av. Corentin-Cariou, 19e. © 01-40-05-80-00; reservations 01-40-05-12-12. www.cite-sciences.fr. Admission to Explora exhibition 7.50€ ($9.40) adults over 25, 5.50€ ($6.90) ages 7–25, free for children under 7; to the Argonaut 3€ ($3.75); to the planetarium 2.50€ ($3.15); to the Géode 8.75€ ($11); to Cinaxe theater 5.20€ ($6.50); to Cité des Enfants 5€ ($6.25). Tues–Sat 10am–6pm; Sun 10am–7pm. Métro: Porte-de-la-Villette.

Maison de l'Air   AIR, IT'S LIFE, announce signs at this museum dedicated to air and all the ways air is of importance to humans. Thought-provoking displays show how air circulates, how birds and winged devices use it to fly, and the effects of air and noise pollution and what's being done in France to curb them. You can visit a small *salle de*

Tips   **A Museum Under Renovation**

The **Musée des Arts d'Afrique et d'Océanie** closed its doors in January 2003 and the collection is now awaiting the completion of the brand-new Quai Branly (by the Eiffel Tower) where it will be housed permanently. The collection is a wonder, including beautiful pieces such as cowrie-covered masks from New Guinea, totem poles from Melanesia, bronze Yoruba sculptures from Nigeria, and rugs from the Magreb. Quai Branly was scheduled to open in 2004, but now, due to construction delays, its much-anticipated *vernissage* has been pushed to mid-2006. To keep up-to-date with the latest developments, consult the museum's website at www.quaibranly.fr.

documentation (research library) and participate in hands-on demonstrations. The museum is up on a hill in the lovely Parc de Belleville. Under the right conditions, the gorgeous views of the city show that Paris is indeed working on its pollution problem. Allow 45 minutes.

27 rue Piat, 20e. ✆ **01-43-28-47-63**. Admission 4€ ($5) adults, 2€ ($2.50) ages 11–18, 1€ ($1.25) children 6–10, free for children under 6 and seniors over 60. Apr–Sept Tues–Fri 1:30–5:30pm, Sat–Sun and holidays 1:30–6:30pm; Oct–Mar daily 1:30–5pm. Métro: Pyrénées or Couronnes.

Parc de Bercy ✿ This spacious park opened in 1997 on what was once the city's wine depot and has several themed gardens, including the Jardin Romantique and the Jardin du Philosophe. Trees shade flower patches, and ducks float on the lake. The Maison du Jardinage has exhibits on wine commerce and classes for garden novices. In honor of its origins, the park has a small vineyard. The new "Meteor" express Métro (line 14) will zoom you here in a flash.

12e. Métro: Bercy.

Parc de la Villette ✿✿ *(Kids)* If you can't abide the thought of Disneyland Paris but the kids are aching for something kidlike to do, this park may be the answer. Baron Haussmann reserved this spot for the city's slaughterhouses; today the "city of blood" has been turned into a park that harbors a "city of music" (see **Cité de la Musique,** p. 206) and a "city of science and industry" (see **Cité des Sciences et de l'Industrie,** p. 207) as well as playgrounds, cinemas, and concert halls. Stretching between the Porte de la Villette and Porte de Pantin, the park was designed by Bernard Tschumi, who included several "follies," small, bright-red buildings that serve as information centers, cafes, children's theaters, and other functions. The park benches and chairs

---

⌒ *Finds* **The Canals of Paris**

It's not Venice, but Paris does have a network of canals that run through the eastern part of the city: **Canal St-Martin, Canal St-Denis,** and **Canal de l'Ourcq** (*"oork"*—pretend you're a seal). For centuries, Paris was short on drinking water; the canals were built to quench its thirst. As time and plumbing progressed, the canals were used for transporting materials to and from industrial northeastern Paris. Once industry left the city, the waterways fell into disuse; it took a small insurrection in the surrounding neighborhood to get the city to abandon plans to make the St-Martin canal into a freeway. Today, Parisians have rediscovered Canal St-Martin, which was a location for the film classic *Hôtel du Nord.* Cafes and boutiques are popping up along the stretch of waterway that cuts through the 10e; the arched bridges and locks make a delightful backdrop for a stroll along the parklike quais. The Canal St-Martin ends at the **Bassin de la Villette,** which has an almost marina-like atmosphere. The waterway continues as the Canal de l'Ourcq, then intersects with Canal St-Denis at Parc de la Villette. A **cruise** through the canals is a wonderful way to visit these little-known neighborhoods. **Paris Canal** offers one that starts on the Seine and ends at La Villette; see "Boat Tours" later this chapter.

were designed by Philippe Starck. Themed gardens include a bamboo garden and one featuring steam and water jets. Then there's that giant, bug-shaped movie theater on legs that moves . . . well, you get the idea. Check the website for the schedule of performances and circus events.

19e. ✆ 01-40-03-75-10. www.villette.com. Daily 6am–1am. Métro: Porte-de-la-Villette or Porte-de-Pantin.

Parc des Buttes-Chaumont   This is one of the four parks Napoleon III commissioned to resemble the English gardens he grew to love during his exile in England. Buttes-Chàumont, on the site of a former gypsum quarry and centuries-old dump, features cliffs, waterfalls, a lake, and a cave topped by a temple.

19e. Métro: Buttes-Chaumont.

11 5 & 6e Arrondissements: The Latin Quarter

Excavations indicate that the ancient Romans made the Left Bank their residential district and the Ile de la Cité their administrative headquarters. The baths at the **Musée National du Moyen Age** and the remnants of an amphitheater at the **Arènes de Lutèce** recall the Roman city of Lutèce, which numbered about 8,000 inhabitants.

The scholarly tradition that began with the Sorbonne in the 13th century is alive today in the Latin Quarter. The district contains not only the famous Sorbonne, but also other extensions of the University of Paris, as well as large high schools and specialized graduate schools.

Nevertheless, you won't find much student life in the noisy snarl of crowds and traffic along the boulevard St-Michel. The pedestrian streets from the quai St-Michel to the boulevard St-Germain provide only a hint of bohemia among the rows of Greek restaurants. Walk through the quieter streets that head south from the quai de Montebello to the **Panthéon** and **rue Mouffetard** and you'll experience the true character of this district. At once studious and carefree, medieval and modern, with university buildings and cobblestone alleys, the Latin Quarter is a pleasant confusion of styles. For greenery, gardens, and playgrounds, head east to the **Jardin des Plantes** or west to the **Jardin du Luxembourg.**

If you've always yearned for the simple village life, visit the market on **rue Mouffetard** (Tues–Sun; Métro: Monge). Although hardly unnoticed by tourists, the area around rue Mouffetard reflects its origins as a 16th-century village. After strolling through the passages Postes and Patriarches and rues Pot-de-Fer and Arbolete, take a break on **place de la Contrescarpe,** one of the city's livelier squares.

Jardin des Plantes ✿   Louis XIII approved the foundation of the Jardin Royal des Plantes Médicinales in 1626, but the botanical gardens' real builders were the king's physicians, who needed an arsenal of medicinal herbs to cure royal maladies. The naturalist Buffon was director of the Jardin des Plantes from 1739 to 1788. The garden was also a favorite place of Jean-Jacques Rousseau. After the Revolution, the **Musée National d'Histoire Naturelle** was created here (see below), and exotic animals were brought in: Elephants arrived in 1795 and giraffes in the 1820s for the zoo. Many, however, were eaten by hungry Parisians during the siege of the city in the Franco-Prussian War.

What you'll see today are straight rows of trees, neat beds of herbs and flowers, a 17th-century maze, a small zoo, and two huge greenhouses: one filled with tropical plants, and the other with cacti. There is also an alpine garden with 2,000 mountain plants from the Alps and the Himalayas.

5e. ℂ **01-40-79-30-00.** Daily sunrise–dusk. Greenhouses: Admission 3€ ($3.75) adults, 1.70€ ($2.15) children under 18. Wed–Mon 1–5pm. Métro: Jussieu, Gare d'Austerlitz, or Censier Daubenton.

Musée de la Sculpture en Plein Air   You may have passed this graceful waterside park on a stroll along the Seine without realizing it's really a museum. Located in the Jardin Tino Rossi, here you will find sculptures by 29 artists, including César, Zadkine, and Stahly.

Quai St-Bernard, 5e. Free admission. Daily 24 hr. Métro: Sully-Morland or Gare d'Austerlitz.

Musée de l'Assistance Publique Hôpitaux de Paris   After a visit here, you'll never take anesthesia for granted again. This museum features more than 8,000 objects that reflect the history of Paris's hospitals since the Middle Ages.

47 quai de la Tournelle, 5e. ℂ **01-40-27-50-05.** www.aphp.fr. Admission 4€ ($5) adults, 2€ ($2.50) children 13–18 and students, free for children under 13. Tues–Sun 10am–6pm. Closed Aug. Métro: Maubert-Mutualité, Cité, or St-Michel.

Musée de l'Institut du Monde Arabe   The architects of this building combined modern materials with traditional Arab designs to create a serene, inviting structure. The south side contains 240 aluminum panels that automatically adjust to allow in the right amount of light. Inside, three floors of galleries display the riches of Arab-Islamic culture from three different regions: the Near East, the Middle East, and the Maghreb. The ninth-floor tea salon and restaurant serves Moroccan food and provides a panoramic view across the Seine. The roof terrace has a spectacular view of Notre-Dame and Sacré-Coeur. The institute often has terrific temporary expositions and concerts.

1 rue des Fossés-St-Bernard, 5e. ℂ **01-40-51-38-38.** www.imarabe.org. Admission 4€ ($5) adults, 3€ ($3.75) children 12–18; free for children under 12. Tues–Sun 10am–6pm. Métro: Jussieu or Cardinal-Lemoine.

Musée National du Moyen Age/Thermes de Cluny   It's difficult not to gawk at the remains of late-2nd- and early-3rd-century baths in one of the Latin Quarter's busiest intersections (the corner of boulevards St-Michel and St-Germain). The baths are part of the Cluny Museum of medieval art and Paris's foremost example of civil architecture from the late Middle Ages.

In the 19th century, the Hôtel de Cluny belonged to a collector of medieval art; upon his death in the 1840s, the government acquired the house and its contents. The exhibits include wood and stone sculpture, brilliant stained glass and metalwork, and rich tapestries. Highlights include jeweled Visigoth crowns, carved ivories from 6th-century Constantinople, and elaborate altarpieces from 16th-century Castille. Don't miss the stunning 15th-century tapestry series of *The Lady and the Unicorn,* an allegory representing the five senses. Allow 2 hours.

(*Moments*   **Le Tango on the Seine**

It's a scene from an old black-and white movie: It's night, the moon is up, we are standing on the banks of the Seine, and the Ile St-Louis is glimmering in the background. Then the music begins and dozens of couples begin to dance the tango. Every Sunday night, when the weather is warm, a group of tango fans bring down a boom box, snap in some Astor Piazzola and voilà, instant *milonga.* Join in if you dare.

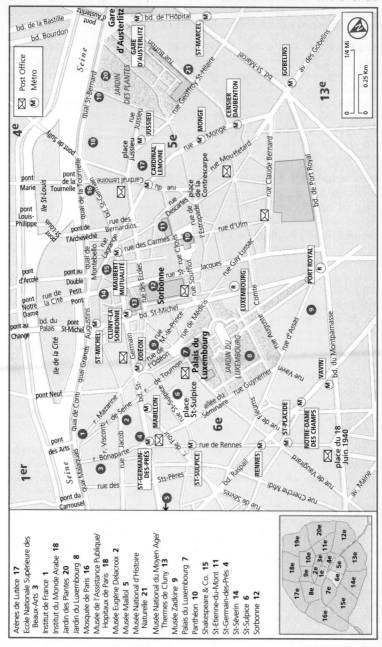

Post Office ⊠
Métro Ⓜ

1/4 Mi
0 0.25 Km

4e
1er
5e
6e
13e

Gare d'Austerlitz

bd. de la Bastille
bd. Bourdon
pont d'Austerlitz
pont de Sully
Seine
quai St-Bernard
quai St-Bernard
JARDIN DES PLANTES
bd. de l'Hôpital
bd. St-Marcel
ST-MARCEL Ⓜ
GARE D'AUSTERLITZ
rue Buffon
rue Geoffroy St-Hilaire
av. des Gobelins
GOBELINS Ⓜ
rue des Gobelins

rue Jussieu
JUSSIEU Ⓜ
place Jussieu
rue Cuvier
rue Monge
MONGE Ⓜ
rue Monge
CENSIER DAUBENTON Ⓜ
rue Mouffetard
rue Claude Bernard
bd. de Port Royal
bd. de Port Royal

Île St-Louis
pont Marie
pont Louis-Philippe
pont St-Louis
pont de l'Archevêché
quai de la Tournelle
pont de la Tournelle
bd. St-Germain
rue du Cardinal Lemoine
CARDINAL LEMOINE Ⓜ
place de la Contrescarpe
rue Descartes
rue de l'Estrapade
rue d'Ulm
rue Lacépède

pont d'Arcole
pont Notre Dame
pont au Double
Petit Pont
rue de la Cité
quai de Montebello
rue des Bernardins
rue Lagrange
rue des Carmes
MAUBERT MUTUALITÉ Ⓜ
rue des Écoles
rue St-Jacques
rue Soufflot
rue Gay Lussac
rue Claude Bernard
Sorbonne
rue des Cloîtres
PORT ROYAL Ⓡ

Île de la Cité
pont au Change
bd. du Palais
ST-MICHEL Ⓜ
pont St-Michel
quai des Grands Augustins
bd. St-Michel
CLUNY-LA SORBONNE Ⓜ
LUXEMBOURG Ⓡ
bd. du Montparnasse
rue Comte
rue d'Assas

pont Neuf
pont des Arts
quai de Conti
r. Mazarine
r. de Seine
r. Visconti
r. Jacob
r. r. Bonaparte
ST-GERMAIN-DES-PRÉS Ⓜ
ODÉON Ⓜ
rue de Médicis
Palais du Luxembourg
JARDIN DU LUXEMBOURG
rue Guynemer
rue Auguste Comte
rue d'Assas
VAVIN Ⓜ

Seine
quai Malaquais
rue des Sts-Pères
MABILLON Ⓜ
bd. St-Germain
r. de Tournon
place St-Sulpice
ST-SULPICE Ⓜ
rue de Rennes
RENNES Ⓜ
ST-PLACIDE Ⓜ
NOTRE-DAME DES CHAMPS Ⓜ
place du 18 Juin 1940
bd. Raspail
rue de Vaugirard
rue du Cherche Midi
av. du Maine
rue de Sèvres
pont du Carrousel
allée du Séminaire
rue de Fleurus
rue de Vaugirard
rue Vavin

① ② ③ ④ ⑤ ⑥ ⑦ ⑧ ⑨ ⑩ ⑪ ⑫ ⑬ ⑭ ⑮ ⑯ ⑰ ⑱ ⑲ ⑳ ㉑

18e 19e 20e
17e 9e 10e 11e 12e
8e 2e 3e 1e 4e 13e
16e 7e 6e 5e
15e 14e

211

6 pl. Paul-Painlevé, 5e. ☎ **01-53-73-78-00**. www.musee-moyenage.fr. Admission 5.50€ ($6.90) adults, 4€ ($5) ages 18–25 and for all on Sun, free for children under 18. Wed–Mon 9:15am–5:45pm. Métro: Cluny-Sorbonne.

Musée Zadkine ☆ Ukrainian sculptor Ossip Zadkine (1890–1967) worked in this house and studio until his death. His works evolved over the years from primitivism, to Cubism, to Expressionism, all executed with a fluid grace. The collection is small, but beautiful—the museum displays several works in brass, wood, and stone. His bronze *To a Destroyed City* (1953) is considered a 20th-century masterpiece (the original is in Rotterdam; a model is exhibited here). Take a break in the tranquil sculpture garden.

100 bis rue d'Assas, 6e. ☎ **01-55-42-77-20**. Free admission to permanent collection; admission to special exhibits 4€ ($5) adults, 3€ ($3.75) for seniors over 60, 2€ ($2.50) for people under 26. Tues–Sun 10am–5:40pm. Métro: Notre-Dame des Champs or Vavin.

Muséum National d'Histoire Naturelle ☆☆ *(Kids)* Located in the Jardin des Plantes, the natural history museum was established in 1793 as an extension of the schools of botany, natural history, and pharmacy founded in the botanical gardens. The museum flowered during the 19th century, becoming a center of research and education, a role it maintains today. Bugs, bones, minerals, meteorites, dinosaurs, fossils, and endangered species are represented in its galleries. Among the more popular exhibitions is the Grand Gallery of Evolution, with its subtle lighting and eerie sound effects that induce a kind of trance, the better to absorb the museum's ecological theme. The exhibits trace the evolution of life and humankind's relationship to nature. Don't miss the endangered and extinct species room, which displays Gabonese monkeys, Sumatran tigers, lemurs of Madagascar, and a mock-up of the dodo bird. English explanations of some exhibits are available. Also part of the natural history museum are the Mineralogical Gallery (minerals, meteorites, and precious stones), the Entomological Gallery (1,500 insect specimens of astonishing variety), and the Paleobotanical Gallery (plant evolution and specimens of fossil plants). You could easily spend a day here if you really wanted to see everything.

57 rue Cuvier, 5e. ☎ **01-40-79-30-00**. www.mnhn.fr. Admission to Grande Gallerie 7€ ($8.75) adults; 5€ ($6.25) students, seniors over 60, and children 4–16. Other museums 5€ ($6.25) adults; 3.50€ ($4.40) students, seniors over 60, and children 4–16. Wed–Mon 10am–6pm. Métro: Jussieu or Gare d'Austerlitz.

Panthéon ☆ Is it a church? Is it a tomb? Few other monuments in Paris have had as versatile a career as the neoclassical Panthéon, whose dome is one of the landmarks of the Left Bank. It has been the final resting place of France's greatest citizens since the 18th century. Louis XV built the Panthéon as a church in thanksgiving to Ste-Geneviève after his recovery from gout. Construction started in 1755, and the architect Soufflot chose a Greek cross design. It was first called the church of Ste-Geneviève, in honor of Paris's patron saint, and a series of paintings by Puvis de Chavannes represents scenes from the saint's life. After the French Revolution, the church was renamed the Panthéon—in remembrance of Rome's ancient Pantheon. All Christian elements were removed, and windows were blocked. The first heroes entombed here—the comte Mirabeau and Jean-Paul Marat, both Revolutionary figures—were later expelled. From 1806 to 1884, officials turned the Panthéon back into a church twice more before finally declaring it a final resting place for some of France's greatest intellectual heroes. Voltaire and Jean-Jacques Rousseau, representatives of the Enlightenment, are buried here, as is Victor Hugo. Also here are the remains of Louis Braille, inventor of the reading system for the blind, and Emile Zola. Most recently, French writer, politician, and adventurer André Malraux was honored by a tomb in the Panthéon. A pendulum suspended from the central dome re-creates Jean-Bernard Foucault's 1851 demonstration proving the rotation of the earth.

Pl. du Panthéon, 5e. ℭ **01-44-32-18-00**. Admission 7€ ($8.75) adults, 4€ ($5) ages 18–25, free for children under 18. Apr–Sept daily 9:30am–6:30pm; Oct–Mar daily 10am–6:15pm. Métro: Cardinal-Lemoine. RER: Luxembourg.

The Sorbonne   Founded in 1253 by Robert de Sorbon, this theological college became the principle center of French higher education. In 1626, Cardinal Richelieu commissioned Jacques Lemercier to rebuild the Sorbonne. The chapel, with the fifth dome constructed in Paris, is the only building surviving from that period. The other buildings, erected between 1885 and 1901, are neither distinguished nor harmonious; instead, the character of the Sorbonne lies in the scholarship of the individuals who have taught and studied here—a tradition that began with such formidable early teachers as Abélard and St. Thomas Aquinas. The list of its great students includes Baudelaire, Musset, Ste-Beuve, and Bergson, joined by such distinguished outsiders as Dante, John Calvin, and Henry Wadsworth Longfellow. In 1469, France's first print-ing press was set up here; during the German occupation, the Sorbonne became one of the headquarters of the Resistance. The courtyard and galleries are open to the pub-lic; in the cour d'Honneur stand statues of Victor Hugo and Louis Pasteur.

47 rue des Ecoles, 5e. Métro: Cluny-Sorbonne.

St-Etienne du Mont ⭐⭐   Just behind place du Panthéon is one of Paris's most extraordinary churches. Completed and consecrated in the 17th century on the site of a 13th-century abbey, the church is a unique blend of late Gothic and Renaissance styles. Sanctified in the name of the city's patron saint, Ste-Geneviève, who saved Paris from the Huns in the 5th century, the church has been a pilgrimage site since the Dark Ages. Ste-Geneviève's original sarcophagus stone, set in an ornate copper-trimmed shrine, is preserved near the chancel. The 16th-century rood screen, embraced by twin spiraling marble staircases, is the only one left in Paris and a stunning display of Renaissance design. The tall, vivid 16th- and 17th-century stained-glass windows in the gallery are breathtaking. The church also contains the tombs of Pascal and Racine.

1 pl. Ste-Geneviève, 5e. ℭ **01-43-54-11-79**. Sept–June daily 8am–noon and 2–7pm; July–Aug daily 10am–noon and 4–7pm. Métro: Cardinal Lemoine.

St-Séverin ⭐   A religious building has stood here since the 6th century. The cur-rent building, begun in the 13th century, is in flamboyant Gothic style, featuring a double ambulatory. The west portal is from the church of St-Pierre-aux-Boeufs on the Ile de la Cité, which was torn down in 1837. Jean Bazaine created the brilliant stained-glass windows behind the altar, which depict the sacraments, in 1966. Also notable is the chapel to the right of the altar, designed by Mansart. It contains a series of etch-ings by Georges Rouault, but is only open to those who wish to pray (others can peek in through the open door). Note the palm tree–shaped vaulting. There are free guided visits every Sunday at 5:30pm.

Rue des Prêtres St-Séverin, 5e. Daily 11am–7pm. Métro: St-Michel.

12 6 & 7e Arrondissements: St-Germain-des-Prés

No neighborhood better expresses the Parisian character—intellectual, argumentative, pleasure-seeking, cosmopolitan. St-Germain has been the cultural and intellectual heart of Paris for centuries. Voltaire exercised his rapier wit at the restaurant (then a café) **Le Procope;** Jean-Paul Sartre expounded his existentialist philosophy at the **Café**

des Deux-Magots and **Café de Flore.** Today, newspeople and photogenic philosopher Bernard-Henri Lévy (known simply as BHL) still gather downstairs at **Brasserie Lipp.**

The scores of bookstores in the neighborhood create an inviting atmosphere for native and expatriate writers. When Sylvia Beach's circle of literary giants moved on, the Beat Generation moved in. Allen Ginsberg, Gregory Corso, and William S. Burroughs found freedom and tolerance here that had eluded them in the United States, as did many African-American writers and musicians.

Artists still frequent the neighborhood for its galleries and art-book shops. Long after Monet and Matisse studied there, the **Ecole des Beaux-Arts** continues to influence young artists. You can visit **Delacroix's studio** and get an overview of the contemporary scene in galleries along **rue de Seine** and **rue Bonaparte.**

Most of St-Germain couldn't be farther from its bohemian past, however. Real estate prices have crept so high that only the wealthiest Parisians can live here. The neighborhood is desirable enough to have entangled several French politicians in scandals for trying to secure apartments here for their relatives or mistresses. As the area has steadily moved up, slick new stores selling luxury products have begun driving out businesses that had been fixtures for decades. In the process, St-Germain is losing its quirky individuality and beginning to resemble any tony Right Bank enclave. For a taste of the old St-Germain, veer off the boulevard St-Germain to the side streets. They are still crammed with art galleries and bookstores, small cinemas that show offbeat movies, theaters, cafes, and plenty of restaurants at all price levels. Certainly for the two essential vacation activities—eating and shopping—there's no better place in Paris.

A favorite Left Bank spot is **place St-Sulpice,** between the church of St-Germain-des-Prés and the Jardin du Luxembourg. Enjoy a coffee on the terrace of the **Café de la Mairie** and admire the picturesque square, which holds the elaborate fountain built by Visconti in 1844 and **St-Sulpice,** one of Paris's most stunning churches. In the summer, dancers perform and musicians play against a backdrop of water from the fountain. Several blocks away, beyond the boulevard St-Germain, the market at **rue de Buci,** 6e (Tues–Sun; Métro: Odéon), is one of Paris's most dynamic, especially on Sunday when the rest of the city is closed. Brunch at one of the outdoor cafes is a great way to start the day.

Ecole Nationale Supérieure des Beaux-Arts   Rodin was rejected, but Degas, Matisse, Monet, and Renoir passed the rigorous entrance exam for the most prestigious art school in the world. Sprawling elegantly over 2 hectares (5 acres) of land in the heart of St-Germain-des-Prés, this complex of breathtaking 17th- to 19th-century architecture provides artistic instruction. Originally established by Mazarin in 1648 as the school of the Royal Academy of Painting and Sculpture, it survived the Revolution and merged with the Academy of Architecture to become the Ecole des Beaux-Arts. A visit to the cloister of the old convent is a must—painted Romanesque arches, tiled mosaic floors, and raised marble murals of the Pantheon friezes surround the medieval garden. The hexagonal chapel, built in 1617, is the oldest part of the school.

14 rue Bonaparte, 6e. © 01-47-03-50-00. Métro: St-Germain-des-Prés.

Musée National Eugène Delacroix ⭐   The hand and spirit of Delacroix (1798–1863), arguably the greatest painter of the Romantic period, is evident in the charm of this intimate studio tucked away in the heart of St-Germain. Commissioned in 1849 to design the chapel of St-Sulpice, Delacroix settled here to be nearer his project. Having completed three masterpieces in the church (*St. Michel Vanquishing the*

Devil, Heliodorus Driven from the Temple, and *Jacob Wrestling with the Angel),* he died. He left behind more than 8,000 paintings, drawings, and pastels, along with journals that he had kept for almost 2 decades.

Three rooms of the apartment are on view: the salon, the library, and the bedroom (where Delacroix died in 1863). The rooms are filled with paintings, drawings, and personal items, including the brilliantly colored *Bouquet de Fleurs,* portraits of family members, and his etching of the *Seated Turk.* A portrait of the Delacroix's governess, Jenny le Guillou, who was by his side when he died, is also on display. You can see the artist's palate and worktable in the studio behind the apartment. Step outside into the lovely, shaded garden, and can sit on benches to contemplate the artist's genius. According to van Gogh, only Rembrandt and Delacroix could paint the face of Christ.

6 rue de Furstemberg, 6e. ℭ 01-44-41-86-50. www.musee-delacroix.fr. Admission 5€ ($6.25) adults, free for children under 18. Wed–Mon 9:30am–5pm (last tickets sold at 4:30pm). Métro: St-Germain-des-Prés or Mabillon.

St-Germain-des-Prés ⋆⋆   The most famous church in the 6e arrondissement is also one of the most important Romanesque monuments in France. Built in the 11th century, St-Germain-des-Prés was an abbey and center of learning during the Middle Ages. At the time of the French Revolution, the monks were expelled and the church was vandalized. Much of it was rebuilt and restored in the 19th century; however, the bell tower dates from the 11th century and is the oldest in Paris. One of the few Parisian churches with a painted interior, the vast arches and subtle light make this a tranquil place. King John Casimir of Poland is buried at the church, as is the heart of René Descartes. A small square at the corner of place St-Germain-des-Prés and rue de l'Abbaye contains Picasso's *Homage to Apollinaire.* Free guided visits are available at the information office *(accueil).*

3 pl. St-Germain-des-Prés, 6e. ℭ 01-43-25-41-71. Daily 8am–7:45pm. Métro: St-Germain-des-Prés.

Fun Fact   **An American Bookseller in Paris**

Born in Baltimore, Sylvia Beach (1887–1962) first came to Paris with her family as an adolescent. In 1917 she met Adrienne Monnier at her bookshop at 7 rue de l'Odéon. Monnier encouraged Beach to open an American bookshop, which she did in 1919, at 8 rue Dupuytren. The shop, Shakespeare & Co., was furnished with flea market gleanings and hand-me-downs, and the walls were bare except for two drawings by William Blake and, later, some photographs supplied by Man Ray. In 1921 she shifted the shop to 12 rue de l'Odéon and moved in nearby with Monnier. Every American and English-speaking writer or artist, from James Joyce to Ernest Hemingway, Gertrude Stein to F. Scott Fitzgerald, visited her shop. She became a great friend to many, going so far as to publish the first edition of Joyce's *Ulysses,* when no publisher would accept it. Later, Bennett Cerf of Random House published the book, and reportedly made at least $1 million. Joyce received a $45,000 advance, but Beach never saw any money—even though she edited and published the original. She claimed not to mind and said she'd do anything for Joyce and his art. Joyce never returned her favors, and when her shop was threatened with closure, it was André Gide who came to her rescue.

St-Sulpice ⓖ★   Though today St-Sulpice is one of Paris's largest and richest churches, it didn't start out that way. Construction began in 1646, but stopped in 1678—only the choir was complete—due to a lack of funds. Finally, Gilles-Marie Oppenord resumed building in 1732 and finished everything except the facade. Jean-François Chalgrin was completing the facade's south tower when funds again ran out. It has never been completed.

When you enter, note the enormous holy-water fonts made of natural shells, with intricately carved pedestals by J. P. Pigalle. Turn right after you enter and you'll come across three of Eugène Delacroix's masterpieces: *Jacob Wrestling with the Angel, Heliodorus Driven from the Temple,* and *St. Michael Vanquishing the Devil,* all completed in 1881.

A bronze meridian line runs along the north-south transept. During both equinoxes and at the winter solstice (at midday), sunlight hits the line, runs along the floor, climbs the obelisk to the globe on top, and lights the cross. The church also houses one of the grandest organs in Paris, built in 1781 by Cliquot.

Pl. St-Sulpice, 6e. ☎ 01-46-33-21-78. Daily 8am–7pm. Métro: St-Sulpice.

13 7e Arrondissement: The Eiffel Tower & Invalides

It's not surprising that a neighborhood containing the **Eiffel Tower** (see "The Top 10 Sights," earlier in this chapter), **Ecole Militaire, Musée d'Orsay,** and **Musée Rodin** is calm and dignified. In fact, the splendor of this area may make you feel like taking a deep bow. East of the **Hôtel des Invalides** is the grand Faubourg St-Germain, with its 18th-century mansions. French political life flutters around the **Assemblée Nationale, Ministère des Affaires Etrangéres,** and various other government offices and embassies. But all is not pomp and circumstance in this prestigious district. The construction of Invalides and the Ecole Militaire in the 17th and 18th centuries encouraged artisans and shopkeepers to populate the area, especially along rues St-Dominique and rue du Champ-de-Mars, and the **rue Cler,** now a car-free market street. Several flamboyant Art Nouveau buildings by Jules Lavirotte provide a dramatic contrast to the generally staid architecture. Examples of his work include 151 rue Cler, 3 sq. Rapp, and 29 av. Rapp.

Ecole Militaire et Champ-de-Mars   The idea of a military academy to train young gentlemen without means originated in 1751 with Mme de Pompadour, Louis XV's mistress. Jacques-Ange Gabriel, the architect of place de la Concorde, produced the Ecole Militaire, the vast building at the other end of the Champ-de-Mars from the Eiffel Tower. Its first illustrious student was Napoleon Bonaparte, who graduated in 1785. His excellent record in mathematics, geography, and fencing made up for his abysmal skills in drawing and dancing.

The Champ-de-Mars was originally used as a parade ground for the Ecole Militaire, but after the Revolution it began to stage fairs and exhibitions, most memorably the Exposition of 1889, which saw the construction of the Eiffel Tower. Beginning in 1928, the esplanade was transformed into a vast park of shaded walks, flowers, statues, and plane trees.

1 pl. Joffre, 7e. Métro: Ecole-Militaire.

Hôtel des Invalides ⓖ★★   Louis XIV, who liked war and waged many, built the Hôtel des Invalides as a hospital and home for veteran officers and soldiers, "whether maimed or old and frail." It still performs that function, and houses offices for numerous departments of the French armed forces.

Attractions in the 7e

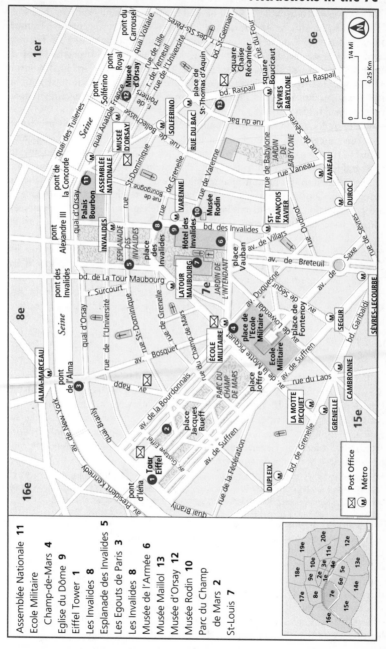

Assemblée Nationale **11**
Ecole Militaire
   Champ-de-Mars **4**
Eglise du Dôme **9**
Eiffel Tower **1**
Les Invalides **8**
Esplanade des Invalides **5**
Les Egouts de Paris **3**
Les Invalides **8**
Musée de l'Armée **6**
Musée Maillol **13**
Musée d'Orsay **12**
Musée Rodin **10**
Parc du Champ
   de Mars **2**
St-Louis **7**

The value of the Invalides goes far beyond its symbolic significance for the French military. The building is an architectural marvel. Its facade, as you approach from the Seine, is majestic, with 16 cannons pointed outward in powerful display. The huge dome, which was regilded in 1989 with 12 kilograms of gold, covers the **Eglise du Dôme** 𝕮𝕮, designed by Hardouin-Mansart. Considered one of the high points of 17th-century art, the dome boasts an openwork skylight rising 107m (351 ft.) from the ground, as well as a cupola fresco inside by Charles de la Fosse, recently restored to its original brilliant colors.

The great dome hovers over the **Tomb of Napoleon** 𝕮, a huge porphyry sarcophagus containing the remains of one of the largest egos of all time. The emperor is buried in six coffins, one inside the other. The first is iron, the second mahogany, the third and fourth lead, the fifth ebony, and the outermost oak. The emperor's remains were transferred to this monumental resting place in 1840, almost 2 decades after his death on the South Atlantic island of St. Helena, where he was exiled following his defeat at Waterloo. A blizzard enveloped Paris on December 15, the day the emperor's cortège made its way from the Arc de Triomphe down the Champs-Elysées to the esplanade. In the 10 days following the funeral, 846,000 people came to pay their respects. The emperor's popularity has dipped since then. A recent poll placed him just ahead of Robespierre and behind six others, including Charlemagne, Jeanne d'Arc, and Clemenceau, on a list of historical figures the French people admire. Also buried here are Turenne, Vauban, and Napoleon's brothers: Joseph, king of Spain, and Jérôme, king of Westphalia. The body of his son, the king of Rome, was transferred here in 1940.

When Napoleon moved into the Eglise du Dome, the church was split into two. The second half, the light-filled **Eglise de St-Louis** 𝕮, is also known as the Church of the Soldiers. Berlioz's *Requiem* was played here for the first time.

If you like military lore, you will want to visit the **Musée de l'Armée** 𝕮𝕮, one of the world's great military museums. It features thousands of weapons dating from prehistory to World War II. You'll see spearheads and arrowheads, suits of armor, cannons, battle flags, booty, and life-size cavalry figures on horseback dressed in full regalia. In 2000, the museum unveiled a new series of rooms devoted to the World War II, with a focus on General de Gaulle and the Free French—perhaps not the most balanced view, but fascinating nonetheless.

Pl. des Invalides, 7e. ⓒ **01-44-42-37-72**. www.invalides.org. Admission 7.50€ ($9.40) adults, 5.50€ ($6.90) students 18–25, free for under 18. Oct–Mar daily 10am–5pm; Apr–Sept daily 10am–6pm. Closed the first Mon of each month. Tomb of Napoleon open until 7pm June–Sept. Métro: Latour-Maubourg, Invalides, or Varenne.

Les Egouts If you followed Jean Valjean's adventures in Hugo's *Les Misérables* or have seen old movies about World War II Resistance fighters, you will want to visit the sewers of Paris. Granted, the subterranean labyrinth is not as beautiful as the city, but the sewers are both very interesting and an engineering marvel. Eugène Belgrand laid them out during the reign of Napoleon III, at the same time that Haussmann was designing his Grands Boulevards. If this kind of thing interests you, get in line for a visit on one of the afternoons when a glimpse is offered. Don't expect the aroma of Chanel No. 5. Allow about 45 minutes, or as long as you can take the smell. Remember that it's substantially cooler down there—take something warm.

Opposite 93 quai d'Orsay/Pont-de-l'Alma, 7e. ⓒ **01-53-68-27-82**. www.egouts.idf.st. Admission 3.80€ ($4.75) adults, 3.05€ ($3.80) students and seniors over 60. May–Sept Sat–Wed 11am–5pm; Oct–Apr Sat–Wed 11am–4pm. Closed 3 weeks in Jan. Métro: Alma Marceau. RER: Pont de l'Alma.

Musée Maillol   Curvaceous, bold, graceful bronze statues of Aristide Maillol's (1861–1944) favorite model, Dina Vierny, are on vivid display in this contemporary-style museum in a renovated 18th-century convent. Discovered at 15, Vierny served as Maillol's exclusive model for 10 years. Inspired by her voluptuous figure, which to him personified femininity, Maillol sculpted nude statues embracing such themes as *The Mountain, The River,* and nymphs playing in harmony. Upon his death, he left all his work to Vierny, who set about establishing a museum dedicated to his work.

The upper floors of the museum display numerous crayon and pastel sketches of Vierny in reclining and seductive postures. A friend of Matisse and Bonnard, Maillol collected their work, which is also exhibited, as are two sculptures by Rodin, works by Gauguin, Degas, Rousseau, and Kandinsky, and Renoir's rendering of *Etude d'une Statuette de Maillol.* The museum features excellent temporary exhibits. Allow 1 hour.

61 rue de Grenelle, 7e. ℰ **01-42-22-59-58**. www.museemaillol.com. Admission 8€ ($10) adults, 6€ ($7.50) students and seniors over 60, free for children under 16. Wed–Mon 11am–6pm (last ticket sold at 5:15pm). Métro: Rue du Bac.

14 6, 14 & 15e Arrondissements: Montparnasse ⧸★

Montparnasse was fashionable even before the Lost Generation made itself at home in its cafes. In the 17th century, students gathered here to read poetry and named the area Mount Parnassus after the Greek mountain consecrated to Apollo and the Muses. The rich promenaded here during the Revolution. Cafes, dance halls, and theaters sprang up in the 19th century and eventually lured artists from touristy Montmartre. Before World War I, Chagall, Matisse, Picasso, Modigliani, and Max Jacob sipped absinthe and argued about art in La Rotonde and La Dôme, while a small group of Russian exiles that included Lenin and Trotsky talked politics over chess at Closerie des Lilas. By the 1920s, the neighborhood had become a haunt of artists, their muses, models, and intellectuals. The opening of La Coupole brought the American literary crowd—Hemingway, Dos Passos, Fitzgerald, and Miller—who liked the wine, the conversation, and the low prices.

The famous old cafes still draw a mix of Left Bank old-timers and tourists, but the rest of Montparnasse has changed dramatically since the old train station was destroyed in 1961 in a 12-year redevelopment project. The Tour Montparnasse, an office building next to the Gare Montparnasse, looms over an increasingly disappointing neighborhood. Though the 206m (688-ft.) tower has been despised since it opened in 1967, the 56th-floor observatory provides a stunning panorama of the city. Crowds are thick in Montparnasse, movie theaters abound, and the main shopping is chain stores on rue de Rennes—a *centre commercial* that includes Galeries Lafayette next to the tower.

Catacombes   ARRETE, C'EST ICI L'EMPIRE DE LA MORT ("Stop, here is the Empire of Death") is the inscription over the door to one of the city's more macabre attractions. The catacombs are not a destination for the fainthearted. About six million skulls and skeletons are stacked in 900m (2,952 ft.) of tunnels, and a visit is bound to provoke uneasy meditations.

Nonetheless, they are fascinating. Around the middle of the 18th century, complaints about the unsanitary, overstocked Cimetière des Innocents reached a crescendo. In 1785, city officials decided to close the cemetery and transfer the bones to this former quarry, where bones from an assortment of other Parisian cemeteries joined them.

The timing was perfect, because officials were beginning to realize that the underground network of limestone, gypsum, and clay quarries had made the city's foundations resemble Swiss cheese. After several serious collapses, in 1777 Louis XVI set up a commission to address the problem. Quarrying stopped in 1813, but Parisians found other uses for the 2,100 acres of tunnels and caves. Smugglers had maps of underground Paris and sometimes dug their own quarries to evade authorities. The revolutionaries of 1848 and the *communards* of 1870 also traveled clandestinely through the network. The Resistance used the quarries during World War II—but only the most secret passages, because the Nazis were aware of the underground system. Today access to the quarries is completely blocked. The only part open to the public is the Catacombes.

Tips for intrepid visitors: Those prone to claustrophobia should think twice about entering, because the dark tunnels close in rapidly and tightly. Equip yourself with flashlights to navigate the poorly illuminated corridors, and proper footwear (sneakers or hiking boots) to grip the rocky, often slick passageways. A hood will protect you from dripping water of dubious origin.

1 pl. Denfert-Rochereau, 14e. ✆ **01-43-22-47-63.** Admission 6.50€ ($8.15) adults, 4.50€ ($5.65) ages 8–26, free for children under 8. Sat–Sun 9–11am; Tues–Sun 2–4pm. Métro: Denfert-Rochereau.

Cimetière de Montparnasse   Originally called the Cimetière du Sud (Cemetery of the South), this cemetery was built in 1824 and features a 15th-century windmill, the Moulin de Charité, as well as sculptures by Brancusi, Rodin, and Bartholdi. Cimetière de Montparnasse is not as eerily removed from the city as Père-Lachaise, but you'll still walk among the graves of the famous, including Bartholdi, Baudelaire, Simone de Beauvoir, Samuel Beckett, Guy de Maupassant, Jean-Paul Sartre, and Maurice Zadkine. Free maps are available at the office by the entrance.

14e. Métro: Edgar Quinet or Raspail.

Fondation Cartier pour l'Art Contemporain   Perhaps it's only natural that such an inspiring building sits across the street from the Ecole Spéciale d'Architecture—it certainly gives students much to appreciate. This almost completely transparent structure, designed by Jean Nouvel, is one of the most striking modern buildings in Paris. Resembling a futuristic greenhouse, it has a glass-and-metal screen that stands between the street and the building, creating an optical illusion that makes courtyard greenery appear as if it's growing indoors. The offices of the Cartier jewelry empire are upstairs where the natural light is, and most of the foundation's contemporary art exhibits are in the artificially lit basement. Some Thursday nights the center is open for "Les Soirées Nomades," an evening of performance art and music; call ahead for dates and details.

261 bd. Raspail, 14e. ✆ **01-42-18-56-51.** www.fondation.cartier.fr. Admission 6€ ($7.50) adults, 4€ ($5) under 25, free for children under 10. Tues–Sun noon–8pm. Métro: Raspail.

Musée Bourdelle ⟨   He spent his life in the shadow of Rodin, but this museum is helping get the word out about sculptor Emile-Antoine Bourdelle, Rodin's assistant. This museum includes the home and workshop of Bourdelle, who lived and worked here from 1884 to 1929. Bourdelle's statues ranged from busts (including some fascinating portraits of Rodin) to titanic monuments such as one to General Alvear. It took him 10 years to create this fabulous horse and rider; the model is in the museum, the actual is in Buenos Aires. Be sure to visit the studio, which has been left untouched since the artist's death. Give yourself at least an hour to peruse the museum and sculpture garden.

18 rue Antoine Bourdelle, 15e. ℂ **01-49-54-73-73**. Admission 5€ ($6.25) adults, free for people under 27 and over 60. Tues–Sun 10am–5:40pm. Métro: Montparnasse-Bienvenüe.

Parc Montsouris *(Moments* Haussmann laid out these gardens in 1868 on Napoleon III's return from England. It resembles an English garden, with copses and winding paths. Swans and ducks gather on the pond, and the bandstand is still in use.

14e. RER: Cité Universitaire.

15 Organized Tours

BUS TOURS

Paris is the perfect city to explore on your own, but if time or leg muscles do not permit, consider taking a tour. The most prominent company is **Cityrama**, 4 pl. des Pyramides, 1er (ℂ **01-44-55-61-00**; www.graylineparis.com; Métro: Palais-Royal–Musée du Louvre). The 1½-hour orientation with a recorded commentary in several languages costs 15€ ($19), free for children under 12 (one free child per paying adult). Guided half- and full-day tours are 39€ ($49) and 92€ ($115), respectively. Tours to Versailles for 60€ ($75) and to Chartres for 53€ ($66) are a good bargain—they eliminate a lot of hassle. Nighttime illumination tours start at 22€ ($28).

Paris's public transit agency, the RATP, has a sightseeing system called **Paris l'Open Tour** (ℂ 01-43-46-52-06; www.paris-opentour.com). This is a "hop-on, hop-off" setup using open-topped yellow buses that take you from highlight to highlight in the city while you listen to recorded commentary in French and English. Three circuits cover all the sights in central Paris and extensions east to Bercy and north to Montmartre—40 stops in all. You can get on and off the bus as many times as you wish; buses pass the stops about every 20 minutes. The buses run daily throughout the year from

---

Tips View from the Bus

If you're feeling adventurous and want a bargain tour, the Paris bus system is clean and efficient, and has routes that could come straight from a guidebook. Bus nos. 21 and 27 take you from the Opéra, to the Ile de la Cité, and on to Jardin de Luxembourg. Bus 29 has a little porch in the back and stops at place des Victoires, the Marais, and place de la Bastille. Bus no. 82 can pick you up at the Eiffel Tower and drop you off in Montparnasse, and bus no. 73 takes you down the Champs-Elysées and drops you at the Musée d'Orsay. If you want a north-south axis, try the 47 (Gare du Nord, Louvre, St-Germain-des-Prés, Montparnasse), and if you want east-west, try our favorite, the 63 (Gare de Lyon, Hôtel de Cluny, St-Germain-des-Prés, St-Sulpice, Invalides, and Trocadéro). *Note:* Have your passes/tickets handy and try to avoid rush hour, unless you don't mind standing. If you have a pass (Paris Visite or Carte Orange—see "Getting Around" in chapter 4), flash it at the driver; if not, remember to stamp your ticket in the machine as you go in. You can get bus tickets for 1.40€ ($1.75) and maps in most Métro stations; each bus stop will have a map showing the route of the bus that stops there. For more information, contact the public transit agency, the RATP (ℂ **08-92-68-41-14**).

Moments   Americans (& Others) in Paris

If you want to feel like an American expat, join Patricia Laplante-Collins at one of her cozy dinner parties for Americans and Europeans (and the rest of the world) in a historic flat on the Ile St-Louis every Sunday. There is always a guest speaker, perhaps a writer, actor, or historian—you name it, Patricia hosts them all. The wine flows freely, the food is often fabulous, and the conversation better. The evening usually begins at 6:30pm. Minimum donation per person: 20€ ($25). Reservations are necessary a few days in advance, preferably by e-mail. 14 rue St Louis en L'Ile, 4e (© **01-43-26-12-88;** parissoirees@noos.fr). Métro: Sully-Morland or Pont Marie.

---

around 9:30am to 6:30pm. A 1-day pass costs 25€ ($31), and the 2-day pass is 28€ ($35). You get a 16% discount on a 1-day pass if you have a Paris Visite pass (1- to 3-day pubic transit pass; 8€–19€/$10–$24). Paris l'Open Tour and Paris Visite passes are on sale at the Paris Tourist Office and the RATP visitor center at place de la Madeleine.

BOAT TOURS

Among the most popular ways to see Paris is a cruise on the Seine. The **Bateaux-Mouches** (© **01-42-25-96-10,** or 01-40-76-99-99 for reservations; www.bateaux-mouches.fr; Métro: Alma Marceau) sail from the pont de l'Alma on the Right Bank. From March through mid-November, departures are usually on the hour and half-hour; in winter 5 to 10 cruises depart daily, depending on demand. The voyage includes taped commentary in six languages and lasts about an hour. It costs 7.50€ ($9.40) for adults, 4.50€ ($5.65) for children 5 to 13 and seniors (over 65); children under 5 ride free.

Bateaux-Parisiens (© **01-44-11-33-44;** www.bateauxparisiens.com; Métro: Iéna) offers similar tours from the pont d'Iéna on the Left Bank very close to the Eiffel Tower, with the added attraction of an onboard cafeteria and evening departures until 10pm (11pm July–Aug). They cost 9.50€ ($12) for adults, 4.50€ ($5.65) for children under 13. **Vedettes Pont Neuf** (© **01-46-33-98-38;** Métro: Pont Neuf) sails from Square du Vert Galant on the Ile de la Cité, and has smaller boats and live guides. It charges 9.50€ ($12) for adults, 4.50€ ($5.65) for children 4 to 12.

Paris Canal (© **01-42-40-96-97;** www.pariscanal.com; Métro: Bastille) offers longer and more unusual tours of Parisian waterways. The 3-hour cruises leave the Musée d'Orsay at 9:30am and end at Parc de la Villette, 19e. The boat passes under the Bastille and enters the Canal St-Martin for a journey along the tree-lined quai Jemmapes. An English-speaking guide is on hand to regale you with local lore as you cruise under bridges and through locks. The boat leaves the Parc de la Villette at 2:30pm for the same voyage in reverse. Reservations are essential. The trip costs 16€ ($20) for adults, 12€ ($15) for seniors over 60, 9€ ($11) for children 4 to 11. Paris Canal also has a 1-day trip that cruises the Seine past Paris and into the countryside and takes a little loop on the Marne; it costs 34€ ($43), not including lunch (no discounts for children).

BICYCLE TOURS

Along with renting bicycles (see chapter 4), **Maison Roue Libre** (95 bis rue Rambuteau; © **08-10-44-15-34;** www.rouelibre.fr; Métro: Rambuteau) also runs **bike**

tours. Tours cost 25€ ($31) for 2 hours for adults, for under 26 the price is 20€ ($25). **Paris à Vélo C'est Sympa** (© 01-48-87-60-01; www.parisvelosympa.com; Métro: Bastille) offers 3-hour bike tours for 33€ ($41) for adults, 28€ ($35) for ages 12–26, and 18€ ($23) for under children under 12. Reservations are required. They also rent bikes for 13€ ($16) a day, 9.50€ ($12) a half-day, or 24€ ($30) from Saturday morning until Sunday evening.

8

Paris Strolls

Examining your life along the Seine, window-shopping in the Marais, getting lost on a winding street in Montmartre . . . there's no greater pleasure than exploring Paris on foot.

This chapter offers walking tours covering some famous districts and sights. As with all walking tours, don't be afraid to improvise—let the spirits of Paris past and present lead you to find what it is you're searching for.

For full descriptions of the sights, see chapter 7.

WALKING TOUR 1   THE MARAIS

Start and Finish:	Church of St-Paul–St-Louis (Métro: St-Paul).
Time:	3 to 5 hours.
Best Time:	Weekdays, when the courtyards of the *hôtels* are open.
Worst Time:	Sunday. Boutiques along rue des Francs-Bourgeois are open, but those everywhere else in Paris are closed; crowds of shoppers limit sightseeing.

This walk takes you through one of Paris's most fascinating neighborhoods, filled with 17th-century *hôtels particuliers* (private mansions) and cutting-edge shops and galleries. Because many of these *hôtels* are used as libraries, archives, or cultural centers, you can enter and admire their courtyards during the week. If you're around for special events or exhibits, explore the opulent interiors. In addition to the striking architecture and trendy stores around place des Vosges, you'll go into the bustling Jewish district, where delis, patisseries, and takeout falafel shops serve a community that has been here for 7 centuries.

After leaving the Métro station, walk to your right (east along rue St-Antoine). You will soon see on your right, the baroque facade of:

① St-Paul–St-Louis

This is the most outstanding church in the Marais. Although the facade is pollution-faded, the inside is luminous.

Turn right when you leave the church. Across rue St-Antoine is the:

② Hôtel de Sully

The 17th-century mansion commissioned by Henri IV houses the Caisse Nationale des Monuments Historiques et des Sites (National Historical Monuments and Sites Commission). It features photography exhibits. Walk through the courtyard into the gardens; on sunny days, you'll find a bevy of people catching some sun. Continue through the courtyard leading to the Orangerie. On the left side of the passage is a bookstore (Librairie Hôtel de Sully) that retains the painted ceiling beams that were a feature of 17th-century mansions.

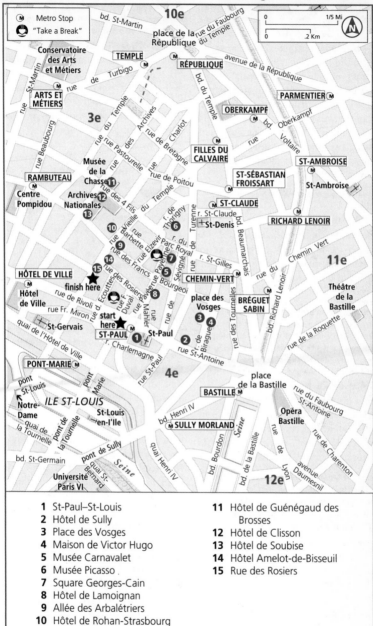

1 St-Paul–St-Louis
2 Hôtel de Sully
3 Place des Vosges
4 Maison de Victor Hugo
5 Musée Carnavalet
6 Musée Picasso
7 Square Georges-Cain
8 Hôtel de Lamoignan
9 Allée des Arbalétriers
10 Hôtel de Rohan-Strasbourg

11 Hôtel de Guénégaud des
   Brosses
12 Hôtel de Clisson
13 Hôtel de Soubise
14 Hôtel Amelot-de-Bisseuil
15 Rue des Rosiers

You'll see an exit on the right of the Orangerie. It takes you on to the:

❸ Place des Vosges

A great architectural achievement, 36 brick-and-stone pavilions rise from arcades surrounding the central square. The buildings were constructed according to a strict plan—the height of the facades equals their width, and triangular roofs are half as high as the facades—producing a symmetrical, harmonious space. The square was the model for Covent Garden in London.

In the southeastern corner of place des Vosges is the:

❹ Maison de Victor Hugo

The author of *Les Misérables* and *The Hunchback of Notre Dame* lived here for several years, during which he wrote "Les Miz" and other works. You can visit his house.

Leave the square at the end opposite the entrance and make a left on rue des Francs-Bourgeois. The facades of many of its stately mansions are worth studying; plaques along the street outline the history of the area. On the corner of rue de Sévigné, you'll see the:

❺ Musée Carnavalet

Begin your visit to the Museum of the City of Paris by admiring the carvings by Jean Goujon that grace the entrance and courtyard. Inside, you'll find a tour through the history of Paris.

Facing the Musée Carnavalet, turn right and continue up rue de Sévigné. Turn left at rue du Parc-Royal to place de Thorigny, and make a right on rue de Thorigny. At no. 5 is the:

❻ Musée Picasso

It houses the largest collection of the master's paintings in the world. You'll be amused by the contrast between Picasso's modern shapes and angles, and the 17th-century residence in which they are housed. Don't miss the lovely garden in back.

Retrace your steps to the corner of rue du Parc-Royal and rue Payenne. Turn right onto rue Payenne. On your left you'll see the:

❼ Square Georges-Cain

This flowery park contains a pediment from the former Palais des Tuileries as well as other remnants of demolished mansions. On your right is the Swedish Cultural Center, in another lovely 17th-century mansion.

> **TAKE A BREAK**
> In warm weather there's outdoor dining in the garden of the **Swedish Cultural Center**, 11 rue Payenne (☎ 01-44-78-80-20). Coffee, tea, and sweets like *pepparkaka* (spice cake) and *kanelbulle* (vanilla cake) are available for 2.80€ $3.50. The center also offers exhibits on Scandinavian topics.

Follow rue Payenne across rue des Francs-Bourgeois until it becomes rue Pavée. At no. 24 is the entrance to one of the oldest mansions of the Marais:

❽ Hôtel de Lamoignan

Built in 1585 for Diane de France, the illegitimate daughter of Henri II, who was made legitimate at age 7 by an adoption that granted her all noble rights. She lived here until her death. The motifs of the goddess Diana decorating the courtyard recall the first lady of the house. Dogs' heads, bows and arrows, and other emblems of the hunt embellish the curved pediments. The building houses the Bibliothèque Historique de la Ville de Paris.

Return to rue des Francs-Bourgeois and turn left. Proceed to no. 38, the:

❾ Allée des Arbalétriers

A typical medieval street with large paving stones and overhanging floors, it was the scene of the crime of the century—the 15th century. In 1407, Charles VI's brother, Louis d'Orléans, was returning home through this alley when he was attacked by men with swords and axes. The killers were hired by Jean the Fearless, duc de Bourgogne. The murder launched 30 years of conflict between the Burgundians and the Orléanists (Armagnacs).

Make a right onto rue Vieille-du-Temple. On the corner is a Gothic turret that's the only remnant of the Hôtel Hérouet, built around 1510. At no. 87 is the entrance to the:

⑩ Hôtel de Rohan-Strasbourg

Along with the Hôtel de Soubise (see no. 13 below), this *hôtel* represents the best that money could buy in 18th-century Marais. Architect Delamair built these linked mansions for the powerful Rohan-Soubise clan. Along with the Hôtel de Soubise, this hotel now houses the National Archives.

At the corner, turn left onto rue des Quatre-Fils, continue to the corner of rue des Archives, and turn right. At no. 60 is the entrance to the Musée de la Chasse et la Nature, lodged in the:

⑪ Hôtel de Guénégaud des Brosses

This imposing manor is the work of the architect François Mansart, uncle of Jules Hardouin-Mansart, who designed the dome of the Hôtel des Invalides and other works for Louis XIV.

Retrace your steps, noticing the 18th-century fountain with the nymph on the southwest corner of rue des Archives and rue des Haudriettes. Continue down rue des Archives. On your left at no. 58 are the towers of the:

⑫ Hôtel de Clisson

The towers are all that remain of the 14th-century Clisson mansion. This is one of the few remnants in Paris of medieval defensive architecture. From here, hot oil was poured out the window onto unwanted visitors.

Continue to rue des Francs-Bourgeois and turn left to find, at no. 60, the:

⑬ Hôtel de Soubise

This may be the architectural highlight of your walk. Stroll the courtyard even if you choose not to visit the Musée de l'Histoire de France.

Continue along rue des Francs-Bourgeois and make a right at rue Vieille-du-Temple. At no. 47 is the:

⑭ Hôtel Amelot-de-Bisseuil

The *hôtel* is also known as the **Hôtel des Ambassadeurs de Hollande,** even though no Dutch ambassadors have ever lived there. Beaumarchais wrote *The Marriage of Figaro* here in 1784. Offices now occupy the ground floor. During working hours you can ring for admission to the outer courtyard and gaze at the sculptures and bas-reliefs, most notably that of Romulus and Remus over the inside entry door.

When you emerge, take a right and then turn left onto:

⑮ Rue des Rosiers

The heart of the old Jewish quarter, the Jewish community in this neighborhood dates from the 13th century—references to the "street of rosebushes" *(rosiers)* appeared as early as 1230. The shops still have signs in Hebrew, and it's the best place in Paris for eastern European cuisine.

WINDING DOWN
At 7 rue des Rosiers is **Jo Goldenberg** (⓪ 01-48-87-20-16), founded by Albert Goldenberg (p. 121.) Lunch here on chopped liver, pastrami, or gefilte fish. The place can get crowded. If you can't get into Jo Goldenberg, stop for falafel at **L'As du Falafel,** no. 34 (⓪ 01-48-87-63-60; p. 121), or any similar place on the way.

Turn right on rue Pavée at the end of rue des Rosiers. On the left at no. 10 is the synagogue built in 1913 by Art Nouveau master Hector Guimard.

At the end of the street is the St-Paul Métro station.

WALKING TOUR 2   MONTMARTRE

Start and Finish: Place des Abbesses (Métro: Abbesses).
Time: 3 to 4 hours, depending on how long you spend in the churches and museums.
Best Time: On a clear day, to enjoy the panoramic view from Sacré-Coeur.
Worst Time: Saturday, when people jam the hilltop streets, and Sunday, when the shops are closed.

This walk will take you along the rustic lanes that inspired artists as diverse as Renoir, Toulouse-Lautrec, Utrillo, and Picasso. This is the Montmartre of windmills and vineyards, of parks and compact cottages half buried in vines and foliage. You'll also take in a panoramic view of Paris from the Sacré-Coeur church, and explore some of the lesser-known attractions on the hill.

Exit the Métro station and begin at the:

❶ Place des Abbesses

This is the centerpiece of an unpretentious, offbeat neighborhood that, although increasingly expensive, still attracts students and artists. Don't let the tourists overwhelm you—Montmartre is one of the oldest and most charming areas of Paris. Notice the entrance to the Métro station: The glass-and-iron shell is one of the few surviving examples of this genre designed by Art Nouveau master Hector Guimard.

Take a right up rue des Abbesses, a lively street of shops, boutiques, cafes, and restaurants. Notice the view of the windmill Moulin de la Galette as you pass rue Tholozé on the right. A few steps farther, rue des Abbesses branches off to the right into:

❷ Rue Lepic

This street climbs to the top of the butte. Currently in a state of disrepair, **no. 54,** on the right, is where Vincent van Gogh and his brother, Theo, lived from 1886 to 1888.

Continue along rue Lepic to:

❸ Moulin de la Galette and Moulin Radet

Early in the 16th century, the first windmills appeared in Montmartre to press grapes from nearby vineyards and grind grain. There were once 13 windmills; two remain. At **no. 75** is the **Moulin de la Galette,** built in 1622. It was an outdoor dance hall in the 19th century, and the subject of a Renoir painting. At the intersection of rue Lepic and rue Girardon is the **Moulin Radet,** now part of a restaurant.

Turn left on rue Girardon and head to its intersection with avenue Junot, where you'll find:

❹ Place Marcel-Aymé

Writer Marcel Aymé lived in the building here until his death in 1967. His novel *Le Passe-Muraille (The Man Who Passed Through Walls)* inspired the sculpture of a man emerging from a wall, executed by actor and Montmartre resident Jean Marais in 1989.

Across rue Girardon on your left is the:

❺ Square Suzanne-Buisson

You can sit on shaded benches in this park, watching games of boules in the warmer months. The statue in the center of the park is of St-Denis, who reputedly washed his decapitated head in the fountain that used to be here.

With the intersection of Girardon to your back, continue along avenue Junot. Peek over the hedges to see a private enclave of historic homes. On your left at no. 25, you'll see:

❻ Villa Léandre

Creeping vines and gardens surround the houses of this cul-de-sac in English style.

Walking Tour: Montmartre

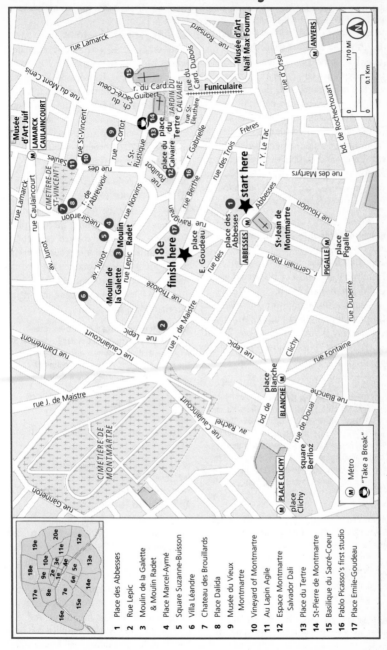

1 Place des Abbesses
2 Rue Lepic
3 Moulin de la Galette & Moulin Radet
4 Place Marcel-Aymé
5 Square Suzanne-Buisson
6 Villa Léandre
7 Chateau des Brouillards
8 Place Dalida
9 Musée du Vieux Montmartre
10 Vineyard of Montmartre
11 Au Lapin Agile
12 Espace Montmartre Salvador Dali
13 Place du Tertre
14 St-Pierre de Montmartre
15 Basilique du Sacré-Coeur
16 Pablo Picasso's first studio
17 Place Emile-Goudeau

Ⓜ Métro
☕ "Take a Break"

Return to avenue Junot, turn left, and go down the hill a few steps. Turn right onto rue Simon-Dereure. At the end of the street on the left is:

❼ Château des Brouillards

This 18th-century mansion was home to the Casadesus family of musicians after 1928. Now abandoned, the château and its front garden retain a haunting beauty.

Take the stairs on the left that lead up to the **allée des Brouillards.** One of the houses behind the foliage on the left was the home and studio of Pierre-Auguste Renoir from 1890 to 1897. His son, Jean, who was born here in 1894, directed the French films *Rules of the Game* and *The Grand Illusion.*

At the end of the allée des Brouillards, you'll arrive at:

❽ Place Dalida

Here you'll see a bust of the French singer Dalida, who lived nearby.

Take the road opposite the allée des Brouillards and follow rue de l'Abreuvoir, a quaint ivy-framed street, to **no. 2.** This is the "little pink house" painted by Utrillo; it was his earliest success.

TAKE A BREAK
At **La Maison Rose,** 2 rue de l'Abreuvoir (✆ **01-42-57-66-75**), Utrillo's subject is now an inexpensive cafe and restaurant. The vine-draped cottages recall a village lane. The cafe does not open before 11am; during the week it is closed from 3:30 to 6pm.

At the end of rue de l'Abreuvoir, cross rue des Saules, looking to your left at the view of Paris, and take a few steps to the right onto rue Cortot, where you'll make a left. At no. 12 is the:

❾ Musée du Vieux Montmartre

Exhibits feature artists who lived and worked in Montmartre.

At the end of rue Cortot, turn left on rue du Mont-Cenis and go down the stairs to rue St-Vincent. Turn left. A little way down the road is the:

❿ Vineyard of Montmartre

This vineyard is a tribute to the days when Montmartre supplied Paris with most of its wine. It produces about 500 bottles of Clos Montmartre red annually. Every year on the first Saturday of October, there's a celebration of the harvest, called the Vendanges. The wine is more notable for its nostalgic value than its drinkability, however.

On your right, down a few steps, is:

⓫ Au Lapin Agile

Dating to 1860, when it was called Au Rendez-Vous des Voleurs ("meeting place of thieves"), the rose-colored cabaret has green shutters and windows adorned with harlequin designs. It's named for a painting of a *lapin* (rabbit) by the artist A. Gill, a copy of which hangs outside this often-photographed spot.

Take a left up rue des Saules. Utrillo often painted the crossroads of rue des Saules, rue St-Rustique, and rue Norvins—although without the souvenir shops. At the intersection of avenue Junot, to your left you'll see rue Poulbot. Follow the curve to no. 11, the:

⓬ Espace Montmartre Salvador-Dalí

This museum houses a permanent display of 330 works by the Spanish artist.

When you leave the museum, go left and up a few steps to place du Calvaire and enjoy the view over Paris. Turn left and you'll come to:

⓭ Place du Tertre

The old town square of Montmartre, it's now overflowing with portraitists and overpriced cafes. If you get your portrait done, go only to the seated artists in the square, not the ones standing on the side streets, who will charge you twice the price. Also, make sure to negotiate the price before the sketch is done, and pay only if the final work resembles the subject. Despite the commercial frenzy, place du Tertre is a typical village square surrounded by 18th-century dwellings.

Continue across the square to the end of rue Norvins, where you'll make a right and arrive at the historic church of:

⓮ St-Pierre de Montmartre

One of the oldest churches in Paris, this is the last remnant of the powerful Montmartre Abbey that once dominated the hill.

When you leave the church, head left along place du Tertre, go downhill, and take the first left, rue Azaïs, to the:

⓯ Basilique du Sacré-Coeur

The gleaming white stone was chosen for its ability to secrete calcium when it rains, making this a self-whitening (and possibly self-dissolving) church. The dome rises 79m (259 ft.) and holds an 8,100kg (19-ton) bell, one of the world's heaviest. Take in the spectacular view over Paris.

Leaving the church, go down the stairs that lead to the *funiculaire* and follow the road, rue du Cardinal Dubois, right. At the second passageway after the *funiculaire*, rue Chappe, take a

left, go down the stairs, and you'll arrive at rue Gabrielle. Turn right. At no. 49 is:

⓰ Pablo Picasso's first Paris studio

He got the space from another Spanish painter in 1900 and supported himself by supplying a Spanish art dealer with a certain number of paintings in exchange for $20 a month.

Follow rue Gabrielle as it turns into rue Ravignan, which leads you to the cobblestoned:

⓱ Place Emile-Goudeau

At **no. 13** on your right is the **Bateau-Lavoir,** a small building that many artists, including Picasso, Modigliani, and Juan Gris, have called home. Here Picasso painted his famous portrait of Gertrude Stein, *The Third Rose,* as well as *Les Demoiselles d'Avignon.* The original building burned in 1970 and was rebuilt in 1978; the studios now house 25 artists and sculptors.

The stairs at the end of the square take you to rue Ravignan. Follow it down to rue des Abbesses, turn left, and you'll be back at the Abbesses Métro station.

WALKING TOUR 3   THE LITERARY & ARTISTIC LEFT BANK

Start:	Café des Deux Magots (Métro: St-Germain-des-Prés).
Finish:	Carrefour de l'Odéon.
Time:	About 3 hours.
Best Time:	Any pleasant, sunny day.
Worst Time:	Monday, when the Buci market is closed.

On this tour, you can sit in the cafes where Hemingway, Sartre, and de Beauvoir sat, and visit Delacroix's studio and museum. In the winding back streets you'll take in Henry Miller's favorite square (pl. de Furstemberg) and see where Picasso, Stein, and Toklas lived. Although the area has become more commercial, the narrow streets are still crammed with galleries, bookstores, and antiques shops, with jazz clubs, theaters, cafes, and restaurants at all price levels.

Begin with coffee at one of three landmark cafes on boulevard St-Germain:

❶ Café des Deux Magots, Café de Flore, or Brasserie Lipp

Pick one of the "golden triangle" of Parisian cafes, which conjure up the glory of St-Germain's literary past.

Café des Deux Magots is across from the church of St-Germain-des-Prés. Founded in 1881, it was named after the statues of two Chinese dignitaries *(magots)* on the wall. In the 1920s it attracted surrealists André Breton and

Raymond Queneau, as well as Hemingway and Ford Madox Ford.

Next door is **Café de Flore.** The oldest of the three, it was founded in 1870. Picasso used to come here from his nearby studio on rue des Grands-Augustins. Later, Sartre and de Beauvoir wrote and instructed budding existentialists at the cafe.

Brasserie Lipp is across the boulevard. A favorite rendezvous since the 19th century, the cafe drew politicians with the *choucroute* (sauerkraut) served in its plush interior.

From Brasserie Lipp, cross boulevard St-Germain, take a right, and walk a few steps to:

❷ St-Germain-des-Prés

This is the oldest of the city's large churches. After viewing the Romanesque and Gothic interior, walk behind the church. You'll find square Laurent-Prâche, a park containing a **Picasso bronze bust of a woman** dedicated to his friend Guillaume Apollinaire.

Return to boulevard St-Germain and cross the street to rue Bonaparte, which lies straight ahead. This street marks the course of the canal that at one time connected the Seine to the moat surrounding the abbey of St-Germain-des-Prés. Today it is a fashionable street, home to many chic stores. Take a left on rue du Vieux Colombier and follow it to:

❸ St-Sulpice

One of Paris's most impressive churches stands in a splendid square boasting an elaborate fountain. When you leave the church, step just to your right onto rue des Canettes.

Take a right onto rue Guisarde, then a left onto rue Princesse. At no. 6 you'll find:

❹ Village Voice

This is perhaps the most literary English-language bookstore in Paris. Contemporary artists, including some French ones, often give readings here. After browsing, step outside and turn left; you'll come to **rue du Four.**

Turn right on rue du Four and follow it to boulevard St-Germain. Directly across the street is rue de Buci. Follow this street for a block or two, until it bears gently to the right, where you'll walk into the splendid:

❺ Marché Buci

Although its heyday was a few decades ago, it's still one of the city's liveliest markets. Here you'll find fish, flowers, *fromage,* and fruit, as well as shop windows filled with mouthwatering pastries.

Go to the end of the market, and after munching on various treats, turn around and backtrack until you reach rue de Bourbon-le-Château. Take a right here and continue to rue de l'Echaudé. When St-Germain-des-Prés's abbey spread over several acres, roads converged here to form the abbey's place of public chastisement, where thieves and criminals were shamed before jeering crowds. Cross rue de l'Echaudé and continue until you reach rue Cardinale, which has changed little since 1700, and take a right. This will bring you to rue de Furstemberg, where you will make a left, leading directly to:

❻ Place de Furstemberg

Named for Cardinal Egon von Furstemberg, abbot of St-Germain-des-Prés in the 17th century, it would be hard to find a more tranquil hideaway. Here's how Henry Miller described it, though, in *Tropic of Cancer:* "Pass the Square de Furstemberg. Looks different now, at high noon. The other night when I passed by it was deserted, bleak, spectral. In the middle of the square four black trees that have not yet begun to blossom. Intellectual trees, nourished by the paving stones. Like T. S. Eliot's verse."

Across the square at no. 6 is the:

❼ Musée National Eugène Delacroix

The French Romantic painter (1798–1863) lived and worked here from 1857 to 1863.

Exiting the museum, go left up rue de Furstemberg to rue Jacob. (As you approach rue Jacob, there are some wonderful fabric shops left and right.) Go left on rue Jacob to:

Walking Tour: The Literary & Artistic Left Bank

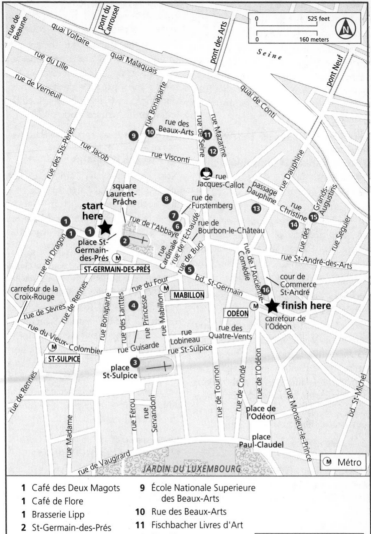

0		525 feet
0		160 meters

1 Café des Deux Magots
1 Café de Flore
1 Brasserie Lipp
2 St-Germain-des-Prés
3 St-Sulpice
4 Village Voice
5 Marché Buci
6 Place de Furstemberg
7 Musée Nationale Eugène-Delacroix
8 No. 20
9 École Nationale Superieure des Beaux-Arts
10 Rue des Beaux-Arts
11 Fischbacher Livres d'Art
12 No. 12
13 Passage Dauphine
14 Gertrude Stein's apartment
15 Rue des Grands-Augustins
16 Cour du Commerce St-André

⑧ No. 20 rue Jacob

This is the former residence of Natalie Clifford Barney (1876–1972), who moved here from the United States in 1909 as a student and stayed for over 60 years. Though virtually unknown in America, Barney was famous for her literary salons, visited by such luminaries as Joyce and Proust.

When you reach rue Bonaparte, turn right and proceed to the:

⑨ Ecole Nationale Supérieure des Beaux-Arts

The most famous of art schools, the Ecole des Beaux-Arts occupies architecturally splendid 17th- to 19th-century buildings. The alma mater of Degas, Monet, Matisse, and Max Weber, the school remains a busy cultural center. Check out the magnificent cloistered garden.

Upon leaving, cross rue Bonaparte and step onto:

⑩ Rue des Beaux-Arts

At **no. 13** is the discreetly elegant **L'Hôtel,** where Oscar Wilde, broke and in despair, died in 1900. "I'm dying beyond my means," the English playwright and author wrote—and he was only paying $10 a month for his room. Multiply that figure by 20 and you can begin to think about a room here now—for a night.

Make another right when you get to rue de Seine. At no. 33 is the art bookstore:

⑪ Fischbacher Livres d'Art

Works on all genres of art, in French and English, are stocked here.

TAKE A BREAK
At the corner of rue Jacques-Callot, you may want to stop at **La Palette,** 43 rue de Seine (✆ **01-43-26-68-15**), a friendly terrace cafe that has been an artists' hangout since it opened in 1903. Colorful murals decorate the interior, and a palette hangs over the bar. The cafe is closed the entire month of August.

Continue on rue Jacques-Callot to rue Mazarine, make a left, and find:

⑫ No. 12 rue Mazarine

This is the site of the theater where Molière made his first stage appearance. In 1623 at age 21, he joined an acting troupe and opened a theater. While he trod the boards here, he is remembered today for his written work.

Turn around and walk back up rue Mazarine, looking on your left for:

⑬ Passage Dauphine

Next to the garage, ring the button marked PORTE and enter the gate (if it is not open). This passageway is an easy, scenic way to get from rue Mazarine to rue Dauphine. Peek into the tea salon on the left side of the passageway.

Cross rue Dauphine and head onto rue Christine. Continue along rue Christine. At no. 5 you'll see:

⑭ Gertrude Stein's apartment

Stein and Alice B. Toklas lived here after leaving 27 rue de Fleurus. Stein's reputation as a writer and art collector was established. On a visit to deliver a housewarming bouquet, Janet Flanner, American correspondent for the *New Yorker,* was asked to inventory Stein's art collection. She found more than 130 canvases, 25 of them Picassos.

Rue Christine ends at:

⑮ Rue des Grands-Augustins

Across the street to the left (just a few steps toward the river) is **no. 7,** where Picasso lived from 1936 to 1955, near his good friend Gertrude Stein. He painted the masterpiece *Guernica* here in 1937, as is noted on the plaque.

Head back up rue des Grands-Augustins (away from the river) to rue St-André-des-Arts, then turn right. Look for Bar Mazet on your left. Right before the bar, go left onto:

⑯ Cour du Commerce St-André

This passage was built in 1776. At **no. 9,** Dr. Guillotin perfected his little invention on sheep before deciding it was fit to use on humans—much to the regret of Marie Antoinette and many others. This was also the site of the **printing shop** to which Jean-Paul Marat (1743–93), the Swiss-born revolutionary, walked in his bathrobe to correct the proofs of *L'Ami du peuple,* the paper he founded.

Charming cafes and restaurants line the cobblestone passageway. Near the rear entrance is **Le Procope,** founded just after the 1689 opening of the Comédie-Française, which used to be across the street.

> **WINDING DOWN**
> **A la Cour de Rohan,** 59–61 rue St-André-des-Arts (**℃ 01-43-25-79-67**), is a cozy tea salon that offers homespun charm along with scrumptious pastries and fine teas.

Exit cour du Commerce St-André onto boulevard St-Germain. The island at the center of the boulevard is carrefour de l'Odéon; here you'll find the Odéon Métro station.

WALKING TOUR 4   THE LATIN QUARTER

Start:	Place Maubert Mutualité (Métro: Maubert-Mutualité).
Finish:	Institute de Monde Arabe (Métro: Jussieu or Cardinal-Lemoine).
Time:	4 to 5 hours.
Best Time:	Tuesday, Thursday, and Saturday mornings, when the markets are open.
Worst Time:	Sunday, when nothing is open.

Ancient streets, walls, and ruins mark this tour through one of the oldest sections of Paris. The Latin Quarter is a true village in a city, replete with picturesque squares and crowds of students dashing to the university (which just happens to be the Sorbonne). The Romans plotted some of the narrow streets 1,000 years ago.

Start your tour at place Maubert Mutualité, where you'll find the:

❶ Market at Maubert Mutualité

Locals have come to this market since the Middle Ages to stock up on fresh products, including fish from Brittany, Saint Marcellin chèvre, fresh bread, and olives (a man from Provence sells over 20 varieties).

After trolling the market, cross boulevard St-Germain at place Maubert Mutualité to rue Lagrange. Follow it toward the river until rue du Fouarre. During the Middle Ages, university lecturers spoke here to students sitting outdoors on straw, or *fouarre.* Cross the street and step to your right. On your left is:

❷ St-Julien-le-Pauvre

One of the oldest churches in Paris, this example of Gothic splendor sits in the lovely park **Square René Viviani.** Originally constructed in the 12th century, it

lies on the pilgrimage route of St-Jacques de Compostelle to Spain. The oldest tree in Paris, an acacia reputedly planted in 1602, still stands in its garden. The church contains a stunning wooden screen, enclosing the beautiful chancel. Many classical concerts take place here.

When you leave the church, turn right and walk along rue St-Julien le Pauvre, a wonderfully preserved medieval street. Near the quai, make a left on rue de la Bûcherie. At no. 37 is:

❸ Shakespeare & Co.

A pilgrimage site for Anglophones, this storied old shop offers a wonderful collection of books in English.

When you leave, head to the right and walk along the quai de Montebello for a lovely view of Notre-Dame (to your left). When you get to rue de l'Hôtel Colbert, turn right. Walk 1 block to rue de la Bûcherie. On the left corner is:

④ Hôtel Colbert

A little historic gem, its prices preclude an overnight stay, so take a quick look at the lovely facade.

At the intersection of rue de l'Hôtel Colbert and rue de la Bûcherie (with your back to the river), turn left onto rue de la Bûcherie.

On your right is:

⑤ Librairie Dobosz

A small Polish bookstore that sells hand-painted pottery at fair prices.

The street turns into rue des Grands Degrés and intersects quai de la Tournelle. Walk along for just a few steps and turn right on rue de Bièvre.

This street follows the course of the river Bièvre, which, in the Middle Ages, flowed directly into the Seine. No. 22 is the former residence of the late French president François Mitterrand. On the right is the Jardin de la rue Bièvre, a lovely spot to catch some morning sun.

Cross boulevard St-Germain. Turn right to cross rue Monge, then walk a few steps and make a left onto rue de la Montagne Ste-Geneviève. Walk up this hill and cross rue des Ecoles. Walk another few minutes until you reach a small square.

TAKE A BREAK
La Madeleine de Proust, 4 rue Descartes (☎ 01-40-51-04-76), is a good place to stop for a quick coffee.

After a breather, climb the hill on rue de la Montagne Ste-Geneviève until you reach a square facing the back of the Panthéon. On your left is:

⑥ St-Etienne du Mont

Built between 1492 and 1626, this hilltop church is a spectacular amalgam of Gothic layout and Renaissance decorative style. The Renaissance rood-screen staircase is the only one left in Paris. Inside is the gold sarcophagus of Ste-Geneviève, the patron saint of Paris and adviser of Clovis. Since the Dark Ages the church

has been a pilgrimage stop for thousands seeking to pay homage to Ste-Geneviève. Racine and Pascal are also buried here.

Upon exiting the church, turn left; at the first street, rue Clovis, make another left. At 3 rue Clovis, you'll see a piece of:

⑦ Philippe Auguste's perimeter wall

Recovered in 1807, this is a section of the 10m-high (33-ft.) wall that once surrounded Paris. After craning your neck to see the stone structure, turn around and walk up the hill, backtracking, until you reach rue Descartes. Make a left.

As you walk a bit over 1 long block, rue Descartes turns into rue Mouffetard. Notice on your left **39 rue Descartes,** where **Hemingway** lived from 1921 to 1925, and **Paul Verlaine** died in 1896.

Continue another short block or so to:

⑧ Place de la Contrescarpe

Officially completed in 1852, this square occupies the site of one of the grand gates to Philippe Auguste's wall. In 1530, 1 place de Contrescarpe, known as the **Cabaret du la Pomme de Pin,** was a stomping ground for writers Rabelais and Ronsard.

Walk a few steps down rue du Cardinal Lemoine. At no. 74 you'll see:

⑨ Ernest Hemingway's apartment

The writer lived here on the third floor with his wife, Haley, from January 1922 to August 1923. This was his favorite neighborhood, as evinced by his other apartment just 1 block away.

Cross through the square and continue along **rue Mouffetard.** Once the road leading to Rome, this street is full of bookshops, small stores, and old houses. In 1938 construction workers at **no. 53** discovered 3,350 gold coins (4 million euros today) from the period of Louis XV, left behind by the king's counselor, Louis Nivelle.

Walking Tour: The Latin Quarter

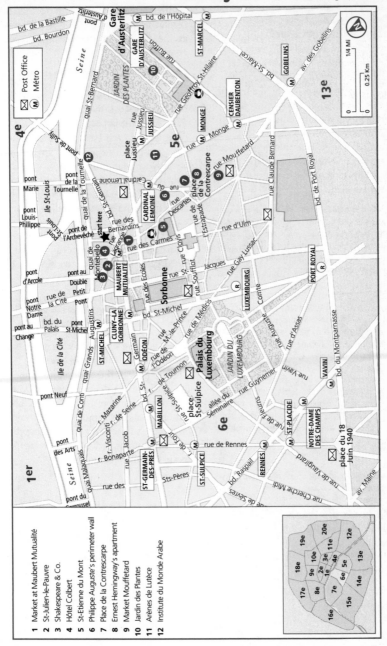

Legend / Map Key:

☒ Post Office
Ⓜ Métro

1/4 Mi
0.25 Km
0

1 Market at Maubert Mutualité
2 St-Julien-le-Pauvre
3 Shakespeare & Co.
4 Hôtel Colbert
5 St-Etienne du Mont
6 Philippe Auguste's perimeter wall
7 Place de la Contrescarpe
8 Ernest Hemingway's apartment
9 Market Mouffetard
10 Jardin des Plantes
11 Arènes de Lutèce
12 Institut du Monde Arabe

Follow rue Mouffetard for a good 5 to 10 minutes until you run into the:

⑩ Market Mouffetard

Nestled in one of the most dynamic neighborhoods of Paris, the market teems with students and academics. It abounds with *primeurs*—perfectly ripe fruits available here before they're in stores and other markets—including cherries galore, strawberries, blueberries, and figs. Every conceivable cheese is for sale, as are sausages, boudin, and tripe. As you explore, look on the left for a small street, rue Daubenton.

Follow rue Daubenton until you reach a confusing intersection with rue Monge. Cross straight through the intersection, where you'll continue on rue Daubenton. Cross rue de la Clef and keep walking until a large green-and-white mosque comes into view on your left.

TAKE A BREAK
The **Salon de Thé de la Mosquée de Paris**, 39 rue Geoffroy-St-Hilaire (✆ 01-43-31-18-14), is a great place to grab a baklava and tea, or, if you've worked up an appetite, *tajine* and couscous. Built in 1920 in gratitude to the North African Muslims for their support in World War I, the mosque, designed in Moorish style, has a patio and a highly decorated interior with long, cozy couches.

After refueling, walk across rue Geoffroy-St-Hilaire. Just a few steps to your right is the entrance to the:

⑪ Jardin des Plantes

The oldest garden in Paris, it was created in 1626 and opened to the public in 1640. The Musée National d'Histoire Naturelle is also here.

After exploring, exit at the corner of rue Cuvier and rue Geoffroy-St-Hilaire—at the far end of the side where you entered.

Cross rue Geoffroy-St-Hilaire to rue Lacépède, and follow it almost 1 block. Take a right on rue Navarre. At the end, cross the street. On your left is the entrance to the:

⑫ Arènes de Lutèce

Built between the 1st and 2nd centuries A.D., these are the ruins of an ancient arena. With the Cluny baths, they are the only remaining ruins of the Gallo-Roman period in Paris. Discovered in 1869, the arena has been restored, revealing a grand Coliseum that seated approximately 15,000 spectators who came to watch gladiators. Now surrounded by manicured gardens, the park attracts Parisians for a more civilized game of boules.

Leave at the exit by rue Monge. Turn right on rue Monge, walk to rue Cardinal Lemoine, and make another right. Cross rue des Ecoles and rue Jussieu. Bearing to your right, follow rue des Fossés St-Bernard to the entrance of the:

⑬ Institut du Monde Arabe

The top floor of this building, an imposing structure of aluminum and glass constructed to promote Islamic culture and art, offers one of the most beautiful views of Paris. It's free, too. From the seventh-floor restaurant, where the terrace is located, drink in the view.

9

Paris Shopping

Presentation is everything in Paris. It's evident from the impeccable way people dress to the meticulous way they arrange every item in their *magasin* (store) windows—from the largest department store to the smallest boutique.

For the visitor and Parisian alike, this makes shopping in the City of Light an

art in itself. So take your time, soak it in, and treat yourself. Don't worry, you'll be able afford that perfect something. And remember, searching some ancient, cobblestone street on a quest to find your gem is part of the joy and mystery of Paris.

1 The Shopping Basics

France adds a 20.6% **value-added tax (VAT)** to the price of most products, which means that most things cost less in the U.S. (For details on getting a VAT refund, see below.) Even French-made goods are not necessarily cheaper here than elsewhere. Appliances, paper products, housewares, computer supplies, CDs, and women's clothing are notoriously expensive. On the other hand, you can often get good deals on cosmetics such as **Bourjois** (a low-priced line made in the same factory as Chanel—it's excellent); skin-care products from **Lierac, Galenic, Roc,** and **Vichy;** and some luxury goods.

The time to find a bargain in Paris is during the twice-annual **sales** *(soldes)* in January and July. If you can brave the bargain-hungry crowds, you just might find the perfect designer outfit at a fraction of the retail price.

Store hours are Monday to Saturday from 9 or 9:30am (sometimes 10am) to 7pm, later on Thursdays, without a break for lunch. Many smaller stores close on Monday or Monday mornings and break for lunch for up to 3 hours, beginning at around 1pm. Small stores may close for all or part of August and some days around Christmas and Easter. Sunday shopping is gradually spreading but is limited to tourist areas. Try **rue de Rivoli** across from the Louvre, **rue des Francs-Bourgeois** in the Marais, the **Carrousel du Louvre,** and the **Champs-Elysées.**

Politeness is important. Always greet salespeople with "Bonjour, madame" or "Bonjour, monsieur" when you arrive. Whether you've bought anything or not, say, "Merci, au revoir," when you're leaving.

If you spend more than 185€ ($231) in a single store (U.K. residents no longer qualify for a VAT refund), you're entitled to a **value-added tax (VAT) refund.** The discount is not automatic. Food, wine, and tobacco don't count, and the refund is granted only on purchases you take with you out of the country—not on what you ship home.

To apply, show the clerk your passport. You'll be given an export sales document (in triplicate—two pink sheets and a green one), which you must sign, and an envelope addressed to the store. Travelers leaving from **Charles de Gaulle** airport may visit the

Europe Tax-Free Shopping (ETS) refund point, operated by CCF Change, to receive an immediate VAT refund in cash; there's a 5€ ($6.25) fee if you take your refund in cash. Otherwise, when you depart, arrive at the airport early, allowing for lines at the *détaxe* (refund) booth at French Customs. If you're traveling by **train,** go to the *détaxe* area in the station before boarding—you can't get your refund documents processed on the train. Give the three sheets to the official, who will stamp them and return a pink and a green copy to you. Keep the green copy and mail the pink copy to the store. Your reimbursement will be mailed by check (in French francs) or credited to your credit card. If you don't receive your refund in 4 months, write the store, giving the date of purchase and location where you submitted the forms. Include a photocopy of your green copy. Department stores that cater to foreign visitors, like Au Printemps and Galeries Lafayette, have *détaxe* areas where clerks will prepare your invoices.

2 The Best Shopping from A to Z

Most of the shops and markets listed here offer good deals throughout the year—especially in January and July.

ANTIQUES

Le Louvre des Antiquaires   As malls go, this one is rather subdued, despite the numerous shops, particularly jewelry stores. From Rolex watches to Jean Cocteau sketches to silver older than the United States, items are pricey at des Antiquaires, but rumor has it that some good deals turn up. 2 pl. du Palais-Royal, 1er. ℂ **01-42-97-27-00.** Métro: Palais-Royal–Musée du Louvre.

Marché aux Puces de la Porte de St-Ouen   If you like flea markets, you'll love this one: It has a lively, festive atmosphere and consists of more than 3,000 indoor-outdoor stalls carrying everything from vintage clothing to valuable art and antiques. Between Porte de St-Ouen and Porte de Clignancourt, 18e. No phone. Métro: Porte de Clignancourt.

Village St-Paul   Located in a courtyard off the delightful rue St-Paul, this 17th-century village is filled with lovely small antiques stores and is a popular destination for Parisian couples on weekend afternoons. The stores are closed Tuesday and Wednesday. 23–27 rue St-Paul, 4e. No phone. Métro: St-Paul.

ART PRINTS

Galerie Documents   If you're interested in old posters, this is the place for you, unless you're into movie posters—they don't sell those. Still, you'll find everything else, from sporting events to old ads for Pernod. 53 rue de Seine, 6e. ℂ **01-43-54-50-68.** Métro: Odéon.

Librarie Elbé   One of the most memorable things you can buy in Paris is a poster, etching, or cartoon to frame when you get home. Some *bouquinistes* (booksellers) along the Seine sell good reproductions, but search for the best price before you buy. If you want something original, this shop sells late-19th- and early-20th-century advertising and railroad posters, as well as etchings and cartoons, at reasonable prices. Everything is filed by category; ask if you can browse before opening a portfolio. 213 bis bd. St-Germain, 7e. ℂ **01-45-48-77-97.** Métro: Bac.

BOOKS

Books, especially in English, are expensive in Paris, though a law prohibiting discounting has been limited to French-language books. If you can't go another day without reading in English, your best bet is one of these secondhand shops.

USED

San Francisco Book Co.   Owners Phil Wood and Jim Carroll stock 20,000 affordable secondhand books in their small 7-year-old store. If you're tired of lugging around a quality fiction or nonfiction title, Phil may even pay you cash for it. 17 rue Monsieur-le-Prince, 6e. ☎ 01-43-29-15-70. Métro: Odéon.

Shakespeare & Co.   English-speaking residents of Paris still gather in this cluttered Anglo-Parisian landmark named after Sylvia Beach's legendary lair. On Sunday afternoons free literary tea salons are often hosted by local celebrities for the bookish group, or those who just want to say they were there. 37 rue de la Bûcherie, 5e. No phone. Métro or RER: St-Michel.

Tea and Tattered Pages   Most of the 15,000 books here are used and sell for around 6€ ($7.50), one of the best deals in town. Like her predecessor, new owner Hilda Cabanel-Evans sells brownies and other "American" goodies that you can munch on in her little tea salon while reading one of your favorites! 24 rue Mayet, 6e. ☎ 01-40-65-94-35. Métro: Falguière or Duroc.

WORTH CHECKING OUT

Abbey Bookshop   Besides offering a few thousand English-language books in this small, two-floor store, the Abbey hosts many events, including readings and Sunday hikes in the country near Paris. 29 rue de la Parcheminerie, 5e. ☎ 01-46-33-16-24. Métro: St-Michel or Cluny-Sorbonne.

Brentano's   This is one of the city's leading English-language bookstores, with a broad fiction and nonfiction stock that includes guides and maps. It usually has a shelf of discounted books—a good thing, because its prices tend to be expensive. 37 av. de l'Opéra, 2e. ☎ 01-42-61-52-50. Métro: Opéra.

Galignani   If you're trying to ease your way into reading in French but still need an English book for moral support, this is the place for you! One of the oldest English-language bookstores on the Continent, Galignani sells a wide variety of books and magazines in both languages. 224 rue de Rivoli, 1er. ☎ 01-42-60-76-07. Métro: Tuileries.

Institut Géographique National   With atlases lining its shelves and an array of other well-crafted navigational items in this two-floor store, Institut Géographique is a delightful place to purchase gifts for your favorite traveler. 107 rue de la Boétie, 8e. ☎ 01-43-98-80-00. Métro: Franklin-D-Roosevelt.

Les Mots à la Bouche   This is Paris's largest and best-stocked gay bookstore, where you can find French- and English-language books as well as gay-info magazines like *Illico, e.m@le,* and *Lesbia.* You'll also find lots of free pamphlets advertising gay/lesbian venues and events. 6 rue Ste-Croix-la-Bretonnerie, 4e. ☎ 01-42-78-88-30. Métro: Hôtel de Ville.

Librarie La Hune   For a slice of existential history, visit this shop, between the cafes Les Deux Magots and de Flore. La Hune has been a center for Left Bank intellectuals since 1945. The selection (mostly in French) is outstanding. 170 bd. St-Germain. ☎ 01-45-48-35-85. Métro: St-Germain.

Village Voice   Quality fiction in English is the highlight of this small store in St-Germain-des-Prés. It stocks an excellent selection of poetry, plays, nonfiction, and literary magazines. Owner Odile Hellier schedules free poetry and fiction readings. 6 rue Princesse, 6e. ☎ 01-46-33-36-47. Métro: Mabillon.

W.H. Smith   W.H. Smith is a great place to go if you're feeling homesick—it's not hard to pretend you're at Barnes & Noble flipping through magazines. Notorious for its high prices, a bargain can still be had here, particularly in its classics department with such greats as F. Scott Fitzgerald's *Tender Is the Night* costing about the same price as a café crème. 248 rue de Rivoli, 1er. ✆ **01-42-61-58-15** or 01-44-77-88-99. Métro: Concorde.

CERAMICS, CHINA & GLASS

Baccarat   The incredible hues of lavender, honeydew yellow, rich burgundy, deep ocean blue, and translucent ivory of Baccarat crystals is truly amazing, but then Baccarat has been producing its world-renowned crystal since the 18th century. This store is also a museum, so even if the prices make you faint, you can still enjoy browsing. There is also a store at 11 pl. de la Madeleine, 8e. ✆ **01-42-65-36-26.** 30 bis rue de Paradis, 10e. ✆ **01-47-70-64-30** or 01-40-22-11-00. Métro: Château-d'Eau, Poissonnière, or Gare-de-l'Est.

Cristal Vendôme   You can shop duty-free for Lalique, Baccarat, and more at this shop, and even ship purchases to the United States—plus, there's a great pic of Hillary Clinton purchasing crystal here! In the Hôtel Intercontinental, 1 rue de Castiglione, 1er. ✆ **01-49-27-09-60.** Métro: Concorde.

La Maison Ivre   If you can afford to redecorate your kitchen in French country, this would be the first place to get dishware. Think mustard-colored pitchers with delicately painted violets or Provençal-inspired blue-and-white ceramic plates that you'll want to hang on your wall, not hide in your cupboard. Be sure to check out the other crafts stores nearby in the heart of this antiques and gallery district (on the Left Bank between St-Germain-des-Prés and the Seine). 38 rue Jacob, 6e. ✆ **01-42-60-01-85.** Métro: St-Germain-des-Prés.

La Tisanière Porcelaine   This store sells discontinued lines by prestigious china and glass makers. You can find some great bargains. 21 rue de Paradis, 10e. ✆ **01-47-70-22-80.** Métro: Chateau d'Eau.

Limoges Centre   If you love Limoges, this is the place. Its wares are discounted from 20% to 60%. Glassware and silverware are on sale, too. Usine Centre, Paris Nord. ✆ **01-48-63-20-75.** Métro: Chateau d'Eau.

Paradis Porcelaine   This store, on a street filled with wholesale china and porcelain stores, stocks a great selection at fantastic prices. 56 rue de Paradis, 10e. ✆ **01-48-24-50-90.** Métro: Poissonnière.

CRAFTS

Viaduc des Arts   When the elevated railroad cutting across the 12e was transformed into the Promenade Plantée, the space beneath was redesigned to accommodate a stretch of artisan shops, galleries, and boutiques. A quick walk from the Bastille, it's worth an hour or two to visit these artists-in-residence, who often work before your eyes. 9–147 av. Daumesnil, 12e. ✆ **01-43-40-80-80.** Métro: Bastille, Ledru-Rollin, Reuilly-Diderot, or Gare-de-Lyon.

DEPARTMENT STORES

Two major department stores—Au Printemps and Galeries Lafayette—offer tourists a 10% discount coupon, good in most departments. If your hotel or travel agent didn't give you a coupon, you can ask for it at the stores' welcome desks—the clerks speak English.

Au Bon Marché   The oldest department store in Paris is my favorite with its magnificent open, circular layout and attention to detail in its displays—not to mention the fabulous clothes it sells! Prices are high, but during the sales, you can find tons of deals. Visit the huge basement supermarket, with its many reasonably priced items; it's the city's largest épicerie, and you can find nearly any kind of food. 24 rue de Sèvres, 7e. ✆ 01-44-39-80-00. Métro: Sèvres-Babylone.

Au Printemps   With its first two floors recently redone, Au Printemps is beginning to shed its "not as nice as Au Bon Marché" image and has donned a new, sleeker look. Plus, its Maison Store is great if you're into home decorating, and for the clothes connoisseur there's a fashion show under the 1920s glass dome at 10:15am on Tuesday year-round and Friday from March through October. 64 bd. Haussmann, 9e. ✆ 01-42-82-50-00. Métro: Havre-Caumartin.

BHV (Bazar de l'Hôtel de Ville)   Near the Marais, BHV is a popular department store among Parisians because of its reasonable prices on everything from clothing to luggage. 52–64 rue de Rivoli, 4e. ✆ 01-42-74-90-00. Métro: Hôtel de Ville.

Galeries Lafayette *(Overrated*   Almost always crowded, the colossal Galeries Lafayette is still worth checking out with its selection of hip new clothes, which are very often at affordable prices. If you're shopping with *les enfants,* you might want to visit the kiddie entertainment center. Also, the sixth-floor self-service cafeteria, Lafayette Café, has good views of the Opéra and the rooftops of Paris. 40 bd. Haussmann, 9e. ✆ 01-42-82-34-56. Métro: Opéra or Chaussée-d'Antin.

La Samaritaine   Located between the Louvre and the Pont Neuf, Samaritaine, which is made up of four buildings, feels and looks more quintessentially French than the other department stores. It also has the best view: Look for signs to the *panorama,* a free observation point, to see Paris from up high. The fifth floor of store no. 2 has a fine, inexpensive restaurant.

Note: As of June 2005, the store has temporarily closed for urgent repairs after the 1906 building (itself a historic landmark) was deemed a fire hazard. It's unclear whether parts of the building will reopen in stages or whether the entire store will remain closed for at least 18 months while the repairs are in progress. 67 rue de Rivoli, 1er. ✆ 01-40-41-20-20. Métro: Pont Neuf or Châtelet–Les Halles.

Monoprix-Prisunic   This chain store is the lifeline of many a Parisian and will become the budget-conscious traveler's best friend. It sells everything from cheese in its grocery section to stylish clothes, including some great finds on sexy lingerie, to Bourjois makeup and even housewares in its attached compact mini–department store. 52, av. Des Champs Elysees, 8e. ✆ 01-53-77-65-65. Métro: Franklin D. Roosevelt.

Tati   This store is a lifesaver when you're broke and need staples like cotton underthings to ward off the Paris dampness—all for about 5.25€ ($6.60) each. Occasionally you can even find some cool outerwear, and when people ask where you bought that "funky skirt," you answer, "Samaritaine, but of course." There are branch stores at 172 rue du Temple, 4e (✆ **01-42-76-04-93** or 01-48-04-56-49); 13 pl. de la République, 3e (✆ **01-48-87-72-81**); and 11 bis rue Scribe, 9e (**01-47-42-20-28**). Another branch, Tati Or, specializes in gold (see "Jewelry," later in this chapter). 4 bd. Rochechouart, 18e. ✆ 01-55-29-50-00. Métro: Barbés-Rochechouart.

FASHION

Fashion is an art in Paris. The Parisian woman does not leave her house without looking completely put together. This doesn't necessarily mean she'll be wearing the cutting edge in fashion. But with her coiffed hair; smart-looking, quality shoes; form-fitting pants or a-cut-above-the-knee-length skirt; and understated, chic top, she looks fabulous—whether she's 18, 28, or 70 years old. Her beauty isn't surface, either; she loves her undies and teddies, and has no trouble finding either because there's a lingerie store on about every corner in Paris.

Simply put, French women take pride in their appearance, and expect it of others; so don't get caught running to Monoprix in your sweats—*unacceptable!*

But don't worry, you don't have to spend a fortune to dress like a Parisian—just ask one! *La femme Parisienne* is savvy; she knows with smart shopping she can afford to look like a million dollars without spending it. Her secret? *Soldes* (sales), *dégriffés* (labels cut out), *stock* (overstock), and *dépôt-vente* (resale).

Some of the best fashion deals are in resale shops that deal directly with showrooms and the industry. Designer clothing that has been worn on a runway or for a fashion shoot is on sale for half price, along with other gently used clothes and accessories. Most *dépôts-vente* are in the stylish 8e, 16e, and 17e arrondissements. A few favorites are listed below.

For overstock, end-of-series, and *dégriffé* clothes, bargain hunters head to the south of Paris. Rue St-Placide (Métro: Sèvres-Babylone) is a street for pennywise shoppers looking for affordable sportswear and men's fashions.

Shops on rue d'Alésia in the 14e (Métro: Alésia) offer last season's Cacharel, Chantal Thomass, Diapositive, Régina Rubens, and Sonia Rykiel, among other midprice lines. Many stores are closed Monday or Monday morning.

DISCOUNT

Anna Lowe   Next to the ritzy Hôtel Bristol, this shop is a find for those who want the best designers—Yves Saint-Laurent, Chanel, Giorgio Armani—at a discount. Shopping is genteel and substantially less uptight than at the same designers' retail shops. Remember, however, that a steeply discounted couture price can still mean an expensive item. 104 rue du Faubourg St-Honoré, 8e. ⓒ **01-42-66-11-32** or 01-40-06-02-42. www.anna loweparis.com. Métro: Miromesnil or St-Phillippe-de-Roule.

La Clef des Marques   This place gives one-stop shopping a new meaning—it's highly recommend for mommies who want to buy everything from chic lingerie to adorable *dégriffé* baby's clothes without having to deal with the immensity of a mall—or the high prices. Don't forget to check out the shoes—they stock a fabulous, funky, offbeat selection. Branches are located at 86 rue Faubourg St-Antoine, 12e (ⓒ **01-40-01-95-15**), and 20 pl. Marché St-Honoré, 1er (ⓒ **01-47-03-90-40**). 124 bd. Raspail, 6e. ⓒ **01-45-49-31-00**. Métro: Notre-Dame des Champs.

Le Mouton à Cinq Pattes   A must for bargain hunters in search of that perfect Stella McCartney dress at a decent—if not awesome—price. There is something for everyone in the family, from men's designer clothes to children's shoes to accessories to express the id in you. If you find something you love, buy it immediately because it may not be there tomorrow. Its four branches are located at: 19 rue Grégoire-de-Tours, 6e (ⓒ **01-43-29-73-56;** Métro: Odéon); 15 rue Vieille du Temple, 4e (ⓒ **01-42-71-86-30;** Métro: St-Paul); 138 bd. St-Germain des Prés, 6e (ⓒ **01-43-26-49-25;** Métro: St-Germain des Prés); and at numbers 8, 10, and 48 rue St-Placide, 6e. (ⓒ **01-45-48-86-26** for all stores. Métro: St-Placide).

L'Habilleur   This place is a gem if you're looking for the absolutely latest in glamour-wear; it offers up to a 70% discount off the very latest designs by Helmut Lang, Dries van Noten, and Martine Sitbon. 44 rue de Poitou, 3e. ⓒ 01-48-87-77-12. www. habilleur.fr. Métro: Filles du Calvaire.

Nip Shop   In the same neighborhood as Réciproque (see below) but much smaller, this *dépôt-vente* has good connections with Yves Saint-Laurent, Sonia Rykiel, and Guy Laroche, as well as lesser-known designers. It has recently begun to carry jewelry and handbags made by these same well-known designers. 6 rue Edmond-About, 16e. ✆ 01-45-04-66-19. Métro: Rue de la Pompe.

Réciproque   You don't come here for the dreary atmosphere, you come for the bargains! The largest *dépôt-vente* in Paris fills its small stores along rue de la Pompe with racks of lightly used clothing for men, women, and children, as well as jewelry, furs, belts, and purses. If you've always dreamed of owning a designer outfit—the sheer number of gently worn Chanel suits is astonishing—you might find one that fits your budget. Still, prices over $1,000 are, sadly, all too common. Midrange labels are also well represented. 89–123 rue de la Pompe, 16e. ✆ 01-47-04-30-28. Métro: Rue de la Pompe.

CHILDREN'S

Bonpoint   The clothes are exquisite, but tend to be something that little Madeleine or Billy might wear for their Sunday best, rather than for play. Also, this *kinder* beauty doesn't come cheap—except for this Left Bank location, where you may find the same merchandise at reduced prices, especially after the yearly sales. 82 rue de Grenelle, 7e. ✆ 01-42-84-12-39. Métro: Rue-du-Bac.

Du Pareil Au Même   This great store is in a lively residential neighborhood where few tourists tread. The clothes are not only adorable but practical, too—overalls, shirts, and jackets your children will live in, and all for an incredibly low price. 59 rue du Commerce, 15e. ✆ 01-48-28-86-76. Métro: Commerce.

Natalys   Part of a French chain with more than a dozen stores in Paris, Natalys sells children's wear, maternity wear, and related products. The clothes have a lot of panache for the price. Branches include 74 rue de Seine, 6e (✆ 01-46-33-46-48), and 47 rue du Sèvres, 6e (✆ 01-45-48-77-12). 92 av. des Champs-Elysées, 8e. ✆ 01-43-59-17-65. Métro: George V.

MEN'S

Parisian men always look sharp, well groomed, and well dressed. The highest end stores for men are located on avenue Montaigne (worth a window-shopping spree) where the lovely tree-lined street is lined with the fanciest fashion houses from Dolce & Gabbana to Calvin Klein and Valentino. Men looking for a bargain head to the rue du Cherche-Midi in the 6e (Métro: Mabillon), where many shops sell designer wear at significant discounts. For the latest fashions without the high prices, many Parisian men shop at Zara (see below).

Blanc Bleu   This quintessential Parisian shop offers bargains on casual wear favored by French men: everything from Lacoste-looking shirts to relaxed but elegant slacks and white sneakers. 5 bd. Malesherbes, 8e. ✆ 01-47-42-02-18. Métro: Madeleine.

Mi-Prix   This is an excellent men's designer clothing store offering steep discounts from such labels as Karl Lagerfeld, Alaïa, Missoni, and Gianfranco Ferré. It stocks clothes for women, too. 27 bd. Victor Hugo, 15e. ✆ 01-48-28-42-48. Métro: Balard or Porte de Versailles.

WOMEN'S

Etam   It seems on every corner there is an Etam, which is a good thing because its clothes are colorful and hip. But one caveat: Most merchandise is in synthetics or synthetic blends. The lingerie store, 47 rue de Sèvres, 6e (✆ **01-45-48-21-33**), has some pretty, affordable nightclothes and undergarments. 9 bd. St-Michel, 5e. ✆ **01-43-54-79-20.** Métro: St-Michel.

Kiliwatch   This bright mish-mash of club clothes and vintage in a slightly psyche-delic setting offers some surprisingly good prices. It stocks everything from wigs to coats, plus a few new designers. A must for club kids. 64 rue Tiquetonne, 2e. ✆ **01-42-21-17-37.** Métro: Etienne-Marcel.

Kookaï   Kookaï is always slightly ahead of the trend in fashionable women's cloth-ing. Fortunately, it has many other branches all over the city. 35 bd. St-Michel, 5e. ✆ **01-46-34-75-02.** RER: Luxembourg.

La City   The look here is young and modern. The selection is limited and everything is synthetic, but the prices are as reasonable as you can get in Paris. Branches at 18 rue St-Antoine, 4e (✆ **01-42-78-95-55**), and 42 rue Passy, 16e (✆ **01-42-88-66-21**). 37 rue Chaussée d'Antin, 9e. ✆ **01-48-74-41-00.** Métro: Chaussée d'Antin.

Mango   With locations throughout the city, this store is popular with young Parisian women for its inexpensive, fashion-conscious clothes, and offers better vari-ety than Etam and La City. 3 pl. 18 Juin 1940, 6e. ✆ **01-45-48-04-96.**

Morgan   Sexy synthetics and blends at low prices for the young female crowd. 16 rue Turbigo, 2e. ✆ **01-44-82-02-00.** Métro: Etienne-Marcel.

1-2-3   The suits, blouses, and sweaters at this chain are handsome, if conservative, at moderate prices. If you're looking for that indispensable black cocktail dress, you'll find a few versions of it at one of their chains around the winter holidays. The 1-2-3 lingerie stores located throughout Paris are decidedly more daring. There is one at 85 rue du Commerce (✆ **01-56-23-16-84**). 42 rue Chaussée d'Antin, 9e. ✆ **01-40-16-80-06.** Métro: Chaussée d'Antin.

Rodier   Stylish knitwear stars at this upscale chain. Prices are high for ready-to-wear, but it's good quality and you can find bargains during sales. 72 av. Ternes, 17e. ✆ **01-45-74-17-17.** Métro: Ternes. Also 47 rue de Rennes, 6e (✆ **01-45-44-30-27**).

Zara *Finds*   Zara originated in Spain over a decade ago and offers fantastic bargains for both men and women. Everywhere you look, you'll find exciting colors with designs that somehow combine sexy, classic, and cutting edge and make the mix work! Zara not only has lots of flair but also has even managed to keep prices affordable for the budget-minded. You'll find locations all over the place, including 2 rue Halévy, 9e, near the Opéra (✆ **01-44-71-90-90** and 01-44-71-90-93), and 38–40 av. des Champs-Elysées (✆ **01-56-59-97-10**). 45 rue de Rennes, 6e. ✆ **01-44-39-03-50.** Métro: St-Germain-des-Prés.

FOOD

Before you load your suitcase, remember that U.S. Customs regulations prohibit importation of cheese that isn't "cured"—which means you may have a problem with anything other than wrapped supermarket cheese. Regulations also bar most meat products, except canned meat that is shelf-stable without refrigeration.

Fauchon *Overrated*   Opened in 1888, Fauchon sells all things gourmet, from exotic spices to the rarest of cheeses to canned foie gras. The number of visitors who flock here is staggering and the staff isn't able to help everybody—but this is a good place to ogle the beautifully packaged foods and not to buy, as prices are quite inflated. Pl. de la Madeleine, 8e. ✆ **01-47-42-60-11.** Métro: Madeleine.

Florence Finkelsztajn   In the center of the Jewish Marais, Florence Finkelsztajn specializes in products from central Europe. The store carries everything from Sacher tortes to eggplant caviar, and its friendly staff informed us they now cater private parties. 24 rue des Ecouffes, 4e. ✆ 01-48-87-92-85. Métro: St-Paul.

Foie Gras Import   On the northern edge of Les Halles, this boutique sells all kinds of canned foie gras (duck or goose liver) at reasonable prices. It also carries pâté, canned snails, dried wild mushrooms, and truffles. These gourmet treats are much cheaper in France than they are in North America and are easy to pack. 34 rue Montmartre, 1er. ✆ 01-42-33-31-32. Métro: Etienne Marcel.

Izraë   If it's unusual, it's probably here: canned food, dried meats, and all kinds of spices, herbs, and grains. If you like buying cool, offbeat culinary gifts, this is the place to go! 30 rue François Miron, 4e. ✆ 01-42-72-66-23. Métro: St-Paul.

Jacques Papin   In the heart of the Buci market, this butcher shop has some of the most ravishingly displayed foodstuffs you'll ever see, including trout in aspic, exquisite pâtés and salads, lobsters, and smoked salmon. Prestige et Tradition, 8 rue de Buci, 6e. ✆ 01-43-26-86-09. Métro: Odéon.

Lafayette Gourmet   In one of the buildings of Galeries Lafayette, the department store, this wonderful supermarket is a great place to have a quick snack at one of its eat-on-the-premises areas or to buy a yummy premade picnic-to-go. Note that the house-brand merchandise, often cheaper than other labels, is of very good quality. 48 bd. Haussmann, 9e. ✆ 01-48-74-46-06. Métro: Chaussée d'Antin.

La Grande Epiceriet   Bright-red tomatoes available in the middle of winter, pumpkin soup that tastes as fabulous as the beautiful bottle it's encased in looks, gorgeous squash—a food museum, is what this is, but better than the Louvre because you can actually buy something! And while a bit of a splurge, there are plenty of things that you can afford, including great gift ideas like the adorable box of Maxim's De Paris Biscuits—only 7€ ($8.75). Au Bon Marché, 38 rue de Sèvres, 7e. ✆ 01-44-39-81-00. Métro: Sèvres-Babylone.

La Maison du Chocolat ✿   La Maison du Chocolat is the best place in Paris to buy chocolate. It contains racks and racks of the stuff, priced individually or by the kilo. Each is made from a blend of up to six kinds of chocolate, flavored with just about everything imaginable. All the merchandise, including the chocolate pastries, is made in the store's supermodern cellar facilities. 225 rue du Faubourg St-Honoré, 8e. ✆ 01-42-27-39-44. Métro: Ternes.

La Maison du Miel   The French are connoisseurs of honey, and this shop offers varieties identified according to the flower to which the bees were exposed. Lemon flower and pine tree have distinct tastes and make fine gifts. 24 rue Vignon, 9e. ✆ 01-47-42-26-70. Métro: Madeleine or Havre-Caumartin.

Le Fleuriste du Chocolat   How many people can say they've eaten a chocolate floral bouquet while gazing out the store window at the Eiffel Tower? Even if you're one of those rare people who hates chocolate, you've gotta go! 49 av. de la Bourdonnais, 7e. ✆ 01-45-56-13-04. Métro: Ecole Militaire.

GIFTS

La Chaise Longue   This boutique is a favorite among Parisians with its wonderful array of gift items that will beautify any home at a reasonable price. So if you're still searching for that impossible-to-find wedding gift, look no further! 8 rue Princesse, 6e. ✆ 01-43-29-62-39. Métro: Mabillon.

La Maison du Square   Located on the lovely rue du Commerce in the 15e, La Maison is a gem where the Parisians in this warm, middle-class neighborhood flock to buy gifts for all occasions. You can purchase everything from exquisite water-filled vase candleholders to small, delicate silver teaspoons—perfect for a housewarming. The prices are fabulous and in true Parisian fashion, the shopkeepers do a lovely job of wrapping each gift. 83 rue du Commerce, 6e. ✆ **01-55-76-92-00.** Métro: Commerce.

HOUSEWARES

Déhillerin   This stop is an absolute must for any cook who takes pride in the quality of his or her cookware, glasses, gadgets, utensils, ramekins, and kitchen appliances. Prices are discounted. 18–20 rue Coquillière, 1er. ✆ **01-42-36-53-13.** Métro: Les Halles.

Verrerie des Halles   With its endless rows of shelves filled with cooking accouterments usually reserved for professionals, this is a cook's dream store. Prices are discounted. 15 rue du Louvre, 1er. ✆ **01-42-36-80-60.** Métro: Louvre-Rivoli.

JEWELRY

Bijoux Burma   The secret weapon of many a Parisian woman, you can find some of the best costume jewelry here. At its François 1er location, you'll find "classic" Jackie O.–style jewelry, and in its rue Castiglione store, the look is more bold and colorful, a bit more "fantasy," as the saleswoman described it. Another branch is at 14 rue Castiglione, 1er (✆ **01-42-60-69-56**). 50 rue François, 8e. ✆ **01-47-23-70-93.** Métro: Franklin-D-Roosevelt.

Crétion   The owner of this boutique, Stephanie Lagièr, handcrafts the beautiful and affordable jewelry on display. She uses a lot of cornflower blue, soft pink, and other dreamy colors in her earring, bracelet, and necklace designs that makes browsing, not to mention buying, a joy. She always has one shelf of jewelry on sale year-round. 23 rue du Bouloi, 1er. ✆ **01-40-41-12-70.** Métro: Les Halles.

Monic   While the display windows break an unspoken French rule and are unkempt, you'll find a wide range of affordable costume jewelry and designer creations at a discount here. Located in the heart of the Marais, you'll want to visit all the other wonderful, colorful, fun stores on this block. Monic is open daily, including Sunday afternoons. 5 rue des Francs-Bourgeois, 4e. ✆ **01-42-72-39-15.** Métro: St-Paul.

Tati Or   Here you'll find 18-carat gold jewelry for up to 40% less than traditional jewelers. It stocks more than 3,000 bracelets, earrings, necklaces, rings, and pins, with about 500 items selling for less than 60€ ($75). 19 rue de la Paix, 2e. ✆ **01-40-07-06-76.** Métro: Opéra.

MALLS & SHOPPING ARCADES

For more on arcades, see "The Arcades" in chapter 7, "Seeing the Sights."

Forum des Halles   The famous wholesale fruit-and-vegetable market located in the heart of the city since 1181 was moved to the suburbs in 1969. In its stead, a monstrous underground mall and subway hub were created, complete with endless crowds and too many shops. Thankfully, the above-ground green iron pavilions where you can stroll are not so hard on the eye. *But beware:* Pickpockets abound and it's probably best to avoid coming here at night when the neighborhood can get a little rough. 1–7 rue Pierre-Lescot, 1er. Métro: Etienne Marcel.

Galerie Vivienne   This is probably the prettiest shopping passageway in Paris. You can buy shoes, sweaters, and rare books, or have afternoon tea at A Priori Thé; see

Salons de Thé (Tea Salons) in chapter 6. 6 rue Vivienne or 4 rue des Petits-Champs, 2e. No phone. Métro: Bourse.

Marché St-Germain *(Overrated)*   You thought you'd escape the Gap! But international chain stores have taken up residence in this modern mall that's out of place in a neighborhood known for bookstores and publishing houses. Visit if you need air-conditioning—otherwise, don't waste your time. 14 rue Lobineau, 6e. Métro: Mabillon.

MARKETS

For a real shopping adventure, visit the **Marché aux Puces de la Porte de St-Ouen,** 18e (Métro: Porte-de-Clignancourt). The Clignancourt flea market features thousands of stalls, carts, shops, and vendors selling everything from vintage clothing to antique paintings and furniture. The best times for bargains are at opening and just before closing. Avoid the stalls selling junk on the periphery, and watch out for pickpockets. Open Saturday through Monday 9am to 8pm.

The market at **Porte de Vanves,** 14e (Métro: Porte de Vanves), is a bit more upscale, but so are its prices. Open Saturday and Sunday 8:30am to 1pm.

More comprehensible, and certainly prettier, is the **Marché aux Fleurs** (Métro: Cité), the flower market on place Louis-Lépine on the Ile de la Cité. Come Monday through Saturday to enjoy the flowers, even if you don't buy anything. On Sunday it becomes the **Marché aux Oiseaux,** an equally colorful bird market.

And don't miss the food markets, including the ones on **rue Mouffetard** in the Latin Quarter, **rue de Buci** in St-Germain, **rue Montorgueil** near the Bourse, and **rue Cler** near the Invalides. All sell the freshest fruits, vegetables, meats, and cheeses. Most open-air food markets operate Tuesday through Sunday 9am to 1pm.

MUSIC

FNAC   This leading home-entertainment chain sells videos, music, electronics, and books, and has a photo-developing service. Prices are 5% lower than manufacturers' suggested retail. (*Note:* This is still more expensive than music prices in the U.S.) 4 pl. Bastille, 12e. ✆ 01-43-42-04-04. Métro: Bastille.

Virgin Megastore   This blockbuster store (part of the British chain) overflows with CDs, videos, books, and stereos. Prices are high, but you can spend hours here listening to CDs for free. One branch is at 99 rue de Rivoli, 1er. 52 av. des Champs-Elysées. ✆ 01-49-53-50-00. Métro: Franklin-D-Roosevelt.

PERFUME

Cambray Fràgres   Here you'll receive discounts on perfumes and cosmetics, and on articles like luggage, watches, and pens. Right next door is the other Cambray Fràgres, where you'll find many young Parisian couples registering their nicely priced wedding china. 9 rue Pasquier, 8e. ✆ 01-44-51-56-15. Métro: Madeleine.

Catherine   This store will give you a 20% to 25% discount, plus a 14% value-added tax rebate at the time of purchase if you spend at least 185€ ($231). 7 rue de Castiglione, 1er. ✆ 01-42-61-02-89. Métro: Tuileries or Concorde.

Freddy Parfums   Near American Express and the Opéra, Freddy has some good discounts: up to 40% on perfumes, handbags, cosmetics, silk scarves, and neckties. 3 rue Scribe, 9e. ✆ 01-47-42-63-41. Métro: Auber or Opéra.

Michel Swiss   In a chic location not far from place Vendôme, Michel Swiss offers famous French perfume brands at excellent prices and immediately discounts the VAT for non-European residents. It also sells watches, neckties, leather goods, silk scarves, pens, and fashion accessories from top designers. 16 rue de la Paix, 2e. © **01-42-61-61-11**. Métro: Opéra.

STATIONERY

Cassegrain   Opened after World War I (young for Paris!), this classic Parisian stationery shop custom-makes leather desk sets to fit your individual needs, engraves handsome business cards, and much more—a perfect place to buy Dad a great gift! 422 rue St-Honoré, 8e. © **01-42-60-20-08**. Métro: Concorde.

TOYS

Au Nain Bleu   Guaranteed to make you nostalgic for your childhood, this beautiful 150-year-old toy store filled with exquisitely crafted toy soldiers, stuffed animals, games, model airplanes, model cars, and puppets is a joy to visit. 406 rue St-Honoré, 8e. © **01-42-60-39-01**. Métro: Concorde.

Jeux Descartes   Can toys be approached scientifically? Some of the salespeople think so! 52 rue des Ecoles, 5e. © **01-43-26-79-83**. Métro: Cluny-Sorbonne.

WINE

Lavinia *(Finds)*   One of the largest wine stores in Europe has only been open since 2002. Sleek, modern, and elegant with hundreds of wine racks holding 6,000 different labels from 43 countries, Lavinia has 15 full-time sommeliers to help you find what you're looking for. Almost 40% of the wines sold here are "New World" wines from Australia, the U.S., and South Africa. The rest, of course, are French. Bargains can be found from time to time. If you buy anything here, you're allowed to take it to the store's restaurant and consume it with your meal at no extra charge. 3–5 bd. de la Madeleine, 1e. © **01-42-97-20-20**. Métro: Madeleine.

Le Jardin des Vignes   The owners of Le Jardin des Vignes know their wine. They even offer oenological lessons. Here you'll find delicious bottles of rare wine, champagne, and cognac, at reasonable prices. They're always receiving new and varied shipments, so stop by often! 91 rue de Turenne, 3e. © **01-42-77-05-00**. Métro: St-Sébastien-Froissart.

Nicolas   The flagship store of this boutique chain, which has more than 110 branches around Paris, offers fair prices for bottles you might not be able to find in the U.S. Another plus, all the stores are known for their excellent, friendly service. 31 pl. de la Madeleine, 8e. © **01-42-68-00-16**. Métro: Madeleine.

10

Paris After Dark

Paris nightlife is incredibly diverse, with everything from tony bars and tea dances to throbbing clubs. If you prefer less-ear-splitting activities, there are a wide variety of classical music events, including chamber-music concerts in cathedrals and recitals in historic halls. Opera fans can head to the mammoth opera house at the Bastille, and ballet lovers can enjoy performances in the 19th-century splendor of the Palais Garnier. There are more than 100 theaters in Paris, presenting works that range from Molière at the Comédie Française to avant-garde premieres at the Théâtre de Soleil. Paris is also a cinephile's dream: Movie theaters abound, including small art houses showing both classics and new, offbeat films by young directors.

If you are in search of ultimate cool, some of the hippest bars and dance clubs are in the 8e and the Marais, which is also the focus of gay nightlife. The Bastille proper has lost much of its caché, but new clubs and bars are appearing farther back near rue de Charonne and rue Keller. In the past few years, rue Oberkampf has exploded with a profusion of bars and restaurants offering a relaxed, "nonscene" scene; the area is still popular. Jazz clubs flourish along rue des Lombards near Les Halles, and for those who can't leave Paris without seeing can-can dancers, the Moulin Rouge and the Lido are still cranking out the goods. But you don't have to pay a cover charge to enjoy some of the city's most wonderful evening activities: walking through the illuminated Cour Carée at the Louvre, catching the fire-eaters outside the Centre Pompidou, or strolling along the Seine and admiring the way the light plays on the Pont Neuf at night.

FINDING OUT WHAT'S ON

Several **publications** provide listings of performances, movies, concerts, and other entertainment. *Zurban* (1€/$1.25) is one of the best, offering listings and articles—in French. You can also consult their website at www.zurban.com for information before leaving home.

Pariscope (.40€/50¢) is a weekly guide with comprehensive listings, including a selection of events in its English-language "Time Out Paris" section. *L'Officiel des Spectacles* (.40€/50¢) is another French-language weekly guide with informative listings. *Nova* (1.50€/$1.90) is *the* magazine for club life. All can be found at any newsstand. The *Paris Free Voice* is an English-language free monthly that spotlights events of interest to English speakers, including readings, plays, and literary evenings at bookstores and libraries. Look for it in English-language bookstores and other Anglophone haunts.

In the following listings, prices are approximate; they vary depending on the day of the week and performer. Call the venue or check its website for information, or consult *Zurban* and other entertainment listings. Many concert, theater, and dance tickets are sold through FNAC stores as well as at the box office. There are a dozen or so

FNAC outlets; the biggest is 74 av. des Champs-Elysées (Métro: George V). You can also purchase tickets by phone at **FNAC** (© **08-92-68-36-22**) or online at www. fnac.fr. If you have your heart set on the opera or ballet, try to reserve before coming to Paris; tickets sell out quickly. You can buy tickets online on some venues' websites or call and your tickets will be available an hour before the performance for pickup using your credit card.

1 The Performing Arts

OPERA & DANCE

Châtelet, Théâtre Musical de Paris   Operas, concerts, recitals, and dance—whatever your choice, you'll find it in excellent form at the Châtelet theater, inaugurated in 1874 and renovated in 1998. International orchestras of the finest caliber play regularly. Check out the Sunday morning concert series for 22€ ($28) per ticket. 1 pl. du Châtelet, 1e. © **01-40-28-28-40**. www.chatelet-theatre.com. Opera tickets 14€–105€ ($18–$131); ballet tickets 14€–60€ ($18–$75); concert and recital tickets 14€–55€ ($18–$69). Métro: Châtelet.

Opéra Bastille   After more than 100 years at the Palais Garnier, the Opéra National de Paris moved to the state-of-the-art performance center at Opéra de la Bastille in 1989. Hughes Galls began directing the opera company around the same time, while American conductor James Conlon took over the orchestra, and they have reclaimed Paris's reputation for operatic excellence. While not as impressively grand as the Garnier, the Bastille offers first-class comfort and magnificent acoustics. Classics such as *Don Giovanni, The Marriage of Figaro,* and *Madam Butterfly* are scheduled for 2006. As tickets can be scarce, plan in advance. Dance performances also take place here; the 2006 season will include Nureyev's *La Bayadere.* Performances begin at 7:30pm. Pl. de la Bastille, 12e. © **08-92-89-90-90**. www.opera-de-paris.fr. Opera tickets 10€–130€ ($13–$163); dance tickets 10€–70€ ($13–$88). Métro: Bastille.

Opéra-Comique/Salle Favart   The Opéra-Comique offers light opera in a beautiful 19th-century theater, the Salle Favart. The Opéra-Comique was created in 1714 to stage theater performances that included song, and evolved into a stage for operas with happy endings. Although smaller than its counterparts—the auditorium is so intimate you can hear people whispering on stage—the interior, completed in 1898, is stunning with Belle Epoque ornamentation. 5 rue Favart, 2e. © **08-25-00-00-58**. Fax 01-49-26-05-93. www.opera-comique.com. Tickets 10€–66€ ($13–$83). Métro: Richelieu-Drouot.

Palais Garnier   The opulent facade of the Palais Garnier (otherwise known as the Opéra Garnier) has had a face-lift and it now beams over the place de l'Opéra in shiny Second Empire splendor. Though it lost a good chunk of its operatic offerings to the Opéra Bastille in 1989, this splendid house is still the home of the Paris Opera Ballet and is mainly dedicated to dance. In 2006 the company will present *William Forsythe and the Trisha Brown Dance Company,* among many others.

The interior, also renovated over the past few years, is a symphony of red, blue, pink, green, and white marble. Chagall painted the ceiling in the auditorium. Be careful when picking seats; all seating is in "boxes," and sightlines can be a problem if you are seated in the rear of the box. Tickets sell out early. Reserve well in advance. Pl. de l'Opéra, 9e. © **08-92 89 90 90**. www.opera-de-paris.fr. Dance tickets 7€–130€ ($8.75–$163); opera tickets 7€–130€ ($8.75–$163). Métro: Opéra. RER: Auber.

Théâtre de la Ville   Once known as the Théâtre Sarah Bernhardt, the Théâtre de la Ville is now a major venue for cutting-edge performances. The schedule offers up an international mix of modern dance and avant-garde theater, including innovators such as Pina Bausch, Jan Fabre, and Sankai Juku. The theater also presents an eclectic array of concerts; world music, classical, and French *chanson* are all on the lineup for 2006. Tickets for big names get snapped up quickly. 2 pl. du Châtelet, 1e. ✆ **01-42-74-22-77**. www.theatredelaville.com. Tickets 15€–22€ ($19–$28). Métro: Châtelet.

CONCERT HALLS & CLASSICAL MUSIC

There are many concerts throughout the year, and many are quite affordable. Look for flyers at most churches announcing times, prices, and locations.

More than a dozen churches schedule **organ** recitals and concerts; tickets are free or inexpensive, 9€ to 25€ ($11–$31). Among them are **Notre-Dame** (✆ **01-42-34-56-10**; Métro: Cité); **St-Eustache,** 2 rue du Jour, 1er (✆ **01-42-36-31-05**; Métro: Châtelet); **St-Sulpice,** place St-Sulpice (✆ **01-46-33-21-78**; Métro: St-Sulpice), which has the largest organ; **St-Germain-des-Prés,** 3 place St-Germain-des-Prés (✆ **01-43-25-41-71**; Métro: St-Germain-des-Prés); **La Madeleine,** place de la Madeleine (✆ **01-44-51-69-00**; Métro: Madeleine); and **St-Louis en l'Ile,** 19 bis rue St-Louis-en-l'Ile (✆ **01-46-34-11-60**; Métro: Pont-Marie). The Sunday concerts at 6pm at the **American Church,** 65 quai d'Orsay (✆ **01-40-62-05-00**; Métro: Invalides), are friendly and inviting.

Free concerts occasionally take place in the parks and gardens; check any of the listing guides for information. **Maison de la Radio,** 116 av. du President-Kennedy, 16e (✆ **01-56-40-15-16**), offers free tickets to recordings of some concerts. Tickets are available an hour before recording starts. The **Conservatoire National de Musique** at the Cité de la Musique, 209 av. Jean-Jaurès, 19e (✆ **01-40-40-46-46**), stages free concerts and ballets by students at the conservatory.

Cité de la Musique The wacky architecture of this music complex might take some getting used to, but the concert program has a universal appeal: chamber music, world music, and new music are all offered here, as well as young people's concerts and a jazz festival. The 2006 lineup includes such diverse offerings as Great Black Music from the Art Ensemble in Chicago, Jazz New Tango, and popular bands from Brazil, among many others. 221 av. Jean-Jaurès, 19e. ✆ **01-44-84-44-84**. www.cite-musique.fr. Tickets 10€–38€ ($13–$48). Métro: Porte-de-Pantin.

Salle Pleyel The Orchestre de Paris plays at the Salle Pleyel from September to late June under the direction of Christoph Eschenbach. There's an impressive lineup of performances from Mozart to Mahler to Rachmaninov. Inquire about the occasional

1-hour free concerts at 6pm Wednesdays. 252 rue du Faubourg-St-Honoré, 8e. ℭ **01-45-61-53-00**. www.orchestredeparis.com. Tickets 9€–80€ ($11–$100). Métro: Ternes.

THEATERS

Most theatrical performances in Paris are, of course, in French. If Racine in the original is too much for you, don't despair; there are a handful of small **English-language theater companies** in Paris. None have a permanent address, but most advertise their periodic performances in the "Time Out" section of *Pariscope* or in the *Paris Voice*. One of these companies, Brava Productions, offers **free staged readings** every Monday at 8pm upstairs at the Café de Flore, 172 bd. St-Germain (ℭ **01-45-48-55-26**. Another option for non-French speakers is to try some of the more avant-garde productions; often these works rely on visuals and a grasp of the language is not always essential.

The theaters listed here are the largest and most well endowed, but there are scads of others. For full listings, consult *Zurban* or *Pariscope*.

Comédie Française   The works of Corneille, Racine, Molière, and other classic French playwrights come alive at this theatrical institution. Created in 1680 by Louis XIV, the troupe moved to its present location in 1799. Not until much later were foreign authors (such as Shakespeare) admitted to the repertoire. Nowadays, schedules vary, with the addition of modern works and plays translated from other languages. If you aren't fairly fluent in French, or aren't familiar with the plays, chances are you will not enjoy the performances. Note that for those under 27, there are last-minute seats for 10€ ($13) in the upper balcony sold 1 hour before the start of performances. 2 rue de Richelieu, 1er. ℭ **01-44-58-15-15**. www.comedie-francaise.fr. Tickets 12€–35€ ($15–$44). Métro: Palais-Royal–Musée du Louvre.

Odéon-Théâtre de l'Europe   Home of the Comédie Française until the Revolution, the Odéon now features productions from all over the Continent, including French works. The theater books shows that veer towards the spectacular—opulent productions of Greek classics, Molière, Brecht, and Robert Wilson are the norm. The 19th-century building is fronted by a grand colonnade, which overlooks a semicircular square. In 2003 the theater began a huge renovation to remove asbestos, install air-conditioning, and provide access for patrons with disabilities; the renovations are due to be completed in late 2005. 1 pl. Paul Claudel, 6e. ℭ **01-44-85-40-40**. www.theatre-odeon.fr. Tickets 8€–30€ ($10–$38); usually sold 2 weeks before performance. Métro: Odéon.

Théâtre des Champs-Elysées   This theater features international orchestras, opera, and ballet companies. Built in 1914, the facade is covered with friezes by Bourdelle, and the interior is decorated with frescos by Vuillard and Maurice Denis. *Don Giovanni* and the *Marriage of Figaro* are both on the 2006 calendar. ***Note:*** One hour

---

⸜Tips⸝ Box Office Lingo

Even if you are fluent in French, you might need some help at the ticket window. If you are offered seats in a *baignoire,* in this case the word means "mezzanine," not "bathtub." Similarly, being placed in the *corbeille* has nothing to do with being thrown in the trash—these are seats in the balcony. Look at the seating plan to avoid linguistic confusion.

before the show, those under 25 get 50% off available tickets. 15 av. Montaigne, 8e. *(C)* 01-49-52-50-50. www.theatrechampselysees.fr. Tickets 5€–126€ ($6.25–$158). Métro: Alma-Marceau.

Théâtre National de Chaillot   Lodged in the Art Deco Palais de Chaillot, this theater's schedule includes a dynamic mix of new plays and classics, as well as concerts and dance performances. There is an amazing panorama of the Eiffel Tower from the bar in the lobby—get there early to have a glass of wine and drink in the view. Pl. du Trocadéro, 16e. *(C)* 01-53-65-30-00. www.theatre-chaillot.fr. Tickets 17€–30€ ($21–$38). Métro: Trocadéro.

2 The Club & Music Scene
NIGHTCLUBS & REVUES
The names Lido, Folies-Bergère, Crazy Horse, and Moulin Rouge conjure up images of Maurice Chevalier, Mistinguett, and saucy cancan dancers. The cancan is still a standard cabaret number, but headlining entertainers have given way to light shows, special effects, canned music, and a bevy of nearly nude women and (sometimes) men. Unlike the predominantly French audiences that used to frequent supper-club revues, today's audiences arrive in tour buses, expecting and seeing a glitzy "international" show. If you're looking for elaborate costumes, special effects, variety acts, and sexy bodies, you will get your money's worth, but it is about the least Parisian experience you can have and still be in Paris.

If you must see a Paris spectacle, do yourself a favor and have dinner somewhere else. For the extra 35€ to 45€ ($44–$56), you can have a much better meal at any of our "Worth a Splurge" suggestions in chapter 6.

Crazy Horse, Paris   This is the most openly erotic program outside the strip joints in Pigalle. Variety acts go on between the femmes fatales with names like Chica Boum, Pussy Duty-Free, and Zany Zizanie. They appear on swing seats or in cages, slithering, writhing . . . you get the picture. Sultry entertainment to some, an expensive bore to others. Shows are at 8:30 and 11pm. 12 av. George V, 8e. *(C)* 01-47-23-32-32. www.lecrazy horseparis.com. Cover and 2 drinks from 49€ ($61) at the bar to 110€ ($138) for orchestra seats and half bottle of champagne; students 49€ ($61) at the bar with 1 drink (no reservations accepted for student rate). Additional drinks from 15€ ($19). Métro: George V.

Lido   The revue *C'est Magique* is a high-tech display of laser lighting, video projections, "flying" dancers, and an ascending stage that periodically delivers befeathered women, fountains, and an ice rink. There are novelty acts, including a magician who does surprising things with birds, but the effect of this hugely expensive show is curiously remote and uninvolving. The food is bland and uninspired, despite the addition of celebrity Chef Paul Bocuse. Shows are at 9:30 and 11:30pm. 116 bis av. des Champs-Elysées, 8e. *(C)* 01-40-76-56-10; reservations from North America 800/227-4884; www.lido.fr. Bar seat 70€ ($88). Show with half bottle of champagne 100€ ($125) Fri–Sat; 80€ ($100) Sun–Thurs (11:30pm show only). Dinner with half bottle of champagne 140€–170€ ($175–$213). Métro: George V.

Moulin Rouge *Overrated*   Perhaps the most famous Paris nightclub, the "red windmill" has been packing in crowds since 1889. Toulouse-Lautrec immortalized the cancan ladies in the 19th century, and performers like Edith Piaf, Yves Montand, and Charles Aznavour made their reputations here. These days, reputation is what the Moulin Rouge mainly trades on. Its current show, *Féerie*, features a giant aquarium, 100 *artistes*, 60 "Doriss Girls," and lots of feathers. Since the release of the 2001 movie

Moments Nighttime Strolls in Paris

Don't underestimate the pleasure of walking around after sunset. When the monuments loom floodlit out of the dark, the city is spellbinding. Approaching the **Eiffel Tower** from the **Palais de Chaillot** and **place du Trocadéro,** across the Seine, or the **Ecole Militaire** and the **Champ de Mars,** is a memorable experience. **Notre-Dame** acquires a golden hue, as does the **Louvre**—the pyramid takes on an outlandish appearance. The **Marais** and **place des Vosges** anchor themselves more strongly in the 17th century after the sun sets. Crowds mill around **place de la Bastille** and wander the **Latin Quarter.** The **Champs-Elysées** glitters as it never does during the day, and the **Arc de Triomphe** becomes truly triumphant as streams of automobile lights careen around it.

with Nicole Kidman, the Moulin has become all the rage with visitors, so make reservations a week or two in advance. Seats at the bar are easier to find and are first-come, first-served. Please note that jeans and sneakers are not allowed and men are expected to wear a shirt and sports jacket (and many wear ties). Pl. Blanche, Montmartre, 18e. ✆ 01-53-09-82-82. www.moulin-rouge.com. Bar seat and 2 drinks 69€ ($86); Sun–Thurs: revue and champagne 95€ ($119) at 9pm, 85€ ($106) at 11pm; dinner from 135€ ($169) at 7pm, otherwise 165€ ($206). Métro: Blanche.

Paradis Latin   In a building designed by Gustave Eiffel, this revue, *Paradis d'Amour,* is the most typically French of them all. The show is less gimmicky than the others and relies more on the talents of its singers and dancers. The master of ceremonies banters in French and English and encourages audience participation. Even the waiters get into the act. Performances are Wednesday through Monday at 9:30pm. 28 rue Cardinal-Lemoine, 5e. ✆ 01-43-25-28-28. www.paradis-latin.com. Revue and half bottle of champagne 80€ ($100); revue and dinner from 114€ ($143). Métro: Cardinal-Lemoine.

CHANSON

No matter how flip or jaded a Parisian may be, he or she will still get mushy about *chanson,* traditional French songs about the ups and downs of life and love. The key here is content—the poetry of the lyrics is much more important than the music. But even if you don't understand the words, an evening spent at a *boîte* listening to French songs can be an engaging, authentically French experience. Tourists are familiar with chanson legends such as Edith Piaf and Jacques Brel, but there are many others, including a new crop of French singers who are putting a new spin on this old tradition.

Au Lapin Agile   True, you may run into the tour-bus crowd here, but, in fact, this famous cabaret is a good place to find French chanson. Once the haunt of Utrillo, Toulouse-Lautrec, and other artists, it later became the jumping-off place for chanson all-stars such as Pierre Brasseur and Annie Giradot. Today, this Montmartre institution continues to nurture new French chansonniers, offering an evening of love songs and ballads in a bohemian atmosphere. Guests are invited to sing along. The show starts at 9:15pm. 22 rue des Saules, 18e. ✆ 01-46-06-85-87. www.au-lapin-agile.com. Cover (includes 1 drink) 24€ ($30); 17€ ($21) students (except Sat and holidays). Additional drinks 7€ ($8.75). Métro: Lamarck.

LIVE MUSIC CLUBS

La Flèche d'Or As with so many venues of the moment in east Paris, it's hard to say what this place is. Is it a cafe? Yes, and it's up and running from 2pm to 2am. Is it a bar? It's that, too, and a hip cultural center that schedules video nights, political debates, art shows, and multimedia projects. Maybe the best reason for trekking here after a visit to the nearby Père-Lachaise cemetery is the live concerts on Thursday, Friday, and Saturday nights. You might find reggae, alternative rock, Celtic rock, or blues rock. Sundays at 5pm there's usually a dance band playing salsa or swing, and on other nights there could be, well, anything. In a former train station, this cavernous space pulls in a funky, artsy, racially mixed crowd. 102 bis rue de Bagnolet, 20e. ✆ 01-43-72-04-23. www.flechedor.com. Cover 3€–6€ ($3.75–$7.50). Métro: Alexandre-Dumas.

Le Cithéa Rue Oberkampf is so hip that you could probably open a carton there and trendy club-goers would come to check it out. Le Cithéa obviously benefits from the street's continuing weekend crowds, but reasonable prices and an eclectic mix of world, jazz, and funk bands Wednesday through Saturday would keep this club sizzling anywhere. There's a DJ when the bands aren't playing, and room to dance if the mood strikes. Open every night from 8pm until 5:30am. 114 rue Oberkampf, 11e. ✆ 01-40-21-70-95. www.cithea.com. Cover (includes 1 drink) 5€–8€ ($6.25–$10). Métro: Parmentier.

DANCE CLUBS

Whether you like dancing to techno, house, salsa, world, classic rock, or swing, you're sure to find it somewhere in Paris. In fact, you might find it all in the same club, depending on the night. In an attempt to please everybody, many clubs change their programming from night to night. The current fad is Latin music, which seems to be everywhere. Sundays are often devoted to afternoon "tea dances" for a gay crowd or *bal musettes* for ballroom dancing.

To party on a budget, go out during the week, when cover charges may be (officially or unofficially) waived. Women often get in free, especially if they're dressed in something slinky, low-cut, short, or all three. Black clothes are de rigueur for men and women, and the ultrahip clubs choose their clientele at the door—dress appropriately if you want to gain entry to these temples of cool. Some of the smaller clubs, in an effort to limit the number of *drageurs* (pickup artists) bothering single women and to maintain a mellow atmosphere, will refuse entry to men if they are not accompanied by a female friend.

Most clubs don't open until 11pm, and the music doesn't stop until dawn. The later you go, the better. But everything can change overnight. What will it be like next season? Who knows, although the French magazines *Nova* and *Zurban* can give you some idea. Also check out *Pariscope's* sections *"Paris la Nuit"* (in French) and "Paris Nightlife" (in English; written by the "Time Out" staff).

Barrio Latino Fusion Latin might be the best way to describe the music at this spacious dance club, where the rhythms are a blend of Caribbean, African, and Top 40. A young, energetic crowd packs this former furniture showroom, whose upper galleries are trimmed with wrought-iron balconies. The airy space has a sort of "Galeries Lafayette Goes to the Tropics" decor, with warm tones on the walls and fringed lamps illuminating velvet couches. Not particularly authentic, but unpretentious fun. 46–48 rue du Faubourg-St-Antoine, 12e. ✆ 01-55-78-48-75. Cover Thurs–Sat 12€ ($15). Métro: Bastille.

Batofar One of the city's more unique clubs is in this bright-red boat moored on the banks of the Seine. Formerly a floating fire engine, Batofar now works as a venue for electronic music (techno, trip-hop, jungle, funk, and so on), and its searchlight sends out signals to the young and restless of eastern Paris, as well great DJs from all over Europe. The boat lures a dressed-down, casually cool kettle of fish; come early, the doors close at 2am. Docked in front of 11 quai François Mauriac, 13e. ℂ 01-56-29-10-00. Cover 8€–12€ ($10–$15). Métro: Bibliothèque or Quai de la Gare.

Bus Palladium   This club is the best bet in Paris for people who can't stand house and techno. Thursday night is devoted to Motown and the groove sound, with DJs Cut Killer and Abdel spinning. On other nights you'll find a heavy emphasis on mainstream rock. What might be a surprise, considering the disheveled neighborhood, is the crowd—well-dressed French yuppies. They like to party, though, and everyone gets down as the night goes on. 6 rue Fontaine, 9e. ℂ 01-53-21-07-33. Cover 20€ ($25). Métro: Blanche.

Caveau de la Hûchette   If you swing, this is a fabulous place to dance to top-quality jazz bands. This club has been on the jazz scene for some 50 years, and dance aficionados come to revel in the great music and friendly ambience. The irreverent crowd is a mix of foreigners and locals of all ages. The music starts at 9:30pm. 5 rue de la Hûchette, 5e. ℂ 01-43-26-65-05. Cover Sun–Thurs 10€ ($13), Fri–Sat 12€ ($15). Métro or RER: St-Michel.

Favela Chic   This temple of all things Brazilian has moved to new, soundproof digs, and draws a hip crowd of *bobos* (bourgeois bohèmes), fashion mavens, chic Brazilians, and other creatures of the night. In theory, this is a restaurant and bar (great *caipirinhas*), but dancing is at the top of everyone's list of favorite things to do. The music is so good the club has come out with its own samba CD. Try to come before or after the dinner rush (around 9pm) to avoid the hoards, but don't come too late—the fun stops at 2am. 18 rue du Faubourg-du-Temple, 11e. ℂ 01-40-21-38-14. No cover. Métro: République.

La Chapelle des Lombards   The festive tropical ambience and diverse music—everything from salsa to funk to reggae—attract a lively crowd to this hip club near the Bastille. To really enjoy this place, you have to dress the part, which means no sneakers or jeans, but rather your sophisticated best. 19 rue de Lappe, 11e. ℂ 01-43-57-24-24. No cover Tues and Wed; Thurs 15€ ($19); Fri–Sat 19€ ($24); free for women 11:30pm–1am. Métro: Bastille.

La Java   If you have a taste for something fun, funky, and authentic, and you like Latin music, this charming dance hall might provide your most memorable night in Paris. A diverse crowd dances without restraint to mostly Cuban and Brazilian music, played by a live band Friday and Saturday nights. There is a *bal musette* Sunday afternoons from 2 to 7pm. 105 rue du Faubourg-du-Temple, 10e. ℂ 01-45-32-57-63. Cover Thurs 10€ ($12); Fri–Sat (includes 1 drink) 16€ ($20); Sun 10€ ($12). Métro: Belleville or Goncourt.

La Locomotive   "La Loco" as it's known here, pulls in a very young, clean-cut, jeans-wearing crowd who come here to dance to a variety of music, lean over the balconies, and sit on cushions on the floor. Graffiti art and psychedelic flowers decorate the walls. This is a big, three-level place; in the lower level you can see an old railway line. 90 bd. de Clichy, 18e. ℂ 08-36-69-69-28. Cover Sun–Thurs 10€ ($13); Fri (includes 1 drink) 18€ ($23); Sat (includes 1 drink) 20€ ($25). Women admitted free Sun before 1am. Métro: Blanche or Clichy.

Le Balajo   Once filled with apache dancers and the sound of Edith Piaf, this venerable 1930s dance hall now echoes with a combination of rock 'n' roll, salsa, and dance music, as well as the *musette* of yesteryear. The international crowd is racially mixed, fun, hip, and wild. The age range is 18 to 80, with the *bal musette* on Thursday and Sunday afternoons drawing older crowds. The third Sunday of the month is "Tango" and draws a mixed aged group. Check the website to see what style music is being offered on a particular night. This is a good place to avoid the hipper-than-thou competition that reigns at so many other clubs. It really gets going around 1am. 9 rue de Lappe, 11e. (C) 01-47-00-07-87. www.balajo.fr. Cover 8€–15€ ($10–$19); *bal musette* Thurs and Sun 8€–12€ ($10–$15). Métro: Bastille.

Le Baron   The doorman will decide whether you'll be allowed in to play with the supermodels, designers, and movie people who frequent this *très chic* club. If that doesn't put you off, dress as fashionably as you can and show up around 1am. It's a plus to be a movie star, or at least act like one. Attitude helps. Inside, this is one of the best parties in town. The DJ spins mostly retro music (nothing more recent than the '80s), and the crowd is mixed in nationality, age, outlook, and sexual preference. If you do get in the door, there's no cover and the drinks start at 10€ ($13). 6 ave. Marceau, 8e. (C) 01-47-20-04-01. Métro Alma-Marceau.

Le Gibus   Formerly one of the most famous rock dance clubs in Paris, this place has changed its style. Artistic director Laurent Cohen books top-level DJs who spin house music for a predominantly, but not exclusively, gay crowd. Wednesday and Friday the music can get quite trancey. Watch for the monthly "Nuits Blanches" parties. 18 rue du Faubourg-du-Temple, 11e. (C) 01-47-00-78-88. www.gibus.fr. Cover Tues 5€ ($6.25); Wed 7€ ($8.75); Thurs 5€ ($6.25); Fri (includes 1 drink) 13€ ($16); Sat (includes 1 drink) 20€ ($25). Métro: République.

Le Queen   Not only the busiest gay disco but one of the hottest clubs in town, this place attracts the wildest of Paris's night people. The crowd is about two-thirds gay, with the remaining third composed of attractive couples, models trying to escape the pickup scene, and straight men clever enough to have figured out where the beautiful women are. To get past stringent admission control at the door, it helps to have a great face and body, or at least the ability to disguise your faults with great clothes. Women usually get in only with male friends, and Sundays and Mondays the crowd is more heavily gay. 102 av. des Champs-Elysées, 8e. (C) 08-92-70-73-30. www.queen.fr. Cover Sun–Thurs (includes 1 drink) 10€–15€ ($13–$19) Fri–Sat (includes 1 drink) 20€ ($25). Métro: George V.

Le Satellit Café   With an intriguing, constantly changing array of world music—one night there's a singer from Madagascar, the next a Cuban funk band—this is one of the livelier and most original nocturnal options in Paris. Sort of a cross between a cafe and a disco, this place attracts a young, cool crowd. A DJ spins danceable exotica when there's not live music. It's very friendly, so almost everyone feels comfortable, even if they sometimes need a selection from the very good wine list (itself a rarity in Paris bars) to get that way. 44 rue de la Folie Mericourt, 11e. (C) 01-47-00-48-87. Cover (includes 2 drinks) 10€ ($13). Métro: Oberkampf or St-Ambroise.

Rex Club   Follow a stairway that seems to lead to the middle of the earth. Everything is gray and high-tech. It's big. There are mirrors. There is smoke that smells like strawberries. One customer is young. Another wears silver clothes. Friday is techno night; house rules on Thursday and Saturday; Wednesday could be anything. The big lure these days is Paris's most famous DJ, Laurent Garnier, who spins house music the second Thursday of the month, a wildly popular event. 5 bd. Poissonnière, 2e. (C) 01-42-36-10-96. Cover Wed varies; Thurs–Sat 13€ ($16). Métro: Bonne-Nouvelle.

JAZZ

Parisians have an insatiable craving for American music, especially jazz, and the scene is vibrant as a new generation develops a taste for the sound. Look through the current *Zurban* or *Pariscope* for the artists you admire. If you don't care who's playing and you're just out for a night of good music, try the following:

Le Baiser Salé   A small club where the jazz sounds are fusion: jazz funk, Latin jazz, and African jazz are some of the mixes on tap. A cool spot, and a good value on Tuesdays when it's free. 58 rue des Lombards, 1er. ✆ **01-42-33-37-71.** Cover 12€–17€ ($15–$21). Métro: Châtelet–Les Halles.

Le Duc des Lombards   It may be crowded, noisy, and smoky, but this club presents some of the most interesting jazz around. A different band plays every night. Repertoires range from free jazz to hard bop—you won't find traditional jazz here. 42 rue des Lombards, 1er. ✆ **01-42-33-22-88.** Cover 17€–23€ ($21–$29). Métro: Châtelet–Les Halles.

Le Petit Journal Montparnasse   The interior here is much more spacious and, in principle, less smoky than at other clubs. Jazz stars Art Blakey, Michel Petrucciani, and Stephane Grappelli have played at this renowned club. Current programming includes jazz, blues, boogie, and, occasionally, French songs. The music starts around 10pm and lasts until 1:30am. 13 rue du Commandant Mouchotte, 14e. ✆ **01-43-21-56-70.** Cover (includes 1 drink) 20€–24€ ($25–$30). Métro: Montparnasse-Bienvenüe.

Le Petit Journal Saint-Michel   This small club offers a lineup that is at least as prestigious as its sister operation in Montparnasse (see above). The Claude Bolling Trio visits regularly, as do the Claude Luter Quintet and the Benny Bailey Quartet. You can dine as well as drink here in a warm, relaxed atmosphere. 71 bd. St-Michel, 5e. ✆ **01-43-26-28-59.** Cover (includes 1 drink) 20€–24€ ($25–$30). Métro: Cluny-Sorbonne. RER: Luxembourg.

Le Sunside/Le Sunset   This club has two parts, with different spaces for different sounds. The ground-level Le Sunside offers acoustic jazz, whereas Le Sunset, in the basement, focuses on electric jazz and world music. This is one of the better-known jazz clubs in Paris, and international artists play here. The rooms are small and space is at a premium—arrive early or buy tickets in advance. 60 rue des Lombards, 1er. Le Sunside: ✆ **01-40-26-21-25.** Cover 12€–20€ ($15–$25). Le Sunset: ✆ **01-40-26-46-60.** Cover 22€–25€ ($28–$31). Métro: Châtelet–Les Halles.

New Morning   When the Lounge Lizards played here, the audience withheld its approval until it was totally seduced by the music. But once the crowd was convinced, the concert lasted until 4am. New Morning is the star of Paris's jazz clubs, and the audience is one of the toughest in the world. The best perform here, from Archie Shepp, Bill Evans, and Elvin Jones to Kevin Coyne and Koko Ateba. Concerts begin at 9pm. If you're set on going a certain night, reserve ahead of time. 7–9 rue des Petites-Ecuries, 10e. ✆ **01-45-23-51-41.** www.newmorning.com. Cover 20€–23€ ($25–$29). Métro: Château-d'Eau.

GAY PAREE

The Marais is the city's main gay and lesbian neighborhood, and rainbow flags flutter over bars and restaurants dotting its narrow streets. Gay dance clubs come and go so fast that even the magazines devoted to them—*e.m@le* and *Illico,* both distributed free in the gay bars and bookstores—have a hard time keeping up. For lesbians, the guide *Exes Femmes* publishes a free seasonal listing of bars and clubs. Also look for nightlife listings in **Têtu.**

Paris's gay and lesbian scene gets a chapter in *Frommer's Gay & Lesbian Europe.* Don't forget to check out the listings for dance clubs earlier in this chapter, which can be heavily gay, depending on the day of the week.

Amnesia Café   This relaxed cafe-bar-bistro is decorated in warm, coppery tones and furnished with easy chairs. The ambience is more friendly than cruisy, and the drinks and food reasonably priced. Restaurant service stops at 5pm when the bar action cranks up. There's a tiny dance floor in the basement that gets hopping at midnight. 42 rue Vieille-du-Temple, 4e. ✆ 01-42-72-16-94. Métro: Hôtel-de-Ville.

La Champmesle   A few blocks east of the avenue de l'Opéra, La Champmesle is a comfortable bar for women. Thursday night (and sometimes Fri–Sat) is cabaret night and it draws a crowd. 4 rue Chabanais, 2e. ✆ 01-42-96-85-20. Métro: Bourse, Pyramides, Quatre-Septembre, or Opéra.

Le Cox   Popular with gay men with an "edge," Le Cox is very busy for happy hour (when the sidewalk gets jammed with rowdy beer drinkers) and later gets more mellow but cruisy. This is definitely not an Abercombie & Fitch crowd, it's more Levis and white T-shirts. 15 rue des Archives, 4e. ✆ 01-42-72-16-94. Métro: Hotel de Ville.

Le Pulp   Formerly L'Entr'acte, this club has made a spectacular comeback and is now the hippest lesbian dance club in Paris. Its decor is like a 19th-century French music hall, and the venue, as the French say, is "cool," with cutting-edge music. Open Thursday to Sunday; don't show up until after midnight. The presence of men is discouraged. What to do if you're a gay male? Go to the side entrance with a "separate but equal facility," **Le Scorp** (✆ 01-40-26-28-30), where *les mecs gais* (gay guys) are welcome. 25 bd. Poissonnière, 2e. ✆ 01-40-26-01-93. Cover Fri–Sat 12€ ($15). Métro: Grands-Boulevards.

Le Quetzal   This colorful bar draws in mostly local guys. For those who prefer their bars not to be cafes, this is the place. It can get quite cruisy later in the evening. 10 rue de la Verrerie, 4e. ✆ 01-48-87-99-07. Métro: Hôtel-de-Ville or Rambuteau.

Les Scandaleuses   This laid-back lesbian bar attracts a diverse mix of women, with styles running from pink-haired punk to denim and flannel. The place is jammed on weekends when Djette Sex Toy spins house and techno. 8 rue des Ecouffes, 4e. ✆ 01-48-87-39-26. Métro: St-Paul.

Open Café   A great spot to people-watch in the heart of the Marais, this popular gay cafe/bar has lots of outdoor seating and is busy from midafternoon to late at night. It's especially popular on warm summer nights, when the crowd spills out onto the surrounding sidewalks. The crowd is mostly male and mixed—everything from American tourists nursing beers to young professionals sipping espresso after a day at work to partying Parisians on their way to the dance clubs. 17 rue des Archives, 4e. ✆ 01-42-72-26-18. Métro: Hotel de Ville.

3 The Bar Scene

In Paris, bars are different. A cafe can function as a bar, a restaurant, or a coffee shop at any given moment of the day or night—they are not reserved for drinking or for nighttime entertainment. Parisians are as likely to drop into a cafe or wine bar for a brandy at breakfast as they are to hang out at night. For this reason, the bars listed below are American-style cocktail bars. Although some open at noon and others after dinner, most bars stay open until 2am. For a more complete listing of traditional cafes and wine bars, see chapter 6, "Great Deals on Dining." ***Note:*** The drinking age in France is 18; if you look young but you're with an adult, bartenders will rarely ask for ID.

Alcazar   If the culinary offerings at this bar-brasserie were equal to the eye-popping decor, this review would appear in our restaurant chapter. Unfortunately, that is not the case. Opened by London tycoon Sir Terence Conran with great fanfare in 1998, this sky-lit bi-level space is stunningly designed. Slicked-up elements of traditional brasserie style, such as banquettes and mirrors, mix with innovations such as a glassed-in kitchen. Admire the decor, then head to the comfortable upstairs bar for a drink and a view over the restaurant. The best time to get here is around 10pm, as it's too quiet before then. Drinks are pricey, but just think of the money you saved by not eating here. After a drink, head downstairs to **Wagg**, the very trendy club with British DJs playing U.K. house music late into the night. 62 rue Mazarine, 6e. ✆ 01-53-10-19-99. Métro: Odéon.

Buddha Bar   A giant, impassive Buddha presides over the very un-Zen-like doings in this cavernous bar and restaurant. From the upstairs balcony you can observe the fashionable diners below or mix with the swanky international crowd at the bar. The music is spacey, the atmosphere is electric, and you'll see your share of pretty people. This place is no longer trendy with Parisians but visiting foreigners continue to flock here. The point is to see and be seen and then say you saw it. 8 rue Boissy d'Anglas, 8e. ✆ 01-53-05-90-00. Métro: Concorde.

Chez Justine   In the midst of the hype of rue Oberkampf, this spot is a reprieve. Chez Justine offers the down-to-earth air of a no-nonsense hangout. A fireplace and couches provide comfort downstairs, and twin mahogany staircases lead to an upstairs dining space that serves French food with a twist. It can get very loud after 10pm, so come early if you want some peace. 96 rue Oberkampf, 11e. ✆ 01-43-57-44-03. Métro: Parmentier.

China Club   This posh spot, just a few steps from the Bastille, exudes the atmosphere of 1930s Shanghai. Stake out a spot at the downstairs bar, which often has live music (with no cover charge), or at the quieter upstairs one, and take in the scene—it seems nearly everyone passes through the China Club at least once. If you hate cigars, avoid the trendy upstairs *fumoir* (smoking room). Prices for the well-made cocktails start at 9€ ($11), but the Chinese food is overpriced. 50 rue de Charenton, 12e. ✆ 01-43-43-82-02. Métro: Bastille.

Comptoir Paris-Marrakech   With a sister restaurant in Marrakech, hip, brash Comptoir certainly knows how to bring a taste of Morocco to Paris. The wide, harem-like space holds cushioned Moroccan seats with throw pillows, and brass-topped tables. A stylish 30-something set looks pretty sipping cocktails from an extensive alcohol menu while munching on tasty North African *tajine* and *pastilla*. World music rhythms set the musical beat. Drink prices go up after 11pm; the house specialty is the Sexy Drink, made with tequila and ginger juice. 37 rue Berger, 1er. ✆ 01-40-26-26-66. Métro: Louvre-Rivoli.

The Cruiscin Lan   This friendly, low-key place is one of the many Irish bars that have sprouted like mushrooms in Paris. Filled with a mix of wayward Anglophones and curious French people, the Cruiscin (that's pronounced "crush-kin") offers a full range of Irish and foreign beers, a great wine list, and a pool table. Come on a Tuesday night to hear some R & B. 18 rue des Halles, 1er. ✆ 01-45-08-99-15. www.irishfrance.com/cruiscinlan. Métro: Châtelet.

Harry's New York Bar Founded in 1911, Harry's is one of Europe's famous bars, and as popular with Americans today as it was in the time of F. Scott Fitzgerald and Gertrude Stein. The Bloody Marys are legendary, and there's an amazing selection of whiskeys. There's also a cabaret-cellar bar downstairs. It's not cheap, of course—cocktails start at 10€ ($13)—but you may want to splurge just so you can lift a glass to the ghost of Hemingway. 5 rue Daunou, 2e. ℰ 01-42-61-71-14. Métro: Opéra or Pyramides.

Hôtel Costes The bar at this gorgeous hotel is a series of intimate rooms filled with plush furniture, potted plants, and beautiful people. Here is where the Parisian chic come to lounge on velvet-covered divans and speak of their weekend in Antibes. Unless you are determined to part with large amounts of cash, don't even think about eating or sleeping here; just hang on to the edge of your chaise longue and enjoy the atmosphere at the epicenter of cool. Drink prices are sobering; cocktails start at 18€ ($23). 239 rue St-Honoré, 1er. ℰ 01-42-44-50-25. Métro: Tuileries.

La Fabrique Dark, simple, sleek, this Bastille haunt with jazzy background music is a favorite for a late-night rendezvous. Beautiful people dressed in black come here to be seen, drink at the minimalist bar, and eat the Alsatian specialty, *Flammekueche* (large, thin-crusted pizzas topped with cream, herbs, and items of your choice). DJs arrive around 11pm, as do the crowds. 53 rue du Faubourg St-Antoine, 11e. ℰ 01-43-07-67-07. No cover Mon–Thurs; cover 10€ ($13) Fri–Sat. Métro: Bastille.

La Perla Even in Paris, the yearning for a margarita might overtake you. If so, come to this popular Marais bar with high ceilings and cooling fans. It takes pride in having the largest collection of tequilas in Europe, and also stocks eight different Mexican beers. You can also get decent Mexican munchies, including nachos and quesadillas. Drinks are half price during happy hour (weekdays 6–8pm); otherwise, margarita prices start at 10€ ($13). 26 rue François-Miron, 4e. ℰ 01-42-77-59-40. Métro: St-Paul.

La Suite What used to be the popular Verandah is a now hip and happening all-white and very minimalist restaurant/bar. Across the street from the now-passé **Barfly** (49 av. George V), this hot spot targets the fashion crowd. Women in Thierry Mugler and men in Armani size each other up along the long bar, then retire to comfortable sofas for further flirtation before tripping off to nearby Le Queen. The intimidating bouncers at the front door only allow entry to those who look ultraglamorous—so dress accordingly or you'll be turned away! The attached restaurant serves seriously overpriced mediocre food. Drink prices start at 20€ ($25). 40 av. George V, 8e. ℰ 01-53-57-49-49. Métro: George V.

Le Bar at The Plaza Athenée When Naomi Campbell is in Paris, this is where she goes. Not surprisingly, this oh-so-trendy bar is also one of the most exclusive (and expensive) bars in the city. But the drop-dead gorgeous blue-lit bar and comfortable and very loungey sofas are delightful for watching the rich and famous sip the signature "regressive cocktails" concocted by the talented barmen. The house specialty is a glass of champagne with a hint of raspberry syrup, which will set you back a whopping 24€ ($30). But if you're in Paris for a night, you may not want to pass up a chance to experience the epitome of glamour. Be sure to dress sharp and arrive before the crowds do at 10pm. 25 av. Montaigne, 8e. ℰ 01-53-67-66-65. Métro: Alma-Marceau or Franklin-D-Roosevelt.

Man Ray This addition to the glitzy bar scene around the Champs-Elysées is known for its star-studded list of proprietors: Johnny Depp, Sean Penn, John Malkovich, and Mick Hucknall (from Simply Red) all have a piece of the action.

An Affordable Night Out in Young & Happening Menilmontant

After erupting onto the scene some years ago, **rue Oberkampf** still rules nightlife in eastern Paris. Longtime residents shake their heads in disbelief and worry that the neighborhood's quirky authenticity may disappear under the swarms of night crawlers that have migrated north from the Bastille. "Too many *banlieusards* go to the Bastille," the owner of Café Cannibale said, referring to Parisians' well-known reluctance to socialize with the suburban crowd.

Most of the people who come here are young, many are students, and most are on a budget. Drinks are not as pricey as elsewhere in the city and you can get decently priced light meals at many of the bars. To spend an evening with the young jeans-and-sneakers Parisians is great to see yet another side of the city.

Starting from Métro Ménilmontant and heading down rue Oberkampf, your first stop is the divey **Le Scherkhan** at no. 144 (✆ **01-43-57-29-34**). Sink into an easy chair under the fangs of a stuffed tiger, inhale the incense, and dream of equatorial Africa.

Across the street at no. 133 (✆ **01-43-57-81-44**), you'll find one of the best happy hour bargains in Paris at the hopping **Gecko Café**, where every day from 6 to 9pm a pint of beer goes for a mere 3.50€ ($4.40) and two-for-one cocktails are on offer.

Stop in at **Le Cithéa** (see "Live Music Clubs" earlier in this chapter) if it's open, or continue to **Café Mercerie** at no. 98 (✆ **01-43-38-81-30**). At the end of the fashionably grungy bar is a tiny back room lined with sofas. Across the street at no. 109 is the famous **Café Charbon**, popular with a young artsy crowd and serving some yummy light meals. Farther down the street at no. 99 is the plush **Mecano Bar** (✆ **01-40-21-35-28**). Old implements on the wall are left over from its days as a tool factory. The spacious back room has a palm tree, a skylight, and murals of seminude ladies lounging about in *fin de siècle* naughtiness. At number 10, **Le Kitch** (✆ **01-40-2194-14**) is the newest addition to the street. Opened in 2004, the place is a haphazard concoction of styles and decor. It's more bohemian than the other bars and serves decent international food like gazpacho and curries.

Backtrack a few steps and turn right onto rue St-Maur to no. 111–113, the **Blue Billard** (✆ **01-43-55-87-21**). The former camera factory is an upscale bar and pool hall, with 22 blue tables under a mezzanine and skylight.

A few steps further is a local favorite, **Les Couleurs** (✆ **01-43-57-95-61**), outfitted with tacky posters, chrome-and-plastic chairs, and rec-room lamps. The campy decor is 1970s, but the sounds are strictly 21st century. Live bands regularly play "free jazz," alternative rock, and anything experimental.

Ostensibly dedicated to Dadaist painter and photographer Man Ray, this chic nightspot draws a sleek, international crowd. Don't look for a sign—a Chinese character and big wrought-iron doors mark the entrance. The downstairs restaurant is dominated by statues of two winged Asian goddesses who appear concerned—possibly about the very iffy food. The upstairs bar area is spacious, and the music leans to jazz. Friday and Saturday nights after 11pm the music takes on a harder edge when the DJ's music of choice is house (with a pricey 20€/$25 cover charge). 34 rue Marbeuf, 8e. ℰ 01-56-88-36-36. Métro: Franklin-D-Roosevelt.

Opus Lounge A New York–style bar with a definite Parisian touch, this is a hidden hot spot in the Marais. Tucked away on a side street, it attracts a mix of bohemians and sophisticates who sit in the plush lounge chairs under modern art (which is for sale). Others hang at the bar and listen to the DJ, who spins house tunes nightly from 6 to 9pm. A dim backroom dining area with velvet seats and wine racks built into the wall provides an intimate setting and decent food. 5 rue Elzévir, 3e. ℰ 01-40-29-44-04. Closed Aug. Métro: St-Paul.

Sanz Sans This Bastille bar is done up with gilt mirrors, red velvet chairs, and ersatz Old Masters on the walls. A trendy young crowd surrounds the U-shaped bar and listens to acid jazz and funk. Those seated in the back of the bar get a high-tech view of the action in the front—a closed-circuit camera projects onto a screen on the back wall. It's very crowded on weekends. The *venir accompagner* (men must come accompanied by a woman) policy applies here, as does a hipster dress code. 49 rue du Faubourg St-Antoine, 12e. ℰ 01-44-75-78-78. Métro: Bastille.

11

Side Trips from Paris

If you can tear yourself away from the glories of Paris, the wonders of **Versailles, Fontainebleau,** and **Chartres** are worth the trips. Along with **Disneyland Paris,** they're the most frequently visited attractions in the Ile-de-France, the suburbs, and countryside surrounding Paris.

If you'll be in Paris a little longer, you may want to visit the gardens in **Giverny** that painter Claude Monet made famous, or venture out for a day of champagne tasting in **Reims.**

If your day trip time is limited, Versailles and Chartres give you more for your money.

1 Versailles ★★★

21km (13 miles) SW of Paris, 71km (44 miles) NE of Chartres

The Château de Versailles (© **01-39-50-36-22;** www.chateauversailles.fr) is astonishing. The over-the-top magnificence of the vast grounds and gardens and the size and wealth of the castle attest to the excessiveness of Louis XIV. The "Sun King" reigned for 72 years, beginning in 1643, when he was only 5. He sought to prove his greatness with a château that would be the wonder of Europe. He hired the best: Louis Le Vau and Jules Hardouin-Mansart, France's premier architects; André Le Nôtre, designer of the Tuileries gardens; and Charles Le Brun, head of the Royal Academy of Painting and Sculpture, for the interior. Construction began in 1661.

Louis XIII built Versailles's first château, a small hunting lodge, between 1631 and 1634, and Le Vau enlarged it. It was still too small to suit the Sun King, so in 1668 Le Vau created an "envelope" and wrapped the old château in a second building. In the meantime, 22,000 men and 6,000 horses tore up the gardens, drained the marshes—often at the cost of their lives—and demolished the forests for Le Nôtre's garden.

(Tips) Word to the Wise: Plan a Picnic

To save money on food, pack a light *piquenique* before you leave Paris. The destinations in this chapter are major tourist centers where meals are overpriced and unremarkable. However, you'll find wonderful picnicking opportunities, so save your food budget for a memorable meal in Paris.

At Versailles, you can eat in one of the world's most magnificent gardens. At Fontainebleau, dine along a canal as ducks and swans glide by. In Chartres, head for the Parc André Gagnon, a short walk northwest of the cathedral. You're not allowed to eat in the gardens of Giverny, but you can dine at the benches next to the parking lot on the grounds.

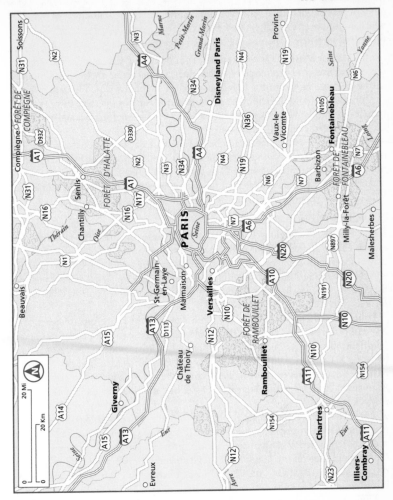

In 1682, Louis XIV transferred the court to Versailles and, to prevent plots against him, summoned his nobles to live with him. An estimated 3,000 to 10,000 people, including servants, lived at Versailles.

When Louis XIV died in 1715, his great-grandson Louis XV succeeded him. The new king continued the pomp and ceremony and made interior renovations until lack of funds forced him to stop. His son, Louis XVI, and his queen, Marie Antoinette, had simpler tastes and made no major changes. But by then, it was too late. On October 6, 1789, a mob marched on the palace and forced the royal couple to return to Paris, and Versailles ceased to be a royal residence.

Napoleon made some renovations, but he never much liked the château. Louis-Philippe, the Citizen King who reigned from 1830 to 1848, prevented the château's destruction by donating his own money to convert it to a museum dedicated to the glory of France. John D. Rockefeller also contributed to the restoration of Versailles, which continues to this day.

GETTING THERE　To get to the palace, catch RER Line C5 at the Gare d'Auster-litz, St-Michel, Musée d'Orsay, Invalides, Pont de l'Alma, Champs-de-Mars, or Javel station and take it to the Versailles Rive Gauche station. From there it is a short walk to the château. Holders of a Eurailpass can use it for the trip. The fare is 2.80€ ($3.50) one-way, and the trip takes about half an hour. For the same price, a regular train leaves the Gare Montparnasse for the Versailles Chantier station, and a free shut-tle bus runs to the palace.

Alternatively, if you're planning to buy a Mobilis 1-day travel ticket, ask for a *billet* covering zones 1 to 4 (Versailles falls in zone 4). It'll set you back 9€ ($11) for the round-trip and unlimited travel in Paris for the day.

Arrive early. Not only is there a lot to see, but more than three million tourists visit Versailles each year—you'll want to get as much of a head start as possible.

TOURING THE PALACE

Kings used the six glorious Louis XIV–style Grands Appartements for ceremonial events. They're named for their ceiling paintings, done by artists from the Royal Acad-emy of Painting and Sculpture. The best-known *appartement* is the Salon of Hercules, which houses Paolo Veronese's painting *Christ at Supper with Simon* and has the finest fireplace in the château. After his death in 1715, the body of Louis XIV lay in state for 8 days in the Salon of Mercury.

Louis XV and Louis XVI and their families lived in the Petits Appartements. Louis XV stashed his mistress, Mme du Barry (and earlier, Mme de Pompadour), in his sec-ond-floor apartment, which can be visited only with a guide. The *appartement* of Mme de Maintenon, Louis XIV's mistress and later his wife, is also here. Attempts have been made to restore the original decor of the queen's bedchamber, which Marie Antoinette renovated with a huge four-poster bed and silks in a pattern of lilacs and peacock feathers.

The Salons of War and Peace flank the most famous room at Versailles, the 236-foot-long Hall of Mirrors. Hardouin-Mansart began work on it in 1678, and Le Brun added 17 large windows and corresponding mirrors. Thirty ceiling paintings represent the accomplishments of Louis XIV's government. The German Empire was pro-claimed here in 1871. On June 28, 1919, the treaty ending World War I was signed in this room.

Louis XVI had an impressive library, designed by Ange Jacques Gabriel, but it didn't seem to influence the dim-witted monarch. The library's panels are delicately carved, and the room has been restored and refurnished. The Clock Room contains Passement's astronomical clock, encased in gilded bronze; it took 20 years to make and was completed in 1753. At the age of 7, Mozart played in this room for the court.

Gabriel designed the Royal Opéra for Louis XV in 1748, although it wasn't com-pleted until 1770. The bas-reliefs are by Pajou, and bearskin rugs once covered the floor. At one time, lighting the place required 3,000 powerful candles. The final restoration of the theater was finished in 1957.

Hardouin-Mansart built the gold-and-white Royal Chapel between 1699 and 1710. Louis XVI, then the dauphin, married Marie Antoinette here when they were just teenagers. After his father's death, Louis XVI and Marie prayed for guidance, feel-ing they were too young to rule the country.

Versailles

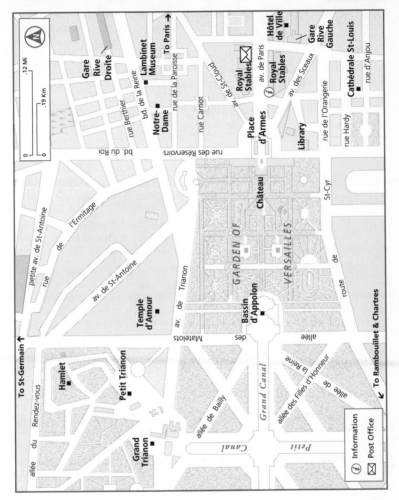

The landscape artist André Le Nôtre laid out the 250-acre Gardens of Versailles. At the peak of their glory, 1,400 fountains splashed. The fountains of Apollo, Neptune, and Latona—the last with statues of people being turned into frogs—are exceptional. Le Nôtre created a Garden of Eden in the Ile-de-France, using ornamental lakes and canals, geometrically designed flowerbeds, and avenues bordered with statuary. On the mile-long Grand Canal, Louis XV used to take gondola rides with his "favorite" of the moment.

A long walk across the park leads to the pink-and-white-marble Grand Trianon, designed in 1687 by Hardouin-Mansart for Louis XIV. It has traditionally housed the country's important guests, although de Gaulle wanted to turn it into his weekend retreat. Napoleon I spent the night, and Nixon slept in the room where Mme de Pompadour died. The original furnishings are gone; today it's filled mostly with Empire pieces.

Gabriel, who designed place de la Concorde, built the Petit Trianon in 1768 for Louis XV. Mme de Pompadour, who died before it was complete, inspired its construction. Not one to waste a good space, Louis used it for his trysts with Mme du Barry. It was Marie Antoinette's favorite residence. Many of the current furnishings, including a few in the bedroom, were hers. Napoleon I presented the Petit Trianon to his sister, Pauline Borghese, but ungallantly took it back and gave it to his new bride, Marie-Louise.

Behind the Petit Trianon is the Hamlet. Marie Antoinette strolled around the thatched farmhouses, enchanted by the simple tasks of farm life—milking cows, milling grain, and fishing in the lake. On October 6, 1789, in a grotto nearby, she heard that a mob from Paris was marching on Versailles. She fled to the château, never to return. Near the Hamlet is the Temple of Love, built in 1775 by Richard Mique, the queen's favorite architect. In the center of its Corinthian colonnade is a reproduction of Bouchardon's *Cupid* shaping a bow from the club of Hercules.

Near the stables is the entrance to the Carriage Museum, which houses coaches from the 18th and 19th centuries, including vehicles used at the coronation of Charles X and the wedding of Napoleon I and Marie-Louise. One sleigh rests on tortoiseshell runners. Admission to the Petit Trianon includes this museum.

HOURS & ADMISSION   From March 26 to October 31, the palace is open Tuesday to Sunday 9am to 6:30pm; the Grand Trianon and Petit Trianon are open the same days 10am to 6pm. The rest of the year, the palace is open Tuesday to Sunday 9am to 5:30pm; the Grand Trianon and Petit Trianon are open Tuesday to Friday 10am to noon and 2 to 5pm, Saturday and Sunday 10am to 5pm. Admission to the palace is 7.50€ ($9.40) adults; 5.30€ ($6.65) for ages 18 to 24 and seniors (over 60), and for all on Sunday; free for those under 18. Admission to the Grand Trianon and Petit Trianon is 5€ ($6.25) adults, 3€ ($3.75) for ages 18 to 24. Admission to the gardens only is 3€ ($3.75). Admission to the park is free for pedestrians, 5€ to 6€ ($6.25–$7.50) per car.

2 Fontainebleau ★★

60km (37 miles) S of Paris, 74km (46 miles) NE of Orléans

The Palais de Fontainebleau (© **01-60-71-50-70;** www.musee-chateau-fontainebleau.fr) has witnessed many great moments in French history. It's most famous for Napoleon's farewell to his Imperial Guard, which he delivered on the horseshoe-shaped stairway before leaving for exile. From the enthronement of Louis VII in 1137 to the fall of the Second Empire, Fontainebleau contains more than 700 years of history. Plus, it's on the edge of the kings' old hunting grounds, the Forêt de Fontainebleau. If you get tired of the grandiosity, you can walk or rent bikes to ride in its 17,000 hectares (41,990 acres).

GETTING THERE   The Montargie line to Fontainebleau departs hourly from the Gare de Lyon in Paris. The trip takes about 45 minutes and costs 9.30€ ($12). Fontainebleau Avon station is just outside the town in the Paris suburb of Avon. From the station, the town bus makes the 3.2km (2-mile) trip to the château every 10 to 15 minutes on weekdays, every 30 minutes on Saturdays and Sundays. The bus costs 1.40€ ($1.75).

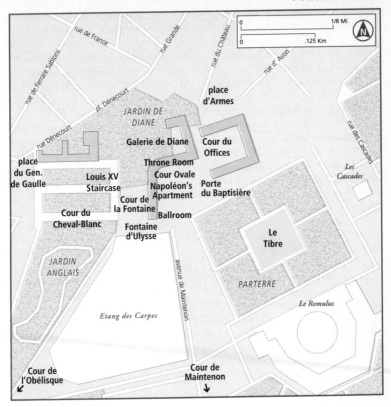

TOURING THE PALACE

It is said that Fontainebleau was built for love. François I built it for his mistress; his successor, Henri II, left a beautiful memorial to the woman he loved, a ballroom decorated with the intertwined initials of his mistress, Diane de Poitiers, and his own. French kings used Fontainebleau as a retreat and hunting ground. François I rebuilt part of the château in the Renaissance style, recruiting Italian artisans to design and craft the interiors. Their work—fresco, stucco, and *boiserie*—can be seen in the Gallery François I, in the ballroom, and on the Duchesse d'Etampes staircase. Painters Rosso Fiorentino and Primaticcio adorned the 63m (207-ft.) long gallery of François I, where the *Mona Lisa* once hung; François bought the painting from da Vinci. Stucco-framed paintings depict mythological and allegorical scenes related to the king's life. The salamander, symbol of the Chevalier King, is everywhere.

At one end of the room is a fireplace supported by two bronze satyrs (made in 1966—the originals were melted down in the Revolution). At the other side is the salon of the musicians, decorated with sculptured garlands. A series of frescoes, painted between 1550 and 1558, depict such subjects as *The Feast of Bacchus*. Rosettes adorn the coffered ceiling.

Make sure to see the racy ceiling paintings above the Louis XV Staircase. Primaticcio decorated the bedroom of the Duchesse d'Etampes with them, and the stairway's architect ripped out her floor and used her bedroom ceiling to cover the staircase. Of the Italian frescoes that were preserved, one depicts the queen of the Amazons climbing into Alexander the Great's bed.

When Louis XIV ascended the throne, Fontainebleau was largely neglected. He wasn't opposed to using the palace for houseguests—specifically Queen Christina, who had abdicated the throne of Sweden. Apparently thinking she still had "divine right," she ordered one of the most brutal royal murders on record—that of her lover, Monaldeschi, who had ceased to please her.

Fontainebleau found renewed glory under Napoleon I. You can walk around much of the palace on your own, but most of the Napoleonic Rooms are accessible only on guided tours, which are in French. Napoleon had two bedchambers: Mirrors adorn either side of his bed in the grander room (look for his symbol, a bee), while the small bedchamber holds a small bed. A red-and-gold throne with the initial N is displayed in the Throne Room. You can also see where the emperor signed his abdication (the document exhibited is a copy).

Minor apartments include those once occupied by Mme de Maintenon, the second wife of Louis XIV. Pope Pius VII, whom Napoleon kept a virtual prisoner, lived in another; still another was Marie Antoinette's. The Chinese collections of Empress Eugénie are on display in the Napoleon III salons.

After a visit to the palace, wander through the gardens, paying attention to the lovely carp pond, with its fearless swans. If you'd like to promenade in the forest, a map of its paths is available for 5.50€ ($6.90) from the Office de Tourisme, 4 rue Royale, near the palace (© **01-60-74-99-99**). You can rent bikes nearby from **A la Petite Reine,** 32 rue des Sablons (© **01-60-74-57-57**), for 14€ ($18) a day, 17€ ($21) on weekends, with a credit card deposit. The Tour Denencourt, about 4.8km (3 miles) north of the palace, makes a nice ride.

HOURS & ADMISSION   The Château de Fontainebleau is open Wednesday to Monday 9:30am to 6pm June to September and 9:30am to 5pm October to May. Admission to the Grands Appartements is 5.50€ ($6.90) for adults, 4€ ($5) for ages 18 to 24 and seniors (over 60) and for all on Sunday. Separate admission to the Napoleonic Rooms is 3€ ($3.75) for adults, 2.30€ ($2.90) for students 18 to 25. Children under 18 enter free.

3 Chartres ★ ★ ★

97km (60 miles) SW of Paris, 76km (47 miles) NW of Orléans

It survived the French Revolution, when it was scheduled for demolition. It withstood two world wars, when volunteers took down all of its 12th- and 13th-century stained-glass windows—piece by piece. You won't fully appreciate that feat, however, until you visit the Cathédrale de Notre-Dame de Chartres (© **02-37-21-56-33**), one of the world's great Gothic cathedrals and one of the finest creations of the Middle Ages. While many come to marvel at its magnificence, the cathedral also draws many pilgrims to see a small scrap of material that is said to have been worn by the Virgin Mary when she gave birth to Jesus.

GETTING THERE   Trains run from Paris's Gare Montparnasse to Chartres. A round-trip ticket costs 25€ ($31); the trip takes 1¼ hours.

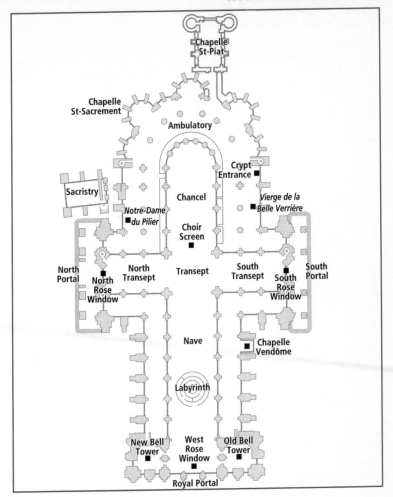

SEEING THE CATHEDRAL

The origins of the cathedral are uncertain; some suggest it was built on the site of an ancient Druid shrine and, later, a Roman temple. There was a Christian basilica here as early as the 4th century. A fire in 1194 destroyed most of what was by then a Romanesque cathedral, but spared the western facade and crypt. The cathedral you see today dates principally from the 13th century, when it was built with the efforts and contributions of kings, princes, church officials, and pilgrims from all over Europe. It was among the first to use flying buttresses.

Begin at the beginning—with the entryway. It's said that Rodin sat for hours on the edge of the sidewalk, contemplating the portal, spellbound by its sculptured bodies draped in flowing robes with amazingly lifelike faces. In the central tympanum, Christ is shown in all his majesty at the Second Coming; his nativity is depicted on the right,

---

Finds **The Best Tour of Chartres**

To get the most out of your visit, consider taking one of the guided tours of the cathedral—especially those by Englishman Malcolm Miller (© **02-37-28-15-58;** MillerChartres@aol.com). He gives tours Monday to Saturday at noon and 2:45pm from Easter to late October, and is sometimes available in winter. Tours cost 10€ ($13) for adults, 5€ ($6.25) for students. Reservations are not necessary for these tours—just show up at the above times. To arrange for a private tour, however, call or e-mail Malcolm in advance of your arrival. Also save some time to stroll around the tranquil town itself.

---

his ascent on the left. Before entering, walk around to the north and south portals, which date from the 13th century. The bays depict such biblical scenes as the expulsion of Adam and Eve from the Garden of Eden and episodes from the life of the Virgin.

Just inside are the Clocher Vieux (Old Tower), with its 105m (344-ft.) steeple dating from the 12th century, and the Clocher Neuf (New Tower). Built in 1134, the New Tower gained an ornamental tower between 1507 and 1513. Jehan de Beauce designed it following one of the many fires that swept over the cathedral. You can climb to the top of the Clocher Neuf, but make sure your shoes aren't slippery—the tower is steep and narrow, and parts lack a railing.

The cathedral is also known for its choir screen; a carved wood piece that took nearly 200 years to complete. The 40 niches contain statues illustrating scenes from the life of Mary. It's in the middle of the cathedral toward the back.

Few visitors ever notice the screen; they're transfixed by the stained-glass windows. Covering more than 3,000 square yards, the glass is unequaled anywhere. It was spared in both wars because of a decision to remove it piece by piece. Most of the stained glass dates from the 12th and 13th centuries.

It is difficult to single out one panel or window of special merit; however, the oldest is the 12th-century *Notre Dame de la belle verrière* (Our Lady of the Beautiful Window, sometimes called the Blue Virgin) on the south side. The color is such a vibrant, startling blue, it's hard to believe the window is nearly 1,000 years old. The three fiery rose windows are spectacular.

Look down in the nave—the widest in France—at the 13th-century labyrinth. Designed for pilgrims to navigate on their hands and knees as a form of penance, it is nearly 300m (984 ft.) long. These days, folding chairs cover much of it. The Virgin of the Pillar, to the left of the choir, dates from the 14th century. The crypt was built over a period of 200 years, beginning in the 9th century. Enshrined is Our Lady of the Crypt, a Madonna made in 1976 that replaced one destroyed during the Revolution.

The **Sancta Camisia,** the relic Mary is believed to have worn during the birth of Jesus, is behind the choir screen in a chapel to the left of the church's treasury.

HOURS & ADMISSION   Entrance to the cathedral is free. It's open daily April through September 7:30am to 7:30pm; October through March 7:30am to 7pm. French-language tours of the cathedral are given in summer Tuesday through Saturday at 10:30am and daily at 3pm; in winter, daily at 2:30pm. Ask at the Chartres tourist office (© **02-37-18-26-26;** www.chartres-tourisme.com) outside the cathedral for information about tours in English and a schedule of Masses.

French-language tours of the crypt start at 11am and 2:15, 3:30, and 4:30pm (also at 5:15pm in summer). The crypt tour costs 2€ ($2.50) for adults, 1€ ($1.25) for ages 18 to 24 and seniors (over 60).

From April to September, the tower is open Monday to Saturday 9:30 to 11:30am and daily 2 to 5:30pm; October to March, Monday to Saturday 10 to 11:30am and daily 2 to 4pm. Admission to the tower is 4€ ($5) for adults, 2.50€ ($3.15) for seniors and students, free for children under 12.

4 Disneyland Paris

32km (20 miles) E of Paris

After evoking some of the most enthusiastic and most controversial reactions in recent French history, Disneyland Paris opened in 1992. It's one of the most lavish theme parks in the world. Set on a 2,000-hectare (4,940-acre) site (about one-fifth the size of Paris) in the suburb of Marne-la-Vallée, the park incorporates the elements of its Disney predecessors but gives them a European flair.

The Disneyland Paris resort is conceived as a total vacation destination, encompassing five "lands"; six massive, well-designed hotels; a campground; and dozens of restaurants, shows, and shops. Visitors from across Europe stroll amid flowerbeds, trees, reflecting ponds, fountains, and a large artificial lake flanked by hotels. An army of smiling and largely multilingual employees and Disney characters—including Buffalo Bill, Mickey and Minnie Mouse, and Caribbean pirate Jean Lafitte—are on hand to greet and delight thousands of children.

GETTING THERE   By **train,** take RER Line A from the center of Paris (Invalides, Nation, or Châtelet–Les Halles) to Marne-la-Vallée/Chessy, a 45-minute ride. The fare is 7€ ($8.75) one-way, 13€ ($16) round-trip. Trains run every 10 to 20 minutes, depending on the time of day. The station is at the entrance to the park.

Shuttle **buses** connect the resort's hotels with Orly Airport (every 45 min. daily 9am–7pm) and Roissy–Charles de Gaulle (every 45 min. daily 8am–8pm). One-way transport to the park from either airport costs 17€ ($21). Within the park, a free shuttle bus connects the hotels with the theme park, stopping every 6 to 15 minutes, depending on the time of year. Service begins an hour before the park opens and stops an hour after closing.

By **car,** take the A4 highway east and exit at PARK EURO DISNEY. Parking at any of the thousands of spaces costs 7€ ($8.75). A series of moving sidewalks speeds you from the parking areas to the park entrance.

For more information, contact the **Disneyland Paris Guest Relations** office on Main Street, U.S.A. (© **01-64-74-30-00;** www.disneylandparis.com).

Value A Time- and Money-Saving Disney Pass

The **RATP Disneyland Resort ticket,** which may be purchased at any RER station in Paris, combines round-trip transportation and 1-day admission to the park. For 41€ ($51) for adults and 33€ ($41) for children 3 to 11, you'll get to skip the long lines when you arrive at the park and go to the "Pluto Cashier" to exchange your ticket for a day pass.

EXPLORING THE PARK

Main Street, U.S.A., abounds with horse-drawn carriages and barbershop quartets. Steam-powered railway cars leave Main Street Station for a trip through a Grand Canyon diorama to **Frontierland,** with its paddle-wheel steamers, the Critter Corral at the Cottonwood Creek Ranch petting zoo, and the Lucky Nugget Saloon, straight from the gold rush era. There, visitors find an array of cancan shows (a dance that originated in the cabarets of 19th-century Paris).

The resort's steam trains chug past **Adventureland**—with its swashbuckling pirates, the Swiss Family Robinson treehouse, and reenacted legends from the *Arabian Nights*—and on to **Fantasyland.** There lies the symbol of the theme park: the Sleeping Beauty Castle (Le Château de la Belle au Bois Dormant). Parading in its shadow are time-tested, though Europeanized, versions of Snow White and the Seven Dwarfs, Peter Pan, Dumbo, Alice in Wonderland's Mad Tea Party, and Sir Lancelot's magic carousel.

Visions of the future dominate **Discoveryland,** whose tributes to invention and imagination draw from the works of Leonardo da Vinci; Jules Verne and H. G. Wells, the modern masters of science fiction; and the original *Star Wars* trilogy. One of the most popular attractions is Space Mountain, a roller coaster that sends riders on a virtual journey from the earth to the moon through the Milky Way.

The **Walt Disney Studios** opened in 2002 and its attractions all revolve around the art of filmmaking, animation, and special effects. *The Stunt Show Spectacular* is a live show featuring real stunt men and women; in the very popular Art of Disney Animation, kids can experiment with their own cartoon creations. The Live TV Production tour is an insider look into the world of television shows, and the Armageddon Tour takes you aboard the space station of the blockbuster movie by the same name.

In addition to the theme park, Disney maintains an entertainment center, **Le Festival Disney.** Illuminated by a grid of lights suspended 18m (60 ft.) above the ground, the complex contains dance clubs, shops, restaurants, bars, a French-government tourist office, a post office, a babysitting service, and a marina. Outside the park are swimming pools, tennis courts, and a 27-hole golf course.

HOURS & ADMISSION   Admission to the park for 1 day is 41€ ($51) for adults, 33€ ($41) for children 3 to 11; children under 3 enter free. Admission for 3 days is 109€ ($136) for adults, 89€ ($111) for children. Off-season (early Nov to early Apr) prices for 1 day are 33€ ($41) for adults, 29€ ($36) for children; prices are 83€ ($104) and 73€ ($91), respectively, for 3 days. Entrance to Le Festival Disney is free; there's usually a cover charge for the dance clubs.

Disneyland Paris is open June 12 to September 12 daily 9am to 11pm; September 13 to June 11 Monday to Friday 10am to 6pm, Saturday and Sunday 9am to 8pm. Hours vary with the weather and season, so call ℂ **01-64-74-30-00** before setting out or consult their website at www.disneylandparis.com.

TOURS   Guided tours in English cost 7€ ($8.75) for adults, 6€ ($7.50) for children 3 to 11. Tours last 3½ hours, and group size is generally 20 or more. The tours offer one of the best opportunities for a complete visit. Ask at the information desk for details.

FOR FAMILIES   Wheelchairs and children's strollers can be rented for 5€ ($6.25) per day, with a 10€ ($13) deposit.

5 Giverny—In the Footsteps of Claude Monet ★★★

81km (50 miles) NW of Paris

Even before you arrive at Giverny, you'll likely already have some idea of what you're going to see, because Claude Monet's paintings of his garden are known and loved throughout the world.

Monet moved to Giverny in 1883, and the water lilies beneath the Japanese bridge in the garden, as well as the flower garden, became his regular subjects until his death in 1926. In 1966 the Monet family donated Giverny to the Académie des Beaux-Arts in Paris. It has since become one of the most popular attractions in France, but even the crowds can't completely overwhelm the magic.

The gardens are usually at their best in May, June, September, and October. Should you yearn to have them almost to yourself, plan to be at the gates when they open. For more information, call ℂ 02-32-51-28-21.

GETTING THERE   **Trains** leave the Gare St-Lazare in Paris approximately every hour for the 45-minute trip to Vernon, the town nearest the Monet gardens. The round-trip fare is about 23€ ($29). From the station, buses make the 4.8km (3-mile) trip to the museum for 2€ ($2.50), or you can go on foot—the route along the Seine makes for a nice walk.

By **car,** take Autoroute A13 from the Porte d'Auteuil to Bonnières, then D201 to Giverny.

HOURS & ADMISSION   The gardens are open April 1 to November 1 Tuesday through Sunday 9:30am to 6pm. Admission to the house and gardens is 6€ ($7.50) adults, 4€ ($5) students, and 3€ ($3.75) children 7 to 12; admission to the gardens only is 4€ ($5).

Some say Monet's influence was responsible for the influx of American artists into the village of Giverny in the late 1880s. Others say that Monet had little contact with the Americans, and the town's beauty captured the hearts of painters like John Singer Sargent and William Metcalf, who began spending their summers there. It's estimated that at one point, more than 50 American artists lived in Giverny. You can see much of their work at the **Musée d'Art Américain Giverny** (ℂ 02-32-51-94-65; www.maag.org), 90m (295 ft.) from Monet's house and gardens. It's open March to November Tuesday to Sunday 10am to 6pm. Admission is 5.50€ ($7) for adults, 4€ ($5) for students and seniors, and 3€ ($3.75) for children 12 to 18.

6 Reims: Champagne Tasting & Culinary Adventures ★★

142km (88 miles) NE of Paris

A mere 90 minutes by train east of Paris will bring you to Reims (pronounced "rahns"), home to one of the most important cathedrals in France, as well as to the rows of champagne vineyards dotting the rolling landscape surrounding the city. Champagne production is so stringently controlled that no sparkling wine produced elsewhere in the world can be labeled "champagne." Reims is home to many of the world's most famous champagne houses and many are open for tours during the week. Reims is so accessible that you could take a morning train from Paris, enjoy a tour and champagne tasting, a one-Michelin-star lunch, and return to the city in time for dinner. If you'd like to splurge for a night here, we've discovered an affordable minichâteau perfect for an overnight stay.

GETTING THERE

By Train   Trains to Reims leave about every 2 hours from the Gare de l'Est in Paris and the round-trip fare is about 43€ ($54). Ask for off-peak round-trip "leisure" tickets to get the best deal, or reserve ahead online at www.voyages-sncf.com. Taxis are plentiful at the station and the 10-minute ride to one of the local champagne houses costs about 7€ to 10€ ($8.75–$13).

By Car   From Paris, head east toward Strasbourg on the A4, exit at Reims Cathedral, and that will bring you to the center of the city.

EXPLORING REIMS

The Cathedral de Reims (pl. du Cardinal-Lucon; ℂ **03-26-47-81-79**) was built in the 13th century, took almost 200 years to complete, and is a masterpiece of Gothic art. Originally used for the anointing of kings, the cathedral was for a time one of the most important monuments in France, adorned with over 2,500 statues (including angels with open wings). Last century's renovations include stained-glass windows created by Chagall.

Tours of the cathedral are offered every Saturday from March 15 to end of October from 10 to 11am and 2 to 5pm; Sunday tours are offered 2 to 5pm. Tours begin on the hour. Please note that the cathedral is completely closed from November 1 to March 14.

CHAMPAGNE TOURS & TASTINGS

The champagne houses described below provide a tour of their ancient cellars dug by the Romans, an up-close view of their current production facilities, and a chance to touch a real vine. To put things in perspective as you walk around: One vine produces roughly 4 kilos of grapes, which in turn translates to one bottle of champagne! (Since the champagne houses are in the middle of the city, most of their grapes are trucked in from the surrounding countryside, but all have a small patch of vines planted for visitors to see.)

Of course, whichever champagne house you choose to visit, the tour always ends with a chilled glass of their house bubbly and a demonstration on the *correct* way to open a champagne bottle. Bottles of champagne at a reduced rate are available for purchase.

Note: Always call at least 1 day in advance to reserve your spot on the tour. English-speaking guides are only available at specific times and it changes daily. Tours are generally held Monday to Friday 9:30am to noon and 2:30 to 5:30pm.

Veuve Clicquot (1 pl. des Droits de L'Homme; ℂ **03-26-89-53-90**) is one of the most popular stops for visitors. The cellars here are a must-see, with bottles dating back to 1904. Veuve Clicquot stores over 40 million bottles of champagne in their cellars. A 1½-hour tour and tasting costs 7€ ($8.75).

Pommery (5 pl. du General Gouraud; ℂ **03-26-61-62-56**) is a good house to visit because of its palatial visitor center and sprawling gardens. A 1-hour tour and tasting costs 6€ ($7.50).

Lanson (66 rue de Courlancy; ℂ **03-26-78-50-50**) is a smaller house but one that offers a much more personalized view of the process of champagne production. You'll get to smell the fermenting wine and even see the labels being smacked on the bottles. A 1-hour tour and tasting costs 5€ ($6.25).

Other popular champagne houses include **Taittinger** (9 pl. St-Nicaise; ℂ **03-26-85-84-33**), **Piper-Heidsieck** (51 bd. Henry Vasnier; ℂ **03-26-84-43-44**), and **Mumm** (34 rue du Champ de Mars; ℂ **03-26-49-59-70**).

Reims

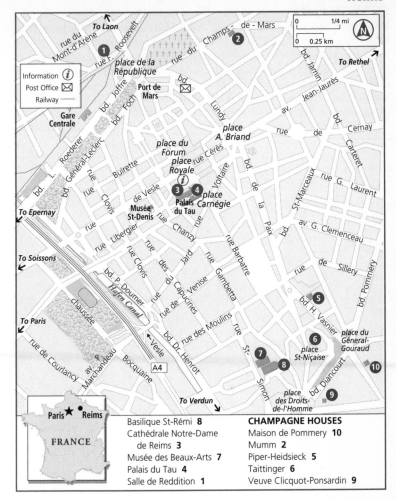

		CHAMPAGNE HOUSES
Basilique St-Rémi **8**		Maison de Pommery **10**
Cathédrale Notre-Dame		Mumm **2**
de Reims **3**		Piper-Heidsieck **5**
Musée des Beaux-Arts **7**		Taittinger **6**
Palais du Tau **4**		Veuve Clicquot-Ponsardin **9**
Salle de Reddition **1**		

WHERE TO EAT

When in Reims you can take advantage of being away from the capital to minisplurge on an exquisite meal at a price much lower than in Paris. Make reservations at **Le Foch** (37 bd. Foch; ℰ **03-26-47-48-22**) in advance. Jacky Louaze and his wife run this tiny, award-winning restaurant across the street from the train station. The 31€ ($39) three-course meal may include salmon marinated in orange rind or a foie gras tart followed by roast duck with wild mushrooms. For dessert, offerings include poached rhubarb with yogurt cheese and seared pineapple with coconut sorbet. The 41€ ($51) five-course meal includes two appetizers and a cheese course. The restaurant is open Monday to Friday from noon to 2pm and 7 to 10pm, Saturday 7 to 10pm, and Sunday noon to 2:30pm. Visa and MasterCard are accepted.

WHERE TO STAY

L'Assiette Champenoise, 40 av. Paul Vaillant-Couturier, 51430 Tinqueux-Reims (© **03-26-84-64-64;** fax 03-26-04-15-69; www.assiettechampenoise.com), is the perfect place for an overnight splurge. Housed in the lovely Château de la Muire surrounded by manicured gardens, this charming hotel has luxurious double rooms for 128€ ($160), a fantastic two-Michelin-star restaurant, a traditional English bar with leather sofas, and an indoor pool. The friendly, English-speaking staff can help you arrange for champagne tastings at smaller, lesser-known vineyards, so be sure to ask. American Express, MasterCard, and Visa are accepted.

Appendix A:
Paris in Depth

In order to understand Paris, you need to know how it evolved from its humble origins on the Ile de la Cité to the thriving metropolis it is today. Battles were fought over this territory, works of art were created, great love stories were lived—and no one knows this better than the Parisian. That is why he or she is always mindful to nurture past glories while creating new ones. The Louvre displays more art than ever, modern sculpture graces the shady paths of the Tuileries gardens, the facades of Notre-Dame and the Pont Neuf are grime free, and the Centre Pompidou has reopened. The city has survived war, revolution, occupation, and political disarray, demonstrating a strength, beauty, and resiliency that will continue to ensure its place as a world capital city well into the second millennium.

1 History 101

IN THE BEGINNING

In the beginning, there was the river. And an island in the river.

Paris began on the Ile de la Cité, where Notre-Dame stands today. Kilometer 0 of the French road and highway system is in place du Parvis Notre-Dame in front of the cathedral.

The Ile de la Cité was ideally situated for the Germanic Parisii tribe that arrived in the 3rd century B.C. The Seine formed a natural moat, was an abundant source of fish, and allowed them to trade with other tribes along the river. The Parisii produced excellent boatmen, a legacy recalled in the city's coat of arms: a boat with the Latin inscription *Fluctuat Nec Mergitur* ("It floats and does not sink"). The settlement was on the main trading route connecting the Mediterranean with northern Europe.

However, the river and the road made handy routes for invaders, too. The island came under attack, first and most successfully by the Romans. Julius Caesar stormed through France in 52 B.C. and made the Parisii settlement an outpost of the Empire. The Romans found it so

agreeable that they stayed 500 years, and the settlement became known as Lutetia Parisiorum (*Lutèce* in French). They built a temple to Jupiter on the site of Notre-Dame, erected administrative buildings where the parvis is now, and installed their governor at the site of the current Palais de Justice. The public baths at the Hôtel de Cluny and the Arènes de Lutèce are the best-preserved remnants of Roman Paris.

St. Denis, the first bishop of Paris and its most famous martyr, introduced Christianity around A.D. 250. After he was beheaded on the mont de Mercure, he reputedly picked up his head and walked over 6km (4 miles). The mont was renamed mont des Martyrs, which over the years became Montmartre. (In another account, a Roman temple to Mars gave Montmartre its name.) A century later, the city was spared a visit by Attila the Hun due to the miraculous intervention of St. Geneviève, later Paris's patron saint.

In 508, Clovis, king of the Franks, made Paris his capital. Around 786, the Carolingian dynasty, whose roots were closer to the Rhine, abandoned Paris for Aix-la-Chapelle and left it unprotected against Viking (Norman) attacks. In 885 and 886, Eudes, comte de Paris, defended the city against the invaders, and his victory led to the rise of a new dynasty. His grandnephew Hugues Capet became king of France in 987, and the Capetians ruled the Ile-de-France region until 1328.

Paris again developed into a capital city. Two Gothic masterpieces, Notre-Dame and the Sainte-Chapelle, were built on the Ile de la Cité, and on the Left Bank, one of Europe's first universities developed: the Sorbonne. The university was founded in 1215, and Thomas Aquinas was among its early professors. Scholars came from all over the continent, as they still do today, to what was then the largest city in the Christian world. Latin was their *lingua franca*—hence the name "Latin Quarter."

The major role France played in the Crusades enhanced the city's reputation as a theological center. St. Louis (Louis IX, 1226–70) personified that prominence; he built the awesome Sainte-Chapelle to house such treasures from the Holy Land as the Crown of Thorns. Philip III and Philip IV further strengthened the monarchy, but the Hundred Years' War (1337–1453) consumed the rest of the 14th century. The English and their Burgundian allies occupied Paris from 1420 to 1436, and Henry had himself crowned in Notre-Dame as Henry VI, king of England and France. After liberating Orléans, Joan of Arc tried to free Paris and was wounded in the thigh. Not until 1453 were the English finally driven out of France.

PARIS IN THE 16TH CENTURY

After the chaos of the Hundred Years' War, the consolidation of the monarchy's power resumed under François I. Although the Renaissance King spent most of his time in the Loire Valley with his friend Leonardo da Vinci, he intended to make the Louvre his official residence and started to transform the medieval fortress into a magnificent palace. Under François, France's prestige grew: Cartier and Verrazano explored the New World, and the Collège de France, with its interest in languages and sciences, was founded in 1530. Politically, François I laid the foundation for the rise of an absolute monarchy, a concept that reached its zenith with Louis XIV.

The period of stability did not last. From 1562 to 1598, the Wars of Religion tore Paris apart. The St. Bartholomew's Day Massacre of thousands of Protestants in 1572 saw Paris awash in blood; on the Day of the Barricades in 1588, Henri III was forced to flee. Protestant Henri of

Dateline

- **3rd century B.C.** The Parisii settle around the area that is now Paris.
- **53 B.C.** Julius Caesar mentions Paris in *De Bello Gallico*.
- **A.D. 250** St. Denis introduces Christianity.
- **360** Julian the Apostate proclaimed emperor of Rome; Lutetia is renamed Paris and becomes imperial capital.
- **508** Clovis, king of the Franks, chooses Paris as his capital.
- **786** Carolingians move their capital to Aix-la-Chapelle.
- **800** Charlemagne crowned Holy Roman Emperor.
- **885–886** Viking invasions; Comte Eudes defends Paris.
- **987** Eudes's grandnephew Hugues Capet proclaimed king.
- **1066** William the Conqueror invades England.
- **1140** St-Denis, the first Gothic cathedral, is built just north of Paris.
- **1163** Construction of Notre-Dame begins.
- **1215** The University of Paris founded.
- **1357** Etienne Marcel's revolt.
- **1420** English occupy Paris.
- **1431** English burn Joan of Arc at the stake in Rouen.
- **1436** End of English occupation.

Navarre, Henri III's heir, laid siege to the city. The Catholic League, led by the Guise family, opposed him and terrorized the city. Henri defeated them but was forced to convert to Catholicism before being allowed to enter Paris in 1594, when he reportedly said, *"Paris bien vaut une messe"* ("Paris is well worth a Mass").

One of France's most beloved kings, Henri IV, restored the country's prosperity and encouraged greater religious tolerance. His statue stands beside the Pont Neuf, the city's oldest bridge, completed during his reign in 1604. He and his minister, the duc de Sully, were responsible for building place Royale (now pl. des Vosges). He also laid out place Dauphine, built the quai d'Horloge, and enlarged the Cour Carrée at the Louvre to four times its previous size. The Edict of Nantes, issued in 1598, protected Protestants' religious rights. For this act and others, Henri IV was assassinated by a Catholic fanatic in 1610.

FROM LOUIS XIII TO LOUIS XVI

Louis XIII assumed the throne and continued the expansion and beautification of Paris. He joined two islands in the river, creating the Ile St-Louis. Marie de Medici, Henri IV's widow, built the Luxembourg Palace, inspired by the architecture of her native Tuscany. Louis XIII's minister, Cardinal Richelieu, founded the

Académie Française, influential in French cultural life even today, and built the Palais Cardinal (later Palais-Royal) and the Jardin des Plantes. Richelieu's successor, Jules Mazarin, endowed the Collège Mazarin in the Hôtel de L'Institut, home today of the Académie Française.

Under Louis XIV, the Sun King, who ruled for 72 years, the centralization of power under the monarchy reached its zenith. Although Louis XIV shunned Paris, establishing his court at Versailles, he contributed to the city's splendor. He added the colonnade to the Louvre, completed the Tuileries Palace, and laid out the Grands Boulevards, place Vendôme, and place des Victoires. He also built the Hôtel des Invalides for sick soldiers, the Observatory, the Gobelins factory, and the Pont Royal. His desertion of Paris alienated the citizens and prepared the ground for the ideas that grew into the French Revolution.

The wars that Louis XIV fought weakened France financially; the trend continued during the reigns of Louis XV (1715–74) and Louis XVI (1774–92). Louis XV laid out the grandiose place Louis XV (later pl. de la Concorde), created rue Royale, and began the Madeleine church. He also erected such edifices as the Ecole Militaire (1751), the Champs-de-Mars, and the church of Ste-Geneviève

- **1515–47** Reign of François I.
- **1530** Foundation of the Collège de France.
- **1562** Start of the Wars of Religion.
- **1572** St. Bartholomew's Day Massacre.
- **1594** Henri IV converts to Catholicism.
- **1598** Edict of Nantes.
- **1604** The Pont Neuf completed.
- **1605** Place des Vosges built.
- **1610** Henri IV assassinated.
- **1635** Richelieu founds Académie Française.
- **1643–1715** Reign of Louis XIV.
- **1789** Storming of the Bastille and the beginning of the French Revolution.
- **1790** The Festival of the Federation.
- **1793** Louis XVI and Marie Antoinette guillotined. The Louvre becomes a public museum.
- **1794** Robespierre guillotined.
- **1799** Napoleon enters Paris.
- **1804** Napoleon crowns himself emperor.
- **1815** Napoleon's defeat at Waterloo. The Bourbons are restored to the throne of France.
- **1830** Louis-Philippe replaces Charles X.

continues

(now the Panthéon). On the Right Bank, people flocked to the gardens of the Palais-Royal and its galleries, which had been added in 1761. In the 1780s, such theaters as the Comédie Italienne, the Odéon, and the Comédie Française thrived. In the literary clubs and cafes, the revolutionary spirit grew. During the reigns of Louis XIV and Louis XV, Paris dominated the Western world, nourishing some of Europe's great architects and intellectuals: the Mansarts, Soufflot, Molière, Racine, Corneille, Gluck, Rameau, Lully, Fragonard, Watteau, Boucher, Voltaire, and Montesquieu. The financial strain of pomp, glamour, and conquest drained the treasury, and in 1788, the king was forced to convene the Estates General—the parliamentary assembly—for the first time since 1614.

FROM THE REVOLUTION TO THE SECOND EMPIRE

The summoning of the Estates General started the chain of events that led to the Revolution. In many ways, Paris was its center. On July 14, 1789, a mob stormed the Bastille, and 3 days later at the Hôtel de Ville, Louis XVI was forced to kiss the new French tricolor. On July 14, 1790, the Festival of the Federation was celebrated on the Champs-de-Mars. About 300,000 people attended a Mass at which the king swore an oath of loyalty to the constitution. Yet radical factions grew. On August 10, 1792, revolutionary troops and a Parisian mob stormed the Tuileries, taking the king prisoner. In 1793, he and Queen Marie Antoinette were beheaded in place de la Concorde. Robespierre directed the Reign of Terror from 1793 until his arrest on July 27, 1794. A reaction ushered in the Directory (1795–99), which ended with Napoleon's coup.

In 1804, Napoleon crowned himself emperor and his wife, Joséphine, empress; he then embarked on a series of campaigns that ended in his defeat at the Battle of Waterloo in 1815. During his reign, he gave Paris many of its most grandiose monuments, notably the Arc de Triomphe, the Arc de Triomphe du Carrousel, and the Bourse. His greatest gift was the Louvre, which he set on its course to becoming an art museum. Here, he displayed the art he had "acquired" in his campaigns; it became the core of the museum's collection.

Although today you can still see traces of Roman and medieval Paris, as well as the city of the 16th, 17th, and 18th centuries, the look that most of us associate with the City of Light dates to the 19th century. Napoleon landscaped the view from the Louvre, extending the perspective past the Tuileries and place de la

- **1832** A cholera epidemic kills 19,000 people.
- **1848** Revolution. Louis Napoleon elected "prince-president." The Second Republic proclaimed.
- **1852** Louis Napoleon proclaimed Emperor Napoleon III.
- **1863** The revolutionary Impressionist exhibit at the Salon des Refusés.
- **1870** The Third Republic proclaimed.
- **1870–71** Franco-Prussian War.
- **1871** The Paris Commune.
- **1875** Construction of the Opéra Garnier completed.
- **1885** Victor Hugo dies.
- **1889** Exposition Universelle in Paris; the Eiffel Tower erected.
- **1900** First Métro line opens.
- **1914–18** World War I.
- **1920** The Unknown Soldier is buried under the Arc de Triomphe.
- **1929** Construction of the Maginot Line.
- **1940** Germany invades France and occupies Paris.
- **1944** Normandy landings; Paris liberated.
- **1946–54** War in Indochina.
- **1958** The Fifth Republic proclaimed; Charles de Gaulle elected president.
- **1960** Most of France's African colonies gain independence.

Concorde to the Champs-Elysées and the Arc de Triomphe. He also built fountains, cemeteries, and the arcades along rue de Rivoli.

After Waterloo and the restoration of the Bourbons, the canals of St-Martin, St-Denis, and de l'Ourcq opened in eastern and northeastern Paris. The population grew at an amazing rate, from 547,000 in 1801 to 2.3 million in 1881. Industrialization and the arrival of the railroad in 1837 fueled the growth. In its wake, industrialization brought change and democratization, which contributed to the two 19th-century revolutions. The first, in 1830, replaced Charles X with Louis-Philippe; the second, in 1848, ushered in Louis Napoleon, first as president of the Second Republic and later, in 1852, as Emperor Napoleon III.

From 1852 to 1870, Napoleon III reshaped Paris with the aid of Baron Haussmann, who razed whole neighborhoods and laid out boulevards and avenues. The displaced population settled in eastern Paris, in the neighborhoods of Belleville and Ménilmontant, which retain a strong working-class flavor. Broad avenues linked the railroad stations, and their intersections became great crossroads like the Etoile, place de l'Opéra, and place de la République. During the Second Empire, the city gained 24 parks, including the Bois de Boulogne and Parc de Monceau; a new sewage system was begun; and the market pavilions at Les Halles were constructed. Much of what is still familiar in the cityscape today originated in the baron's vision.

In this Paris, with its cafes, music halls, and theaters, the artistic giants of the day lived and worked—Balzac, Baudelaire, Dumas, Hugo, Sand, Chopin, Berlioz, Delacroix, Ingres, Daumier, and Manet, to name only a few. Famous courtesans reveled in their social prominence, and one, La Paiva, amassed such a fortune that she was able to open a palace on the Champs-Elysées. The life that filled the boulevards survives in the paintings of Manet, Renoir, Degas, Toulouse-Lautrec, and the other Impressionists. The city was the art capital of Europe, and a series of International Exhibitions from 1855 to 1900 showcased its achievements. The Eiffel Tower, built for the 1889 expo as a temporary structure, caused a sensation, and despite much controversy, it was allowed to remain standing, the tallest structure in the world at the time. The first Métro line opened in 1900, and the Grand Palais and the Petit Palais were unveiled for the exposition of that year.

- 1962 Algeria becomes independent.
- 1968 Strikes and student demonstrations. De Gaulle resigns.
- 1969 The old central markets at Les Halles transferred to Rungis.
- 1970 RER (Réseau Express Régional) train inaugurated.
- 1977 Centre Georges Pompidou opens.
- 1981 François Mitterrand elected president.
- 1989 Bicentennial of the French Revolution. The Louvre pyramid and the Opéra Bastille inaugurated.
- 1991 Edith Cresson becomes France's first female prime minister.
- 1992 Disneyland Paris opens in suburban Marne-la-Vallée.
- 1995 Jacques Chirac, former mayor of Paris, becomes president.
- 1996 Bibliothèque Nationale de France opens in southeast Paris.
- 1997 Lionel Jospin takes office as prime minister.
- 1998 The French host the World Cup soccer title, and its team, the Bleues, win it— the first time the French have won the championship.
- 1999 Two storms with hurricane-force winds hit France, ravaging millions of trees,

continues

FROM THE PARIS COMMUNE TO WORLD WAR I

The empire ended disastrously in the Franco-Prussian War (1870–71), during which Paris was again occupied, Alsace and Lorraine were lost, and Napoleon III was captured and exiled. A communist uprising occurred shortly after the Prussians withdrew in March 1871. In two months, it was bloodily suppressed, but not before a mob torched the Tuileries Palace, burning all but the Pavillon de Flore. The last of the Communards were executed at Père-Lachaise, and a Third Republic was established; it lasted 60 years.

Under the Third Republic, French painters and writers made the country a world center of art and literature. The death of writer Victor Hugo in 1885 marked the change from the Romantic era to the modern era. Hugo had been the great symbol of France; his body lay in state at the Arc de Triomphe. But signs of change were apparent in the more realistic works of Manet, Courbet, and Zola. In particular, Manet's *Déjeuner sur l'herbe,* shown at the Salon des Refusés in 1863, caused a scandal not only for its subject, but also because of its technique. In 1874, Manet, Pissarro, Renoir, Cézanne, Monet, Morisot, Degas, Sisley, and 21 other artists, calling themselves the Société Anonyme, held their first exhibition. Their paintings were greeted with revulsion and dismissed. The artists were dubbed madmen, and a critic in *Charivari* referred to the show as the "exhibition of the impressionists"—a name that stuck. The same disgust greeted a second exhibition in 1876; one critic even suggested that someone should "try to explain to M. Renoir that a woman's torso is not a mass of decomposing flesh with those purplish green stains which denote a state of complete putrefaction in a corpse."

By the 1890s—in Paris, at least—Impressionism had arrived. In 1895, Samuel Bing opened his shop L'art nouveau Bing, and "Art Nouveau" became synonymous with the fluid, sinuous style that dominated the first decade of the 20th century. It survives at such grand restaurants as Maxim's (1890) on rue Royale and Laperousse on the quai des Grands Augustins, and at the few remaining Métro entrances designed by Hector Guimard. The experimentation continued, giving birth to cubism (1907–14), dadaism (1915–22), and surrealism and Art Deco in the 1920s.

By the turn of the 20th century, Paris had 27,000 cafes, about 150 cafe concerts, and thousands of restaurants. Shop girls, milliners, barmaids, prostitutes, and

including 10,000 in Versailles, destroying thousands of homes and cutting off power to parts of France.

- 2000 Spectacular fireworks at the Eiffel Tower herald the millennium. The French Bleues win the Eurocup soccer title, the first team in the history of the sport to win both a World Cup and a Eurocup soccer title.

- 2001 The French win the Eurocup title for the second year in a row.

- 2003 France opposes the war with Iraq, causing a significant decline in U.S. visitors. President Jacques Chirac's approval rating hits an all-time high of 85%.

- 2005 Tourism booms again with high occupancy rates at all hotels and American

visitors returning in droves. Paris loses bid to host the 2012 Olympic Games.

other workers flocked to the cafes along the Grands Boulevards and in Montparnasse and Montmartre. Montmartre, in particular, became the favorite gathering place of artists such as Manet, Monet, and Renoir.

The cafe concert was a late-19th-century invention at which people ate and drank while they watched a show, commented throughout, and often joined in the singing. Mistinguett and Maurice Chevalier started their careers in such places, the most famous of which were the Folies Bergères and the Moulin Rouge in Montmartre. We know the dancers and other characters who frequented the Moulin Rouge—including Colette, La Goulue, and Jane Avril—from the posters, pastels, and oils of Toulouse-Lautrec.

The party ended in August 1914, when the troops marched off singing the "Marseillaise." Paris was not occupied, but France paid a heavy price in World War I, losing 8.4 million men. The peace treaty returning Alsace and Lorraine to France was signed in the Hall of Mirrors at Versailles. French premier Georges Clemenceau exacted heavy war reparations and insisted on imposing a tough treaty on the Germans, which some historians believe led directly to World War II.

FROM 1920 THROUGH WORLD WAR II

Between the wars, Paris became a magnet for writers and artists from all over. In the United States, Prohibition had passed in 1919, and nativism and isolationism dominated the political scene. Paris, by contrast, was fun, cheap (by American standards), and the art capital of the world. Americans came in droves—F. Scott Fitzgerald, Henry Miller, Ernest Hemingway, Gertrude Stein, Natalie Barney, and many more. They gathered in Montparnasse cafes such as Le Dôme, Le Select, and La Coupole, all still operating today.

And Americans were not the only ones—James Joyce, Marc Chagall, and George Orwell came as well. In the '40s and '50s, the bohemian focus moved to St-Germain, where intellectuals like Jean-Paul Sartre and Simone de Beauvoir frequented the Les Deux Magots, Café de Flore, and Brasserie Lipp, all still thriving on boulevard St-Germain.

The 1930s saw economic depression through Europe, German rearmament, and the appeasement of Hitler. In May 1940, Germany invaded the Netherlands, Luxembourg, and Belgium, and broke through France's defensive Maginot Line. The Germans occupied Paris on June 14, 1940, establishing their headquarters at the Hôtel Lutétia on boulevard Raspail. The Vichy government, led by Marshal Pétain, in theory ran unoccupied France but, in fact, collaborated with the Germans. Gen. Charles de Gaulle became leader of the Free French and organized le Maquis (the Resistance) throughout the country, proclaiming in a famous radio broadcast from London that France had lost a battle but not the war.

The Allies landed in Normandy in June 1944. On August 24, General Leclerc entered Paris, followed 2 days later by General de Gaulle, who paraded down the Champs-Elysées. By the end of the year, the Germans had been expelled from France and de Gaulle was heading a provisional government before the official proclamation of the Fourth Republic.

THE POSTWAR YEARS

The Fourth Republic saw the violent end of colonial French rule around the world. In the late 1940s, some 80,000 soldiers died fighting the revolt in Madagascar. In the mid-1950s, France abandoned Indochina in the hope that the United States would defeat the Chinese-funded revolutionaries. In North Africa, Morocco and Tunisia won their independence, but the French would not let go of Algeria, which was a *département,* technically a part of France. The Algerian war of liberation was a bloody conflict that led to the collapse of the Fourth Republic. Refugees from Algeria flooded France. In 1958, de Gaulle was recalled to head the Fifth Republic and to resolve another Algerian crisis created when a right-wing military coup threatened France. In 1962, after a referendum in France proposed by de Gaulle, Algeria gained its independence.

The writer André Malraux was de Gaulle's minister of cultural affairs from 1958 to 1969. He protected and restored such districts as the Marais, which had fallen into disrepair. Elsewhere in the city, modern architecture took over. The Maison UNESCO, in the 7e arrondissement, and the Maison de la Radio, on the Seine in the 16e, were built in 1958 and 1960, respectively.

The decade ended with more turmoil. In 1968, workers were striking around the country; in Paris, students took to the streets, rebelling against France's antiquated educational system. Some political analysts date the more recent changes in French attitudes toward modernization from 1968. De Gaulle was swept from power, and in 1969, Georges Pompidou became president.

In 1970, the Réseau Express Régional (RER express train) was inaugurated, heralding a new era of *grands projets.* Four years later, the Montparnasse Tower was completed; Saul Bellow described the skyscraper as "something that had strayed away from Chicago and had come to rest on a Parisian street corner." Many Parisians responded that it should have stayed in Chicago. Further outrage greeted the destruction of the old market at Les Halles in 1969; it was replaced by a large hole that became an underground shopping mall in 1979. By the time it was extended to include a swimming pool, a 15-screen cinema, and a film archive (in 1986), Parisians were tired of it; they have

effectively left it to the homeless, drug dealers, and pickpockets. Other 1970s architectural adventures proved more successful. Parisians confronted the multicolored inside-out design of the Centre Pompidou in 1977 and grew to accept and even love the structure.

François Mitterrand, France's first postwar socialist president, was elected in 1981. After a disastrous experiment with textbook socialism, the president adopted a policy of economic growth coupled with the preservation of France's beloved social safety net. His imperious manner earned him the nickname *Dieu* (God), but the modernization of France's infrastructure marked his term—or reign. The first 275-kmph (170-mph) TGV (Train à Grande Vitesse) went into service in 1983, cutting the 462km (286-mile) Paris-Lyon route to 2 hours. The dream of a rail link to Britain was realized in 1994 with the opening of the Chunnel under the English Channel.

In 1989, France celebrated two great birthdays: the bicentennial of the Revolution and the centennial of the Eiffel Tower, both symbols of hope, progress, and change. Since then, the political and economic situation has declined. The unemployment rate has edged upward and become a major preoccupation.

Although former Paris mayor Jacques Chirac won the presidency in 1995 with a promise to jump-start the economy, growth remained stagnant, and the ranks of the jobless multiplied. Confrontations with labor unions, such as the transit workers' strike that paralyzed Paris at the end of 1995, revealed a bitter mood. Hoping for a mandate to institute reform, Chirac called an election in 1997, but the strategy backfired. The Socialist Party won, and the president was forced to "cohabit" with Prime Minister Lionel Jospin, the leader of the opposition. The cohabitation has worked out well. Enjoying strong growth, the Socialist government has managed to trim the unemployment rate, and it solidified its popularity by implementing a 35-hour workweek, with the hopes that this might encourage companies to hire more people because employees would be working fewer hours. So far, this reduced-hours experiment has not yielded the desired results, but some say that it is too soon to declare it a failure.

Meanwhile, the single European currency plan went into effect on January 1, 2002, with the euro replacing the franc in a rare and breathtaking display of glitch-free bureaucracy. Of course, France is one of the few European nations that still displays prices in francs (albeit in hardly visible lettering) below euro prices. Prices on the whole have inched up since January 2002, when every single item sold in France changed from francs to euros. Vending machines, for example, conveniently replaced 5F coins with 1€ coins, a 13% increase—and this applied to most everything in the country, with businesses, naturally, rounding *up* when the euro took effect. The economy is still dealing with high unemployment, but the mood is upbeat and Paris is as clean and vibrant as ever since the election of the first openly gay mayor, Bertrand Delanoe, who has been in office for several years now.

In 2003, France's opposition to the U.S.–led war in Iraq caused a significant drop in American visitors. Hotels reported record-low occupancy rates, and exports to the U.S. slowed dramatically. That said, however, the French had never stood behind their president as they stood in the spring of 2003: A whopping 85% percent supported Jacques Chirac. Peace demonstrations were frequent, nonviolent, and countrywide. But the soaring approval rate did not last very long, as the focus soon shifted back to the economy. Several general strikes took place in April and May 2003, slightly dampening the spirit of camaraderie that had swept across the country during the first major war of the new millennium.

By 2005, France's opposition to the Iraq war seemed to have been long forgotten as U.S. visitors returned in droves. Hotels were, once again, reporting near-full capacity for the summer tourist season and the Paris Air Show at Le Bourget held in June 2005 was very well attended.

In May 2005, French voters overwhelmingly rejected the proposed European Union constitution. Turnout for the referendum was huge—about 70% of the eligible voters came out and 55% of the people said "non." Thus the E.U. was plunged into one of its worst crises and the future of the constitution is very uncertain. By voting no, the French also registered their discontent with President Chirac's center-right government. Barely a week after the vote, Chirac fired his prime minister and replaced him with the man who was France's chief spokesman against the war in Iraq. Dominique de Villepin took over from Jean-Pierre Raffarin in a ceremony at Matignon, the prime minister's official residence, on May 31, 2005. President Chirac's second term ends in 2007.

2 Parisian Art

Art in Paris is not merely French art. Many French movements—Impressionism is only one—began or developed here, but that's only part of the picture. Generations of artists from all parts of the world have thrived in Paris. Though the stereotype of the painter starving *La* *Bohème*-style in a Montmartre garret may be a thing of the past, the city's museums and galleries hold enough art for several lifetimes of viewing. From Egyptian, Assyrian, and Greco-Roman art at the Louvre; through realism, Impressionism, and Art Nouveau at the Musée d'Orsay;

to the modern masters at the Centre Pompidou, Paris offers a wealth of art.

Don't bypass the small museums; often less crowded than their larger, more famous counterparts, they hold their own wonders. Also look for special exhibitions such as those regularly held at the Louvre and the Grand Palais, and shows by contemporary artists at private galleries on both sides of the Seine.

The history of art in Paris is inseparable from that of art in France. Since medieval times, French artists have found inspiration in Paris and the surrounding areas. In their famous devotional book *Les très riche heures (The Very Prosperous Hours),* the Limbourg brothers, 15th-century illuminators, represented the blue skies of the Ile-de-France region as well as some recognizable Parisian scenes.

From the Renaissance to the 19th century, French artists created an astoundingly rich body of painting. In the 16th century, Jean Clouet and his son François combined the traditions of Gothic art with native French styles, producing paintings remarkable for their design. In the 17th century, Nicholas Poussin studied in Italy and, inspired by Italian painters as well as by the art of ancient Greece and Rome, became one of the foremost neoclassical artists. The delicate paintings of Antoine Watteau dominated the first half of the 18th century. The second half belonged to Jean-Honoré Fragonard; with his soft palette, his works represent the pinnacle of rococo art in France. After the Revolution, classicism reigned supreme, with such artists as Jacques-Louis David and Jean-Auguste-Dominique Ingres. Eugène Delacroix later became the master of romantic painting. None of these artists, however, paid much attention to representations of Paris. The city became the center of world art as well as an important subject for the Impressionists in the second half of the 19th century.

The critics and the public were at first scandalized by the art of those painters later described as Impressionists whose works were often rejected by the official Salon. They created their own Salon des Refusés. At the 1874 Salon des Refusés, Monet exhibited his *Impression: soleil levant (Impression: Rising Sun);* a disrespectful critic derived the term "Impressionism" from the painting's title. Impressions were what many of the painters had in mind—not simply to paint an object, but to capture the impression it produced. The Impressionists argued that every vision of the object occurs in a particular light, at a particular time, and that what the eye perceives is not simply the object. They brought light and color to the foreground and even represented shadows as areas of color. Artists such as Monet, Renoir, Pissarro, Sisley, Seurat, Gauguin, and van Gogh painted their impressions of Paris, and because of them we have a better artistic record of Paris in the late 19th century than we do of any of the preceding centuries.

From this period on, Montmartre is especially well represented. At the turn of the 20th century, Toulouse-Lautrec painted the Moulin Rouge and its cancan dancers, and in the first half of the 20th century, Maurice Utrillo devoted his art to capturing the modest streets of the district.

In the 20th century, internationalization marked the Parisian art scene. Picasso, Chagall, Modigliani, and Cuban painter Lam all worked here, and their works are exhibited in Paris's world-class museums of modern art, Musée National d'Art Moderne at the Centre Pompidou and Musée d'Art Moderne de la Ville de Paris.

Appendix B:
Glossary of Useful Terms

Useful French Words & Phrases

BASICS

English	French	Pronunciation
yes/no	**oui/non**	wee/nohn
okay	**d'accord**	dah-*core*
please	**s'il vous plaît**	seel voo *pleh*
thank you	**merci**	mehr-*see*
you're welcome	**de rien**	duh ree-*ehn*
hello (during daylight hours)	**bonjour**	bohn-*zhoor*
good evening	**bonsoir**	bohn-*swahr*
goodbye	**au revoir**	o ruh-*vwahr*
What's your name?	**Comment vous appellez-vous?**	ko-mahn voo-zapleh-*voo*
My name is . . .	**Je m'appelle . . .**	zhuh ma-*pell*
Happy to meet you.	**Enchanté(e).**	ohn-shahn-*teh*
Miss	**Mademoiselle**	mad-mwa-*zel*
Mr.	**Monsieur**	muh-*syuh*
Mrs.	**Madame**	ma-*dam*
How are you?	**Comment allez-vous?**	kuh-mahn-tahl-eh-*voo*
Fine, thank you, and you?	**Très bien, merci, et vous?**	treh byehn, mehr-*see* eh voo
Very well, thank you.	**Très bien, merci.**	tre byehn mehr-*see*
So-so.	**Comme ci, comme ça.**	kum-*see* kum-*sah*
I'm sorry/excuse me.	**Pardon.**	pahr-*dohn*
I'm so very sorry.	**Désolé(e).**	deh-zoh-*leh*

GETTING AROUND/STREET SMARTS

English	French	Pronunciation
Do you speak English?	**Parlez-vous anglais?**	par-leh *voo*-zahn-*gleh*
I don't speak French.	**Je ne parle pas français.**	zhuh ne parl *pah* frahn-*seh*
I don't understand.	**Je ne comprends pas.**	zhuh ne kohm-*prahn* pah

English	French	Pronunciation
Could you speak more slowly?	**Pouvez-vous parler un peu plus lentement?**	Poo-*veh* voo par-*leh* uh puh ploo lahn-te-*mahnt*
Could you repeat that?	**Répetez, s'il vous plaît.**	*reh*-peh-teh seel voo *pleh*
What is it?	**Qu'est-ce que c'est?**	kess-kuh-*seh*
What time is it?	**Qu'elle heure est-il?**	kel euhr eh-*teel*
Pardon?	**Pardon?**	par-*dohn*
Help!	**Au secours!**	oh seh-*coor*
How? *or* What did you say?	**Comment?**	ko-*mahn*
When?	**Quand?**	kahn
Where is . . . ?	**Où est . . . ?**	ooh eh
Who?	**Qui?**	kee
Why?	**Pourquoi?**	poor-*kwah*
here/there	**ici/là**	ee-*see*/lah
left/right	**à gauche/à droite**	ah goash/ah drwaht
straight ahead	**tout droit**	too drwah
I'm American/ Canadian/British.	**Je suis américain(e)/ canadien(e)/ anglais(e).**	zhuh swee za-meh-ree-*kehn*/ca-nah-*dyehn*/ahn-*gleh (glehz)*
I'm going to . . .	**Je vais à . . .**	zhuh veh ah
I want to get off at . . .	**Je voudrais descendre à . . .**	zhuh voo-*dreh* deh-*sohn*-dreh ah
I'm sick.	**Je suis malade.**	zhuh swee ma-*lahd*
I have a headache.	**J'ai une mal de tête.**	zheh oon mal duh tet
airport	**l'aéroport**	leh-roh-*pohr*
bank	**la banque**	lah bahnk
bridge	**le pont**	luh pohn
bus station	**la gare routière**	lah gahr roo-*tyehr*
bus stop	**l'arrêt de bus**	lah-*reh* duh boohs
by means of a bicycle	**en vélo/par bicyclette**	ahn *veh*-loh/par bee-see-*clet*
by means of a car	**en voiture**	ahn vwa-*toor*
cashier	**la caisse**	lah *kess*
driver's license	**permis de conduire**	per-*mee* duh con-*dweer*
elevator	**l'ascenseur**	lah sahn *seuhr*
entrance (to a building or a city)	**la porte**	lah port

English	French	Pronunciation
exit (from a building or a freeway)	une sortie	oon sor-*tee*
ground floor	rez-de-chaussée	reh-duh-shoh-*seh*
highway to . . .	la route pour . . .	lah root poor
hospital	l'hôpital	loh-pee-*tahl*
insurance	les assurances	leh zah-sur-*ahns*
luggage storage	consigne	kohn-*seen*-yuh
museum	le musée	luh moo-*zeh*
no entry	sens interdit	sehn zehn-tehr-*dee*
no smoking	défense de fumer	deh-*fahnz* duh fu-*meh*
on foot	à pied	ah pyeh
one-way ticket	aller simple	ah-*leh* sam-pluh
police	la police	lah po-*lees*
round-trip ticket	aller-retour	ah-*leh* re-*toor*
second floor	premier étage	pruh-*myeehr* eh-*tazh*
slow down	ralentez	rah-lahn-*teh*
store	le magasin	luh ma-ga-*zehn*
street	la rue	lah roo
subway	le Métro	luh meh-*troh*
telephone	le téléphone	luh teh-leh-*phun*
ticket	un billet	uh *bee*-yeh
ticket office	vente de billets	vahnt duh bee-*yeh*
toilets	les toilettes	leh twa-*lehts*

NECESSITIES

English	French	Pronunciation
I'd like . . .	Je voudrais . . .	zhuh voo-*dreh*
a room.	une chambre	oon *shahm*-bruh
the key.	la clé (la clef).	lah cleh
I'd like to buy . . .	Je voudrais acheter . . .	zhuh voo-*dreh* ahsh-*teh*
aspirin.	des aspirines.	deyz ah-speeh-*reen*
cigarettes.	des cigarettes.	deh see-gah-*ret*
condoms.	des préservatifs.	deh preh-sehr-va-*teef*
contraceptive suppositories.	des ovules contraceptives.	days oh-*vyules* kahn-trah-cep-*teef*
a dictionary.	un dictionnaire.	uh deek-syoh-*nehr*
a gift (for someone).	un cadeau.	uh kah-*doe*
a purse.	un sac.	uh sahk
a map of the city.	un plan de ville.	uh plahn duh *veel*
matches.	des allumettes.	deh zah-loo-*met*
a lighter.	un briquet.	uh bree-*keh*

English	French	Pronunciation
a newspaper.	**un journal.**	uh zhoor-*nahl*
a phone card.	**une carte téléphonique.**	oon cart teh-leh-fo-*neek*
a road map.	**une carte routière.**	oon cart roo-*tyehr*
shoes.	**des chaussures.**	deh shoh-*soohr*
soap.	**du savon.**	doo sah-*vohn*
socks.	**des chaussettes.**	deh shoh-*set*
a stamp.	**un timbre.**	uh *tam*-breh
How much does it cost?	**C'est combien?/ Ça coûte combien?**	seh com-*byehn*/sah coot com-*byehn*
That's expensive.	**C'est cher/chère.**	seh share
That's inexpensive.	**C'est raisonnable/ C'est bon marché.**	seh reh-soh-*nah*-bluh/ seh bohn mar-*sheh*
Do you take credit cards?	**Est-ce que vous acceptez les cartes bancaires?**	es-kuh voo zak-sep-*teh* leh kart bahn-*kehr*

TIME PHRASES

English	French	Pronunciation
Sunday	**dimanche**	dee-*mahnsh*
Monday	**lundi**	*luhn*-dee
Tuesday	**mardi**	*mahr*-dee
Wednesday	**mercredi**	*mehr*-kruh-dee
Thursday	**jeudi**	*zheu*-dee
Friday	**vendredi**	*vahn*-druh-dee
Saturday	**samedi**	sahm-*dee*
Yesterday	**hier**	yehr
Today	**aujourd'hui**	oh-zhoor-*dwee*
This morning	**ce matin**	suh mah-*tehn*
This afternoon	**cet après-midi**	set ah-preh mee-*dee*
Tonight	**ce soir**	suh *swahr*
Tomorrow	**demain**	duh-*mehn*

Index

See also Accommodations and Restaurant indexes, below.

The Ultimate Guide for People
Who Love Good Value!

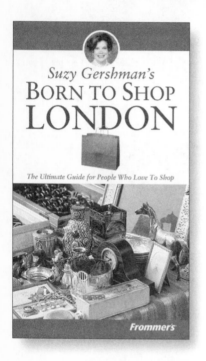

Check out the complete list of Born to Shop Guides:

- France
- Italy
- Hong Kong, Shanghai & Beijing

- London
- New York
- Paris

FROMMER'S® NATIONAL PARK GUIDES

Algonquin Provincial Park
Banff & Jasper
Family Vacations in the National
  Parks

Grand Canyon
National Parks of the American West
Rocky Mountain

Yellowstone & Grand Teton
Yosemite & Sequoia/Kings Canyon
Zion & Bryce Canyon

FROMMER'S® MEMORABLE WALKS

Chicago
London

New York
Paris

San Francisco

FROMMER'S® WITH KIDS GUIDES

Chicago
Hawaii
Las Vegas
New York City

Ottawa
San Francisco
Toronto

Vancouver
Walt Disney World® & Orlando
Washington, D.C.

SUZY GERSHMAN'S BORN TO SHOP GUIDES

Born to Shop: France
Born to Shop: Hong Kong, Shanghai
  & Beijing

Born to Shop: Italy
Born to Shop: London

Born to Shop: New York
Born to Shop: Paris

FROMMER'S® IRREVERENT GUIDES

Amsterdam
Boston
Chicago
Las Vegas
London

Los Angeles
Manhattan
New Orleans
Paris
Rome

San Francisco
Seattle & Portland
Vancouver
Walt Disney World®
Washington, D.C.

FROMMER'S® BEST-LOVED DRIVING TOURS

Austria
Britain
California
France

Germany
Ireland
Italy
New England

Northern Italy
Scotland
Spain
Tuscany & Umbria

THE UNOFFICIAL GUIDES®

Beyond Disney
California with Kids
Central Italy
Chicago
Cruises
Disneyland®
England
Florida
Florida with Kids
Inside Disney

Hawaii
Las Vegas
London
Maui
Mexico's Best Beach Resorts
Mini Las Vegas
Mini Mickey
New Orleans
New York City
Paris

San Francisco
Skiing & Snowboarding in the West
South Florida including Miami &
  the Keys
Walt Disney World®
Walt Disney World® for
  Grown-ups
Walt Disney World® with Kids
Washington, D.C.

SPECIAL-INTEREST TITLES

Athens Past & Present
Cities Ranked & Rated
Frommer's Best Day Trips from London
Frommer's Best RV & Tent Campgrounds
  in the U.S.A.
Frommer's Caribbean Hideaways
Frommer's China: The 50 Most Memorable Trips
Frommer's Exploring America by RV
Frommer's Gay & Lesbian Europe

Frommer's NYC Free & Dirt Cheap
Frommer's Road Atlas Europe
Frommer's Road Atlas France
Frommer's Road Atlas Ireland
Frommer's Wonderful Weekends from
  New York City
Retirement Places Rated
Rome Past & Present

THE NEW TRAVELOCITY GUARANTEE

EVERYTHING YOU BOOK WILL BE RIGHT, OR WE'LL WORK WITH OUR TRAVEL PARTNERS TO MAKE IT RIGHT, RIGHT AWAY.

To drive home the point, we're going to use the word "right" in every single sentence.

Let's get right to it. Right to the meat! Only Travelocity guarantees everything about your booking will be right, or we'll work with our travel partners to make it right, right away. Right on!

Here's a picture taken smack dab right in the middle of Antigua, where the guarantee also covers you.

The guarantee covers all but one of the items pictured to the right.

Now, you may be thinking, "Yeah, right, I'm so sure." That's OK; you have the right to remain skeptical. That is until we mention help is always right around the corner. Call us right off the bat, knowing that our customer service reps are there for you 24/7. Righting wrongs. Left and right.

For example, what if the ocean view you booked actually looks out at a downright ugly parking lot? You'd be right to call – we're there for you. And no one in their right mind would be pleased to learn the rental car place has closed and left them stranded. Call Travelocity and we'll help get you back on the right track.

Now if you're guessing there are some things we can't control, like the weather, well you're right. But we can help you with most things – to get all the details in righting,* visit **travelocity.com/guarantee**.

*Sorry, spelling things right is one of the few things not covered under the guarantee.

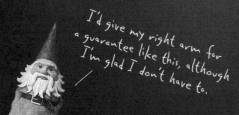

I'd give my right arm for a guarantee like this, although I'm glad I don't have to.

travelocity
You'll never roam alone.